A HISTORY OF
ROMAN
ART

A HISTORY OF
ROMAN
ART

STEVEN L. TUCK

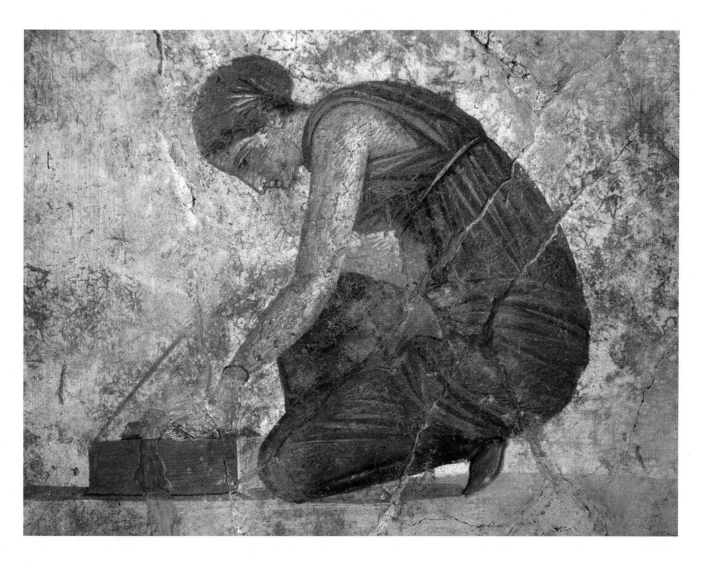

WILEY Blackwell

This edition first published 2015
© 2015 Steven L. Tuck

Registered Office
John Wiley & Sons, Ltd, The Atrium, Southern Gate, Chichester, West Sussex, PO19 8SQ, UK

Editorial Offices
350 Main Street, Malden, MA 02148-5020, USA
9600 Garsington Road, Oxford, OX4 2DQ, UK
The Atrium, Southern Gate, Chichester, West Sussex, PO19 8SQ, UK

For details of our global editorial offices, for customer services, and for information about
how to apply for permission to reuse the copyright material in this book please see our
website at www.wiley.com/wiley-blackwell.

The right of Steven L. Tuck to be identified as the author of this work has been asserted in
accordance with the UK Copyright, Designs and Patents Act 1988.

Library of Congress Cataloging-in-Publication Data

Tuck, Steven L., author.
  A history of Roman art / Steven L. Tuck.
     pages   cm
  Includes bibliographical references and index.
  ISBN 978-1-4443-3025-0 (cloth) – ISBN 978-1-4443-3026-7 (pbk.)
1. Art, Roman.   I. Title.
  N5740.T83 2015
  709.37–dc23
                                            2014029770

A catalogue record for this book is available from the British Library.

Cover image: Detail of slave from a fresco in the House of Punished Love, Pompeii,
1st century CE. Museo Archeologico Nazionale, Naples, Italy / © Samuel Magal,
Sites & Photos Ltd. / The Bridgeman Art Library

Set in 10/13pt Minion by SPi Publisher Services, Pondicherry, India
Printed and bound in Singapore by Markono Print Media Pte Ltd

1   2015

This book is dedicated to ELIZABETH TUCK *and* EMILY TUCK.
More than mere witnesses to the years of work that went into it,
they endured – with great patience – my long answers to the innocent question,
"How is it going?" They also endured endless questions from me about images, adverbs,
and grammar in general. Emily read much of the book in manuscript
prior to publication, an act of pietas if ever there was one.

BRIEF CONTENTS

CONTENTS

ILLUSTRATIONS

PREFACE

The obvious question is why we might need a new book on Roman art. We seem tolerably well stocked with them. I began writing this book because the options for textbooks on Roman art, organized chronologically as I taught my classes, were limited. Factor in the need for many illustrations at a reasonable cost and the options were even more limited. It seemed that an alternative book with those features that emphasized the context of art within Roman social structure and politics and the contributions of various styles to Roman art would fill a niche. Below I outline some of the elements that make up the book and were part of what we perceived would set the book apart.

One of the goals of the book is to integrate the arts into a discussion of the broader cultural context in which they are created. As such the social, political, and cultural milieux will be critical to a full understanding of the art. Each chapter, therefore, has some discussion of the non-art events in the world that affected the form of the arts. These are brief but designed to make the sequence of changes far less arbitrary. A second goal is to avoid what many introductory art history texts convey as a sense of inevitability. Some narratives seem to imply a trajectory of improvement: as artists get better, art improves and new techniques for portraying the human form and landscape, linear perspective, etc. are invented or discovered and then things get better, before they fall apart in the Middle Ages. In this book we reject that perspective. It is necessary to study what might be termed the leading styles of particular periods. Nevertheless, these are not presented as inevitable developments over previous styles. They don't exist as evolutionary models or improvements. The changes that occur in the art of a particular period represent the response of the visual world to the needs of its makers: artists, patrons, audience, and their selection for their ability to convey the selected lessons or messages to the audience. Some specifics on the book might illustrate this approach.

First, the title. I wanted to be as accurate as possible and call it "An Extremely Biased and Capricious History of Roman Art which Can't Possibly Take into Account All of the Constantly Changing Themes, Subjects, Styles and Developments in the Vast Roman World over a 2000 Year Period." My long-suffering editors were dubious, pointing out that it wouldn't fit on the spine of the book. We compromised on the title you read on the cover. The point is that there is no *the* History of Roman Art. There are many. This is one. In it we have taken a broad view of the definition of Roman art and have created an inclusive look at the cultures that contributed to the Roman system in order to understand and appreciate the full range of influences that created, transmitted, received, and adapted Roman art across the centuries and continents.

The book is, straightforwardly if perhaps uncreatively, organized chronologically. Although certain media, subjects, and themes are traced across the entire book, this organization seemed to serve the needs of students better than a thematic one. Each chapter has some consistent features as well.

Timeline. Each chapter starts with a timeline of key events during the period covered. Non-art events, selected to provide some context for the art, are distinguished from works of art.

Marginal glosses. There is a running glossary keyed to the first use of a Latin word or technical term also collected in a full glossary at the back of the book. Most of these are technical terms in art and architecture, e.g. cella, orthogonal planning, atmospheric perspective; some are words in Latin or English that my long-suffering editors agreed to include if I added them to the glossary, e.g. apotropaic, *adventus*.

A series of features in each chapter is designed to focus attention on information that provides context for the art, its creation, use, or meaning. These include five categories of sidebars, at least three of which will appear in each chapter:

◆ **Tools & Techniques.** Covers artistic technique, materials, and so forth. Examples include cameo glass technique, use of concrete, artistic workshops.

◆ **More on Myth.** Provides a quick introduction to a myth central to the art, e.g. Serapis, Seven against Thebes.

◆ **Ancients on Art.** These quotations allow readers to engage, in translation, ancient testimony about this material.

◆ **Form & Function.** Examines an aspect of Roman life in relation to some of the art or architectural pieces described, e.g. analysis of amphitheaters, bath complexes, the Forum Romanum.

◆ **Historical Context.** Includes information on specific events, e.g. Dacian wars, the Jewish Revolt, and particular individuals, e.g. Antinous, Valerian.

Each chapter also has three larger box features. **Art and Literature** explores these intersections in each period. **A View from the Provinces** spotlights art from outside Rome to ensure the perspective is not exclusively a Rome-centered one. **Scholarly Perspective** provides an opportunity to problematize the work by exploring a scholarly debate, perspective, or approach to the art. This gives the reader a case study in how we know what we know and how professionals develop the way we understand the arts of ancient Rome. The goal is not to isolate the scholarship, which actually permeates the entire narrative, but to concentrate on a single issue with a particular work of art or narrow collection of evidence.

Each chapter ends with **Suggestions for Further Reading**. These represent a small selection of recent, accessible, excellent scholarship including both articles on more limited topics and books. One work is keyed to the **Scholarly Perspective** box and also listed at the end of that box. A **Guide to Further Reading** with additional books and articles arranged thematically can be found at the back of the book with the glossary.

Finally, the book is supplemented with online content including additional images of many of the monuments to allow instructors to illustrate views or details of works of art not limited to those in the book.

NOTE TO STUDENTS

This note is designed to help you get the most out of the book by pointing out its approach, some of the features, and offering a time-honored strategy for success.

It is hard to overestimate the importance of Rome and Roman art to the modern western world. More than you may be aware, you are living in a world largely created by people who deliberately emulated the Romans. Forms of government, law, architecture, the arts, and infrastructure have all been modeled on the Roman versions. And, like our world, the Romans shared a visually based, international, multicultural culture. This is why Roman art carries such significance. In fact, the visual arts served the Romans, as they serve us, as the primary means of communicating (think of how many corporate logos you can instantly recognize and you'll get an idea of the role of the visual in defining our world). You should be aware of the critical role art played in the Roman world, a world that is largely non-literate, spread over three continents, and composed of a myriad of local cultures with unique and exclusive customs, traditions, laws, and beliefs. Taking a look at the map you can see the Roman Empire at its height covering an area from Scotland to Saudi Arabia and from Morocco to Armenia.

This means that the visual messages projected by the art and architecture of the Roman world carry a critical set of information allowing the Romans to understand and navigate their world, goals you have as well. It matters because art represented the way people across the Roman Empire communicated their ideas, values, beliefs, and identities. These were all embedded in the art and could be unpacked by a Roman, and sometimes intentionally by a non-Roman, audience, and, with some guidance from this book, by one today as well. And, of course, the subjects and forms they selected are still with us today. Now, about the features in the book and that promised strategy for success.

If you'll forgive some advice from a stranger, allow me to suggest a plan. When faced with a chapter, consider starting with the timeline and pictures. There are many pictures and, while we encourage you to read every word here, time spent looking at the pictures, truly studying the images of the art itself, is time well spent. Note that the captions each end in the date of the work. With a little practice you can teach yourself to glance down at that and start connecting images and dates from the beginning. So, look first at the timeline and pictures, only after that read the chapter, taking time to glance aside at the definitions in the margin. Finally, ideally following a class in which the material is covered, return to a visual review by looking at the pictures a second time. About those pictures: you should know that there is an inherent tension in the selection of images for each chapter and thus period. The tension is between works of art that are characteristic and those that are cutting edge, leading to trends that will be developed in later periods or places. What you have before you is a mix of these two groups. It's not all about the pictures though. We want you to read the text and to aid you in that we have created the marginal glossary as well as a number of sidebars and box features. These are pulled out to give them special emphasis and although it would be easy to skip them and just keep skimming the main text, you'll find that stopping to read them will help your understanding of the main text.

Just a couple more things about the book before we launch into the art. The goal for the Preface, Note to Students, and Introduction is to introduce you both to this book and to provide a brief orientation to Roman art history. The Introduction on Roman art history is designed to provide some examples of the defining qualities of Roman culture and the way art intersects with them. It would, however, be a separate book, actually two of them as Stewart and Hölscher demonstrate below, to write on the Roman social system and the means by which art in the Roman world operated

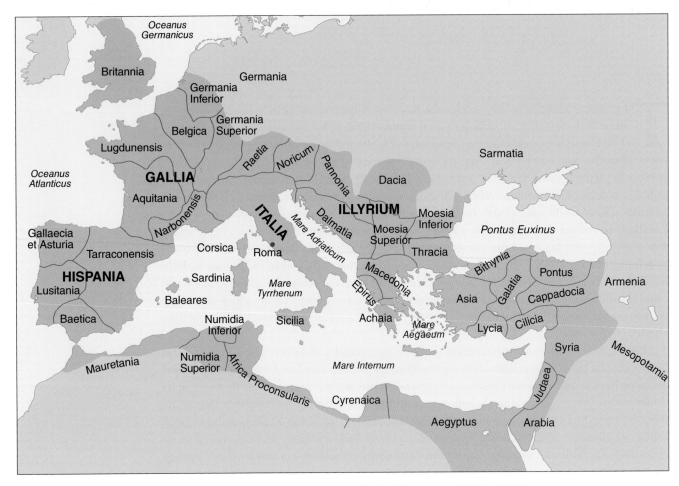

0.1   Map of full extent of Roman Empire under Trajan, *c.* 115 CE. Drawing by Jani Niemenmaa/Wikimedia Commons.

as a symbolic system to convey values. The best takeaway from this is awareness that the Roman world operated with different rules than our own, that those rules need to be learned, and that art can be a key to learning them and to seeing how the Romans reinforced the rules. As you go through the book, you can apply this lesson to the material, asking what it tells us about Roman culture, Roman values, and Roman arts. Then you will have taken a huge step not just toward learning Roman art, but to thinking like an art historian. And that brings us to the art itself and its history and study.

ACKNOWLEDGMENTS

First and foremost I owe great thanks to the Wiley Blackwell editorial team. As mentioned above the editors have been truly long suffering. The entire team: Haze Humbert, Deirdre Ilkson, Allison Kostka, and Ben Thatcher were instrumental in the final form, content, and appearance of the book. I am grateful to them all for their thoughtful insights. A tremendous number of friends and colleagues were generous with their ideas, suggestions, images, bibliography, and expertise on many areas of Roman art. Listing their names is a sure way to omit someone. Nevertheless, I want to thank in particular Jacquelyn H. Clements, Kathleen Coleman, Nancy de Grummond, John J. Dobbins, Jane DeRose Evans, Garrett Fagan, Pedar Foss, Elise A. Friedland, Andrew Goldman, Alison Griffith, Theresa Huntsman, Amy K. Leonard, Deborah Lyons, Elizabeth Marlowe, Denise Eileen McCoskey, Stephen Nimis, John Pollini, Anton Powell, Daniel Resheter, David Romano, Irene Romano, Peter Rose, Melanie Grunow Sobocinski, Lea Stirling, Zara Torlone, Francesca Tronchin, Anthony Tuck, and Jeffrey Wilcox.

WALK THROUGH TOUR

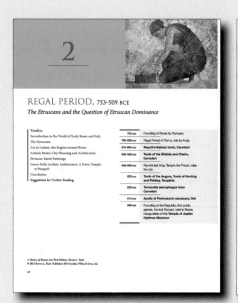

Feature: Timelines
Timelines are included at the start of each chapter to give the reader a snapshot of relevant events.

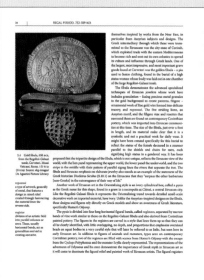

Feature: Key terms and glossary
Key terms are given in bold, defined in the adjacent margin, and included in a complete glossary at the end of the book.

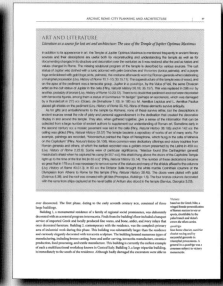

Art and Literature
Art and Literature feature boxes explore contemporary Roman descriptions of the art from each period and the reception of works and styles.

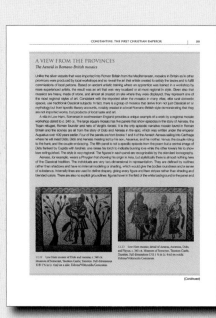

A View from the Provinces
A View from the Provinces feature boxes spotlight art from outside Rome, providing the reader with an awareness of art across the expanse of the Roman world.

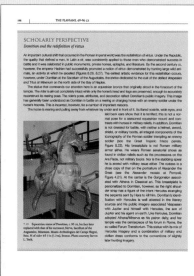

Scholarly Perspective
Scholarly Perspective feature boxes examine a scholarly debate, perspective, or approach to the art, giving readers a case study in how we know what we know and supporting a critical understanding of the art of ancient Rome.

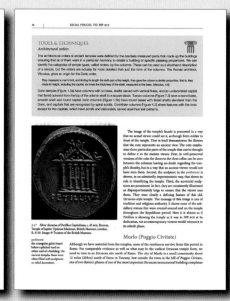

Tools & Techniques
Tools & Techniques sidebars provide readers with insight into the artistic techniques and materials used to create the art.

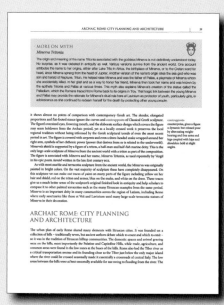

More on Myth
More on Myth sidebars highlight specific myths central to the art, giving the reader the necessary background to recognize and interpret mythological figures and stories depicted in art and architecture.

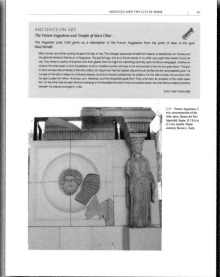

Ancients on Art
Ancients on Art sidebars include quotations that enable readers to engage with ancient testimony about the material.

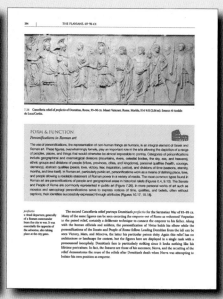

Form & Function
Form & Function sidebars examine social contexts, the functionality of art and buildings, and their relationship with the everyday lives of Romans.

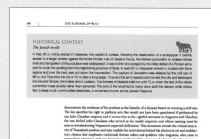

Historical Context
Historical Context sidebars provide the reader with a solid foundational knowledge of specific events that influenced art of the period.

Suggestions for Further Reading
Suggestions for Further Reading appear at the end of each chapter and include a selection of recent, accessible scholarship to help readers embark on further study.

Guide to Further Reading
A Guide to Further Reading is included at the end of the book and contains additional recommended books and articles.

TIMELINE

753 BCE	Founding of Rome by Romulus
753–509 BCE	Regal Period of Rome, rule by kings
670–650 BCE	**Regolini-Galassi tomb, Cerveteri**
600–550 BCE	**Tomb of the Shields and Chairs, Cerveteri**
535–509 BCE	Rome's last king, Tarquin the Proud, rules the city
530 BCE	**Tomb of the Augurs, Tomb of Hunting and Fishing, Tarquinia**
525 BCE	**Terracotta sarcophagus from Cerveteri**
510 BCE	**Apollo of Portonaccio sanctuary, Veii**
509 BCE	Founding of the Republic; first public games, the *ludi Romani*, held in Rome; **inauguration of the Temple of Jupiter Optimus Maximus**
480 BCE	**Tomb of the Diver, Paestum**
474 BCE	Battle of Cumae, Greeks defeat Etruscans
470 BCE	**Tomb of the Leopards, Tarquinia**
396 BCE	Romans besiege and defeat Veii, one of the twelve major Etruscan cities
390 BCE	Gallic sack of Rome
386 BCE	**"Servian wall" built around Rome**
364 BCE	First theatrical performance in Rome
338 BCE	Ostia, Rome's first colony, established
300 BCE	**Bronze bust of a man "Brutus"**
273 BCE	Colonies at Paestum and Cosa founded
264 BCE	The first gladiatorial games in Rome at the funeral of Junius Brutus Pera
264–241 BCE	First Punic War
218–202 BCE	Second Punic War
212 BCE	Sack of Syracuse
211 BCE	Triumph of Marcus Claudius Marcellus
168 BCE	Battle of Pydna, victory of Aemilius Paullus over Perseus of Macedon
c. **150** BCE	**Basilica of Pompeii constructed**
146 BCE	Destruction of Carthage and Corinth

91–88 BCE	Social War
89 BCE	Siege of Pompeii by Sulla
80 BCE	Founding of Roman colony of Pompeii by Sulla; **House of the Faun renovated; amphitheater begun at Pompeii**
73–71 BCE	Revolt of Spartacus
62 BCE	**Pons Fabricius built**
61 BCE	Pompey's Triple Triumph
55 BCE	**Pompey's Theater, first permanent theater in Rome, built**
46 BCE	**Forum of Caesar dedicated**
44 BCE	Assassination of Julius Caesar
40 BCE	**Decoration of Mysteries Suite in the Villa of the Mysteries**
31 BCE	Battle of Actium, Octavian/Augustus defeats Antony and Cleopatra
28 BCE	**Mausoleum of Augustus begun; Temple of Apollo dedicated**
27 BCE	Octavian takes the name Imperator Caesar Augustus; Livy's monumental History of Rome begins appearing
20 BCE	**Original of the Prima Porta Augustus statue**; recovery of the military standards from Parthia
19 BCE	Death of Roman poet, Vergil, publication of his *Aeneid*
15 BCE	Vitruvius writes his book on architecture; **earliest examples of Third Style wall painting; construction of Caesarea Maritima**
14 BCE	**Basilica Aemilia reliefs**
13 BCE	**Ara Pacis Augustae vowed**
12 BCE	Augustus becomes Pontifex Maximus; **Via Labicana portrait**
9 BCE	**Ara Pacis Augustae inaugurated**
2 BCE	**Forum Augustum inaugurated**
14 CE	Death of Augustus; succession of Tiberius
14–37 CE	Tiberius as emperor
20–26 CE	Tiberius resides at Sperlonga; **sculpture group created**
37–41 CE	Caligula as emperor
37 CE	**Portrait of Caligula**
41–54 CE	Claudius as emperor
43 CE	Invasion of Britain
c. 51 CE	**Grand Camée; Ravenna relief**

52 CE	**Porta Maggiore gate constructed**
54–68 CE	Nero as emperor
59 CE	Amphitheater riot at Pompeii
62 CE	Earthquake along the Bay of Naples that extensively damaged Pompeii; **Domus Transitoria of Nero**
after 62 CE	**Temple of Isis and House of Octavius Quartio rebuilt at Pompeii**
64 CE	Great fire in Rome; **Domus Aurea of Nero begun**
69–79 CE	Vespasian as emperor
71 CE	Flavian Triumph for Jewish War
75 CE	**Temple of Peace dedicated**
79–81 CE	Titus as emperor; **portrait of Titus as magistrate**
79 CE	**Sacellum of the Augustales, Herculaneum**; Eruption of Mt. Vesuvius and destruction of Pompeii, Herculaneum, Oplontis
80 CE	**Inauguration of the Colosseum**; fire and plague hit Rome
81–96 CE	Domitian as emperor
81 CE	**Arch of Titus dedicated**
92 CE	**Domus Flaviana, Flavian Palace, built**
93 CE	**Cancelleria reliefs**
ca. 94 CE	**Tomb of the Haterii**
96–98 CE	Nerva as emperor
98–117 CE	Trajan as emperor
103 CE	Trajan's new harbor of Portus at Ostia begun
106 CE	Conclusion of the Dacian War; conquest of Petra and Nabatean kingdom
109 CE	**Adamclisi victory monument built**
112 CE	**Forum of Trajan inaugurated**
113 CE	**Column of Trajan dedicated**
114 CE	Parthian war begun; **Arch of Trajan, Beneventum**
117–138 CE	Hadrian as emperor
118 CE	**Villa of Hadrian begun**
120 CE	Hadrian's Wall begun
126 CE	**Pantheon completed**
130 CE	**Hadrianic roundels**
138–161 CE	Antoninus Pius as emperor

140 CE	**Baths of the Seven Sages, Ostia**
147 CE	**Faustina the Younger portrait bust**
160 CE	**Hercules sarcophagus**
161–180 CE	Marcus Aurelius as emperor
161–169 CE	Lucius Verus co-emperor with Marcus Aurelius
161–166 CE	Parthian War
161 CE	**Column of Antoninus Pius**
165 CE	Plague sweeps Rome; **Alcestis sarcophagus**
176 CE	**Arch of Marcus Aurelius begun**
180–192 CE	Commodus as emperor; **Portonaccio sarcophagus**
192 CE	**Column of Marcus Aurelius completed; Commodus bust**; Commodus appears in the Colosseum as Hercules
193 CE	Civil War and Year of the Six Emperors
193–211 CE	Septimius Severus as emperor
193 CE	**Julia Domna portrait from Gabii**
197 CE	Invasion of the Parthian Empire
200 CE	**Painted portrait of Severan family**
203 CE	Severan family's triumphal entrance into Lepcis Magna; **Arch of Septimius Severus dedicated in Rome; Forma Urbis Romae begun; Julia Domna portrait from Ostia**
204 CE	Celebration of the 950th anniversary of Rome; **Arch of the Argentarii erected**
211–217 CE	Caracalla as emperor
216 CE	**Baths of Caracalla dedicated; Farnese Bull and Farnese Hercules sculptures**
218–222 CE	Elagabalus as emperor
222–235 CE	Alexander Severus as emperor
c. 225 CE	**Achilles and Penthesilia sarcophagus**
238 CE	**Acilia sarcophagus**
244–249 CE	Philip the Arab as emperor; **portrait bust of Philip the Arab; Synagogue at Dura Europus**
249–251 CE	Decius as emperor; **portrait of Decius**
250 CE	**Mattei Lion Hunt sarcophagus**
253–260 CE	Valerian as emperor
260 CE	**Relief of Emperor Valerian kneeling before Shapur I**

260–270 CE	**Good Shepherd sarcophagus**
270–275 CE	**Aurelian wall built around Rome**
284–305 CE	Tetrarchy founded with Diocletian and Maximian as joint rulers
298–303 CE	**Arch of Galerius, Thessaloniki**
c. 300 CE	**Tetrarchs porphyry statue group; Villa of Piazza Armerina built**
303 CE	Tetrarchs visit Rome; **Decennalia monument dedicated**
306 CE	**Baths of Diocletian dedicated**; Constantine declared emperor at York
310 CE	**Basilica at Trier built**
312 CE	Battle of the Milvian Bridge; **Arch of Constantine begun; Basilica Nova completed**
313 CE	Edict of Milan issued legalizing Christian worship
315 CE	**Colossal portrait of Constantine from the Basilica Nova**
324 CE	Final defeat of Licinius and unification of empire under the rule of Constantine
330 CE	**Porphyry sarcophagus of Constantina; Lullingstone mosaic**; founding of Constantinople
336–337 CE	**Bronze portrait of Constantine**
340 CE	**Low Ham Villa and mosaic**
359 CE	**Sarcophagus of Junius Bassus**
476 CE	Abdication of Romulus Augustulus, last emperor of the Western Empire
955–983 CE	Otto II, Holy Roman Emperor
1453 CE	Fall of Constantinople to Ottoman Empire
1806 CE	Arc de Triomphe commissioned in Paris
1865 CE	**Apotheosis of Washington fresco**

ABOUT THE WEBSITE

www.wiley.com/go/romanart

The *Roman Art* companion website features resources created by the author to help you use this book in university courses, whether you're an instructor or a student.

FOR INSTRUCTORS AND STUDENTS

- ✦ **Glossary**
- ✦ **Timeline**

FOR INSTRUCTORS

- ✦ **Additional images of works of art discussed in the book**
- ✦ **Sample lessons, assignments, and related educational resources**

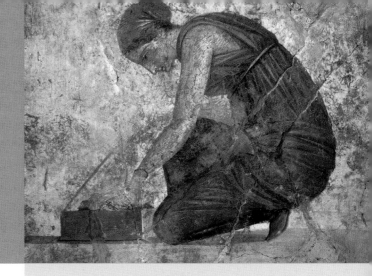

INTRODUCTION TO ROMAN ART HISTORY

A History of Roman Art, First Edition. Steven L. Tuck.
© 2015 Steven L. Tuck. Published 2015 by John Wiley & Sons, Ltd.

provenance
the place of origin or earliest known history of something. In art it can refer to the chain of ownership of a piece from origin to the present day.

This introduction is (as the Roman dictator Sulla called Roman government) a bit of "a two-headed dog." It is designed to introduce you, the reader, to both Roman art and the study of art history. In other words, to some of the overarching themes and forms of the art that follow as well as some of the ways that art historians operate and analyze that art. Let's start with the controversies.

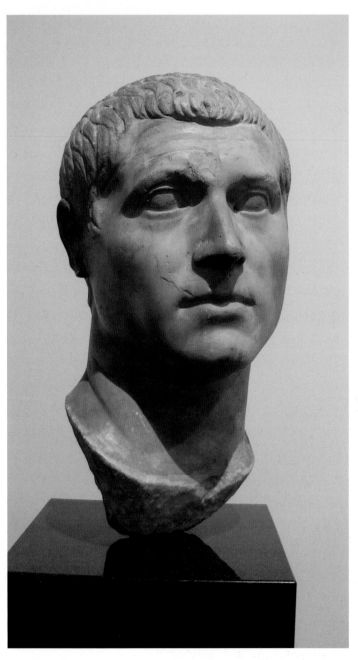

1.1   Julio-Claudian man, portrait from Pyramid Hill Sculpture Park Ancient Sculpture Museum, Hamilton OH. Photo courtesy Steven L. Tuck.

CULTURAL PROPERTY CONTROVERSIES

As I write this, and no doubt as you read it as well, one of the major controversies in art history and archaeology is over matters of cultural property. Museum professionals, academics, legal authorities, law enforcement officers, and diplomatic corps around the world have debated the question of who owns the past. Works that made their way into museum collections from the art market, such as the example below, legally purchased in an auction in New York at Sotheby's or Christie's and now in a small museum, are gaining increased scrutiny from foreign governments and art historians.

Some governments have called for the return of all such objects arguing that their **provenance**, the chain of ownership from the ground to the present day, cannot be proven and they might be the result of looting and illegal export. Art historians are drawn into this debate as they wrestle with issues of whether museum acquisition or even publication of these objects encourages the looting of archaeological sites by creating or encouraging the market in this material. Add to that the problem of fake or forged objects and it becomes very complicated and potentially controversial to handle objects that have recently come to light through the art market. Some have advocated for cut off dates that would prohibit the study and publication of recently acquired works while others have gone so far as to argue that professionals should only publish works with unbroken strings of legal ownership. Virtually all professionals, no matter where they stand in the debate, agree that we must be aware of and acknowledge issues of poor provenance. We should be aware that the lack of precise provenance information does limit what we can say about particular works. The example above could be from any one of a number of contexts: a tomb, a house, or a dedicatory statue in a public space such as a forum. Each one of those spaces would carry its own meaning and change how the work was viewed in antiquity and, given its provenance on the art market, we will never know that. But we will never know that for the vast majority of ancient art, even works that have eyewitness accounts of their excavation. Factor in the lack of documentation even for indisputably legitimate works such as the Portland Vase (Figure 5.27) and Ficoroni Cista (Figure 3.17) with long chains of ownership and it is clear that we cannot limit ourselves only to a discussion of works whose exact placement from the ancient world is transmitted to us. There are, however, works that should be and currently are being questioned, challenging our assumptions about what we know with confidence.

DATING DILEMMAS IN ROMAN ART HISTORY

Most dates assigned to works of art from the Roman world are not absolute. That is, they are not linked to a firm calendar, but are relative, determined by comparing an art work to one or more other examples with more or less similar characteristics. This gives us a series of relative, and sometimes very insecure, dates all based on some key works of art. When the dates of those key works are questioned, it has the potential to throw the whole system off. A case study in that issue is one of the most iconic works of Roman art, the Capitoline Wolf statue. This bronze statue of the she-wolf that saved Romulus and Remus, on display in Rome since 1471, has long been a staple work of art history texts. It has been republished and discussed for over two hundred years as an Etruscan masterpiece of the fifth century BCE.

Some authors have argued that it was in fact the same piece of sculpture mentioned by the Roman politician/author Cicero in the first century BCE. Since 2006, however, the scholarly world has reevaluated this based on a number of arguments including the type of casting process and the results of scientific tests such as thermoluminescence dating. These combined with reexamination of the style of work have led to new conclusions that the wolf is actually a medieval work, not an Etruscan one, perhaps dating to the thirteenth century CE. Thus, if they are correct, this work was misdated by as much as 1800 years and is eliminated as an ancient piece of sculpture, let alone a famous one. This sort of reevaluation is an important part of art historical study and it means that the field is constantly changing.

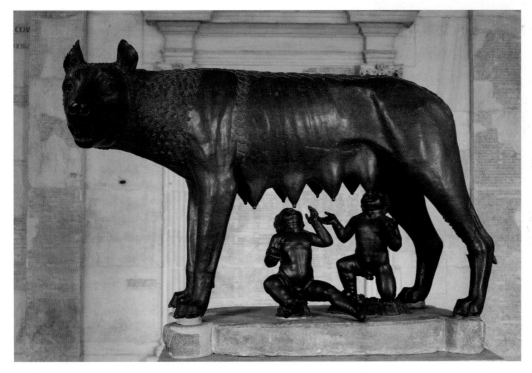

1.2   Capitoline She-wolf statue, 5th cent. BCE or 13th cent. CE, Musei Capitolini, Rome. H 29 ½ in (75 cm) L 44 ¾ in (114 cm). Photo courtesy Steven L. Tuck.

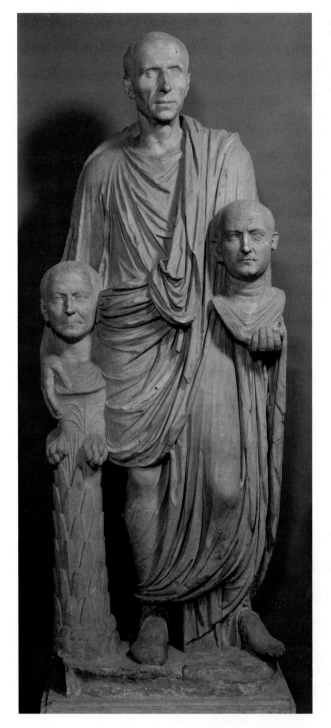

1.3   Statue of Roman man with busts of ancestors, "Barbarini Togatus," 1st cent. CE and 16th cent. CE. Musei Capitolini Centrale Montemartini, Rome. H 5 ft 5 in (1.65 m). Source: © 2014. Photo Scala, Florence. Courtesy of Soprintendenza di Roma Capitale.

RESTORATION ISSUES IN ROMAN ART HISTORY

A somewhat hidden problem in the study of Roman art is the role of reconstructions or restorations. Most works that survive are damaged in some way leading to restoration or reconstruction, particularly prior to museum display. What is not readily apparent is that the resulting work then represents a series of conclusions made by the restorers and not an ancient work of art per se. In effect, reconstructions mask the tremendous number of uncertainties and suppositions scholars are faced with. In previous centuries the goal of restoration was to make an object look new so that the actual ancient portion could not be distinguished from the more recent repairs.

An excellent example of this is the statue that has been displayed and published in many art history texts as a Roman man holding the busts of his ancestors. It is a great piece for teaching about ancestor busts, dynastic display, and Roman piety. The problem is that the statue is actually a pastiche of fragments of a number of ancient statues, some male, some female, and close examination suggests that it bears no resemblance to any original ancient work. As such, it really tells us nothing about the form, meaning, or display of ancient art. But it says much about the restoration of ancient art since the fifteenth century and how that has changed our view of the Roman world. With that in mind, we need to cover some cultural elements of the Roman world that we might assume are identical to the same elements in our world, but are not. Awareness of these cultural constructions and their effect on art is critical to our full understanding of the art as they are frequently embedded in the art. It will be impossible to cover all of the cultural differences between ourselves and the Romans. A few examples, however, should make the point that the Romans do not live in our world. Their world has its own culturally constructed values and artistic forms that reflect those.

THE ROLE OF ELITES IN PUBLIC ART AND ARCHITECTURE

In the modern western world most major public works are paid for by government at a variety of levels. Taxes are collected to pay for infrastructure from roads and bridges to water supply and drainage systems, and for all manner of public buildings from court houses to entertainment venues. Public officials administer these things and are paid salaries for their jobs. In the Roman world none of these steps were part of the culture. Taxes did not cover infrastructure projects; they were simply too low. Instead, elite Romans personally paid for all of the categories of projects listed above. In return their names were attached to the projects. This had been the case in Rome for a long time. The pattern was established at least as early as the last king of Rome, Tarquinius Superbus

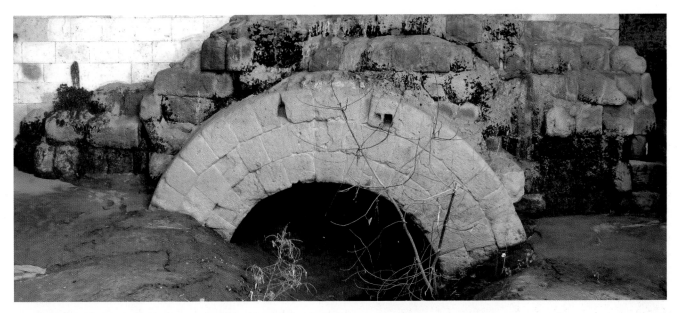

1.4   Cloaca Maxima (Great Drain) outlet to the Tiber, Rome, *c.* 510 BCE. Photo courtesy Steven L. Tuck.

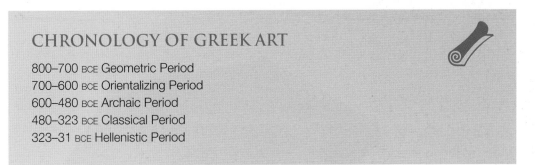

CHRONOLOGY OF GREEK ART

800–700 BCE Geometric Period
700–600 BCE Orientalizing Period
600–480 BCE Archaic Period
480–323 BCE Classical Period
323–31 BCE Hellenistic Period

(535–509 BCE). He commissioned the great Temple of Jupiter Optimus Maximus on the Capitoline Hill. More importantly for the development of Roman urban space, he also began the Cloaca Maxima, the Great Drain, that drained water from all the low areas of the city between the hills. This allowed Romans to build in the areas that would become, for example, the Forum Romanum and later imperial fora.

This also set the precedent for later Romans at all levels that the expectation was for them to commission public art and architecture for the entire community. Rome's great early highway, the Via Appia, was named for the man who paid for it, Appius Claudius Caecus. There was a critical side-effect to this expectation for Roman art. Statues of those who used their wealth on behalf of the community were created and placed in the community, extending their reputation and image.

ITALIC VERSUS CLASSICAL STYLES AND FORMS I: TEMPLES

It might first be helpful to point out that the Romans also differed from other ancient people in their art and architectural forms. Contrasting Greek and Roman temples makes a good visual case for that difference. This Roman style temple is often referred to as **Etrusco-Italic** because of its use in many cultures and communities in central Italy.

Etrusco-Italic refers to architecture, especially temples, shared by cultures of central Italy. The temples generally featured tall podiums, deep front porches, wide roofs, small cellas, and rooftop sculptures.

(a)

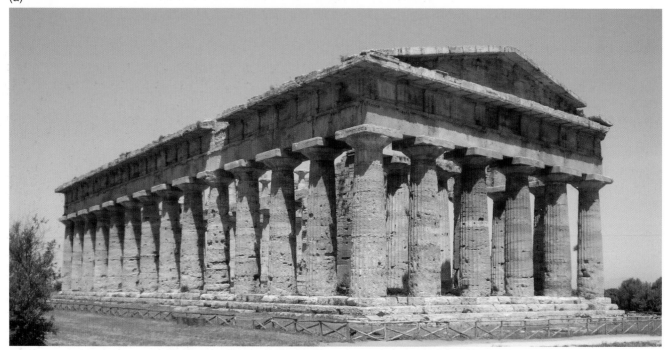

(b)

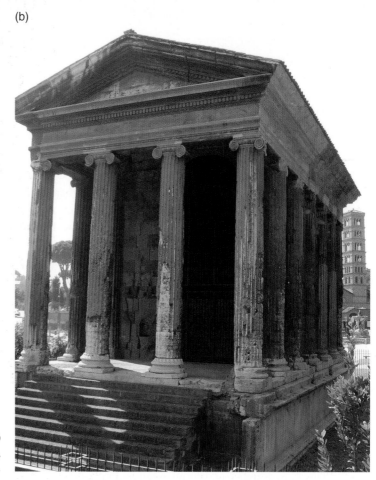

1.5a and 1.5b   Greek Temple of Hera, Paestum, *c.* 450
BCE, compared with Roman Temple of Portunus, Rome,
c. 150 BCE. Photos courtesy Steven L. Tuck.

Greek temples were generally very large buildings; this example is 197 ft (60 m) in length. Roman temples, based on the traditions of the Etruscans, were generally much smaller, here 85 ft 4 in (26 m) in length. The Greek temple is raised on a three-step platform while the Roman one has a tall 7 ½ ft (2.3 m) podium. This changes the relationship of the temple to the viewer as the Greek temple is accessible from all sides while the Roman one is strictly frontal and forces anyone approaching to do so from one direction. It essentially channels anyone viewing or engaging with the temple into a single point of view. By contrast, the Greek temple is **peripteral** with a colonnade that extends to all four sides allowing approach from every direction and actually shielding the building within so that the front and rear are virtually indistinguishable. Probably as a result of their frontality Roman temples were more often found on hills projecting the religious and cultural identity of a community.

peripteral
refers to a building, usually a temple, with a single row of columns surrounding it.

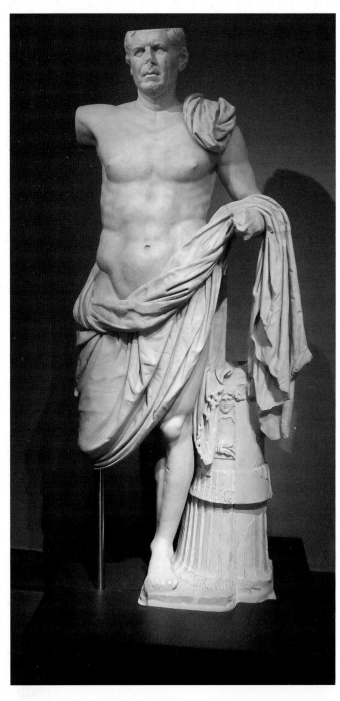

ITALIC VERSUS CLASSICAL STYLES AND FORMS II: PORTRAITURE

Many art history texts which cover the Roman world use a terminology of plebeian, a term referring to the Roman lower class, art versus patrician, referring to the Roman upper class, art. The former is used to refer to art whose characteristics largely follow the style and conventions of the native Italic works while the latter, patrician, refers to Classical, Greek-inspired, works. This concept and the associated terms plebeian and patrician are not used in this book. It applies a set of class distinctions to the art that is simply not accurate. When we note the Italic (the preferred term here rather than plebeian) style of a relief dedicated by a Roman emperor, to refer to it as plebeian is absurd. These are not classes of art or people, but choices of styles that in fact do not exist in an Italic versus Greek dichotomy, but as a range of options in which in many cases elements of the styles are blended to serve the needs of the artist and patron and to speak to the viewer in a new way. Some of the best examples of this deliberate use of Greek or Italic antecedents can be found in Roman portraiture, which demonstrate the meanings inherent in much of the art. Portraits as symbols of communication, especially under the principate (period of rule by a *princeps*, colloquially known as an emperor) represent a dialogue between the ruler and the ruled. This is particularly true when they are not set up by emperors but by others. In some cases this means that they reflect an acceptance of the cultural, political, and social premises of Roman artistic display.

Roman art can be seen, despite the style of a particular work, as a semantic system that conveys various meanings and values in a visual way. This makes sense in a society covering a vast geographical

1.6 Victorious general from Tivoli, Italy, *c.* 75–50 BCE. Museo Nazionale Romano Palazzo Massimo, Rome. H 6 ft 1 in (186.5 cm). Photo courtesy Steven L. Tuck.

and cultural area with a very low literacy rate and no better means of mass communication than the visual. The arts helped to create and transmit a Roman cultural identity across the Roman world. The style may or may not be a component of this, but the work can also, through its elements of subject, form, and structure, convey a variety of meanings.

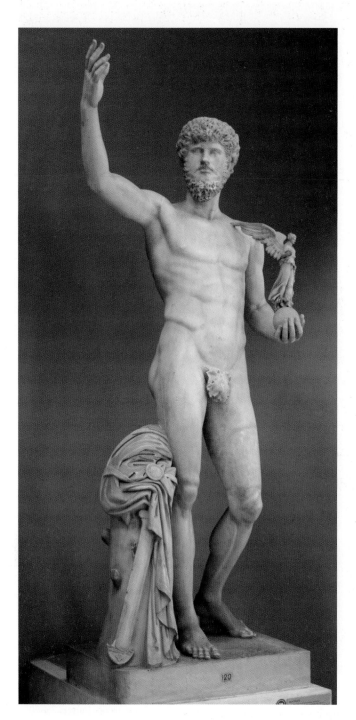

1.7 Emperor Lucius Verus as victorious athlete, *c.* 169 CE, Rome. Musei Vaticani, Rome. Photo courtesy Steven L. Tuck.

To many modern viewers the image of a victorious general – the subject is confirmed by the use of a set of body armor as a strut supporting the left leg – might resemble the "after" photo for an exercise program. It seemingly incongruously combines an idealized, youthful, bulky, muscular body with a craggy, lined face with sagging skin and a wrinkled neck. To a Roman observer it indicates two separate sets of artistic conventions, and therefore cultural values, combined in a single work of art. The craggy portrait face is the Italic tradition conveying the qualities of dignity and maturity of the depicted man, while the muscular youthful body shows the Hellenistic Greek heroization of rulers from the Greek world after the death of Alexander the Great. Together, they merge into a new form of Roman portraiture in the first century BCE. The imagery of victory was important in the Roman world and their readiness to adopt Greek conventions demonstrates the fluidity of the Roman system and its basis on the personal choices of subjects, artists, and patrons.

While modeling the sort of analysis you will find later in the book, mention should be made of the importance of literary reference to our understanding of art. You might think this statue reflects only the personal preference of the person portrayed as a victorious general. In fact, it is only one in a long line of statues that demonstrates broader Roman cultural values as the Roman politician and author Cicero makes clear in his work *De Officiis* (Concerning Duties 1.61):

When, on the other hand, we wish to pay a compliment, we somehow or other praise in more eloquent strain the brave and noble work of some great soul. Hence there is an open field for orators on the subjects of Marathon, Salamis, Plataea, Thermopylae, and Leuctra [famous battles], and hence our own Cocles, the Decii, Gnaeus and Publius Scipio, Marcus Marcellus, and countless others, and, above all, the Roman People as a nation are celebrated for greatness of spirit. Their passion for military glory, moreover, is shown in the fact that we see their statues usually in soldier's garb.

Another example of the blending of iconography and projected message is in the statue of a Roman emperor, Lucius Verus, as a victorious athlete. The semantic expression in the statue of Lucius Verus communicates a number of lessons. It is portraiture (giving as the Roman writer, Pliny the Elder, says, "an accurate likeness"), ruler imagery, and a victory monument of a successful military leader (the sword and military cloak near his right foot), but also utilizes the vocabulary of the victorious Greek athlete in its nudity. Roman viewers, depending on their level of visual literacy, could engage the image and any or all of these lessons from it. The fully heroic nudity of Lucius Verus is in contrast to the draped figure from Tivoli. In this case the convention seems to have changed in

the more than two hundred years between the two sculptures as nudity is now socially acceptable in an image for a Roman elite male celebrating victory.

Almost a hundred years after the statue of Lucius Verus, the image of another Roman emperor, Trebonianus Gallus, shows another shift in the form and meaning of these victory images. In the case of the Gallus statue, it retains the heroic nudity that first entered Roman art three hundred years earlier from Greek conventions of ruler representation. But here the Greek sculptural proportions, either the Hellenistic ones of the Tivoli general or the Classical ones of Lucius Verus, are abandoned in favor of a completely different set of proportions. The figure has, by Classical conventional terms, a tiny head and undeveloped musculature. But rather than conclude that these features are the result of poor art, as has been argued in the past, it is probably a deliberate attempt to exploit the traditional imagery of the victorious ruler/athlete with an image that conveys the massive power of the emperor over his pretensions of Classical cultural connections. The issue of judging art and its values and class connections is an important topic and one that art historians debate, as did the Romans.

FEMALE PORTRAITURE AND EMBEDDED VALUES

In 1711 in southern Italy workmen digging a well hit a set of ancient statues that were part of the remains of the city of Herculaneum, destroyed by the eruption of Vesuvius in 79 CE. Two of these have become known as the Large and Small Herculaneum Woman statues. Both of the standing women are dressed in a combination of a dress and mantle, the traditional dress for elite Roman women. The Large Herculaneum Woman has her mantle pulled up to cover her head, a sign of piety. The Small Herculaneum Woman seems to be younger, possibly unmarried, and pulls her mantle around her body in a gesture of modesty.

If these were unique statues, they might not be worth discussing here, but they are not. Far from it. In fact, more than 180 copies or variations of the Large Woman type and 160 of the Small Woman type are now known along with a number of variations in relief on tombstones and sarcophagi. The majority have individualized facial features, some amounting to portraits, indicating that the types were widespread throughout the Roman world. Their popularity derived at least in part from their ability to convey elite female values through the figures' poses and dress.

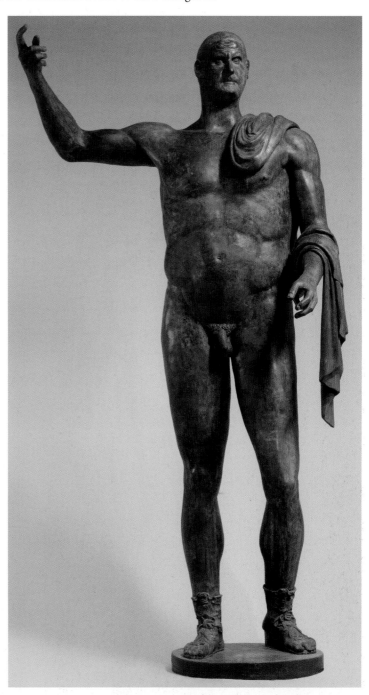

1.8 Trebonianus Gallus bronze portrait, 251–253 CE, in the Metropolitan Museum of Art, New York. H 95 in (241.3 cm). Source: © 2014. Image copyright The Metropolitan Museum of Art/Art Resource/Scala, Florence.

(a)

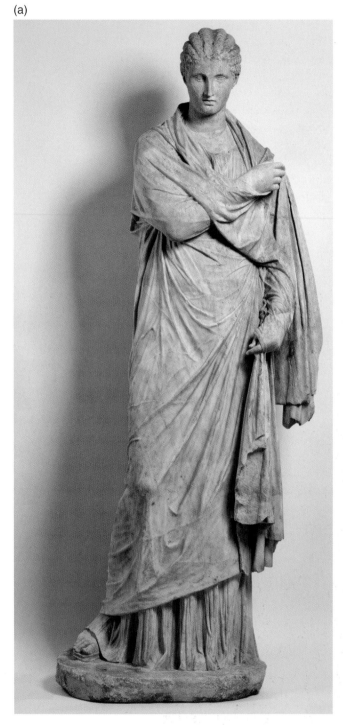

(b)

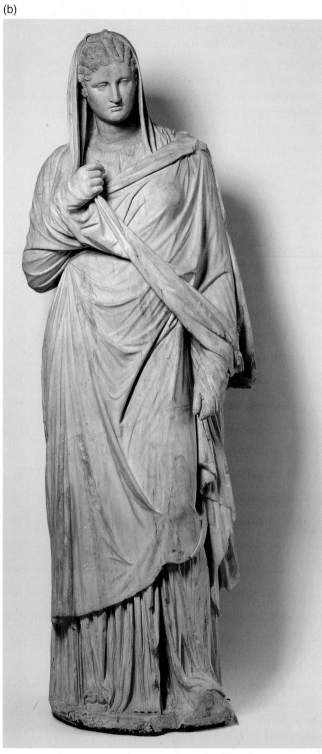

1.9a and 1.9b Small Herculaneum Woman Statue, 1st cent. CE, Skulpturensammlung, Staatliche Kunstsammlungen Dresden, H 71 ¼ in (1.8 m), and Large Herculaneum Woman Statue, 1st cent. CE, Skulpturensammlung, Staatliche Kunstsammlungen Dresden, H 78 in (1.98 m). Source: ©Skulpturensammlung, Staatliche Kunstsammlungen Dresden. Photos: Ingrid Geske.

ROMANS JUDGING ROMAN ART: VALUES AND CLASS

On the issue of judging art, its projected values, and the class connections it conveys, we need to avoid bringing our own class values and judgments with us as we examine the art. However, we need to be aware of and take into account ancient Roman class conventions and judgments. For this, the study of the art can be greatly helped by ancient literary sources in which authors comment on the art, its meaning, and contemporary attitudes towards it. Nowhere is that made more explicit than for still life paintings. A property in Pompeii, labeled on the outside in a for rent sign as the Praedia (estate) of Julia Felix, was decorated on the interior with a series of wall paintings. A number of these featured panels of still life scenes in which the images concentrated on food products. But these were food products of two particular types. One of these is *obsonia* and the other is *xenia*.

To us the subjects of the paintings might seem generic, which they were, and unworthy of comment other than whether they reflected the use of space. We might expect that these food scenes would be found in or around food preparation, storage, or serving areas, notably the latter, perhaps dining rooms. That does not seem to be the case for the Romans, who did not carry the same

obsonia
literally spoils or prizes, prepared food as a subject for painting in Hellenistic art.

xenia
guest gifts, a class of paintings described by the Roman architectural author Vitruvius, including provisions such as poultry, eggs, vegetables, fruit, and the like.

1.10 Still life paintings, Praedia of Julia Felix, Pompeii, *c.* 70 CE. Museo Archeologico Nazionale di Napoli. H 28 ¾ in (73 cm). Photo courtesy Steven L. Tuck.

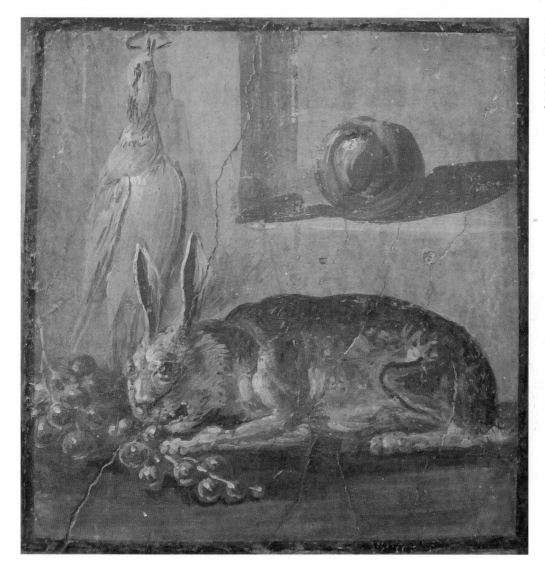

triclinium
Roman dining room laid out for nine diners reclining on three couches (in Greek: *tri cline*) from which the room gets its name.

tablinum
a room in the Roman house off the atrium and directly opposite the front door. It was the major formal reception room, used to receive clients and conduct business.

paradeisos
a walled park where wild animal hunts took place. A Persian concept adopted by the Greeks after the conquests of Alexander the Great.

unspoken expectations of space and use and decoration that we do. The subjects, however, carried connotations of class to a Roman viewer. Pliny the Elder, a contemporary author from the area writing on painters and paintings, notes (*Natural History* 37),

> We must now, however, make some mention of those artists who acquired fame by the pencil in an inferior style of painting. Among these was Piræicus, inferior to few of the painters in skill. I am not sure that he did not do injustice to himself by the choice of his subjects … His subjects were barbers' shops, cobblers' stalls, jackasses, eatables, and the like, and to these he was indebted for his epithet of "Ithyparographos," "Painter of Low Subjects."

In this digression, Pliny makes it clear that the painter could be skilled, but his subject is inferior and among those low forms was still life. Such a judgment is critically important evidence for us of what the Romans thought of painting and while we are historians of art, not critics of it, that in no way means that we should not be aware of the Roman attitudes towards art. For the Praedia of Julia Felix, the painting subjects provide valuable evidence that the estate was used by non-elites, perhaps rented for special events or existing as a sort of membership-only club for Pompeii's newly wealthy sub-elite inhabitants, often called the "middle class," to use a term that perhaps applies better to our world than to theirs. The idea of art as conveying class, status, and social and political rank and pretensions is also clear from tombs. One of the best examples of this, the Tomb of Vestorius Priscus, is also from Pompeii.

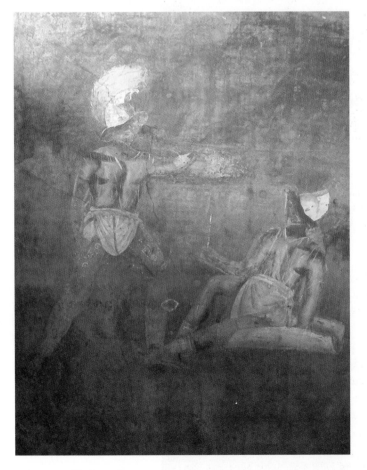

1.11   Gladiator fresco, Tomb of Vestorius Priscus, Pompeii, 75/76 CE. Photo courtesy Steven L. Tuck.

ART, CONTEXT, AND SOCIAL STATUS I: THE TOMB OF VESTORIUS PRISCUS

The Tomb of Vestorius Priscus, who was buried outside the Vesuvian Gate at Pompeii in 75/76 CE, is decorated with art that encourages our awareness of the theme of personal aggrandizement in Roman public art. The images in the central panels on the inner surfaces of the tomb's enclosure walls show a range of high status iconography designed to create an identity of the deceased as an important man in Pompeii defined by his public service and connections. The six major panels include a large silver table service of the type found on display in a *triclinium*, a high status banquet or symposium – likely also taking place in a *triclinium*, a pair of gladiators, Vestorius Priscus standing in the *tablinum* of his house – the room where he would receive clients, Priscus seated surrounded by attentive listeners, and a *paradeisos*. The outdoor scenes of Priscus and an audience and the *paradeisos* are joined by the pair of gladiators, essentially one of only three episodes outside of his home that represent his political and social status.

The gladiators probably represent one component of a set of games he hosted as *aedile* (a low level public official) at Pompeii, most likely in the year he died. That panel shows the connections between local elites and games that they sponsored, and demonstrates the close ties between their games and personal identity. Hosting games was as

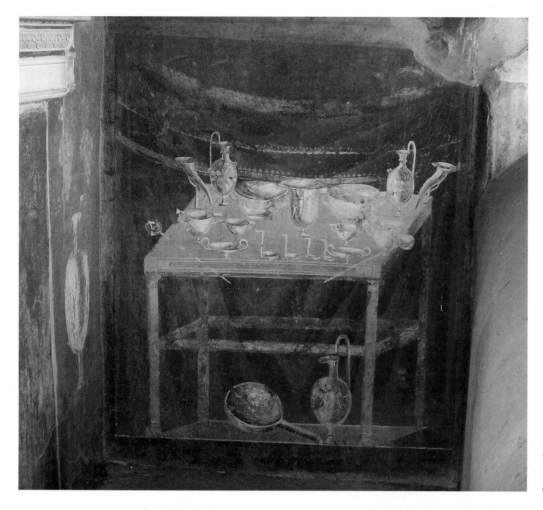

1.12 Silver service fresco, Tomb of Vestorius Priscus, Pompeii, 75/76 CE. Photo courtesy Steven L. Tuck.

important for a Roman politician as hosting dinners and receiving clients. The use of spectacle imagery in the domestic sphere also reinforces these conclusions about its critical role in projecting personal values and identity. The most common composition is a pair of gladiators engaged in combat as seen in the painting from the Tomb of Vestorius Priscus. The gladiators are almost universally armed and armored in ways that conform to the known categories of gladiators, giving these otherwise generic scenes a specificity that is probably important to the patron or audience. These images seem to represent one of three stages in gladiatorial combat: the initial clash with both combatants on their feet facing each other, an intermediate stage when one combatant is disarmed, on the ground or facing possible defeat, or the conclusion of a bout with the defeated either subdued, wounded and surrendering, or dead.

Three of the images are domestic and reinforce Priscus as a host, receiving clients and welcoming guests, while the silver service establishes his pretensions to high status domestic display. As modern viewers of this, we need to be aware that this seemingly circumstantial imagery is, or at least could be, something different than it appears. In the matter of images that convey status, we must remember that they are symbolic, not documentary. There is no evidence that Priscus had a silver service that looked like this, or, if he did, that it was on display in his home. This painting represents that Priscus is the type of person who would have this sort of display. It projects his status, not his ownership, much like the scene of Priscus surrounded by attentive listeners indicates status, but is not thought to reflect any particular episode. The emphasis on the spaces and decor of his home brings us to another issue, that of the place of the home in the Roman elite world. This represents another cultural gulf between ourselves and the Romans.

ART, CONTEXT, AND SOCIAL STATUS II: THE ROMAN HOUSE

One of the key issues to understanding Roman art is that of context. While we often divide the world between public and private spaces, with offices and shops as the default public spaces and home the private one, the Roman conception is more complex. In the Roman world high status authors spoke of the distinction between *otium* and *negotium*. Rather than business taking place in offices and private gatherings at home, the situation in the Roman world is that *negotium* took place in the home as well, but in certain spaces accessible and adjacent to the **atrium**. A quote from the Roman architectural writer Vitruvius can help make this point clear. Vitruvius, discussing the Roman house in his book *De Architectura* (6.5.1), notes,

> We must determine the situation of the private rooms for the master of the house, and those which are for general use, and for the guests. Into those which are private no one enters, except invited; such are bed chambers, dining rooms, baths, and others of a similar nature. The common rooms, on the contrary, are those entered by any one, even unasked. Such are the vestibule … the peristyle, and those which are for similar uses.

When we examine the layout and rooms of a Roman house, we need to think in Roman terms of public and private, not modern ones. Rather than the default that house = private space, it is critical to think as a Roman would and to distinguish the common rooms from others. For an elite Roman house, the front door would have been open throughout the daylight hours and anyone who wished was allowed in. According to Velleius Paterculus (2.14.3) when the architect working for Livius Drusus, Tribune of the Plebs in 91 BCE, promised to make his new house on the slope of the Palatine above the Forum "completely private and free from being overlooked by anyone," Livius replied, "No, you should apply your skills to arranging my house so that whatever I do should be visible to

otium
Latin term for leisure, it includes time spent on reading, writing, and academic activities, including rest. Often associated with the Roman villa as the space for *otium*.

negotium
Latin term for business (literally "not leisure"), including both public and private business.

atrium
the main or central room of a Roman house, usually directly accessible from the front door.

(a)

1.13a Cutaway of Roman *atrium* house. Reproduced with the permission of QA International, www.ikonet. com from the book *The Visual Dictionary*. © QA International, 2003. All rights reserved.

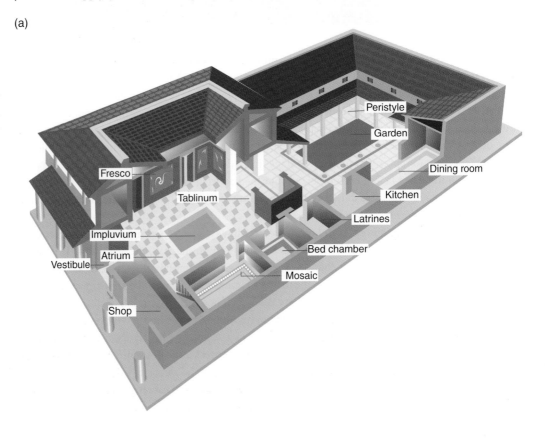

(b)

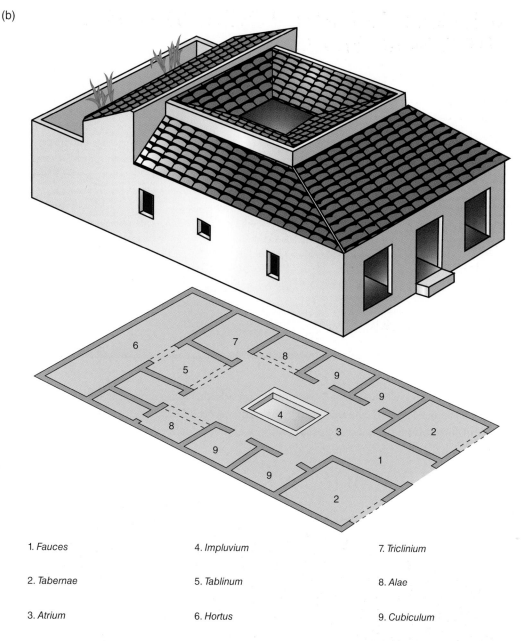

1. *Fauces*

2. *Tabernae*

3. *Atrium*

4. *Impluvium*

5. *Tablinum*

6. *Hortus*

7. *Triclinium*

8. *Alae*

9. *Cubiculum*

1.13b   Plan of Roman *atrium* house: T. Langhammer/Wikimedia Commons.

everybody." As a result the decor of the front rooms was designed in much the same way a public building was, with a notion of the expected audience. It became a stage to present a public image of the family to those passing on the street and to those who chose to enter. Much of the family's public image derives from the public service, either civic or military, of the men in the family. The *atrium* was decorated with their military trophies and achievements, busts of ancestors who had served the state, and this became the means of projecting status. That led to embellishments such as on this house found at Pompeii.

A wreath called a ***corona civica*** dominates the space above the front door. A wreath on the front of a house may say nothing to us, but to the Romans it was special. This is the wreath granted to a Roman citizen for saving the life of another citizen in battle. It was placed above the door to his home and marked out everyone in this domestic space through their association with the honoree of the wreath. The first Roman emperor, Augustus, had a wreath like this marking his front door as well. The benches on either side of the front door are a common feature flanking the doors of wealthy

corona civica

the civic crown, a wreath of oak leaves, a tree sacred to Jupiter, awarded to Roman citizens who saved the lives of other citizens in battle

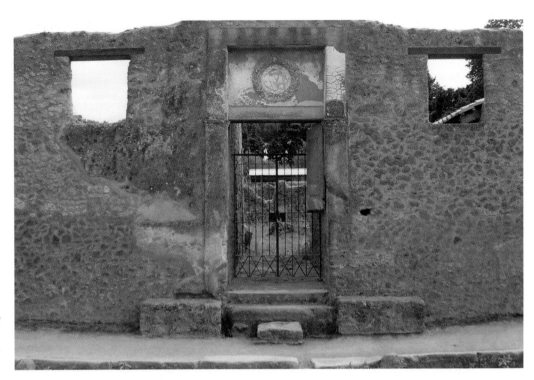

1.14 Facade photo of Roman house, Pompeii. Photo courtesy Steven L. Tuck.

houses at Pompeii. We believe that those with business in the house or visiting it could use them to wait for an audience with the homeowner. Visually, they serve, like the wreath, to mark an elite home, distinguishing it from the houses of people without as much public service.

NARRATIVE MOMENT

Finally, it will be useful here to introduce among these concepts, the concept of narrative in art. Much of Roman art tells stories to the viewer and the ways in which those stories were told can differ dramatically. Ability to recognize narrative moments and the types of narrative used by artists can help art historians to analyze works and the meaning intended by the artist. For those stories illustrated by a single episode the moment selected falls into one of four categories: the initial moment of a story, the anticipatory moment (prior to the climax), the climactic moment, or the post-climactic moment. Each gives a very different image and makes its own demands upon the viewer. The initial moment of the story only implies the further story to come. For example, the relief of a religious ceremony to found a Roman colony (Figure 3.21) need only show a Roman priest plowing while wearing his formal attire to convey the idea of the city about to be founded. The anticipatory moment relies on dramatic tension rather than explicit action to allude to a story. The colossal sculpture group of the blinding of the Cyclops, Polyphemus (Figure 6.7) illustrates the moment just before he is blinded. The climactic moment is often the moment of the greatest action as the battle relief of the monument of Aemilius Paullus (Figure 4.31) uses to great effect. The post-climactic scene often allows artists to concentrate on the emotional effect of an event or its outcome. The relief of the Emperor Trajan being crowned by Victory herself (Figure 8.24) carries with it the notion of the battles won without showing them more directly.

The various solutions for telling a story with multiple scenes were developed by Greek artists as they worked to create recognizable mythological narration. The major conventions are episodic, continuous, and synoptic narrative. Episodic narrative consists of a story told in a series of separate episodes, usually, but not invariably, arranged in chronological order. The Hadrianic Hunting Tondi

(Figure 8.27) with their paired scenes of hunting and post-hunt sacrifice are episodic. Continuous narrative tells a story in one work of art usually with the same characters portrayed repeatedly to create a sequence. The repeated figures are not separated by borders as are episodic scenes. The Column of Marcus Aurelius (Figure 9.14) exemplifies one of the longest continuous narratives in Roman art. Synoptic narrative occurs when different elements or symbols of a story are placed in one image together to give a synopsis of the overall story. Sometimes devices such as placing the climactic scene in the foreground indicate the narrative sequence. The pediment relief sculpture from Temple A, Pyrgi (Figure 3.5) illustrates synoptic narrative. The figures in the lower foreground represent the climax of the story while those in the background fill out the narrative with pre- and post-climactic secondary events from the same story.

Although these names are not applied explicitly to every work in the following chapters, that's not to say that they cannot be. You are encouraged to ask which narrative moment a work represents and how that decision affects the presentation and meaning of the art. Your answers to these and other questions on the themes covered can serve as some of the building blocks of art historical studies.

SUGGESTIONS FOR FURTHER READING

John R. Clarke, *Art in the Lives of Ordinary Romans: Visual Representation and Non-Elite Viewers in Italy, 100 B.C.–A.D. 315* (Berkeley 2003). Examines the art designed for and sometimes created by slaves, former slaves, foreigners, and the free poor in the Roman world.

Christopher H. Hallett, *The Roman Nude: Heroic Portrait Statuary 200 B.C.–A.D. 300* (Oxford University Press 2005). Surveys the many examples of male and female nude portrait and sets them in cultural context. Investigates the origins and Roman understanding of these portraits using nudity as an important form of costume.

Tonio Hölscher, *The Language of Images in Roman Art* (Cambridge University Press 2004). If you don't believe me that Roman art operates as a semantic system that expresses values, this book will convince you. Gives a great deal of attention to the role of Greek art in later Roman art.

Elizabeth Marlowe, *Shaky Ground: Context, Connoisseurship and the History of Roman Art* (Bristol Classical Press 2013). The recent crisis in the world of antiquities collecting has prompted scholars and the general public to pay more attention than ever before to the questions of archaeological findspots and collecting history for newly found objects. This book argues that the question of archaeological origins should be the first one asked not only by museum acquisitions boards but by scholars as well.

Peter Stewart, *The Social History of Roman Art* (Cambridge University Press 2008). The character of Roman art history has changed in recent years. More than ever before, it is concerned with the role of art in ancient society, including the functions that it served and the values and assumptions that it reflects. Focusing on selected examples and themes, this book sets the images in context, explains how they have been interpreted, and points out where we have gone wrong in our interpretations of Roman art.

Jennifer Trimble, *Women and Visual Replication in Roman Imperial Art and Culture* (Cambridge University Press 2011). Focuses on the "Large Herculaneum Woman" statue type to assess how sameness helped to communicate a woman's social identity. The author demonstrates how visual replication in the Roman Empire thus emerged as a means of constructing social power and articulating dynamic tensions between empire and individual localities.

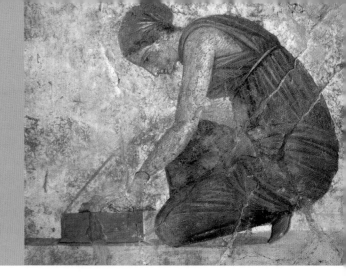

REGAL PERIOD, 753–509 BCE

The Etruscans and the Question of Etruscan Dominance

753 BCE	Founding of Rome by Romulus
753–509 BCE	Regal Period of Rome, rule by kings
670–650 BCE	**Regolini-Galassi tomb, Cerveteri**
600–550 BCE	**Tomb of the Shields and Chairs, Cerveteri**
535–509 BCE	Rome's last king, Tarquin the Proud, rules the city
530 BCE	**Tomb of the Augurs, Tomb of Hunting and Fishing, Tarquinia**
525 BCE	**Terracotta sarcophagus from Cerveteri**
510 BCE	**Apollo of Portonaccio sanctuary, Veii**
509 BCE	Founding of the Republic; first public games, the *ludi Romani*, held in Rome; inauguration of the **Temple of Jupiter Optimus Maximus**

A History of Roman Art, First Edition. Steven L. Tuck.
© 2015 Steven L. Tuck. Published 2015 by John Wiley & Sons, Ltd.

INTRODUCTION TO THE WORLD OF EARLY ROME AND ITALY

This chapter will cover the roughly 250 years during which Rome was ruled by kings. It will establish the role of the kings in creating expectations that government and elite individuals would act as patrons of public art, architecture, and spectacle in the Roman world. Based on the chapter title and works listed in the timeline an astute reader might be wondering as they begin this chapter where exactly the Romans are in this. In fact, they may have the same question when they finish the chapter. How is this Roman art? It's a fair question since much, in fact the majority, of the art in the chapter isn't Roman by any strict definition. That is, it was not necessarily made by Roman artists or for Roman art patrons. It is, however, the art that surrounded the early Romans, defined their cultural outlooks, and that which they themselves (as stated by later Roman authors) were inspired to imitate and use to define their world. It is the art from areas that shortly will be under the military, economic, and cultural control of the Romans. The extent of influence that the Etruscans and other peoples of early Italy had on Roman culture is a source of considerable scholarly debate. What is not debated is that the Romans attributed much of their culture including art and architecture to the Etruscans and other advanced cultures around them. In addition Etruscan art serves a number of useful purposes for our study of ancient art. It demonstrates cultural interaction and engagement while providing evidence of how and where Greek artistic trends and influences permeated ancient Italy. The premier example of this is the early inclusion of Greek mythological imagery in the arts of ancient Italy. Etruscan art also provides evidence of the common culture of ancient Italy and the many ways that the ancient Italians, Romans included, defined and illustrated their world and world views. The art and architecture of the earliest periods of Roman culture already demonstrate many cultural values that define the Romans in later times. Their inclusive culture, welcoming foreign influences especially in the areas of religion and art, starts early. Also found early is the use of public art and architecture by elites to define and celebrate their status and contributions to the community through the type and grandeur of their public monuments.

The traditional date for the founding of Rome, 753 BCE, places the formation of the city in a period of dramatic change and an explosion of urban development in ancient Italy. The first Greek colony in the west, Cumae, just north of the Bay of Naples, was founded in approximately 775 BCE. The Etruscans responded in about 770 BCE by founding the nearby city of Capua in an attempt to check Greek control over Campania and the spread of Greek colonies. In both, they failed. Rome, therefore, had its origin in a world dominated by two civilizations, the Greeks and the Etruscans, who were rapidly expanding throughout Italy to control its rich resources and to exploit its critical geographical position in the Mediterranean for their own purposes. The Italian peninsula is situated as the perfect crossroads for travel both east–west and north–south across the Mediterranean. Many people entered and occupied this remarkable crossroads, including Greeks and Phoenicians from the eastern Mediterranean, Italic peoples like the Romans and their neighbors the Latins, Samnites who occupied the Apennine mountains in the center of Italy, and the Etruscans whose homeland in modern Tuscany and Umbria gave them a base for expansion south leading to contact and conflict with the Greek colonies of southern Italy and Sicily. Given this geography it would be amazing if the Romans did not absorb ideas from the advanced and expansionist cultures that literally surrounded them. In fact, the Etruscans are considered by many scholars to have contributed the most to the development of Roman culture. The Romans themselves made this point, attributing much that defined them to the Etruscans, making them the subject of study by Roman scholars such as Livy (59 BCE–17 CE), Varro (116–27 BCE), and the Roman emperor Claudius (reigned 41–54 CE), who wrote a twenty-volume history of the Etruscans.

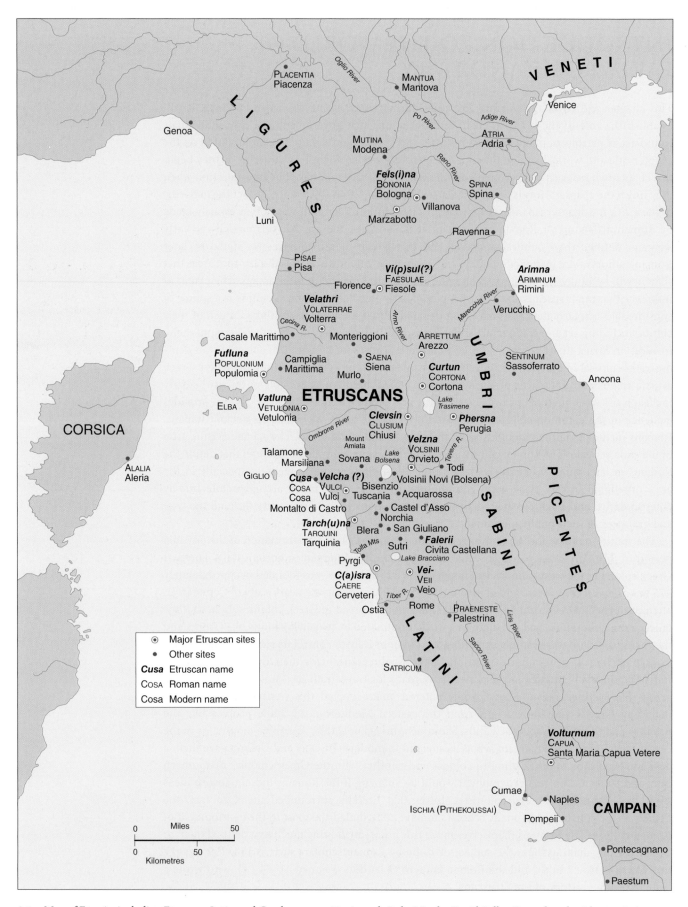

2.1   Map of Etruria, including Etruscan, Latin, and Greek communities in early Italy. Map by David Fuller. Reproduced, with permission, from *Etruscan Civilization: A Cultural History* by Sybille Haynes, © 2000 the J. Paul Getty Trust.

THE ETRUSCANS

The Etruscans were the advanced civilization whose homeland, Etruria, bordered Latin territory and the area of Rome itself. The word most often used in modern books to describe the Etruscans is "mysterious." Their origins, language, government, myths, and many of their cultural habits and customs are imperfectly known and the source of great speculation by both ancient and modern authors. Take the issue of origins for example. Ancient authors debate whether the Etruscans were emigrants to Italy from the eastern Mediterranean (like the Greeks and Phoenicians) or whether they represent a stage of cultural development of the area's native inhabitants. Those authors used evidence such as burial practices and shape of Etruscan footwear to compare the Etruscans to other people perhaps related to them. Modern scholarship contributes linguistic and genetic analysis to this discussion. The result of this scholarship is not unanimous agreement on the origins of the Etruscans. We do, however, know far more than we used to thanks largely to archaeology, especially excavations of their necropoleis, cities of the dead.

These sites are important, as their actual cities, largely fortified hilltop communities, lie under currently occupied cities such as Siena and Orvieto. In a pattern similar to their Greek contemporaries, the Etruscans formed a loose confederacy of individual city-states with a shared language, religion, and culture, but without political unity. The city-states of southern Etruria including Caere (Cerveteri), Tarquinii, Vulci, and Veii developed beginning in the eighth century BCE into a formidable group of communities controlling vast territories including, at least briefly in the sixth century BCE, Rome itself. Rome came eventually to absorb all of Etruria by the third century BCE, but not before the Romans themselves absorbed many elements of Etruscan culture, a pattern that would repeat itself later as the Romans encountered and conquered other areas in Italy and beyond.

Etruscan art is largely known from grave goods and the wall paintings that decorated the tombs themselves in the extensive necropoleis found outside their communities. In addition to the tomb material, some art, notably sculpture, has been found in sanctuaries and in one well-preserved and excavated Etruscan domestic complex at Poggio Civitate, Murlo. The major categories of Etruscan art included tomb paintings, bronze statuary, gold jewelry, and terracotta works including free-standing sculpture, relief plaques, and decorative vessels. In all of these media we see a number of consistent patterns. First, the Etruscans were, if not originators, then innovators in portraiture. They created a well-developed portrait tradition of images that transcended the generic. They created what has been termed true portraiture, capturing the image as well as character of the person portrayed, in other words, art that showed both what someone looked like as well as what they were like.

One of the larger patterns identified in Etruscan art was a close connection to the current subjects, materials, and style trends in Greek art in the city-states of southern Italy and Sicily. Clearly the Etruscans were aware of the latest styles, valued Greek art, and may have imported it as well as invited Greek artists to work in Etruscan communities. This Greek art profoundly changed Etruscan art, both initially and as styles developed, perhaps only a generation behind the leading styles and subjects in Greek art. This was a critical early source of Roman exposure to Greek art as the subjects, styles, and media of Greek art were transmitted to Rome via Etruria centuries prior to the Roman conquest of Greek city-states. Because many cities founded by the Etruscans are still occupied today, we can study their architecture and city planning only partially through those sites, but more directly at their necropoleis.

Etruscan architecture and city planning

One of the best sites to study Etruscan grave goods, tomb decoration, and the development of architecture and city planning is the Banditaccia necropolis at the Etruscan city of Caere (modern Cerveteri). The necropolis is the largest surviving one in the Mediterranean, containing thousands of tombs organized along roads with gutters, drains, and sidewalks, all elements taken from Etruscan urban planning. The tombs date from the eighth to the third centuries BCE with the earliest examples

necropolis (pl. necropoleis) from Greek, literally "a city of the dead." Refers to the extramural cemeteries often mimicking real cities organized by family tombs shaped like houses, sometimes with roads, sidewalks, and drains.

(a)

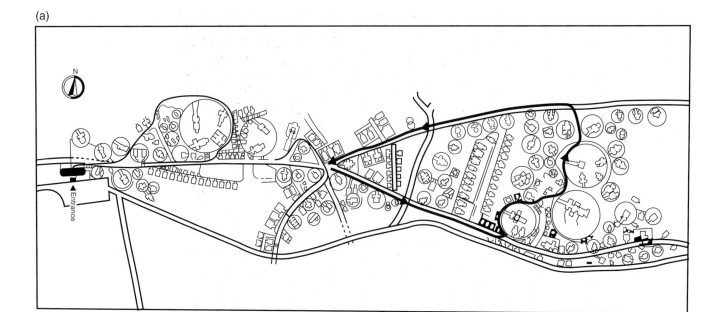

(b)

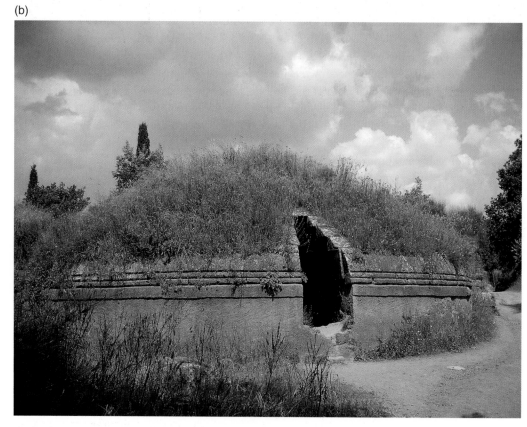

2.2a and 2.2b Plan of the Etruscan Banditaccia necropolis, Cerveteri and photo of tumulus. (a) Plan: M. Cristofani, G. Nardi, M.A. Rizzo, Caere 1. Il Parco Archeologico, Roma, 1988. Consiglio Nazionale delle Ricerche. (b) Photo courtesy Steven L. Tuck.

tumulus
a type of tomb with a mound raised over it. Etruscan examples cover chamber tombs that belonged to extended families. Large tumuli resemble small hills.

being large circular grass-covered mounds, a type referred to as a **tumulus**. These had interiors of carved tombs, often three or four to a mound, carved out of the volcanic bedrock.

The tombs are generally organized with a central passage leading to a series of chambers that are believed to imitate the room size, shape, and organization in Etruscan houses. Many of the tombs are carved to resemble the timber framing and other perishable materials that actual Etruscan houses were constructed with. Most have elements that were necessary in a real house including a central

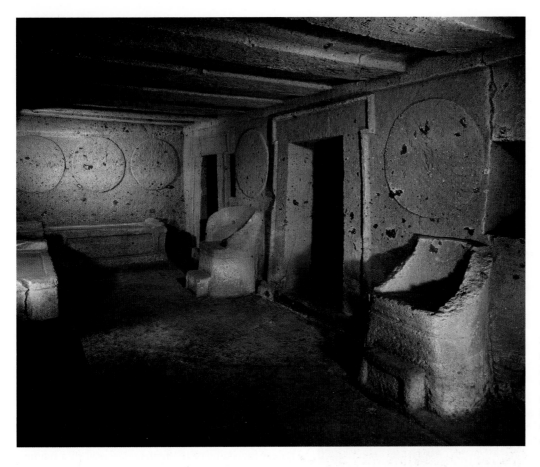

2.3 Tomb of the Shields and Chairs plan, Banditaccia necropolis, Cerveteri, *c.* 550 BCE. Source: © 2014. Photo Scala, Florence. Courtesy of the Ministero Beni e Att. Culturali.

ridge beam that runs along the length of the roof with timber joists attached to it, all supported by columns and pillars. The decoration often imitates domestic furnishings as well, with carved beds and chairs.

Two design features found repeatedly in the tombs are seen in contemporary Etruscan and later Roman building practice in both houses and temples. The first feature is that the tombs/houses are organized symmetrically with a long axis placing the entrance at a short end and the rooms clustered at the far end. The second feature is a tendency towards tripartite organization, with rooms often appearing in groups of three, as in the Tomb of the Greek Vases, and wall niches to hold bodies are also found in threes, as in the Tomb of the Reliefs. Both of these design features are found together in the Tomb of the Shields and Chairs. The tomb seems to be designed to reflect Etruscan domestic architecture. Although carved out of solid rock, it has elements of wood construction: ceiling beams, door frames, and moldings. The layout includes features found in later Roman houses (see Figure 4.17, Plan of the House of the Faun) including the central hallway leading into a single common room, which will become the atrium in the Roman house. Opposite the entrance is a three-room suite with a wider central room flanked by two smaller side rooms, features that reflect tripartite temples as well as the Roman *tablinum*. Finally, the carved chairs and shields reflect the two outlets for elite male competition: warfare, symbolized by the shields, and government service, symbolized by the chairs conferred upon community magistrates.

Etruscan Orientalizing art

The art of this period, exemplified by the fibula in Figure 2.4, is known as **Orientalizing**. The material (imported gold), subjects, and decorative motifs follow the Orientalizing style popular in Greece in the seventh century BCE. These elements of the work are based on Greek models that were

Orientalizing
style of art based on ideas, forms, and materials from the Near East and Egypt. In Greek art, it dominates the period 700–600 BCE.

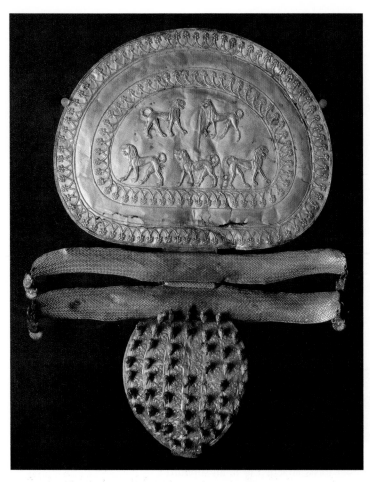

2.4   Gold fibula, 650 BCE, from the Regolini-Galassi tomb, Cerveteri. Musei Vaticani, Rome. 1 ft ½ in (31 cm). Source: akg-images/ De Agostini Picture Library.

repoussé
a type of artwork, generally of metal, that features a design in raised relief created through hammering the material from the reverse side.

register
division of an artistic field into parallel columns or rows. These, usually horizontal bands, act as groundlines and aid in creating narrative.

themselves inspired by works from the Near East, in particular from Assyrian subjects and designs. The Greek intermediary through which these were transmitted to the Etruscans was the city-state of Corinth, which exploited trade with the eastern Mediterranean to become rich and sent out its own colonies to spread its culture and influence through Greek lands. One of the largest, most impressive, and most important grave goods found at Cerveteri was the golden fibula – a pin used to fasten clothing, found in the burial of a high status woman whose body was laid out in one chamber of the large Regolini-Galassi tomb.

The fibula demonstrates the advanced specialized techniques of Etruscan jewelers whose work here includes granulation – fusing precious metal granules to the gold background to create patterns, filigree – ornamental work of fine gold wire formed into delicate tracery, and **repoussé**. The five striding lions, an Assyrian motif, and the filigree vine and rosettes that surround them are found on contemporary Corinthian pottery, which was imported into Etruscan communities at this time. The size of the fibula, just over a foot in length, and its material make clear that it is a symbolic and not a practical work for daily wear. It might have been created specifically for this burial to reflect the status of the female deceased in a manner parallel to the shields and chairs for men, each signifying high status in a gendered way. It has been proposed that the tripartite design of the fibula, which is not unique, reflects the Etruscan view of the world, with the lion panel representing the upper world, the lower panel the underworld, and the two strips in the middle with their pattern of parallel zigzag lines the rivers that separate the two. The fibula and Etruscan emphasis on elaborate jewelry also stands as an example of the statement of the Greek historian Diodorus Siculus (8.18.1) on the Etruscans that they "surpass the other barbarians [non-Greeks] in the extravagance of their way of life."

Another work of Etruscan art in the Orientalizing style is an ivory cylindrical box, called a pyxis as the Greek name for this shape, found in a grave in a necropolis at Chiusi, a central Etruscan city. Like the Regolini-Galassi fibula it represents the Orientalizing trend towards detailed small-scale decorative work on imported material, here ivory. Unlike the Assyrian-inspired designs on the fibula, these designs and figures rely directly on Greek models and show an awareness of Greek literature, specifically Homer's *Odyssey*.

The pyxis is divided into four long horizontal figural bands, called **registers**, separated by narrow bands of vine work similar to those on the Regolini-Galassi fibula and also derived from Corinthian painted pottery. The figures in the registers are carved in a style that lines them up so that they can all be clearly identified, with little overlapping, no depth, and proportions that emphasize oversized heads on squat bodies in a very careful style that will later be referred to as Italic, but seen here in early Etruscan art. In addition to figures of animals and monsters, types seen on contemporary Corinthian pottery, two of the registers are filled with scenes from Homer's *Odyssey* with the escape from the Cyclops Polyphemus and the monster Scylla clearly represented. The representations of the adventures of Odysseus and his men demonstrate the importance of Greek myth in Etruscan art as it will come to dominate the figural relief and painted work of Etruscan artists. The figural registers also exemplify the introduction of Greek narrative techniques into Etruscan art as the story is told by lines of figures divided by bands in an episodic narrative technique. The prominent ship in the upper register may supply some indication of the popularity of this story and its spread throughout ancient Italy at this time of colonization, naval exploration, and international trade between Etruscans, Greeks, and Phoenicians around the Italian peninsula. The Orientalizing phase in Etruscan art represents the earliest introduction of Greek subjects and Near Eastern influence into the art of the Italian peninsula. These subjects, materials, and styles were transmitted to the Romans through the Etruscans who, because of their extensive trade networks, were a conduit for foreign influences into Rome from alphabetic writing to Greek mythology.

Etruscan sculpture and portraiture

In addition to the arts that were heavily influenced by Greek and eastern models, the Etruscans developed a number of artistic traditions, notably works in bronze and terracotta, free from foreign influence particularly in their early phases. These local forms were critical in the development of Roman art, notably the portrait tradition and the promotion of elite male martial identity. The development of portraiture in Etruscan art is linked to their burial practices, a tradition seen in later Roman art where portraits are a prominent part of tombs and memorials. The Etruscans practiced cremation with the ashes of the deceased placed in an urn. Many of these in the seventh century BCE were closed vessels in bronze or terracotta topped by an anthropomorphic (human-shaped) lid. When first excavated they were called canopic urns because of their resemblance to the Egyptian vessels with headed lids used in mummification burials.

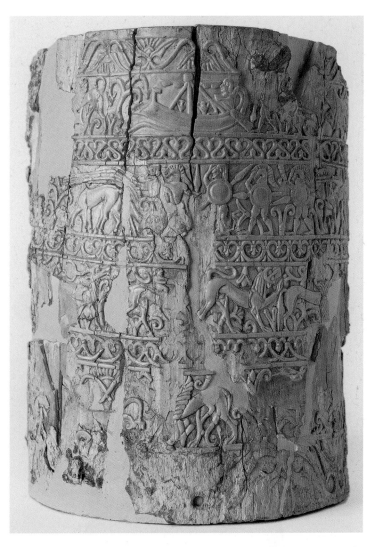

2.5   Ivory pyxis, 650–600 BCE, Pania burial, Chiusi. Museo Archaeologico Nazionale, Florence. H 7 ½ in (19 cm) D 5 ¾ in (14.6 cm). Source: The Art Archive/Archaeological Museum Florence/ Mondadori Portfolio/Electa.

These human-headed urns developed from the earlier type of an urn topped by a bronze helmet indicating the warrior status and male gender of the deceased. They later developed by stages, for example the handles became arms, and the urns became full hollow statues with the ashes placed inside, leaving no doubt that they provide a very early type of portraiture and are meant to convey an image of the deceased. The body, lid, and chair in which it rests are all made separately, in this example in terracotta. In many cases the chair is bronze, sometimes decorated with relief work. The chairs are a known Etruscan image that they passed down to the Romans and signify elite male status and may be thrones or, more likely, represent the chairs used by magistrates in local government. The individualized face is intended to represent the male whose ashes rest within the urn. The holes over the face are for the attachment of a mask. Funeral masks were another Etruscan custom adopted by the Romans, particularly to transmit the images of elite males through the family. As an early form of portraiture it signifies the priority of this art in conveying the status and rank of the deceased to the family and other spectators of later generations. Etruscan terracotta sculpture becomes more artistically and technically sophisticated and increasingly symbolic, as a piece from a century later shows.

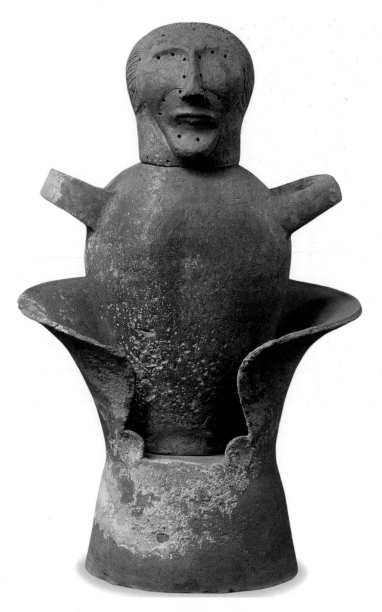

Perhaps the most celebrated work of Etruscan terracotta sculpture is a sarcophagus for a married couple found in a tomb in the Banditaccia necropolis at Cerveteri. It is evidence of the rapid changes in Etruscan art from the small scale (18 inches tall) urn from Chuisi to this sarcophagus that is large enough for lifesize sculptures on its lid. While it appears to be a work of sculpture in the round, it is really better understood as a very high relief work with the feet and legs in shallow relief and the figures from the waist up in very high relief. That emphasis on the upper body and face is an Etruscan convention. A great deal of attention is paid to surface detail and pattern, seen in the treatment of the fabric they wear as it wrinkles, drapes, and folds around their bodies. Their eyes, hair, and the man's beard are also very much surface additions. All of these elements rely on the model of Greek Archaic sculpture from the almond-shaped eyes, pointed chins, and noses to the shape of the beard and the hair that falls in locks shaped like Tootsie Rolls®, a standard component of contemporary Greek sculpture.

Partially due to the use of terracotta, which allows greater surface detail and more unsupported limbs than marble would, the figures are very expressive, lying together on the couch with the man's right arm across his wife's back and resting on her right shoulder. The gestures of their hands show the Etruscan interest in accurately portraying the details of nature, in this case the very difficult task of showing how hands move in a variety of gestures. The gestures themselves are significant as the deceased were probably each holding objects related to funerary ritual such as small perfume flasks, garlands, wine cups, or eggs, all found in other funerary imagery. The portrayal of a couple illustrates Etruscan social customs with husband and wife dining together on a banqueting couch in contrast to the elite Greek practice which at that time showed two males on a couch, not a man and woman.

The capacity of Etruscan sculptors to exploit terracotta for dynamic and detailed sculpture is seen in the large-scale works from the Portonaccio Sanctuary at Veii, a southern Etruscan city near Rome. The sanctuary contained temples to, among other deities, Minerva and Apollo. The roofline of the Temple of Apollo was decorated with at least four over-lifesize statues of Greek deities: Apollo, Leto, Hermes, and the hero Hercules. The Apollo is the best preserved and demonstrates the Etruscan adaptation of Greek Archaic sculpture, in many ways comparable to the Cerveteri sarcophagus.

Unlike a contemporary Greek figure, which would be nude, the Apollo is dressed in a tunic and cloak. It still echoes Greek proportions from the period, however. The figure's surface is covered with a great deal of decorative design, including the precise folds of his garments, the muscles and shin bone of his lower legs, his facial features, and his Tootsie Roll hair. Even the support between his legs is finished with an Ionic volute design, the spiral found on Greek column capitals in Ionia. The figure was certainly created by an Etruscan sculptor inspired by the works found in east Greek communities in Ionia (the Greek areas in what is today western Turkey), showing the international nature of

2.6 Terracotta "canopic" urn, 625–600 BCE, Chiusi. British Museum, London. H 18 in (45.7 cm). Source: © The Trustees of the British Museum. All rights reserved.

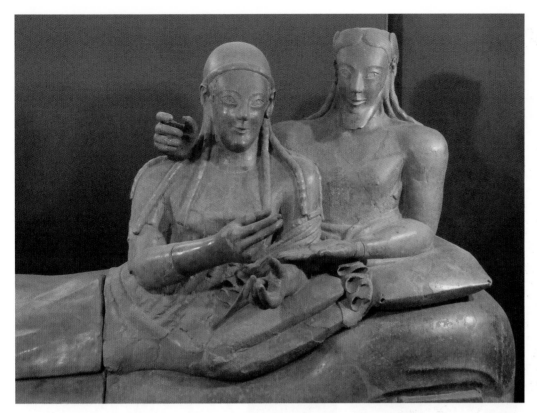

2.7   Couple sarcophagus from Cerveteri, *c.* 525 BCE. Museo Nazionale Etrusco di Villa Giulia, Rome. Terracotta, 3 ft 9 in x 6 ft 2 in (1.14 m x 1.9 m). Photo courtesy Steven L. Tuck.

the art of this period. The figure is more dynamic than surviving contemporary Greek works, due both to Etruscan style and the use of terracotta. Apollo strides forward with his legs reflecting the long step he takes as his arms swing as well, his now broken right arm probably ended holding out one of his attributes such as a lyre or perhaps just reaching forward with a bow in his lowered left hand. The sculptor of this group is believed to have been Vulca of Veii, the only Etruscan artist whose name is known. He is also credited with the contemporary statues at the Temple of Jupiter Optimus Maximus on the Capitoline Hill in Rome.

ART IN LATIUM, THE REGION AROUND ROME

Immediately south of Etruria lies the territory of Latium where Rome was founded. Its proximity to Etruscan territory exposed it early to Etruscan artistic influences and Greek subjects carried through Etruscan works. One of the Latin communities, Lavinium, had long ties to Rome. According to popular Roman mythology it was founded by the Trojan refugee Aeneas, whose heirs went on to found Rome itself. Located in Latin territory south of Rome, Lavinium was, like Veii, home to a large sanctuary outside the walls of the city itself. Here, in a sanctuary dedicated to Minerva, rites of passage for local children passing through adolescence and into adulthood were performed. One of the dozens of terracotta statues from the sanctuary is of the goddess Minerva herself. In fact, it is possibly the cult statue from the temple and not just subsidiary decoration or a votive placed in fulfillment of a vow.

The statue is a large-scale terracotta work of a standing Minerva wearing her helmet, the aegis – the serpent-fringed snakeskin she wears over her dress as a form of armor, the Gorgoneion or Medusa's head on her chest, and carrying a shield. Unlike the slightly earlier Apollo of Veii (Figure 2.8)

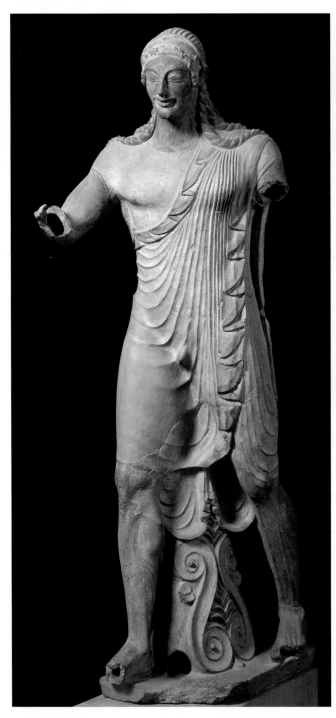

2.8   Apollo of Portonaccio Sanctuary, Veii, 510 BCE. Museo
Nazionale Etrusco di Villa Giulia, Rome. Terracotta. 5 ft 9 in
(1.75 m). Source: © Araldo de Luca/Corbis.

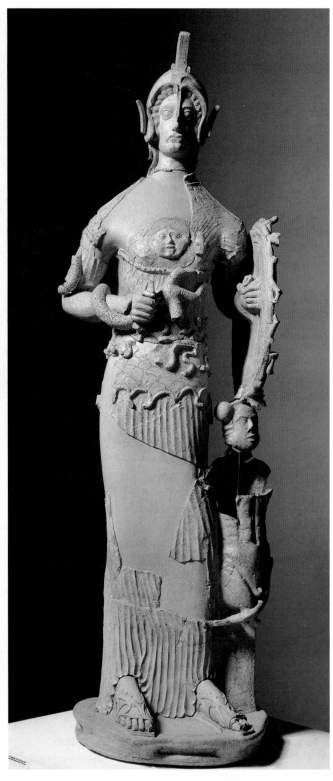

2.9   Minerva Tritonia from Lavinium, Latium, 5th cent. BCE, in the
Museo Civico Archeologico Lavinium, Pratica di Mare. Terracotta,
6 ft 5 in (1.96 m). Source: Getty Images/De Agostini Picture Library/
G. Nimatallah.

it shows almost no points of comparison with contemporary Greek art. The slender, elongated proportions and flat-footed stance ignore the curves and **contrapposto** of Classical Greek sculpture. The figure's oversized eyes, frowning mouth, and the elaborate surface design which covers the figure may seem holdovers from the Archaic period, yet as a locally created work it preserves the local regional tradition without being informed by the Greek sculptural trends of even the most recent period in art. The figure is covered with serpents and even a three-headed snake wrapped around her right arm, symbols of her chthonic power (power that derives from or is related to the underworld). Minerva's shield is supported by a figure of a triton, a half-man and half-fish marine deity. This is the only large-scale sculpture of Minerva from the ancient world with a triton as part of the composition. The figure is associated with Minerva and her name, Minerva Tritonia, as used repeatedly by Vergil in his epic poem *Aeneid* written in the late first century BCE.

As with most marble and terracotta sculpture from the ancient world, the Minerva was originally painted in bright colors. On the vast majority of sculpture these have completely disappeared. On this sculpture we can make out traces of paint on many parts of the figure including yellow on her hair and shield, red on the triton and armor, blue on the snake, and white on the dress. These traces give us a much better sense of the sculpture's original finished look in antiquity and help scholars to compare it to other painted terracottas such as the many Etruscan examples from the same period. Minerva is an important deity in many communities across the region of Latium, including Rome where early sanctuaries like those at Veii and Lavinium used many large-scale terracotta statues of Minerva in their decoration.

contrapposto
counterpoise, gives a figure a dynamic but relaxed pose by alternating weight-bearing and free arms and legs coupled with hips and shoulders held at slight angles.

ARCHAIC ROME: CITY PLANNING AND ARCHITECTURE

The urban plan of early Rome shared many elements with Etruscan cities. It was founded on a collection of hills – traditionally seven, but ancient authors debate which to count and which to omit – so it was in the tradition of Etruscan hilltop communities. The domestic spaces and animal grazing were on the hills, most importantly the Palatine and Capitoline Hills, while trade, agriculture, and common areas were found in the low zones at the bases of the hills. Rome also had the Tiber river as a critical transportation avenue and its founding close to the Tiber just below the only major island where the river could be crossed seasonally made it essentially a crossroads of central Italy. The low areas between the hills were at best seasonally available for use owing to flooding from the river. The

A VIEW FROM THE PROVINCES
Decorative Italic armor from Picenum

The sixth and fifth centuries BCE saw the beginnings of Roman expansion through Italy. Under their kings the Romans won their first major victories in wars against the Etruscans. They also attacked and took a number of neighboring towns including Collatia, Gabii, and Suessa Pometia and warred against the Volsci, Aequi, Rutuli, and Sabines as they moved into central Italy. As they expanded and conquered neighboring territory, the cultural differences between Rome and its neighbors lessened as they began to share cultural traits. The early Roman expansion into central Italy makes it difficult to identify local or regional cultures of that area as they were absorbed and their cultural habits blended with the Roman. The influence of local cultures, however, is visible in Roman art and confirms that Roman art was not exclusively inspired by the Greeks and Etruscans. The few surviving pieces of art from these local cultures prior to Roman conquest demonstrate skilled work in a variety of regional styles.

This bronze disk is one of three that were originally joined together to make an Italic breastplate, probably of the Picentes, a people of central Italy along the Adriatic coast. This type of armor is known in central Italy from art as well as grave goods and consisted of two disks arranged over the chest and one over the stomach all supported and connected by leather bands or a linen garment. The bold, somewhat abstracted figure of a monstrous animal was created in repoussé. It fills the round field and is defined by a simple outline with only a few internal lines to define body volume and movement. Its open mouth, fang-like teeth, bird-like claws each with three talons, and snake tail are all designed to intimidate an enemy warrior. The horned serpent tail has parallels in Celtic art but the entire beast is without direct antecedents in art or mythology outside of central Italy. The almost heraldic presentation and abstract design could mean that it was a totem or symbolic figure referring to the owner or it could be in the category of **apotropaic** images found in cultures across the Mediterranean.

2.10   Bronze Italic disk, 7th cent. BCE, one of three from a breast plate, 9 ¾ in (24.8 cm). Saint Louis Art Museum, Museum Purchase 53:1922.

apotropaic
literally "to ward off evil," usually with designs, often grotesque, frightening, and incorporating serpents, placed on the outsides of buildings or objects to protect those within from harm.

geography of the area resulted in the growth of the Forum Boarium, the cattle market adjacent to the banks of the Tiber and the road that crossed the river, and the Forum Romanum, the central and most important urban civic and commercial space in Rome.

Under the kings from the origins of Rome in 753 BCE almost to the founding of the Republic in 509 BCE the area that would develop into the Forum Romanum had no substantial buildings in it; it was low ground and at the best of times had swampy patches. The lowest collection of buildings was found on the west side and included the Temple of Vesta and the Regia, the official house of the kings, their headquarters for religious rituals. These were on a spur of the Palatine Hill just above the swampy areas. Below and north of them was the Forum necropolis. Here was found one of the earliest burial sites for Romans on the edge of the city.

Like Etruscan burials, these were cremations. Unlike Etruscan tombs, these burials were individual affairs with the cinerary urn and some grave goods placed in a shaft dug next to the road that would

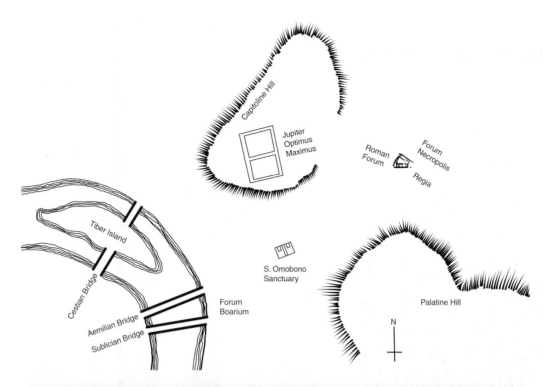

2.11 Rome, plan of Palatine and early Rome with cemeteries, Forum Romanum (including Regia) and Boarium marked. Drawing courtesy Steven L. Tuck.

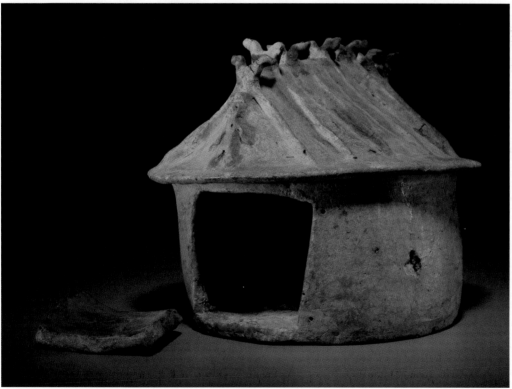

2.12 House urn, 7th cent. BCE, Forum Romanum, Rome. Terracotta. H 11 in (27.9 cm). Source: Photograph © John Deane. Lent by the Republic of Italy, 2010.

become the Via Sacra (the Sacred Way). Sometimes the urn and goods were first set in a large terracotta jar then placed in the ground. The urn that held the ashes of the deceased was shaped like a house from the period, here created out of terracotta. These demonstrate what the early houses would have looked like and connect Rome culturally to other sites in Latium with similar urns. Based on the urns and excavations on the Palatine Hill in Rome, we can conclude that the house would have

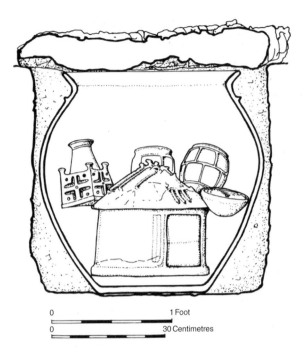

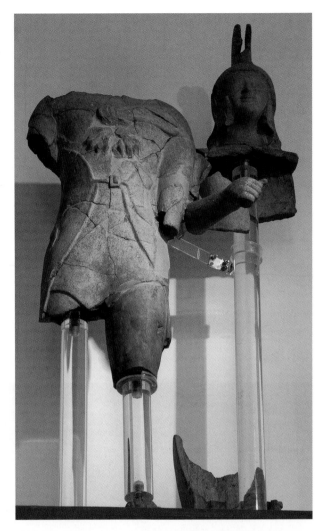

2.13 Cross section drawing of cremation burial tomb from the Forum necropolis, Via Sacra, Rome, Antiquarium Forense. Soprintendenza Speciale per i Beni Archeologica di Roma. Reproduced with permission.

been a single-room structure constructed out of wattle and daub (woven branches for support covered with thick layers of mud plaster). The broad roof designed to shed water away from the mud walls was built from a timber frame covered with thatching. The single door into the house was always at the short end, creating an interior space that was organized along the long axis and symmetrically, compo-

2.14 Temple of Fortuna acroterion of Hercules and Athena, 570–540 BCE, Sant'Omobono Sanctuary, Rome. Musei Capitolini; Centrale Montemartini, Rome. 4 ½ ft (1.35 m). Source: Jeremy Thorpe, photo 2009.

nents of Etruscan and later Roman domestic architecture. Analysis of the remains in the house urns shows that they were male. This is a remarkable departure from Etruscan cultural practice of family burial in larger tombs or tomb groups, but it demonstrates a common culture with other Latin communities as well as later Roman culture of the historic periods. House-shaped urns reflect not only the shapes of houses but also the status and identity of elite males as heads of households. Men in death were defined by their relationship to the community as heads of households and buried together in the area that becomes the urban space for elite male political activity where the Senate and courts will meet.

The Forum Boarium between Rome's hills and the Tiber river was probably the area that saw more traffic and certainly more trade than any other in early Rome. On the lower slope of the Capitoline near the Tiber was an archaic sanctuary datable to the sixth century BCE. It consisted of two temples, identified as those of Fortuna and Mater Matuta, both of which were Etrusco-Italic in style. Each small temple was set on a high podium with a frontal set of steps and a deep porch leading to a door on the short end, all elements they had in common with Etruscan religious architecture. Like the houses on the hills, they were probably originally built of perishable materials including broad timber roofs which were covered in terracotta tiles and terracotta decorative components, to protect the perishable structures from rain. Many of these early terracotta elements survive.

The most important of these terracotta sculptural features is a three-quarter lifesize **acroterion** sculpture group of Minerva and Hercules. Set together on a single base on the ridgeline of the Temple of Fortuna, the same location as the Apollo of Veii (Figure 2.8) statue on that temple, it was designed to be viewed by those approaching the temple so that the figures faced and looked down on those who entered the temple. The group is recognizable from their standard attributes. Minerva wears a helmet and carries a spear while Hercules has his lionskin tied around him as a cloak. Minerva has the archaic smile of Greek sculpture of this period and her Greek-inspired proportions show more in common with Etruscan sculpture than with the Minerva of Lavinium (Figure 2.9). The specific form

acroterion
a decorative ornament, such as a statue, placed on the roof of a temple, usually above the front pediment but could also be spaced along the ridgeline.

SCHOLARLY PERSPECTIVE
Is the concept of Etruscan Rome a myth?

A major scholarly debate concerning this period is the extent of Etruscan influence on Archaic Rome. Ancient historians refer to the last three of the seven kings of Rome as Etruscans. Traditionally L. Tarquinius Priscus (616–579 BCE) was an Etruscan immigrant, succeeded by Servius Tullius (578–535), and followed by the final king, Tarquinius Superbus (535–509). Tarquin is well known as an Etruscan name, found in the city of Tarquinia. But the question remains, how Etruscan was Rome itself? Many elements follow patterns familiar from Etruscan communities including the city's urban design as a community on fortified hilltops, and its monumental architecture, notably the style of its early temples. Yet the argument has been made that these do not represent Etruscan influence but a common culture found throughout central Italy. The Samnites, for example, built hilltop communities. If that is the case, then the tradition of tracing many Roman practices back to the Etruscans should be questioned as it may represent ancient Roman authors' attempts to give greater authority and antiquity to their cultural practices by attributing them to the most advanced civilization in the region. To say that the toga, religious practices, and the chair used by Roman magistrates (to name but a few examples) are Etruscan is to reinforce their power. The evidence is mixed, however. The material from the Sant'Omobono sanctuary is important to this debate. The acroterion of Hercules and Minerva is not unique. Similar examples are found at a variety of sanctuaries in the region including Veii, Caere, Pyrgi, and Satricum, all Etruscan communities except Satricum, which was a Latin community with close ties to Rome. It can be argued either that the pattern emerged in Etruscan communities and spread with their influence over the cities of Rome and Satricum, or that the spread represents a cultural practice common to Etruscans and Latins alike. The lack of precise dates from the excavations makes it impossible to determine the sequence of these statues' creation.

Additional evidence cited in debate comes from inscriptions including some from the Sant'Omobono sanctuary. Perhaps the most important inscription for the notion of Etruscan Rome is an inscribed ivory lion plaque, probably dedicated to the deity in the sanctuary. The plaque bore an Etruscan inscription, *Araz Silqetenas*, and an elite Etruscan name known from Tarquinia, *Spurianas*. The Etruscan name, association with Tarquinia, and luxury imported material all correspond to Etruscan Orientalizing art. An Etruscan inscription reading *uqnus* inscribed on an Etruscan vessel was found in a votive pit in the sanctuary as well. These inscriptions provoked much interest not simply because of their early date (late seventh–early sixth century BCE), but also because they provide evidence of Etruscan contact with Rome and support conclusions of an Etruscan Rome during the sixth century BCE for some scholars. An early Latin inscription reading *ouduios*, on a broken fragment of Etruscan pottery, was also discovered in the sanctuary, leading other scholars to argue that the presence of Etruscans in the city does not necessarily require us to conclude that they dominated the community. In fact, this sanctuary, outside the walls of the city, could provide evidence of Rome at its early period as a sophisticated community made up of people from various ethnic groups in the region, evidence of Rome's cultural inclusiveness well known from later periods. None of this requires an Etruscan Rome, but a Rome as open to influence from Etruria as it was from Greece and many other cultures whose contributions are now indistinguishable in the cultural makeup of Rome.

T.J. Cornell, *The Beginnings of Rome: Italy and Rome from the Bronze Age to the Punic Wars (c.1000–264 BCE)* (Routledge 1995).

of Hercules' lionskin cloak with the buckled belt around his waist can be traced to the sculpture of the eastern Mediterranean island of Cyprus, showing that the Orientalizing tradition penetrated Roman art as well. Minerva, in the Greek Athena, was the patron deity who aided the hero Hercules in many of his adventures and eventually led him to Mount Olympus to join the gods in his **apotheosis**. This statute group shows that apotheosis, which had a political meaning. The contemporary ruler of Athens, the tyrant Pisistratus (ruled 561–527 BCE), identified himself with Hercules and claimed the aid and support of Athena. In one spectacular display of political theater he drove a chariot onto the Athenian acropolis in the company of a young woman dressed like Athena, a symbolic apotheosis for the tyrant. He also used the image of Hercules and Athena in public art as part of his political propaganda. Scholars believe that the later kings of Rome bolstered their rule as Pisistratus had done with lavish public building programs and other aspects that connected them to the people and the gods at the cost of their aristocratic opponents. It is possible that this temple represented an important location in the succession of kings, where they came to commune with the goddess, probably by spending the night in the temple, and so reinforced their authority to rule by association with the divinity. The decoration of the sanctuary and its major renovations prior to the founding of the Republic in 509 BCE has reinforced the notion for many scholars of its direct association with the kings of Rome.

apotheosis
to become a god, often shown as the elevation to divine status through bodily ascension or the moment the figure is welcomed into the company of the gods.

triumphal procession
victory parade granted by the Senate to a conquering general, who rode in a *quadriga*. It began at the city gates and concluded at the Temple of Jupiter.

2.15 Temple of Jupiter Optimus Maximus, plan. Sailko / Wikimedia Commons.

Temple of Jupiter Optimus Maximus

The Temple of Jupiter Optimus Maximus is without a doubt the most important temple in ancient Rome. It represents the culmination of the massive public building programs of the last kings. It also became the central religious space in the community for over a thousand years as here the consuls offered their first public sacrifices, the senate met in assembly, it was the last stop of the **triumphal procession**, and the repository of Rome's foreign relations archives. This was the temple replicated at Roman colonies for hundreds of years as a symbol of Roman religious culture. The temple, dedicated to Jupiter Optimus (Best) Maximus (and Greatest) was founded on the Capitoline Hill under the final king, Tarquinius Superbus (Tarquin the Proud). Although named only for Jupiter it actually held cult spaces for Juno and Minerva as well, initiating the so-called Capitoline Triad. Its location on one of the two most important of the hills – along with the Palatine – meant that it dominated the surrounding area and served as an image of Rome to whoever approached the city either by the Tiber or the road that ran along it. The temple was, for its time and for some two centuries afterwards, one of the largest in the entire Mediterranean world. It measured 220 ft (61 m) by 180 ft (55 m), 80 percent of the area of a football field.

In form the temple followed the Etrusco-Italic style rather than the Greek tradition. It was almost square rather than rectangular and built on a 16 ft (5 m) tall podium, instead of the low, three-step platform of the Greek temple. The temple was approached by a single flight of stairs

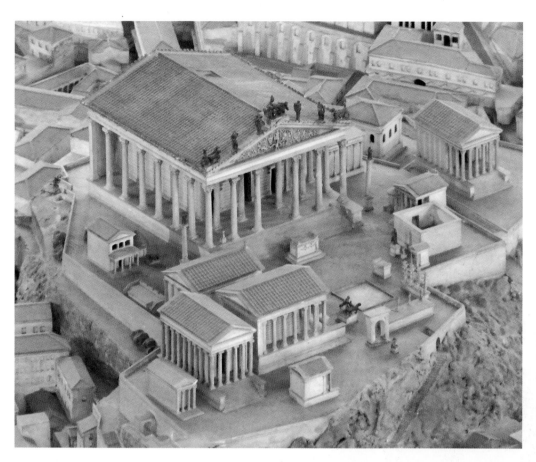

2.16 Temple of Jupiter Optimus Maximus, model. Museo della Civiltà Romana, Rome. Source: Sovrintendenza Capitolina ai Beni Culturali – Archivio Fotografico Museo della Civiltà Romana.

across the south-facing front, unlike Greek temples which were accessible from all sides. Its construction out of perishable materials such as timber and not the marble of Greek temples had a great influence on its form. The **cella**, divided into three separate shrines for the three deities, measured only about 100 ft (28 m) square. This occupied only the rear half of the top of the platform. The front half was taken by a porch that covered as much area as the cella. This pattern is a holdover from earlier buildings made entirely of perishable materials that needed broad roofs to direct water away from timber structures and mud walls. The roofing system was terracotta and the temple was topped by a series of terracotta acroteria probably similar to those from the sanctuaries at Veii and Sant'Omobono. The cult statue was terracotta as well and it and the acroteria were the work of an Etruscan sculptor, Vulca of Veii.

Beyond the foundation and some votives, not much is preserved of the temple. But, in addition to being the most important and largest of Rome's temples, the Temple of Jupiter Optimus Maximus was also a frequent subject of artists and authors. It was also the first temple ever to appear on Rome's coinage. For these reasons it makes an interesting case study in using Roman coin imagery and ancient sources to reconstruct a building, particularly one like the temple with few actual remains extant. The coins represent apparently objective images of the temple that are presented as accurate accounts of how it looked. In reality the needs of those authorizing the coinage as well as the limited field on a coin mean that the image is necessarily reduced to what the coin's sponsor felt were the essential elements. The result is an image that by design emphasizes key building features selected to transmit certain messages about the temple. These images also show the limits of usefulness in reconstructing a building. For example, elements that modern scholars use to define temple types, such as column type and number, and decorative features, were not portrayed consistently by ancient artists. The coins of the temple variously show Tuscan, Doric, or Corinthian columns, demonstrating their indistinct imagery.

cella
the inner room of a temple. It served primarily to house the cult statue. It could also hold votive objects and ritual items such as vessels and braziers.

TOOLS & TECHNIQUES
Architectural orders

The architectural orders of ancient temples were defined by the precisely measured parts that made up the buildings ensuring that all of them were in a particular harmony to create a building of specific pleasing proportions. We can identify the categories of temple types, called orders, by the columns. These can be used as a shorthand description of a temple, but the orders are actually far more detailed than just the form of the columns. The Roman architect, Vitruvius, gives an origin for the Doric order,

> They measured a man's foot, and finding its length the sixth part of his height, they gave the column a similar proportion, that is, they made its height, including the capital, six times the thickness of the shaft, measured at the base. (Vitruvius, 4.6)

Doric temples (Figure 1.5a) have columns with no base, shafts carved with vertical flutes, and an undecorated capital that flared outward from the top of the column shaft to a square block. Tuscan columns (Figure 7.3) have a round base, smooth shaft and round capital. Ionic columns (Figure 1.5b) have round bases with fluted shafts slenderer than the Doric, and capitals that are recognized by spiral scrolls. Corinthian columns (Figure 4.3) share features with the Ionic except for the capitals, which have scrolls and elaborately carved acanthus leaf patterns.

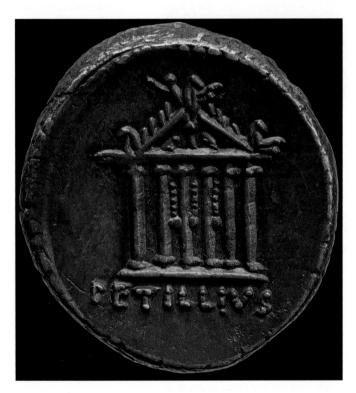

2.17 Silver denarius of Petillius Capitolinus, *c.* 43 BCE. Reverse, Temple of Jupiter Optimus Maximus. British Museum, London. R. 9119. Image: © Trustees of the British Museum.

pediment
the triangular gable found below a pitched roof on either end of a building. On ancient temples these were often filled with sculptures or relief decoration.

The image of the temple's facade is presented in a way that no actual viewer could see it, as though from midair in front of the temple. That in itself demonstrates the illusion that the coin represents an ancient view. The coin emphasizes three particular parts of the temple that can be thought to define it to the ancient viewer. First, in well-preserved versions of the coin the doors to the three cellae can be seen between the columns leaving no doubt regarding the temple's identity, but in a way that an ancient viewer would not have seen them. Second, the sculpture in the **pediment** is shown, in an admittedly impressionistic way, that shows its role in identifying the temple. Third, the acroterial sculptures are prominent. In fact, they are consistently illustrated as disproportionately large to ensure that the viewer sees them. They were clearly a defining feature of this old, Etruscan-style temple. The message of this image is one of tradition and religious authority. It shows none of the subsidiary statues that were erected around and on the temple throughout the Republican period. Here it is almost as if Petillius is showing the temple as it was in 509 BCE at its dedication, not as contemporary viewers would witness it in its rebuilt phase.

Murlo (Poggio Civitate)

Although we have material from the temples, none of the residences survive from this period in Rome. For comparable evidence as well as what may be the earliest Etruscan temple form, we need to turn to an Etruscan site north of Rome. The city of Murlo is a small community about 12 miles (20 km) south of Siena in Tuscany. Just outside the town is the hill of Poggio Civitate, site of two distinct phases of one of the most important Etruscan monumental building complexes

ART AND LITERATURE
Literature as a source for lost art and architecture: The case of the Temple of Jupiter Optimus Maximus

In addition to its appearance in art, the Temple of Jupiter Optimus Maximus is mentioned frequently in ancient literary sources and their descriptions are useful both for reconstructing and understanding the temple as well as for documenting changes in its structure and decoration over the centuries as it was restored after fire and as tastes and values changed in Rome. The missing sculptural program of the temple is described by various sources. The cult statue of Jupiter was clothed with a tunic adorned with palm branches and **Victories** (*tunica palmata*), and a purple toga embroidered with gold (*toga picta, palmata*), the costume afterwards worn by Roman generals when celebrating a triumphal procession (Livy, *History of Rome* 10.7–10; 30.15.11). The superstructure of the temple was of wood, and on the apex of the pediment was a terracotta group, Jupiter in a ***quadriga***, by the Vulca of Veii, the same Etruscan artist as the cult statue of Jupiter in the cella (Pliny, *Natural History* 28.16; 35.157). This was replaced in 296 BCE by another, probably of bronze (Livy, *History of Rome* 10.23.12). There is no doubt that pediment and roof were decorated with terracotta figures, among them a statue of *Summanus "in fastigio"* (perhaps an acroterion), which was damaged by a thunderbolt in 275 BCE (Cicero, *de Divinatione* 1.10). In 193 BCE M. Aemilius Lepidus and L. Aemilius Paullus placed gilt shields on the pediment (Livy, *History of Rome* 35.10). None of these elements survive antiquity.

As for gifts and embellishments to the temple by Romans, none of these survive either, but the descriptions in ancient sources reveal the role of piety and personal aggrandizement in the dedication that created the decorative display in and around the temple. They also, when gathered together, give a sense of the information that can be collected from a large number of ancient authors to supplement our understanding of Roman art. Sometime early in the second century BCE a mosaic pavement was laid in the cella (Pliny, *Natural History* 36.185) and in 142 BCE the ceiling was gilded (Pliny, *Natural History* 33.57) The temple became a repository of works of art of many sorts. For example, paintings are recorded, "Nicomachus painted the Rape of Persephone, which hung in the cella of Minerva on the Capitolium" (Pliny, *Natural History* 35.108). More common were dedicatory offerings and victory trophies from Roman generals and others, of which the earliest recorded was a golden crown presented by the Latins in 459 BCE (Livy, *History of Rome* 2.22.6). Some were of particular significance, "Marcius found [the Carthaginian general] Hasdrubal's shield when he captured his camp [in 207 BCE]; this shield hung above the doors of the Capitoline Temple right up to the time of the first fire [in 83 BCE]" (Pliny, *Natural History* 35.14). The number of these dedications became so great that in 179 BCE it was necessary to remove some of the statues and many of the shields affixed to the columns (Livy, *History of Rome* 40.51.3). In 80 BCE the Dictator Sulla brought the white marble Corinthian columns of the Olympieion from Athens to Rome for this temple (Pliny, *Natural History* 36.45). The doors were plated with gold (Zosimus 5.38), and the roof was covered with gilt tiles (Procopius, *Buildings* 1.5). The four bronze columns decorated with the rams from ships captured at the naval battle of Antium also stood in the temple (Servius, *Georgics* 3.29).

ever discovered. The first phase, dating to the early seventh century BCE, consisted of three large buildings.

Building 1, a monumental residence of a family of regional social prominence, was elaborately decorated with an acroterial program in terracotta. Finds from the building's floor included a banquet service of imported Greek and locally produced fine wares, and bone, antler, and ivory inlays that once decorated furniture. Building 2, contemporary with the residence, was the complex's primary area of industrial work during this phase. This building was substantially larger than the residence and curiously elegantly decorated with terracotta sculpture. The building housed numerous types of manufacturing, including bronze casting, bone and antler carving, terracotta manufacture, ceramics production, food processing, and textile manufacture. This building is currently the earliest example of such a multifunctional workshop known in Central Italy. Building 3, a large tripartite building, is immediately to the south of the residence. Although badly damaged the excavators were able to

Victory
based on the Greek Nike, a winged female personification of Roman success in war or sports, identifiable by the palm branch and victor's crown she often carries.

quadriga
four-horse chariot, used for chariot racing and by successful generals in triumphal processions. A general in a *quadriga* was a common subject in victory monuments.

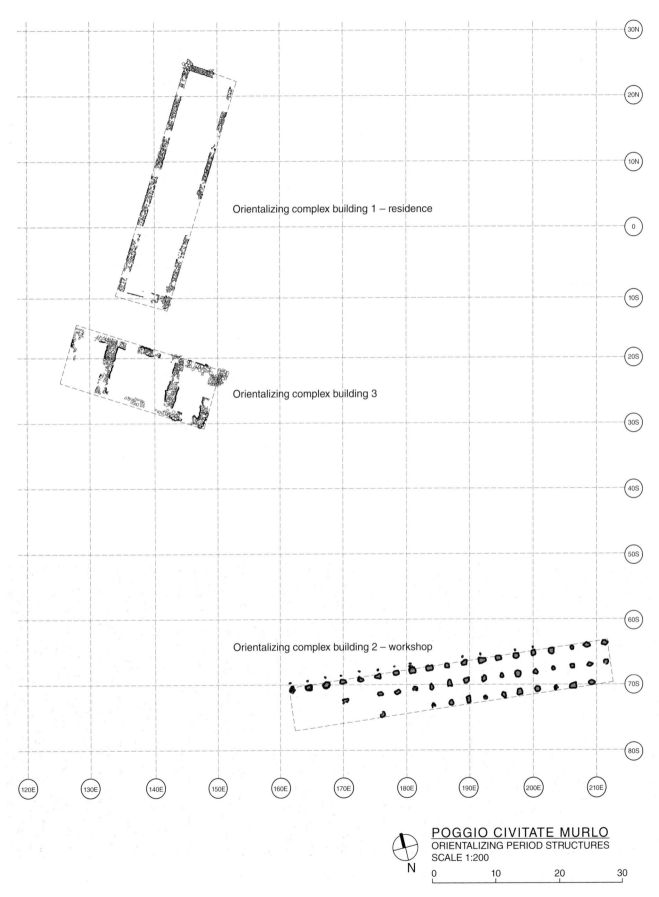

Orientalizing complex building 1 – residence

Orientalizing complex building 3

Orientalizing complex building 2 – workshop

POGGIO CIVITATE MURLO
ORIENTALIZING PERIOD STRUCTURES
SCALE 1:200
N
0   10   20   30

2.18   Murlo (Poggio Civitate) plan of Orientalizing phase buildings, *c.* 675–600 BCE. Drawing courtesy Anthony Tuck.

reconstruct a building with a large central cella flanked by two chambers precisely half the dimensions of the central room. Both the building's tripartite form and examples of luxurious inscribed vessels found in the central cella suggest this building was an early example of a temple, making it one of the earliest examples of monumental religious architecture in Italy known to date. The tripartite cella is a familiar feature from later Etrusco-Italic temples including the Temple of Jupiter Optimus Maximus.

Constructed almost immediately after the destruction by fire of the phase 1 complex, the Archaic period phase 2 consisted of a massive four-winged building enclosing central and southern courtyards. Each wing was 197 ft (60 m) in length and a western defensive work extended that facade an additional 98 ft (30 m). This remarkable building, far larger than any known in the Mediterranean for its time period, has been the subject of considerable debate as to its function. Theories include its use as a political meeting hall, a religious sanctuary, a palace and even an Etruscan version of an agora. Currently, the excavators believe that the building combined the functions of the disparate structures of the earlier phase into a single edifice. Architecturally notable is the central room organization on the west wing opposite the main entrance. It consists of an open room flanked by two small closed rooms with a water basin set in front of it in the courtyard. The entire three room and basin arrangement is mirrored in later Roman domestic architecture such as the Regia, the official residence of the kings on the edge of the Forum Romanum, and the atrium house where the *tablinum*, an open room facing the main entrance of the house, is flanked by a pair of rooms and faces a pool or basin of water (Figure 4.18 Plan of the House of the Faun). This Archaic complex may be the ultimate origin of that core of the Roman domestic space.

Like the buildings of the earlier complex, this structure was also elaborately decorated with terracotta acroterion sculpture in the round that sat along the pitch of the roof. In addition, frieze plaques were nailed to exposed wooden beams, protecting them from the elements. Terracotta gorgon antefixes, upright ornaments along the eaves of the tile roof, decorated the building's perimeter while a line of locally produced terracotta relief plaques ornamented the courtyard. The images on these plaques, representing a horse race, banquet, procession, and assembly, reveal much about Etruscan culture and central Italian art in the sixth century BCE.

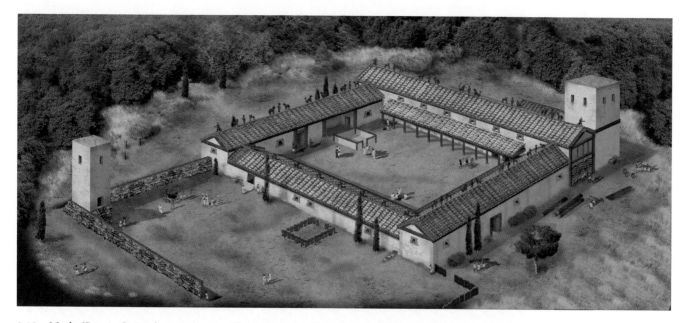

2.19 Murlo (Poggio Civitate) reconstruction illustration of Archaic phase buildings, *c.* 600–590 BCE. Illustration courtesy Anthony Tuck.

Architectural terracotta plaques, Murlo

All four of the scenes use artistic conventions most familiar from Greek Orientalizing period works showing disproportionate figures in profile and without settings participating in a variety of high status special event activities. Three of these, the horse race, banquet, and procession, have earlier parallels in Greek and Near Eastern art. Each also represents an event associated with Etruscan elite culture, notably seen in Etruscan tomb paintings of slightly later date. Most scholars conclude that the scenes do not contain specific elements that might indicate that they narrate stories such as Greek myths. Rather, they are generally interpreted as generic images of elite ceremonial experiences.

Horse races were a common element of Italic religious festivals. The horse race plaques show three riders on horses riding to the right away from a feature that shares the attributes of a turning post as seen in Greek horse racing imagery. The top of the feature is a cauldron, a large vessel of the type described in the *Iliad* as a prize for a chariot race during funeral games.

The banquet scene, with elements that have parallels in Greek and Near Eastern art from this period including the Greek style banqueting furniture, includes a variety of figures in a **hierarchy of scale** with the high status banqueters reclining in pairs on couches in larger scale than the lower status attendants, musicians, and cup bearers.

The pairs of reclining figures are participating in an activity that reinforces elite status and self-identity with the posture and size of the banqueting men and women along with their activity serving to convey their position in society. The event may mirror the types of banquets that took

hierarchy of scale
an artistic convention in which higher status or more important figures are portrayed as larger than lower status or subsidiary figures in a scene.

2.20 Murlo (Poggio Civitate) terracotta plaque of horse race, *c.* 580–575 BCE; artist's reconstruction of fragmentary plaques. Original dimensions L 21 ½ in (55 cm) H 9 ½ in (24 cm). Illustration courtesy Anthony Tuck.

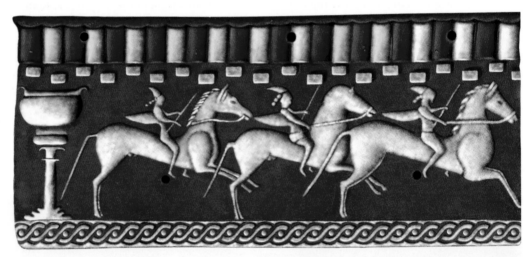

2.21 Murlo (Poggio Civitate) terracotta plaque of banquet scene, *c.* 580–575 BCE; artist's reconstruction of fragmentary plaques. Original dimensions L 21 ½ in (55 cm) H 9 ½ in (24 cm). Illustration courtesy Anthony Tuck.

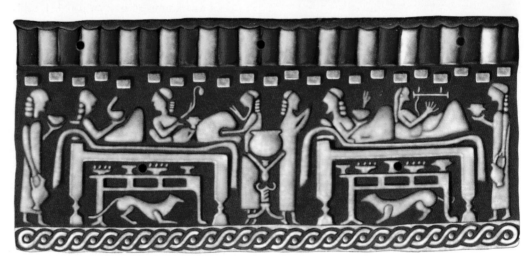

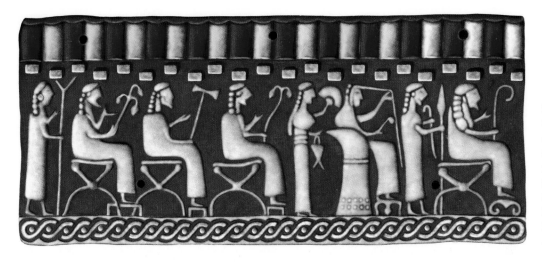

2.22 Murlo (Poggio Civitate) terracotta plaque of assembly scene, *c.* 580–575 BCE; artist's reconstruction of fragmentary plaques. Original dimensions L 21 ½ in (55 cm) H 9 ½ in (24 cm). Illustration courtesy Anthony Tuck.

place in the complex, but should not be considered as documenting Etruscan daily life. The drinking cups and bowls held by the banqueters, for example, are ceremonial vessels found on Greek and Near Eastern reliefs and so the entire event may have religious significance. A notable Etruscan departure from the Greek and Near Eastern source material is the presence of many women in the scene suggesting their importance in Etruscan ritual.

Different from the other three scenes is the assembly relief that does not seem to portray an event in high status Etruscan life. Each plaque has five seated and three standing figures. As with the banquet scene posture and hierarchy of scale indicate the elite status of the seated figures while the smaller-scale standing figures interspersed between them are clearly servants, one, a woman, holding a recognizable fan and vessel.

Of the seated figures, four are male and seated on folding chairs with footstools. The fifth figure, third from the right, is a woman seated on a more elaborate chair, again showing the high status of women in Etruscan culture. Each seated figure holds a different attribute, suggesting that this is an assembly of the gods, a motif found in later Greek art such as the Parthenon frieze. The two seated figures on the right are distinguished by more elaborate footstools while the woman pulls her veil before her face, a gesture that in later art indicates a bride at the wedding. That would make this scene a *hieros gamos*, a holy marriage, either representing the myth or a reenactment of it performed by local political and religious authorities. These two figures may be the local equivalent of Zeus and Hera (Jupiter and Juno in the Roman world) while the male deity with the axe is perhaps Hephaestus (Vulcan). While the material from Murlo is important for our understanding of early Italic art and architecture, the best evidence comes from the interiors of Etruscan tombs, particularly their well-preserved paintings.

hieros gamos
from Greek, literally "holy marriage," may refer to a marriage between a god and goddess, for example Jupiter and Juno, or to a ritual re-enactment of that by elites.

ETRUSCAN TOMB PAINTINGS

Etruscan tomb paintings are our most important source for the art of painting in central Italy before 200 BCE. These brilliantly colored scenes reveal much about Etruscan culture as well as about the development of the styles and subjects of art through a four-hundred-year period. Many of the best-preserved and most artistically significant tomb paintings are found at the site of Tarquinia, one of the most important of the twelve Etruscan cities and one whose position to the south and near the coast exposed it earlier to Greek influence.

The wall paintings in the Tomb of the Bulls demonstrate much about Etruscan art as well as showing its cultural inclusiveness. The painting on the center panel of the wall in the main room of the tomb shows an Etruscan composition familiar from later works. The wall is divided into three

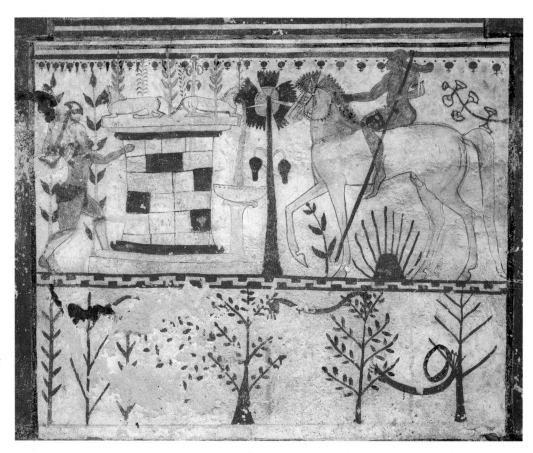

2.23 Wall painting of Achilles and Troilus, main wall of the antechamber, Tomb of the Bulls, Tarquinia, 560 BCE. Source: The Bridgeman Art Library.

horror vacui
from Latin meaning "fear of empty space," the filling of the entire surface of a work with details, often ones that are extraneous to the narrative or the main scene.

panels both vertically and horizontally. The central panel is dominated by a figural scene, a convention that carries over into later Roman wall painting.

Two features distinguish the work from contemporary Greek art. First is the emphasis on nature and the natural world. The lower panel below the central register shows four trees, possibly symbolic of the four seasons and the passage of time. The central scene itself has landscape and vegetal elements while a narrow frieze above this shows bulls in a field along with Etruscan couples. Second, we see the Etruscan application of *horror vacui*. In the Tomb of the Bulls the central panel is crowded with plants and other natural objects that spring up from the ground, sides of the panel, on top of the altar, and fill the space under the horse's legs.

The extent of foreign influence, however, is strongly seen in the painting. The bulls in the upper frieze have human faces and resemble bulls in Sumerian and Assyrian art. The central panel is a scene from Greek mythology in which the Greek hero Achilles, on the left, ambushes the mounted Trojan prince, Troilus, at a fountain and murders him.

In addition to the story, the painting owes much to Greek artistic conventions. The figures conform to Greek proportions of the Archaic period and display the Greek convention of red skin tone for men in contrast to pale skin usually reserved for women. The narrative moment is also a Greek one, the anticipatory moment prior to the violence of the fight itself. This convention emphasizes the anticipated conflict rather than the violence in a way familiar from Greek tragedies where the violence was implied or took place off stage.

The Tomb of the Augurs provides one of the earliest Etruscan tomb paintings illustrating what will be a common motif in the medium: funeral games. The large-scale fresco paintings on the interior of the tomb take as their subjects the events of Etruscan funerary ritual. We see mourners flanking a doorway that may be that of the tomb itself or the door into the Etruscan underworld. Some figures perform religious rituals, the Augurs who give their name to the tomb are priests shown

MORE ON MYTH
Troilus

Scenes from the Trojan War are among the most popular images of Greek myth in Etruscan and Roman art. Troilus was one of the sons of King Priam and Queen Hecuba. As his name suggests, containing the root of the name Troy, he was symbolically tied to the city of Troy and his identity and existence connected to that of the city. On hearing of a prophecy that Troy would not fall if this young prince reached the age of twenty, Achilles, encouraged by the goddess Athena, is determined to kill him early in the war. Knowing that Troilus regularly left the city to water his horses at a fountain near the sanctuary of Apollo, Achilles hid himself near the fountain-house. He waited until Troilus and his sister, Polyxena, who was at the fountain getting water, were off their guard, then attacked. Troilus managed to leap on to one of the horses but swift-footed Achilles caught him, dragged him off, and killed him, thus ensuring that Troy would fall. In some versions of the story, Achilles kills him at the altar of Apollo, setting up his own death since the arrow that killed him was guided by Apollo in retribution for this act of impiety. Troilus and Polyxena are often presented as ideal young people, innocent and ambushed while performing idealized gender-appropriate tasks of caring for horses and fetching water.

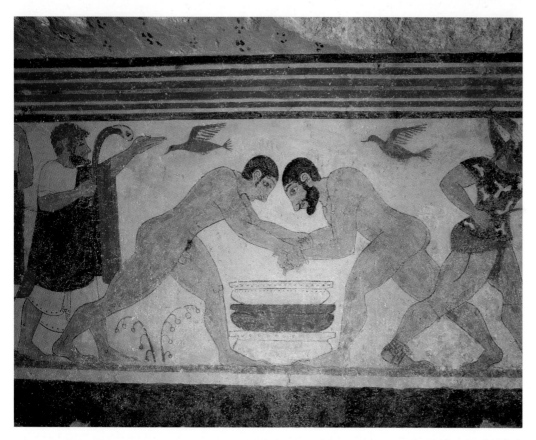

2.24 Wall painting of events from funeral games, Tomb of the Augurs, Tarquinia, 530 BCE. Source: © The Art Archive / Alamy.

examining the flights of birds to predict the future. One wall has two sets of figures performing in funeral games. On the right side is a man in a costume holding a leash that leads to a collared dog that is attacking another man who is armed with a club, but whose head is covered with a bag. This is evidence of the origins of gladiatorial combat in the blood sacrifices of Etruscan funeral games. The central pair of figures in the wall are wrestlers, showing the reliance on Greek models for Etruscan art. These figures participating in a Greek athletic contest are also drawn in Greek style

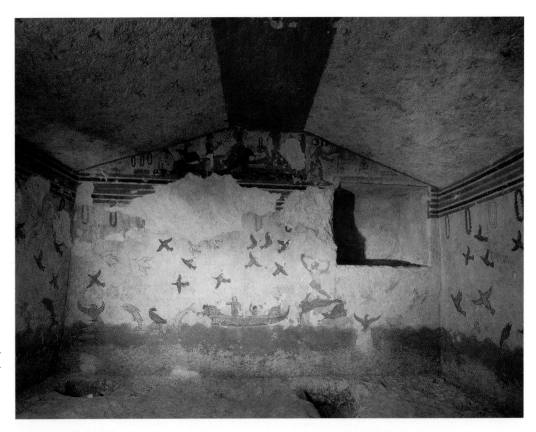

2.25   Elite dining and outdoor scenes, wall painting from back wall of the burial chamber, Tomb of Hunting and Fishing, Tarquinia, 530 BCE. Source: © The Art Archive / Alamy.

with Archaic proportions, notably the thickset figures of Greek art from the Peloponnesus and southern Italy, and the mix of profile figures with frontal eyes. Between the figures is a stack of cauldrons, a Greek prize for athletic events. The entire field is crowded showing Etruscan *horror vacui* still at work.

The portrayal of elite activities and the natural world combine in a wall painting that seems more Etruscan and less Greek than the earlier examples. The back wall of the burial chamber in the Tomb of Hunting and Fishing has two major figural scenes. The first, in the pediment just below the roof, is a banquet scene with a couple reclining at a meal attended by smaller scale servants, musicians, and cup bearers. The man and woman are shown with Greek conventions of skin tone of white for the woman and red for the man, but the notion of a man and woman dining in a pair is Etruscan as seen on the Murlo terracotta plaques discussed above. The major scene on the wall is one of men in the natural world. Four men in a small boat are fishing, having dropped lines into the water while around them dolphins leap. The sky above their heads is filled with birds flying away from the center of the panel, perhaps in response to the man on a rock to the right shooting them with a sling. The birds, boat, and dolphins show a bold use of solid blocks of color undermining any naturalism of the outdoor scene. Although the subject shows outdoor space it has no depth and like other paintings the subjects are lined up in the foreground as if on stage. The set of images appears to show daily life activities, but may in fact show events at least symbolically linked to death and funerary ritual. The banqueting couple are thought to show either a funeral or an underworld banquet. The left-hand wall in the burial chamber is dominated by an outdoor scene of water and rocks. A young man is diving into the water from a multicolored rock while in the mid-distance, on a boat, a spectator seems to applaud. Scholars conclude that the image is a symbol of the transition from life into the afterlife made with the dive downward into the water. This is not a Greek notion and so like the banqueting pair and the hunting and fishing scenes shows the emphasis on Etruscan iconography over Greek in the late Archaic period.

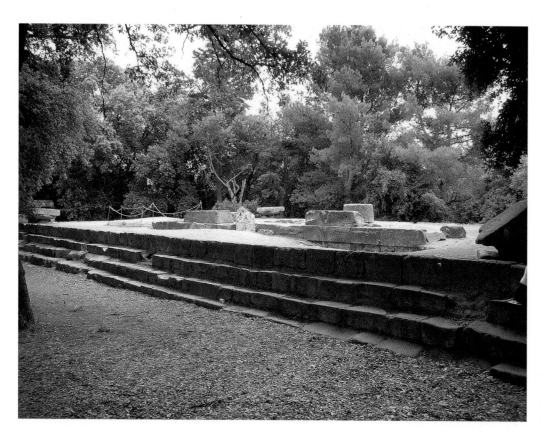

2.26 Remains of the Doric temple in the Triangular Forum, Pompeii, 600–550 BCE. Note the podium, parts of the cella walls, and the Doric capitals on the left corners of the podium. Photo courtesy Steven L. Tuck.

GRECO-ITALIC ARCHAIC ARCHITECTURE: A DORIC TEMPLE AT POMPEII

Many of the themes of this period with combined Greek, Etruscan, and Italic cultural elements and peoples come together in the largest temple ever built at Pompeii, the Doric temple in the Triangular Forum. The city of Pompeii was in its infancy when this temple was built on a platform on the southern edge of the city where its presence dominated the view of the city to those approaching from up or down the Sarno river valley or from the port of Pompeii below. The Doric temple seems an unusual choice for a hilltop community like Pompeii with very Etrusco-Italic urban planning and sanctuaries as seen in the contemporary sanctuary of Apollo.

It is a very traditionally Greek style temple on a low three-step platform with steps and a surrounding colonnade on all sides. The surviving capitals are Doric and provide evidence of the architectural order as well as the proportions of the temple. As a building form it demonstrates the architectural inclusiveness of the Italians in the sixth century with their willingness to build a massive Greek temple as a defining public building in their community. Judging by the surviving decoration, which consists of a stone relief and a terracotta plaque, the temple was associated with and possibly dedicated to Minerva. The terracotta work has been compared to that found at Cumae, a Greek colony on the north side of the Bay of Naples, and Capua, an Etruscan colony further north in inland Campania. It may be included in that set of temples from central Italy of this period decorated with images of Minerva. The cella may have had two cult spaces, leading some scholars to conclude that the worship here included Hercules as well, strengthening the connections to the sanctuaries at Sant'Omobono in Rome and elsewhere with images of Minerva and Hercules together.

CONCLUSION

The art of the Orientalizing and Archaic periods (to use the designations for this period familiar from Greek art) in Rome and central Italy shows a number of lively trends and developments. Already at this early phase we see the characteristic Roman cultural inclusiveness influencing its art. Foreign traditions from the region, Etruscan and Italic, poured into Rome and Roman art and can be seen in the forms of architecture and sculpture. In these the buildings and terracotta decoration at Murlo are vital evidence. These were joined by influences from further away, Greece and the Near East, that were to be as powerful in shaping Roman art to come. The tension between Italic and Greek art is one that we will be following throughout the coming chapters as various artists and patrons take decisions to adopt one or the other style for a variety of reasons, some personal and others based on context. Many of the styles and subjects of later Roman art owe their forms to the Etruscan reliance on tripartite divisions in art and architecture and their subjects to the use of Greek mythology. The Etruscan tomb paintings provide the best evidence for large-scale painting in early Italy as well as exemplifying the art and culture of Italy as it reacted to Greek art and artists. Roman cultural traits are exemplified by the art of the period as well. The expectation that Roman elites, especially her ruling officials, would dedicate large-scale works of art and architecture is established by the Temple of Jupiter Optimus Maximus. The Tomb of the Shields and Chairs shows the reliance on public service for elite male identity, a notion found in Rome in the house urns of its earliest phases. Finally, the connections between all of these cultures are demonstrated by the images of Minerva (Greek Athena) and Hercules found at Rome and at communities from Pompeii in the south to Etruscan cities in the north. In the next chapter we continue developing these themes with two important developments. The Roman kings were overthrown in 509 BCE and the Roman Republic established. Since different forms of government have different needs in public art and architecture, this political change drives artistic change. The expansion of Rome into more of Italy in the early Roman Republic introduced the Romans to some new artistic subjects and media, for example bronze sculpture, while beginning their conquest of Italy.

SUGGESTIONS FOR FURTHER READING

Albert Ammerman, "On the Origins of Forum Romanum." *American Journal of Archaeology* 94: 627–645 (1990).

Albert Ammerman, "Environmental Archaeology in the Velabrum, Rome: Interim Report." *Journal of Roman Archaeology* 11: 213–223 (1996). This work has been critical in developing our understanding of the city of Rome at its earliest phases. In particular it shows the sequence of the creation of urban public spaces in the Forum Romanum, Capitoline, Palatine, and Forum Boarium.

T.J. Cornell, *The Beginnings of Rome: Italy and Rome from the Bronze Age to the Punic Wars (c.1000–264 BCE)* (Routledge 1995). This magisterial book explores the relationship between Rome and surrounding communities with special emphasis on the question of how Etruscan Rome was in this period. His arguments rely heavily on the art and architecture of the archaic period.

Richard Daniel De Puma and Jocelyn Penny Small, eds., *Murlo and the Etruscans: Art and Society in Ancient Etruria* (University of Wisconsin Press 1994). This collection of essays explores many of the critical elements of this very important Etruscan site. Separate essays address the subjects and interpretations of the architectural phases of the complex as well as the terracotta decoration from the buildings.

R. Ross Holloway, *The Archaeology of Early Rome and Latium* (Routledge 1996). Examines the material culture of early Rome based on the critical archaeological finds including the tombs, Palatine houses, Forum Boarium sanctuaries, and terracotta sculptures from across Latium. He draws connections between these sites and finds to explore issues of early Roman culture.

P.S. Lulof, "Archaic Terracotta Acroteria Representing Athena and Heracles: Manifestations of Power in Central Italy." *Journal of Roman Archaeology* 13: 207–219 (2000). Contextualizes the Athena and Heracles acroteria as only one example of this subject in central Italy at this time. Discusses possible meanings of these terracottas and their use in reinforcing elite power in these communities.

Elena Marini, "A Study of the Architectonic Development of the Great Funerary *Tumuli* in the Etruscan Necropolises of Cerveteri." *Etruscan Studies* 13: 3–28 (2010). Takes a developmental approach to the study of the elite tombs around the Etruscan city of Caere (Cerveteri). Categorizes the necropoleis as well as touching on the commercial relations of these families and the city within the wider Etruscan world.

Nigel Spivey, *Etruscan Art* (Thames and Hudson 1997). Provides a thoughtful and well-illustrated survey of Etruscan art including its reliance on and connections to the art of Greece and the eastern Mediterranean and its relationship to Rome.

Stephan Steingräber, *Abundance of Life: Etruscan Wall Painting* (J. Paul Getty Museum 2006). This book traces the stylistic and iconographic evolution of Etruscan wall paintings over the span of five hundred years and analyzes what they reveal about Etruscan daily life, religion, funerary rites, and belief in the afterlife. The earliest paintings, with their colorful scenes of banquets, hunts, and athletic games, gave way, in the later tombs, to scenes whose darker subjects seem to reflect the collapse of the Etruscan world.

Nancy Winter, *Symbols of Wealth and Power: Architectural Terracotta Decoration in Etruria and Central Italy, 640–510 B.C.* (University of Michigan Press 2009). Rarely has a book been more aptly titled. In addition to their role in architecture, terracottas were used to project wealth, power, and cultural identity at sanctuaries across central Italy in this period, as Dr. Winter's thorough, well-written work concludes.

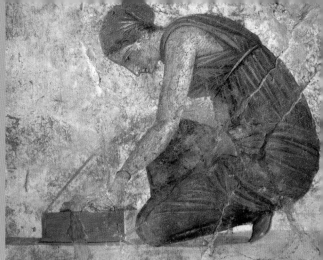

3

THE EARLY REPUBLIC, 509–211 BCE
The Spread of Roman Power and Forms

509 BCE	Founding of the Republic; first public games, the *ludi Romani*, held in Rome; **dedication of the Temple of Jupiter Capitolinus**
480 BCE	**Tomb of the Diver, Paestum**
474 BCE	Battle of Cumae, Greeks defeat Etruscans
470 BCE	**Tomb of the Leopards, Tarquinia**
396 BCE	Romans besiege and defeat Veii, one of the twelve major Etruscan cities
390 BCE	Gallic sack of Rome
386 BCE	**"Servian wall" built around Rome**
364 BCE	First theatrical performance in Rome
338 BCE	Ostia, Rome's first colony, established
300 BCE	**Bronze bust of a man "Brutus"**
273 BCE	Colonies at Paestum and Cosa founded
264 BCE	The first gladiatorial games in Rome at the funeral of Junius Brutus Pera
264–241 BCE	First Punic War
218–202 BCE	Second Punic War

A History of Roman Art, First Edition. Steven L. Tuck.
© 2015 Steven L. Tuck. Published 2015 by John Wiley & Sons, Ltd.

INTRODUCTION TO EARLY ROMAN REPUBLICAN ART

The first phase of the Roman Republic demonstrates the rise of Roman public art and architecture in forms that will become familiar to you from later periods including portraiture, tomb decoration, and high status personal possessions. The traditional founding date of the Roman Republic and the overthrow of the kings in 509 BCE may seem an arbitrary date to mark a new period in the history of Roman art. Yet the close connection between government forms and the needs of public art and architecture meant that this new form of government ushered in new forms of artistic expression. Just as the kings needed art and architecture that reinforced their positions, so did the families and individuals who were to rule Rome under Republican government. With more participation at high levels in government and military leadership Roman artists responded with tomb decoration that celebrates the achievements of Roman elites and portraiture that preserves their images. Urban planning develops cities deliberately designed around the public spaces necessary for members of the community to gather for civic functions. At Rome this planning is manifested in the forum – a public square designed for civic activities – decorated with art (as we will see in subsequent chapters) that reinforces those activities. This can be portrait sculptures of civic and military leaders, monuments celebrating military victories, and civic buildings with decorative programs that reinforce community values.

The chapter also explores the continuing influence of Etruscan art in works of sculpture and painting. As the Romans began to expand power at first through their region, Latium, and then all of Italy they encountered numerous local peoples and regional cultures. While many of these shared common qualities with the Romans, others brought new forms, materials, and concepts of art into the Roman world. In contrast to most ancient peoples, the Romans welcomed this foreign material. Roman cultural inclusiveness and absorption of former enemies becomes a hallmark of their society. The results of this cultural practice in art continue throughout the Republican period and into later periods as well. The elite male values of public civil and military service seen in the Etruscan Tomb of the Shields and Chairs easily transferred to the new Rome where aristocrats competed in these same areas. Their competitions were marked and celebrated by forms of art and architecture in both their homes and public areas of the city. A demonstration of this cultural transference is found in the Roman siege and defeat of the Etruscan city of Veii, one of the twelve major Etruscan cities. In the account in Livy's *History of Rome* (5.22), the Roman commander, Marcus Furius Camillus, prays to the gods before battle:

> Pythian Apollo, guided and inspired by your will I go forth to destroy the city of Veii, and a tenth part of its spoils I devote to you. You too, Queen Juno, who now dwells in Veii, I beseech, that you would follow us, after our victory, to the City [Rome] which is ours and which will soon be yours, where a temple worthy of your majesty will receive you.

Note that the Roman commander invokes a Greek god in seeking the divine support for his attack. The result of his prayer is the relocation of a goddess from an Etruscan city into Rome itself. Such cultural transference is exemplary of the Roman policy throughout the Republic and it had a direct and profound impact on Roman art. The Romans made their own contributions and some of the greatest works of art and architecture blend Roman and foreign influence. Some of the greatest Roman innovations of the early Republican period are seen in the colonies of Ostia, Paestum, and Cosa. New urban forms combined Roman architecture and building materials and Greek city planning to create Rome's first planned cities.

A brief historical survey of the Early Republic

While a comprehensive history of Rome is outside the scope of this book, the facts of Roman conquest provide important context to the development of Roman arts. The period can be considered the rise of Rome, but also the decline of the Etruscans. Their absorption by the Romans can be illustrated in a few dates and events. In 474 BCE the Battle of Cumae occurred, a naval battle off the west coast of Italy at the site of the first Greek colony at Cumae. The Greeks of southern Italy defeated the Etruscans. In 415 BCE the Etruscans supported the massive Athenian military expedition to conquer Sicily. The expedition was the greatest military disaster in Athenian history and was another major loss for the Etruscans. In 390 BCE the southernmost Etruscan city, Veii, fell to the Romans in a siege. This battle weakened all of Etruria as many communities had poured support into Veii. Finally, the three Samnite Wars saw the Etruscans join the Samnites against Roman expansion. The third war ended in 290 BCE with the defeat of this allied group of Samnites, Etruscans, and other peoples of Italy. Rome quickly began to occupy their territories with colonies that created a permanent Roman presence throughout much of Italy.

By the end of this period Rome controlled Italy from the Po river valley in the far north to the end of the Italian peninsula in the south, "from the Po to the toe." This rapid expansion and cultural dominance has a near contemporary witness in Greek historian Polybius (*c.* 200–118 BCE), who captured the importance of this period in powerful terms (1.1.5–6),

> For who is there so worthless and lazy that he would not wish to know how and under what kind of government the Romans have brought under their sole rule almost the whole of the inhabited world in less than fifty-three years; for nothing like this has ever happened before. Or who can be so devoted to any other subject of study that he would regard it as more important than the acquisition of this knowledge?

Through the chapter the Etruscan art survey continues with examinations of their artistic media and subjects. If Roman gains are reflected in their art, it shouldn't be a surprise that Etruscan losses are reflected in theirs. A shift occurs in tomb painting subjects as demons, death, and the underworld come to dominate just as the Etruscan world is being taken over by the Romans. Meanwhile we see the first of what can be called true portraits and historical narratives in Italic art. These are two of the subjects that come to dominate Roman art in later periods and both enter their art in the Early Republic.

Greek wall painting: Tomb of the Diver, Paestum

Since Greek art comes to dominate Roman art in later periods in all media including painting, it makes sense to examine the earliest and best-preserved example of Greek monumental painting, which is in southern Italy. The Tomb of the Diver is a Greek underground tomb from their colony at Poseidonia (later referred to by its Roman name, Paestum). For its location, see Figure 2.1.

The Tomb of the Diver consists of five slabs of local limestone. Four of these, two long and two short, are arranged on edge to make the walls of the tomb while the fifth was laid flat to make the tomb's roof. All were plastered and painted on the interior. All four walls were illustrated with a coherent

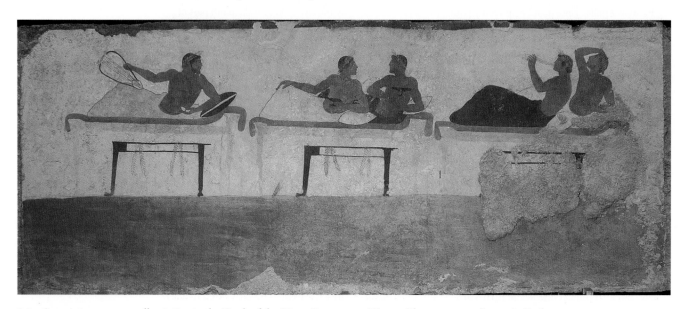

3.1 Symposium scene, wall painting in the Tomb of the Diver, Paestum, *c.* 480 BCE. Photo courtesy Steven L. Tuck.

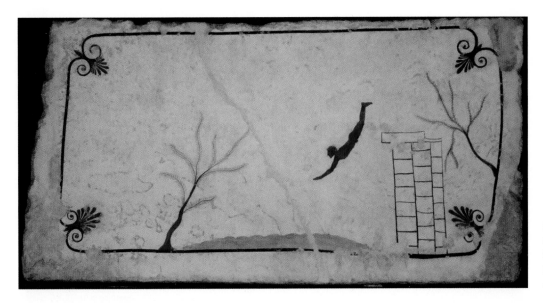

3.2   Diver scene from the roof slab, wall painting in the Tomb of the Diver, Paestum, *c*. 480 BCE. Photo courtesy Steven L. Tuck.

banquet scene of a **symposium**. One short end shows a young cupbearer and table holding a large wine crater. The other has a young flute-playing girl leading a couple of guests, an older bearded man and younger man. The long walls are filled with elite males reclining on dining couches. Each wall has three couches, two of which show other couples composed of an older and a younger man, in two cases clearly loving couples, demonstrating the Greek concept of male same-sex love defined by a relationship between an older and a younger man. The third couch has one older, bearded man on each, one with a lyre. The lyre is an important component of the symposium and elite male identity as lyric poetry was sung or recited accompanied by the lyre. A lyre was left in this tomb as one of the very few grave goods. The subject of the wall paintings reinforces the elite status of the tomb's occupant, certainly a local high-status man, by connecting him to Greek male culture across the Greek world.

Although 480 BCE is the conventional date for the start of the Classical period in Greek art, these paintings are solidly in the late Archaic tradition. All of the figures use the Greek gender convention of red skin for males and white for females. The bodies are not integrated, but composed of separate parts so that when one part moves, the rest of the body does not. There are no successful oblique views, the faces are all pure profile views, and the internal details are defined by lines rather than shadow to create volume. The forms are all painted in blocks of solid color without shading. The roof scene introduces something new to Greek art, evidence of Etruscan motifs, proving that the artistic influences flowed in both directions.

The scene on the interior of the flat roof shows a young man diving off of a platform into a body of water below. His form follows Greek conventions including skin tone and ideal proportions for the slender young man. The scene, however, is unique in Greek art. It seems to come from Etruscan art and is identical in subject to the diver in the earlier Tomb of Hunting and Fishing, from the Etruscan necropolis at Tarquinia (Figure 2.25). The meaning of the scene is metaphorical. As in the Etruscan tomb of fifty years earlier, it shows the passage of the deceased from life to death and from this world into the underworld. Found here in a Greek tomb in a community on the boundary between Greek and Etruscan lands it seems to indicate the cultural transference that took place along the frontier as Etruscan beliefs in the afterlife (or, at least, images of the passage into it) are adopted by the Greeks. Similarly, the transfer of Greek styles and motifs continues into Etruscan art, but with adaptations for Etruscan cultural values.

Etruscan tomb painting of the fifth century BCE

That transfer of Greek styles and motifs into Etruscan art was addressed in the previous chapter in tomb painting. Here, we can see the same trend, but with definite limits to its spread as Etruscan subjects show that Greek material is adapted and not adopted wholesale. The back wall of the burial

symposium
a Greek elite male drinking party at which men would recline on couches to drink wine, listen to entertainment, sing, or discuss philosophical, cultural, or political topics.

chamber of the Tomb of the Leopards at Tarquinia is dominated by a large banquet scene. Its subject and composition rely closely on Greek models. Like the banquet panels in the Tomb of the Diver, it has three couches, each holding two elite diners while servants stand at the feet of two of the couches. Greek conventions of profile faces, blocks of color, gendered skin tone, and Archaic body proportions are used as are the garlands indicating a celebration. The overall composition of the wall, however, relies on Etruscan conventions with its tripartite division both horizontally and vertically and the use of red lines to define the registers and act as groundlines in the upper zones.

3.3 Banquet scene, wall painting in the Tomb of the Leopards, Tarquinia, 470 BCE. Photo courtesy Steven L. Tuck.

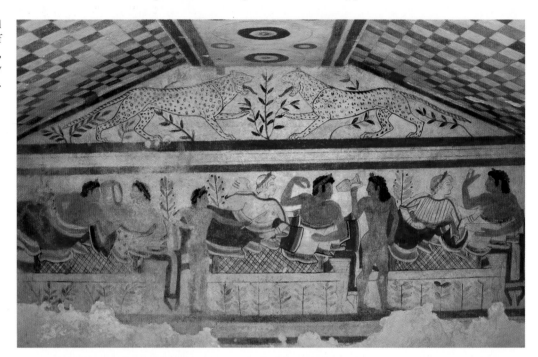

3.4 Dancers, wall painting from the Tomb of the Triclinium, Tarquinia, 470 BCE. Photo courtesy Steven L. Tuck.

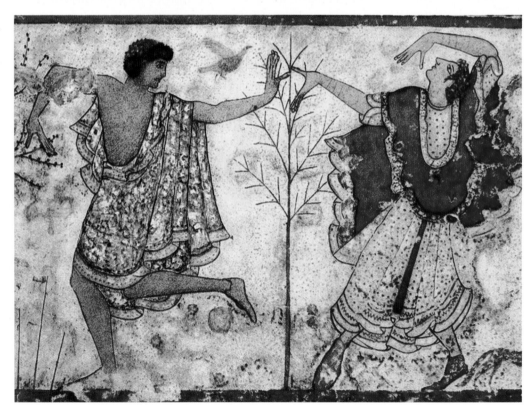

The subject is not a symposium, however, but a banquet of male–female couples, probably married couples, indicating Etruscan cultural adaptation of the Greek original. Other Etruscan conventions applied to the scene include hierarchy of scale with the small-scale servants showing their lower status. Horror vacui is also seen, with plants filling the spaces between the legs of the dining couches and, nonsensically, sprouting above and behind the couches. Another contemporary tomb from Tarquinia shows the dynamic nature of Etruscan art.

SCHOLARLY PERSPECTIVE
Can we understand the meaning of Etruscan tomb paintings?

The study of the art of the earlier periods of Roman and Etruscan culture is not for those with a low tolerance for ambiguity. One of the thorniest problems in understanding Etruscan and early Italian art is determining the meaning of the scenes on the wall paintings in Etruscan tombs. Of the little, imperfectly understood, Etruscan writing that survives none of it sheds light on these images. There are no direct descriptions or analysis of the scenes from ancient authors. We are left with comparisons between these and parallel images in contemporary cultures and using what we know of Etruscan beliefs and behaviors from other evidence. The ubiquitous banquets found on wall paintings, terracotta sarcophagi, cinerary urns, etc. are perhaps the most divisive images for scholars. All scholars conclude that the banquets portray the deceased and not just generic images as we saw in the Greek Tomb of the Diver. But some feel that these high status social gatherings are idealized images of the type of events that would have punctuated Etruscan life while others see them as merely symbolic of the status, or presumed status, of the deceased and therefore they may not reflect any actual event but stand only as a shorthand for Etruscan elite life. A third school concludes that these are banquets of eternity and that the images are actually of banquets in the underworld at which the deceased, family, and friends partake in a feast, the imagery of which depicts the happy afterlife they will have in eternity marked by feasting, music, dancing, and games. These scholars point to the correspondences between the food in the paintings and the actual food left in tombs such as grapes, pomegranates, honey, eggs, olives, and amphorae of wine.

Almost as contentious are the scenes of games. We know that various games and athletic contests were held at funerals to honor the deceased. Literary sources also report the origins of gladiatorial combat at funerals as a blood sacrifice for the dead. But the images that survive of these games from the tombs themselves seem altogether too grand to be held in honor of each of the deceased. We are faced with the same conclusions as with the banquets. Either they represent idealized versions of the actual events held at the funeral of the deceased, hypothetical events that reflect the status of the dead, or images from the afterlife as the banquets are. Supporting the notions that they reflect some element of real life is the testimony of grave goods and later authors that these sorts of events were held at funerals. On the other side, however, is the authority of the Roman poet, Vergil, whose description of the underworld (*Aeneid* 6.638–695) exactly matches many of these images:

> they came to the pleasant places, the delightful grassy turf of the Fortunate Groves, and the homes of the blessed. ... Some exercise their bodies in a grassy gymnasium, compete in sports and wrestle on the yellow sand: others tread out the steps of a dance, and sing songs. ... Look, he sees others on the grass to right and left, feasting, and singing a joyful paean in chorus, among the fragrant groves of laurel . . .

Vergil's description solves the problem of all of these scenes except the darker underworld scenes of the later Etruscan periods, but he could have been relating an earlier, more positive time. Of course, he is a Roman writing five hundred years after some of this imagery and not an Etruscan. By comparison, we wouldn't accept anything written today by an American as firsthand testimony for the English Renaissance. No theory has or is expected to receive universal acceptance, but through the process of debate and marshaling evidence and arguments we believe that we will continue to come closer to understanding this art.

Stephan Steingräber, *Abundance of Life: Etruscan Wall Painting* (J. Paul Getty Museum 2006).

The dancers from the Tomb of the Triclinium at Tarquinia demonstrate the continuity of influence of Greek Archaic artistic style and subjects in Etruscan art. This pair of dancers derives from Greek models of dancing followers of the god Dionysus. Here there is no Dionysiac iconography, but figures dancing, probably on their way to or from a banquet on the adjacent wall, which may be either an idealized banquet in this life or one in the underworld – scholars are not certain on this point. The figures show the Greek conventions of gendered skin tone and the Archaic conventions of profile faces and legs and frontal torsos as well as nonintegrated bodies with arms and legs in apparent motion that have no effect on the symmetry of their torsos or other body parts. The pair is separated by the traditional Etruscan plant life that fills the backgrounds of many tomb wall paintings. Greek influence in Etruscan art continues to extend into terracotta work, one of the media Etruscans were most famous for mastering in the ancient world.

Etruscan terracotta plaque, Pyrgi

One of the best examples of Greek subjects in Etruscan art of this period is found at the coastal Etruscan sanctuary site at Pyrgi, 30 miles (50 km) north of Rome. This major sanctuary developed into a large complex in the sixth century and was the site of Etruscan and foreign interactions. Some of these were military while others were religious and diplomatic. The latter were exemplified by gold plaques in Etruscan and Phoenician (the language of the Carthaginians) displayed in the sanctuary that recorded a treaty between the two enemies of the Greeks.

Shortly after the disastrous Battle of Cumae in 474 BCE, the Etruscans built Etrusco-Italic style Temple A at the sanctuary. Despite their loss to the Greeks, Greek myth is the preferred subject and artistic style for the largest decorative element of the temple. A large, very high-relief terracotta plaque filled the pediment at the rear of the temple. It illustrates one of the most dramatic scenes in the Greek myth of the Seven against Thebes, the duel between Tydeus and Melanippus, who are seen at the bottom of the relief locked in deadly combat, the mortally wounded Tydeus eating the brain of his enemy.

3.5 Pediment relief sculpture from Temple A, Pyrgi, 460 BCE. Museo Nazionale Etrusco di Villa Giulia, Rome. H 57 ½ in (146 cm). Source: © 2014. Photo Scala, Florence. Courtesy of the Ministero Beni e Att. Culturali.

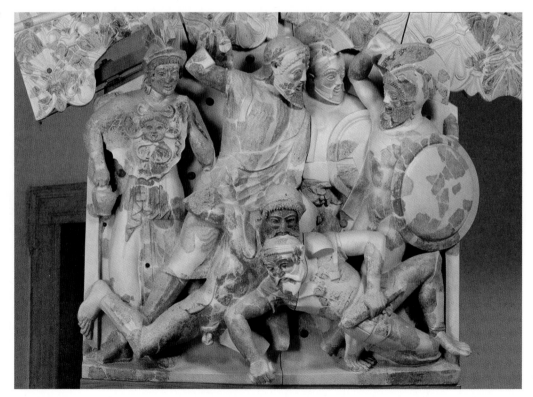

MORE ON MYTH
Seven against Thebes

This myth develops from the story of Oedipus. Having killed his father and married his mother, Oedipus and his mother/wife had three children, sons Eteocles and Polynices, and daughter Antigone. When they discover their crime, his wife hangs herself and Oedipus blinds himself. Unable to rule Thebes any longer, it falls to his sons who agree to share power, ruling in alternate years, Eteocles first. After the year is over Eteocles refuses to step down and Polynices recruits an army from Argos with seven captains, the Seven against Thebes, to take the city and overthrow his brother. The seven each faced a defending captain and his forces at one of the seven gates to the city, which included Tydeus and Melanippus who kill each other in horrific fashion. Eteocles and Polynices meet and fight before the walls of the city where they slay each other in battle. This mythical fratricide was the subject of a play by Aeschylus that was produced about 467 BCE in Athens. Images of Eteocles and Polynices and their mutual and simultaneous deaths are found on many works of Etruscan art, notably bronze mirrors and terracotta cinerary urns.

The upper register is filled with three figures: the gods, Athena on the left and Zeus in the center, striking down another attacker, Capeneus, with his thunderbolt. Both Capeneus and Tydeus had outraged the gods and were therefore killed. In an act of hubris, overbearing pride, Capeneus swore that even Zeus could not prevent him scaling the wall of Thebes. Tydeus' cannibalism is an obvious impiety for which Athena withholds his promised immortality. In representing the scene, rarely found in Greek art, but popular among the Etruscans like other images of the cycle, the artist has chosen the moment of climactic narrative rather than the more common Greek anticipatory narrative that would hint at the horror to come but not show it explicitly. Here the horror is clear and the message that the gods will punish acts of impiety is fitting for a major sanctuary and may have been directed at visiting Greeks and Carthaginians as well as Etruscans.

LUCANIAN TOMB PAINTING, PAESTUM

The Greek colony of Poseidonia, like many of the communities along the west coast of Italy including Pompeii, was overrun in the late fifth century BCE by incursions of Italic people from the center of Italy. In the case of Poseidonia, the Lucanians occupied the city starting about 425 BCE and bringing their own culture to dominate but also absorb the Greek one that was already there. From this point on we refer to the city as Paestum. The extent of cultural change that occurred is reflected in a quote on loss from a Greek author, Aristoxenus, in his work *Promiscuous Banquets*,

> We act in a manner similar to the people of Paestum who dwell in the Tyrrhenian Gulf; for it happened to them, though they were originally Greeks, to have become at last completely barbarized . . . and to have changed their language, all the rest of their national habits. But one Greek festival they do celebrate even to the present day [third century CE], in which they meet and recollect all their ancient names and customs and bewail their loss to one another, and then, when they have wept for them, they go home.

In the immediate aftermath of the Lucanian occupation of Paestum we might expect more Greek influence to remain. Looking at the Lucanian tomb paintings we can see some evidence of it. The Lucanian tombs differ from the Tomb of the Diver in shape though all are underground tombs. They consist of four slabs of local limestone used for walls, but the short ends are shaped with triangular tops to hold a pair of roof slabs that make up a standard sort of gabled roof. They also differ in subject. The most revealing subjects in the Lucanian tomb paintings are funerary rituals, including the earliest images of gladiatorial combat in art.

Lucanian tomb paintings with human figures are found by 390 BCE, with the earliest images of funerary ritual among the paintings dated to 380 BCE. This demonstrates the key role funerary ritual played in celebrating the lives of the deceased and the piety of their survivors in preparing an appropriately elaborate tomb. The wall paintings from Tomb 90a, dated to about 370 BCE, preserve funerary games in three pairs of figures on two walls. On one wall we see a pair of charioteers driving two horse chariots past a column. On the other a column separates the two scenes of different events. On the left a pair of boxers pummel each other until blood flows freely to the accompaniment of a

3.6 Funerary games of boxers and gladiators, wall painting from Tomb 90a, Paestum, 370 BCE. Museo Archeologico Nazionale di Paestum. Photo courtesy Steven L. Tuck.

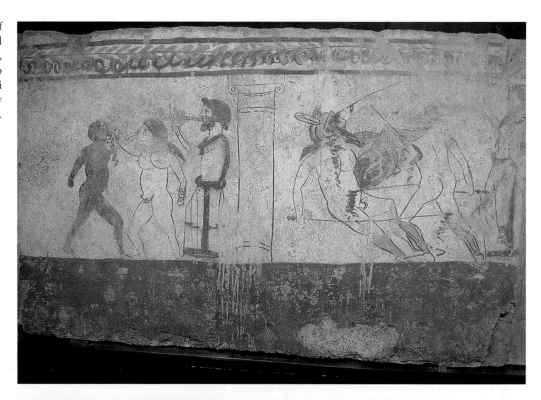

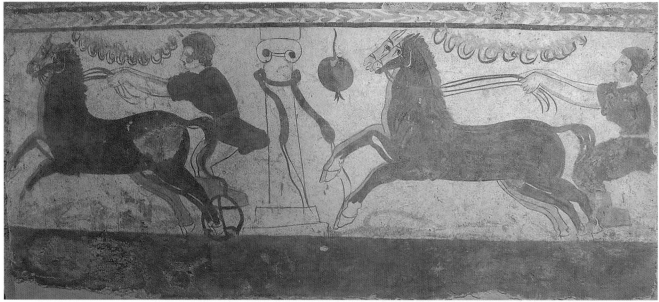

3.7 Funerary games of charioteers, wall painting from Tomb X, Paestum, 350 BCE. Museo Archeologico Nazionale di Paestum. Photo courtesy Steven L. Tuck.

flute player. On the left a pair of gladiators, armored with helmets and greaves and armed with spear and shield, also fight until blood flows freely, watched by a figure who may be a supervising official. The emphasis on blood flow is significant and sets these apart from the athletic contests known from Greek funeral games where blood flow was not the object of the competition. Here the blood seems to be a sacrifice to the dead, over whose tomb they might have fought so the blood soaked the ground above the deceased, perhaps as a sacrifice to the gods of the dead easing their passage. These scenes likely do not illustrate the actual games for this individual, but represent the idealized version, operating as a sort of promise to the deceased witnessed by those attending the funeral.

Greek cultural and artistic elements are seen in the many chariot scenes. The notion of chariot racing as a component of funeral games is found in Greek culture back to the eighth century BCE and it is certainly from the Greeks that the Lucanians adopted this motif. Most of the images show light two-horse chariots being driven by charioteers, in some cases wearing helmets. That the image is a ritual is clear from the details such as the garland around the column, the garlands that fill the field above the horses, and the large hovering pomegranate next to the column. The pomegranate is associated with death and rebirth in Greek iconography as in the story of Persephone eating pomegranate in the underworld. The garlands and pomegranate, therefore, make it clear that the context is not just ritual, but funerary ritual. The artist has created bold images with a sense of motion with the charioteers leaning forward as their tunics flow behind them. The horses' front hooves are off the ground about to touch down as they gallop.

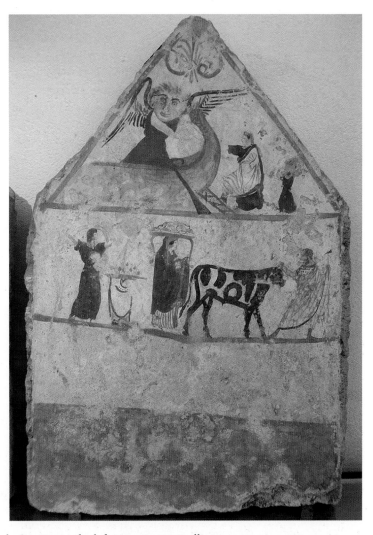

dado
the lower portion of the wall of a room, often distinctly decorated with panels or painted in contrasting colors.

Throughout the fourth-century BCE Lucanian tombs we see the development of clear and exclusive male and female gender roles illustrating the ideal qualities of the deceased. Women are often portrayed as fulfilling their duties in the domestic sphere while men hunt wild animals, fight in war, display their armor, or are celebrated by funerary blood sports. The source for the vast majority of the imagery of female domestic duties is Greek art. Exact and earlier parallels for many scenes of women spinning wool or selecting jewelry from boxes can be found in Athenian grave stones. Other images, however, seem to have more complex origins and meanings.

The short, gabled end of a Lucanian woman's tomb from the mid-fourth century BCE demonstrates the complexity in many of these artistic programs. The slab is divided into four registers, starting from the bottom a red **dado**, an Etruscan method of denoting the base of a wall, then a blank register, then two figural registers. The first shows a segment of the funeral itself as the procession moves to the right towards the tomb. Starting at the left is a mourner pulling her hair or striking her head in grief, a woman carrying a tray of food, a woman with a table piled with loaves of bread on her head, a cow for sacrifice, and finally a man, probably a priest, leading the cow and carrying a hammer, which he will use to perform the sacrifice.

The uppermost register shows a scene that is unique in all of ancient Italic art. With a small mourner, probably a young girl, behind her, the deceased herself, although it must surely be only her spirit, steps forward onto a boat reaching out her hand to the welcoming arms of a truly monstrous figure. The

3.8 Scenes of woman's funeral and travel into the underworld, wall painting from Tomb 47, Paestum, 360 BCE. Museo Archeologico Nazionale di Paestum. Photo courtesy Steven L. Tuck.

chthonic
literally "of the earth," refers to anything, usually a god or other powerful being that dwells under the earth or draws its power from the earth.

psychopomp
psychopompos, literally "guide of souls," a descriptor of the god Mercury who guided the souls of the newly dead into the underworld.

figure, standing above the steering oar of the boat, is clearly the figure that guides the woman's spirit into the underworld. It is not the male ferryman Charon of Greek mythology, however. It is a female, judging by her white skin and dress. She has a pair of large, spread wings and a truly enormous head that most resembles a gorgon. She must be a variant on the Vanth, a winged, female Etruscan **chthonic** figure that supervised and aided the passage of the deceased into the underworld. Vanths are found on many forms of Etruscan funerary art, from wall paintings to terracotta urns, where they generally stand beside the deceased at the moment of death or are shown guiding them in some conveyance (horse, wagon, or chariot, for example) on the journey into the underworld, a role known as the **psychopomp**. This conflation of Greek and Etruscan iconography demonstrates the rich cultural mixing of ancient Italy as a Lucanian woman is celebrated in her tomb paintings with a Greek style procession and her mourners comforted with an image of her passage to the underworld that makes use of a mixture of Greek and Etruscan iconography of that passage. Male identity develops its own forms of imagery in these tombs as well and leads to what may be some of the earliest representations of historical events in Italic art.

As noted above, elite male identity in Lucanian tomb paintings differs from elite female identity. Males are often celebrated by scenes that create visual records of their masculine excellence, what in Greek would be called *arête* and in Latin *virtus* (we do not know the Lucanian word). Generic scenes such as the departing warrior motif – an armed, mounted man leaving for battle, lion hunts, gladiatorial matches, or displays of armor – all reinforce generalized notions of male identity without making statements of particular activities on the part of the deceased. One tomb has such a detailed and circumstantial painting that it is thought to represent an actual historic event in which the deceased participated and may move past generic forms of heroization into a record of history. The scene on the long side of Tomb 114 shows the moment prior to the start of battle. On the left we see an army lined up with shields in formation. Behind them is a specific topographical detail, a mountain with a herd of cattle behind it. To the right is another army lined up facing them. One figure in this line stands out by his size, facial features, and helmet. He is larger and taller than the other warriors in rank, his face closely resembles that of the departing warrior on the adjacent short end slab and he wears a Lucanian helmet known from tombs rather than the generic cone of his fellow warriors. Perhaps this scene shows an actual battle, perhaps in response to a cattle raid from the hills just to the

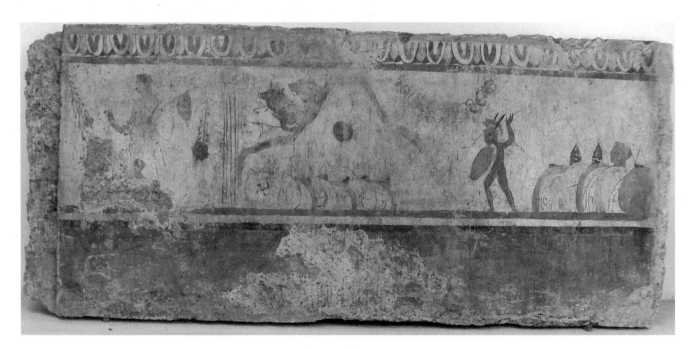

3.9　Historical battle, tomb painting from Tomb 114, Paestum, 320 BCE. Museo Archeologico Nazionale di Paestum. Photo courtesy Steven L. Tuck.

A VIEW FROM THE PROVINCES

Poseidonia/Paestum: Cultural crossroads of southern Italy

One could argue, in fact I'm just about to, that the site of Poseidonia/Paestum represents a superb example of the artistic cross-fertilization and succession of influences that we find contributing to Roman art, particularly in the Early Republican period. Founded by Greek colonists from Sybaris in *c.* 600 BCE, its territory extended as far north as the banks of the Sele river across which was the furthest extent of Etruscan expansion. It was essentially on the frontier between Greek and Etruscan territory. Some of the Greek art and architecture from the colony is purely Greek, for example, the spectacular and well-preserved temples (see Figure 1.5a). Other art from the Greek period, such as the Tomb of the Diver (Figures 3.1, 3.2), shows a mix of Greek and Etruscan subjects and styles and it challenges the traditional notion of Etruscan art as a receptor of Greek influence, where clearly in this case those roles are reversed. It forces us to consider a different model, one of an artistic cross-pollination.

With the occupation of the city by the Lucanians *c.* 425 BCE we see a new cultural layer added to the local dynamic but not apparently replacing it. This is best seen in the Lucanian tombs whose grave goods include Lucanian armor but also Greek vases and personal objects such as items used in the Greek gymnasium. The paintings from the Lucanian tombs in the fourth and third centuries BCE depict subjects and styles familiar from Greek art including the Greek iconography of death with pomegranates, chariot races as components of funeral games (Figure 3.7), and elite males and females portrayed with the same dress, jewelry and accessories as contemporary Greeks on their grave markers (Figure 3.8). It may not be a surprise that Greek influence permeates this art when they apparently continued to live in the city under the occupying Lucanians, but the very notion that the occupying people adopted the culture of the occupied is not an inevitability. Note that very little of the culture of early American colonies shows such an adoption of Native American art and representation.

In addition to the Greek subjects and styles, Etruscan influences permeate the art of the Lucanian and, to a lesser extent, Greek period at Poseidonia/Paestum. The roof slab painting in the Tomb of the Diver features an Etruscan motif of transition to the underworld (Figure 3.2) while the wall paintings in the tomb feature a red dado, which seems to be an Etruscan innovation. That dado and other elements of composition in the Lucanian tomb paintings also derive from Etruscan examples. Some of the Lucanian tomb subjects also seem to be Etruscan in origin. The blood sports that are such prominent features of the tomb paintings including boxing, but most importantly the various gladiatorial pairs (Figure 3.6) reflect an activity seen in earlier permutations on the walls of Etruscan tombs and which the surviving literary sources also attribute to the Etruscans. When the Romans establish their colony here in 273 BCE it places them in direct contact with this rich and complex artistic tradition. Examining a Roman work such as one of their earliest surviving tomb paintings we can separate the threads of all three cultures from their art at Paestum: the Greek decorative frieze along the top of the wall, the historical event in the central field as seen in Lucanian tombs, and the Etruscan dado at the base of the wall.

east of Paestum, that the deceased fought in. His side is led by another unusual figure. Standing in front of the army is a tall male, naked but for a shield and a type of Lucanian helmet, who raises a spear against the enemies. This seems to be the Italic god, Mars, who leads the army. The Italic artistic convention of mixing gods and mortals in a single scene is one we will see often later in Roman art. Here we believe we see that convention in an early historical event.

Etruscan tomb painting of the fourth century BCE

Etruscan tomb painting of the fourth century BCE demonstrates two major changes from the idealized images of banquet and elite status activities seen in the earlier sixth and fifth centuries BCE. First, the subjects become darker, and the mood changes from a celebration of life to mourning of death.

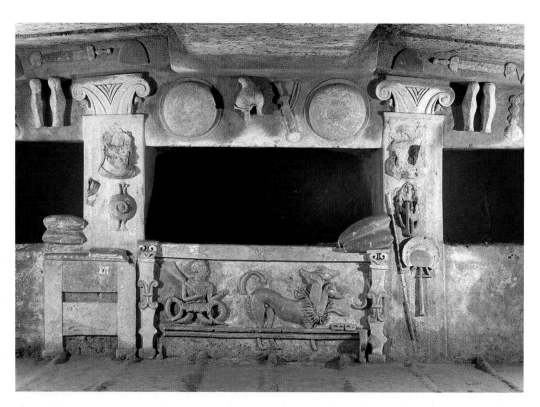

3.10 Carved and painted reliefs, Tomb of the Reliefs, Cerveteri, 4th cent. BCE. Source: © 2014. Photo Scala, Florence. Courtesy of the Ministero Beni e Att. Culturali.

Some scholars conclude that this reflects the political and military upheaval in the Etruscan world at the time. Second, in this period true portraits make their first appearance in Etruscan painting.

The Tomb of the Reliefs shows us much about Etruscan art and culture in the fourth century. It demonstrates the continued Etruscan expertise with terracotta work, the expansion of Greek material into new areas, and the Etruscan response in art to their steady loss of territory to Rome. The tomb is a large underground tomb with a passage leading down into a single large room surrounded by niches cut to resemble beds, in which bodies were to rest with their stone pillows carved out of the bedrock as well. In normal Etruscan domestic pattern, three niches line the back wall of the room. The walls and piers of the room are covered with brightly painted terracotta reliefs. Most of these are of household objects such as drinking vessels, hand tools, kitchen implements, and so forth. Military gear including helmets, shields, greaves, and swords are carved over the rear niches, suggesting that these high status beds were reserved for the adult males in the family. Notably this is contemporary with the great wars between the Etruscans and Romans for domination of central Italy, both wars that were not going the Etruscans' way. That loss might be reflected in the reliefs below the central bed. Here are two demons of the underworld, Charun and Cerberus, the three-headed dog who guards the underworld's entrance in Greek mythology. Suddenly we begin to see an emphasis on the dark figures of the underworld, demons and monstrous figures who indicate a shift, if not in Etruscan belief about the underworld, then in their imagery of it. The tombs at Tarquinia prove that this trend is not limited to Cerveteri, but extends through the Etruscan world.

The Tomb of Orcus seems to reflect the increasing emphasis on the dark side of death that we see during the course of the fourth and third centuries BCE in Etruscan art. Images of demons, often tormenting people in the underworld, are found throughout the tomb. Gone are the funeral games and dancing figures of the earlier periods. Banquets are overseen by demons. Another new form of representation emerges at this period, portraiture. The deceased were named in earlier inscriptions on their urns and niches, but in the late fourth century BCE names are attached to specific figures who seem to be painted to show the visage and character of the deceased, the earliest Etruscan portraits. These were initially somewhat generic, but show attempts at individualism as well as recent artistic developments.

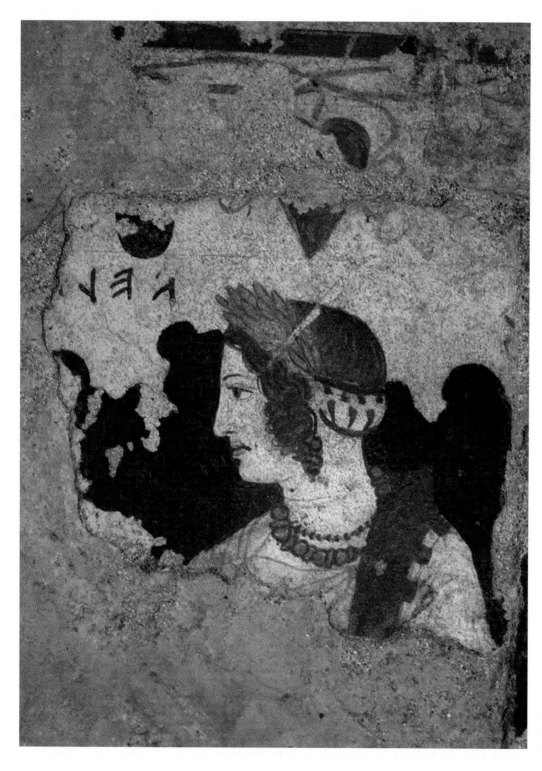

3.11 Portrait of Velia, tomb painting, Tomb of Orcus, Tarquinia, 330 BCE. Photo courtesy Steven L. Tuck.

The occupant of this tomb is Velia, a noble Etruscan woman. She stares ahead with a solemn expression. She is richly attired in an elaborate dress and earrings and necklaces of types known from Etruscan jewelry. She wears a gold wreath on her elegantly arranged hair. The wreath is a type found in the tombs of southern Italy associated with Greek cults, indicating a belief in life after death. The very realistic depiction of the eye, shown from the side rather than frontally as in earlier period Etruscan painting, is a clear indication of the artist's knowledge of late fourth-century BCE Greek models.

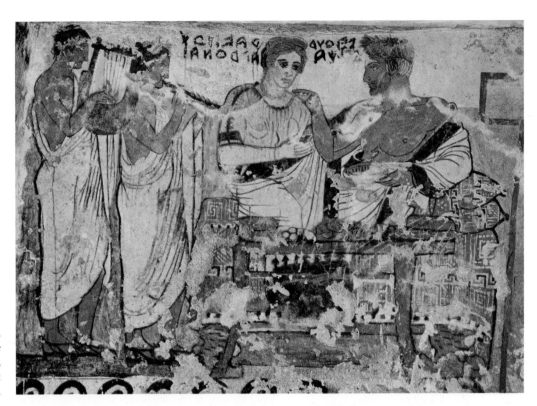

3.12   Banqueting couple, wall painting from the Tomb of the Shields, Tarquinia, 325 BCE. Source: © INTERFOTO/Alamy.

The elements of Greek art, elite identity, portraiture, and the mourning impulse in Etruscan art come together in a modified banquet scene from the Tomb of the Shields, also from Tarquinia. The name of the tomb comes from the large golden shields painted on the back wall, but the majority of the paintings are scenes from the lives of the Velcha family, the tomb's occupants.

The many paintings of generations of members of the Velcha family show them in a variety of poses and situations that reinforce the family's status including at least one banquet scene. On the back wall, one of the most privileged locations in the tomb, there is a banquet, with the two banqueters identified by painted captions. Larth Velcha reclining on his couch with his wife Velia Seitithi, who is handing him an egg, a common symbol of rebirth or life after death found in Etruscan tombs and tomb paintings. Two smaller-scale musicians who stand at the foot of the couch attend them, traditional Etruscan figures in Italic hierarchy of scale. Unlike the earlier ideal banquets, this one is somber, with Velia looking mournfully at her husband while he places his right hand on her shoulder in a gesture of comfort. She is portrayed in three-quarter view, a fourth-century BCE Greek artistic refinement, with her face about halfway between frontal and profile view. The wall paintings in the tomb combine the iconography of death and that of elite life in new ways. The same notion of combined identity is developed in another Tarquinian tomb of an elite family, the Tomb of the Typhon, perhaps thirty years later.

A wall painting from the Tomb of the Typhon shows a procession of sixteen figures featuring humans – presumably the deceased, relatives and retainers – along with demons with many of their standard attributes: snakes, torches, and hammers. The figures are lined up in rows to indicate space as the back rows rise up the wall. Their faces are individualized and the artist used a range of frontal, profile, and three-quarter views to add variety and a sense of depth to the composition. The form of the procession is such that it could be the journey of the deceased, dressed as and with the attributes of a magistrate, to the underworld with demons, family, priests, and retainers accompanying him, reinforcing his status. That combination of the natural and supernatural is found throughout Italic and later Roman art. Rather than detracting from the historicity of an occasion it served to highlight the significance of an event with the divine in attendance. This might, however, be a different sort of

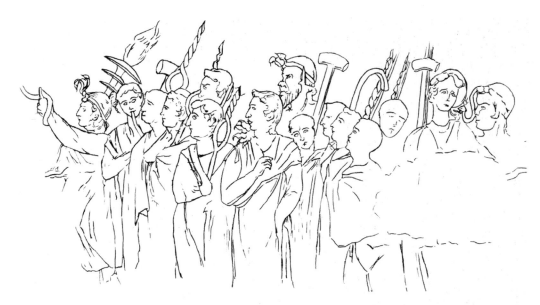

3.13 Processional scene, Tomb of the Typhon, Tarquinia, late 3rd cent. BCE, drawing by Jacquelyn Clements. Drawing courtesy Jaquelyn Clements and Nancy de Grummond.

procession. It could be the funeral itself and not a spiritual journey to the underworld, but to the tomb. The demons and infernal figures might be priests dressed to represent them. The Roman historian Livy records that sort of pageantry occurring prior to a battle between Romans and Etruscans from Tarquinia in 356 BCE. He writes (7.17.3) that the Romans were thrown into panic because leading the Etruscan troops came "priests bearing serpents and blazing torches before them . . . [which] utterly dismayed the Roman soldiers with the extraordinary sight." Note that the attributes are the same as those in the wall painting, which blurs the lines between historic and symbolic in this art. The use of symbols as well as the emphasis on procession are found in the earliest example of Roman tomb painting so far known. It is notable that no historical scenes were painted on Etruscan tombs until their wars with Rome. Scholars continue to debate the direction of possible influence, whether from Rome or from Etruria. One thing is clear. By the third century BCE, historical paintings were found in the tombs of Etruscans, Romans, and Lucanians.

Roman tomb painting of the Early Republic

The earliest discovered historic Roman wall painting was found in a tomb outside the walls of Rome. The painting shows a number of key similarities to both Etruscan and Lucanian tomb paintings, but also elements that are recognizably Roman, conveying a clear picture of the celebration of the life of an elite Roman whose military achievements won fame for his family.

The major figure in the painting is a bearded man on horseback wearing a plumed helmet, belted white tunic, and boots and leading a small procession. The procession includes two men on foot immediately behind his horse. They are toga-clad, bearded, and probably represent middle-aged magistrates. The final two figures are unbearded young men on horseback. The procession faces a sixth man standing along the left edge of the painting wearing a toga with a portion of it pulled over his head, *capite velato*. He holds a staff in his right hand and a vessel of some kind in his left. As we read the scene, it depicts a returning victorious general leading a procession back to the city of two walking magistrates, possibly the consuls for the year, and mounted members of his army. It may be an early form of triumph, although it has none of the key elements known from triumphs in the later Republican period. The iconography is similar to the much later images of imperial *adventus* (Figure 7.25). The religious figures are key because the general must undergo ritual purification before he enters the *pomerium*, the sacred boundary of Rome. The figure on the left is clearly a priest wearing his toga as one did in preparation for a sacrifice or performing other sacred ritual. The general seems to have his right hand raised in a gesture of speaking or acclamation as seen on later *adventus*

capite velato
Latin, meaning "with covered head," referring to the act of covering one's head while performing a sacred ritual.

adventus
arrival ceremony conducted by civil and religious officials, usually after a military campaign, welcoming a commander or emperor back into Rome. These occurred formally at the city gate.

pomerium
the sacred boundary of Rome. In legal and religious terms Rome consisted only of that part of the city within it. Burials were forbidden inside the *pomerium*.

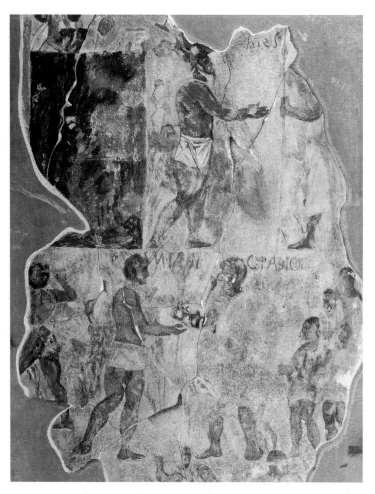

3.14 Tomb of Q. Fabius, wall painting from a tomb on the Esquiline Hill, Rome, *c.* 300–250 BCE. Musei Capitolini, Rome. H 34 ¼ in (87 cm). Source: © De Agostini/Superstock.

episodic narrative
a narrative structure in which a series of events or episodes occur with the same main character, generally portrayed in each episode.

coins and reliefs including the Cancelleria reliefs (Figures 7.25, 7.26, 8.24). Whether this painting represents a triumph or an *adventus*, the name of the deceased and the occasion are lost to us.

The painting style, layout, and composition are very similar to Lucanian tombs from Paestum, with a solid red dado covering the lower portion of the wall and used as a groundline for the figural scene, which proceeds with no landscape elements or Etruscan *horror vacui*. The subject, however, is not found in the painted tombs from Paestum or Etruria though it is closer to the processions in later Etruscan tombs. The figures are not captioned, raising the question of whether this is a generic scene or historic event. We may never be certain, as many forms of Roman ritual are very generic, with processions as a particularly flexible motif used to celebrate a host of major life events including triumphs, funerals, weddings, etc. A slightly later Roman tomb has more precise detail and is thought to represent documented historical events.

A small chamber tomb found outside the walls of Rome yielded this remarkable if fragmentary painting. Preserved is a section with two of the four registers of painted decoration from the tomb chamber, thought to be less than 10 percent of the original painted surface. In the upper register only a right leg and left foot remain, probably those of a soldier, comparing them to the figures in the register below. The second register preserves a fortified city on the left with civilians, men wearing togas, looking over the walls. Standing in front of the city is a pair of large-scale figures who fill the register. The one next to the city is a soldier wearing armor, a cloak, carrying a shield, and extending his right hand to the second man facing him. The second figure wears a toga and carries a spear. Between them near the spear tip is a painted caption that names these men as Fannius on the left and Fabius on the right. The third register also has a pair of men meeting, this time with five smaller-scale spectators to the right while to the left a man in combat faces a missing opponent to the left, clearly part of another scene. The left figure of the pair is armed and armored, extending his right hand to the right figure, a toga-clad man holding a spear and extending his hand as well, perhaps in an oratorical gesture. Another fragmentary inscription identifies this pair as M. Fannius and Q. Fabius. Finally, the fourth register shows a fragment of a battle taking place before a walled city.

The togate figure of the pair, and the occupant of the tomb, is thought to be Q. Fabius Maximus Rullianus, who was elected consul five times between 322 and 295 BCE and who celebrated a triumph in 322 BCE. He captured Sentinum during the Second Samnite War and died sometime after 280 BCE. Fannius is therefore a Samnite commander, and his armor is consistent with that found in Samnite and Italic tombs of the period, as well as on tomb paintings from Paestum. Here the pair is negotiating a Samnite surrender, possibly of Sentium after the battle held before the city in 295 BCE, won by the Romans. In terms of art we see many Italic conventions including hierarchy of scale, emphasis on status through details of dress, use of captions, and circumstances of history such as the walled city. What is new here is an **episodic narrative**, in which the same figures appear repeatedly in different episodes in the story. Scholars believe that the design of this narrative reflects the paintings that we know were painted and displayed as part of Roman triumphal processions. Here, that imagery of triumph is transferred to the tomb where it would be viewed by a more restricted

ART AND LITERATURE
Working together to paint a picture of the Roman triumph

In some cases, as in the Temple of Jupiter Optimus Maximus addressed in chapter 2, literature provides critical evidence for art and architecture that is lost to us. In the case of Roman triumphs, the victory parades of successful generals and their armies, art and literature work together to allow us to better understand a kinetic spectacle that is performed once and then gone forever. Thanks to both artistic and literary sources we have a good picture of the Roman triumph, its key features, and the roles of various components of society in it. The triumph seems to have developed in complexity over time and perhaps with each procession but some elements were standard. The first of these was the Roman Senate led by the toga-clad magistrates, notably the consuls, which showed the role of civic government in the military victory being celebrated. Another component was the vast display of captured material including things that were of intrinsic value as well as those of symbolic value (Figure 7.24), representing the captured nation or people and demonstrating the benefits of the victory. Florus (1.13.26) describing the triumph of Curius Dentatus in 275 BCE says, "if you looked upon the procession, you saw gold, purple statues, pictures and all the luxury of Tarentum." Captured warriors (Figure 12.9) were also paraded through the streets as Florus (1.13.26) again relates, "if you looked at captives, they were Molossians, Thessalians, Macedonians, Bruttians, Apulians and Lucanians." Along with those were the children and entire households of rulers demonstrating that Rome's victory was over a people or system and not just an army in the field. This is recorded by Plutarch's account (*Aem. Paul.* 33) of the triumph of Aemilius Paulus of 167 BCE in which the children of the Macedonian king, Perseus, were a feature, "Then, at a little interval, came the children of the king, led along as slaves, and with them a throng of foster-parents, teachers, and tutors, all in tears, stretching out their own hands to the spectators and teaching the children to beg and supplicate." The captive king or enemy commander himself was a special highpoint as Plutarch (*Aem. Paul.* 34) makes clear. The triumphant general, dressed in a special toga and usually riding in a chariot as Festus (*de verb. Sign.* 228) describes for the triumph of T. Papirius Cursor in 272 BCE (Figures 7.25, 9.13), came near the end of the procession accompanied by his family, notably male offspring (Figure 10.29) and followed by military officers, Roman citizens rescued from slavery, and his victorious army (Figure 8.23). The procession began outside the *pomerium* where the general waited for the Senate to vote in favor of a triumph, passed through the streets along a set route, and then culminated at the Temple of Jupiter Optimus Maximus (Figures 2.17, 9.13). There on the Capitoline Hill animal sacrifices (Figure 4.32), dedications, and prayers were made to Jupiter. The tradition of victory dedications dates back at least as far as Appius Claudius in 495 BCE according to Pliny (*NH* 35.12). Frequently a banquet was held for all who fought, as Livy (24.16.19) records for the victory of Tiberius Sempronius Gracchus in 214 BCE.

audience, but conveying the same values celebrating the military achievements and contributions of a Roman elite male.

Etruscan and central Italian bronze sculpture

In addition to the Etruscan achievements in terracotta sculpture already noted, they had a great number of artists who worked in bronze as well. Because bronze is easily melted down and reused only a fraction of the original Etruscan bronze sculpture survives. What we do have, however, demonstrates a sophisticated and highly developed series of sometimes Greek-informed bronze workshops turning out a full range of works in regional schools for many centuries. Even a brief survey of this material makes clear its quality and the Etruscan desire to capture both human and animal forms as truly as possible, which the Greeks referred to as **mimesis**.

A large-scale, nearly complete, hollow-cast bronze **votive** from an Etruscan sanctuary is one of the finest bronze statues to survive from antiquity. Called the Mars of Todi, for its findspot at the

mimesis
literally "to imitate" in Greek, especially refers to the goal of accurate representation of the human and natural world in art.

votive
something offered in fulfillment of a vow. These range from small statuettes to pieces of armor or altars or temples, all demonstrating the piety of the dedicant.

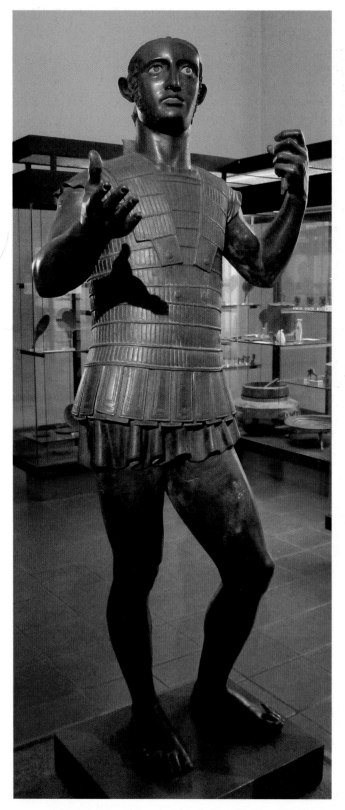

3.15   Statue of Mars from Todi, *c.* 400 BCE. Musei Vaticani, Rome. Bronze, H. 4 ½ ft (141 cm). Photo courtesy Steven L. Tuck.

sanctuary of Todi, it is likely not a god, but an idealized image of the warrior who dedicated it. According to the dedicatory inscription, his name was Ahal Trutitis.

It represents a warrior wearing armor and a, now missing, helmet, portrayed in the act of pouring a libation from a cup held in his extended right hand, while with the left he holds a spear that he leans on. The statue is one of the most Classicizing works of Etruscan art. Elements of the Classicizing include his stance, proportions, and facial features. He stands in the Greek contrapposto pose with his weight primarily on his right leg and left arm, giving his body a weight shift seen in the diagonal line of his hips. This weight shift was a convention of Greek art starting from the middle of the fifth century BCE, as part of Greek artists' attempts to portray the human form as it was in nature, both relaxed and in motion. The figure's proportions and facial features also owe a great deal to Classical sculpture although the details of the face and the style of armor are very Etruscan. This type of high status sculpture was always rare and, after the Romans defeated the Etruscans, much of it was taken to Rome by the conquerors. More common and representative of art in the lives of ordinary Etruscans are the small-scale works that fortunately survive in larger numbers.

Beginning in the fourth century BCE we see dramatically increasing evidence of votive deposits at Etruscan sanctuaries. This is not to say that votives weren't dedicated earlier ("absence of evidence is not evidence of absence" is a favorite axiom of archaeologists), but that they now appear in more permanent materials such as bronze and terracotta. This could reflect increasing wealth, devotion or, perhaps most likely, desperation among the Etruscans as their homelands are under attack by Roman forces and they in turn appeal to the gods.

Most of these votives are cast images of the gods who were the objects of devotion. One such example is this solid cast bronze statuette of Hercules, probably from Cerveteri. Hercules was popular in Etruscan art and here he carries all of his major attributes: club, bow, and lion skin, leaving no doubt of his power and identity. The face and the careful patterning of the lion skin he wears as well as his even and symmetrical ribs retain traditional Archaic elements of Etruscan art. The dramatic pose, however, with one deeply bent knee, along with his robust physique are elements of Greek Late Classical sculpture of the fourth century BCE. An inscription dedicating the statuette to Hercules is chiseled in Etruscan on the right leg.

In addition to hollow and solid cast bronzes, the Etruscans and central Italians were masters at engraving. This incised or engraved work probably transferred from the Etruscan jewelry industry. It moved from soft metals like gold to harder metals like bronze, where the technique was used to create complex figural works of great sophistication including complex engraved scenes on bronze mirrors. These mirrors are found in tombs and reveal Etruscan adaptation of Greek myths and their use on the accessories that established elite female identity. Of the hundreds of examples of engraved work that survive, the Ficoroni Cista is easily one of the finest. Excavated at the town of Praeneste, about 21 miles (35 km) east of Rome, it was one of 118 *cistae* (containers that held cosmetics, jewelry, and other items for female adornment) found in tombs there. The technical complexity of the form is surprising. In addition to shaping the round bronze container, it was engraved and solid cast feet and handles were made separately and attached to it in the final step. Notably for our study it was inscribed by the maker who not only made it in Rome, but made a point of stating that. The inscription on the handle reads "Novios Plautios Romai med fecid/ Dindia Macolnia fileai dedit" (Novios Plautios made me in Rome/Dindia Macolnia gave me to her daughter). This is rare and critical evidence of the high level of these forms made by artists in Rome in the fourth century BCE. It also shows the spread of Greek myths to Rome and the association of this form with Roman women. In fact, it is the earliest work of Roman art owned and perhaps commissioned by a woman that survives.

The exterior body of the *cista* is covered with a detailed engraving of nineteen figures in a fully realized landscape in a single scene that wraps around the entire vessel. The full height of the field is utilized as figures sit, stand, or recline in the landscape, encouraging the eye to move, taking in the entire image. The proportions, composition, and style of the figures exemplify knowledge of contemporary Late Classical Greek motifs and artistic conventions, particularly those known from landscape painting and reliefs. The figures are viewed from a variety of perspectives, each one in fact is a unique image of the nude human male form as Novios Plautios displayed his mastery of contemporary standards of Greek art.

The scene tells one episode in the story of the Argonauts, the heroes who accompanied Jason on the quest for the Golden Fleece. Amycus challenged any boxer who wanted to get water from his spring; Pollux accepted the challenge and beat him so that the other Argonauts could drink. Here he is tying Amycus to a tree as Minerva and Hercules look on; the rest of the Argonauts are resting, and his twin brother, Castor, is training at boxing with his punching bag. Some scholars conclude that the engravings on the Ficoroni Cista reproduce a lost fifth-century BCE painting by Mikon, painted for a sanctuary in Athens and known from descriptions by the author Pausanias. The issue of copying versus adaptation is a contentious one in scholarship; see Tools & Techniques: Reproducing sculpture in the Roman world in chapter 5 for a brief discussion. The narrative moment depicted is the post-climactic one after the match is over, therefore concentrating attention on Pollux's victory. A very different narrative moment, displaying the climactic action of a fight, gives another bronze its remarkable energy.

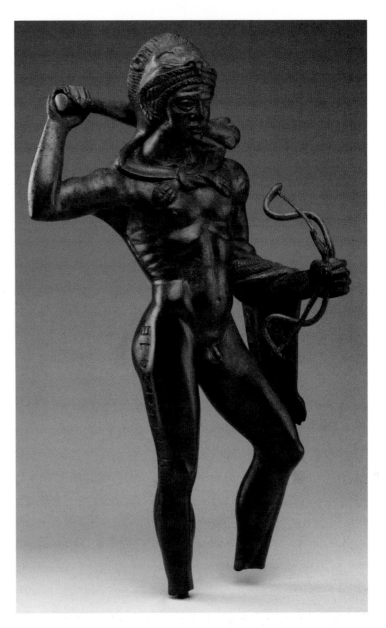

3.16 Bronze statuette of Hercules, *c.* 400–350 BCE, probably from Cerveteri. H 9 ½ in (24.2 cm). Toledo Museum of Art (Toledo, Ohio), Purchased with funds from the Libbey Endowment, Gift of Edward Drummond Libbey, 1978.22. Photography credit: Tim Thayer.

TOOLS & TECHNIQUES
Votive statuettes in the ancient world

Votive statuettes in bronze or terracotta were common, mold-made, mass-produced works of art that filled sanctuaries across the ancient world. In whichever medium, artists used molds to cast works in either bronze or terracotta. Terracotta was technically easier and used cheaper material, but the steps are largely the same. The work is cast in a mold, usually two pieces of terracotta clamped together. Once the bronze had cooled or the terracotta dried, shrunk, and pulled away from the mold, the statuette was removed. At that point it was trimmed of flash (extraneous bits of material that seeped into the seams of the mold), perhaps polished, and put up for sale. Molds would eventually wear out, but could be recut periodically as well. Some artists set up shop outside major sanctuaries, but others traveled from sanctuary to sanctuary following the calendar of religious festivals, either bringing votives with them or producing them on site. In this way, works by particular artists could be spread across a region. There is evidence that these artists could represent significant economic activity. *Acts* 19.24–25 records those who made their living supplying votives to a major sanctuary fearing for the loss of their good living with the rise of Christianity and its threat to the pagan sanctuaries.

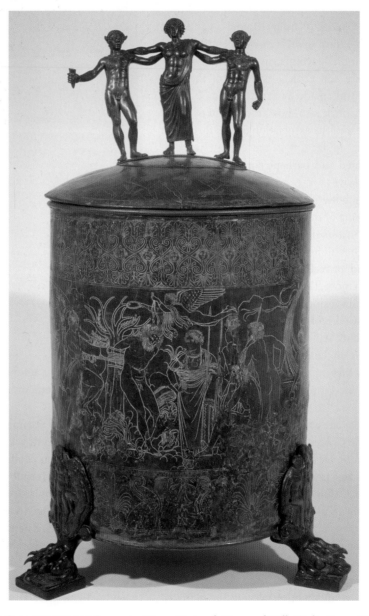

3.17   Ficoroni Cista, 350–330 BCE, Praeneste. Museo Nazionale Etrusco di Villa Giulia, Rome. Bronze, H 2 ½ ft (76 cm). Source: akg-images / Pirozzi.

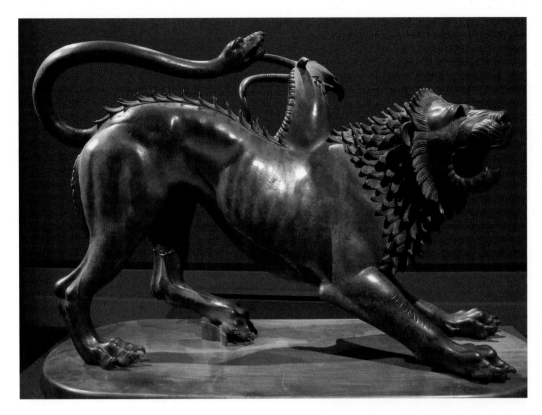

3.18 Bronze chimera from Arezzo, 4th cent. BCE. Museo Archaeologico Nazionale, Florence. H 31 ½ in (80 cm). Sailko / Wikimedia Commons.

The chimera, seen here in a large-scale Etruscan bronze from Arezzo, is a monstrous figure from the Greek myth of the hero Bellerophon, who fought it mounted on the winged horse, Pegasus. Greek authors as far back as Homer describe the monster as lion in front, snake behind, and goat in the middle. Here the artist has interpreted it as a lion with a snake's tail and a goat's head and neck projecting from the side. The artist has created a work with great potential energy as the lion is crouched with its mouth open, apparently roaring and ready to strike with its mane and back hair bristling. The chimera is wounded with a gash on the neck of the drooping goat head and another on the lion's left flank, but it continues the battle. The composition of the figure seems designed to encourage the viewer to move around it, the first large-scale work of Etruscan art that encouraged that sort of active engagement. The lion looks upward, we assume at Bellerophon on Pegasus, so perhaps it was originally part of a larger group that included the hero as well. The inscription on its right foreleg is a dedication to the Etruscan god, Tinia, meaning that it was a votive object. Since it was discovered in 1553 buried with other bronzes just outside the city of Arezzo, it was possibly in a votive deposit from a sanctuary.

Not all Etruscan bronze sculptures were votives. Many works were probably made for domestic, civic, or funerary use instead. Since we lack excavated Etruscan civic or residential spaces, sanctuaries and tombs are our best sources for examples of these works. One portrait bust, from *c.* 300 BCE, may have been made for one of these locations, but since it was donated to the Musei Capitolini in 1564 and its findspot is unrecorded, we will never know. It has been long known, for no good reason, as Brutus, its assumptive identity as the founder of the Roman Republic who overthrew the kings in 509 BCE. That identification is baseless, but the notion that it represents a specific individual is probably accurate. It is considered to be an excellent example both of bronze work and of the art of portraiture in central Italy of the late fourth century BCE. The tight-lipped, middle-aged figure looks ahead in a way that reinforces his dignity, a key quality for men, while not adopting the Greek ideal of youthfulness for his features. In fact the work has modeling in the flesh of the face that indicates forehead wrinkles, bags under the eyes, and deep grooves that run from the nose to the corners of his mouth. The work shows a severe man and was probably displayed in a house and later a tomb much like the painted portraits of ancestors found in Etruscan tombs of the late fourth century BCE. Here we see the Italic tradition of portraiture and the values of elite males together with the local artistic tradition without explicit Greek influence or imitation. The bust represents not just a mature man, but a mature art.

ROMAN ARCHITECTURE AND URBAN PLANNING

The Roman siege and defeat of Veii in 396 BCE weakened the Etruscan alliance to the point that the Gauls of northern Italy were able to move unimpeded through Etruscan territory and attack and sack Rome in 390 BCE. This attack had a profound effect on many areas of Roman culture, not the least of which was architecture and urban planning. Once the Romans paid the required tribute, the Gauls departed and the Romans began building the first walls that enclosed the entire city, the so-called Servian Walls, named because they were mistakenly associated with the Roman king Servius Tullus of the sixth century BCE.

The Servian Walls represent the largest public works and examples of extant architecture from fourth-century BCE Rome. Although originally large and impressive, only small sections can be found

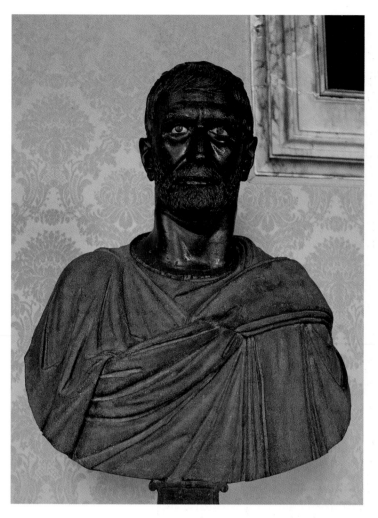

3.19 Bronze bust of a man "Brutus," Musei Capitolini, Rome. The head and neck (H 12 ½ in, 32 cm) are ancient, *c.* 300 BCE, in a 16th-cent. CE draped bust (total H 29 in, 74 cm). Photo courtesy Steven L. Tuck.

sulcus primigenius
The ritual furrow plowed to mark the *pomerium* and the subsequent line of walls at Rome by Romulus and later by other Romans at Rome and its colonies.

around the city of Rome today. They were the first walls to enclose all seven hills of Rome, an area that dwarfs other contemporary cities. They were constructed of small 2 ft (*c.* 60 cm) tall blocks of tufa, a local volcanic stone, and originally stretched 6.8 miles (11 km) and rose to a height of *c.* 33 ft (10 m). Pierced by sixteen gates, they were never tested in a major siege. Ancient sources and masons' marks on the stones themselves confirm the import of Greek masons to perform much of the work on the walls.

Building a wall like this was a major architectural undertaking, with the need to create an entire defensive complex including platforms for siege engines, ditches, and other components. It was also a religious undertaking because the wall was placed along the *pomerium*, the sacred boundary of the city. Establishing that boundary required a ritual in which priests and magistrates yoked a team of oxen together and plowed a furrow that became the line of the city. That ritual, called the *sulcus primigenius*, is associated with Romulus and the first walls of Rome. Images of this ceremony are found on Roman coins. In Etruscan art they date back as far as the fifth century BCE in a bronze statuette votive group found at Arezzo.

A limestone relief of debated date from a public building at the Roman colony of Aquileia shows the ritual that took place at the colony there in 181 BCE. It is thought to show the founder of the colony, L. Manlius Acidinus, performing the ceremony. The team of oxen is guided by a man in a tunic while five priests in togas follow, one of whom, presumably Acidinus, drives the plow. The furrow becomes the line of the city walls and the plow is lifted up where the gates will be placed to reserve in an unbroken strip that area for roads leading into the city.

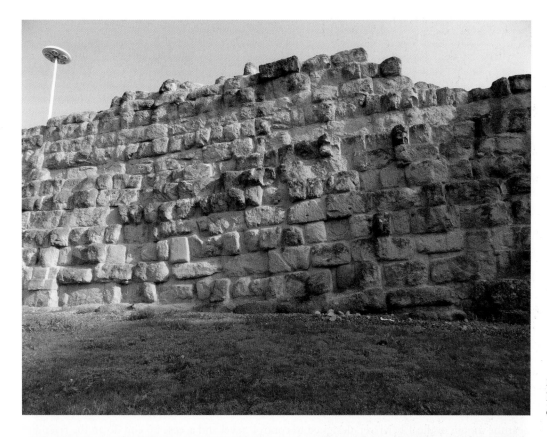

3.20 "Servian Wall," Rome, *c.* 386 BCE. Photo courtesy Steven L. Tuck.

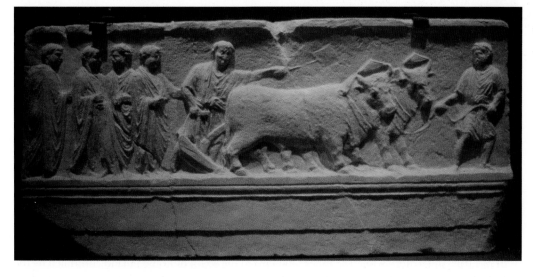

3.21 Limestone relief of *sulcus primigenius* for a Roman colony, 2nd cent. BCE? Museo Archeologico Nazionale di Aquileia. H 17 ¼ in (44 cm) L 37 ⅜ in (95 cm) W 3 ½ in (9 cm) Photo courtesy Steven L. Tuck.

Ostia: Rome's first colony and planned community

Ironically, thanks to the Gallic sack of 390 BCE and the subsequent piecemeal resettling of Rome, the city itself does not reflect Roman urban planning. In fact, the Roman historian Livy describes the period after the Gauls left (5.55) saying,

> they began to rebuild the City in a haphazard way. . . . In their haste, they took no trouble to plan out straight streets; as all distinctions of ownership in the soil were lost, they built on any ground that happened to be vacant. That is the reason . . . why the form of the City resembles one casually built upon by settlers rather than one regularly planned out.

HISTORICAL CONTEXT
Pomerium

In a passage describing the reign of the Roman king, Servius Tullius (578–535 BCE), the Roman historian Livy (1.44) describes the origins and use of the *pomerium*:

> For the space which the Etruscans of old, when founding their cities, consecrated in accordance with auguries and marked off by boundary stones at intervals on each side, as the part where the wall was to be carried, was to be kept vacant so that no buildings might connect with the wall on the inside (which now they generally touch), and on the outside some ground might remain virgin soil untouched by cultivation. This space, which it was forbidden either to build upon or to plow, and which could not be said to be behind the wall any more than the wall could be said to be behind it, the Romans called the "pomoerium."

It is clear from the description that the *pomerium* was not just a sacred boundary but a practical one and the edict that clear space be maintained around the walls was to facilitate defense in case of attack, robbing attackers of cover.

To understand Roman urban planning, we need to examine the colonies that Rome created during the turbulent period of the fourth and third centuries BCE, starting with her first colony at Ostia in 338 BCE. Colonies were a form of military occupation as they were placed in newly conquered territory, but they were also a cultural occupation. Where the Romans went their culture came with them and to analyze the components of Roman colonies is to understand Roman cultural values and priorities, which they imposed on occupied territory as they settled it.

Ostia, whose name derives from the Latin word for mouth, was founded at a critical crossroads near the mouth of the Tiber river, designed to control travel and access up and down the river and the roads. Its founding during the conflicts with the Samnites and Etruscans demonstrates the importance Rome put on control of the Tiber and roads in the area. The oldest settlement that has been found is the so-called *castrum*, meaning fort. It was a rectangular, military fortress (636 x 412 ft) (194 x 125.7 m), with walls of large tufa blocks. Remains of the walls have been excavated around the later forum, which is at the center of the original foundation. The two main streets, crossing at right angles and leading to four gates in the center of each of the four city walls, were called *Cardo* and *Decumanus*. *Cardo* is the main north–south road and *Decumanus* the main east–west road. The form of the colony has led some to argue that Roman urban design was based on military models. It seems more likely that both military and civilian planning relied on the same spatial organization including central focus and symmetrical arrangement.

Maritime colonies at Cosa and Paestum, 273 BCE

In 273 BCE Rome simultaneously founded two important coastal colonies in an attempt to annex territory from her enemies and project her control on the Tyrrhenian sea. Cosa was in the north in the heart of Etruscan territory while 186 miles (300 km) to the south of Rome in land controlled by the Lucanians was the colony of Paestum. Unlike Ostia, Paestum was established on the site of a thriving city that had been there since 600 BCE. In that way, its plan demonstrates Roman projected identity as well as selective cultural inclusiveness. The plan of Paestum shows the central feature of the new colony was a rectangular forum, demonstrating the centrality of public life in the Roman world.

The Romans adjusted the road plan to create a major crossroads at the forum and destroyed the Greek and Lucanian civic public buildings as they destroyed the public institutions associated with them. In their place they laid out a forum 656 x 197 ft (200 x 60 m) surrounded by temples, markets, shops, and civic buildings, a basilica for legal cases, and specialized buildings for meetings of local bodies such as the city council. Just off the forum are venues for public entertainments, including a bath complex and an amphitheater, though both post-date the founding of the colony. The major Greek temples and their large sanctuaries to the north and south of the forum continued in use, while west,

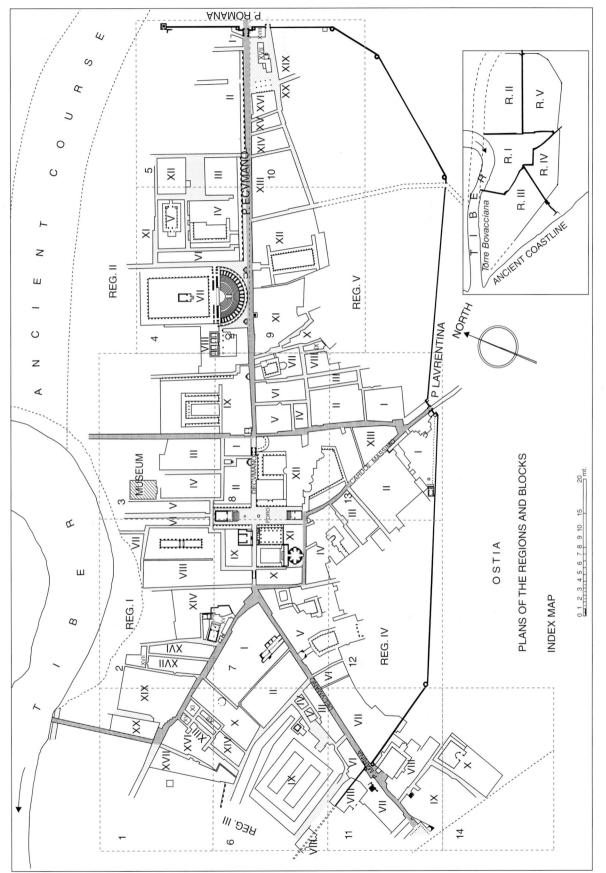

ANCIENT COURSE

T I B E R

REG. II

REG. V

P. ROMANA

P. DECVMANO

MUSEUM

DECVMANO

FORO

CARDO MASSIMO

P LAVRENTINA

REG. I

REG. III

REG. IV

NORTH

INDEX MAP

R. II

R. V

R. I

R. IV

R. III

T I B E R

Torre Bovacciana

ANCIENT COASTLINE

OSTIA

PLANS OF THE REGIONS AND BLOCKS

0 1 2 3 4 5 6 7 8 9 10 15   20 mt.

3.22   Ostia, plan of Roman colony centered on forum, 338 BCE. Soprintendenza Speciale per i Beni Archeologica di Roma. Reproduced with permission.

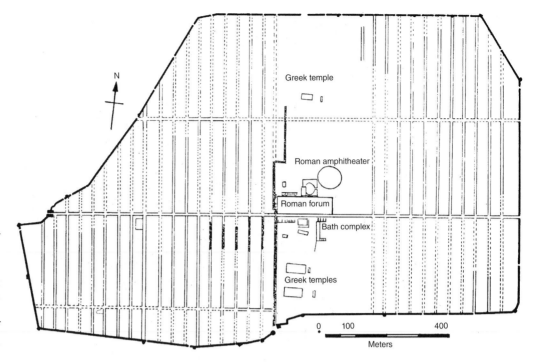

3.23 Paestum, plan of Roman colony, 273 BCE. Ferdinando Castagnoli, Orthogonal Town Planning in Antiquity, figure, street plan of Paestum, © 1967 Massachusetts Institute of Technology, by permission of The MIT Press.

orthogonal planning
the type of city plan in which the streets run at right angles to each other, forming a grid.

and probably east, though it has not been excavated yet, were blocks of Roman houses. The layout of colonies reveals the Roman aesthetic of order, symmetry, and axiality as seen in the individual buildings as well. Their decisions on what to build, destroy, and renovate also reveal deeper cultural values.

The simultaneous colonial foundation at Cosa on Etruscan coastal land 87 miles (140 km) north of Rome provides key evidence of Roman colonization, urban design, and architecture during the third century BCE. In particular Cosa seems to answer the question of what Rome would look like if it had been planned in the Republican period. It seems to be an idealized version of Rome that, in contrast to Paestum, was founded on empty land. The outline of the city walls is irregular, matching the hilly terrain. Nevertheless, inside the city strict order is imposed with **orthogonal planning**, a grid plan with a series of blocks at right angles, which creates the urban structure. This form of planning was found in earlier Greek colonies in southern Italy. Romans may have first encountered it there or, as with so much Greek influence, through the Etruscan use of this form of planning. The forum at Cosa is not centrally located, probably owing to the terrain, but takes up a four-block area and is flanked by major streets that run to gates in the city walls. The forum is surrounded by typical religious and civic buildings with a well-preserved temple, early basilica, and meeting houses for local bodies as at Paestum. Notably, the forum was also surrounded by large private homes that must have belonged to the elite members of the colony. This arrangement is known at Rome from the period, but only in literary references. At Cosa we can see the Roman idea of elite display as their homes and lives were part of the fabric of the public space along with civic buildings.

The southwest corner of the colony is dominated by a separately fortified high hill, referred to by the excavators as an arx or citadel, on which were two temples that dated to the early days of the colony. One was an Etrusco-Italic style temple on a tall podium with a deep front porch and a triple cella. It was clearly Cosa's Capitolium, their temple of Jupiter, Juno, and Minerva, copying the most important temple in Rome.

Its presence here reflects the same design notion as at Rome, using the most important temple to create a visual display of the culture of the people who inhabit the area. Visible from a distance it would have announced to those in the region that this was now Roman territory. These buildings and the urban plans of the colonies demonstrate the state of Roman architecture and urban planning in the period before Hellenization, Greek-inspired design, comes to dominate Roman public art and buildings.

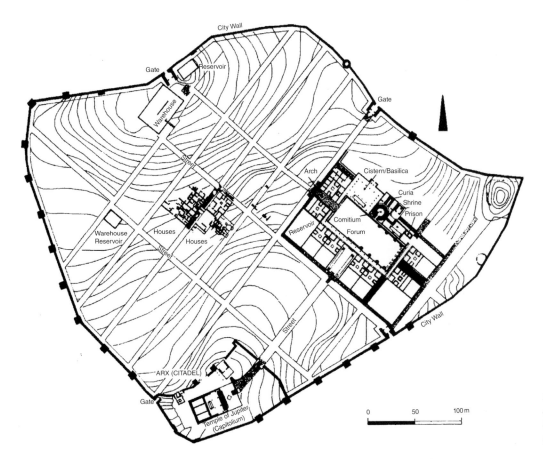

3.24 Cosa, plan of Roman colony, 273 BCE. Clementsalvi/Wikimedia Commons.

FORM & FUNCTION

The Forum Romanum in the Republican period

Any Roman forum fulfilled a variety of functions and served the needs of all classes in the community from the highest to the very lowest. The evidence for this period from the Forum Romanum is sparse as it was constantly rebuilt following fires, floods, and desires to create more lasting and elaborate buildings and monuments. A satiric but possibly somewhat accurate account of the Forum Romanum and its populace at about 200 BCE is found in the Roman playwright Plautus' work, *Curculio* 4.1:

> If you wish to meet a perjurer, go to the Comitium; for a liar and braggart, try the shrine of Venus Cloacina; for wealthy married wasters, the Basilica. There too will be harlots, well-ripened ones, and men ready for a bargain, while at the Fish-Market are the members of eating clubs. In the lower forum citizens of repute and wealth stroll about; in the middle forum, near the Canal, there you find the merely showy. Above the Lacus Curtius are those bold, garrulous, spiteful fellows who slander others and are open to slander themselves. Below the Old Shops are those who lend and borrow upon usury. Behind the Temple of Castor are those you would do well not to trust. In the Vicus Tuscus are those who sell themselves. In the Velabrum you'll find a baker, butcher or fortune teller.

CONCLUSION

In a period of almost exactly three hundred years, Rome went from a small city in central Italy ruled by a king to a Republic that controlled almost the entire Italian peninsula. During the course of this expansion and change in government, it is natural that its art and architectural forms changed along the way. The early and most deeply embedded influence in that change was Roman contact with the Etruscans to the

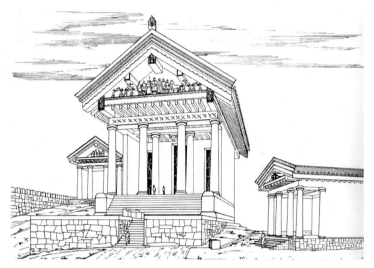

3.25 Cosa, reconstruction drawing of arx dominated by their Capitolium, 273 BCE. After fig. 5, Frank E. Brown, *Roman Architecture*. New York, 1961. Reproduced with permission from the American Academy in Rome.

north. From the Etruscans they absorbed many of the components of Etrusco-Italic art from the form of their temples to the development of portraiture and many of these took place in the native media of bronze and terracotta. The tombs of the period, Greek, Etruscan, Lucanian, and Roman, provide the best evidence of large-scale art in their mural paintings. The images of rituals and underworld journeys show the underlying beliefs of these cultures while illustrating the transmission of artistic styles and iconography between the cultures of central Italy. The movement of art seems to be in all directions as a remarkable artistic cross-fertilization occurs. In the third century BCE we see the Romans begin to define their art in ways that reflect their local culture. In the colonies of Paestum and Cosa in particular we see the projection of Roman culture into areas formerly held by foreign people and the transmission of Roman forms and values into the wider world begins at a larger scale.

SUGGESTIONS FOR FURTHER READING

Frank Edward Brown, Emeline Hill Richardson, and L. Richardson, *Cosa III: The Buildings of the Forum: Colony, Municipium, and Village* (Pennsylvania State University Press for the American Academy in Rome 1993). This represents one of the best excavated, published, and understood Roman colonies. Its foundation date in the third century BCE gives us unique evidence of Roman urban design and public architecture in the Republic.

Jane DeRose Evans, ed., *A Companion to the Archaeology of the Roman Republic* (Wiley-Blackwell 2013). Among the thirty-seven essays in this volume are many that cover topics from the art, architecture, and city planning of this period, including chapters on Cosa, Paestum, and the use of art and architecture to create a Roman identity.

Peter J. Holliday, *The Origins of Roman Historical Commemoration in the Visual Arts* (Cambridge University Press 2002). Analyzes the formative Roman practice of visualizing history to commemorate the achievements of the elite in the Early and Middle Roman Republic.

Angela Pontrandolfo Greco, Agnès Rouveret, and Marina Cipriani, *The Painted Tombs of Paestum* (Pandemos 2004). This short volume gives an overview of the Lucanian tomb paintings and their development over the centuries. It charts the changing styles and subjects of these important works of Italic art. It also includes a brief chapter on the Greek Tomb of the Diver.

Anna Maria Sgubini Moretti, *The Villa Giulia National Etruscan Museum: Short Guide* (L'Erma di Bretschneider 2001). This work provides a well-written short introduction to many of the most important works of Etruscan art, held in one of the best museum collections in the world. The illustrated chapters also give context to the objects from key Etruscan sites such as Veii, Cerveteri, and Pyrgi.

Michael Thomas and Gretchen E. Meyers, eds., *Monumentality in Etruscan and Early Roman Architecture: Ideology and Innovation* (University of Texas Press 2012). With a chapter focusing on the Temple of Jupiter Capitolinus this volume covers a range of building types that developed in early Roman architecture.

Nancy Thomson de Grummond, *Etruscan Myth, Sacred History, and Legend* (University of Pennsylvania Museum of Archaeology and Anthropology 2006). Relying heavily on Etruscan art, the author provides a case study for the importance of art in aiding scholars in revealing aspects of Etruscan society that are otherwise lost to us.

Mario Torelli, ed., *The Etruscans* (Rizzoli 2001). This is a wide-ranging series of chapters by experts in their various fields on a host of Etruscan topics. It includes excellent chapters on sculpture and bronzes along with chapters on the most important Etruscan museums at the Villa Giulia in Rome, the Vatican Collection and the National Archaeological Museum in Florence.

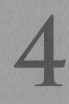

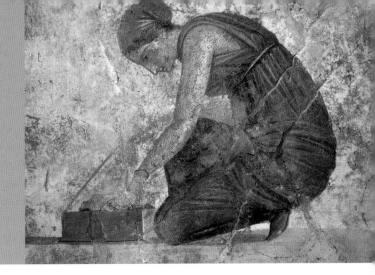

4

THE LATER REPUBLIC, 211–31 BCE
The Origins of a Hellenistic Roman Culture

212 BCE	Sack of Syracuse
211 BCE	Triumph of Marcus Claudius Marcellus
168 BCE	Battle of Pydna, victory of Aemilius Paullus over Perseus of Macedon
c. 150 BCE	**Basilica of Pompeii constructed**
146 BCE	Destruction of Carthage and Corinth
91–88 BCE	Social War
89 BCE	Siege of Pompeii by Sulla
80 BCE	Founding of Roman colony of Pompeii by Sulla; **House of the Faun renovated; amphitheater begun at Pompeii**
73–71 BCE	Revolt of Spartacus
62 BCE	**Pons Fabricius built**
61 BCE	Pompey's Triple Triumph
55 BCE	**Pompey's Theater, first permanent theater in Rome, built**
46 BCE	**Forum of Caesar dedicated**
44 BCE	Assassination of Julius Caesar
40 BCE	**Decoration of Mysteries Suite in the Villa of the Mysteries**
31 BCE	Naval Battle of Actium; Octavian (Augustus) defeats Mark Antony and Cleopatra

A History of Roman Art, First Edition. Steven L. Tuck.
© 2015 Steven L. Tuck. Published 2015 by John Wiley & Sons, Ltd.

INTRODUCTION

Rarely in history can one draw such a clear line as we can, and as the Romans did, between the art of two periods. In this case these periods are the Early and Later Republic. The line here is marked by the triumph of Marcus Claudius Marcellus following the sack of Syracuse in 212 BCE. One of the most successful generals in Roman history, Marcellus served as a military commander for almost twenty years against Gallic armies, the Carthaginians, and their allies in southern Italy and Sicily. After Hannibal defeated the Roman army at the Battle of Cannae in 216 BCE, the Senate turned to Marcellus to help secure Rome and her allies against further Carthaginian attacks. He besieged and finally sacked the Greek city of Syracuse. For this the Senate voted him a triumph. This triumph brought for the first time works of Greek art and architecture into Rome in large amounts. The explosion of Greek art and architecture into the Roman world and the consequent changes in the arts in all media provides the theme for the chapter. It may seem that we have examined Greek subjects and styles in Roman art in earlier chapters. We have. But the difference here is one of scale. Greek material becomes so prevalent in the Later Republican period that Rome essentially begins to transform into a Greek city. This chapter examines the First Style wall decoration of the House of the Faun at Pompeii, based on Greek palace architecture. It then introduces the Second Style wall paintings of the villa at Oplontis and the Villa of the Mysteries with their reliance on Greek spaces and antecedents for inspiration. The period includes the introduction of the quintessential Roman building form of the basilica, based on Greek columned halls. Some traditional forms, such as Roman temples, were also augmented with Greek decorative and design elements during this period. Since a number of these temples were built to commemorate victories and triumphs, the Romans were using the architectural style of a conquered people to decorate the buildings celebrating their conquest.

Not every work of art, however, so fully embraced the explosion of Greek art and architecture. In terms of innovation, the Roman invention of concrete becomes the major new distinguishing characteristic of Roman architecture. The creation of and ability to exploit concrete construction led to dramatic changes in the architecture that developed in this period. Finally, the Roman arch also makes its appearance in quintessential buildings such as bridges, temple platforms, and amphitheaters.

The final part of the chapter addresses the rise of the public art of rule. Almost the entire first century BCE was dominated by the struggles of powerful Romans who sought sole rulership over the Roman world. This series of political and social upheavals, punctuated by civil wars, changed the entire Roman world. The Roman dictator Sulla seized control of Rome to thwart his political enemies and to gain command over foreign wars. He was followed by a series of men, notably Crassus, Pompey, and Caesar, who looked to Sulla as a model and fought to impose their own rule on Rome. We see echoes of these efforts in the propagandistic art and building projects of Julius Caesar and Pompey the Great with their artistic programs in Rome inspired by the urban forms of Hellenistic kings. The decisions taken by these patrons of art and architecture of the first century BCE set a lasting precedent for the Roman emperors to come.

ARCHITECTURE AND URBAN PLANNING

The introduction of Greek forms does not lead immediately to the abandonment of Etruscan ones, but Greek elements are added to the traditional Roman and Etruscan in a very consistent way. Perhaps the earliest surviving work of art in Rome that shows strong Greek influence is the sarcophagus of Lucius Cornelius Scipio Barbatus, a prominent Roman government official and general. Although not itself a work of architecture, it demonstrates the addition of Greek architectural features on an otherwise local form of art.

ART AND LITERATURE
Greek art comes to Rome: The triumph of Marcus Claudius Marcellus

In 214 BCE Marcellus besieged the city of Syracuse, the largest and wealthiest city in Sicily, which had joined Hannibal's war on Rome following the defeat at Cannae. The siege lasted until 212 BCE when the Roman forces finally took and sacked the city. From that victory Marcellus brought to Rome not just the traditional money and slaves but – for the first time – large amounts of Greek art and architecture. Plutarch relates in his *Life of Marcellus*:

> Marcellus . . . to illustrate his triumph, and adorn the city, carried away with him a great number of the most beautiful ornaments [temples] of Syracuse. For, before that, Rome neither had, nor had seen, any of those fine and exquisite rarities. (21)

This description seems to match the other literary accounts of traditional Roman victory displays. Prior to 212 BCE the major objects exhibited in victory were captured arms and armor and military standards from defeated units brought back and displayed mainly in houses and a few public areas throughout the city. In this way, Marcellus' decision to bring back Greek art and architecture is unprecedented in scale and form. It marked a cultural shift from previous notions of appropriate and desirable monuments to military success in the type and locations where they were put on view.

> Whence Marcellus was more popular with the people in general, because he had adorned the city with beautiful objects that had all the charms of Grecian grace and symmetry. . . . They blamed Marcellus . . . as it seemed now to celebrate victories and lead processions of triumph, not only over men, but also over the gods as captives; then, that he had diverted to idleness, and vain talk about curious arts and artificers, the common people, which, bred up in wars and agriculture, had never tasted of luxury and sloth . . . so that now they misspent much of their time in examining and criticizing trifles. And yet, notwithstanding this reprimand, Marcellus made it his glory to the Greeks themselves, that he had taught his ignorant countrymen to esteem and admire the elegant and wonderful productions of Greece. (Plutarch, *Life of Marcellus*, 21)

The account in Plutarch makes it clear that the conservative forces in Rome resisted these innovations. The common people, perhaps the primary beneficiaries of these new forms of public art, supported these innovations as it would be generations until Greek art was found in large amounts in the homes of Rome's poorer citizens. In addition to the opposition based on tradition there seems to be a strong class-based resistance to Marcellus' innovation, as Plutarch makes plain, since now the common people learned to appreciate art and luxury and, it apparently follows, sloth. One presumes that the wealthy elite had at least limited opportunities to incorporate this material already in the privacy of their homes, but they feared the effect on the lower classes. The historian Livy's account is much the same. In his book *Ab urbe condita*, 25.40 Livy states that

> He removed to Rome the ornaments of the city, the statues and pictures in which Syracuse abounded; they were, it is true, spoils taken from the enemy and acquired by the laws of war, but that was the beginning of our admiration for Greek works of art, which has led to the present [200 years later when Livy is writing] reckless spoliation of every kind of treasure, sacred and profane alike.

The remarkable aspect of these accounts is not that they agree with each other, although that is important. It is that they agree so precisely with the evidence that survives from the art and architecture itself. Looking at the art we can see a dramatic difference after 212 BCE in terms of the amount of Greek influence found in these works of art. It seems that the works brought to Rome by Marcellus inspired the Romans in their own creation and construction.

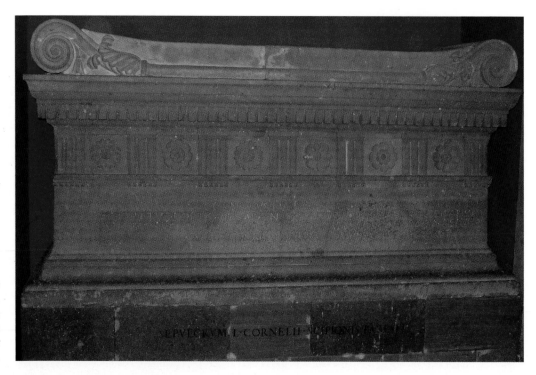

4.1 Sarcophagus of Scipio Barbatus, *c.* 200 BCE, Rome. Musei Vaticani, Rome. Tufa, H 4 ft 7 in (1.4 m) L 9 ft 1 in (2.77 m). Photo courtesy Steven L. Tuck.

triglyph-metope frieze
element of Doric architecture with rectangular panels (metopes), often used for sculpture, separated by projecting blocks (triglyphs) with three vertical portions separated by two channels.

dentil frieze
a series of closely spaced projecting rectangular blocks that make a molding on a building usually at the top of the wall just below the roofline.

lectus
Roman couch used by the elite to recline while dining, sleeping, and to display the body in a funeral.

pseudoperipteral
refers to a building that mimics the peripteral colonnades that completely surrounded Greek temples. It has a porch with free-standing columns but engaged half columns around the sides and back.

Although he died in 280 BCE, his sarcophagus dates from *c.* 200 BCE when members of the family renovated the family tomb and placed distinguished ancestors in more elaborate sarcophagi. This practice shows the continued importance of ancestors to elites in the period and the new use of Greek art to distinguish them. A Greek Doric **triglyph-metope frieze** dominates the decoration of the sarcophagus. The metopes are filled with rosettes carved in relief. A **dentil frieze** runs above that and then a curved molding. The sarcophagus lid is designed to evoke the cushion on a *lectus* and so carries over an allusion to the Etruscan visual concept of the deceased reclining on the lid (see Figure 2.7). The lid is elaborated with additional Greek architectural features: volute spirals and acanthus details found on Ionic and Corinthian architecture. The overall decorative program relies on Greek architecture for its inspiration, but since it is carved in local volcanic tufa with a Latin inscription across the front, it seems to be the product of a Roman workshop.

Architecture

The general development in architecture in this period is the injection of Greek, specifically Hellenistic elements, onto the traditional Italic forms. Greek styles are not adopted completely. For example, large Greek temples do not replace Etrusco-Italic temples, but components of their design are added to the traditional building styles. The greatest change Hellenistic design made to Roman architecture is found in sanctuaries and urban design, but the earliest is in smaller-scale buildings such as temples. The second-century BCE temples demonstrate that the Greek influence extended into architecture as well. Perhaps the best single example of this is the Temple of Portunus in Rome between the Tiber river and the Forum Boarium.

In form it is a traditional Italic style temple: a rigidly frontal small (85 ft 4 in, 26 m) building on a high (7 ½ ft, 2.3 m) podium with front steps and a deep porch, all made of the local materials, travertine and volcanic tufa. The decorative features are all Greek, however. These include Ionic columns supporting the roof over the porch. Engaged half columns wrap around the building attached to the walls of the cella in a style called **pseudoperipteral**, meaning that they mimic the Greek peripteral colonnades that completely surrounded their temples with free-standing columns. These create the illusion of a surrounding colonnade as one of the earliest attempts to soften the frontality of the Italic temple, making it appear more Greek.

The Temple of Hercules Victor, as it is known in Rome, built almost adjacent to the Temple of Portunus, shows the extent of Hellenistic influence in a different way. The temple is the earliest surviving marble building in Rome and was probably dedicated by Lucius Mummius after his defeat of the Greeks and destruction of the city of Corinth in 146 BCE. Its design is based on round Greek temples, a form found in sanctuaries across the Greek world that became widespread in the fourth century BCE. It is round and peripteral with a surrounding colonnade of twenty Corinthian columns. The marble walls of the cella are carved in rectangular blocks with smooth faces and drafted edges that outline each block, a Hellenistic convention. As with Greek temples, it is surrounded by steps, violating the frontality seen in Italic temples.

Not all temples of the second century BCE are as completely Greek as Hercules Victor, possibly because of its Greek deity and dedication in honor of a victory over the Greeks. Nonetheless, Hellenistic architectural features are found in contemporary temples in Rome at the Forum Holitorium and the Largo Argentina sanctuaries where more traditional Italic temples boast pseudoperipteral engaged colonnades and even round cellae, but with the old-fashioned high front steps of older Roman temples.

About 25 miles outside of Rome in the small town of Tivoli are two adjacent temples from the late second century, one round and one rectangular, that demonstrate the mix of Italic, Greek, and Roman elements.

The rectangular one is of the traditional Italic form on a high podium. Here, however, the podium is of concrete, a new development for temples. The podium is faced with travertine slabs, the same material as the cella walls. The cella is pseudoperipteral, creating the illusion of a Greek Ionic temple. The round temple next to it, called the Temple of Vesta, also sits on a high podium. Its podium and cella are completely constructed of concrete, with the cella covered with **opus incertum**. The Greek elements include a colonnade of fluted Corinthian columns surrounding the cella, and above that a frieze of ox heads connected by heavy garlands. Wide marble frames define the door and windows matching the color of the colonnade.

The integration of Hellenistic elements is not restricted to temples in this period. The oldest surviving **basilica** at Pompeii also shows this combination of Italic and Greek design. The basilica, a large roofed, columned hall designed as a multiple use public building, had its origin in the Forum Romanum in 184 BCE. The name basilica, derived from the Greek word for king (*basileos*), demonstrates the building form's inspiration in the royal audience halls found adjacent to palaces and public spaces in Hellenistic cities.

The basic form is a rectangle whose interior is divided into a broad nave that runs the length of the building flanked by side aisles defined by lines of columns that support the timber roofing system. A second story walkway extended above the side aisles and contained a line of windows providing light source for the interior. A second line of windows pierced the wall that rose above the colonnades. This line of **clerestory** windows, a feature of Hellenistic buildings, is

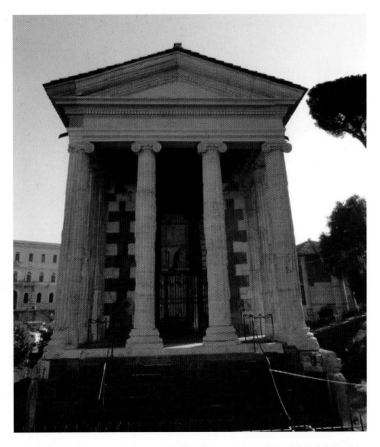

4.2   Temple of Portunus, Rome, *c.* 150 BCE. Photo courtesy Steven L. Tuck.

opus incertum
a facing of irregularly shaped, fist-sized tufa stones commonly applied to concrete structures in the late second and early first centuries BCE.

basilica
a Roman building characterized by a central hall with flanking aisles and often a porch on one end and a raised tribunal on the other, often used for law courts.

clerestory
the upper level of a building, seen in basilicas, that rises above the roof level of the outside aisles. Pierced with windows it floods the central aisle with light.

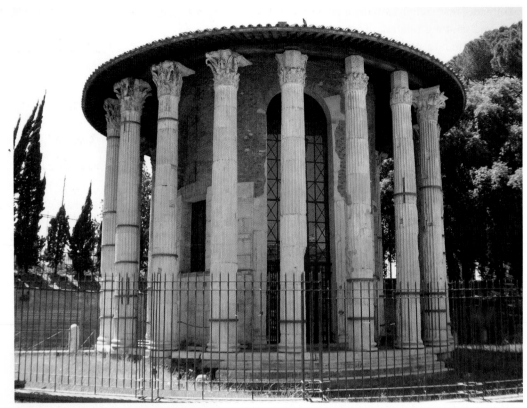

4.3 Temple of Hercules Victor, Rome, *c.* 150 BCE. Photo courtesy Steven L. Tuck.

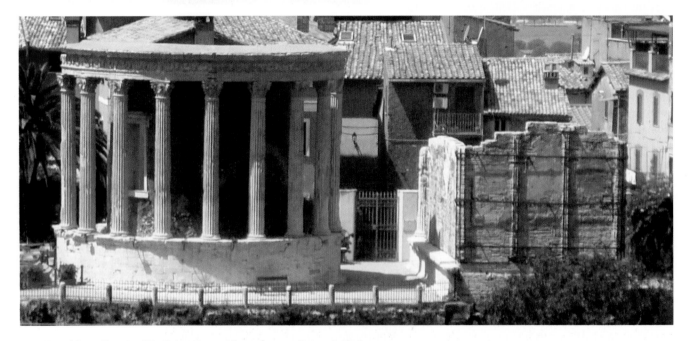

4.4 Republican Temples, Tivoli, *c.* 100 BCE. Photo courtesy Steven L. Tuck.

found in Roman architecture for the first time in second-century BCE basilicas. The basilica at Pompeii, measuring 196 by 79 ft (60 by 24 m), is well enough preserved that the two-story design is clear, with large Ionic engaged columns lining the wall on the first floor and slender Corinthian columns on the second.

The building opens onto the forum on one of the short ends. The short end opposite it is dominated by a two-story tribunal. This stage-like platform on which presiding magistrates sat as they supervised trials was the focus of the building and was therefore more elaborately distinguished in its design. The ground floor of the tribunal has a line of Corinthian columns that distinguish it from the Ionic columns of the rest of the basilica. This use of architectural features to highlight a particular part of the interior of a building is found in Greek temples in the Classical period (480–323 BCE) and makes its way to secular buildings in the Hellenistic period. The second story of the tribunal is finished with a triangular pediment like the front of a Greek temple or large tomb, further reinforcing the importance of this part of the building and focusing attention here with another element of Greek design.

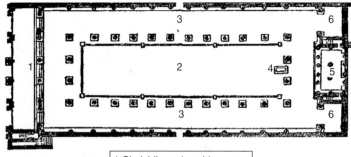

1 Chalcidicum (porch)
2 Nave
3 Aisle
4 Pedestal for honorary statue
5 Tribunal
6 Space for public officials

4.5 Basilica plan, Pompeii, *c.* 150 BCE. Illustration from 1911 *Encyclopædia Britannica*, article BASILICA.

Greek urban planning and sanctuary design

In addition to the Hellenistic elements in individual buildings, Greek design is found in Roman urban planning. The large religious sanctuaries of the late Republican period owe their forms to a combination of Hellenistic planning and Italic materials, notably the exploitation of concrete in these new immense constructions. The origins of Hellenistic design can be readily seen at the Greek city of Pergamon, a powerful Hellenistic kingdom closely allied with Rome against other Greek states.

(a)

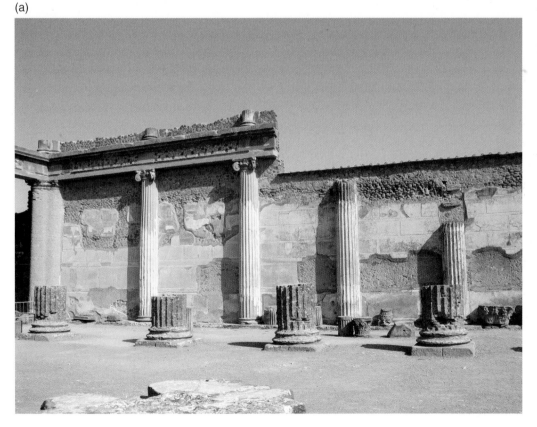

4.6a and 4.6b Basilica interior, Pompeii, *c.* 150 BCE. Photos courtesy Steven L. Tuck.

(b)

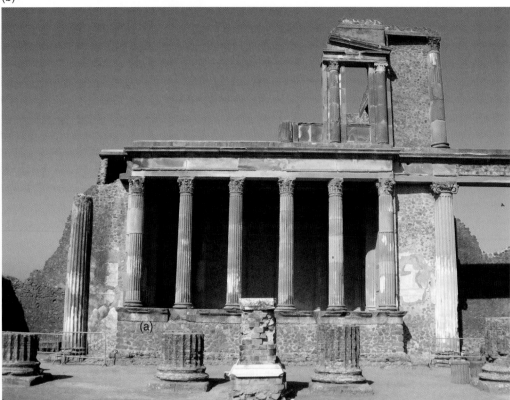

4.6   (*Continued*)

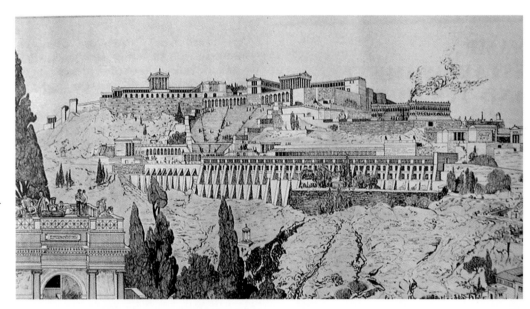

4.7   Plan, city of
Pergamon, *c.* 133 BCE.
Koch, M., and Kips, A.,
1886. Pergamon Panorama,
based on reconstructions
by Bohn, R. Ernst
Fabricius, 1997.

barrel vaults
a cylindrical architectural
feature formed by extending
an arch along an indefinite
length, creating a solid
roofing system that is
essentially a continuous arch.

In fact, its last king willed the entire kingdom to Rome upon his death in 133 BCE. Pergamon
was built on a rugged mountainous spot in western Asia Minor (modern Turkey). The site
required the use of large terraces to create level areas big enough for major public buildings. These
terraces were found on top of the acropolis as well as on the slopes down into the lower city. In
some instances the front of a terrace projected out beyond the line of the hill and was finished in
a line of **barrel vaults**. The terrace itself was finished on the back and sides by a three-sided

TOOLS & TECHNIQUES
Opus caementicium: *Roman concrete, materials and methods*

The Roman invention of concrete was one of the most important architectural innovations in history. It allowed completely new types and forms of architecture, with new shapes and scales of building developing over time. Roman concrete consisted of two parts: aggregate and mortar. The aggregate is the particulate material that creates the mass in concrete. Roman builders used many aggregates including various stones, brick, or ceramics of a range of sizes depending on need. Larger and heavier aggregate is found in foundations and other load-bearing parts of buildings, while lighter ones were used for roofs and upper walls. The mortar consists of water, lime, and, ideally, Pozzolana, a volcanic sand from the area of the Bay of Naples. Pozzolana cured quickly into a hard concrete that could also set underwater (a quality termed hydraulic), a boon for creating Roman harbors. No reinforcing materials such as iron bars found in modern concrete were used. Concrete took curvilinear shapes impossible to make with traditional materials. Wooden forms were constructed and the concrete mix was dumped in and set to shape before the forms were removed. The exposed surfaces of Roman concrete were generally faced with small blocks of stone or courses of brick.

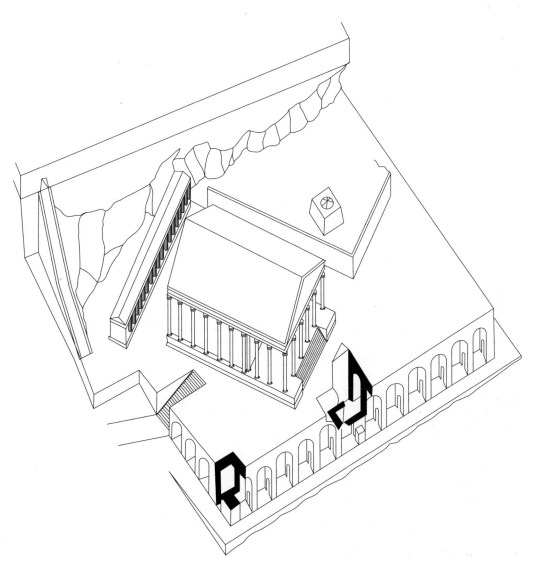

4.8 Sanctuary plan, Terracina, *c.* 100 BCE. Alberto Berengo Gardin in *The Roman Empire: Volume 1: From the Etruscans to the Decline of the Roman Empire*, Henri Stierlin, Taschen (1997), fig. 32. Reproduced with permission from A. B. Gardin.

portico that framed the structure on the terrace, sometimes a temple or large altar. These terraces created dramatic units in the city, often set at angles to each other, enhancing the dramatic elements of the design while creating features that dominated the skyline in the city. These design elements are found in Italic architecture in locations outside of Rome, at Tivoli, Palestrina, and Terracina.

Terracina, a town along the western, Tyrrhenian, coast of Italy and served by the Via Appia, was a strategically important natural promontory that dominated the coastline, coastal plain, and the ancient roads for many miles. On the top of the promontory was a late second- or early first-century BCE sanctuary thought to have been dedicated to Jupiter Anxur.

It was created on a massive terrace platform supported by an immense substructure all formed of concrete faced with opus incertum. The substructure of the terrace consists of two lines of barrel-vaulted *cryptoportici* over 113 feet (35 m) in length. The outer one presents an arcaded facade that runs along the front of the promontory in a line of high arches without any overtly Greek elements such as engaged columns.

The top of the terrace holds the late Republican pseudodipteral temple, set at a dramatic angle to the front of the terrace and the arcade. It is framed across the back by a portico as seen in Hellenistic sanctuaries. Here the scale and form of the complex were made possible by using concrete.

Another late Republican sanctuary that combined Hellenistic design and Roman building materials in an even more ambitious program is the Sanctuary of Fortuna Primigenia at Praeneste (modern Palestrina), a small town about 20 miles east of Rome. Where Terracina consisted of one large terrace on the top of a mountain, the Sanctuary of Fortuna at Praeneste covers the side of a mountain in a series of at least five levels, all terraced and cut into the mountain in work started after 82 BCE under the patronage of the Roman general Sulla. The organization of the space owes its inspiration to Hellenistic design with the key part of the sanctuary, a massive terrace, supported by a concrete substructure with a line of barrel vaults across the front.

cryptoportici
a vaulted covered passageway, usually open along one side, that creates the support for a building above. Often used to create large platforms for a Roman temple or villa.

4.9 Temple platform arcade, Terracina, *c.* 100 BCE. Photo courtesy Steven L. Tuck.

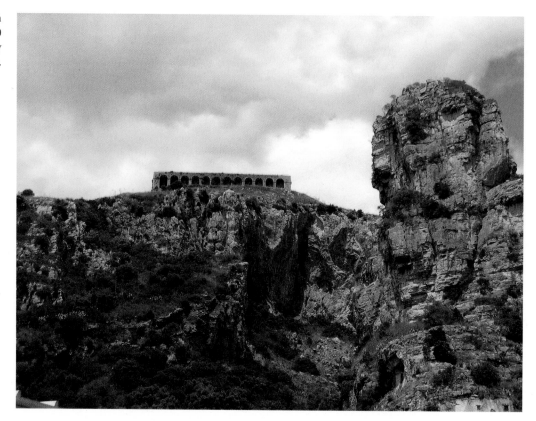

(a)

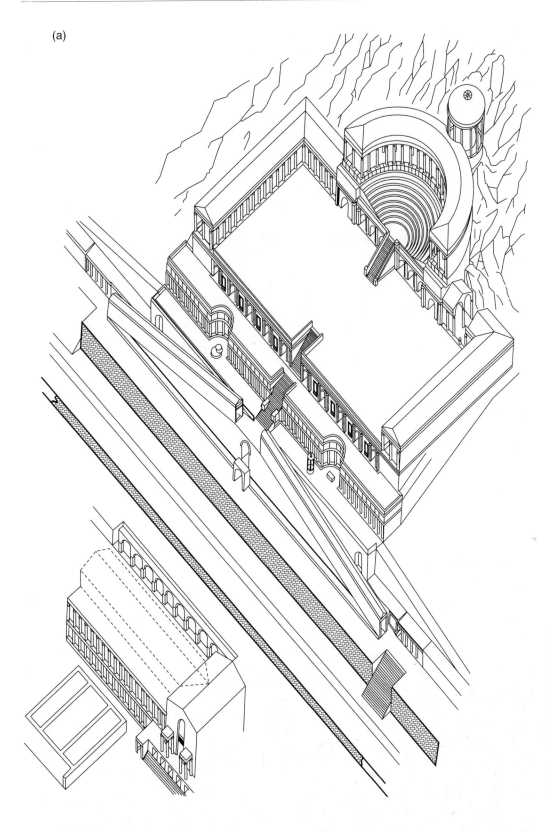

4.10a and 4.10b
Sanctuary of Fortuna
Primigenia, Praeneste, *c.* 80
BCE, plan and photo detail.
(a) Plan from *Roman
Architecture*, by Frank
Brown. Copyright © 1961,
1990 by George Braziller,
Inc. Reprinted by permission of George Braziller,
Inc., New York. All rights
reserved.

(b)

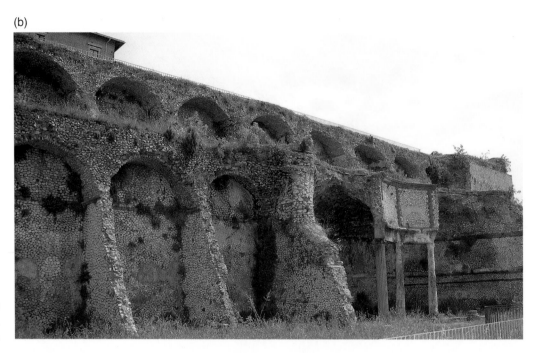

4.10b (b) Photo courtesy Steven L. Tuck.

This leads to a theater-shaped semi-circular staircase that finally terminates at the very top in a small round temple, similar to the earlier one at Tivoli (Figure 4.4). The terrace is framed by a three-sided portico while the theatral staircase feature is topped by a semi-circular one. A series of stairways, terraces, and a remarkably large pair of roofed ramps lead up from the valley floor below where the town of Praeneste was. Its design reflects a key element in Roman religious observance: procession. The movement of people from the edges to the central shrine of a sanctuary, often in a large group including priests, sacrificial animals and their attendants, worshippers, and other such as musicians, was a standard event and this sanctuary seems designed for such movement. The entire complex is grand in scale, very axial and symmetric in plan, and makes extensive use of Hellenistic design and Roman concrete construction to create the largest religious sanctuary ever built in ancient Italy. We date it perhaps twenty years after Terracina because it retains the opus incertum facing but utilizes more ambitious design and engineering.

The limits of Hellenistic influence and the flexibility of concrete construction in Roman architecture can both be seen at Pompeii where the amphitheater demonstrates Roman building materials and Roman building form together. Like Pompeii's basilica the amphitheater is the oldest of its type surviving from the Roman world. After the Roman colony was founded at Pompeii in 80 BCE, the colonists began to alter the city into a more specifically Roman space.

Previously constructed buildings were renovated into Roman forms as seen in the theater, forum, and Temple of Jupiter, while new Roman public buildings such as the covered theater and amphitheater were added to the assemblage of public buildings. The amphitheater was constructed in the early years of the colony by two Roman magistrates. Compared to the Colosseum and later amphitheaters, it is a simpler building without any subterranean rooms or tunnels under the arena floor for gladiators, animals, or equipment. It also has only modest tunneling under the superstructure of the seating area and only two large entrances that cut through the structure on the main axis of the oval to give access to the arena and to the lower rows of privileged seating. Most spectators reached their seats from the two exterior double staircases. Like later amphitheaters it is oval, in this case measuring 500 x 350 ft (150 x 105 m). It was also all constructed from concrete and makes use of arches and vaults to support the building.

A line of shallow concrete vaults ran around the exterior at ground level supporting the superstructure and the staircases with opus incertum-faced concrete and providing the only visual

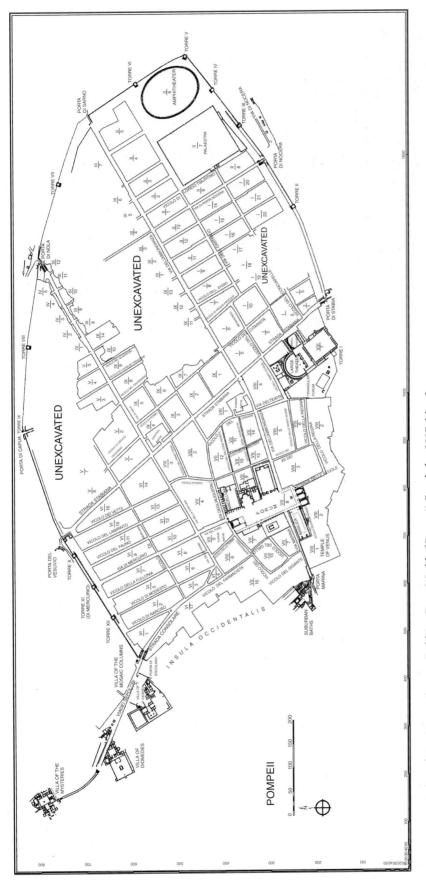

POMPEII

UNEXCAVATED

UNEXCAVATED

AMPHITHEATER

PALAESTRA

FORUM

TEMPLE OF VENUS

BASILICA

LARGE THEATER

TRIANGULAR FORUM

INSULA OCCIDENTALIS

SUBURBAN BATHS

PORTA MARINA

VILLA OF THE MYSTERIES

VILLA OF DIOMEDES

VILLA OF THE MOSAIC COLUMNS

PORTA DEL VESUVIO

PORTA DI CAPUA

PORTA DI SARNO

PORTA DI NOLA

PORTA DI NOCERA

PORTA DI STABIA

PORTA DI ERCOLANO

TORRE V
TORRE VI
TORRE VII
TORRE VIII
TORRE IX
TORRE X
TORRE XI (DI MERCURIO)
TORRE XII
TORRE I
TORRE II
TORRE III DI NOCERA
TORRE IV

STRADA STABIANA
STRADA CONSOLARE
VIA DI MERCURIO
VICOLO DEI VETTI
VICOLO DEL LABIRINTO
VICOLO DEL FAUNO
VICOLO DELLA FULLONIA
VICOLO DI MODESTO
VICOLO DI NARCISO
VICOLO DEL FARMACISTA
VICOLO DEL GIGANTE
VIA DEL FORO
VIA MARINA
VIA DELL'ABBONDANZA
VICOLO DELLE SCUOLE
VIA DELLA REGINA
VICOLO DELLA REGINA
VIA DEL TEATRI
STRADA STABIANA
VIA DI PORTA NOCERA
VIA DI CASTRO
VICOLO DEL EFEBO
VICOLO DI PAQUIO PROCULO
VICOLO DI TESMO
L'OREO TIBURTINO
VICOLO DI
CITHARISTA
VICOLO STORTO
XII DEI

N

0 50 100 150 200

4.11 Pompeii, plan of city, 80 BCE. Source: Dobbins-Foss, *World of Pompeii*, Routledge 2007, Map 2.

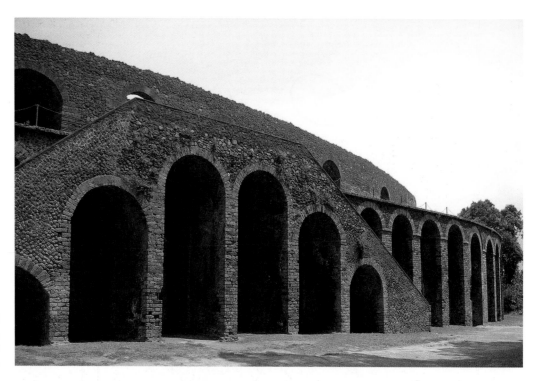

4.12 Amphitheater exterior, Pompeii, 80 BCE. Photo courtesy Steven L. Tuck.

HISTORICAL CONTEXT

Amphitheaters, a microcosm of the Roman world

Amphitheaters, the oval buildings (the name means double theater) that housed Roman spectacle, were a Roman invention. Their use reflected Roman cultural values and class structure. All those who entered an amphitheater literally took their places in the Roman world as the seating area was divided into sections, the lowest for the highest ranking Romans such as senators, public priests, government officials, and patricians all dressed in togas. The middle section was for the second class of Romans, the equestrians, and the upper section for the plebeians, the lowest class. Women, slaves, and foreigners stood in upper galleries. Those on the floor of the arena were outside the Roman system: slaves, non-citizens, and condemned criminals. The events in a typical day of games began with wild animals hunted by professional hunters, often in a themed hunt emphasizing conquest of foreign animals as metaphors for foreign lands and people. During a lunch break executions either of criminals or prisoners of war might take place, reinforcing Roman justice and control over threats to the state. The main event, gladiatorial combat, concluded a day's events. As a gift from an elite Roman, usually a politician, spectacles were accompanied by music, a parade, prize ceremonies, and distributions of free items to the spectators.

interest on the exterior, which had no Greek decorative features. The amphitheater held perhaps 20,000 spectators and the simple design meant that the special effects of trapdoor entrances seen in later spectacles at Rome were not found here. The design also meant that the animal hunts held in the arena largely consisted of bulls, boars, and bears with none of the very popular big cats possible.

Another common building form of the Late Republican period is the stone bridge. The earliest surviving example from Rome, the Pons Fabricius, bridged the Tiber at Rome. Dated to 62 BCE, the

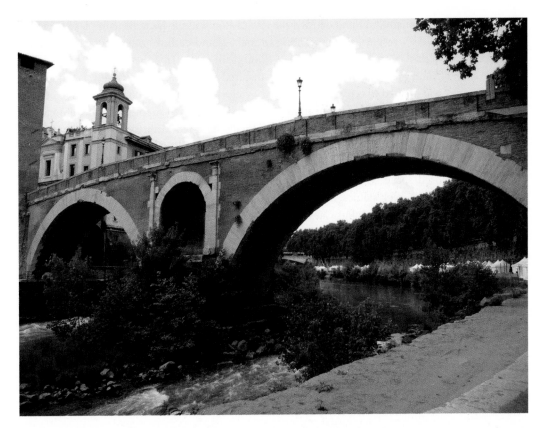

4.13   Pons Fabricius, Rome, 62 BCE. Photo courtesy Steven L. Tuck.

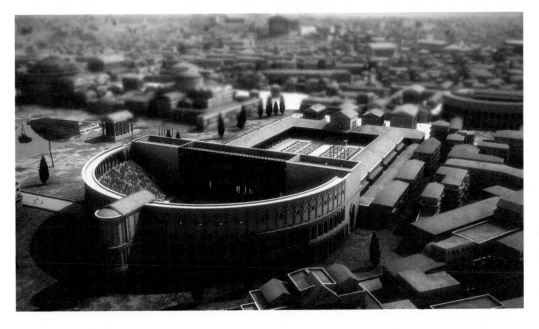

4.14   Theater of Pompey, 55 BCE, reconstruction of the complex, Rome Reborn. © 2012 by Frischer Consulting, Inc. All rights reserved.

bridge is named for the man who commissioned it, Lucius Fabricius, the *curator viarum* (caretaker of roads). It connects the left bank of the river with the island and replaced an earlier wooden bridge on this location. The bridge was built of two varieties of local stone, tufa and peperino, and faced with travertine. In design it relies on the power of the arch. It has two wide arches that are anchored by a central support in the middle of the Tiber incorporating its own smaller arch. The bridge is 201 ft (62 m) long, and the arches are each 79 ft (24.25 m) long and 18 ft (5.5 m) wide.

Given its population and building density, the city of Rome itself was a difficult place for large-scale construction. As a result, patrons wanting to make grand gestures often looked outside the walls of the city to the Campus Martius, the vast flood plain of the Tiber between the banks of the river and the Via Flaminia. The earliest Hellenistic-inspired complex, that of Pompey, is found here.

The complex was created to celebrate the military victories of Pompey the Great, which literally reached from one end of the Mediterranean to the other. Pompey had suppressed a revolt in Spain, helped destroy the revolt of Spartacus in Italy, and finally defeated Mithridates VI of Pontus and cleared the Mediterranean of pirates from Cilicia. Rather than a traditional Republican victory temple, he built a Hellenistic style complex dedicated in 55 BCE. It consisted of a rectangular colonnade creating an enclosed space. Within it were garden spaces and walkways decorated as a sort of museum with famous Greek statues, a statue of Pompey himself, a public latrine, a *curia* where the Senate could meet – and where Julius Caesar was assassinated, the first permanent theater in Rome, and a temple of Venus Victrix (Venus of Victory). The theater was designed as a set of steps leading to the temple, which was placed at the top of the *cavea* or seating area, a design found at the Sanctuary of Fortuna Primigenia at Praeneste. Pompey's was always the most important theater in Rome. The multiple elements of the complex demonstrate the increasing scale of construction

4.15 Forum Romanum, Rome, plan of late Republican buildings, *c.* 44 BCE. Drawing courtesy Jane DeRose Evans.

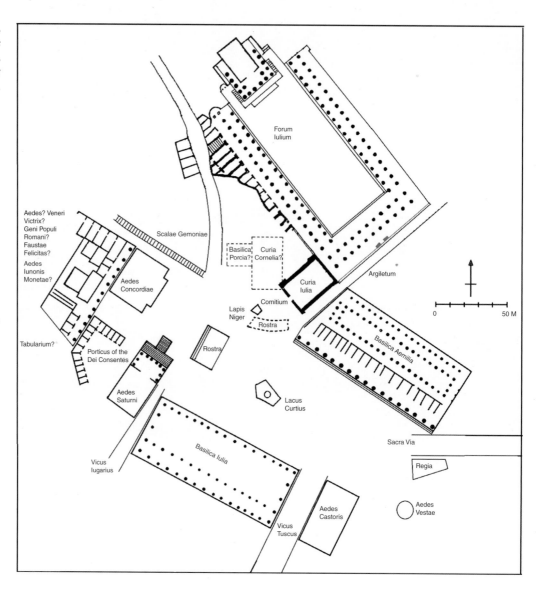

commissioned by the powerful generals of the Late Republic. It serves as a transitional monument between the Republican tradition of temple construction and the grand patronage of the imperial period. It also seems to have inspired what might be considered the first of the imperial fora, the Forum of Julius Caesar.

Julius Caesar, Pompey's rival for power at the end of the Republic and enemy in the civil war of 49–44 BCE, built an extension onto the Forum Romanum. It was inspired by Hellenistic urban

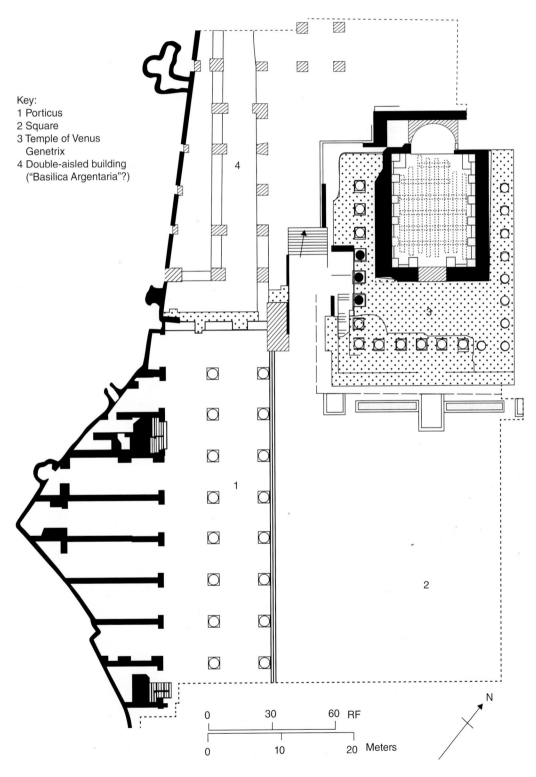

Key:
1 Porticus
2 Square
3 Temple of Venus
  Genetrix
4 Double-aisled building
  ("Basilica Argentaria"?)

4.16 Forum Iulium, dedicated 46 BCE, reconstruction. J. Toms in *Rome: An Oxford Archaeological Guide*, Amanda Claridge, Oxford University Press (2010), fig. 61, based on data from 1960.

planning and designed to compete with Pompey's building program in the Campus Martius. Started in 54 BCE and dedicated in 46 BCE, his forum set the pattern for the four imperial fora that were to follow. It was enclosed within a rectangular wall and framed by porticoes. The overall design was largely symmetric and axially organized with an entrance on one short end and a temple on the other short end opposite facing the entrance. It held a variety of buildings for many functions including legal, religious, and commercial, yet had an integrated decorative program. Often called the Forum of Caesar, we refer to it by its Latin name, Forum Iulium.

The Forum Iulium repeated elements of Pompey's complex including a *curia*, open plaza, public latrine, porticoes, and a temple to Venus. Here the temple was dedicated to Venus Genetrix (Latin for "founder of a family"), reinforcing Caesar's claim of descent from the Trojan hero, Aeneas. The forum also hosted statues by Greek artists as well as a statue of Caesar. It had no theater attached, but Caesar had started one a short distance away. Elements not in Pompey's complex include shops, a basilica, and paintings and carved gems that were placed on display here, giving the forum a museum aspect that was repeated in following imperial fora.

ROMAN WALL PAINTING IN THE LATE REPUBLIC

While we have scant surviving Roman tomb painting from earlier periods, our earliest extensive evidence of Roman wall painting comes from the Late Republican period, and it is from this point that we can trace the development of wall painting in an unbroken line in one area of the Roman world. This is largely the result of the eruption of Mt. Vesuvius in 79 CE and the consequent destruction of Pompeii, Herculaneum, and surrounding small communities and villas. The wall paintings on these structures make up the majority of evidence we have of this art from the Roman world. The early excavation of Pompeii and other sites, however, made dating these works of art almost impossible. In 1882 August Mau proposed a scheme that we still use today in a more refined form. He divided the wall paintings by date into four styles. Still called First through Fourth Styles, this scheme is used for organizing and dating Roman wall paintings from 200 BCE up to 79 CE. The dates for the four styles are

> First Style, 200–80 BCE
>
> Second Style, 80–15 BCE
>
> Third Style, 15 BCE–50 CE
>
> Fourth Style, 50–79 CE

Notably the First Style is during the pre-Roman period at Pompeii when it was a community of Samnites, an Italic people related to the Romans of the region of Samnium, who had settled Pompeii and other communities in the area in *c.* 425 BCE. The origins of First Style painting are connected with the pattern of Greek artists and ideas coming into Italy in the period beginning in 200 BCE when elite Romans and other Italians became the great patrons of art. Evidence makes it clear that the artists entering Italy are of the highest level and come from the most advanced cities in the Greek world. For wall painting we have literary evidence of the emigration of Greek artists to Italy in the second century BCE from Alexandria, arguably the most important city at the time for patronage of the arts:

> Ptolemy [VI Philometor, 186–145 BCE] the king of Egypt, after being driven out of his kingdom by his own brother, arrived at Rome in the wretched condition of an ordinary man accompanied by one eunuch and three slave boys, and when he perceived along the road the lodgings of Demetrius the Topographer [landscape-painter], he sought out this man and took lodging with him, since the latter had been entertained by him many times during his residence in Alexandria. (Diodorus Siculus 31.18)

peristyle
refers to a structure with columns that enclose it, such as a peristyle temple with columns on all four sides of the exterior or a peristyle courtyard with colonnaded porches on all four sides.

This anecdote shows at least one of the best, most sought-after Greek artists relocating to Italy in the second century BCE. In this case, the artist is a painter who had worked for the king of Egypt. This sets up a mechanism by which the patterns of Greek palaces became the ideal models for Roman elite residences. Another mechanism was when Romans traveled into Greek lands and saw this material firsthand. We see two distinct approaches to this palace model in the first two phases of Roman wall paintings.

First Style wall painting, 200–80 BCE

The earliest of the wall painting styles in ancient Italy, First Style, is a wall treatment that imitates the look of the actual wall construction in Hellenistic Greek palaces. Heavy layers of plaster were spread over rubble walls and then carved and painted to resemble blocks of cut stone, giving walls the look of grand marble construction. A brief description of the style and its development was recorded by the architect, Vitruvius: "Hence those of the ancients who first used polished coats of plastering, originally imitated the variety and arrangement of inlaid marbles. Afterwards the variety was extended to the cornices, and the yellow and red frames of panels" (*De Architectura* 7.5.1).

As First Style wall painting developed it added to the simple illusion of courses of rectangular blocks cut with smooth faces and drafted edges. Color was used to distinguish different faux marbles and expensive imported stones such as porphyry and onyx. The plaster was cut to closely resemble actual construction, with large simulated blocks along the base of the wall for a foundation topped with smaller blocks laid in courses as were the real stones. Eventually other architectural features such as engaged columns and cornices were created in plaster as well, adding to the illusion of grand architecture.

First Style is found on a relative handful of buildings at Pompeii including the largest house, the House of the Faun, which at 33,000 square ft (3,050 sq. m) is essentially a Greek Hellenistic palace.

The facade of the House of the Faun uses Corinthian pilasters on either side of the front entrance to formalize it. The same feature is found at the *tablinum* on the opposite side of the atrium directly across from the front door. These are found again flanking the second *tablinum* off of the **peristyle** that held the Alexander the Great mosaic. The result is to create a line of high status spaces beginning at the front door.

The First Style was also used in public buildings such as the interior of the basilica at Pompeii. It is important to note that the modern distinction between public and private did not apply in the Roman world and that many of the spaces in these houses covered with First Style painting, such as the front halls, atrium, *tablinum*, and reception rooms, were considered public spaces. We should also note the difference in perspective between Roman and modern

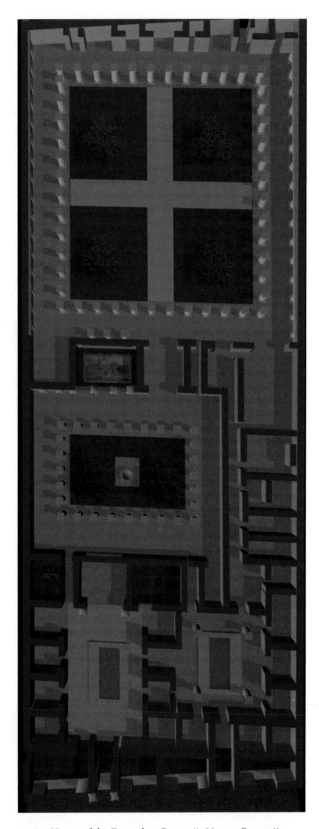

4.17 House of the Faun plan, Pompeii, 80 BCE. Pompeii: Daily Life in an Ancient Roman City, © 2010 The Teaching Company. Reproduced with permission of The Teaching Company, www.thegreatcourses.com.

orthostates
squared stone blocks of
greater height than depth.
These upright standing
stones were used to make
the bases of walls and then
topped with courses of
smaller cut stones.

loggia
a roofed gallery open on one
side and generally supported
by columns, often found on
an upper floor of a building.

views of decor. To many of us, designing our house to conform to a palace might seem pretentious. To the Romans it was aspirational. Not a statement of aspiring to be a king, but of the values and social status of the highest levels of society.

Although based on Greek palace architecture, First Style painting has key Etruscan elements as well. The resulting style in fact violates the structural logic (and the laws of physics) of the Greek forms and instead shifts the elements to conform to the Etruscan tripartite wall division, both horizontally and vertically with the main focus on a central zone/register. A dado or socle, an element of Etruscan wall design, is inserted under the line of **orthostates** visually raising this apparent base for the wall into the air. The orthostates in the central register are broken up by narrow blocks that reflect later divisions of the wall into scenes divided by verticals such as columns, trees, etc. Coloring is not consistent or coherent. Despite the illusion of stone construction the colors selected for stones do not necessarily conform to real building stones but instead match the blocks of color found in Etruscan tomb paintings (see Tomb of the Bulls, Figure 2.23) One of the best preserved examples of First Style and its Etruscan components is found in the House of Sallust at Pompeii from *c.* 100 BCE.

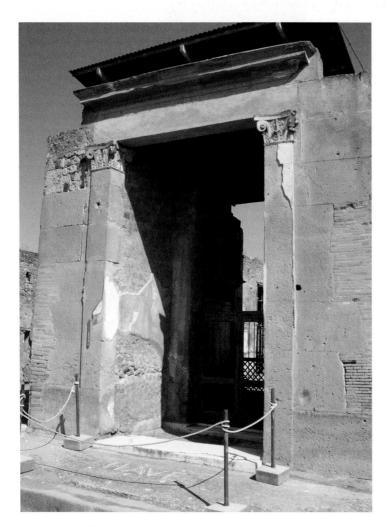

The plain dado, orthostates, and upper courses of blocks are all clearly carved in plaster and painted a variety of rich colors to evoke the image of a wall made not of rubble but of large blocks of imported stone, although the colors do not imitate actual stones. The upper zone of the wall is not preserved. For that element a cubiculum, bedroom, in the House of the Ship Europa at Pompeii provides excellent evidence.

Here the upper zone of the wall is carved as a small-scale colonnade creating the illusion of a second story **loggia** or small peristyle walkway. Real such walkways are known from grander houses such as the House of the Faun. Here, however, they demonstrate the trend in Roman wall painting of illusionistic or **trompe l'oeil** piercing appearing first in the upper zone of the wall before being applied to the lower registers.

The grand if relatively simple wall paintings of First Style houses seem to show a coordination between wall decoration and the elaborate floor mosaics in the period in which one of the leading styles of floor mosaics is Greek. These polychrome mosaics differ from the predominantly black and white Italic mosaics, generally have Greek subjects, and large, mainly mythological, images that dominate the centers of the floors in elite residences. One of the most spectacular of these is the Alexander mosaic from the House of the Faun.

It shows Alexander the Great in battle against the Persian king Darius and is thought to be a revised copy of a famous painting from *c.* 300 BCE by the Greek artist Philoxenos of Eretria. It measures just

4.18 House of the Faun facade, Pompeii, 80 BCE. Photo courtesy Steven L. Tuck.

over 19 x 10 ft (5.8 x 3.1 m) and contains over a million and a half **tesserae**. As with many Hellenistic works, the emphasis here goes beyond portraiture and the historical event and concentrates the viewer's attention on two elements. First, it emphasizes visual effects such as

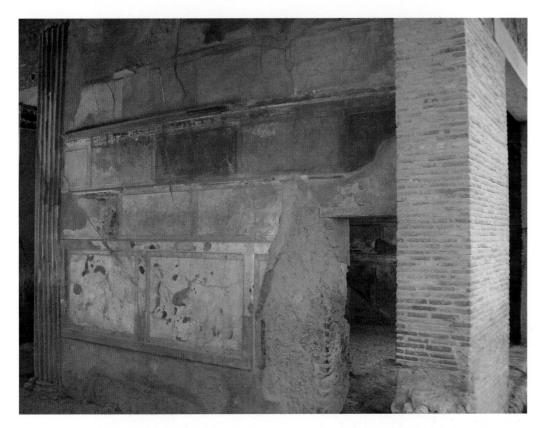

4.19 First Style wall painting, House of Sallust, Pompeii, *c.* 100 BCE. Photo courtesy Steven L. Tuck.

foreshortening, lines of sight, and reflections in the bronze shield in the foreground. Second, it foregrounds the emotional reaction to the events in the attack including the relatively prominent Darius reaching back towards one of his dying bodyguards. The pain and anguish on the faces of the Persians are characteristic of Hellenistic art. This Alexander imagery in a house decorated like a Hellenistic palace conveys the influence of Alexander as a subject through this period in Roman art.

Second Style wall painting, 80–15 BCE

Second Style wall painting followed immediately from First Style in about 80 BCE and can be considered a direct development from it. The origins of Second Style wall painting are a subject of scholarly discussion. Current theories place the origins of Second Style either at Pompeii or at Rome. The correspondence between the founding of the Roman colony and the date of Second Style both in 80 BCE leads to the conclusion that it originated at Pompeii and was instigated by the influx of Roman colonists into an area which already had a strong tradition of Greek-inspired painting with First Style. The money, tastes, and needs for display of the colonists provided the impetus for the change to the new style. The earliest extant example, however, is found at Rome in the House of the Griffins on the Palatine Hill, at the time one of the most prestigious residential areas in the city. To some scholars it seems more likely that the style developed among the wealthy elite in Rome and was carried by them to Pompeii where, thanks to the preservation of the city by the eruption of Vesuvius, we have the best evidence for it.

Second Style is a form of illusionistic painting that achieves architectural forms and space by pictorial means. While First Style was itself a form of relief plaster work that emphasized solidity of the wall, Second Style opened up the wall, creating space in front of and beyond it using trompe l'oeil

trompe l'oeil
literally, "to fool the eye." A technique in art to create the optical illusion of objects existing in three dimensional space.

tesserae
small handcut cubes of stone used to make mosaics.

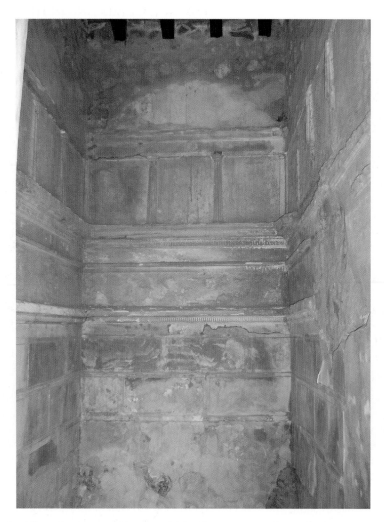

4.20 First Style wall painting, *c.* 100 BCE, House of the Ship Europa, Pompeii. Photo courtesy Steven L. Tuck.

4.21 Alexander mosaic, 80 BCE, House of the Faun, Pompeii. Museo Archeologico Nazionale di Napoli. Photo courtesy Steven L. Tuck.

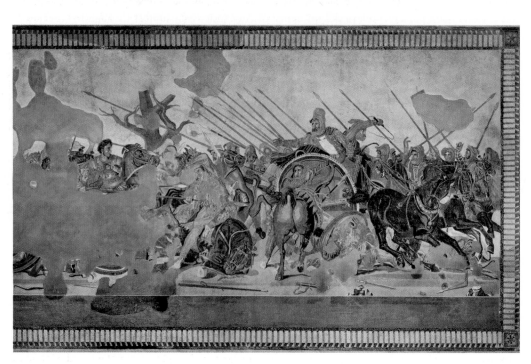

SCHOLARLY PERSPECTIVE
The inspiration(s) for Second Style wall painting

The inspiration for the style is a point of scholarly debate. The contemporary architect, Vitruvius, once again provides us with a description that addresses that issue, but doesn't entirely solve the problem. In fact, the vagueness of his wording has led to further confusion. The inspirations for Second Style wall painting are a subject of scholarly discussion partially because of the poorly dated, limited surviving examples and partially because of the references to it in the work of Vitruvius.

> From which they proceeded to the representations of buildings, columns, and the projections of roofs. In spacious apartments, such as *exedræ*, on account of their extent, they decorated the wall with scenery, after the tragic, comic or satyric mode; and galleries from their extended length, they decorated with varied landscapes, the representations of particular spots. In these they also painted ports, promontories, the coasts of the sea, rivers, fountains, straits, groves, mountains, cattle, shepherds, and sometimes figures representing gods, and stories, such as the Trojan battles, or the wanderings of Ulysses over different countries, and other subjects, founded on real history. (Vitruvius, *De Architectura* 7.5.2)

Most scholars now agree that Vitruvius' statement of the use of scenery design to decorate large walls is accurate. They see the composition of the enormous full wall paintings deriving from the design of Roman theater buildings, the *scaenae frons*. These buildings made up the backdrop of Roman stages and generally consisted of a two-story facade with three entrances on the ground floor; balconies on the second floor for cast members occasionally to use when playing gods; and alternating projecting and receding elements such as balconies and porticoes allowing entrances and exits on stage as well as some visual interest for spectators. This notion of the inspiration for Second Style from theater buildings makes sense as far as it goes. Vitruvius does not, however, mention the Greek, Hellenistic inspiration for these building forms. In fact, it's only when we look at other sources and the works themselves that we can see that component clearly. The *scaenae frons* design itself clearly has elements alluding to Hellenistic palace design. The shields with Macedonian sunburst patterns found on many Second Style wall paintings are only the most obvious example while much of the architecture including wall surfaces, four panel doors, and use of landscape paintings over doorways is found earlier in Macedonian royal tombs from Vergina. So, we are forced to conclude that Vitruvius is providing only one source, perhaps in an attempt to make the painting style seem more Roman. Since it is a style that he approves of, it is natural that he would de-emphasize the foreign origins. The inspiration for Second Style is quite possibly found in both theater and Hellenistic palace designs. Elements of both are seen in overall composition as well as details (mask, shields, architecture).

Vitruvius' references to landscape paintings of particular spots and to the wanderings of Ulysses in the description of painting are also somewhat problematic for scholars. Mythological subjects are not found in surviving examples of the main fields of Second Style wall paintings. They do, however, correspond exactly to the subsidiary paintings we find in either the upper or flanking zones of Second Style walls. If the last part of his description of figure painting refers to the introduction of these in the subsidiary panels of walls then it matches the existing evidence, although some scholars argue that what we call the earliest phases of Third Style are really late Second and reflect what Vitruvius is describing. This is currently a minority opinion.

Bettina Bergmann et al., "Roman Frescoes from Boscoreale: The Villa of Publius Fannius Synistor in Reality and Virtual Reality." *Metropolitan Museum of Art Bulletin* 62.4 (Spring 2010).

techniques to create an illusion of the spatial extension of the wall. The goal of First Style was to turn a rubble wall into a marble one with plaster and paint. The goal of Second Style was to use paint to make that wall dissolve entirely.

A number of elements defining Second Style are found in its first phase, 80–40 BCE, and are illustrated by a room in the House of the Griffins, Rome. These include the breaking down of the enclosing space

scaenae frons
the elaborate background for a Roman theater stage, usually two or three stories in height with multiple entrances, balconies, and alternating projecting and receding elements articulated with columns.

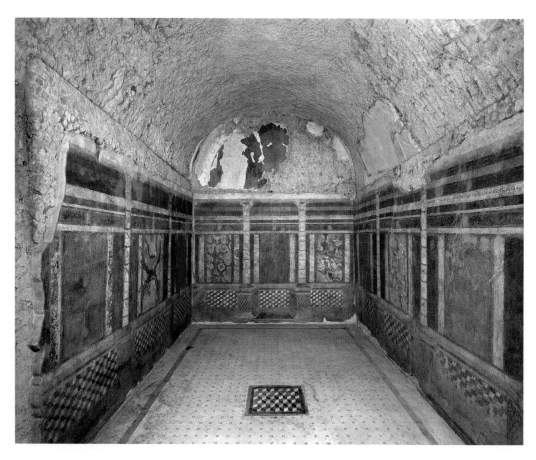

4.22 House of the Griffins, Palatine Hill, Rome, 80–40 BCE. © 2014. Photo Scala, Florence/ Luciano Romano. Courtesy of the Ministero Beni e Att. Culturali.

entablature
architectural term for the part of the building above the columns including cornice, moldings, and friezes.

imbrication
an overlapping pattern like roof shingles or fish scales.

of the room and the imitation wall pushed to the background by a screen of columns often resting on a continuous podium or individual pedestals, all carrying an illusionistic **entablature**.

Projection and recession are achieved by shading and perspective. Illusionistic motifs (**imbrication**, cubes in three-dimensional perspective, etc.) are moved from the floor mosaics of First Style to the dado and central panels of Second Style. The composition of the wall continues the largely tripartite wall division seen earlier in the Italic tradition both horizontally and vertically. But the first steps are taken towards centralized organization by treating the central panel differently than the flanking panels. In terms of color, polychromy continues with the blocks of color as well as imitation stones including marbles, alabaster, and agate.

In the second phase of Second Style, recognizable by 40 BCE, the upper zone of the wall appears to recede and has the illusion of windows that allow further architecture to be viewed in the distance. This spatial recession seems to begin in the upper registers before moving as well into the central zone of the wall. Similarly, we see the first appearance of figure painting in Roman mural decoration, starting in the upper zones of the wall and gradually coming to be a major subject.

At the villa at Oplontis on the Bay of Naples some of the grandest and highest quality Second Style paintings were preserved by the eruption of Vesuvius. This villa includes one room with a tremendous integrated scene of illusionistic sanctuary architecture. The scene centers on a door into a sanctuary with a large tripod as the focal point. Since the tripod was most famously associated with the oracle of Apollo at Delphi, who sat in one to recite her pronouncements, the painting suggests a sanctuary of Apollo.

Large-scale columns on a projecting plinth create a foreground while the portico in the sanctuary recedes on both sides with both linear and visual perspective used to reinforce the sense of depth. Theater masks and landscape panel paintings are seen on the edges of the work as further items of visual interest.

The best preserved wall in the atrium of the villa is painted with a large scene of an illusionistic room that contains more complex space than the earlier House of the Griffins. It serves to extend the space of the atrium in a grand form of architecture with flights of steps leading from the real floor of the room to doors in the illusionistic wall. The wall is organized with faux central and right-hand doors while the true door into the room is on the viewer's left completing the expected tripartite composition.

(a)

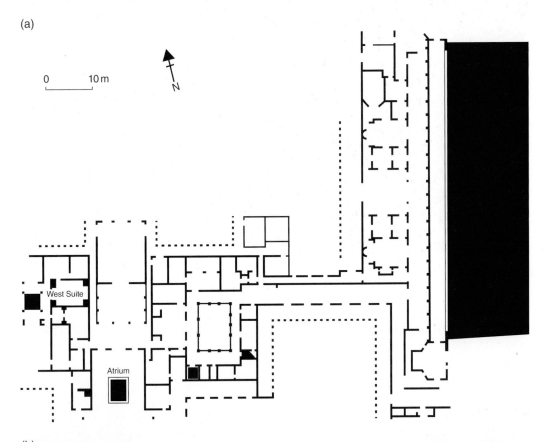

4.23a and 4.23b Villa at Oplontis plan paired with Villa Maritima painting from House of Marine Venus, Pompeii. (a) Plan: Experiencing Rome: A Visual Exploration of Antiquity's Greatest Empire, © 2008 The Teaching Company. Reproduced with permission of The Teaching Company, www. thegreatcourses.com. (b) Photo courtesy Steven L. Tuck.

(b)

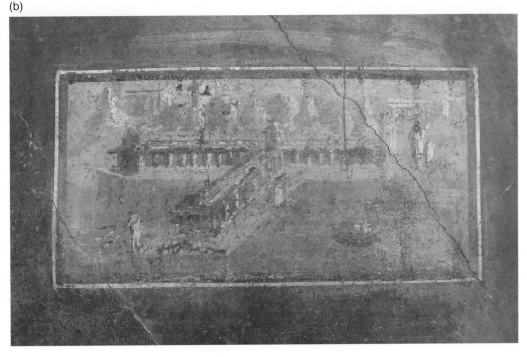

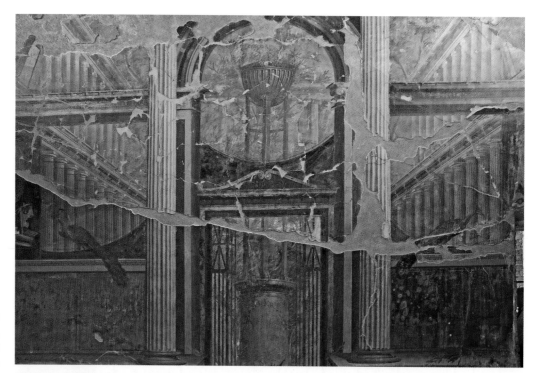

4.24 West Suite, villa at Oplontis, wall painting, *c.* 40 BCE. Photo courtesy Steven L. Tuck.

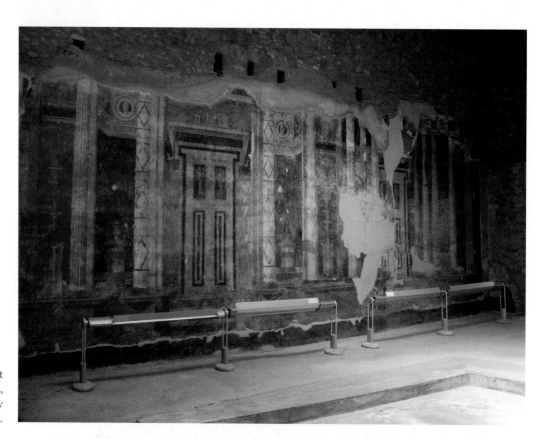

4.25 Atrium, villa at Oplontis, wall painting, *c.* 40 BCE. Photo courtesy Steven L. Tuck.

Heavy, realistically proportioned architecture gives a sense of authenticity while furniture set in front of the illusionistic wall further integrates the atrium and serves as foreground elements to the projecting and receding wall behind. The upper zone of the wall sports both illusionistic portrait shields, described by Pliny the Elder as a type captured in battle against the Carthaginians, and Macedonian shields, perhaps evoking those captured in the wars in the previous century against Perseus and other Greek kings. The image aspires to the architecture and decor in a Greek palace but also alludes to the military victory decorations found in the atrium of a Roman house of the highest level of society.

Another variety of Second Style is found in the Villa of the Mysteries just outside of Pompeii. Some rooms have very similar wall paintings to those at Oplontis while those in room 5 differ dramatically. The illusionistic stone wall and red-ground central register operate as a backdrop for a single line of large-scale figures. The importance of the figures in this room goes beyond their use in illustrating this variety of wall painting. They are the only cycle of illustrations we have of the various stages of initiation into the worship of the god Dionysus. The space they decorate is believed by many scholars to be the actual chamber where initiations took place, making it a very rare find from the ancient world. The villa itself was a working winery, but the room we will concentrate on, room 5, was found in the farthest corner from the agricultural area. It was part of the most distant and

(a)

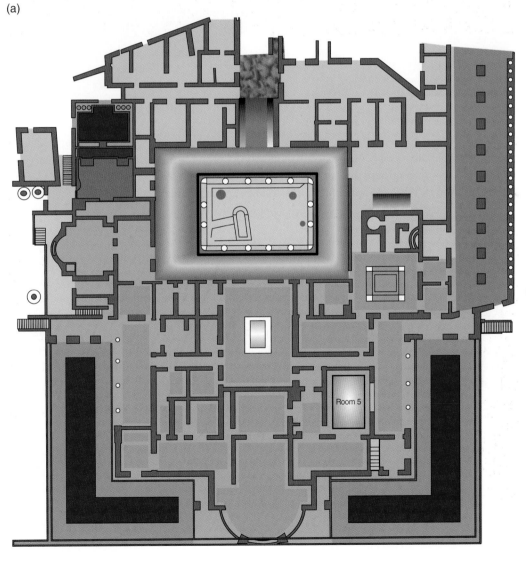

4.26a and 4.26b Plan and exterior photo, Villa of the Mysteries, Pompeii, 40 BCE. (a) Plan: Pompeii: Daily Life in an Ancient Roman City, © 2010 The Teaching Company. Reproduced with permission of The Teaching Company, www.thegreatcourses.com.

Room 5

(b)

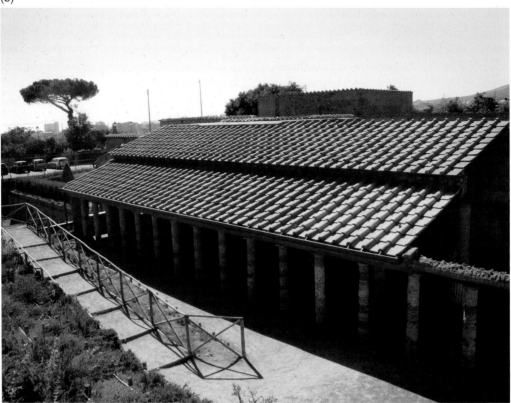

4.26b (b) Photo courtesy Steven L. Tuck.

restricted suite of rooms from the entrance on the opposite side of the complex. Some scholars believe that the suite was space restricted to members of the family that owned the villa, perhaps only to women. The figure groups are not in what we presume the order of initiation was because that order is broken by the compositional priority to place the most important figures and events in the center of the back wall opposite the entrance: Dionysus and two images that represent the culminating epiphany of the initiation.

On the left wall as one enters the room are three groups of figures retaining the traditional Etrusco-Italic tripartite organization and placing the most important figure in the central panel. To the far left is a group, overseen by a Roman matron, that shows the reading of the sacred text observed by a woman with a tray of food for the subsequent celebratory meal after the initiation concludes. In the center is the initiate, a woman on the eve of her wedding, seated with her back to us washing her hands in a standard form of ritual purification prior to a religious rite. To the right is a group of satyrs and Silenus, followers of Dionysus, who, given the bases they stand on, probably represent statues rather than participants. The final figure is a woman reacting as she observes part of the ritual on the opposite wall.

The rear wall also has three groups and a single figure at the end. On the left are two satyrs manipulating a third into seeing a mask instead of his reflection in the bottom of a wine cup, a form of epiphany in which his reflection stands for his nature. The central pair is Dionysus sprawled on the lap of his wife, Ariadne, as they oversee the initiation. The third group shows the initiate again, now on her knees about to lift the cloth off a herm, an old-fashioned, rural form of statue of Dionysus. The final figure is a Vanth, a figure who oversaw major life transitions in Etruscan mythology, wielding a switch as she whips the initiate on the right-hand wall.

The final wall on the right has only two figure groups as the center is dominated by a large window. The first set shows the initiate, her head in the lap of another woman, undergoing an ordeal, a

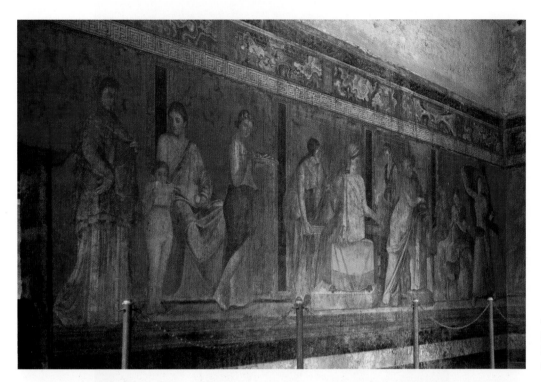

4.27 Left-hand wall, room 5, Villa of the Mysteries, Pompeii, 40 BCE. Photo courtesy Steven L. Tuck.

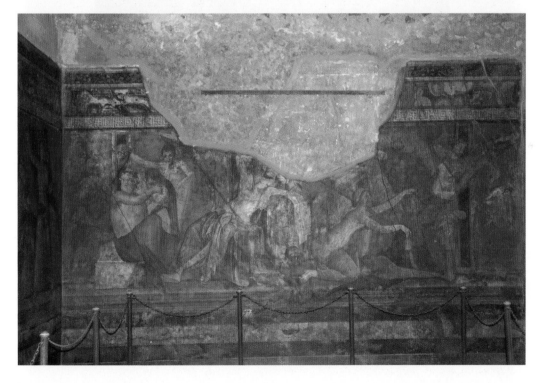

4.28 Rear wall, room 5, Villa of the Mysteries, Pompeii, 40 BCE. Photo courtesy Steven L. Tuck.

standard component of intiation, as the Vanth whips her back while music plays. The final group shows the initiate seated on an elaborate chair fixing her hair in the characteristic style of a Roman bride while another woman stands behind her. These two women are flanked by Eros figures. The one to the left holds a jewelry box with a mirror in the lid for the initiate's use while arranging her hair. The final, pendant figure, is a Roman matron, apparently the same one who starts the sequence on the left wall still supervising the entire process.

(a)

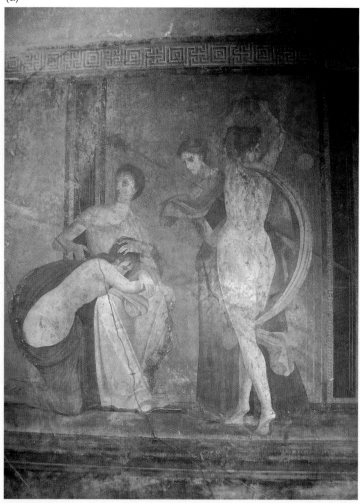

(b)
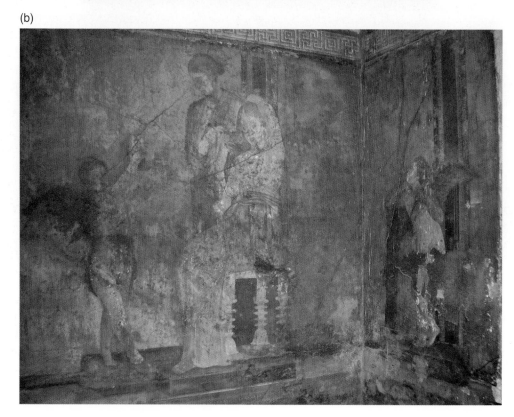

4.29a and 4.29b Right-hand wall, room 5, Villa of the Mysteries, Pompeii, 40 BCE. Photos courtesy Steven L. Tuck.

A VIEW FROM THE PROVINCES
The monument of Aemilius Paullus at Delphi

The Roman love of Greek art and appreciation for Greek culture seems to have accelerated during the second century BCE after the sack of Syracuse and other victories against Greek cities and armies. One mechanism for the transmission of Greek art to the Roman world is found in this monument, the first commissioned by a Roman general in the aftermath of one of these wars that was sculpted by Greek sculptors. This may, in fact, constitute a pivotal moment in popularizing Greek sculptural style among the Roman elite. Aemilius Paullus' permanent triumphal monument was erected in the sanctuary of Apollo at Delphi. Here, he commissioned a memorial to the Roman victory, using an unfinished monument to the defeated Macedonian king, Perseus.

The completed monument was made of a rectangular pillar over 29 feet (9 m) in height with a dedicatory inscription near the base and a statue of Paullus on a rearing horse on the top. A relief frieze depicting the critical battle of Pydna was placed at the top of the pillar running on all four sides of it. The two armies, consisting of men on foot and on horseback, fight in the frieze with no landscape or other context. Figures fill the relief and are organized into groups of combatants, often with a dead or dying warrior lying on the ground filling the space beneath a pair of warriors.

The figures show great energy with many diagonals, rearing horses, and individual combats. The design and some individual figures seem based on Athenian reliefs from the fifth century BCE, especially the battle reliefs on the Temple of Athena Nike on the Athenian Acropolis. If so, they could be evidence of the transmission of these figural and compositional conventions into the Roman world. The depictions of some figures may provide historical detail as well.

The iconography of the scene with details of armor and weapons allowed viewers to distinguish the two sides, the Macedonian round shields and Roman long oval ones are one means of doing so, as are the various forms of armor. One of the long sides of the frieze is dominated by a riderless horse that doubtless alludes to the start of the battle. An oracle had declared that whichever side started the battle was fated to lose. So, both armies waited. Eventually a horse broke out from the Roman lines, crossed to the Macedonian army and as men from both sides tried to capture it, fighting broke out. Paullus responded to the Macedonian attack and the Romans won the battle. The riderless horse is a visual reminder of the start of the battle even as the battle itself rages around it. The historical portrayal is not precisely chronological, but based on Greek synoptic narrative that places various episodes together in the same scene, a type of narrative seen later in the census and sacrifice frieze of the so-called Altar of Domitius Ahenobarbus.

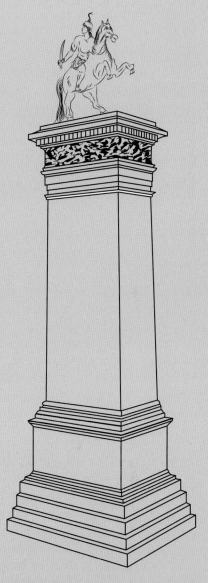

4.30 Victory monument of Aemilius Paullus, Delphi, *c.* 167 BCE, drawing. Heinz Kähler, *Der Fries vom Reiterdenkmal des Aemilius. Paullus in Delphi* (Monumenta Artis Romanae, v). Berlin: Gebr. Mann, 1965. Frontispiece.

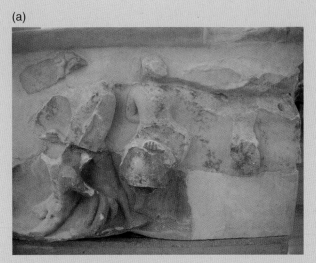

(a)

(b)

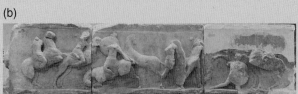

4.31a and 4.31b Victory monument of Aemilius Paullus, Delphi, *c.* 167 BCE, photo of relief, Archaeological Museum, Delphi. H 1 ft ¼ in (31 cm). Photos courtesy Steven L. Tuck.

One figure group on the short ends consists of a Roman cavalryman whose horse is at a dramatic diagonal. He carries a Roman sword and is apparently swinging it against a Macedonian soldier who covers his head with his round shield. The rider's face differs from all of the others in the scene with qualities that seem to be elements of portraiture. He has the face of a mature man with sagging skin under his chin, possibly a double chin. This is thought to be a portrait of Paullus himself, then about sixty years old. If so, the monument, carved by a Greek artist, includes two of the most important genres of sculpture in the Late Republic, historical relief and portraiture. It certainly set the pattern for scenes of battle found on commemorative Roman reliefs in later periods.

LATE REPUBLICAN SCULPTURE

In contrast to painting and architecture, which embraced Hellenistic styles, late Republican sculpture resisted such influences. Perhaps this is due to the use of sculptures to present images of traditional Roman public accomplishment, which encouraged artists to retain a conservative style. Nevertheless, there are developments in the period and indications of integration of Hellenistic style into public art. The largest surviving relief sculpture of the late Republican period is the so-called Altar of Domitius Ahenobarbus. It is composed of four panels that were not an altar, but probably originally surrounded a monumental statue base.

Three of the reliefs, carved in Greek marble, show a scene from Greek mythology, the wedding procession of Neptune and Amphitrite. All three panels are filled with sea creatures including tritons, nereids, seahorses, and seabulls. The wedded couple sit in a double cart drawn by tritons. The style is Hellenistic, based on the sculptural workshops at Pergamon, with very close stylistic parallels to the reliefs on the Great Altar from the middle of the second century BCE. The figures fill the frame, occasionally even spilling over the edges. They are cut in very deep relief with round bodies full of anatomical detail including full bodied snake and animal figures as seen on the Great Altar. The Hellenistic interest in dramatic composition, movement, and expression are found in the repeated use of curving and twisting forms, diagonals, and groups of figures connected by overlapping figures and looping reins.

(a)

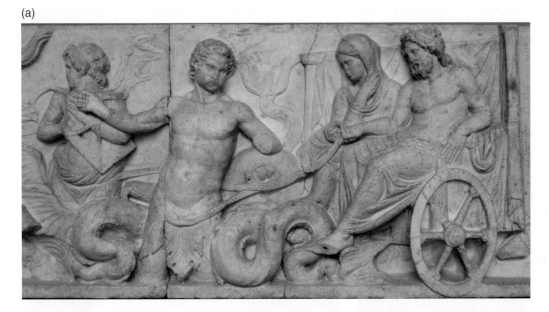

(b)

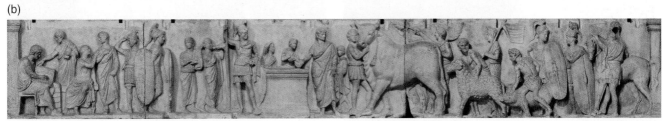

4.32a and 4.32b   "Altar of Domitius Ahenobarbus" reliefs, *c.* 100 BCE, Rome. Musée du Louvre, Paris and the Staatliche Antikensammlungen, Munich. H 32 in (81.3 cm), marble. Source: (a) Bibi Saint-Pol/Wikimedia; (b) Marie-Lan Nguyen/Wikimedia Commons.

The fourth panel differs in almost every way. It is carved in pure white marble in a traditional Roman style and the subject is one of Roman public life. The distinctions seem to have been a deliberate attempt to highlight this side of the monument. The scene, a census and sacrifice to Mars, shows the tradition of Roman historical relief sculpture. The event is presented in a documentary way with the census scene on the left, then an altar flanked by Mars and the presiding magistrate, while a *suovetaurilia* fills most of the right side of the panel. The figures are all carved in smaller scale than the Hellenistic ones on the remainder of the monument. Roman Republican features include the subject, hierarchy of scale, and the combination of divine and human figures in a single scene. Rather than the drama and movement of the wedding procession, here the scene is dignified and demonstrates public accomplishments, both features of the portraiture of the period as well.

Etruscan portrait traditions continued to affect Roman art in the period as well. An excellent example is the votive portrait bust of a man from the early part of the first century found at the Manganello Temple, Cerveteri. This terracotta portrait is painted with red skin tone following Greek and Etruscan conventions of gender representation. It is an image of a middle-aged man with close-cropped hair and slightly prominent ears and nose, forehead wrinkles, and distinct nasolabial folds that run from his nostrils to the corners of his mouth. The figure, apparently a portrait of a specific individual, is calm with a closed, straight mouth displaying maturity and dignity, important virtues for a Roman man.

Many of the same features can be seen on an approximately contemporary rare surviving bronze portrait, even more rarely named in an Etruscan inscription, Aulus Metellus. It demonstrates the continuation of the Etruscan sculpture traditions of bronze work and portraiture, here seen in a

suovetaurilia
a sacrifice made up of a bull, sheep, and pig, traditionally made to Mars, it was one of the oldest and most sacred Roman rituals.

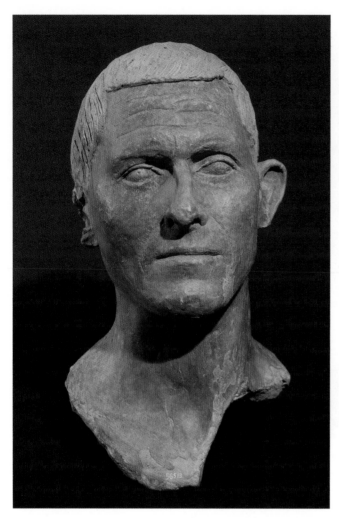

4.33 Head of a man from votive deposit, Manganello, Cerveteri, *c.* 100 BCE. Museo Nazionale Etrusco di Villa Giulia, Rome. H 1 ft (30.5 cm), painted terracotta. Source: Museo Etrusco di Villa Giulia, Rome, Italy/The Bridgeman Art Library.

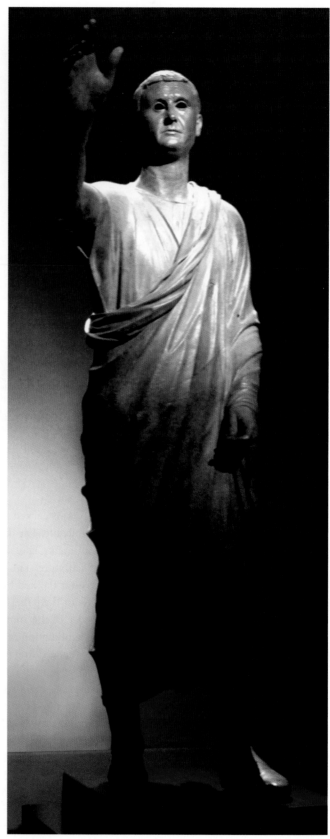

4.34 Aulus Metellus, bronze, *c.* 90 BCE. Museo Archaeologico Nazionale, Florence. H 71 in (180 cm). Corneliagraco/Wikimedia.

large-scale Roman sculpture. He stands, one hand extended in a gesture of speaking, wearing a toga and Roman senatorial boots. The image is an adult Roman defined by his public identity and accomplishments, here as in the census relief in the civic arena as opposed to the military. The face has elements of the Manganello portrait with its short hair, lined forehead, and crow's-feet. But the receding hairline, full cheeks, and close set eyes make it clearly a portrait. There is little explicitly Greek about the figure other than a subtle contrapposto stance.

Another approach to portraying ideal male qualities is seen on a marble portrait bust from Verona from the middle of the century. It is in a style called **veristic** in which every element of aging is magnified into a hyper-realistic image with deep wrinkles and folds of skin, larger than ideal nose and ears, sunken cheeks, and receding hair. The origin of this style and the motivations behind it are unclear, although it might have developed as a backlash against Greek Classicizing imagery or as a way of emphasizing traditional character traits thought to be lost in the chaotic period of the Late Republic. The popularity of the style may also be connected to the Roman practice of displaying death masks of distinguished male ancestors at a time when more families were claiming such ancestors for themselves. Whatever the reason, it becomes popular in the Late Republican period as a means of illustrating great virtues of maturity and dignity. In many ways it served the same purpose as idealized portraiture, not only to show what someone looked like, but to portray their character in the image.

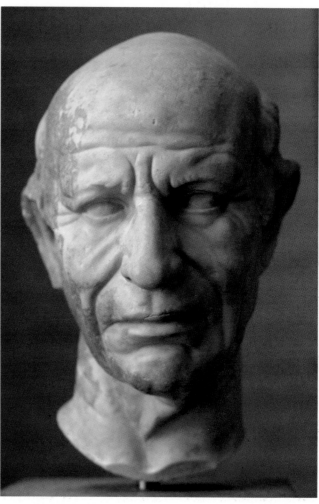

4.35 Veristic portrait of a Roman man, *c.* 50 BCE, lifesize, Verona. Staatliche Antikensammlungen, Munich. Bibi Saint-Pol/ Wikimedia.

veristic
from the Latin *verus* meaning "true," refers to a style of exaggerated naturalism or hyper-realism found in Roman portraits, often to emphasize the age-dependent virtues of the subject.

The combination of these two traditions, the Italic veristic and the Greek ideal, can be seen in the portrait of a victorious general from the Temple of Hercules at Tivoli from 75–50 BCE (Figure 1.6). Carved from Greek marble the general stands wearing only a mantle with his breastplate on the ground next to him as a support and in very frontal contrapposto with an idealized and heavily muscled body. The general's broad proportions match Hellenistic figures as in the Neptune and Amphitrite wedding procession. His head however reveals veristic portraiture with a lined forehead, bags under his eyes, creases and wrinkles at the corners of his eyes and mouth, and sagging skin under his chin and on his neck. The image is one that combines two traditions of elite ideal representation using the Greek conventions to portray his accomplishments as a victorious general and the Italic veristic to portray his personal qualities of maturity and dignity.

CONCLUSION

The period of the Later Republic in Roman art demonstrates the extraordinary changes that can occur in a culture in a relatively short period of time when the people of that culture willingly and deliberately embrace outside elements. Given the long Roman tradition of an inclusive culture, the embrace of Greek art, architecture, and urban planning may not seem unusual or even notable, but its scale and effect were. The wholesale adoption of Greek artistic subjects, material, media, conventions, and forms led to remarkable changes in every facet of Roman art. Even the traditionally Etruscan works such as terracotta portraits display Greek elements during this period. Perhaps the most interesting changes occur in domestic and religious architecture. In examples such as the Temple of Portunus and the House of the Faun we can see the application of Greek material onto the forms and spaces of Italic architecture. The tremendous variations in this application can be traced throughout the period as the integration of Greek material spreads through Roman art. In addition to the profound changes that wholesale adoption of Greek art brought about, the same period saw the introduction of Roman concrete. The use of this new material allowed the Romans to create architecture of a size, shape, and design previously impossible. It opened up their buildings to light and led to some of the most imaginative and innovative works in world architecture, culminating in the masterpiece of Roman concrete construction, Hadrian's Pantheon (Figure 8.11). Still, traditional Italic forms persist. These are seen in the basilica, amphitheater, and bridge with their local materials, use of the arch, and emphasis on Roman civic identity.

The explosion of Greek art forms – styles and subjects – is an important innovation of the period and arguably traced to the great amounts of art that came into Rome with the military victories of Marcellus, Paullus, and other triumphant generals. The shift to Hellenistic architectural vocabulary in temples and large-scale sanctuaries is another innovation and arguably an even more remarkable development. From the sanctuaries of Terracina and Praeneste to the Theater of Pompey, Greek urban design becomes the leading means of conveying the very traditional concept of piety throughout Roman Italy. These two innovations together spark the design of the Imperial fora as the way forward for Roman public art and architecture, and the culminating monuments of the Later Republic foreshadow the massive redesign of the city of Rome under its first emperor, Augustus.

SUGGESTIONS FOR FURTHER READING

Bettina Bergmann et al., "Roman Frescoes from Boscoreale: The Villa of Publius Fannius Synistor in Reality and Virtual Reality." *Metropolitan Museum of Art Bulletin* 62.4 (Spring 2010). A thoughtful case study on Roman wall painting contextualizing the paintings, house, and finds. Includes a discussion of the theories of the origins and influences on Second Style painting.

John R. Clarke, *The Houses of Roman Italy, 100 B.C.–A.D. 250: Ritual, Space, and Decoration* (University of California Press 1991). In case studies of seventeen excavated houses, Clarke demonstrates how patterns of Roman decoration signal the cultural, religious, and social imprints of the people who lived with them.

John J. Dobbins and Pedar W. Foss, eds., *The World of Pompeii* (Routledge 2007). A collection of essays that covers virtually every aspect of the ancient city of Pompeii including its urban plan, architecture, and arts. Many of the chapters focus on domestic architecture and decoration, subjects for which Pompeii provides substantial unique evidence.

Linda Fierz-David, *Women's Dionysian Initiation: the Villa of Mysteries in Pompeii* (Spring 1988). An analyst and colleague of C.G. Jung, Linda Fierz-David explores what an initiation ceremony in the ancient world for women might have been all about using the fresco of the Villa of the Mysteries as her starting point.

Anne Laidlaw, *The First Style in Pompeii: Painting and Architecture* (L'Erma di Bretschneider 1985). The only book-length study in English of this period and material. Explores the development of Roman wall painting at the earliest phase at Pompeii and the intersections between painted wall treatment and the architecture it is based on and attached to.

Donatella Mazzoleni, *Domus: Wall Painting in the Roman House* (J. Paul Getty Museum 2004). This lavishly illustrated book includes chapters on many of the most important and well-preserved houses at Pompeii including the villa at Oplontis, the Villa of the Mysteries, House of the Faun, and House of the Griffins.

J.W. Stamper, *The Architecture of Roman Temples: the Republic to the Middle Empire* (Cambridge University Press 2005). This book examines the development of Roman temple architecture including the temples' formal qualities, the public spaces in which they were located, and how they accommodated changing political and religious contexts.

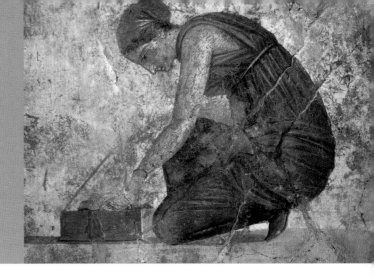

THE AGE OF AUGUSTUS, 31 BCE–14 CE

The Art of Empire

31 BCE	Battle of Actium, Octavian/Augustus defeats Antony and Cleopatra
28 BCE	**Mausoleum of Augustus begun; Temple of Apollo dedicated**
27 BCE	Octavian takes the name Imperator Caesar Augustus; Livy's monumental History of Rome begins appearing
20 BCE	**Original of the Prima Porta Augustus statue**; recovery of the military standards from Parthia
19 BCE	Death of Roman poet, Vergil, publication of his *Aeneid*
15 BCE	Vitruvius writes his book on architecture; **earliest examples of Third Style wall painting; construction of Caesarea Maritima**
14 BCE	**Basilica Aemilia reliefs**
13 BCE	**Ara Pacis Augustae vowed**
12 BCE	Augustus becomes Pontifex Maximus; **Via Labicana portrait**
9 BCE	**Ara Pacis Augustae inaugurated**
2 BCE	**Forum Augustum inaugurated**
14 CE	Death of Augustus; succession of Tiberius

A History of Roman Art, First Edition. Steven L. Tuck.
© 2015 Steven L. Tuck. Published 2015 by John Wiley & Sons, Ltd.

It is out of fashion among some historians to write about great men and to assign dramatic or long-term cultural changes to their influence. So, this chapter will be unfashionable to some. There seems no way around the fact that Augustus directly and personally changed the Roman system of government. As noted under the Regal and Republican periods in previous chapters, public art and architecture conform to the needs of those paying for them, notably the government. So, as government changed, the subjects and styles of art and architecture changed forever. It is almost impossible to accept that this sickly, balding man, who on occasion wore platform shoes, and professed to be the son of a god, became the model for rulers throughout Roman and world history. Nonetheless, he did and the role of art and architecture in his public image was an important part of that. So, we start this chapter with a brief biography of the man who became Rome's first emperor and whose entire life, from 63 BCE to 14 CE, gave its name to an age, voted into the calendar by the Roman Senate, The Age of Augustus.

AUGUSTUS

Born Gaius Octavius in 63 BCE, the future emperor lost his father at the age of four. But it was his mother, the niece of Julius Caesar, who provided the key connections that launched his career. By 44 BCE at the age of eighteen he had served under Julius Caesar in Spain and was participating in the preparations to invade Parthia when Caesar was assassinated on March 15, 44 BCE. Caesar had adopted him in his will, a common Roman practice, and his adopted name was now Gaius Julius Caesar Octavianus, Octavian as he was then known. After Caesar's murder he found himself the very junior partner with Caesar's trusted lieutenant Mark Antony and Aemilius Lepidus. These three struggled for power against Caesar's assassins: Brutus and Cassius, the Senate, and Cicero. Despite Cicero's attempts to control him, Octavian reached a power-sharing agreement with Antony and Lepidus called the Triumvirate, rule by three men. By 42 BCE the three had masterminded the defeat of Brutus and Cassius in battle, the murder of Cicero and other opponents, and a takeover of Roman government.

The triumvirs each struggled for greater authority and sole rule over the Roman world from separate areas: Octavian from Italy, Lepidus from Africa, and Antony from the east. By 36 BCE Octavian had defeated Sextus Pompeius, son of Pompey the Great, in a series of naval battles and seized control of Lepidus' armies, securing their loyalty to himself and mastering the western Roman world. The contest to control the entire Roman Empire was now between Octavian and Antony, who had begun to live openly in Alexandria with Cleopatra, the queen of Egypt, with whom he had a number of children. Antony and Cleopatra appeared as Hellenistic monarchs and even performed a triumph in Alexandria, a serious blow to the unique position of Rome as capital. In 32 BCE Octavian had Antony's will taken from the Vestal Virgins and published, hoping to discredit him in the eyes of Romans. It revealed Antony's wish to be buried at Alexandria. He now looked less like a man corrupted by an exotic, beautiful woman and more like a traitor. The Senate gave Octavian a declaration of war against Cleopatra and his forces met the combined army and fleet of Antony and Egypt in Greece. The decisive naval battle occurred at Actium on September 2, 31 BCE. Antony and Cleopatra committed suicide shortly thereafter when Octavian's forces reached Alexandria. Now, after almost a century of civil and political unrest and four major civil wars, Octavian was sole ruler of the Roman world. He wished, in a culture with a long aversion to kingship, to maintain that sole rule, found a dynasty, and avoid Caesar's fate. He accomplished all of these with the support of his public art and architecture program as well as changes in his personal image and Roman government.

The most critical date for all of these changes is 27 BCE. In an act of political theater worked out with the Senate, Octavian made a point of giving up his power as Triumvir, reasserting the power of the Senate and other traditional offices, and accepting only Republican titles and offices while not actually relinquishing any true power. He continued to exercise personal control over the armies and the treasury. He also had a final name change. Gone was Octavian; he was now Imperator Caesar

Augustus. Imperator, a Republican title for a conquering general, became his first name. Caesar was now his family name. His cognomen, the name friends and close associates used, he changed to Augustus, meaning worthy of worship. He held a variety of offices including consul and tribune, but the title he seemed to prefer was *princeps*, meaning First, in this case, First Citizen. From that title the period of the emperors is often known at the principate. Because Augustus lived to be 76, he outlived many of his planned heirs. He finally settled on Tiberius, stepson by his wife Livia, along with his sole surviving grandson, Agrippa Postumus.

THE PORTRAITS OF AUGUSTUS

Rome saw under Augustus the search for a style that would reflect the new agenda and public image of the new regime. In portraiture he settled on a new style of Classicizing portraiture. Images of Augustus, his heirs, and finally many other Romans were carved imitating the Classical style of sculpture from the golden age of Athens in the fifth century BCE. The youthful ideal images of the imperial family under Augustus reinforce both the notions of the new golden age as well as the needs of the dynasty to create an imagery of dynastic succession, something the Romans had never before needed. Almost identical facial features and hairstyles convey a sense of family. Republican veristic imagery filled the needs of projecting one type of value system, emphasizing maturity, dignity, and experience, while Classicizing portraits under Augustus projected another, competing, system of ideal individuals, eternally youthful and reflecting the new golden age in Rome.

A full standing portrait of Augustus from the Via Labicana in Rome portrays him wearing a toga with his head covered, a style known as *capite velato*. This indicates that he is performing a religious ritual, probably a sacrifice. The image conveys piety and may date to after 12 BCE when Augustus became Pontifex Maximus, Chief Priest of Rome. It represents the tendency under Augustus to portray him in traditional ways, not emphasizing his extraordinary powers.

The head, neck, and veiled portion of the toga are carved from a separate piece of finer Greek marble, not the Italian marble of the rest of the statue. The proportions are Greek, with the figure over seven and a half heads in height, giving it the proportions advocated by the Classical Athenian sculptor, Polykleitos. He stands in a variation of the Athenian contrapposto. The most telling Greek element is found in his idealized features. Although over fifty years old when the statue was made, he looks to be in his early twenties, which is consistent with his youthful public images. He is recognizable by his broad forehead, long nose, thin lips and narrow chin, features that are all smooth, sharply carved, and repeated on the many surviving portraits of Augustus. The most characteristic feature is the

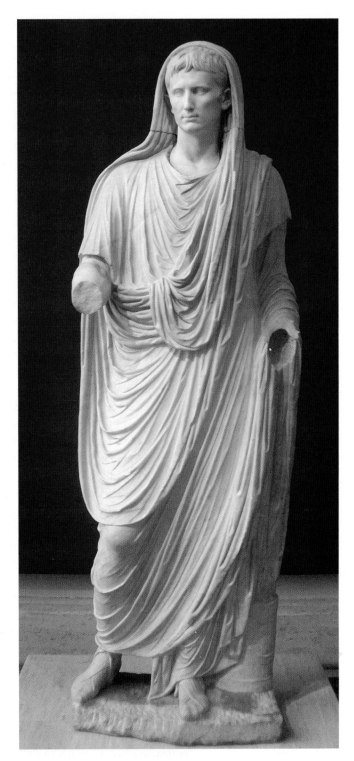

5.1 Augustus as Pontifex Maximus, from the Via Labicana, Rome, *c.* 12 BCE. Museo Nazionale Romano Palazzo Massimo alle Terme, Rome. Marble, 6 ft 9 in (2.06 m). Photo courtesy Steven L. Tuck.

HISTORICAL CONTEXT/FORM & FUNCTION
The Doryphoros of Polykleitos

The fifth-century BCE sculptor, Polykleitos, developed a new canon for human figure sculpture. He worked out his own set of ideal proportions for the body based on the theory that to achieve perfection every part must be in exact proportion. This meant that, for example, the measurement of a finger related in a certain way to all of the fingers, those to the palm, the palm to the forearm, and everything to everything else in the body. He then created a statue that demonstrated his notion of the perfect visual expression. That statue, surviving in later Roman versions, is known as the Doryphoros (the spearbearer). It shows the balance of Polykleitos' new system as the figure is balanced between stepping and standing still, between motion and rest. The integration of the parts of the body is seen in the contrapposto with the right hip and left shoulder both raised as the right leg and left arm bear weight, giving the figure a rhythm designed to accentuate its realism. The Doryphoros was very influential in ancient art, serving as the starting point for human sculpture for hundreds of years and resulting in many remaining versions as it was studied, copied, and adapted by Greek and Roman sculptors alike.

arrangement of his hair. He has a cap of hair that is parted on the left and falls into layered comma-shaped locks. This organization is consistent on many of Augustus' portraits and is based on the Doryphoros of Polykleitos, an iconic fifth-century BCE Athenian statue.

The most important extant portrait of Augustus is the Prima Porta statue, found at the villa of his wife, Livia, at Prima Porta just north of Rome. Even more closely based on the Doryphoros it shows the emperor with the same idealized Classicizing proportions, facial features, and hairstyle as the Via Labicana statue. Here Augustus stands with his right arm outstretched in a gesture of address (*adlocutio*) similar to the Aulus Metellus statue (Figure 4.34) while his feet, head, and line of his hips match the pose of the Doryphoros.

adlocutio
a public address by an emperor to the army or citizens, shown by the right arm raised in salute.

He is wearing a cuirass, the breastplate of a victorious general, as seen earlier as a support on the general from Tivoli (Figure 1.6), placing this image in the tradition of Late Republican sculpture. Here the cuirass is decorated in three registers with groups of figures that celebrate the achievements and aspirations of Augustus' rule, including its geographical extent.

Tellus, or Mother Earth, cradling two babies anchors the lowest zone. Apollo riding a griffin and Diana on a stag flank her and allude to the geographical extents of the empire to the north and east. Caelus, god of the sky, dominates the upper register while just below him is the sun god, Sol, in his chariot following his sister Aurora, the dawn. The central register consists of two pairs of figures. On left and right are seated captives, one for Gaul and one for Hispania, commemorating Augustus' military victories in those provinces to the north and west. The central standing pair consists of a Roman man in armor on the left receiving a Roman military standard handed over by a Parthian on the right. This pair celebrates a major foreign policy achievement for Augustus, the recovery in 20 BCE of the standards lost to the Parthians by the Roman general Crassus in 53 BCE when his entire army was wiped out. These may be personifications of the empires or the actual individuals who were involved, Tiberius for the Romans and Phraates IV for the Parthians. Augustus celebrated the return as a military, not a diplomatic, victory and even erected a triumphal arch in celebration. The support for the statue is a cupid riding a dolphin alluding to Augustus' proclaimed descent from Venus. Altogether the statue and its decoration proclaim Roman power over the world as Jupiter promised in Vergil's national epic, *The Aeneid* (1.390), "To the Romans I grant empire without end." His feet are bare as a signal of his own divinity, a feature that may have been altered when the statue was copied into marble from the original bronze after his death. The original would not have made such a visual proclamation of divinity during Augustus' lifetime.

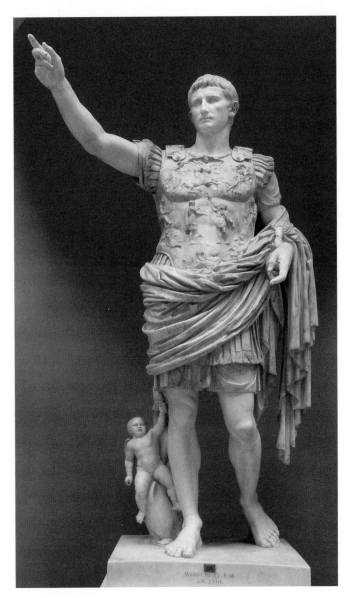

5.2   Prima Porta Augustus, from the villa of Livia at Prima Porta north of Rome, copy of *c.* 14 CE from an original of 20 BCE. Musei Vaticani, Rome. Marble, 6 ft 8 in (2.04 m). Photo courtesy Steven L. Tuck.

TOOLS & TECHNIQUES

Reproducing sculpture in the Roman world

Famous sculptures, like the Doryphoros by Polykleitos or portraits of Roman emperors, were routinely replicated and distributed throughout the Roman world. Roman sculptors, working in marble, used various techniques to produce versions of Greek originals, often cast in bronze. Plaster casts were made from original sculptures and used along with careful measurements to create versions of Greek masterpieces. Still, the Roman creations are not slavish copies. Roman sculptors introduced important variations that reflect artistic tastes and political and cultural values of their own periods, the function of the statues in their Roman contexts, and the realities of their different medium. Goddesses like Venus often bear contemporary hairstyles; postures and gestures were inverted, creating pendants of the same sculptural type to flank doorways; and marble versions of bronze originals required added supports, designed as tree stumps, animals, or drapery, to stabilize the stone statues. This phenomenon has impacted the study of ancient art enormously. Some scholars try to reconstruct lost bronze originals, melted down for their valuable metal and attested only in literary sources, from extant Roman copies. Only recently have "Roman copies" been studied as works of art in their own right, reflecting their Roman artistic, architectural, and cultural contexts.

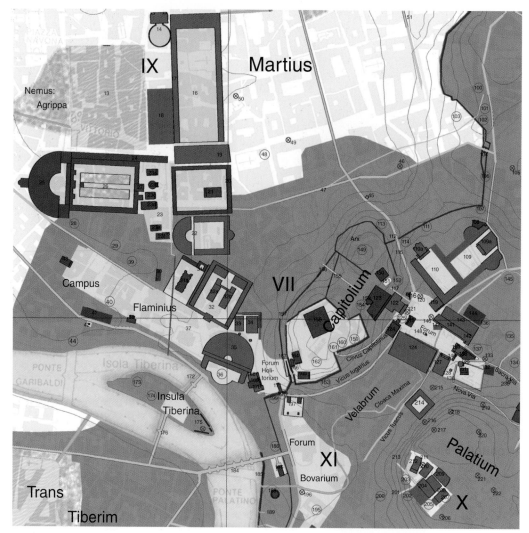

5.3 Augustan building program in Rome, buildings built or heavily restored under Augustus marked in grey. Buildings in the northern Campus Martius (Mausoleum, Ara Pacis, Horologium) not shown, 44 BCE–14 CE. Digital Augustan Rome, http://digitalaugustanrome.org, courtesy D.G. Romano and N.L. Stapp.

AUGUSTUS AND THE CITY OF ROME

According to the second-century CE biographer of the emperors, Suetonius (*Aug.* 28), Augustus declared, "I found Rome built of brick and left it covered in marble." His statement reflects his massive building and rebuilding plans in the city. In many ways he altered Rome into a Hellenistic style capital of a great empire with new temples and public buildings. He also created vast new urban zones both within and outside the old walls, radically changing the size and form of the city. Much of this was made possible by the work of his right hand man, Marcus Agrippa. The key zones were the Campus Martius, the Palatine Hill, and the Forum Augustum.

The Campus Martius

The broad floodplain of the Tiber, the Campus Martius, was kept for military training in the Republic partly because floods from the Tiber made building on it problematic. Agrippa's new flood control system, however, transformed this vast area on the outskirts of the city, making it suitable as a new urban zone between the river and the Via Flaminia. Augustus exploited this land by creating two large-scale building complexes, the largest in Rome built by a single family. In the south were the new voting enclosures, the enormous Baths of Agrippa, the model for the later immense imperial baths,

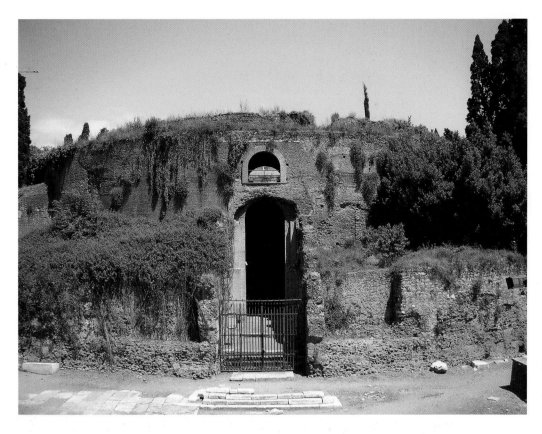

5.4 Mausoleum of Augustus, 28 BCE, exterior view. Photo courtesy Steven L. Tuck.

and the Pantheon of Agrippa. The front porch of this round temple faced north creating a visual connection to the second set of buildings in the northern Campus Martius. These consisted of the Horologium (a huge sundial), the Ara Pacis (the altar of peace), and the Mausoleum of Augustus, the earliest of his buildings in Rome.

The Mausoleum of Augustus was begun by 28 BCE and its size and design manifested Augustus' plans for a dynasty. Its entrance faced south, aligning with the porch on the Pantheon, probably creating a visual–spatial connection between the traditional gods and those divine members of Augustus' household. The building was a massive work with a central concrete drum surrounded by concentric circles of concrete walls and lower concrete retaining walls creating greater height for the monument. The mausoleum was topped with soil and plants to resemble a tumulus, the traditional Etruscan burial mound (see Figure 2.2), perhaps most directly copying the mound tomb of Aeneas at Lavinium.

It was about 295 ft (90 m) in diameter and 132 ft (42 m) in height. Such huge dimensions were probably to ensure that it became and remained the major landmark of the city from the Tiber or the Via Flaminia. The name, Mausoleum, suggests that it was compared to the tomb of Mausolus, an Asian king whose enormous burial monument, the original Mausoleum, was one of the seven wonders of the ancient world. The outer wall was faced with white travertine, a local stone similar to marble later used to face the Colosseum. Here its use as a facing may be, along with the name, another Greek element. The first ashes placed in its niches belonged to Marcellus, Augustus' heir, who died in 23 BCE. Many other members of the family followed including Augustus himself in 14 CE and Augustus' wife, Livia, after her death in 29 CE. The last emperor interred in the Mausoleum was Nerva in 98 CE. The monument was finished with a statue of Augustus on the top, two obelisks from Egypt flanking the door, and two bronze columns on which were carved the *Res Gestae Divi Augusti*, the Achievements of the Divine Augustus, an account of his public works written by Augustus himself, serving as a form of obituary. The area around the building was landscaped into a public park for Romans to enjoy. The scale and complexity of the display created by the Mausoleum

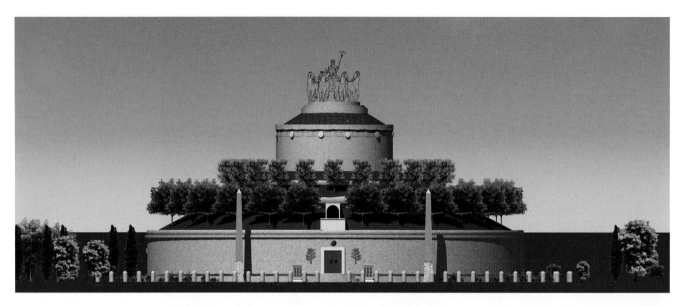

5.5   Mausoleum of Augustus, 28 BCE, reconstruction. Illustration courtesy John Pollini.

HISTORICAL CONTEXT
The Res Gestae *of Augustus*

The Emperor Augustus left behind a unique, untitled document. Called the *Res Gestae* or *Things Accomplished* from its opening words, it was the list that Augustus himself wrote and left in the keeping of the Vestal Virgins that tells all of his accomplishments while in office. The biographer Suetonius, in his *Life of Augustus*, recorded that the emperor wished it to be inscribed on bronze tablets and set up in front of his mausoleum so it became part of his public monument. It includes lists of battles fought, money spent, and religious rituals performed for the Roman state. For the study of Roman art and architecture it is valuable for dating major works from his public art program. It is the only source that gives the dates for the Ara Pacis as well as listing the buildings built and restored by Augustus throughout Rome, including his Forum Augustum and eighty-two temples that he restored. It also records the earliest public decorations that celebrated the emperor, "by decree of the Senate the door posts of my house were wreathed with laurel and a Civic Crown fixed over my door and a golden shield was set in the Curia Julia" (34). That shield was inscribed with four virtues that would be a sort of motto: courage, clemency, justice, and piety.

make clear how much Augustus valued his new dynasty. That theme along with Roman history and statements of foreign and domestic policy shaped the decoration of the next monument in the northern Campus Martius, the Ara Pacis.

Ara Pacis Augustae

The Ara Pacis Augustae, Altar of Augustan Peace, demonstrates the new Classicizing style of public art under Augustus. It also represents the most important surviving work of public art from the period celebrating what Augustus presented as traditional Roman values, piety, family, foreign conquest, and honoring Rome's founders. The marble altar, pledged in 13 BCE and inaugurated in 9 BCE, was commissioned by the Senate to commemorate the peace Augustus had brought to the Roman world and set up near the Via Flaminia. The altar has a long and remarkable history since antiquity. Thanks to the silt from many floods of the Tiber in the Middle Ages, it was eventually

Roma   Tellus Italiae

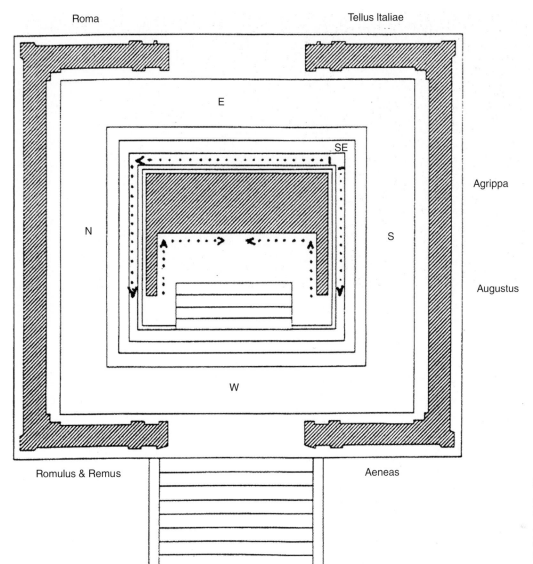

E

SE

N   S

Agrippa

Augustus

W

Romulus & Remus   Aeneas

5.6   Plan, Ara Pacis
Augustae, Rome, 13–9 BCE.
Museo dell'Ara Pacis, Rome.
Area enclosed by the wall
38 ft (11.6 m) x 34 ft 5 in
(10.6 m). Drawing courtesy
John Pollini.

buried over 36 feet below modern ground level. Pieces of it, often very small pieces, have been excavated since 1568 and placed in numerous collections. The last major excavation campaign was in 1937 when, preparing for the 2000th anniversary of the birth of Augustus, about half the altar was recovered. This was previously thought impossible since it was below the water table and under the foundations of a major Renaissance building. But special equipment allowed excavators to freeze the ground water and surrounding soil, dig out the altar fragments and shore up the building above to avoid collapse. The altar as we see it today is heavily restored from pieces found over a period of three hundred years.

The most important element for art history was the marble wall that surrounded the altar precinct defining the sacred area. The interior of the wall was carved to resemble a fence with garlands suspended over it. The exterior, however, was covered with reliefs that conveyed powerful messages about Augustus' policies. These exterior reliefs are organized into two registers. The entire lower register is divided into panels of plants sacred to Apollo, largely acanthus, and presented in a formal, symmetrical way to reinforce notions of abundance and order under Augustus. Despite the formal presentation all of the species of plants, even those which would not appear together in nature, are flowering and thriving simultaneously under the rule of Augustus. The animal world is represented,

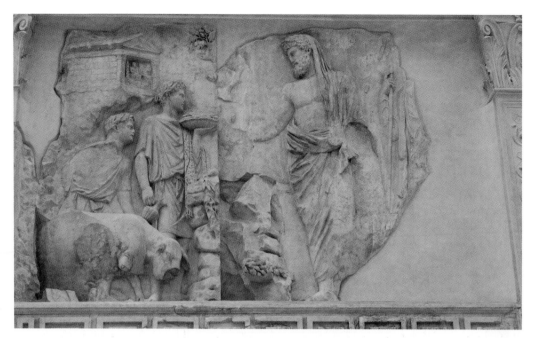

5.7   Aeneas sacrificing panel, Ara Pacis Augustae, Rome, 13–9 BCE. Museo dell'Ara Pacis, Rome. Marble. Photo courtesy Steven L. Tuck.

as a variety of animals inhabit the plants. The upper registers displayed figural scenes, those on the east and west mythological and the north and south historical. The north and south walls had no doors so were filled by large, unbroken reliefs that depicted processions of Romans. Scholars debate whether these represent the vowing or dedication of the altar, but in either case they provide an ideal image of Roman religious activity, as all of the crucial components of Roman civil and religious offices are seen preparing for a sacrifice. Two doorways, on the east and west sides, pierced the wall and allowed access to the altar.

The east and west wall panels were clearly designed to reflect each other. On the west a relief of the discovery of Romulus and Remus was on the left of the door and on the right was a scene of Aeneas sacrificing.

The panel reflects a famous event as described in Vergil's national epic poem, the *Aeneid*. In book 8 of the poem, Aeneas is told in a dream that he will find a white sow and by sacrificing her and her litter he will ensure the founding of Rome. The east side had two panels dominated by female personifications. To the right was Roma enthroned and surrounded by captive enemy arms and armor. To the left was a complex figure with many attributes of abundance who probably represents Italy under Augustus.

The central figure personifies the land flanked by supporting personification figures of air and water and her identity is reinforced by the fat babies in her lap (now heavily restored), the lush plant life and healthy farm animals in the panel. Visually and spatially the panels interact and reflect each other. The Romulus and Aeneas panels place the viewer between Rome's two founders, an arrangement that echoes the placement of Romulus and Aeneas statue groups in the Forum Augustum where they flank the temple of Mars Ultor. The Aeneas panel is opposite Italy, the land to which he brought Roman culture, while Romulus is opposite Rome, the city he founded. Both of these mythological panels follow the conventions of Hellenistic mythological reliefs and paintings. This is clear in the use of landscape elements to create context and, notably in the Aeneas scene, a sense of space receding into the distance where we see the temple on the hill.

The long panels on the upper registers of the north and south sides show lines of Romans in procession for a religious function, probably a sacrifice. Although the north side is in the worst shape and heavily restored, most of the south side is legible. Unlike the mythological panels that follow the Hellenistic conventions for mythological scenes these follow the Classical conventions of processional art.

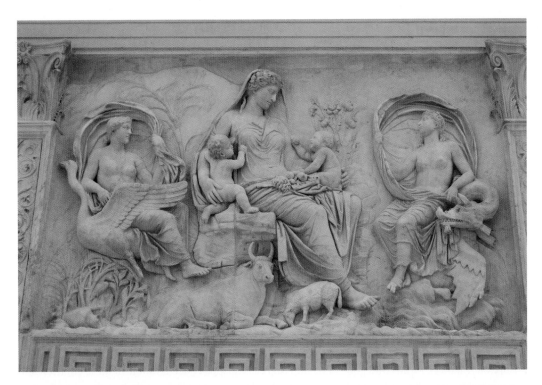

5.8 Tellus/Italia panel, Ara Pacis Augustae, Rome, 13–9 BCE. Museo dell'Ara Pacis, Rome. Marble. Photo courtesy Steven L. Tuck.

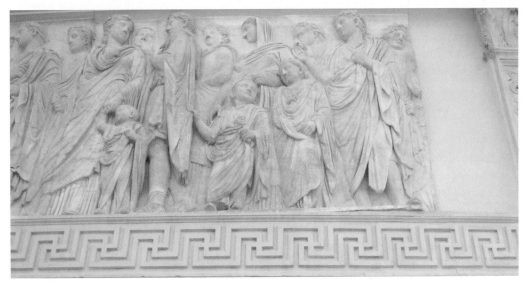

5.9 South procession relief showing the family of Augustus, Ara Pacis Augustae, Rome, 13–9 BCE. Museo dell'Ara Pacis, Rome. Marble. Photo courtesy Steven L. Tuck.

The figures all appear to be walking along the bottom of the register in a procession but there are no architectural or landscape features to give context. The composition uses overlapping figures for a sense of some depth, but with the application of **isocephaly** it creates depth with the conventions of background figures who are offset in shallow relief and in profile. The style comes from Athenian art of the fifth century BCE and bears a strong resemblance to the procession frieze on the Parthenon in Athens. Groups of priests, their helpers, and bodyguards are seen, but the unprecedented element is the inclusion of Augustus' extended family. In the Republican period, women and children had no place on this type of historical relief as can be seen from the Altar of Domitius Ahenobarbus census scene (Figure 4.32).

The family of Augustus was critical for his dynastic plans and therefore needed to be displayed as a legitimate part of his rule. They were also models of his domestic program, which featured an

isocephaly
artistic convention of portraying figures, whether seated or standing, with all of their heads on the same level.

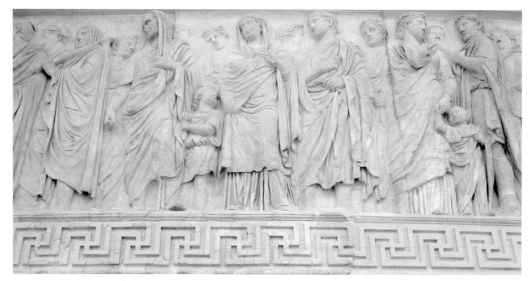

5.10 Children on south procession panel detail, Ara Pacis Augustae, Rome, 13–9 BCE. Museo dell'Ara Pacis, Rome. Marble. Photo courtesy Steven L. Tuck.

torque
large neck ring, often made of twisted strands of gold wire, worn by elite ancient Celts or Gauls.

bulla
amulet worn by Roman boys like a locket designed to protect them from harm until they came of age and stopped wearing it.

emphasis on marriage and offspring particularly among the upper classes. One, however, of the child figures is clearly non-Roman. He has long curly hair, wears a tunic, diadem, and a **torque**, not a toga and **bulla** as do the Roman boys. He is one of the hostage sons of foreign kings brought to Rome to ensure their fathers' loyalty and good behavior. Marcus Agrippa collected some of these children and this boy holds on to Agrippa's toga. The subject and style are matched here with the Athenian Classical sculpture used for processions. This integrity argues that the patron or designers are thoughtfully using past styles to evoke particular forms or periods. The themes of Rome's mythical founders, foreign policy, and the style of Classical art are used for a very different subject in the Forum Augustum – war and empire.

Forum Augustum

The Forum Augustum, an addition to the Forum Romanum, was not on the same scale as the building program in the Campus Martius, but was still very important and linked to it in promoting Augustus' rule. Much of the complex from the pavements to the upper stories was constructed using richly colored marbles from the edges of Roman territory. Here these recognizable stones served as a symbol of Roman control over the expanse of the world. Pliny the Elder included the forum in his list of the finest buildings in the world. Its design was based on the Forum Iulium with the basic elements of an open piazza with a temple at the rear and a surrounding portico and enclosing wall. The design veers from the symmetrical, which was preferred by Romans, because Augustus purchased the property rather than using the power of government to force anyone off their land. Someone refused to sell so the rear of the forum has a room on the left not repeated on the right. Although it wasn't dedicated until 2 BCE the forum had its origins in the civil wars of forty years earlier.

Augustus vowed the large temple, dedicated to Mars Ultor, during the war against Caesar's assassins to avenge the death of his adopted father. The dedication of the temple to Mars Ultor (Ultor is Latin for "avenger") not only reflects his motives, but reinforces both his personal virtue of *pietas* (piety or devotion) and the legitimacy of his rule as Caesar's son and heir. The relief in the pediment and the statue group in the temple further reinforced Augustus' ties to Caesar. These displays included images of Mars, the deified Julius Caesar, and Venus Genetrix, the founder of the Julian family and the goddess worshipped in Caesar's forum.

The form of the statues is preserved in a relief found at Carthage (in modern-day Tunisia), a Roman colony founded by Julius Caesar. The relief perhaps directly copied this sculptural display much as other elements of Augustus' building and decorative program were copied in public spaces

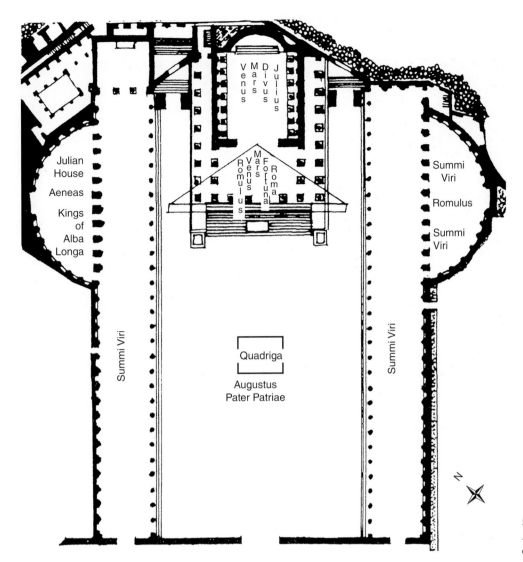

Venus
Mars
Divus
Julius

Romulus
Venus
Mars
Fortuna
Roma

Julian
House

Aeneas

Kings
of
Alba
Longa

Summi
Viri

Romulus

Summi
Viri

Summi Viri

Summi Viri

Quadriga

Augustus
Pater Patriae

N

5.11 Plan of Forum
Augustum, 2 BCE. Drawing
courtesy John Pollini.

5.12   Forum Augustum,
Temple of Mars Ultor, 2
BCE. Photo courtesy Steven
L. Tuck.

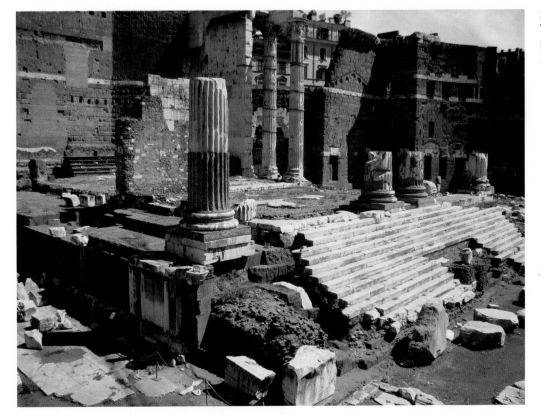

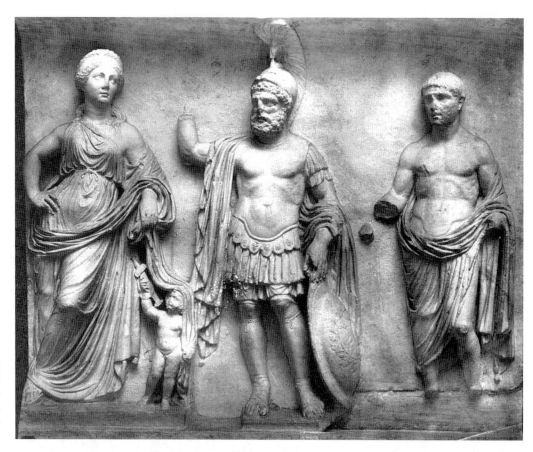

5.13 Algiers relief of Mars Ultor, Venus Genetrix, and Caesar, Augustan. Algiers Museum of Antiquities, Algeria. Marble. Photo courtesy John Pollini.

exedrae
in architecture semi-circular recesses or bays often roofed with a half dome.

caryatid
a female figure used in place of a column to support the entablature of a building.

around the Roman world. The theme of the temple is *pietas* and also Augustus' double divine descent from Venus and the god Caesar. The figure of Caesar is barefoot, a symbol of his divinity. It is missing the star originally attached to his forehead, a reminder of the comet that appeared during his funeral games, proclaiming his apotheosis.

Dominated by a temple of Mars, it is hardly a surprise that the decorative theme of the Forum is war. Here Augustus took the sort of decorative display found in the atrium of a Roman house (in particular, images of ancestors and trophies from war) and created a hall of fame display for all Romans. The wall around the forum is lined with niches that were filled with lifesize statues. This display was called the *summi viri*, the highest men, and exhibited many famous Roman generals including Marcus Claudius Marcellus and Aemilius Paullus. None of the statues survive, but some descriptions and the plaques that listed their names and accomplishments do. The statue presentation culminated in two large **exedrae** (the remains of an adjacent second pair, probably destroyed to make room for later fora, were discovered in excavations begun in 1999). In the largest niches in the backs of the exedrae facing each other were Romulus on one side and Aeneas on the other, the same figures who flanked the entrance to the Ara Pacis Augustae. Famous Julio-Claudian descendants of Aeneas filled the niches in the exedra with him while the mythical kings of Alba Longa attended Romulus.

The attic story of the portico above the colonnade illustrates both Augustus' proclaimed golden age and cultural appropriation of Classical art from Athens. The area is composed of panels the center of each of which is filled with a shield decorated with the head of Zeus Ammon, father of Alexander the Great, making a visual link between Augustus and Alexander as world conquerors descended from gods. **Caryatids**, copied from originals on the Erechtheion, a Classical temple in Athens, separate the panels.

The forum became not just a hall of fame, but a museum to Roman military might as captured armor, weapons, and unit standards were displayed here. Among the first were the Roman standards Augustus recovered from the Parthians, the event illustrated on the breastplate of the Prima Porta

ANCIENTS ON ART

The Forum Augustum and Temple of Mars Ultor

The Augustan poet Ovid gives us a description of the Forum Augustum from the point of view of the god Mars himself.

Mars comes, and at his coming he gave the sign of war. The Avenger descends himself from heaven to behold his own honors and his splendid temple in the forum of Augustus. The god is huge, and so is the structure: in no other way ought Mars dwell in his son's city. That shrine is worthy of trophies won from giants; from its might the Marching God fitly open his fierce campaigns, whether an impious foe shall assail us from the eastern world or whether another will have to be vanquished where the sun goes down. The god of arms surveys the pinnacles of the lofty edifice, and approves that the highest places should be filled by the unconquered gods. He surveys on the doors weapons of diverse shapes, and arms of lands subdued by his soldiery. On this side he sees Aeneas laden with his dear burden [his father, Anchises, son, Ascanius, and the household gods from Troy], and many an ancestor of the noble Julian line. On the other side he sees Romulus carrying on his shoulders the arms of the conquered leader, and their famous deeds inscribed beneath the statues arranged in order.

(Ovid, *Fasti* V.550–566)

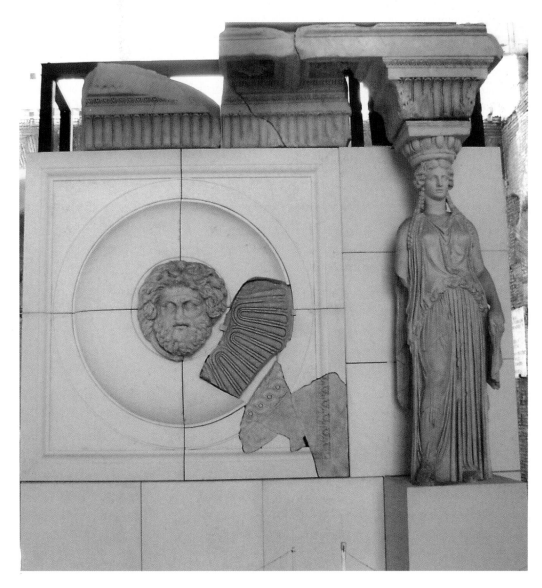

5.14 Forum Augustum, 2 BCE, reconstruction of the Attic story, Museo dei Fori Imperiali, Rome. H 7 ft 6 in (2.3 m), marble. Photo courtesy Steven L. Tuck.

Augustus statue (Figure 5.2). These exhibits extended and reinforced the theme of warfare and created a setting for military ceremonies for the next three centuries.

The Palatine Hill

The third major space transformed by Augustus was the Palatine Hill, long a residential district for the elite, with ties to Romulus, whose house was preserved there. Under Augustus its religious character was expanded with new temples and re-emphasized cult activities to compete with the Capitoline Hill. His residence here was the start of a string of imperial houses that grew into the great palace that eventually took over the entire hill. (The word palace derives from the name Palatine.) But Augustus started small, building a modest house close to the House of Romulus, making an association between them once again. His house was designed to be a section of the sanctuary of Apollo that he built on the hill close to the Temple of Victory, making visual associations with that as well. The sanctuary contained the first temple of the Greek god Apollo inside the walls of Rome as well as libraries, porticoes, and room for the Senate to meet.

Temple of Apollo Palatinus

Vowed at the battle of Actium in 31 BCE and dedicated in 28 BCE, it was the first temple in Rome constructed completely out of marble (above the concrete core of the podium). The Roman poet Propertius notes the origins of much of the marble from conquered foreign lands, suggesting that Romans were expected to equate the materials with Roman control over these formerly hostile territories. Thanks to later robbing of this valuable stone, almost nothing is left except elements of the decorative program, which provide a great example of the use of Greek myth as political metaphor. These fragments combined with contemporary descriptions give a sense of the image and effect of the sanctuary.

A marble relief from Rome seems to illustrate the walled sanctuary and the Temple of Apollo, shown with Corinthian columns, some of which have been found in fragments in the sanctuary, and a great deal of sculptural decoration.

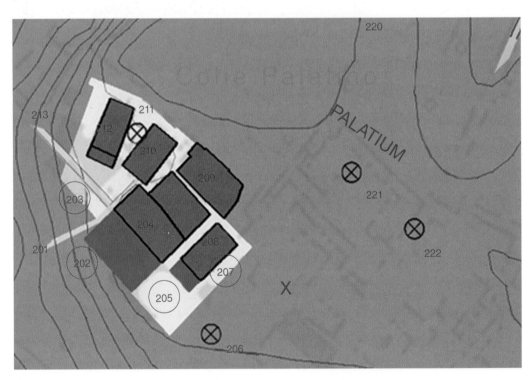

5.15 Augustan buildings on the Palatine Hill, 28 BCE, detail of Figure 5.3. Digital Augustan Rome, http://digitalaugustanrome.org courtesy D.G. Romano and N.L. Stapp. Key to major buildings:
202 House of Romulus
204 House of Augustus
205–208 Sanctuary of Apollo
210 Temple of Victory
212 Temple of Magna Mater

ANCIENTS ON ART

Propertius, Elegy 2.31 on the Temple of Apollo Palatinus

You ask why I came to you so late. Apollo's golden colonnade was opened today by great Caesar. Such a great sight, laid out with columns from Carthage and between them the crowd of daughters of old Daneus. And, about the altar, stood four of Myron's cattle, carved statues of oxen, that seemed to live. Here in the midst, dearer to Phoebus Apollo than his own Ortygian country, the temple reared in bright marble on top of which were two chariots of the Sun, and the doors of Libyan ivory, beautifully made. One door told the sad story of the wretched Gauls hurled from Parnassus' peak. The other the death of Niobe, daughter of Tantalus. Next the Pythian god himself was singing, in flowing robes, between his mother and sister. Here Apollo seemed to me more beautiful than the true Phoebus, lips parted in marble song to a silent lyre.

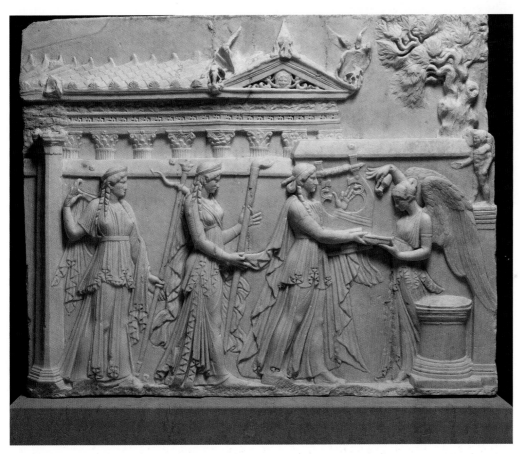

5.16 Archaistic relief of Apollo, Diana, and Leto from the Temple of Apollo Palatinus, Rome, 28 BCE. Galleria Albani e collezione archeologico, Rome. Marble. Source: Photo Johannes Laurentius. © 2014. Photo Scala, Florence/ BPK, Bildagentur für Kunst, Kultur und Geschichte, Berlin.

It also shows Apollo, his sister Diana, and their mother Leto all standing in front of the sanctuary accepting a sacrifice. These match the statues Propertius says were in the sanctuary, including Apollo with his lyre. All are carved in a style called **Archaistic**. The style was probably selected to impart a sense of tradition and the dignity of age to the sanctuary. The figures stand in walking profiles and wear garments that flare out around them in flat folds, a standard characteristic of Archaic art. That was not the only Archaic-inspired element in the sanctuary decoration.

The interior of the portico was lined with a large number of very old-fashioned terracotta plaques of the type that protected the wooden components of Archaic temples from the elements. Reliefs molded in the style of Archaic (sixth century BCE) Athenian art covered these, including one showing

Archaistic
a style of art imitating or reviving elements of Greek Archaic art (600–480 BCE). It was a popular revivalist style in Roman free-standing and relief sculpture.

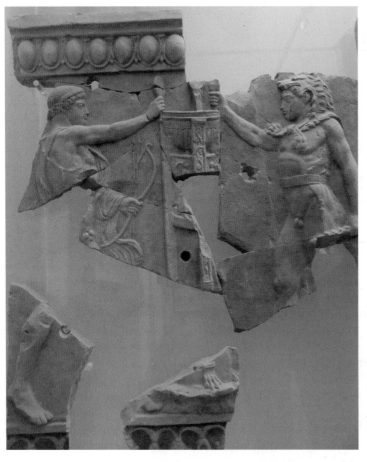

5.17 Terracotta plaque of Apollo and Hercules from the Temple of Apollo Palatinus, Rome, 28 BCE. Museo Palatino, Rome. H 30 in (76 cm) W 24 ½ in (62 cm). Photo courtesy Daniel Resheter.

herms
a type of Greek statue, originally of Hermes, with a squared stone pillar supporting a carved upper body and head; used as boundary markers in Greek cities and sanctuaries.

a Greek myth of Apollo struggling against Hercules for control of the tripod, a sacred symbol of Apollo from his sanctuary at Delphi.

The figures are designed in a style reminiscent of Archaic art with a static, formal composition and no real sense of struggle between them. Here the myth of Apollo's ultimate success in this contest is used as a metaphor for the civil war against Mark Antony. Apollo, Augustus' patron deity and sometimes proclaimed father, is victorious against Hercules, Mark Antony's protector. In fact, in some versions of the myth Apollo not only saved the tripod but after Zeus broke up the struggle Hercules was sold into slavery for a year. Roman tradition kept Augustus from putting images of the defeated Antony in his public art, but mythological metaphor was acceptable.

Another major part of the decoration was a group of fifty statues of the Danaids as Propertius mentions in his elegy. In Greek mythology the Danaids were the fifty daughters of Danaus. To settle a dispute for the throne, and on orders from their father, they married the fifty sons of Aegyptus and on their wedding night all but one of them killed their husbands. In the Greek myth they were punished for this gross act of betrayal and impiety for all eternity in the underworld. The setting of the story in Egypt, the fact that it involved the Egyptian royal family, and that one of the Danaids was named Cleopatra would all have served to encourage viewers to associate this myth with Antony and Cleopatra and to draw a parallel between their betrayal and that of the Danaids.

Three of the fifty survive, although badly damaged and now restored. In form, they are **herms**. Here the Danaids are in an Archaistic style resembling the female statue of the sixth century BCE in Athens, the Kore (maiden figure), in their hairstyles, dress, facial features, and detailed decorative surfaces. Even the arm position, with one hand holding their skirts, derives from the Athenian Kore. The other arm is broken off each one but originally carried a vessel for water, an allusion to their punishment in the underworld, which was to endlessly fetch water to fill a container that constantly leaked, an impossible task. They are carved in black marble, probably to more closely resemble Egyptian statues carved from a similar black basalt to reinforce their Egyptian connection. The Archaic sculptures from the Temple of Apollo represent the last attempt to revive this style in imperial art at Rome. Augustus and his successors abandon it in favor of the Classical.

House of Augustus

Augustus was very careful to avoid appearing as a king, the mistake that cost Julius Caesar his life. That meant that his house was small and comparatively modest compared to the grand palaces and villas of late Republican Romans. In fact it was not only modest in size, but its decoration rejected the grand, pretentious imagery of Hellenistic palaces and sanctuaries seen in First and early Second Style wall painting. Rather than images of kingship it favored walls with smaller architectural frameworks and larger copies of panel paintings.

In many ways wall painting in the House of Augustus ushers in key components of the Third Style. The architectural framework seen in earlier Second Style decoration as at the villa at Oplontis

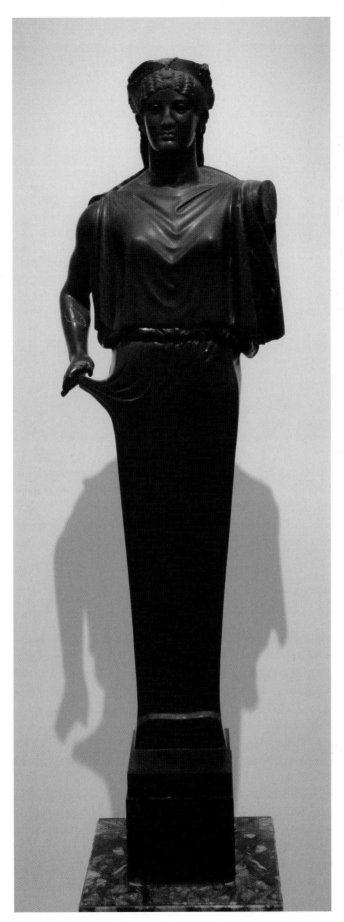

5.18 Black marble herm of Danaid from the Temple of Apollo Palatinus, Rome, 28 BCE. Museo Palatino, Rome. H 47 ¼ in (120 cm). Photo courtesy Daniel Resheter.

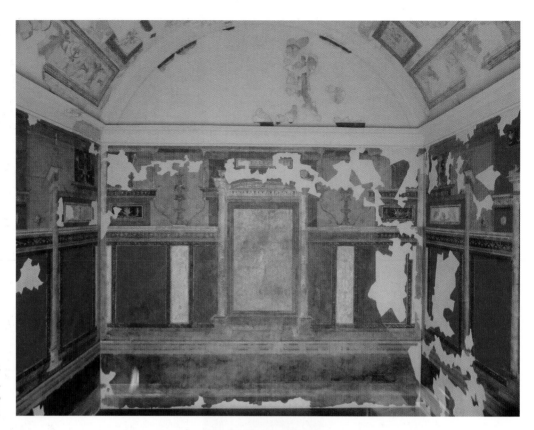

5.19   Wall painting, *c.* 28
BCE, House of Augustus,
Palatine Hill, Rome. Photo
courtesy Daniel Resheter.

(Figure 4.25) here does not frame large windows or vistas into sanctuaries. Instead, the central elements of the walls are faux panel paintings. The architecture acts more as elaborate picture frames than to create spaces that extend the room and that one might enter. The background of the side panels of the walls are blocks of color with subsidiary decoration including candelabra, smaller panel paintings, and painted objects such as vases and theater masks. Many of these elements develop more fully in Third Style wall paintings.

THIRD STYLE WALL PAINTING

The next phase of Roman wall painting, Third Style, is closely tied to the household of Augustus. The earliest building with many elements of the style is the Villa Farnesina in Rome, believed to be the home of Augustus' daughter, Julia, and her husband, Marcus Agrippa. The full expression of this style is seen slightly later in a villa at Boscotrecase near Pompeii, which was covered by the eruption of Vesuvius. It was thought to be the home of Julia and Agrippa's last child, Agrippa Postumus, who was born after his father's death in 12 BCE.

Third Style shows a renunciation of the architectural illusionism of Second Style in favor of panel paintings, perhaps inspired by real Greek panel paintings and decorative ornament. These become the focus of the walls in the style as they developed from the subsidiary paintings along the very edges of Second Style compositions and their size and subjects expanded as they became more prominent in the newly organized space of the wall. The style emphasizes various landscape scenes with and without figures including villas, porticos, gardens, woods, groves, hills, fishponds, canals, rivers, and seashores. The addition of figures is one of the hallmarks of Third Style and may be the innovation of the painter Studius, the most famous painter of the period.

This result and its distance from Second Style are achieved in a number of ways. The style rejects spatial illusionism in favor of surface effects (reinforcing the solidity of the wall again). It uses a decorative framework of structural implausibility, created from materials such as wood, ivory, gold, and glass all taking the place of normal architectural materials and the proportions of the architecture are exaggerated in their thinness and height. The projecting podium of Second Style gives way to (or reverts to the First Style convention of) a flat dado or socle. Colors shift to reds, yellows, blacks, and whites, often in large blocks of color creating empty space in the flanking panels of the wall. This also emphasizes the central panel, which retains illusionistic architecture but the picture in it is explicitly a framed panel.

Third Style painting at Oplontis

The villa at Oplontis demonstrates the spread of this style beyond Rome and the family of Augustus. A room identified as a *caldarium* was painted just after 10 BCE with zones of red and yellow paint over a deep red dado. The attic or upper zone contains very fine architecture, peacocks, horizontal panel paintings of sacred landscapes and a figure, perhaps a poet, seated under a pergola playing a lyre.

The relationships between all of these elements are not reconciled. Is the figure alive, a statue, or a deity? Are the panel paintings and peacocks illusions or related to him, assuming he is there and not a faux painting himself? Is the spindly architecture supporting a real or faux garland? The answers to these questions do not seem to have concerned the painters and those with a low tolerance for ambiguity would do well not to consider them for too long. The central panel contains an architectural frame creating an **aedicular niche** with a coffered rounded top. Inside it is a very large, vertically oriented panel painting inspired by the Hellenistic style. It shows a landscape with a hazy blue background using the **atmospheric perspective** technique to convey depth. The scene is Hercules in the Garden of the Hesperides, one of his final labors, where he retrieved the golden apples that bring life after death. The labor was full of conflict and struggle, none of which is seen here. The apples rest on a rude altar to the right while Hercules approaches in front of a large vertical tree, a standard feature in Third Style landscapes. Here the scene has no action, but evokes the garden scene and the narrative without overwhelming the landscape, which seems to be the true subject.

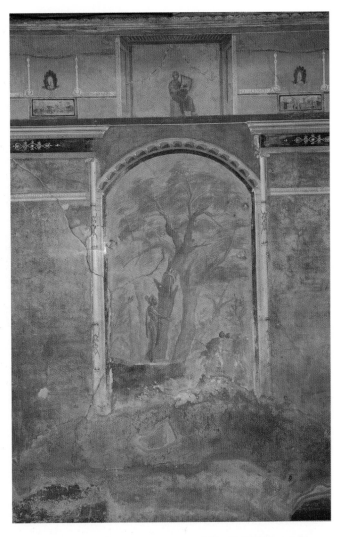

5.20 Third Style painting, villa at Oplontis, *c.* 10 BCE. Photo courtesy Steven L. Tuck.

caldarium
hot room in a Roman bath complex. It usually featured a heated pool and radiant heat from the walls and floor.

aedicular niche
a structural framing device in architecture that creates a space designed like a shrine, usually with a frame surround and roof structure above.

atmospheric perspective
artistic device to create a sense of depth in painting by shifting the background colors to the blue side of the spectrum and painting distant objects paler.

THE EMULATION OF AUGUSTAN ART

The villa at Oplontis demonstrated the reception and ready adoption of an Augustan style of art with Third Style wall paintings. Other works in and out of Rome illustrate further adoption of the styles created by and under the emperor as well as the limits of their adoption as some conservative trends in Italic art remain.

One of the best examples of the power of art of the Age of Augustus is found at Pompeii. The largest building on the forum of Pompeii is the Building of Eumachia. It was named for the local priestess who, as the dedicatory inscription makes clear, paid for it with her own money. The inscription also makes its debt to the family of Augustus explicit since the description of the building

ART AND LITERATURE
Contemporary reactions to Third Style wall painting

It is rare in the field of Roman art that we have surviving contemporary reactions to the art and even rarer to have more than one. We have two long written reactions to Third Style wall painting: one, the architect Vitruvius, writing in 15 BCE when the art was new, and the other, Pliny the Elder, about a century later. Vitruvius loved Second Style with its realistic illusionistic architecture that recreated the forms and proportions of actual architecture. Third Style he hates with a fiery passion. I imagine him shaking his head, if not his fist, at the new style as he describes (7.5) it in his work on architecture:

> But these paintings, which had taken their models from real things, now fall foul of depraved taste. For monsters are now painted in frescoes rather than reliable images of definite things. Reeds are set up in place of columns, as pediments, little scrolls, striped with curly leaves and volutes, candelabra hold up the figures of aediculae, and above the pediments of these, several tender shoots, sprouting in coils from roots, have little statues nestled in them for no reason, or shoots split in half, some holding little statues with human heads, some with the heads of beasts.

Clearly the playfulness, abstraction, and alterations to the realistic architecture of Second Style are too much for Vitruvius. The substitution of decorative features for architecture is a point of particular annoyance to him. Interestingly for us, virtually every detail that he mentions can be found in surviving examples of the style. The paintings from the House of Augustus incorporate the reeds, candelabra, shoots, and coils that Vitruvius objects to so strongly. The reason for his distress is found in the next passage:

> Now these things do not exist nor can they exist nor have they ever existed, and thus this new fashion has brought things to such a pass that bad judges have condemned the right practice of the arts as lack of skill. How, pray tell, can a reed really sustain a roof, or a candelabrum the decorations of a pediment, or an acanthus shoot, so soft and slender, loft a tiny statue perched upon it, or can flowers be produced from roots and shoots on the one hand and figurines on the other? Yet when they see these deceptions, people never criticize them, but rather take delight in them, nor do they ever notice whether any of these things are possible or not. Minds beclouded by feeble standards of judgment are unable to recognize what exists in accordance with authority and the principles of correctness.

For Vitruvius, these new forms are just wrong because they do not depict things of this world. What may in fact be worse than the art itself is what it reveals about taste. Vitruvius is firm about what constitute "the principles of correctness" and it is not Third Style. This harsh judgment of a style linked so closely to the family of Augustus from an author also linked to them is remarkable.

In sharp contrast is Pliny the Elder's description of the style in his *Natural History* 35.37. Pliny does a thorough job here surveying the major subjects of the paintings that filled the central and side panels of Third Style walls. Pliny credits key elements of the style to the innovations of a particular named painter, Studius.

> Studius too, who lived in the time of the late Emperor Augustus, must not be allowed to pass without some notice; for he was the first to introduce the fashion of covering the walls of our houses with most pleasing landscapes, representing villas, porticos, ornamental gardening, woods, groves, hills, fishponds, canals, rivers, sea-shores, and anything else one could desire; varied with figures of persons walking, sailing, or proceeding to their villas, on asses or in carriages. Then, too, there are others to be seen fishing, fowling, or gathering in the vintage. … It was this artist, too, who first decorated our uncovered edifices with representations of maritime cities, a subject which produces a most pleasing effect, and at a very trifling expense.

Pliny's repeated mention of villas along with gardens, porticoes, and so forth may explain one element of the popularity of the style. It allowed patrons to make an aspirational display. The villas, gardens, and so forth that they could not afford themselves could be displayed, demonstrating their identity with and value for elite culture. Pliny also shares two reasons for their popularity. First, they amuse the viewer, and second, and this may account for the popularity and longevity of the style, it was cheaper. The main part of the wall is a block of color with only small areas painted with detailed scenes. It is a far cry from the work necessary to create the successful spatial illusion of a good Second Style wall.

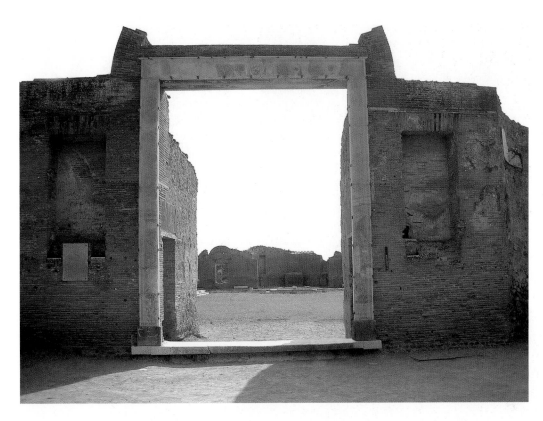

5.21 Doorway of the Building of Eumachia, Pompeii, after 7 BCE. Marble. Photo courtesy Steven L. Tuck.

complex matches that of one in Rome dedicated by Augustus' wife, Livia. The existence of this building and its dedication by a woman is based on the new public role of women that Livia modeled in Rome. In form the building contains elements taken from other components of the Augustan building program in the city.

The marble frieze that framed the front door was carved with the same subjects, style and using the same type of marble as the lower acanthus panels on the Ara Pacis Augustae. Niches in the building facade, perhaps the two flanking the doorway, contained statues of Romulus and Aeneas, the same pair that were carved in relief flanked the entrance to the Ara Pacis Augustae in Rome as well as in the two most prominent statue niches in the Forum Augustum.

The Age of Augustus emphasized the founders of Rome but also much of its early history. This was largely driven by the monumental history of Rome (literally translated, *Since the City's Founding*) written by the historian Livy and published in parts starting in 27 BCE. It told the stories of Rome's founding along with moral lessons and judgments for contemporary readers. It was almost immediately popular, made Livy a celebrity, and led to illustrations in art especially of the legendary and mythological stories of Rome's early years. Some of these are seen on a marble frieze from the interior of the Basilica Aemilia, on the north side of the Forum Romanum.

Considered by Pliny the Elder as one of the most beautiful buildings in Rome, it was first built in 179 BCE but restored periodically because of damage from fire, including in 14 BCE under Augustus. The badly damaged frieze illustrates scenes from the early history of Rome, recognizable from accounts in Livy's history. These include the rape of the Sabine women, battle scenes, the building of the walls of a city in Italy overseen by a goddess, and the death of Tarpeia. Livy in his first book of the history recounts how Tarpeia betrayed Rome to its attacking enemies, the Sabines, in exchange for what they wore on their left arms (meaning their metal bracelets). When she let them into the city, they crushed her to death with their shields, which they also wore on their left arms. It was considered a fitting punishment for a traitor and the event also appeared on Augustan coinage. The frieze is carved in a very recognizable style based on a fifth-century BCE Classical

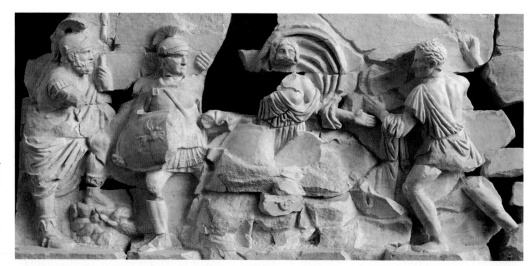

5.22 Marble frieze of Tarpeia, *c.* 14 BCE, from the Basilica Aemilia, Forum Romanum, Rome. H 30 in (76.2 cm). Marie-Lan Nguyen/Wikimedia Commons.

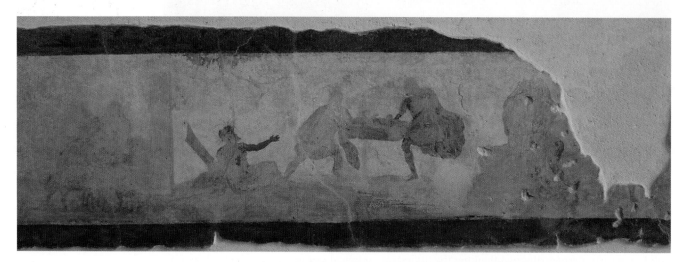

5.23 Roman history painting, Tomb of Statilius Taurus, *c.* 15 BCE, Rome. Museo Nazionale Romano Palazzo Massimo, Rome. H 15 in (38 cm) x L *c.* 32 ft (9.7 m), fresco. Photo courtesy Steven L. Tuck.

battle frieze in the Temple of Apollo at Bassae in Greece, which included the same composition, high relief, dramatic poses, and landscape elements.

The small (9 ½ ft x 6 ft 4 ½ in; 2.9 x 1.95 m) tomb of one of the most prominent Roman politicians of the Age of Augustus, Statilius Taurus, also shows this emphasis on Rome's early history. Taurus served as consul multiple times under Augustus, celebrated a triumph, held the city of Rome for Augustus during the latter's absence, and also built the first stone amphitheater in Rome. The interior of his tomb was decorated with a painted frieze illustrating scenes from Rome's early history and mythical founders, events featured in Livy's history and consistent with Augustus' own program of public art.

Painted in a Hellenistic technique it includes battle scenes, meetings between military leaders and two episodes of the construction of city walls, one overseen by a goddess. These cities are probably Lavinium and Alba Longa, founded by the Trojan refugees, Aeneas and his son Ascanius. The final scene shows the twins Romulus and Remus in a basket being lowered into the Tiber on orders of the usurper Amulius. The personification of the Tiber reclines to the left along the riverbank while shepherds and other pastoral figures fill the landscape on the edges of the scene, providing further context for this event that by tradition took place on the base of the Palatine, just below the houses of Romulus and Augustus.

TRADITIONAL ITALIC STYLE IN THE AGE OF AUGUSTUS

Not everyone adopted Augustan subjects or styles, however. Another tomb just outside the walls of Rome shows a relief that provides a very different image of social status and cultural identity under Augustus, that of freedmen. It belonged to Marcus Vergilius Eurysaces, who became wealthy in his profession of baker and contractor, presumably supplying bread to the Roman army. His 33 ft (10 m) tall tomb structure is one of the largest tombs of a sub-elite Roman ever found in Rome and consists of, starting from the bottom, a high base, a lower section designed like a series of vertical cylinders, a cornice with an inscription, an upper zone with three rows of open holes, and, finally, just below the roof, a frieze.

The significance of the cylinders and holes is debated by scholars, but they seem to represent dough-kneading machines, so that the tomb's shape reflect the subject of the decorative frieze. The frieze wraps around the three surviving sides of the tomb and documents all of the stages in breadmaking. This unique monument is decidedly different in subject from the public friezes of military victories or men fulfilling the duties of their public office. Here the same sort of Italic documentary style seen in historical reliefs illustrates the steps in breadmaking from purchasing grain, to grinding it in mills turned by donkeys, preparing dough, and then baking and selling the finished bread. The style of the relief is also Italic.

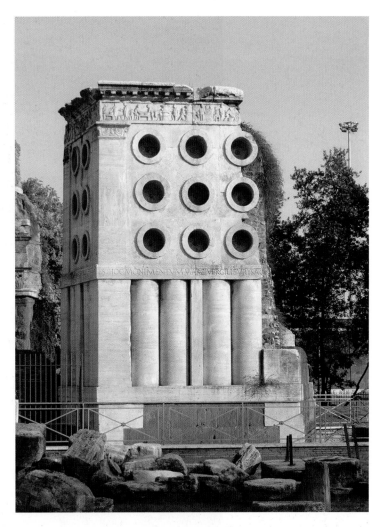

5.24   Tomb of Eurysaces, c. 20 BCE, Rome. Travertine-faced concrete. Photo courtesy Steven L. Tuck.

The figures are dressed appropriately for their stations and activities, with the lower status workers in tunics instead of togas and those working the hot ovens without shirts or tunics. Each figure, as in public reliefs of public office, fulfills his job in a straightforward way. The relief also uses hierarchy of scale so that the viewer can readily tell which of the flatly carved, rather static figures are the most important. Notably absent are any Hellenistic elements such as landscape or indicators of depth or setting or figures in dramatic diagonal poses showing motion. The subject and style seem unaffected by the Greek artistic trends taking place in the capital.

An even more conservatively Italic tomb relief is found at Amiternum, a regionally important town in the Apennine mountains northeast of Rome. Two reliefs carved in local limestone from a tomb depict elements of funerary ritual. One relief shows a standard image of gladiatorial combat. The other relief is a unique image of a Roman funeral procession taking place.

Composed and carved in a traditional Italic style it illustrates all of the main features and figures of the event in the same way that a historical relief or painting would. The figures are all carefully arranged so they can be distinguished and their role in the ritual is clear from their dress, position, and actions. Most notably groundlines are used to support groups of figures in the upper zone of the register, filling the entire frame with the procession in a convention that breaks up the image visually but makes it clear that all are participating in the ritual. The largest of these groups includes the

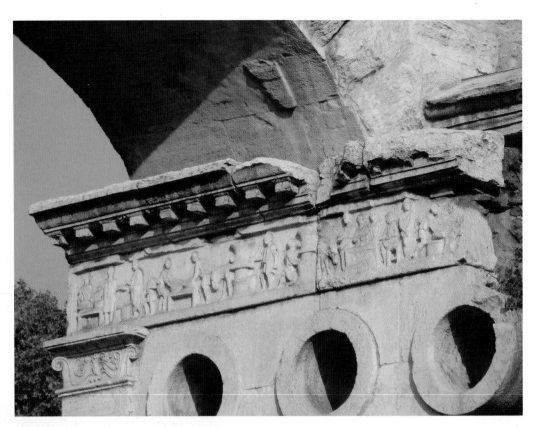

5.25   Detail of baking frieze, Tomb of Eurysaces, *c.* 20 BCE, Rome. H 23 in (58.4 cm), travertine. Photo courtesy Steven L. Tuck.

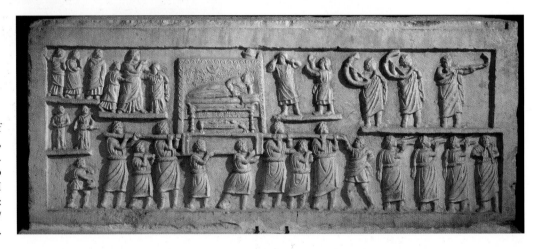

5.26   Tomb relief of funeral procession, Augustan. Amiternum. Museo Archeologico dell'Aquila. Limestone, H 2 ft 2 in (66 cm). Source: © Universal Images Group/ Superstock.

deceased (or an effigy as found on Etruscan sarcophagi) reclining on his funerary bed with its mattress and pillow while a shroud, decorated with moon and stars, is pulled away to reveal the body. Eight pallbearers carry him. Depth is shown with those on the near side much larger than the ones in the background. Members of the family flank the body on their groundlines actively mourning, weeping, holding each other, gesturing and tearing their hair. Behind the body follow smaller-scale figures, probably members of the extended family, smaller both because they are further from the body and because of their lesser importance. Groups of musicians lead the procession, with four double flute players on the bottom register and three horn players above them. Behind the flautists is a figure looking back and gesturing to the pallbearers, thought to be the *designator*, the professional who arranged the procession. The use of these Italic conventions including hierarchy of scale, individual groundlines, and the static, repetitive representation of key figures in the scene is not found in Augustan art in Rome, but makes an appearance in imperial art under the Antonine emperors of the second century CE, probably best seen on the base reliefs of the Column of Antoninus Pius (Figures 9.11, 9.12).

SCHOLARLY PERSPECTIVE
The identification of the figures on the Portland Vase

It seems that no work of Roman art has generated more scholarly debate than the Portland Vase, a cameo glass vase of the highest quality art yet with no origin, date, or names attached to it. Naturally the lack of definites has only fueled scholarly speculation and the theories identifying the figures on this work of art of the Age of Augustus provide a case study in iconography and academic analysis. They also demonstrate the limits of our ability to understand unique works of ancient art when the imagery lacks attributes and the piece has no context. The relief frieze consists of only seven figures in two groups, four on one side (figures A–D) and three on the other (figures E–G) in scenes separated by the handles of the vase.

All of the figures were carved in the style of Athenian Classical art of the fifth century BCE. On one side a youthful male figure on the left stands in front of a section of a colonnade and steps forward, led by a flying infant, as a woman

(a) figures A–D

(b) figures E–G

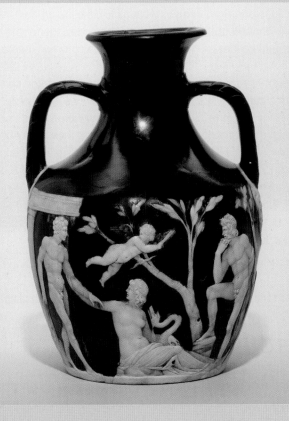

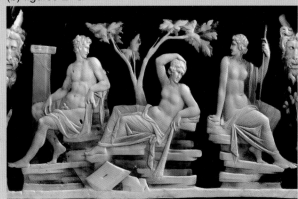

5.27a and 5.27b   Portland Vase, from Rome, Augustan. British Museum, London. Cameo glass, H 9 ½ in (24 cm). Source: © The Trustees of the British Museum. All rights reserved.

(Continued)

on the ground reaches up to take his arm. The head of a serpent-like figure rises from her lap. A bearded, mature man on the right oversees the scene. On the other side two figures, a youth and a seated woman with a staff, sit with their backs to a woman but their heads turned towards her as she reclines on a pile of rocks as her left hand snuffs out a torch against the rocks.

Scholars have generated over fifty-five theories on the identities of the figures and cannot even agree whether the figures represent a single scene, two scenes from the same story, or two separate stories which may be mythological, historical, or allegorical. With no captions and few certain attributes to go on, other than the flying infant, which everyone agrees is Cupid, the theories look to the details of the figure groups, the landscape elements, notably the species of trees, and the serpent-like figure for clues. Theories fall into one of two categories: either the frieze is a scene from Greek myth or it is based on Augustan propaganda. For each theory a key piece of evidence is the identity of the serpent figure.

Previous theories assign the figures to the myths of Dionysus or Theseus. However, the Greek myth that has dominated debate more recently is the wedding of Peleus and Thetis, a famous event in Greek mythology. A version of this theory holds that one side illustrates the marriage of Peleus and Thetis and the other refers to Achilles, their son. The mortal Peleus (A) enters the world of the gods through an archway led by Cupid (B) and grasps the arm of the sea goddess Thetis (C) identified by the sea monster in her lap. The bearded figure (D) is Poseidon, god of the sea or Nereus, Thetis' father, overseeing the match. On the other side Achilles (E), son of Peleus and Thetis, has died in the Trojan War and in the afterlife is rewarded with Helen (F) while Aphrodite (G) looks on giving her blessing. This theory relies on recognizing the serpent as a sea monster, Achilles as sitting next to a tomb marker, the tree behind Helen as a plane tree, associated with her, and the torch she carries giving her identity from the Greek word for torch, *helene*. It does not explain why neither Poseidon nor Aphrodite has their attributes nor the obscurity of that Achilles and Helen tradition.

A theory bridging the Greek and Roman worlds in a way seen in other Augustan art accepts the Peleus and Thetis scene on one side, but identifies the group on the other as figures in Roman myth, Aeneas (E), the Trojan hero who came to Italy, Queen Dido (F), of Carthage who tragically fell in love with him, and Venus (Aphrodite), the mother of Aeneas who created the love between the two. The two separate scenes are then connected by a common theme to appeal to a sophisticated elite Roman audience.

Another theory is that it illustrates a myth that was important to Augustus as it proclaimed that he was the son of Apollo, who coming to Augustus' mother, Atia, in the form of a snake, was her lover. In this theory we see Apollo (E) when he first catches sight of Atia (F) under the influence of Venus Genetrix (G) the aspect of Venus worshipped under Caesar and his descendants. On the other side we have the actual moment of the consummation of their love. Apollo (A) advances out of his sanctuary guided by Cupid (B) and links arms with Atia (C). The serpent in her lap references Apollo's form in the myth while to the right Romulus (D), the founder of Rome, witnesses the event that will lead to the birth of Augustus, the second founder of Rome. Why Atia (F) is holding a torch and why the figures of Apollo, Venus, and Romulus lack their standard attributes are not answered. Also, if Apollo and Atia are both presented on each side, why aren't the figures identical? It is clear that we aren't about to run out of theories on the meaning of the Portland Vase figures. It may be that some pieces of art simply defy our full understanding without additional evidence.

W. Gudenrath, K. Painter, and D. Whitehouse, *Journal of Glass Studies* 32: 14–188 (1990).

CONCRETE ARCHITECTURE

In the Late Republican period, concrete became the key material for creating large temple platforms, terraces, sanctuary complexes, and other types of buildings on a scale not seen before. Concrete's usefulness in creating innovative structures began to be explored in the Age of Augustus. As outlined in chapter 4, concrete could be shaped by forms where it would cure and hold whatever shape was required. This made it ideal for vaults and domes. The largest domed building until Hadrian's Pantheon was built was part of the bathing complex at Baiae on the north side of the Bay of Naples.

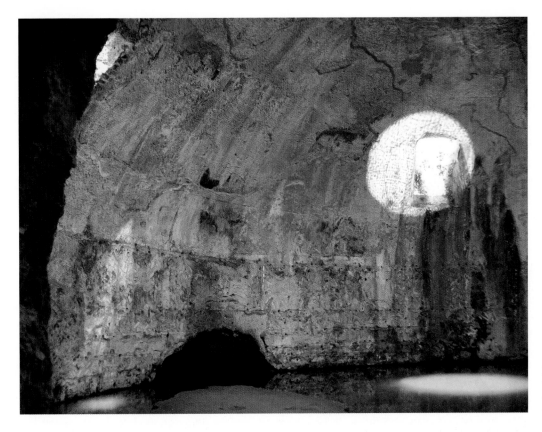

5.28 "Temple of Mercury" at Baiae on the Bay of Naples, Augustan. Concrete, D 71 ft (21.5 m). Photo courtesy Steven L. Tuck.

This bath structure was created with a dome 71 ft (21.5 m) in diameter, a large and unprecedented concrete building and the first massive true dome in world architecture. Although only half the size of Hadrian's Pantheon, the so-called Temple of Mercury (which was not its ancient name as it was neither a temple nor had any association with Mercury) has many of the features of the later work including the concrete material, shape of a true hemispherical dome, and use of an **oculus**. Later domed buildings were added to the bath complex at Baia and it seems clear that this area, the source of the pozzolana volcanic ash critical in manufacturing concrete, is where architects worked out the properties and methods of concrete dome and vault construction seen on a grander scale in the baths and public buildings in Rome.

oculus
from the Latin meaning "eye," refers to a circular open skylight in the center of a dome to provide light into the building.

CONCLUSION

The Age of Augustus was, as in so many other areas, a revolutionary one for art. The creation of a ruling dynasty and new public roles for women created new artistic needs and opportunities that could be explored and exploited by artists and patrons alike. The new dynastically similar images for the family of Augustus reflect their political needs, while the emulation of the Livia's buildings in Rome by Eumachia at Pompeii expresses the success of the new Augustan social system as well. Augustus' reliance on Athenian styles of art, utilizing both Archaic and Classical forms in his work, demonstrates the experimentation taking place in the period along with the search for a style that would resonate with Roman audiences. The eventual success of the Classical style shows its power and appeal to audiences across the Roman world. This is not to say that it drove out all other styles. The Italic style of Roman historical narrative may have been out of fashion in the imperial workshops, but it was still found in the tomb reliefs of Amiternum while the Hellenistic style was used in the privately commissioned Basilica Aemilia reliefs and the painted frieze in the tomb of Statilius Taurus, although these last two works did rely on the Augustan subject of early Roman

A VIEW FROM THE PROVINCES

Caesarea Maritima

The potential for concrete construction is seen in its repeated use to create the largest complexes ever attempted in Roman architecture in one of the most difficult building environments in the world: harbors along the sea coast. The first large-scale artificial harbor in the Mediterranean was built at Caesarea by King Herod. Called Sebastos, Greek for Augustus, it demonstrates concrete construction, Roman imperial ideology, and became a model for the form and decoration of harbors around the Mediterranean.

Situated on an otherwise bare stretch of coast, the harbor was only possible because of the potential of concrete construction. Large concrete blocks were created and lowered into the sea where they continued to set. Concrete is ideal for this purpose as it can be shaped based on the forms it is dumped into and it sets even underwater, the chemical reaction that hardens it continuing. The material and technology for this work came from the Bay of Naples where it had been worked out in the earlier part of the century. Here it was applied on a much grander scale in a completely artificial harbor for the first time.

The decorative program of the harbor takes Hellenistic models, notably that of Alexandria, the greatest harbor in the Mediterranean up to that time, and adapts them for a display honoring the family of Augustus. This becomes a pattern seen in later Roman harbors, notably at Portus and Leptis Magna. The name of the harbor and the city attached to it are perhaps the most obvious elements of this honor, using the name of the emperor for the facility itself. The largest built element of the harbor was the lighthouse, modeled on the Pharos at Alexandria. The Pharos was a large multi-stage tower used as a fire platform with an inscription and probably statues naming and honoring King Ptolemy and Queen Berenice. Placed on the right of entering ships, here at Caesarea the lighthouse was named for Drusus, brother of the future emperor Tiberius and father of the emperor Claudius. Although they do not survive, it seems clear that the statues that flanked the harbor mouth were a form of imperial family display of a type known from

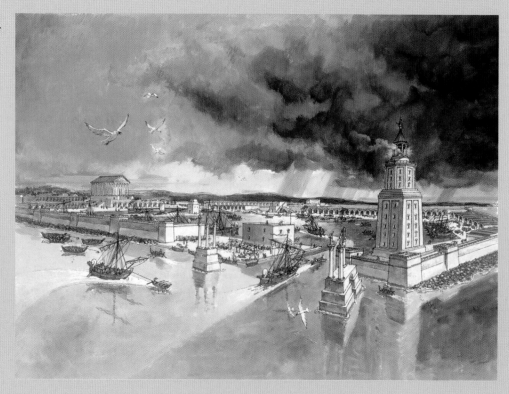

5.29 Caesarea Maritima, painting of Herodian harbor, *c.* 15 BCE. Source: Robert J. Teringo/National Geographic Creative.

many other contexts. Given the date of the harbor completion, *c.* 15 BCE, the six statues probably included Augustus' other step and adopted sons Tiberius, Lucius, and Gaius along with his wife Livia and daughter Julia.

Augustus himself was not part of the statue group since his cult statue, accompanied by his divine consort, Rome, was in the large harborside temple that dominated the inner basin of the harbor. The temple's location was influential for the religious decorative program of future harbors. Its pairing of Augustus and Rome modeled on Zeus and Hera set a pattern that made its way from the eastern Mediterranean to the west by the time of Augustus' successor Tiberius. The pairing is also seen on the Gemma Augustea (Figure 6.3) found at Rome.

ANCIENTS ON ART

Caesarea Maritima described by Josephus

By virtue of expenditure and initiative, the king [Herod] triumphed over nature and constructed a harbor larger than the Piraeus … He had blocks of stone [concrete] let down into twenty fathoms of water, most of them measuring fifty feet in length by nine in depth and ten in breadth, some being even larger. Upon this underwater foundation he constructed above the surface a mole two hundred feet broad; of which one hundred were built out to break the surge, this portion was called the breakwater, while the remainder supported a stone wall encircling the harbor. From this wall arose, at intervals, massive towers, the loftiest and most magnificent of which was called Drusion after the stepson of Caesar (the Emperor Augustus). There was a row of arched recesses where newly-arrived crews could land, and in front of these was a circular terrace forming a broad walk for those disembarking. … At the harbor-mouth stood colossal statues, three on either side, resting on columns … On a rise facing the harbor mouth stood Caesar's temple, remarkable for its size and beauty; it contained a colossal statue of the emperor, not inferior to the Olympian Zeus, which served for its model, and another of the goddess Rome, rivalling that of Hera at Argos. The city Herod … gave the name of Caesarea. (Flavius Josephus, *Jewish War*, 1.408–15 adapted)

history for their subjects. The success of any dynasty or artistic legacy is arguably found in its later reception. It is under the Julio-Claudian emperors from Tiberius to Nero that we see the art of the Age of Augustus as it is transmitted, altered, and, in some forms, rejected in favor of new forms that convey different messages.

SUGGESTIONS FOR FURTHER READING

Elizabeth Bartman, *Portraits of Livia: Imaging the Imperial Woman in Augustan Rome* (Cambridge University Press 1999). This book documents and explores the origins of imperial female imagery and how Livia's image became the model for imperial women for centuries to come. Her portraits created a public image for women in Rome for the first time and promoted the cultural programs of Augustus and the dynasty that they established.

Eve d'Ambra, ed., *Roman Art in Context: an Anthology* (Prentice Hall 1993). This collection contains four influential articles on Roman sculpture. The first reveals the ancient process of reading a sculpture, two analyze the sculptural reliefs of the Ara Pacis, and one deconstructs the decorative program of the Temple of Apollo under Augustus.

William Gudenrath, Kenneth Painter, David Whitehouse, *Journal of Glass Studies* 32: 14–188 (1990). This entire issue of the journal is devoted to the Portland Vase including its creation, history, and iconography. Appendix V traces all of the previous interpretations.

Lothar Haselberger in collaboration with D.G. Romano, ed. E. Dumser, *Mapping Augustan Rome.* Journal of Roman Archaeology Supplementary Series 50 (2008). This work creates a visual synopsis of what is known about the city of Rome c. 14 CE – a pivotal phase of Rome's transformation into an imperial capital. It includes large-scale maps of the city refounded by Augustus as well as written entries on each of the major buildings, complexes, and neighborhoods touched by Augustus' work to recreate the capital.

Ellen Perry, *The Aesthetics of Emulation in the Visual Arts of Ancient Rome* (Cambridge University Press 2005). Arguing that the scholarship on this topic has not appreciated Roman values in the visual arts, this book examines Roman strategies for the appropriation of the Greek visual culture. A knowledge of Roman values explains the entire range of visual appropriation in Roman art, which includes not only the phenomenon of copying, but also such manifestations as allusion, parody, and, most importantly, *aemulatio*, successful rivalry with one's models.

John Pollini, *From Republic to Empire: Rhetoric, Religion, and Power in the Visual Culture of Ancient Rome* (University of Oklahoma Press 2012). John Pollini explores how various Republican artistic and ideological symbols of religion and power were taken over or refashioned to convey new ideological content in the visual culture of the new imperial Rome.

Rolf Winkes, ed., *The Age of Augustus: Interdisciplinary Conference Held at Brown University, April 30–May 2, 1982* (Center for Old World Archaeology and Art, Brown University; Institut Supérieur d'Archéologie et d'Histoire de l'Art, Collège Érasme 1985). Contains essays by a variety of experts on portraiture, historical reliefs, the tomb of Eurysaces, public art in Rome, and architectural programs under Augustus. Issues of Augustan propaganda and his use of the arts run through many of the contributions.

Paul Zanker, *The Power of Images in the Age of Augustus* (University of Michigan Press 1988). Perhaps the most important book to read on Augustan public art, politics, and history. More than a survey of propaganda, Zanker demonstrates how virtually all of the arts were used under Augustus to promote his programs of cultural and governmental renewal. A key element is his discussion of the changing art and its political messages throughout the forty years of Augustan rule.

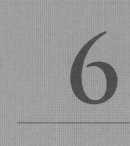

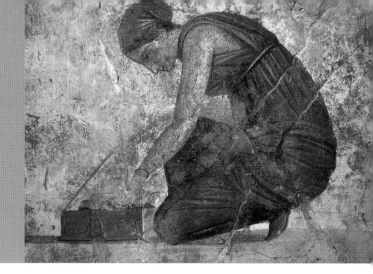

THE JULIO-CLAUDIANS, 14–68 CE
The Rise of Roman Dynastic Art

14–37 CE	Tiberius as emperor
20–26 CE	Tiberius resides at Sperlonga; **sculpture group created**
37–41 CE	Caligula as emperor
37 CE	**Portrait of Caligula**
41–54 CE	Claudius as emperor
43 CE	Invasion of Britain
c. **51 CE**	**Grand Camée; Ravenna relief**
52 CE	**Porta Maggiore gate constructed**
54–68 CE	Nero as emperor
59 CE	Amphitheater riot at Pompeii
62 CE	Earthquake along the Bay of Naples that extensively damaged Pompeii; **Domus Transitoria of Nero**
after 62 CE	**Temple of Isis and House of Octavius Quartio rebuilt at Pompeii**
64 CE	Great fire in Rome; **Domus Aurea of Nero begun**

A History of Roman Art, First Edition. Steven L. Tuck.
© 2015 Steven L. Tuck. Published 2015 by John Wiley & Sons, Ltd.

INTRODUCTION

The death of Augustus in 14 CE marked the final death of the Roman Republic since Augustus' new form of government now included dynastic succession, establishing a monarchy in all but name. As a monarchy, the principate (rule by a *princeps*, commonly referred to as emperor) required new forms of art and architecture to bolster its rulers. Under the Julio-Claudians, the four emperors (Tiberius, Caligula, Claudius, and Nero) who claimed rule due to their lines of descent from Augustus, we see major new forms of art and architecture, most notably dynastic portraiture and imperial palaces. Julio-Claudian emperors used dynastic portraiture, their great contribution to Roman art, to connect themselves to their predecessors and to associate themselves and their families with those deities whose power, myths, or attributes were politically or ideologically useful. Starting with the emperor Tiberius, palaces, official residences of the emperors, were created as a radical architectural development in ancient Rome where they offered the opportunity for innovative design and decor. Nero's great palaces, the Domus Transitoria and the Domus Aurea, represent the revolutionary changes that the new system of government brought about in art and architecture. While the disparate needs of each emperor shaped his artistic program, it would be a mistake to view these as matters of whim or just personal preference; each emperor's artistic program was as much an act of imperial policy as administrative actions or military decisions.

Still, many of the same themes from previous periods continue to inform Roman art during this innovative era. Scenes from Greek mythology comprise the major decorative subject in the residences as seen at Pompeii and it is clear that Rome's cultural inclusiveness encouraged the spread of Greek and Egyptian culture in terms of subjects and motifs, as well as artistic conventions. In addition, the traditional Italic forms and subjects are not abandoned. During this period we see deliberate selections from a range of artistic and architectural conventions to fulfill specific purposes in projecting cultural identity.

TIBERIUS, 14–37 CE, AND CALIGULA, 37–41 CE

Tiberius, the adopted son of Augustus, was born to Livia in 42 BCE and named for his father, Tiberius Claudius Nero. After Livia's marriage to Augustus, Tiberius was raised as their child and found great success as a young man commanding Roman forces in battle in a variety of provinces. A tremendously skilled general, he expanded and solidified Roman power and was an effective administrator outside of Rome. Following the deaths of all of his prospective heirs, Augustus adopted Tiberius and named him his heir. As emperor his name became Tiberius Julius Caesar Augustus. His first acts as emperor in deifying Augustus and vowing a temple to him, as well as his later commissions of imperial art, demonstrate an awareness of the need to continue his links to Augustus and to reinforce his succession in this new form of government.

Caligula, as Gaius Julius Caesar Germanicus was to become known, was born in 12 CE, the son of Germanicus and Agrippina. He received his nickname, meaning "little boots," from his father's soldiers during the German campaigns (14–16 CE) when he accompanied his father dressed in a miniature military outfit. Following his father's death Caligula lived with his mother or one of a number of relatives until he joined Tiberius' household in 31 CE. He succeeded his great uncle and adopted grandfather, Tiberius, upon the latter's death in 37 CE. His own reign of just less than four years was marked by an initial period of almost universal joy followed by fear at his increasingly erratic and violent behavior, leading to his assassination and, following his death in 41 CE, some destruction of his monuments and images by those hostile to him or just eager to distance themselves from his problematic rule.

Portraiture

In his portraiture, Tiberius relies heavily on the prece-dent established by Augustus. Although his portraits do reflect his own physical features, they also reference Augustus in their Classical idealism and serve to create dynastic imagery through the implied resemblances of father and son. These elements can be seen in a por-trait of Tiberius found in a Roman city in Egypt but of a type certainly dictated centrally from Rome, which distributed model portraits of emperors to the prov-inces to be copied by locals who wished to set up their own statues of emperors. These models were updated periodically as the emperor aged. Long-lived emperors and their families could have a variety of portraits on display across the Roman world showing them at dif-ferent ages. The portrait was discovered along with portraits of Augustus and Livia, which suggests it was part of a dynastic group. These family portrait groups are known from the Republican period, but under the Julio-Claudians they serve an explicitly political func-tion that family portraits did not serve under the Republic. Now, they were necessary to establish the relationship between emperor and adopted heirs. Portraits of female members of the family were also included giving them a public role they did not have under the Republic.

Tiberius is sculptured with a high forehead, large eyes, and rather long nose and small mouth, with nota-bly protruding lower lip – all characteristics of his many varieties of portrait types. The smooth skin,

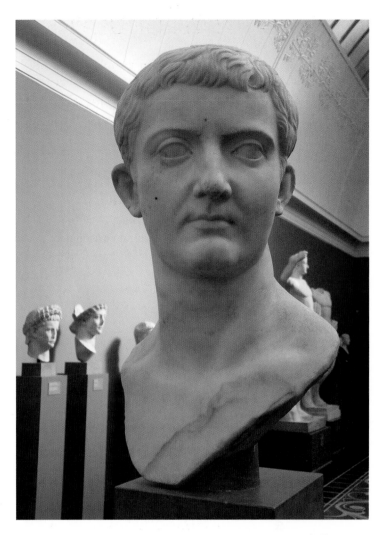

6.1 Portrait of Tiberius, after 4 CE, from the Fayum in Egypt. Ny Carlsberg Glyptotek, Copenhagen. H 18 ½ in (47 cm), marble. Photo courtesy Steven L. Tuck.

calm, idealized features, and cap of hair with its overlapping layers of locks, comma-shaped side-burns, and arrangement of bangs with an off-center part are all modeled on the portraiture of Augustus. The use of Augustan imagery would have conveyed to a Roman audience that Tiberius shared characteristics and qualities of his predecessor. Since his right to rule came directly from Augustus it was important that Tiberius reinforce his connection to him.

A portrait of Caligula, Tiberius' nephew and successor, discovered in Asia Minor also demon-strates the continuity of Julio-Claudian dynastic portraiture. Notable here are the same Classical calm, high forehead, layered locks, and large eyes seen in the portraits of Tiberius. These elements are paired with individual features of deeper, closer set eyes and a protruding upper lip found con-sistently on Caligula's surviving portraits. The paint that originally colored all of these marble por-traits is partially preserved here on the left eye with its distinct pupil, iris, and lashes. Although, as preserved, it gives the emperor an imbalanced look that reinforces his reputation for insanity, in antiquity the complete painting would have created a more lifelike image.

Dynastic monuments

In addition to dynastic portrait groups composed of marble or bronze free-standing statues, the political needs of the Julio-Claudians also informed the creation of small-scale pieces of dynastic art for imperial display and presentation to political supporters. The Gemma Augustea and the

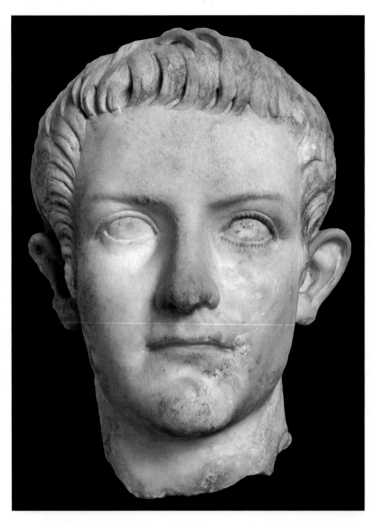

6.2   Portrait of Caligula, 37 CE, from Asia Minor. Ny Carlsberg Glyptotek, Copenhagen. H 11 ¾ in (30 cm), marble. Photo courtesy Steven L. Tuck.

Boscoreale cups serve to link Tiberius to the deified Augustus and to proclaim his ancestry and authority to rule as well as his military achievements. These are among the highest quality works of art promoting dynastic succession, a key contribution of the Julio-Claudian dynasty to Roman art.

The Gemma Augustea is a large, 7 ½ x 9 in (19 x 22.8 cm), sardonyx cameo carved into a statement of imperial power and dynasty. The field of the gem is divided into two registers. The lower one shows the aftermath of a Roman military victory including bound and defeated captive barbarians while Roman soldiers raise a trophy. The barbarians are somewhat generic, having no arms or attributes of specific tribes, but the inclusion of a Scorpio, Tiberius' birth sign, in the design may indicate that the cameo depicts one of his victories. The upper register is more complex in its imagery and, while the identities of some figures are subject to debate, the overall themes are clear. Here the deified Augustus with a personified Roma as his consort, the largest and central figures in the upper register, are seated on a double throne in the manner of Jupiter and Juno. Augustus is crowned with a laurel of victory and additional enemy shields and armor are piled under their feet. The eagle under the throne indicates the support of Jupiter whose regent on earth was Augustus. Capricorn, Augustus' birth sign, replaces the sun. A set of four deities fills the register to the right and, while their specific identities are debated, they are clearly personifications of geographical areas; one holds a cornucopia representing the abundance of the Roman world under Augustus' rule. To the left of the throne Tiberius, dressed in a toga and laurel wreath and holding a scepter, steps down from a triumphal chariot driven by Victory herself and approaches the throne. Between the chariot and the throne is a standing male in military dress, probably Germanicus, who announced Tiberius' Illyrian victory in Rome. The human Tiberius and Germanicus report on this Roman conquest to the divine Augustus and Roma who quite literally occupy a sphere above the terrestrial, a dramatic change from the very human images of Augustus made during his own lifetime (Figure 5.1).

The Boscoreale cups, a set of silver decorative cups with chased exterior decorative panels, were found in the ruins of a villa covered by the eruption of Vesuvius in 79 CE. They were probably given as gifts to the owner of the villa under Tiberius. The cups are understood to be small-scale copies of large public reliefs in Rome that do not survive. Cup A is decorated with two scenes divided by its handles.

The scene we see features Augustus in the center of the panel seated on a Roman magistrate's chair approached by figures from both sides. To the right Mars leads seven captive figures, personifications of captive peoples or provinces, towards the emperor. To the left are four divine figures. At the far left is Virtus, the personification of male military achievement. Next is her companion Honos, the personification of male civic achievement, holding a cornucopia showing Roman prosperity under Augustus. To the right is a small Eros accompanying Venus who personally hands Augustus a statue of winged Victory to surmount the globe he holds in his extended right hand. This image of personal virtues and global power reflects the famous statement of Jupiter from Vergil's *Aeneid* in which he

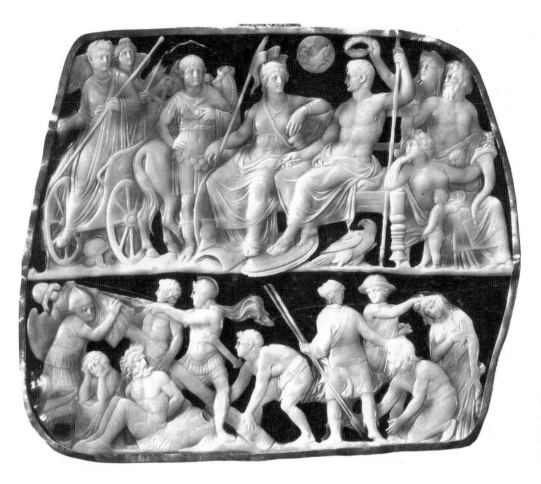

6.3   Gemma Augustea,
c. 15 CE. Kunsthistorisches
Museum, Vienna. Sardonyx,
7 ½ x 9 in (19 x 22.8 cm).
Photo courtesy John Pollini.

TOOLS & TECHNIQUES

Cameo carving

Cameo is a type of carving that creates figures or scenes in raised relief. In antiquity artists used natural materials, generally layered stones such as agate, carnelian, and sardonyx. These naturally layered stones have bands of alternating colors. Artists would lay out a design usually on the lightest layer, but sometimes on two or more layers for greater depth and detail, and carve figures or a scene into that. As they carved they would remove the light material revealing the dark band that lay beneath. The result was a figure or scene in light stone and raised relief with a dark background behind. Some of these scenes were large and involved as many as twenty figures in multiple registers all carved in as many as five layers of hard stone with simple hand tools and no magnification. Beginning under Augustus glass cameos were also made. For smaller cameos such as rings these could be produced by fusing together two cast sheets of glass of contrasting colors. Larger glass cameos, such as vessels, required covering a blown glass vessel, usually cobalt blue, with an overlay, generally white, which was then carved in the cameo technique (see the Portland Vase, Figure 5.27).

promises the Romans *imperium sine fine*, empire [power] without end. Thanks to this type of public art, Romans were trained to draw the connection between world power and the personal virtues of elite men who created their empire.

The second cup is decorated with a single event, a triumphal procession of Tiberius in two stages, but here the fields are joined by figures and background that fill the spaces under the handles of the

(a)

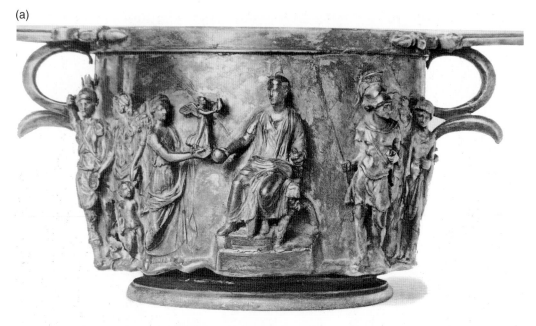

(b)

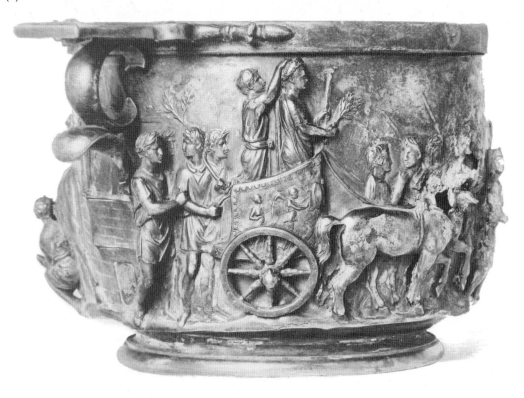

6.4a and 6.4b Boscoreale cups A and B, after 10 CE, Boscoreale. Musée du Louvre, Paris. H 4 ¾ in (12 cm), silver. Photos courtesy Steven L. Tuck.

cup. The best-preserved side shows Tiberius in a triumphal *quadriga* dressed in a toga and holding a scepter and laurel branch with a victory wreath held suspended over his head by a slave. Soldiers from his victorious army follow the chariot while others fill the field behind the four horses pulling the chariot. Sacrificial attendants precede the chariot leading cattle to the sacrifice on the opposite side of the cup. Here the badly damaged figure of Tiberius is presiding over the sacrifice of a bull standing between the altar and a temple that fills the right end of the relief field. The temple probably represents that of Jupiter Optimus Maximus, the terminus of the triumphal procession on the

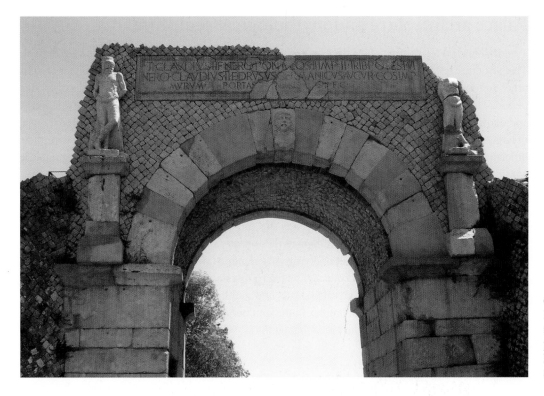

6.5 City gate, Saepinum, Italy decorated with inscription, bound prisoners, and protome head, 15 CE. Photo courtesy Steven L. Tuck.

Capitoline Hill in Rome. Together the cups reinforce the themes of the Gemma Augustea, namely the divinity of Augustus and the terrestrial military accomplishments of Tiberius that extended Roman *imperium* and fulfilled Jupiter's promise.

The city gate at the Roman colony of Saepinum in central Italy reveals the extensive propaganda needs of the Julio-Claudian dynasty. Romans were used to seeing public pronouncements of elite individuals working on their behalf. They had not been accustomed to thinking in terms of dynastic succession in which family members naturally inherited power from older generations. Art was used to indoctrinate them to this new reality. The gate demonstrates that use along with the expectations of public building by the emperor's family who are now the accepted patrons of public benefaction across the Roman world. The sculptural components of the single passage arched gate are extremely traditional. The central panel bearing an inscription is flanked by bound captives in high relief, a type recognizable from triumphal images on monuments and coins. Their generic images mean that they could be from among any of Rome's enemies although, given their context, they might reference Tiberius' successful campaigns. Above the gate projects a human **protome** bust, a form of gate decoration whose frontality has long Italic roots, a characteristic feature of Etruscan city gates with the best-preserved example still visible at Volterra. The bust is probably apotropaic, designed to ward off evil from the city. The largest element of the display is the dedicatory inscription listing Tiberius and his nephew and adopted son, Germanicus, defined by their personal relationship and extensive imperial titles as having paid for the colony's gates, towers, and walls.

Taken as a whole the display creates a projection of power that conveys distinct messages of Roman power and identity to different audiences. To Romans, both citizens and non-citizen subjects, it conveys a message of security, stability, and infrastructure under the responsibility of the ruling dynasty at Rome, whose names and titles at least some could read. Those resisting Roman power such as foreigners and outlaws might instead identify with the bound captives and the severed head above the gate, taking away from the display a message altogether more cautionary and forbidding.

protome
a form of art that consists of a frontal view of an animal head or human bust.

Palace architecture and mythological sculpture

Tiberius constructed the first real palace on Rome's Palatine Hill, from which the word palace derives. That structure is completely covered by later buildings and, as a result, very poorly understood. His other residences, however, reveal some information about Roman architecture and decor at this period. The emperor spent a considerable part of his rule outside of Rome at his villas at Sperlonga and on the island of Capri on the edge of the Bay of Naples. These are villas in the traditional sense of large-scale rural elite dwellings, but they have a new component of identity consistent with their official function. As the residence of the ruler under the new form of government they should be considered as palaces and not only as private residences.

The most dramatically situated of these was the so-called Villa Iovis on a high cliff on the edge of Capri, one of reputedly twelve villas Tiberius had built on the island. Its design demonstrates Roman architects' ability to overcome the deficits of any site, including one such as this with sheer cliffs on half the sides, no water source, no building materials on site, and a narrow and perilously steep road as the only access to the irregular and rocky site. Tremendous water cisterns dominate the center of the complex to store any rainwater collected by the roof system, providing the only water source for the palace. The arrangement of rooms also shows how architecture can create a form of climate control with the hot rooms of the bath complex in the southwest corner of the villa and the ambulatories in the north and west to capture the prevailing winds as well as to take advantage of the spectacular views of the Bay of Naples.

Imperial Villa dining room at Sperlonga

Tiberius' other identified villa at Sperlonga on the Tyrrhenian coast south of Rome hosted the most spectacular surviving sculptural display from any imperial residence. The centerpiece of the villa is a grotto dining room, set in a real cave that seems to set the pattern for later dining spaces built in Roman villas with artificial or evocative grottos.

The cave serves as a setting for several sculpture groups. All were discovered in 1957 broken into thousands of fragments, which are still being reassembled, but four distinct groups have been

HISTORICAL CONTEXT
Tiberius at Sperlonga

The grotto is the location of a famous event in which the emperor Tiberius narrowly escaped serious injury from a roof collapse in the cave.

He retired to Campania, and almost everyone firmly believed and openly declared that he would never come back, but would soon die there. And both predictions were all but fulfilled; for he did not return again to Rome, and it chanced a few days later that as he was dining near Tarracina in a villa called the Grotto, many huge rocks fell from the ceiling and crushed a number of the guests and servants, while the emperor himself had a narrow escape. (Suetonius, *Life of Tiberius* 39)

While they were dining at a villa called The Cave, in a natural cavern between the sea at Amyclae and the hills of Fundi, there was a fall of rock at the cave-mouth. Several servants were crushed, and amid the general panic the diners fled. But Sejanus [commander of his guard], braced on hands and knees, face to face, warded the falling boulders off Tiberius. That is how the soldiers who rescued them found him. (Tacitus, *Annals* 4.56)

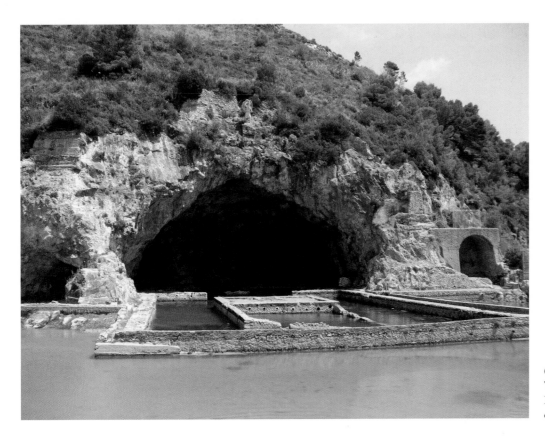

6.6 Grotto dining room of Tiberius, villa at Sperlonga, Italy, *c.* 25 CE. Photo courtesy Steven L. Tuck.

identified and their original locations determined. Two are colossal groups in the dramatic Hellenistic ornate style of Pergamon with large-scale figures surrounded by lifesize men. These are thought by some scholars to date to the time of Augustus, although there is no evidence that he ever resided at the villa.

In a recess at the back of the cave is the largest sculpture group illustrating a scene well known from book 9 of Homer's *Odyssey*. It shows the blinding of the Cyclops Polyphemus by Odysseus and his men who surround his sprawling figure in his cave home. The group represents the anticipatory moment in the narrative, just prior to the plunging of the fiery brand into the eye of the drunken Cyclops. Figures tense and prepare to react to the chaos that will immediately follow. The entire composition relies on long diagonals to create a sense of energy and tension.

The second group in the center of the pool shows the episode, in book 12 of Homer's *Odyssey*, of Scylla attacking Odysseus' ship from her cave and carrying off and consuming some of his few surviving companions, notably the steersman who is lifted bodily off the ship by Scylla's grip on the top of his head. Here the furor of the attack is in full view as the climactic narrative moment is used to full effect as men fight for their lives against Scylla and the dogs that grow out from her waist. The Scylla group is particularly notable because it bears a plaque naming the sculptors as Hagesandros, Athanodoros, and Polydoros of Rhodes. These are the same artists that Pliny the Elder credits with the sculpting of the Laocoon statue, discovered in Rome in 1506 and one of the most famous Greek sculptures to survive from antiquity. In fact, the Sperlonga groups bear great similarities to the Laocoon. The same tremendous energy, struggle, dynamic composition, and narrative moment of the Scylla group are seen in the Laocoon and his sons' fight for life against the serpents sent by Athena. In addition, the face of the Laocoon is very close to that of the Odysseus figure in the Polyphemus group with its open mouth, wild locks of hair, and deeply chiseled beard and expressive brow.

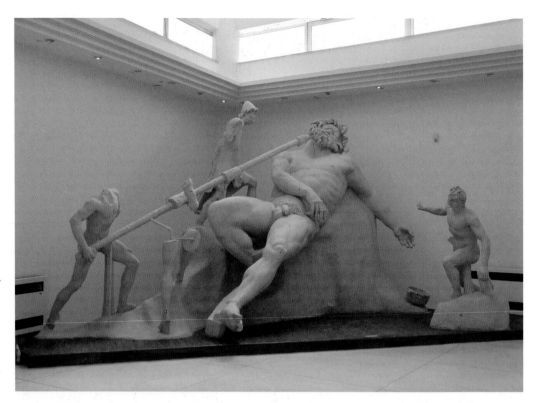

6.7 Sculpture group of Polyphemus, grotto dining room of Tiberius, villa at Sperlonga, Augustan/ Tiberian. Museo Archeologico Nazionale, Sperlonga. Photo courtesy Steven L. Tuck.

6.8 Sculpture group of Scylla, grotto dining room of Tiberius, villa at Sperlonga, Augustan/ Tiberian. Museo Archeologico Nazionale, Sperlonga. Photo courtesy Steven L. Tuck.

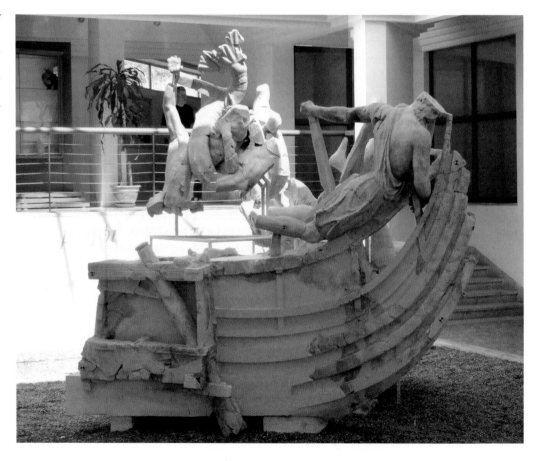

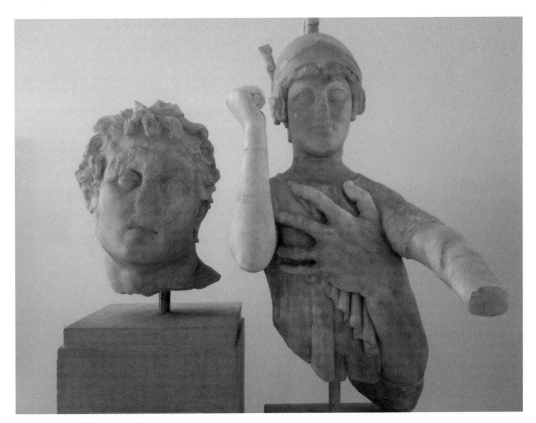

6.9 Sculpture group of Palladium, *c.* 25 CE, grotto dining room of Tiberius, villa at Sperlonga. Museo Archeologico Nazionale, Sperlonga. Photo courtesy Steven L. Tuck.

These Sperlonga sculptures reveal much about Roman residential art including the dominance of Greek mythology in domestic space, and the selection of sculpture – and probably all interior decor – to reinforce the spaces in which they are set. Sperlonga is an extreme example of a trend that we can trace back to the Late Republic. We have a series of letters from Cicero to his friend Atticus asking for thematically appropriate Greek sculptures for various spaces in his villa. At Sperlonga episodes from Greek myth that occurred in caves are displayed in a cave. The use of the space for dining is reinforced in these dining scenes that also operate as socially normative cautionary tales. They illustrate inappropriate dining behavior, a subject found on mosaic floors in lower status Roman dining rooms. Tiberius is known to have enjoyed raising mythological questions at dinner and the decoration of the space may have been designed to inspire such conversation.

The non-colossal sculptures at Sperlonga are not as well preserved but the two groups that flank the pool in the grotto are the so-called Pasquino group and the Palladium group. The Pasquino group, named for a statue of the same group on display in Rome, illustrates a soldier recovering the body of another soldier, lifting it from the ground. The Palladium group shows the capture of the ancient statue of Pallas Athena from Troy, a critical talisman of Trojan and then Roman culture and religion. In both cases these have been analyzed as scenes from the Trojan War cycle. The Palladium group is identified with an episode in which the Greek heroes Diomedes and Odysseus steal the statue. If correct, this links them thematically to the colossal groups that are images of Odysseus and his journey home following the Trojan War.

It is possible as well that these sculpture groups all operate as mythological metaphors for recent events in the lives of the patrons who commissioned them. The figures of Scylla and Polyphemus were used by Sextus Pompey, son of Pompey the Great, as symbols on his coins and public images during his failed civil war in which he was defeated by Augustus. If they refer to Sextus they could be operating as a reminder of Augustus' early victory on display for his guests who would be expected to recognize the scenes and perhaps the association. The Pasquino and Palladium groups might also be metaphors for parallel acts in Tiberius' life. His most famous act of piety was personally retrieving his dead brother's body from where he died on campaign in Germany. Tiberius also returned the Palladium to the temple of Vesta, which he rebuilt after a devastating fire. These groups might have been designed to add to the original colossal groups and to extend the use of the space for mythological metaphor.

SCHOLARLY PERSPECTIVE
Homer's Odyssey *or* Vergil's Aeneid? *Literary inspiration for Sperlonga sculptures*

The colossal sculptures of Scylla and the blinding of Polyphemus from Sperlonga have almost since their discovery been judged by scholars to illustrate the famous episodes of these events in Homer's *Odyssey*. More recently scholars have questioned this association for a number of reasons. Primarily, the details of some figures and the compositions seem to conform better to the accounts of these events in Latin literature, specifically in Vergil's *Aeneid*. The Blinding of Polyphemus sculpture group varies in some key ways from Homer's version, which describes five men gathered around Odysseus while the account in book 3 of the *Aeneid* reflects the position of the Cyclops, the number of men, and their arrangement surrounding him. That may be a subtle difference, but the Scylla shows even clearer correspondence with Vergil's version. Homer describes her in book 12 of the *Odyssey* as having twelve misshapen feet and six necks and heads and three rows of teeth in each of the six mouths. In book 3 of the *Aeneid* she is described very differently, as a girl, human in shape above the waist and with wolves around her belly and dolphin legs, essentially identical to the Sperlonga sculpture. In addition, the action matches Vergil's account with the prostrate steersman ripped off the ship by Scylla. Thus far no consensus has developed between these two views and the lifesize figures are even more strongly contested.

In Greek mythology the Palladium was stolen by Diomedes and Odysseus, but in the Roman tradition it was brought to Rome by Aeneas. As preserved this group does not make the direction of action clear, so it could be argued that it extends either the Greek tradition or the Roman one. The Pasquino group is even more fragmentary and stories of the Trojan War are full of men carrying deceased comrades from the field of battle. If these are Greek heroes it could represent Menelaus retrieving the body of Patroclus, Ajax with the body of Patroclus, or Ajax with the body of Achilles. An alternate Roman theory focuses on Aeneas killing Lausus in book 10 of the *Aeneid* and lifting, with his right arm, the body of the boy from the ground. Certainly this figure is using his right arm and the dead figure is smaller and more slender than the standing one. These arguments have not created a scholarly consensus either. Additional support for Vergil's *Aeneid* as the source is a passage in book 1 in which the Roman hero Aeneas mentions the two episodes of Polyphemus and Scylla while addressing his men at dinner to reassure them of the future with references to dangers past. This speech, book 1: 198–207, reads in part,

> Trojans, this is not our first taste of trouble. You have suffered worse than this, my friends, and God will grant an end to this also. You faced Scylla's fury in her thundering crags and braved the Cyclops' rocks. Recall your courage and put aside your fear and grief … endure and save yourselves for happier times.

Certainly the civil war with Sextus Pompey would count as troubles past and the dining context is identical. That Augustus or Tiberius was associating himself with Aeneas is consistent with early Julio-Claudian image making. In fact, the imperial biographer Suetonius records Tiberius' successor, Caligula, quoting this exact passage in a dining context. The ultimate source or inspiration for the sculptures might illuminate their meaning for the patron or the intended message for an audience of guests. In this case the scholarly world is still debating the issue of Greek versus Roman epic as the ultimate source.

Anne Weis, "Odysseus at Sperlonga: Hellenistic Hero or Roman Heroic Foil?" in N.T. de Grummond and B.S. Ridgway, eds., *From Pergamon to Sperlonga: Sculpture and Context* (University of California Press 2000), 111–165.

CLAUDIUS, 41–54 CE

With the assassination of Caligula on January 24, 41 CE, his uncle, Tiberius Claudius Nero, was selected as the next emperor by the **Praetorian Guard** who discovered him hiding behind a curtain in the palace fearing his own assassination. Instead of killing him, they named him emperor. As the last surviving Julio-Claudian male, Claudius was named emperor almost by default, but he seems to have been a very competent ruler. His family had disregarded him as a political threat largely on account of his physical problems (an unknown medical condition left him lame and with symptoms of neurological problems such as twitching and stuttering). Nevertheless, he was clearly intelligent, even scholarly, writing extensively about Roman and Italic history. He was tutored by the historian Livy and went on to write his own histories of the Republican period and the Etruscans. In his search for a model for his rule, the Republican period was key and many of his administrative actions and benefactions seem to have been based on plans of Julius Caesar, for example his invasion and occupation of Britain. This focus on the Republican period informed his art and architectural commissions including the use of traditional Italic style, muting the emphasis on Classical art seen under Augustus, Tiberius, and Caligula.

Praetorian Guard
the bodyguard of the Roman emperors, formed by Augustus. They guarded the emperor, his palaces, and sometimes acted to remove or create emperors.

Portraiture

Claudius' portraiture follows the Julio-Claudian tradition in many key ways while retaining his own individual traits, such as his protruding ears. Similarities include the proportions, hairstyle, and general and deliberate resemblance to his forebears. Nevertheless, there are elements of Republican and Italic veristic style most notably in his face.

His portraits abandon the ageless look of Augustus and Tiberius and reintroduce signs of aging including pronounced nasolabial grooves, a creased forehead, bags under his eyes, and, most notably in later portraits, loose skin around his jaw and neck. The colossal marble portrait now in the Vatican with the attributes of Jupiter demonstrates these features and his reliance on Late Republican forms with a veristic head combined with an idealized Hellenistic inspired body. Even so, the image is one that reinforces the power of the *princeps* and his position as Jupiter's representative, a variation of the message seen in the upper register of the Gemma Augustea.

Britain, which came under Roman power under Claudius, provides examples of the artistic dialogue that took place in the provinces. The bronze portrait of Claudius, found in Suffolk in Britain and theorized to have come from an equestrian statue from the Roman colony at Colchester (Camulodunum), demonstrates the regional variation of imperial portraiture. Claudius' ears and a clearly Julio-Claudian hairstyle are combined with a smoother, arguably more abstracted face, a style that comes to dominate Roman portraiture in later

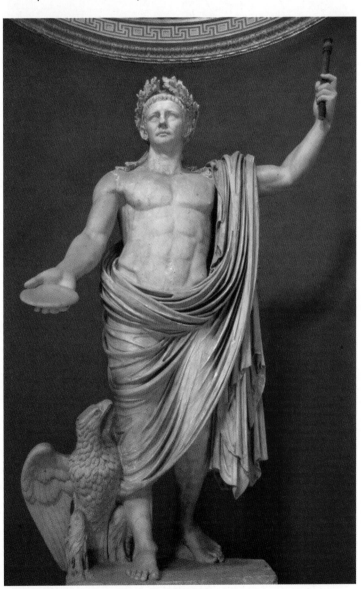

6.10 Portrait of Claudius with attributes of Jupiter, 42 CE, Lanuvium, Italy. Musei Vaticani, Rome. H 8 ft 4 in (2.54 m), marble. Photo courtesy Steven L. Tuck.

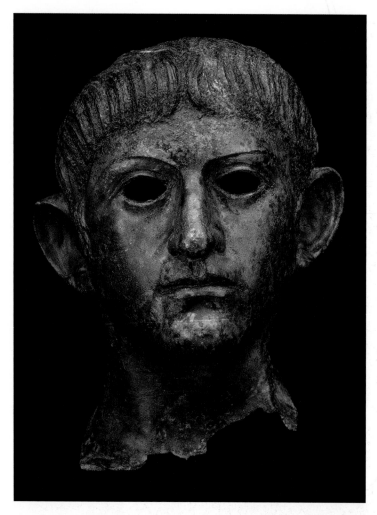

6.11 Bronze head of Claudius, *c.* 50 CE, found at the River Alde at Rendham, Suffolk, perhaps originally from Colchester. British Museum, London. H 11 ¾ in (30 cm). Source: © The Trustees of the British Museum. All rights reserved.

centuries. The adoption of Julio-Claudian styles of portraiture in Britain is seen in a funeral relief of a soldier, Marcus Favonius, who died at Colchester before 60 CE. His tombstone features a high relief image of him standing with a Julio-Claudian hair style with hints of the style in his facial features. The tombstone itself served to project Roman political and military authority in the new province. The inscription mentions the Roman army, but more powerfully the image of a Roman soldier would be recognizable as the most tangible symbol of occupation even if the Claudian elements weren't identified.

Dynastic monuments

Claudius, especially given his succession by violence and without public selection by his predecessor, had the need for dynastic monuments to reinforce his position and connect him back to the dynasty while promoting his own offspring as possible successors.

Grand Camée

One of these monuments is the largest presentation cameo surviving from antiquity, the Grand Camée, which is difficult not to compare to the Gemma Augustea, on which it might have been based. The date of the gem is based on the identities of the figures, which scholars continue to debate. Some scholars favor a Tiberian date, others a recutting from an original made under Tiberius, and still others conclude that it should be dated to the time of Claudius. The gem perhaps dates to the period just after Nero's adoption and is a component of a program to solidify his position in the dynasty. The only real evidence is the gem itself, its figures and carving, both of which are more complex, and therefore perhaps later, than the Gemma Augustea. Its five layers of sardonyx are carved into three major registers of relief decoration showing the developing need for Julio-Claudian dynastic display to equally emphasize its past, present, and future.

The lowest register is crowded with captive barbarians in the aftermath of a successful Roman battle. The date of the gem is based on the identity of the figures in the central register, surrounded by the other individuals and figuratively the world. They have been identified as an enthroned Tiberius and his mother, Livia, with Germanicus standing before them being appointed to the office of *quaestor* in 26 CE. This seems unlikely as the office is not so grand as to seem to demand such a commemoration nor does the standing figure look like Germanicus. Instead, here we follow the alternative school of thought that the central group depicts a divine Claudius, holding a scepter as in the colossal Vatican portrait, enthroned with his fourth wife, Agrippina. One of the captive barbarians sits at their feet. Before the throne are Claudius' children and heirs representing the future of the dynasty. Foremost, in military dress as if taking credit for the victory in the register below, is Nero, adopted by Claudius when he married Agrippina, accompanied by his wife and stepsister, Octavia, who turns to look at him. The close correspondence between these figures and other, accepted, images of them makes the date of the gem likely 50 CE. Behind them are Claudius' younger children, Britannicus and Antonia. In the upper register are key deceased members of the family. Claudius'

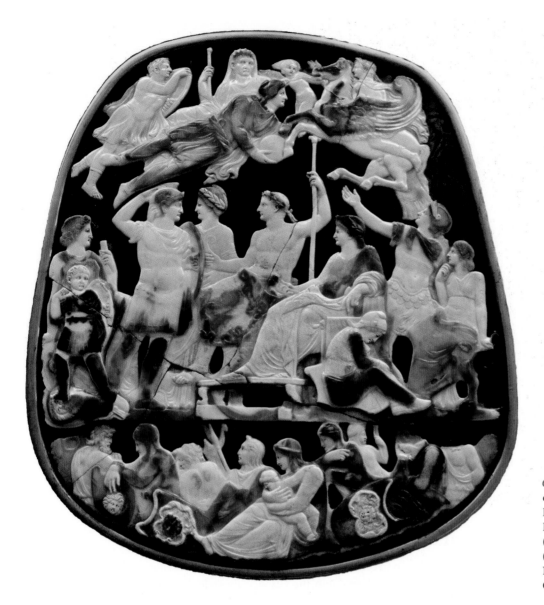

6.12 Grand Camée, *c.* 50 CE. Cabinet des Médailles, Bibliothèque Nationale, Paris. Sardonyx, H 12 ¼ in (31 cm) W 10 ⅜ in (26.5 cm). Marie-Lan Nguyen/Wikimedia Commons.

mother, Antonia, bears the attributes of Venus Genetrix including a cupid accompanying her at her left shoulder and ascends on the back of Aeternitas, the personification of eternity. Behind her, bearing a shield, is her deceased eldest son, Germanicus, while facing them across the gem ascending on Pegasus is her husband and Claudius' father, Drusus.

Claudius needed to bolster his position by associating himself with the extended dynasty especially by drawing visual connections between himself, Julius Caesar, and Augustus in his public art program. An example of this display is found on a fragmentary marble relief from Ravenna modeled on imperial portrait groups of free-standing statues known from across the Roman world. All of the figures display Classicizing proportions and most stand with very pronounced contrapposto. Italic elements include a hierarchy of scale rather than Classical isocephaly, as well as the combination of portrait heads on idealized bodies.

Five figures are preserved on the relief in various poses and with a range of attributes; all are barefoot, a conventional representation of their divinity. To the far right stands the tallest figure, Augustus, crowned with the *corona civica* with a scepter or spear in his right hand and a thunderbolt in his left while resting his left foot on a globe, displaying the *imperium sine fine* granted to him by Jupiter.

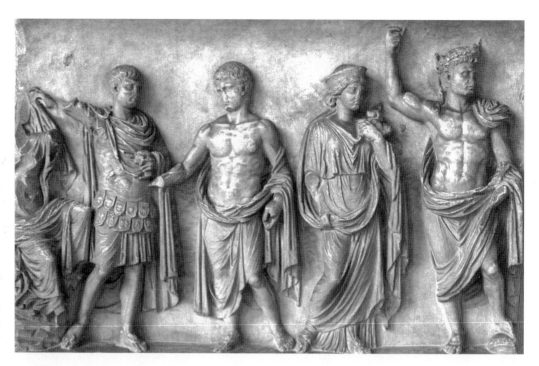

To the left is a Julio-Claudian woman, probably Livia, with the attributes of Venus Genetrix, as the founder of the dynasty. The central figure is Divus Julius, recognizable by the star on his forehead, a symbol associated with him since the comet appeared during his funeral games. The cuirassed figure to the left of him might be Germanicus or Drusus. The final seated figure is another female with drapery based on styles from fifth century BCE Athens. She is probably Claudius' mother, Antonia. The relief serves to create a link between Claudius and Augustus, the founder of the dynasty, by equating Claudius' parents with Augustus and Livia.

Historical reliefs

Historical reliefs, common in earlier periods, are rarer under Claudius, but one outstanding example shows the intrusion of Italic forms into the Classicizing style. The so-called *Vicomagistri* relief records a procession of sacrificial attendants accompanying the *vicomagistri*, a group of priests (*magistri*) who were responsible for rituals that protected the *vici*, the neighborhood districts of Rome. They worshipped at shrines erected at the boundaries of their districts, usually at significant

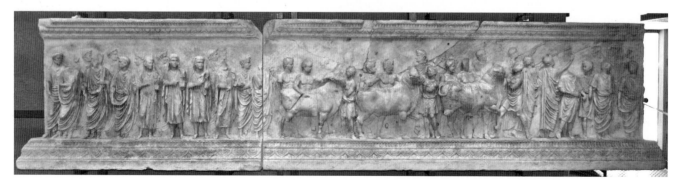

6.14 Relief from the Altar of the *Vicomagistri*, Rome, Claudian. Musei Vaticani, Rome. Marble, H 3 ⅜ ft (1.04 m) L 5 ¾ ft (1.76 m). Photo courtesy John Pollini.

A VIEW FROM THE PROVINCES
Shrine for the worship of the emperors at Aphrodisias

A sanctuary complex excavated at Aphrodisias in Caria provides superb evidence of the spread of the worship of emperors in the Julio-Claudian period, its reception by people in a distant, Greek-speaking city, and the imagery of this new cult in the statues and sculptural reliefs that decorated the sanctuary. The sculptures offer a picture of the emperor and Roman power seen from the Greek East, evidence found nowhere else in the eastern provinces. The complex, known as a Sebasteion, was designed for the worship of the deified emperors, the current emperor, Nero, and Aphrodite, worshipped both as patron of the city and as Venus Genetrix, founder of the Julio-Claudian family who traced their descent from her son, Aeneas.

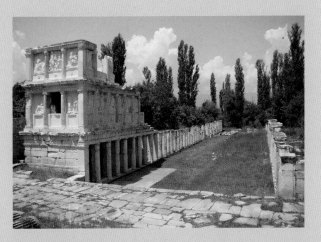

6.15 Sebasteion at Aphrodisias, Turkey, 1st cent. CE. View down the length of the complex. Note the restored three-story facade on the left with copies of the relief panels inserted. Photo courtesy Francesca Tronchin.

The complex consists of a long rectangular paved area (46 x 295 ft; 14 x 90 m) entered by a monumental gateway on one of the short ends; the opposite end stops at the steps of the imperial temple. The facade of the gateway had niches that originally held large marble statues, now missing. Their inscribed bases survive and identify the subjects as members of the Julio-Claudian family and their mythical ancestors. The wide selection of members of the imperial family, including Tiberius Claudius Drusus, the son of the emperor Claudius, who died young in the 20s CE, suggests a desire by the local benefactors to honor the entire family as a dynastic unit. The enclosed area is flanked by two three-story porticoes decorated with 180 large relief panels in the upper two stories.

This assemblage, the largest component of the sanctuary decoration, can be analyzed by subject: Greek mythology, allegorical representations, and imperial images, or by theme: the Roman Empire, the Greek world within it, and the imperial family. Images of myth filled the second story of the facade including very common scenes such as Leda and the Swan, Demeter, Bellerophon and Pegasus, Orestes, Meleager and the boar, Lapiths and Centaurs, Achilles, Apollo, and Hercules. Judging from the lack of inscriptions on the panels, viewers were expected to recognize the scenes without captions.

The third story panels included allegorical and imperial subjects, categories with much overlap. Many of the surviving allegories are single, standing, draped women, all identified as ethnic generalizations by distinct dress or attributes. Each represents a people conquered and made part of the Roman Empire, giving the sanctuary a visual definition of the physical extent of Roman power. Such displays are known from Rome beginning with Pompey and survive from the time of Hadrian, but have never before been found in a provincial city. In addition to the ethnic figures, personifications of abstractions such as Day and Ocean were part of the display, giving the sense of a theme of *imperium sine fine* as found at Rome.

The imperial family panels consist of eleven extant reliefs, which include Augustus, Livia, Tiberius, Claudius, Agrippina, and Nero. Two of the best-preserved reliefs demonstrate the incorporation of the ethnic figures and imperial portraiture into powerful images of Roman conquest. The Claudius and Britannia panel, celebrating his

(Continued)

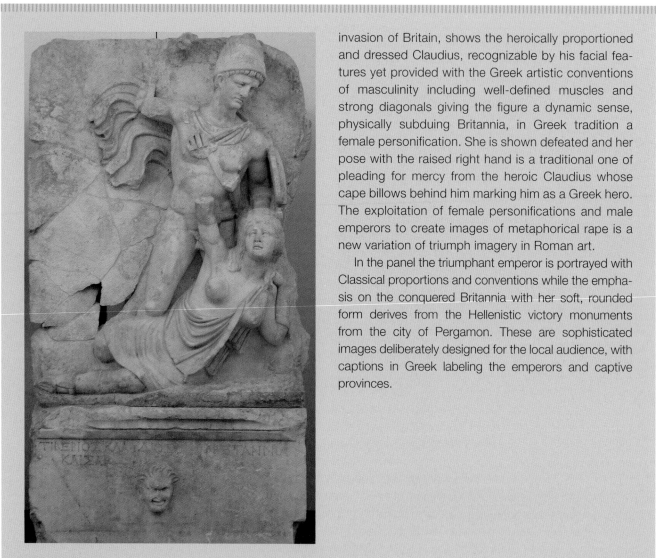

invasion of Britain, shows the heroically proportioned and dressed Claudius, recognizable by his facial features yet provided with the Greek artistic conventions of masculinity including well-defined muscles and strong diagonals giving the figure a dynamic sense, physically subduing Britannia, in Greek tradition a female personification. She is shown defeated and her pose with the raised right hand is a traditional one of pleading for mercy from the heroic Claudius whose cape billows behind him marking him as a Greek hero. The exploitation of female personifications and male emperors to create images of metaphorical rape is a new variation of triumph imagery in Roman art.

In the panel the triumphant emperor is portrayed with Classical proportions and conventions while the emphasis on the conquered Britannia with her soft, rounded form derives from the Hellenistic victory monuments from the city of Pergamon. These are sophisticated images deliberately designed for the local audience, with captions in Greek labeling the emperors and captive provinces.

6.16   Relief of Claudius conquering Britannia, Sebasteion at Aphrodisias, Neronian. H 65 in (165 cm) W 53 in (135 cm) D 17 in (43 cm). Photo courtesy Francesca Tronchin.

crossroads. In this relief a group in procession demonstrates Claudian sculptural style in frontality as well as in hairstyles and facial features. Notable is the appearance of beards here as well when all of the highest status Romans are clean-shaven. The composition utilizes Italic conventions to display the *vicomagistri* by having the second row of figures elongated with their heads above the front rank but their feet completely absent, violating Classical proportions as well as the convention of isocephaly. It is clearly important that they are visible to the viewer and that their participation (presumably by number rather than identifying them by facial features) is recorded.

Architecture

Little architecture that can be assigned to Claudius survives although he is securely associated with the foundation of Portus, the artificial harbor of Rome at the mouth of the Tiber, a project envisioned by Julius Caesar. Perhaps the largest Claudian architecture extant is the Porta Maggiore in Rome.

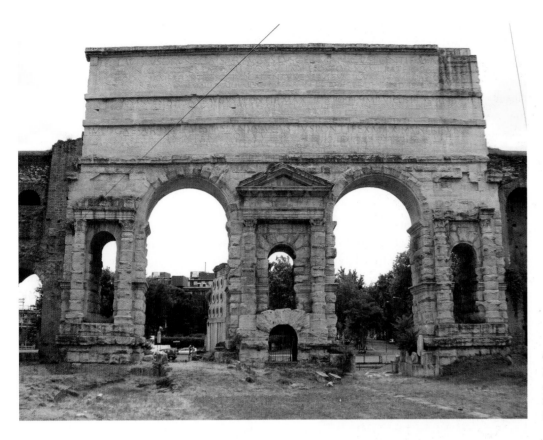

6.17 Porta Maggiore, Rome, 52 CE, with rusticated block masonry, white travertine. Photo courtesy Steven L. Tuck.

This city gate was originally built by Claudius in 52 CE and serves as a bridge over the road for the aqueducts that meet and enter the city at this point. Like the city gate at Saepinum and the later Porta Nigra at Trier (Figure 12.3) it created a grand monument that proclaimed the boundaries of the city to all who arrived on this road. The aqueducts themselves served to announce the power and generosity of Claudius. It was later incorporated into the third-century CE city defenses. The Claudian architecture is deliberately old-fashioned. The blocks are rusticated, that is, the edges are smoothed but the sides are roughly chiseled to give a sense of age. The resulting heaviness emphasizes the mass and solidity of the construction while implying age, probably an allusion to Republican architecture, the period of Claudius' scholarly interest and the one that also provided the clearest contribution to his sculptural style. Other examples of this style include a Claudian colonnade with rusticated column drums at Portus and the platform of the Temple of the Deified Claudius of Neronian date.

NERO, 54–68 CE

Nero Claudius Caesar was born Lucius Domitius Ahenobarbus in 37 CE to Agrippina the Younger and Gnaeus Domitius Ahenobarbus. After his mother became Claudius' fourth wife he was adopted by Claudius in 50 CE. His succession in 54 CE at the age of seventeen ushered in a period of good government apparently largely administered by Seneca, the stoic philosopher, and Burrus, commander of the guard. Nero's murder of his mother, Agrippina, in 59 CE and Seneca and Burrus' fall from power in 62 CE left the Roman world in Nero's hands directly and removed the restraining influences on his behavior. Now free to act as he wished, he openly began to pursue his interests in music, theater, and poetry along with chariot racing. Meanwhile terrible events such as the earthquake of 62 CE along the Bay of Naples and the great fire of Rome in 64 CE led to consequent building booms in both of these areas and further opportunities in Rome for Nero to explore his vision in architecture. Nero's rule after the great fire became marked by increasing instability in his personal and political life including construction of his Domus Aureus (Golden House) in 64 CE. His suicide in 68 CE following provincial revolts ushered in a short civil war of 68–69 CE, bringing the Julio-Claudian dynasty to a close. A note on the dates of the Pompeian material in this chapter: some of these are placed here rather than under the Flavians (next chapter) because of their reliance on Neronian forms and the likelihood that they were conceived of and started by 68 CE, six years after the earthquake.

Portraiture of Nero

The portraiture of youthful Nero follows Julio-Claudian examples, especially the patterns of Caligula and Claudius. Once he comes to power and asserts his control after 58 CE, we see changes in his portraiture that defy the dynastic patterns. It is thought that he is asserting connections to his blood family, the Domitius Ahenobarbus, perhaps as part of his wishes to rule without the interference or influence of his adopted family, the Julio-Claudians.

What is indisputable is that his image becomes heavier with an increasingly massive neck and fleshy face featuring rounded cheeks and a double chin. The Julio-Claudian bowl cut is replaced by a new coiffure with thick waves of hair and bangs that lie like a series of parallel commas across his forehead, which may reflect his actual hairstyle as described in extant literature such as Suetonius' biography (51), "He was utterly shameless in the care of his person and in his dress, always having his hair arranged in tiers of curls, and during the trip to Greece also letting it grow long and hang down behind."

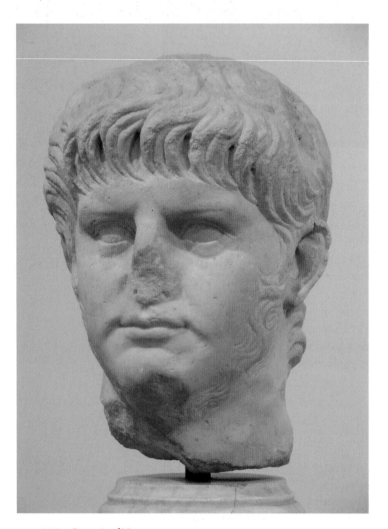

6.18   Portrait of Nero, 59 CE, Palatine Hill, Rome. Museo Palatino, Rome. H 1 ft 1 in (33 cm), marble. Photo courtesy Steven L. Tuck.

Portraiture of Julio-Claudian women

Outside of cemeteries public portraits of women were almost unprecedented in Rome prior to the founding of the principate. Pliny the Elder mentions only three mythical or mytho-historical portraits of Roman women in public civic space before the time of Augustus. Men were celebrated for their contributions to the state, but women, barred from public office, lacked the outlets for public service. Consequently, by the time of the Julio-Claudian dynasty there was no tradition of public images of women and therefore no dress or attributes that conveyed official status. The iconography of imperial women had to be created from nothing and its form established to serve the needs of the dynasty, meaning that the portraits of imperial women reflect the ideology of imperial rule and the new public positions of women in this system of government.

The earliest imperial women granted public statues were Augustus' wife, Livia, and sister, Octavia. The portraits of Livia provide ample evidence for the range of images created to establish an imperial identity for Livia and to bolster the regimes of her husband and son. This was often achieved through creating divine associations between Livia and various divinities, elevating Livia above other mortal women and equating her with particular goddesses. In a few of the over a hundred extant examples that survive, Livia is portrayed with the ideal youthful features seen in the portraiture of Augustus, but also with the attributes of the Roman agricultural goddess Ceres. Portraits from Rome and Puteoli (the second city of Italy on the Bay of Naples) are over-lifesize images of Livia dressed as a Roman matron in *stola* and *palla*, dress and mantle. She bears in her left hand a cornucopia and in her right probably a sheaf of wheat, and wears a crown of flowers. The example from Rome adds to the floral crown a ritual headband worn by the priestesses of Ceres. A cameo gem in the Kunsthistorisches Museum, Vienna combines the *stola*, veil, and crown with the poppies and wheat of Ceres as well, giving us evidence that this display was used in multiple images in a variety of media. The divine guise used for Livia consists of a number of elements that would have resonated with the Roman audiences such as the floral crown and veil combination from Paestum. The crown alludes to the abundance of Ceres and the veil to her role as matron, wife of Augustus and mother of Tiberius, under which emperors these versions were created.

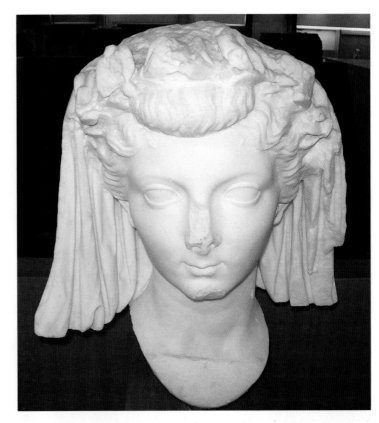

6.19   Portrait of Livia Augusta, mother of Tiberius, Paestum, early Tiberian. Museo Archeologico Nazionale di Paestum. Marble. Photo courtesy Steven L. Tuck.

The consistency in the use of divine imagery among Julio-Claudian imperial women is demonstrated in the portrait of Antonia Minor, mother of Claudius, found in the remains of a dining room/grotto in an imperial villa at the site of Punta Epitaffio on the edge of the Bay of Naples. Like the earlier villa at Sperlonga, the dining room was dominated by a statue group of Odysseus and his men in the cave of the Cyclops Polyphemus. A variety of imperial portraits that made up a group resembling the Ravenna relief filled the wall niches in the room. The image of Antonia Minor wears an intricate tracery diadem and the dress and attributes of Venus Genetrix, including the Eros on her left shoulder. The iconography is familiar from the Ravenna relief but was utilized by the dynasty in the Forum of Julius Caesar as well as on the pediment of the Temple of Mars Ultor, dedicated by Augustus. Here, the imagery is Claudian and redirects divine founder imagery from Livia to Antonia, her successor in this role. A portrait of Claudius' father Germanicus was found with it, making a clear statement of the needs of Claudius to bolster his imperial position and that of his branch of the family.

The needs of an imperial dynasty are not only to aggrandize predecessors. Descendants need to be incorporated into the visual system as well and if they have equal claims to the throne then it is necessary to elevate one of them to reinforce the position of the ruler. Also in the dining room display at the Punta Epitaffio villa is a statue of a minor girl of the Julio-Claudian dynasty. Her hair style combines elements of the coiffure of Claudia Antonia, the eldest daughter of the emperor Claudius, with those of Nero, and evidence suggests that she is Claudia Augusta, the daughter of Nero, who died at the age of three and was deified by Nero. Her body shape is plump and pre-pubescent. Other than her hairstyle, her only other attribute is a moth she holds in her extended hand, referencing the figure of Psyche, whose name in Greek means both spirit and butterfly or moth.

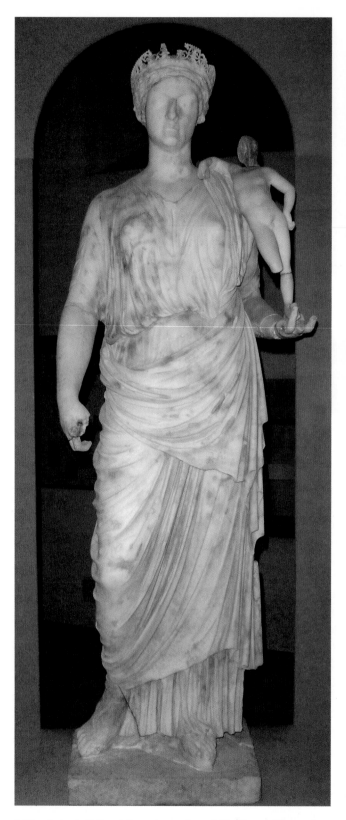

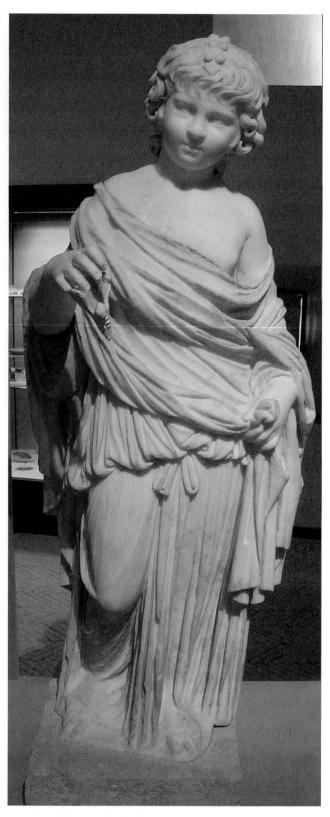

6.20 Antonia (Minor) Augusta, mother of Claudius, as Venus Genetrix statue, *c.* 50 CE, imperial villa at Punta Epitaffio, Italy. Museo Archeologico dei Campi Flegrei, Baia. H 5 ft (1.55 m), marble. Photo courtesy Steven L. Tuck.

6.21 Claudia Augusta as Psyche statue, *c.* 64 CE, imperial villa at Punta Epitaffio, Italy. Museo Archeologico dei Campi Flegrei, Baia. H 3 ft 11 in (1.2 m), marble. Photo courtesy Steven L. Tuck.

Palace architecture

It is impossible to separate Nero's palace architecture and the interior decor it introduced. Both of these components represent revolutionary moments in Roman art and architecture and seem designed to reinforce each other. Nero's first palace, the Domus Transitoria or Passageway Palace, was designed to link imperial properties on the Palatine and Esquiline hills. Only two suites of rooms remain, but these hint at its revolutionary architecture and the beginnings of what is termed the Roman architectural revolution, which we see more fully in the Domus Aurea, Nero's second palace.

The design rejected traditional rectangular rooms and **post and lintel architecture**, instead utilizing concrete to create barrel vaults lifting the ceilings of rooms, freeing up interior spaces from supporting walls, and allowing high windows so that raking light poured into the rooms. The interiors were designed with water features such as fountains and pools, which added visual interest, light, and helped cool the rooms. Rooms were decorated with cut marble floors and wall paintings with large amounts of white background, which also emphasized the available light.

post and lintel architecture a building system with a horizontal feature (lintel) supported by two vertical features (posts or columns) to create open space such as rooms or doorways.

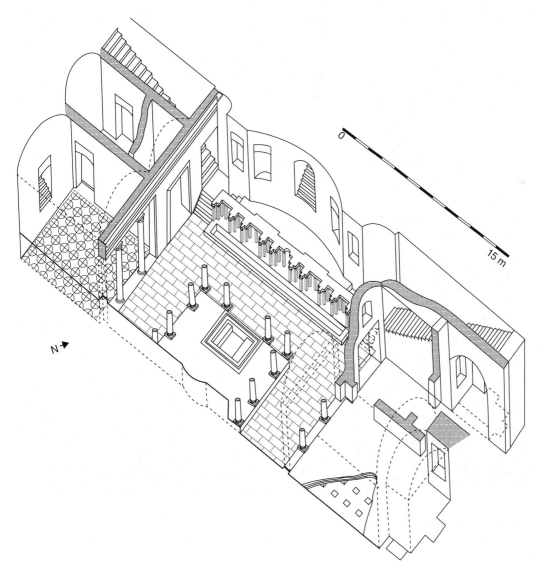

6.22 Plan of the Domus Transitoria, Rome, 62 CE. Roman Imperial Architecture, J.B. Ward-Perkins, Yale University Press, 1970. Drawing by Sheila Gibson.

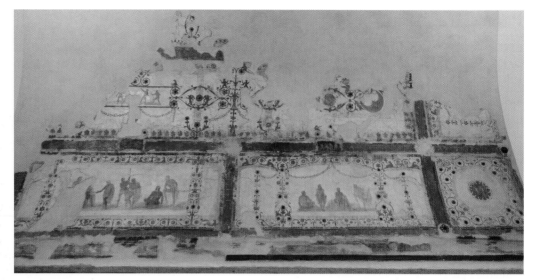

6.23 Ceiling painting from the Domus Transitoria, Rome, 62 CE. Museo Palatino, Rome. Photo courtesy Steven L. Tuck.

One of these paintings shows the innovative white ground design that ushered in one phase of the Fourth Style of Roman wall painting. Fourth Style painting was more eclectic and complex than the previous styles. In some ways it incorporates elements of all three. From First Style we see the faux imported stones, now relegated largely to the dado. From Second Style, the illusionistic space and architecture, now found in subsidiary sections of wall such as the attic story and side panels. From Third Style, the use of faux framed panel paintings as the central features in many walls. Lighter and brighter colors now replace the darker colors of Third Style, however, though the wide variations found in Fourth Style include all of the earlier color palettes as well.

In the Domus Transitoria example of wall painting, the wall was divided into rectangular fields with fine-lined tracery borders with figures and animals as seen in Third Style painting. A new element of design, embedded gems, a feature of Nero's wall treatments described by the historian Tacitus, also reflected light and added color to the composition without darkening it. The subject is Homeric and the style for this mythological scene is Hellenistic Greek with short brushstrokes creating impressionistic figures defined by varying shades of browns. The Hellenistic style is appropriate as one of the first Greek painters who moved to Italy was a Greek of the Hellenistic period, Demetrius Topographus, Demetrius the Landscape Painter. That style had been used for such paintings for over a century by this time.

Domus Aurea, Nero's Golden House

After the great fire of 64 CE, Nero rebuilt his palace on a grand scale. At the time, many Romans believed that Nero's desire to build a new palace motivated him to set the fire himself. The Domus Aurea, Golden House, that replaced the Domus Transitoria was designed by the architects Severus and Celer and took over the center of Rome, covering perhaps three hundred acres and dominating four of the fourteen neighborhoods. The front portico was a mile long and the entrance was marked by a statue of Nero over a hundred feet tall. When the house was completed Nero was reported to have remarked, "Now at last I can begin to live like a human being" (Suetonius, *Nero* 31).

One of the central features was a rotating banquet hall described by the biographer Suetonius. The architects of the Domus Aurea developed the use of brick-faced concrete architecture found in the earlier Domus Transitoria. As far as we can tell, this was the most ambitious and innovative

(a)

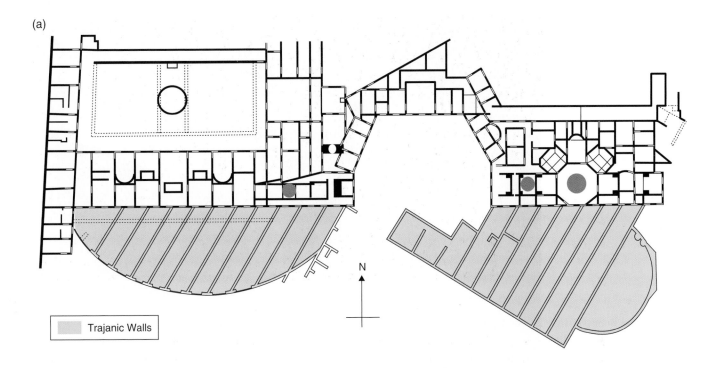

Trajanic Walls

N

(b)

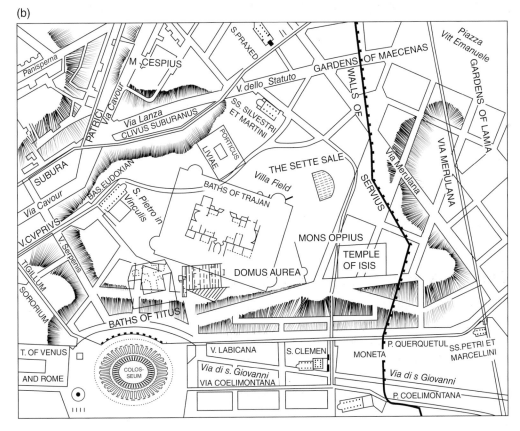

6.24a and 6.24b Plan and map, Domus Aurea, Rome, 64 CE. (a) Plan: ARCHAEOLOGIS. (b) Map: Pianta della Regio III, Isis et Serapis, Lanciani, R., *The Ruins & Excavations of ancient Rome*, London 1897. Macmillan. Fig. 136.

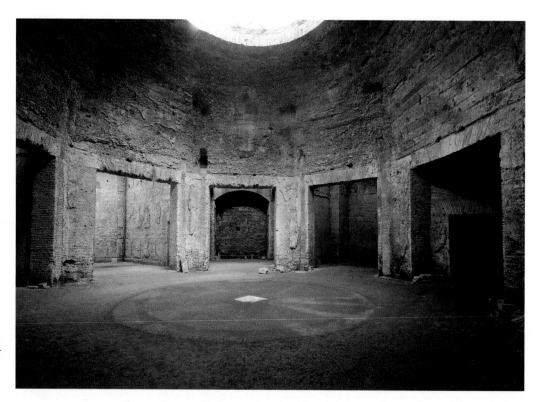

6.25 "Dining room" in the Domus Aurea, Rome, 64 CE. Source: © 2014. Photo Scala, Florence. Courtesy of the Ministero Beni e Att. Culturali.

use of concrete so far and arguably a major building in the Roman architectural revolution, the Roman building revolution that exploited concrete to create new forms that emphasized height, light, round over square spaces, and the use of color and water in room interiors. In the Domus Aurea the architects used concrete to create novel rooms roofed experimentally with vaults, half vaults, and segmented domes. Once again, light filled the halls and suites of rooms from windows and transoms, almost all of which occurred at dramatic angles, creating raking light throughout the complex for an unprecedented size and scale of domestic architecture.

The Fourth Style interior fresco painting that covered most of the walls and vaulted ceilings was attributed in antiquity to a painter whose name is uncertain, either Famulus or Fabulus. He is said to have painted while wearing a toga, an improbable feat which tells us at least about his desire to celebrate his Roman citizenship, itself unusual in a Roman wall painter, when the majority of known artists were low status. The best-preserved paintings, such as the ceiling in room 119, show a white ground composition divided into concentric rectangular zones, often further defined by raised stucco work, with a central rectangular field for a figural painting. Like the Domus Transitoria the subjects are almost exclusively related to the Trojan War.

The panel of Achilles on Skyros displays elements of Hellenistic Greek painting conventions in skin tone, use of dramatic diagonals, and atmospheric perspective. The composition seems to be based on Hellenistic battle scenes as seen in the Alexander mosaic in the House of the Faun at Pompeii (Figure 4.21) and the relief on the Aemilius Paullus monument at Delphi (Figure 4.31). Some of the wall paintings, such as the long corridor 50 painting, create architectural frames that are superficially or distantly related to the *scaenae frons*, the multi-story decorated backdrop of the Roman theater stage. This virtual architecture does not reproduce an actual stage building, but uses units of projecting and receding bays with figures to fill the long and tall wall space with a two-story facade of multi-story columns and doorways filled with figures. The illusion of real space and architecture is shattered by the high blank dado panel at the base of the wall, which raises the structure over three feet off the floor.

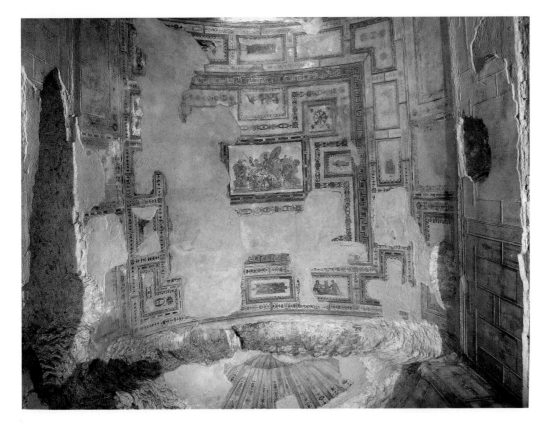

6.26 Ceiling painting of Achilles on Scyros, Room 119, Domus Aurea, Rome, 64 CE. Photo courtesy Steven L. Tuck.

PUBLIC BUILDINGS AND INTERIOR DECORATION, POMPEII

Arguments persist among scholars about how representative or unique Pompeii is as a Roman site. Nevertheless, it is clear that it preserves many of the same motifs, subjects, and styles of interior decoration seen at the imperial level in Rome, but instead in sub-imperial domestic and public spaces. The earthquake of 62 CE also provides a critical *terminus post quem* for dating much of the decoration, providing valuable evidence for Neronian period art outside of Nero's own palaces. At Pompeii the macellum, Stabian Baths, and sanctuary of Isis all display various elements of Neronian painting and wall decoration, defined here at Pompeii as Fourth Style, the final phase of painting in the sequence identified and named by August Mau.

The concept of decoration that reflects, reinforces, or extends the activities and behavior in a particular space is found in the macellum, the food market, in the northeast corner of the forum at Pompeii. Although badly damaged by the eruption of 79 CE, the interior wall paintings along the west side are well enough preserved to read the decorative program in the space. The wall is divided into tripartite zones both horizontally and vertically with a supporting dado, central panel, and upper attic zone in each of the three parts of the wall. Between each of the three zones are apparent openings filled with perspective architecture in which stand human figures, as in the *scaenae frons* painting in the long corridor at the Domus Aurea. The upper zones are filled with still life paintings of poultry, fish, bread, fruit, and flowers, many laid out on counters, seemingly echoing the actual products available in the stalls and shops below. The central panels are black fields with wide red borders each of which has a mythological panel painted in the center. The subjects of the two best-preserved paintings include Odysseus and his loyal wife Penelope in one panel and Zeus' punished lover Io and her guardian Argus in the other. The theme seems to be female virtue and the intent is

terminus post quem literally "time after which" referring to the notion that a datable object or event only tells us the date after which something might have occurred.

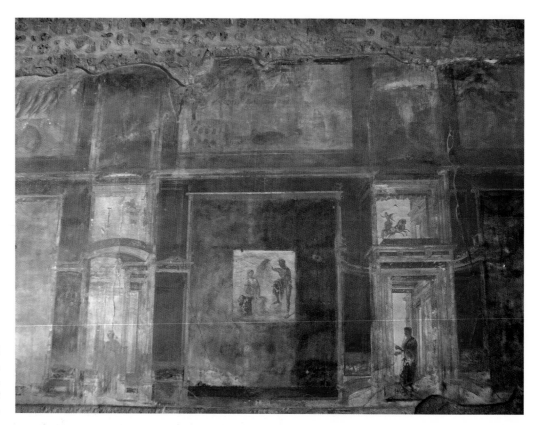

6.27 Wall paintings of still life and mythological scene, macellum, Pompeii, *c.* 64 CE. Photo courtesy Steven L. Tuck.

thought to be socially normative. A largely female audience doing their marketing would be confronted with large panels representing positive and negative female roles from Greek mythology, the positive Penelope rewarded while the negative Io was punished.

Painted stucco decoration, Stabian Baths, Pompeii

The Stabian Baths complex was one of the three main public bath complexes uncovered at Pompeii. The complex is organized around a large open area, a *palaestra*, which served as an exercise ground with porticoes on three sides providing shade for walking and lounging. The largest unbroken and exposed stretch of wall is on the west side of the *palaestra* and is highly visible to those entering the complex from the main entrance on the south side.

The wall is filled with a large integrated decorative work in stucco relief of a two- or three-story architectural framework of the *scaenae frons* type with alternating projecting and receding units of slender architecture creating illusionistic spaces. Many of these spaces are filled with stucco figures, ornaments, or painted scenes. The entire wall was originally brightly painted in panels of red, black, blue, and yellow reminiscent of the corridor at the Domus Aurea. In this instance gods are recognizable among the figures, notably Jupiter occupying the panel just above an open doorway, a very prominent location in the composition. The decoration clearly relies on Neronian models and illustrates the transmission of wall decoration from the highest status Roman residence into a public facility in a Roman colony.

Sanctuary of Isis, Pompeii

The sanctuary of Isis at Pompeii provides the best-preserved example of a cult site to this deity whose worship developed in Egypt and spread throughout the Roman world. Interest in Egypt and Egyptian art seems to have picked up momentum after Augustus brought Egypt into the Roman Empire in

(a)

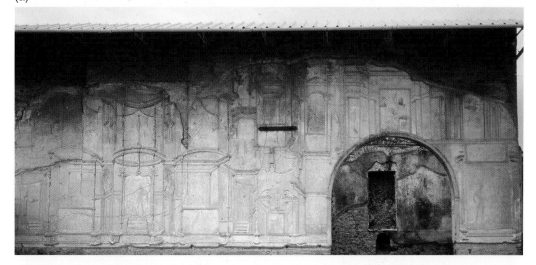

(b)

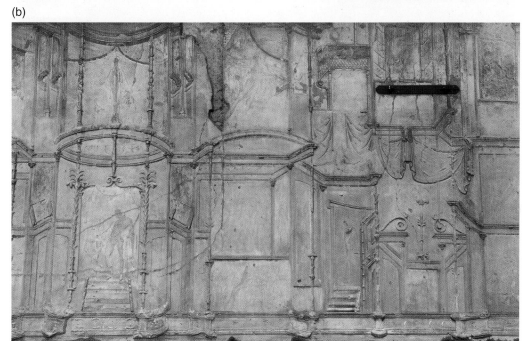

6.28a and 6.28b Stucco wall treatment, Stabian Baths, Pompeii, *c.* 64 CE. (a) Photo courtesy Steven L. Tuck; (b) Source: akg-images / Erich Lessing.

30 BCE. This may be because of increased access or because of emulation of Egyptian motifs in the domestic spaces of the Augustan household. The sanctuary also gives us the firmest evidence for post-earthquake construction and decoration at Pompeii; its dedicatory inscription cites the damage to the sanctuary in the earthquake as the reason for the rebuilding by N. Popidius Celsinus.

Much of the structure of the temple and associated buildings is in brick, which was originally coated with a thick layer of stucco creating the image of a grander complex of cut stone masonry. As in the Stabian Baths the stucco was painted and created decorative schemes that reflect the most recent trends in Roman art. A small building in the southeast corner of the sanctuary is a walled, roofless enclosure with a single door flanked by stucco pilasters under the front **arcuated pediment**. The building probably served as a baptistery as it contained a tank believed to hold the Nile water important in the rites of Isis.

arcuated pediment also known as a Syrian pediment, combines the standard triangular pediment with a semi-circular arch which usually fills the center of the pediment.

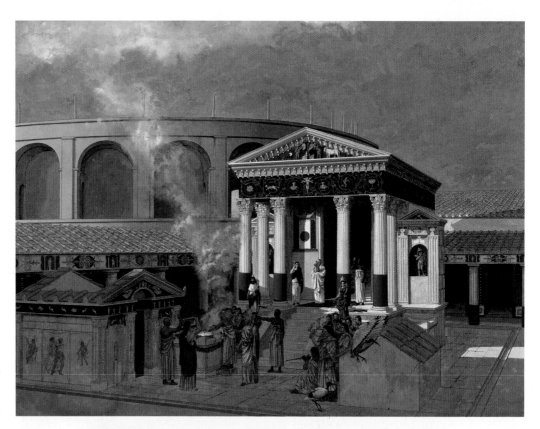

6.29 Sanctuary of Isis, Pompeii, *c.* 62 CE, reconstruction. Source: akg-images/Peter Connolly.

biclinium
a Roman dining room or space with two dining couches rather than the usual three found in a *triclinium*.

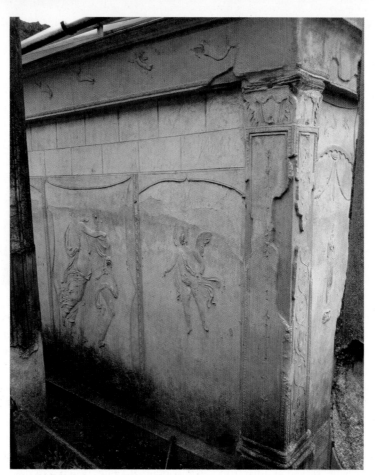

6.30 Sanctuary of Isis, Pompeii, exterior of baptistery, *c.* 62 CE. Photo courtesy Steven L. Tuck.

ART AND LITERATURE
Latin literature and Roman domestic decoration

Scenes from Greek mythology make up the dominant figural subject in Roman mosaics and wall paintings and are also an important component of sculpture. This heavy reliance on Greek myths has raised a number of questions. What were expectations of audience recognition of the stories, and their familiarity with the range of Greek myth, especially in the absence of captions? What are the meanings of these in interior decor? Can we trace the sources for the stories, more specifically whether the scenes represent generic representations, scenes from pattern books copied by artists, or illustrations of specific versions of the stories from particular works of literature? Material from Pompeii aids us in answering these questions. A wall painting from the House of Siricus, Pompeii shows a scene with all of the elements taken from *Aeneid* 12.398–429 in which the wounded Aeneas stands as described by Vergil, leaning on his great spear surrounded by his men, his son Iulus crying while the physician Iapyx probes the wound with forceps. In the background Venus descends, drawn by his pain, bringing the healing herb dittany. That at least some of the population of Pompeii was familiar with the text of the *Aeneid* is clear from the over sixty graffiti from the walls of the city that quote Vergil, the majority from his *Aeneid*. While we cannot know for certain what a viewer or reader would have taken away from reading a graffito, the use of these scenes in domestic contexts indicates that they are for more than casual viewing. They might have been objects for extended discussion or used as a starting point for reflections on mythological or literary topics.

Poetic literacy at Pompeii is not limited to Vergil; passages from a number of poems by Ovid are also found among Pompeian graffiti. In addition, domestic decor also reflects the works of Ovid in a number of spaces, notably those associated with dining and those that self-consciously emulate the villas of patricians. The best example of this may be the House of Octavius Quartio at Pompeii, a property heavily renovated in the Neronian period with a new arrangement of rooms and an elaborate display of wall paintings and over twenty marble and bronze statuettes. The rear two thirds of the lot became effectively a miniature villa in form and decoration. Unlike a patrician, who could afford both a house in town and a rural villa, Octavius Quartio apparently has only this property. An upper terrace runs along the back of the house creating a transitional area with spaces for walking and dining between the interior rooms of the house and the garden in the lower terrace.

The terrace terminates on the east end in a nymphaeum, a dining complex incorporating a *biclinium*, statues, paintings, and water features. The two wall paintings that flank the central grotto statue niche are images of Greek myths sharing the theme of unrequited or doomed love. More precisely the versions here seem to reflect those in Ovid's *Metamorphoses*. On the left is Narcissus staring at his reflection, from *Metamorphoses* 3.339–510, and on the right is a panel painting of Pyramus and Thisbe, a story told in *Metamorphoses* 4.55–166. The west end of the terrace

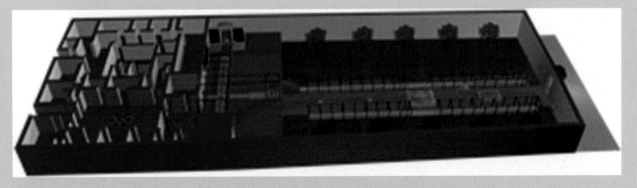

6.31   House of Octavius Quartio, Pompeii, after 64 CE, plan. *Experiencing Rome: A Visual Exploration of Antiquity's Greatest Empire*, ©2008 The Teaching Company. Reproduced with permission of The Teaching Company, www.thegreatcourses.com.

(Continued)

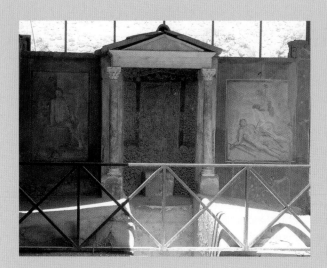

6.32   House of Octavius Quartio, Pompeii, *biclinium* with Narcissus, Pyramus and Thisbe paintings, after 64 CE. Photo courtesy Steven L. Tuck.

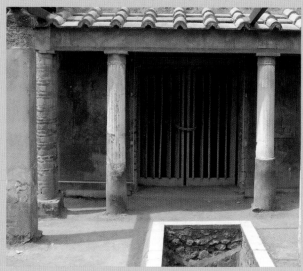

6.33   House of Octavius Quartio, Pompeii, images of Diana and Actaeon, after 64 CE. Photo courtesy Steven L. Tuck.

terminates in a doorway flanked by murals of Diana and Actaeon, as with the paintings on the east end reinforcing the outdoor and hunting imagery of the terrace along with the theme of unrequited love. These are also found in Ovid, *Metamorphoses* 3.165–205.

The exterior of the building is richly covered in stucco reliefs, some of which refer to Egypt and Isis, others of which reference water, and some are apparently purely secular. The separate parts of the building and the decorative panels are defined by red borders and stucco tracery work that contains slender decorative motifs featuring architectural and vegetal elements, the latter including leaves and garlands, elements introduced in Third Style wall painting. Two Egyptian figures on the front in relief stand behind small altars. The best-preserved side of the building is divided into the standard three figural panels. The two flanking panels are filled by hovering Eros figures while

MORE ON MYTH
Actaeon and Pyramus and Thisbe in Ovid's Metamorphoses

Actaeon was a hunter in Greek mythology who became the hunted. Once while in the woods hunting he accidentally came upon the virgin goddess, Diana, bathing. Having seen the naked goddess she punished him for that transgression by turning him into a stag, which his dogs then tore apart. In some versions of the myth he also fell in love with Diana, making the story one of unrequited love. The story of Pyramus and Thisbe was doomed rather than unrequited love. This couple, the prototypes for Romeo and Juliet, were young lovers forbidden by their parents to marry. They decide to run away and agree to meet one night at a mulberry tree. Arriving first, Thisbe sees a lioness and flees, dropping her veil. The lioness, her mouth bloody from a kill, pounces on the veil, ripping and staining it with blood. Pyramus arrives, sees the veil, thinks Thisbe is dead and stabs himself with his sword. When Thisbe returns, she finds her dying lover and kills herself with the same weapon. The gods then change the mulberry fruit to a blood red color in their honor.

the central panel is a floating pair of lovers, perhaps Dionysus and Ariadne, a motif unrelated to the worship of Isis but found elsewhere in contemporary wall decoration, for example in the largest room in the House of the Vettii, also at Pompeii.

CONCLUSION

The dominating art historical contribution of the Julio-Claudian period is the creation of a Roman public dynastic art. As the successors of Augustus endeavored to define themselves, their values, and their imperial identities, a rich array of art was created in a wide range of media including free-standing and relief sculpture, carved gems, and silver vessels. The sculptures from the Sebasteion at Aphrodisias demonstrate the reception of these themes in the provinces. The palaces of the Julio-Claudians introduced a new building type into Roman architecture, the official residence of the *princeps*. In addition the palaces of Nero, the Domus Transitoria and Domus Aurea, launched the building development known as the architectural revolution, new forms of buildings utilizing domes and rounded walls and roofing systems with increased light and interior emphasis all made possible by the use of concrete. The other major trend in interior decor is Neronian style wall painting as found across the public and domestic spaces of Pompeii. Scholars are still debating whether it represents direct emulation of Nero or just current fashion, but there is no doubt of the pattern. The dynasty ends with the suicide of Nero in 68 CE. The civil war of 68–69 CE in which four emperors were declared by armies in the provinces leads to the rise of a new dynasty, the Flavian.

SUGGESTIONS FOR FURTHER READING

Larry F. Ball, *Domus Aurea and the Roman Architectural Revolution* (Cambridge University Press 2003). This thorough study of Nero's grand palace includes a needed comprehensive analysis of its masonry and design along with the abundant ancient literary evidence. Highlighting the revolutionary innovations of the Domus Aurea, Ball outlines their implications for the development of Roman concrete architecture.

John R. Clarke, *Art in the Lives of Ordinary Romans: Visual Representation and Non-elite Viewers in Italy, 100 B.C.–A.D. 315* (University of California Press 2003). This splendidly illustrated book brings to life the art of ancient Romans of the sub-elite classes: slaves, ex-slaves, foreigners, and the freeborn working poor. Chapters 3–9 are largely concerned with material from Pompeii and the Julio-Claudian period.

Nancy T. de Grummond and B.S. Ridgway, eds., *From Pergamon to Sperlonga: Sculpture and Context* (University of California Press 2000). A significant collection of essays that explore important sculptural groups and the meanings of their display in the Roman world with emphasis on the sculptures from the imperial villa at Sperlonga.

Charles Brian Rose, *Dynastic Commemoration and Imperial Portraiture in the Julio-Claudian Period* (Cambridge University Press 1997). Rose examines the production of Julio-Claudian dynastic imagery charting the public presentation of the first imperial dynasty in both Rome and across its provinces. Throughout, the levels of imperial control and local initiative involved in the designing of dynastic monuments are assessed demonstrating the tensions that provincial dedicators encountered during their production.

R.R.R. Smith, *Aphrodisias V: The Marble Reliefs from the Julio-Claudian Sebasteion* (Philipp von Zabern 2012). Documents and analyzes the large repertoire of Julio-Claudian marble reliefs from the shrine dedicated to the worship of the imperial cult. Includes the mythological, ideological, and portrait reliefs that decorated the complex.

Francesca Tronchin, "Art, Nature, City, Country and the Problem of Villa Imitation." *Rivista di Studi Pompeiani* 21: 63–75 (2011). Challenges the standard thinking that non-elite houses, like that of Octavius Quartio, were a banal imitation of upper-class villas and suggests alternate, more nuanced perspectives on these spaces that combined art, nature, and urban elements.

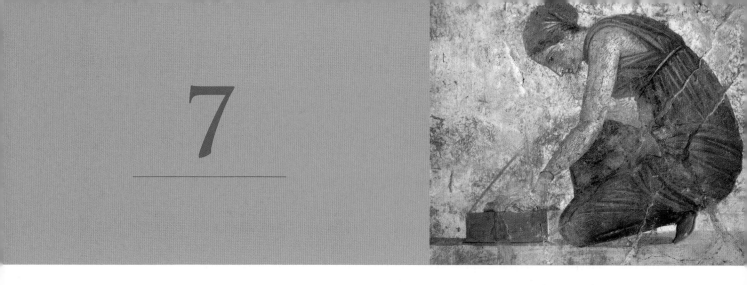

7

THE FLAVIANS, 69–96 CE

Civil War, Disaster, and Response

69–79 CE	Vespasian as emperor
71 CE	Flavian Triumph for Jewish War
75 CE	**Temple of Peace dedicated**
79–81 CE	Titus as emperor; **portrait of Titus as magistrate**
79 CE	**Sacellum of the Augustales, Herculaneum**; Eruption of Mt. Vesuvius and destruction of Pompeii, Herculaneum, Oplontis
80 CE	**Inauguration of the Colosseum**; fire and plague hit Rome
81–96 CE	Domitian as emperor
81 CE	**Arch of Titus dedicated**
92 CE	**Domus Flaviana, Flavian Palace, built**
93 CE	**Cancelleria reliefs**
c. 94 CE	**Tomb of the Haterii**

A History of Roman Art, First Edition. Steven L. Tuck.
© 2015 Steven L. Tuck. Published 2015 by John Wiley & Sons, Ltd.

The civil war of 68–69 CE seemed to have immediate, but not lasting, impact on the art of the Roman world. The key trends in art and architecture that developed under Claudius and Nero continued, and the tensions between Classical and Italic styles persisted, as demonstrated by the range of official art completed under the three Flavian emperors. The art of the Flavian dynasty represents a range of responses to the need for imperial art including some immediate changes. The veristic and self-consciously Republican portraiture of Vespasian (69–79 CE), founder of the dynasty, is married with the old-fashioned architecture of the Colosseum and Temple of Peace. This program of traditional work under Vespasian and his eldest son and heir, Titus (79–81 CE), is abandoned for the lavishly Classicizing style of his second successor son, Domitian (81–96 CE), whose art and architecture returns to many Neronian styles and types. The Arch of Titus and the *sacellum* paintings from the imperial cult site at Herculaneum reveal the exploitation of both Italic and Greek style in painting and sculpture. The art and architecture of Domitian ushers in the styles and forms popular in the second century CE and so deserves detailed attention. His palace complex, with its innovative concrete architecture, is the focus of **Art and Literature**. The statues from the *sacellum* of the imperial cult at Misenum, built under Domitian, provide a case study in imperial commemoration and the earliest evidence of the changing definition of *virtus*. This represents a key development in imperial art and ideology and is the subject of **Scholarly Perspective**. **A View from the Provinces** introduces arena mosaics from North Africa, focusing on the Zliten mosaic, bolstered by a quotation from the *Satyricon* describing this decoration.

CIVIL WAR OF 68–69 CE

Nero's suicide in 68 CE spelled an end to the Julio-Claudian dynasty. More than this, it ushered in a brief civil war in which rival claimants to the position of *princeps* came to power only to be killed by other rivals and former supporters. In March of 68 CE Servius Sulpicius Galba, governor of Hispania Tarraconensis, declared himself the representative of the Roman Senate and people, effectively revolting against Nero and the government in Rome. Nero's weak response to this and other revolts encouraged the Praetorian Guard to support Galba and the Senate to declare Nero a public enemy, leading to his suicide in June. However, Galba's rule in Rome lasted only until January of 69 CE when, faced by additional revolts among the legions, he attempted to bolster his position by adopting a successor. He decided against choosing his supporter, Marcus Salvius Otho, who responded by securing the support of the praetorians who murdered Galba on January 15. Otho faced another rival for power in Vitellius, whose legions in Germany had declared him emperor in January of 69 CE also. After being defeated in battle by Vitellius in April 69, Otho committed suicide in an apparent attempt to avoid further bloodshed. Aulus Vitellius reached the city in July, received the support of the Senate and took office.

Meanwhile Titus Flavius Vespasianus, an experienced general sent by Nero to crush the Jewish revolt, had been gathering support among the eastern governors and armies and was declared *princeps* by his troops on July 1, 69 CE.

He would be the fourth and final emperor declared in 69 CE, a year that has come to be known as the year of the four emperors. Vespasian sent subordinates from battling the Jewish revolt in the east into Italy and Rome. These subordinates fought against the forces loyal to Vitellius in Italy, allowing Vespasian to distance himself from the war, the destruction of the city of Cremona and the burning of the Temple of Jupiter Optimus Maximus on the Capitol in Rome. Vespasian's troops killed Vitellius on December 20, 69 CE, following which the Senate conferred the usual powers on Vespasian, dating them from July 1 when his troops had hailed him as imperator.

A surviving partial copy of the document conferring power on Vespasian (the *Lex de Imperio Vespasiani*) provides strong corroboration of the uncertainty of his succession and helps to demonstrate the weakness of his position as the founder of a dynasty based on winning a civil war. The law specifies his right to perform acts that would not have been questioned if performed by any Julio-Claudian emperor and it names him as the rightful successor to Augustus and Claudius, the two deified Julio-Claudians who served as the model emperors and whose naming must be seen as foreshadowing Vespasian's expected deification. This document reveals the critical insecurity of Vespasian's position and may explain the motivations behind his choices in art and architecture, choices that emphasize traditional Roman values and qualities. Like Augustus, who came to power from winning a civil war, Vespasian emphasized his conquest of a foreign foe. For Augustus it was the Parthians who returned the standards. For Vespasian, the Jewish War could be spun as a foreign conflict rather than a major internal revolt whose victory led to the destruction of a great city in the empire. Vespasian follows Claudius' pattern and returns to a Republican style of art and architecture, perhaps establishing a connection with Claudius and certainly with Roman traditional imagery.

VESPASIAN AND TITUS, 69–81 CE

Unlike any of the Julio-Claudians, or the previous emperors declared during the civil war, Vespasian had two grown sons, providing him with a clear line of succession. This first true father–son succession would become an important theme in Flavian art. Because of their emphasis on Vespasian and Titus as a single ruling unit and because the sculpture and buildings of Vespasian were conceived of, continued, or completed under the brief rule of his successor, Titus, it is almost impossible to separate works of art and architecture into those of Vespasian or Titus. We will therefore address their two reigns together.

Vespasian was sixty years of age when he won the civil war and was declared *princeps* by the Senate. He had no dynastic basis for his rule, the treasury was empty, and he had no political constituency outside of the military. To compensate for these problems, Vespasian made sure that the Roman people could experience the tangible benefits of his rule. He built support in Rome and across the empire through the projection of a personality that was affable, traditional, and dedicated to building infrastructure. That building benefited the largest number of Romans possible through construction jobs as well as the completed buildings, at least some, for example the Colosseum, paid for by the spoils from the Jewish War. These policies were continued and to some extent completed by his heir and eldest son, Titus.

Titus had long been his father's most trusted and closest assistant. This position trained him for his succession but also angered many as he acted as commander of Vespasian's guard. As guard commander Titus removed his father's political opponents by a variety of methods including forged incriminating letters.

Titus' rule as imperator was short-lived and marred by natural disasters and community tragedies. He ruled only from June 79 to September 81 CE, during the course of which he personally and directly supervised relief efforts following the eruption of Vesuvius in August 79 and a great fire followed by an outbreak of the plague that hit Rome in 80. Titus' reactions to these disasters and his general government of Rome made him a very popular ruler during his lifetime and it is probable that his popularity continued to grow after his death. He also oversaw the dedicatory games in the Colosseum in 80 CE, perhaps scheduled in part to reassure Romans of the stability of government and the future of Rome.

Portraiture

Vespasian's portraiture marks a clear rejection of Julio-Claudian Classicism. Instead of the idealized images of that dynasty, Vespasian embraces Republican veristic portraiture, appearing as the 60-year-old ruler he was, with a balding head, deep nasolabial grooves, closely set eyes with crow's feet, and wrinkles across his forehead and neck. These features seem to echo Suetonius' account (*Vesp.* 20) of a comic, asked to make a joke about Vespasian, focused on his famous appearance of crow's feet and wrinkles and answered, "I will, when you have done relieving your bowels." His thin mouth seems to portray some of his good humor and the self-deprecating wit, recorded by many sources, that induced him to utter as his last words, "I think I am becoming a god." There is no doubt that this portraiture is a political image designed to distance Vespasian from the Julio-Claudians. On his death in June of 79 CE, Vespasian was immediately deified and succeeded by his eldest son and namesake, Titus Flavius Vespasianus, known as Titus, then forty years old.

There is so much consistency in images of Titus that we can conclude that his portraits derive from a small number of originals, perhaps only one that was circulated as a model. The portraits of Titus not only demonstrate a change from the Julio-Claudians in terms of facial features, but also in terms of proportions. No full-length portraits survive of Vespasian during his life, but with Titus we can see the stout Flavian proportions and the further rejection of Classicizing Julio-Claudian images. Compare the portrait of Titus as a magistrate to the Augustus as Pontifex Maximus (Figure 5.1) and the squat and broad proportions of the Titus statue are clear. By preferring a veristic style of portraiture, he identifies himself, not as an idealized ruler, like Augustus, but as his father's successor. As his enduring popularity attests, the message of continuity and traditional values must have resonated with the Roman people.

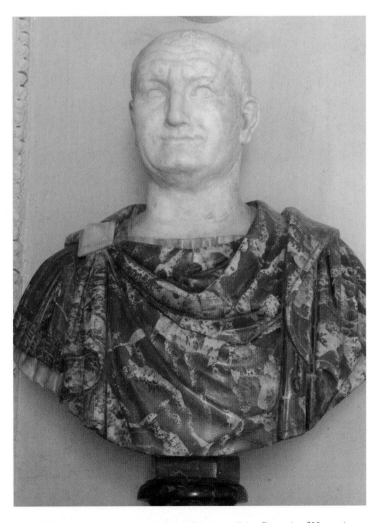

7.1 Portrait of Vespasian, 70–79 CE. Musei Capitolini, Rome. Marble, H 27 in (69.5 cm). Photo courtesy Daniel Resheter.

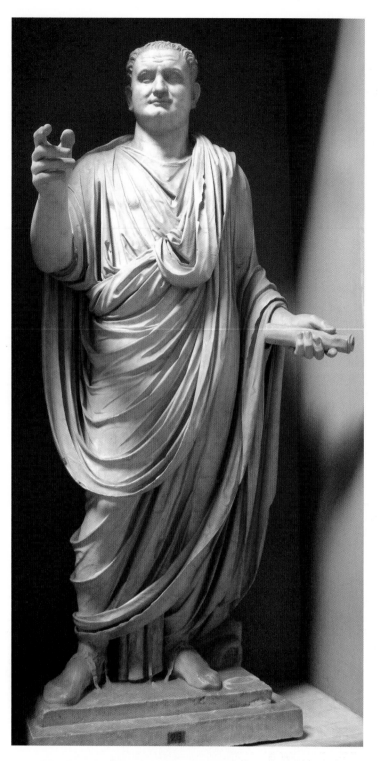

7.2   Portrait of Titus, 70–80 CE, Rome. Musei Vaticani, Rome. Marble, H 6 ft 5 in (1.96 m). Photo courtesy Steven L. Tuck.

Architecture

Despite the dire condition of the treasury at the start of Vespasian's rule, he, and later Titus, began to raise taxes to support a massive public building campaign in Rome. The theme of this campaign seems to have been to create new spaces and venues for public entertainment; to distance themselves from Nero by repurposing some of the land and buildings in his Domus Aurea estate; and to create buildings that were self-consciously conservative in form, reflecting the Republican references in their personal portraiture.

The Colosseum

The greatest and one of the first of these buildings was the Flavian Amphitheater, better known as the Colosseum, for its proximity to the Colossus Neronis, a 120 foot tall bronze statue of Nero on the grounds of his Domus Aurea. The Colosseum was not the first permanent amphitheater in Rome, but it was the largest, grandest, and most important. It was built on the site of a lake that was a prominent feature on the grounds of the Domus Aurea. The construction of the building, which was unprecedented in the Roman world for its scale and architectural sophistication, was amazingly rapid and the bulk of the work was done between 72 and 80 CE, when the hundred days of inaugural games were held under Titus.

Architecturally the Colosseum is complex and sophisticated, particularly in its development of the use of concrete as a structural support for large-scale buildings with great unsupported spaces. It is an ellipse measuring 617 ft (188 m) on its long axis, 512 ft (156 m) on its cross axis and 159 ft (48.5 m) in height, while the arena floor, also an ellipse, measures 282 ft (86 m) by 177 ft (54 m). While it contains a skeleton of locally quarried travertine blocks, the building material that made the amphitheater possible was concrete. The concrete construction utilized great concrete piers and vaults allowing for both the unprecedented size of the building and large tunnels and passageways throughout the substructure of the seating area. The network of tunnels and stairs freed up space, enabling the approximately 45,000 spectators to move quickly to and from their seats by following the numbers that were on each entrance token. This innovative interior was paired with a very conservative and traditional facade, making it consistent with the projected identity of the Flavian art and architecture program.

The facade presents a four-story travertine building, with the lower three stories each consisting of eighty arches in an arcade. Half columns carved in the blocks separate the arches: Tuscan on the ground floor, Ionic on the second, and Corinthian on the third. The facade is very traditional in form and seems to deliberately echo the Theater of Marcellus and perhaps the Theater of Pompey

(a)

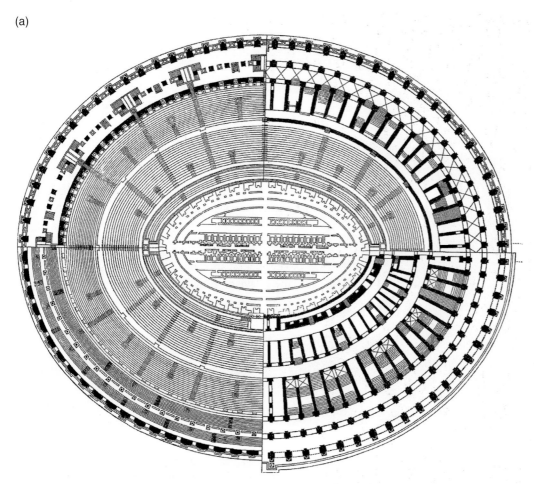

(b)

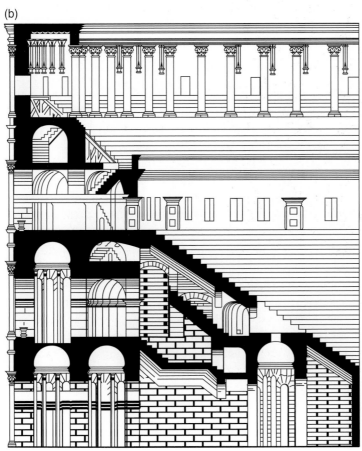

7.3a and 7.3b Colosseum, Rome, dedicated in 80 CE, plan and elevation drawings. (a) Plan: *Dictionnaire des Antiquités Grecques et Romaines*, vol. I, Paris 1877, p. 245, fig. 272. (b) Elevation drawing: Lexikon der gesamten Technik (Dictionary of Technology), 1904, Otto Lueger.

7.4a and 7.4b
Colosseum, Rome,
dedicated in 80 CE, facade
and detail of entrance
arcade. Photos courtesy
Steven L. Tuck.

(a)

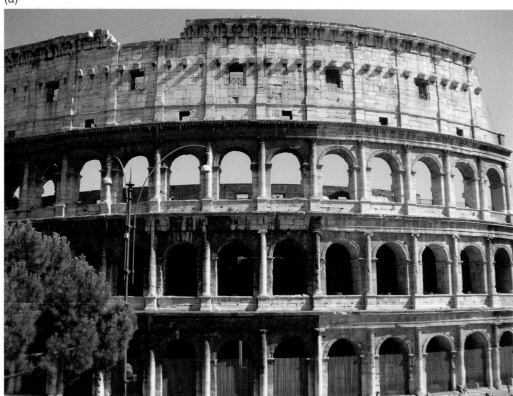

(b)

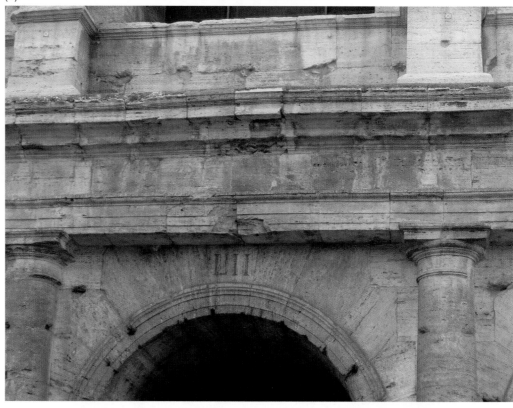

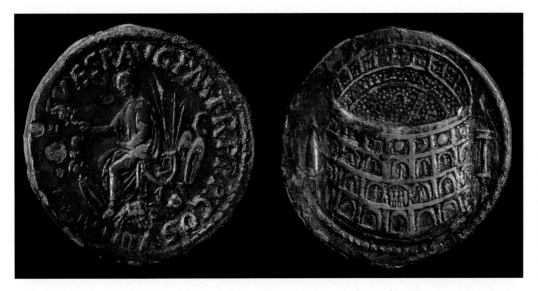

7.5 Colosseum, Rome, sestertius of the amphitheater struck at Rome under Titus showing sculptures in the 2nd and 3rd floor arcades, 80 CE. Source: © The Trustees of the British Museum. All rights reserved.

(Figure 4.14) before that. From images of the Colosseum on contemporary coins and a relief from the Tomb of the Haterii, as well as the amphitheater at Capua (a slightly later copy of the Colosseum), we can suppose that the arches on the second and perhaps third floor were originally used to display sculptures.

Surmounting all this is a high attic story decorated with Corinthian pilasters with a rectangular window between every other pair. The major entrances on the long and short axes were apparently reserved for use by performers and high status spectators and perhaps further defined by projecting pediments that each may have held a *quadriga*, visible on the coin. The travertine facade, awning to shade the seats, decorative stuccowork on the interior, huge number of entrances, and sculptural display all suggest a building designed for grandeur as well as spectator comfort. The building form, with the substructures below the arena floor, allowed for the full range of spectacular entertainments including animal hunts, prisoner executions, gladiatorial matches, *naumachiae* (naval battles), and other forms of spectacle in service of the state. The building and its spectacles seem designed to convey particular themes including the power of the Flavian emperors and their control over the resources of the empire as well as the benefits their rule brings to Romans across the city.

The Baths of Titus

Also built on the grounds of the Domus Aurea, almost adjacent to the Colosseum, were the Baths of Titus, which were dedicated with the amphitheater in 80 CE. Their form is not well understood and they have almost entirely disappeared, but the little known about them confirms that the Baths were a massive concrete complex, like the Colosseum built on a tremendous scale. Additionally, like previous imperial bath complexes of Agrippa and Nero, the Baths were designed with suites of rooms organized around a central hall in bilaterally symmetrical groups. By building the Baths of Titus on a portion of the Domus Aurea, the Flavians were repurposing the private lands seized by Nero and returning them to public use, creating a public entertainment complex of which the Colosseum was only one component.

Templum Pacis

About 200 metres away from the Baths of Titus was a complex that should best be understood as the third of the imperial fora – after those of Julius Caesar and Augustus, the Templum Pacis or Temple of Peace. Also not well preserved, the complex was paid for by the spoils of the Jewish war waged by Vespasian and Titus and was dedicated by Vespasian in 75 CE. Over ten times the size of the Ara Pacis Augustae, it is thought to have been inspired by Augustus' celebration of peace following his

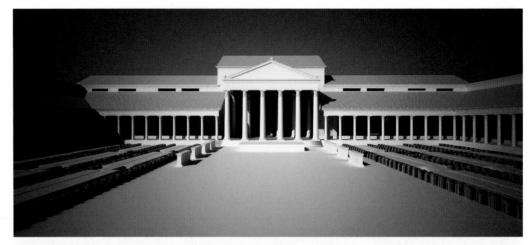

7.6 Reconstruction of the Templum Pacis, Rome, dedicated in 75 CE. Rome Reborn. © 2012 by Frischer Consulting, Inc. All rights reserved.

ANCIENTS ON ART

The museum displays in the Templum Pacis

When the triumphal ceremonies were over, as the Roman empire was now firmly established, Vespasian made up his mind to build a temple of Peace. This was completed with remarkable speed and surpassed all human imagination. Not only did he have unlimited wealth at his disposal; he also adorned it with paintings and statues by the greatest of the old masters. In fact, in that temple were collected and deposited all those works that men had hitherto travelled over the whole world to see, longing to set eyes on them even when scattered in different lands. There too he laid up the golden vessels from the Temple of the Jews. (Josephus, *The Jewish War* 7.5.7)

. . . a bronze bull stands by it, the work, I think, of Pheidias the Athenian or of Lysippus. For there are many statues in this quarter which are the works of these two men. Here, for example, is another statue which is certainly the work of Pheidias; for the inscription on the statue says this. There too is the calf of Myron. For the ancient Romans took great pains to make all the finest things of Greece adornments of Rome. (Procopius, *Gothic War* 8.21.11–14)

own civil wars. Like Augustus, Vespasian came to power as a result of civil war and so a triumphal monument over his opponents, fellow Romans, would not have been accepted. A celebration of peace was again the answer, and the form was again inspired by Greek models of urban space.

Here the major temple was to Pax while the complex contained a library and, in the open area of the colonnaded square, lines of fountains. The museum aspect of the forum primarily housed spoils from Jerusalem taken in the Jewish campaign and Greek sculpture removed from the Domus Aurea. Both Josephus and Pliny the Elder write about the Templum Pacis and Pliny calls it one of the three most beautiful buildings in Rome. The Temple of Peace, like the Flavian entertainment buildings, further reflects the desire to return Neronian art and land to the people, and the continuing benefits of Vespasian's rule.

Pompeii and Herculaneum

The eruption of the volcano Vesuvius began on August 24, 79 CE and destroyed many communities, farms, and villas across the south side of the Bay of Naples. Ironically, the very means of their destruction preserved them for eventual discovery, excavation, and study over the past 250 years. While it is clear that the three days of chaos during the eruption led to enormous death and disorder, these finds are still the closest we have come to uncovering ancient houses, shops, and public spaces as they were used and inhabited in the Roman world. Because of this, the material from Vesuvian

HISTORICAL CONTEXT
Pliny's account of the eruption of Vesuvius

The eruption of Vesuvius was also the only major natural disaster in the ancient world with an eyewitness account; Pliny the Younger, nephew of Pliny the Elder, admiral of the Roman fleet, recorded his observations of the event from the fleet headquarters at Misenum on the north edge of the Bay of Naples. His description of the actual eruption in one of two letters (*Epistles* 6.16, 20) to the historian Tacitus is notable as it records the early phase of the event prior to the rain of ash and pumice and great pyroclastic flows (fast moving currents of superheated gas) that eventually entombed the communities:

> A cloud was ascending, the appearance of which I cannot give you a more exact description of than by likening it to that of a great pine tree, for it shot up to a great height in the form of a very tall trunk, which spread itself out at the top into a sort of branches. It appeared sometimes bright and sometimes dark and spotted, according as it was either more or less impregnated with earth and cinders. (Pliny, *Ep.* 6.16)

lands represents unique and valuable evidence of daily life, the arts, and the architecture of Roman communities of the late first century CE. It is worthy of our extended attention for the lessons it conveys about this period.

The destruction of Pompeii and Herculaneum, the largest cities affected, differed dramatically. Pompeii was initially covered by up to 30 feet (14 m) of ash and pumice and later sealed by the pyroclastic flows, meaning that excavation here was easy and the majority of the material rapidly cleared away. In contrast Herculaneum was covered by flows that solidified into approximately 65 ft (20 m) of material of the consistency of concrete, encasing the city and making excavation very slow and painstaking. There are also differences between the ancient communities themselves. For example, on the one hand, Herculaneum generally lacks some things that are characteristic of Pompeii such as wheel ruts, stepping stones across streets, and painted election and gladiatorial announcements. On the other hand, there are elements more common to Herculaneum than Pompeii, such as regular rectangular blocks indicating orthogonal planning and a higher use of marble and window glass in buildings.

Herculaneum

Herculaneum was the smaller of the two cities, with an estimated population of only five thousand and comprising only twenty city blocks compared to over ninety at Pompeii. It was almost certainly originally a Greek colony and that influence continued throughout its existence, as Herculaneum has no clear early Etruscan or Italic phase. Much of its economy was probably based on fishing and yet its paved roads, orthogonal planning, multiple public baths, high use of marble, and a number of luxurious villas including the Villa of the Papyri, probably at one time the home of Julius Caesar's father-in-law, indicate more than just a small fishing village.

The wall mosaic of Neptune and Amphitrite from the small *nymphaeum* garden *triclinium* in the House of Neptune and Amphitrite provides a spectacular example of the Greek-themed luxury found at the city. As a wall mosaic, it was a costlier decoration than a floor mosaic and the use of **polychromy** rather than the traditional Italic black and white mosaic technique makes it a bolder decoration and one that is more integrated with the wall paintings that flank it in the small garden space. The figures of Neptune and Amphitrite stand before a yellow background in poses familiar from Greek Classical sculpture. Surrounding them is an arrangement of subsidiary decoration including flanking columns. Above them is a scalloped shell-shaped faux apse that heightens the illusion that the figures are set into a niche in the wall. This design of the mosaic reinforces the overall decoration of the *triclinium* with the center of the flanking wall articulated by an actual statue niche with an apse.

polychromy
the use of many colors in decoration, especially in architecture and sculpture. Refers to the brightly painted multi-colored buildings and sculptures of the ancient world.

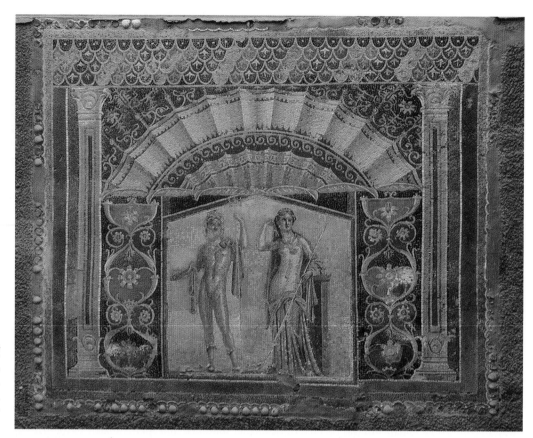

7.7 Wall mosaic of Neptune and Amphitrite, House of Neptune and Amphitrite, Herculaneum, *c.* 70 CE. Photo courtesy Steven L. Tuck.

7.8 Overall view, Sacellum of the Augustales, Herculaneum, 79 CE. Photo courtesy Steven L. Tuck.

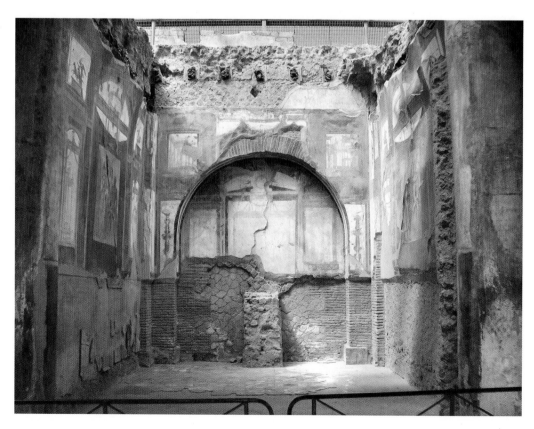

At a key intersection in the city was a shrine to the cult of the emperors, the Sacellum of the Augustales – the shrine for the local priests (*Augustales*) of the emperors, which operated as a cult site for the worship of the deified emperors as well as an outlet for wealthy freed slaves to create a public image for themselves as high class Romans had done for centuries. Such cult sites were found in communities across the Roman world and served a social as well as religious function. In the case of Herculaneum, the Sacellum closely matched the layout of one excavated at Misenum on the north side of the Bay of Naples. The decoration here, however, is remarkable for what it reveals both about artistic styles on the eve of Herculaneum's destruction, and the ways in which imperial ideology was transmitted to and reflected by the local populace. The layout of the Sacellum includes a large fore-court with a set of three rooms along one wall. The flanking rooms supported cult functions, while the center one was the shrine itself. The decoration of the shrine is important because the layout with a single statue base makes it clear that it was done to honor the deified Vespasian while a shrine to the Julio-Claudian cult would contain a larger number of bases, so that it was completed during Titus' reign, sometime between June and August 79 CE. The floor and walls including the dado were covered with **opus sectile**, a more expensive marble treatment than mosaic. The wall paintings show an aesthetic of the latest style, Fourth Style, with illusionistic architecture with details of chariots in the upper windows on the attic stories of background buildings providing a triumphal theme. The lavish use of blue, a rare and expensive pigment, indicates that no expense was spared.

opus sectile
literally "cut work." Refers to the decorative use of cut stone, usually colored imported marble, in patterns to create decorative floor and wall treatments.

The sidewalls of the shrine are each dominated by a single panel painting with a scene from the life of Hercules, the mythical founder of the city. On the viewer's left is a seated Hercules with Juno and Minerva anticipating his apotheosis and welcome into the company of the gods on Mount Olympus. On the right is a scene of Hercules challenging a river guardian who attempted an abduction of Deianeira. This figure of Hercules is the clearest of the two and it looks as though the model for him was the current emperor, Titus. Note the same broad face and wrinkled forehead, receding hairline, closely set eyes, and thick neck. Titus, like Hercules, is the mortal son of a god using his rule and power to bring benefits to those on earth with the expectation of being reunited with his father in the afterlife as he is rewarded with apotheosis and deification. Hercules is a metaphor for the emperor Titus.

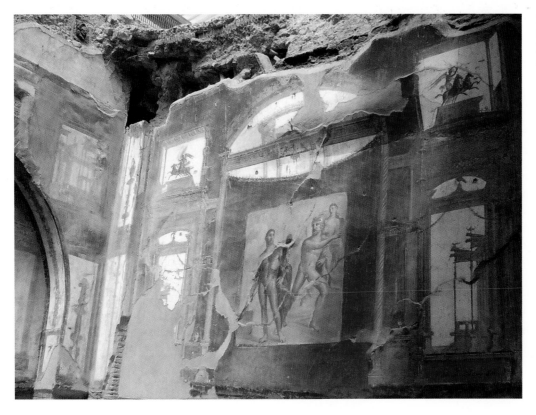

7.9 Hercules painting, Sacellum of the Augustales, Herculaneum, 79 CE. Photo courtesy Steven L. Tuck.

Pompeii

Pompeii provides us with the best-preserved evidence for Roman painted buildings, both public and domestic. While it may not represent houses and public buildings across the entire Roman Empire, it has allowed us to study the entire range of art that was used to decorate Roman houses including especially the wall paintings which are found nowhere else in such numbers or such tremendous preservation. This material combined with the surviving details of names and status of owners and patrons of the art not only allows us to reconstruct the arts, but also the meaning of the arts in the lives of ancient Romans. One of the best decorated, preserved, and studied houses at Pompeii, in fact from the entire Roman world, is the House of the Vettii, believed to be the home of Aulus Vettius Conviva and Aulus Vettius Restitutus, brothers and former slaves. Following the earthquake that rocked Pompeii in 62 CE, the house was remodeled. Here we can explore the projection of a sub-elite commercial identity in the wall paintings, and gain insight into the world after the earthquake, a time when the patricians were being usurped by the nouveau riche in Pompeii.

Finally, the house gives us a sense of these particular former slaves and their attitudes toward the Roman system as new members of the establishment. Thanks to its preservation and careful excavation, we can explore this house and investigate how members of the Roman wealthy sub-elite class lived. What we see is a commercial identity presented to guests through the organization of rooms, sculpture, and especially the unparalleled high-quality wall paintings, from the front door to the reception rooms surrounding the garden in the rear of the house.

The post-earthquake reorganization of space in the house, apparently still in progress when Vesuvius erupted, removed the *tablinum*, the formal reception space, across the atrium from the front door. This opened the house to a peristyle garden, which was surrounded by the highest status rooms, making the garden, not the atrium, the best-decorated and most important reception area. As the architect Vitruvius tells us, men who have no need to host clients have no need for a *tablinum*; here we see that statement fulfilled. Contrast this with the House of the Faun (Figure 4.17), which was twelve times as large with two major *tablina*.

The foyer at the main entrance is dominated by a painting of Priapus, representing a commercial rather than patrician identity. The figure is also apotropaic, designed to keep away evil, a common attribute of entrance decoration that often incorporated phallic imagery.

HISTORICAL CONTEXT
Roman class and the patron–client system

The Roman social system consisted of a number of rigidly defined classes, from slaves at the bottom, to plebeians (common Romans), equestrians (an intermediate class), and patricians (elite Romans) at the top. The system, particularly after modifications made by Augustus, allowed for some social mobility. Freed slaves could serve in local communities as priests of the emperors (*Augustales*), their sons could be military commanders, and the sons of equestrians might have the chance to enter the Senate. This created a social safety valve so that all could benefit from and see advancement in the system. The patron–client relationship held the classes together. In it elite Roman men were patrons of lower status clients, providing their clients with a voice in government and economic help such as jobs or a small allowance. In return, the clients attended the patron daily at dawn at his home. They also supported the political aspirations of a patron by voting as he indicated and accompanying him into the forum when he was called to council or other meetings. In theory both groups benefitted when the patron prospered. Their connection was lifelong and in some cases ran across generations.

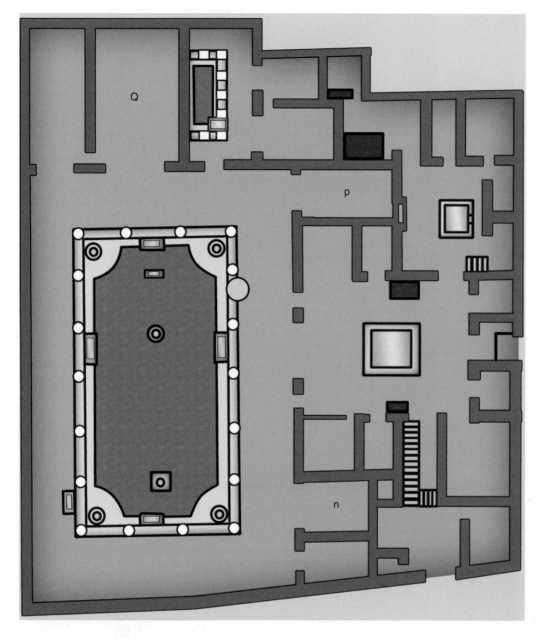

7.10 Plan of the House of the Vettii, Pompeii, renovations *c.* 75 CE. Pompeii: Daily Life in an Ancient Roman City, © 2010 The Teaching Company. Reproduced with permission of The Teaching Company, www.thegreatcourses.com.

Imagery of abundance surrounds the god Priapus including the money bag in the pan scale and the cornucopia of fruit spilling out behind him. His oversize phallus balancing the bag of money is another, very male, statement of abundance. It is an image of prosperity not of noble pretention. Again the House of the Faun with its initial decoration of Greek temple facades and faux marble makes an effective contrast in intent. The Priapus painting was originally repeated by a fountain sculpture of the same figure in the peristyle garden. The identical pose along the axis created a visual link between the vestibule and the garden beyond, the terminal destination in the house for guests.

The peristyle garden itself is crammed with statuettes and fountains imitating an elite villa on a small scale. It acts as the most important node or point of social intersection in the house surrounded as it is by the best-decorated reception spaces.

One reception room is decorated as a ***pinacotheca*** with three panel paintings of Pasiphae, Ixion, and Ariadne, all thematically linked Greek myths that reinforce religious authority.

pinacotheca

literally a picture gallery. In Roman houses a room decorated with mural paintings that replicate Greek panel paintings, often copies or variations of famous pictures.

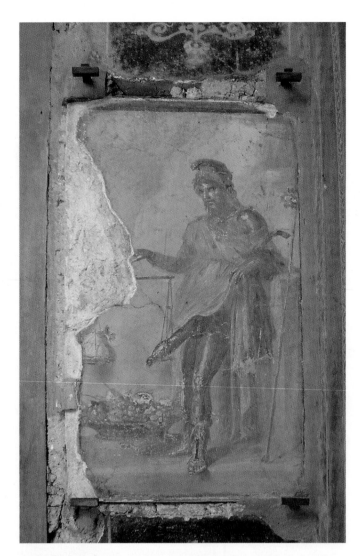

7.11 Priapus painting, front foyer, House of the Vettii, Pompeii, *c.* 75 CE. Photo courtesy Steven L. Tuck.

7.12 *Pinacotheca* n, House of the Vettii, Pompeii, *c.* 75 CE. Photo courtesy Steven L. Tuck.

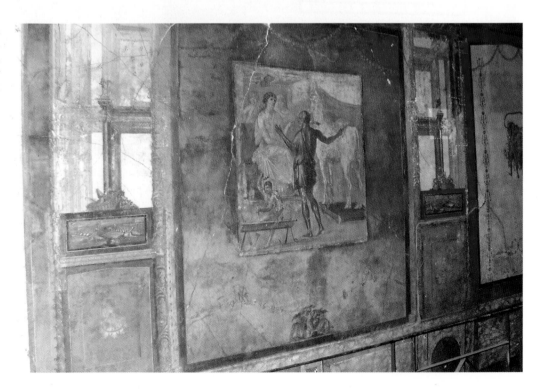

MORE ON MYTH
The Cretan cycle of myths

Minos, the king of Crete, angered the sea god, Poseidon, by withholding a bull from sacrifice to the god. In punishment Poseidon struck Minos' wife, Pasiphae, with a passion for the bull that she consummated with the help of Daedalus, who created a wooden cow she could climb into. She gave birth to the half man, half bull Minotaur, which was kept in a labyrinth built by Daedalus. Minos forced the Athenians to give a tribute of seven boys and seven girls every nine years as sacrifice to the Minotaur. The Athenian hero, Theseus, came to Crete to stop the practice. With the help of Ariadne, daughter of Minos and Pasiphae, who gave him a sword and a ball of string to trace his route in the labyrinth, he killed the Minotaur and made his way out of the labyrinth. He then escaped the island of Crete with Ariadne, who had fallen in love with him and betrayed her own family. On their way back to Athens, they stopped at Naxos where Theseus abandoned the sleeping Ariadne. She was discovered by the god Dionysus, who fell in love and married her.

In each myth those who transgress against their duties or the authority of the gods are punished, often in horrible ways. It was common for scenes of Greek myth to be displayed as metaphors of contemporary events, individuals, or situations. As we know that one of the Vettius brothers was a priest of the cult of the emperors, this reinforcement of religious authority might reflect their feelings on the Roman system, a system that originally enslaved the brothers, but under which they now thrive.

The paired reception room is dominated by three Fourth Style mural paintings of the infant Hercules strangling the serpents sent to kill him, Pentheus being killed by the Bacchae, and Dirce punished by her stepsons, each with the same theme of religious authority bolstered by punishment of the transgressors. These paintings may be based on Greek originals with the Hercules a copy of a famous fifth-century BCE work by Zeuxis. All show stories where the will of Zeus or his authority was tested and those who tested it, whether his sister and wife Hera, the king of Thebes, or a Greek queen, are thwarted or punished. Again, religious authority and piety are central elements in this didactic and moralizing decor.

The final and largest reception space is painted in Pompeiian red with paired lovers hovering in space filling the center of each panel of the wall. The detailed narrative decoration is in a frieze separating the dado from the main wall panels with scenes of putti undertaking a range of tasks. Here the Cupid figures are performing a number of commercial or industrial activities related to love such as jewelry and perfume making, and garland stringing. They also appear, however, as fullers, the textile cleaners of antiquity. This unusual scene, more typical of paintings found at an actual fullery, shows the key steps in cleaning fabric and may reflect the source of the brothers' wealth.

The House of the Vettii provides an opportunity to explore the domestic space and decor of the new rich in the Roman world. While their decoration reflects the subjects and spaces found in elite dwellings – Greek mythology, elaborate dining and garden spaces – the themes do not. Where a Roman senator would emphasize his ancestry

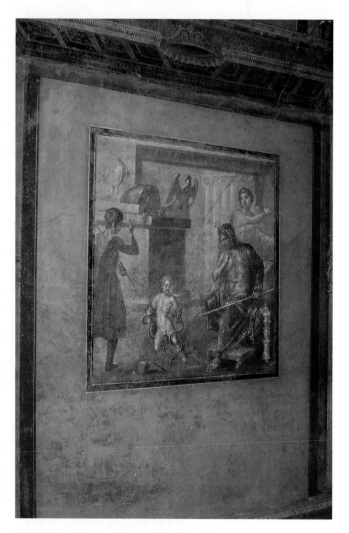

7.13 *Pinacotheca* p, House of the Vettii, Pompeii, *c.* 75 CE. Photo courtesy Steven L. Tuck.

and literary pretensions, the Vettius brothers celebrate their wealth, status as upholders of the Roman religious system, and the notions of love and Dionysus combined with sly references to their commercial ventures. It provides evidence of a social revolution that took place in Pompeii and across the Roman world in the first century as the new rich took their places as beneficiaries of the Roman system.

In addition to what can be learned from the domestic spaces at Pompeii, the art in public, commercial, non-domestic spaces is also illuminating. The *lupanar*, or brothel, at Pompeii is the best-preserved example of this type of building from the Roman world and its design and decoration offer

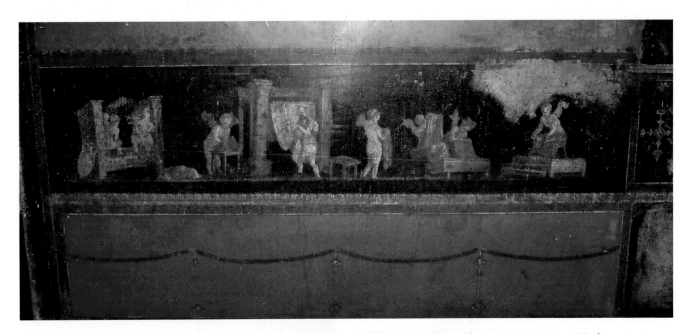

7.14   Cupids as fullers, painted frieze, reception room Q, House of the Vettii, Pompeii, *c.* 75 CE. Photo courtesy Steven L. Tuck.

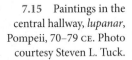

7.15   Paintings in the central hallway, *lupanar*, Pompeii, 70–79 CE. Photo courtesy Steven L. Tuck.

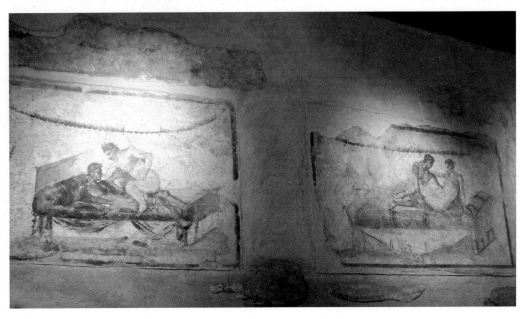

A VIEW FROM THE PROVINCES

A North African arena mosaic from Zliten

The Roman villa at Zliten, a large villa near the coast in the province of Africa Tripolitania (modern Libya) in North Africa, was excavated in 1913–1914 and since then the date of its mosaics has been the source of a great deal of controversy. Some scholars want to identify the figures with historical events in the early first or middle third century CE, but with no evidence outside the mosaic that supports either conclusion. The usual accepted date for the floor we are examining is late first century CE, based on the figures and hairstyles, making it among the earliest mosaics of Roman Africa. The floor is a large square 11 ½ ft (3.53 m) each side.

The center of the floor consists of sixteen alternating squares laid in rows of four. Small mosaic roundels of varieties of fish and shellfish within square frames alternate with high quality square opus sectile panels containing geometric patterns. This is framed by an entire opus sectile frame. Outside of all of this is a figural border with scenes of events in a day of arena games all on a white ground with no setting. Clearly identifiable are *venationes* (animal hunts) including

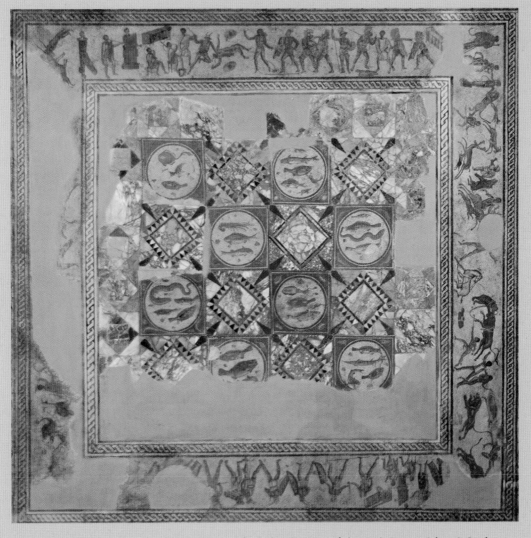

7.16   Floor mosaic from a Roman villa, Zliten, Libya, Flavian. L 11 ½ ft (3.53 m). Source: Sebastià Giralt.

(Continued)

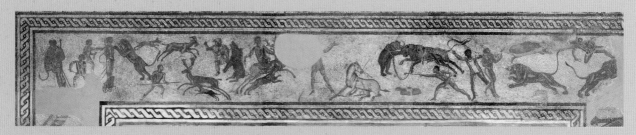

7.17   Detail of arena events, floor mosaic from a Roman villa, Zliten, Libya, Flavian. Source: akg-images/Gilles Mermet.

deer and ostriches, prisoner executions, and – unusually for Roman Africa – many gladiators, along with the musicians and the arena attendants known from other arena images and literary accounts.

The gladiators take up two sides of the border and are clearly the major event of the day with very precise representation of the types of gladiators, pairing of combatants, and circumstances of their refereed bouts. The prisoners in the mosaic are being executed by *damnatio ad bestias*, condemnation to the animals. Two are bound to stakes mounted on little carts pushed by attendants towards leopards while another is driven by whip blows towards an attacking lion. The prisoners look remarkably similar in height, skin tone, and hairstyle to some of those in the arena supervising their execution; they are figures from the region, generally thought to be Garamantes, people of the southern edge of Roman territory along the Sahara, who were the object of a military expedition commanded by Valerius Festus under Vespasian in 70 CE and recorded by Pliny in his *Natural History* 5.36–8.

The circumstantial details of specific events and pairings of gladiators lead to the conclusion that this illustrates a specific set of games, probably in the amphitheater of Lepcis Magna a short distance away from the villa and almost certainly sponsored by the owner of the villa who commissioned this mosaic as a record of his beneficence. The mosaic would serve as a constant reminder to the patron as well as to his guests of his generosity. In contrast to other provinces where they are very rare, many arena and spectacle mosaics are found in Roman Africa. The strongly regional notion of appropriate decor for domestic interiors is confirmed by a passage in Petronius' *Satyricon* (30) in which he mocks just this sort of interior decoration in the home of a freedman in southern Italy. In that passage a survey of the domestic decoration of the nouveau riche Trimalchio concludes with the punchline, "I began to ask the porter what pictures they had in the hall. 'The Iliad and the Odyssey,' he said, 'and the gladiator's show given by Laenas,'" making it clear to his audience of elite Romans that domestic decoration of a gladiatorial show was just another example of the bad taste of the freedman. That may have been true for Italy, but it was not for Roman North Africa.

unique insights into daily life. The grim reality of the *lupanar* with its small cells, stone beds, and pillows contrasts strikingly with high quality evocative wall paintings in the hall of the building. These panel paintings are in the latest post-Neronian painting style and display Greek Hellenistic conventions of ideal beauty and luxurious surroundings. The couples in each panel follow the conventions of Greek art with bronze, muscular men and pale, rounded women, as though each pair is Apollo and Aphrodite. The settings are also luxurious with garlands, rich tapestries, and bedding and expensive beds of turned wood, all in sharp contrast to the reality within the establishment. The paintings are clearly evocative and aspirational, not documentary. Nonetheless, the fact that the most utilitarian space is painted in such a historically informed style reflects the extent of the influence of Greek aesthetics in Roman art.

DOMITIAN, 81–96 CE

Domitian (Titus Flavius Domitianus) became *princeps* upon the premature death by a fever of his brother, Titus, a death he was later suspected of hastening. Despite his skills as a successful general and competent administrator, Domitian suffered from a poor reputation during his lifetime that only worsened after his death. The Senate condemned his memory and his legacy was further maligned by the works of writers under successor emperors, such as Suetonius, who were desperate to distinguish their patrons from the tyrant Domitian. However, Domitian ruled longer than his deified father and elder brother combined and therefore left more works of art and architecture at the end of his reign. Nonetheless, after his assassination by members of his own household in 96 CE, his images were destroyed or altered, no posthumous portraiture was made, and the few images that survive were created in his lifetime.

Portraiture

Domitian's portraiture reflects some Flavian elements familiar from his father and elder brother: a full face, deep set eyes, and hooked nose. Domitian's hair is fuller than the other Flavians, despite the fact that he was bald in real life, a feature that scholars attribute to his vanity. The comma-shaped locks that frame his forehead, especially in later portraits, may be a reference to Julio-Claudian portraiture and thus a political statement associating him with past emperors who adopted this style, or by this time they may only represent a convention of a full head of hair that began with the Julio-Claudians but has now lost any political meaning.

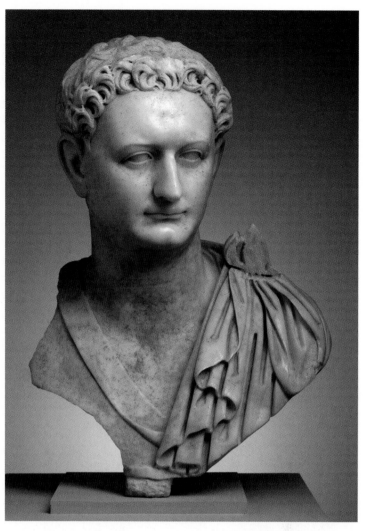

7.18 Portrait bust of Domitian, *c.* 90 CE, Rome. Marble, H 23⅝ in (59.2 cm). Toledo Museum of Art (Toledo, Ohio). Purchased with funds from the Libbey Endowment, Gift of Edward Drummond Libbey and with funds from the Florence Scott Libbey Bequest in Memory of her Father, Maurice A. Scott, 1990.30. Photography credit: Tim Thayer.

Female portraiture under Domitian is probably best exemplified by the bust in Figure 7.20, taken to be a portrait of an aristocratic Roman woman of the period. The emphasis on her beauty and her coiffure in particular reflects Domitian's conservative social program, which encouraged women in domestic pursuits. Her intricate hairstyle reflects her virtue as a wife, enhancing her personal appearance and therefore her husband's reputation. The masterful use of a chisel and particularly of the drill to carve the locks of her elaborate hair create a work of great volume that foreshadows the marble portraiture of the second century, differing from it only in undrilled pupils and the softer finish on this portrait's flesh.

Two posthumous portraits of former emperors also come from the Sacellum of the Augustales at Misenum. The marble statues of Vespasian and Titus found in situ in niches in the interior of the Sacellum provide a case study in imperial commemoration. Each appears as an idealized nude divine figure with a supporting cuirass of the type found in late Hellenistic sculpture and occasionally in late Republican commemorative portraiture (Figure 1.6) with the heavy musculature of the late Hellenistic and the stout body proportions of other Flavian portraiture. These heavy, almost identical bodies are each combined with a head that reflects the conventions of veristic portraiture of the Flavians with broad faces, wrinkles, close-set eyes, and receding hairlines.

SCHOLARLY PERSPECTIVE
Domitian and the redefinition of virtus

An important cultural shift that occurred in the Roman imperial world was the redefinition of *virtus*. Under the Republic, the quality that defined a man, in Latin a *vir*, was consistently applied to those men who demonstrated success in battle and it was celebrated in public monuments, private homes, epitaphs, and literature. By the second century CE, however, the emperor Hadrian had successfully promoted a notion of *virtus* demonstrated by hunting large wild animals, an activity at which he excelled (Figures 8.26, 8.27). The earliest artistic evidence for this redefinition occurs, however, under Domitian at the Sacellum of the Augustales, the shrine dedicated to the cult of the deified Vespasian and Titus at Misenum on the north side of the Bay of Naples.

    The statue that commands our attention here is an equestrian bronze that originally stood in the forecourt of the temple. The rider is almost completely intact while only the horse's head and legs are preserved, enough to accurately reconstruct its rearing pose. The rider's pose, attributes, and decoration reflect Domitian's public imagery. This image has generally been understood as Domitian in battle on a rearing or charging horse with an enemy soldier under the horse's hooves. This is incorrect, however, for a number of important reasons.

    The horse is rearing and pulling away from whatever lay under and in front of it. Its flared nostrils, wide eyes, and laid back ears show that it is terrified; this is not a normal pose for a seasoned equestrian mount and contrasts with horses in military reliefs. In addition, Domitian is not dressed for battle, with neither a helmet, sword, shield, or military boots, all integral components of the iconography of the Roman soldier trampling an enemy soldier (see the Great Trajanic Frieze panels, Figure 8.22). His breastplate is not Roman military armor either. He wears Roman senatorial shoes as found in civilian reliefs such as the processions on the Ara Pacis, not military boots. Nor is the stabbing spear he is armed with military issue either. The cuirass is a close copy of that on the portraiture of Alexander the Great (see the Alexander mosaic at Pompeii, Figure 4.21). At the center is the Gorgoneion associated with Athena in Classical art. This breastplate is personalized to Domitian, however, as the right shoulder strap has a figure of the infant Hercules strangling the serpents sent by Hera to kill him. Domitian's identification with Hercules is well attested in the literary sources and his public imagery associated Vespasian with Jupiter and himself with Hercules, the son of Jupiter and his agent on earth. Like Hercules, Domitian adopted Athena/Minerva as his patron deity, and her temple was the centerpiece of his forum in Rome, the so-called Forum Transitorium. This statue with its mix of Hercules imagery and a combination of military and civilian dress conforms to the conventions of slightly later hunting imagery.

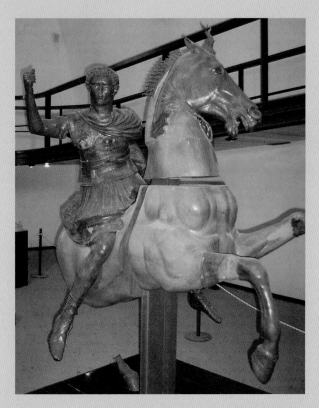

7.19 Equestrian statue of Domitian, *c.* 95 CE, his face later replaced with that of his successor, Nerva, Sacellum of the Augustales, Misenum. Museo Archeologico dei Campi Flegrei, Baia. H of rider 4 ft 3 in (1.3 m), bronze. Photo courtesy Steven L. Tuck.

Domitian was known as a skilled hunter who put on public performances and kept a wild animal park outside of Rome for hunting performances, including lion and deer hunts, inspired by the labors of Hercules. The figure should be reconstructed as a lion hunt with the emperor thrusting with a spear at the crouching lion under the front hooves of his rearing horse, like all horses terrified of large cats, reined in by the emperor holding the reins with his left hand. The equestrian statue marks an important milestone in Roman art. It provides the earliest extant evidence of imperial hunting imagery and of the redefinition of *virtus* away from the military sphere into the field of hunting. The association of *virtus* with hunting is found in wall paintings, mosaics, reliefs, and sculpture groups from the second to the fifth centuries CE. This equestrian bronze represents a key development in imperial art and ideology illustrating a profound cultural change that occurs under the principate.

Steven L. Tuck, "The Origins of Imperial Hunting Imagery: Domitian and the Redefinition of *Virtus* under the Principate." *Greece & Rome* 52.2: 221–245 (2005).

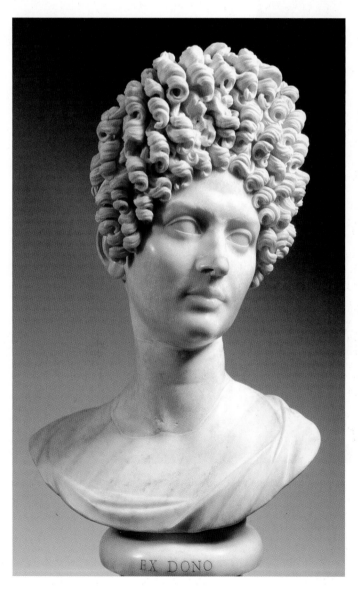

7.20 Portrait bust of a Flavian lady, *c.* 90 CE, Rome. Musei Capitolini, Rome. H 25 ¼ in (64.1 cm), marble.
Source: © The Art Archive/Alamy.

(a)

(b)

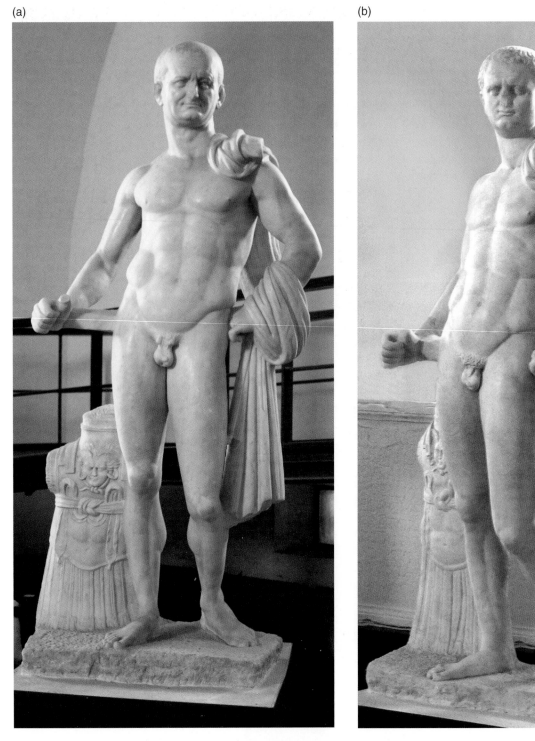

7.21a and 7.21b   Portraits of the deified Vespasian and Titus, Sacellum of the Augustales, Misenum, *c.* 95 CE. Museo Archeologico dei Campi Flegrei, Baia. H of each with base 7 ½ ft (2.3 m), marble. Photo courtesy Steven L. Tuck.

Historical reliefs

Arch of Titus

One of Domitian's first public works was a triumphal arch honoring his brother, Titus, following Titus' premature death in 81 CE. The arch was constructed over the Via Sacra at the highest point on the Velia and, along with the Colosseum and the Baths of Titus, on the grounds of the Domus Aurea, so it belongs to the collection of buildings redirecting that land to public use. The dedicatory inscription names the Senate and People of Rome as the dedicators, but Domitian's role was probably critical as the arch celebrated the entire Flavian dynasty in its original sculptural program, now only partially preserved.

The single passageway arch is decorated with two large panel reliefs in the passage that reproduce scenes from the joint triumph of Vespasian and Titus in 71 CE following their victory in the Jewish War. The panels demonstrate the state of historical relief sculpture under the Flavians and the integration of both Greek and Italic sculptural traditions into public historical relief sculpture.

The Spoils relief panel seems to show some of the most recognizable spoils from the Jewish Wars being carried by attendants in tunics in the triumphal procession, each object preceded by a *tabula ansata*, a plaque that named the object for the spectators. From the right a table with ritual objects and the Menorah, a

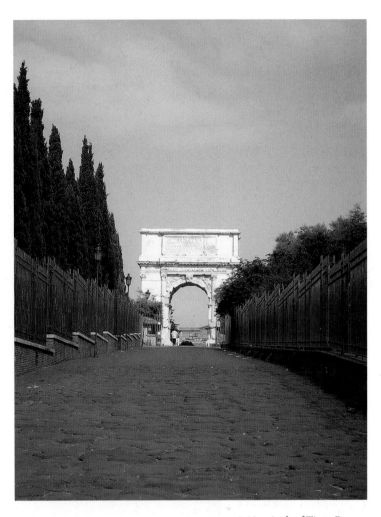

7.22 Arch of Titus, Rome, overall view up the Via Sacra (Sacred Way), after 81 CE. Photo courtesy Steven L. Tuck.

seven-branched candelabrum, are both identifiable. These were probably selected as they would have been recognized by the Roman populace from the triumph itself, the description of it by Flavius Josephus, or by their later display in the Templum Pacis. The portrayal of an historical event is consistent with the Italic tradition, as is the use of architecture to provide context and the illusion of space; here in the archway the procession passes through on the right, which may be another triumphal arch or this one portrayed anachronistically. The attendants, however, display Greek sculptural conventions including their elongated proportions, isocephaly, and the use of shallow profile faces on the figures in the background to indicate depth. Many of the elements, such as contextualizing architecture and sculptural conventions of overlapping, are familiar from the Triumph of Tiberius on the Boscoreale cup B (Figure 6.4).

The Chariot panel also shows a scene from the triumphal procession of 71 CE, but here the subject is Titus himself standing in a *quadriga*, a four-horse chariot, and holding a scepter and palm branch. In addition to his twelve lictors, the bodyguards of a Roman magistrate with *imperium*, and a number of divine figures are also present, marking a clear difference from the Triumph of Tiberius on Boscoreale cup B (Figure 6.4). Rather than a slave, Victory herself crowns the victorious Titus with a laurel wreath. Virtus, the personification of martial prowess, holds the head of the leading horse while personifications of the Senate and People of Rome, each now heavily damaged, flank the chariot to the front and back respectively. This combination of human and divine in the same scene might seem to lessen its historical impact but to a Roman audience they represent familiar elements from their sculptural tradition and would serve to reinforce the power of the event rather than to undermine it. As with the Spoils relief Greek sculptural conventions are used, notably isocephaly and

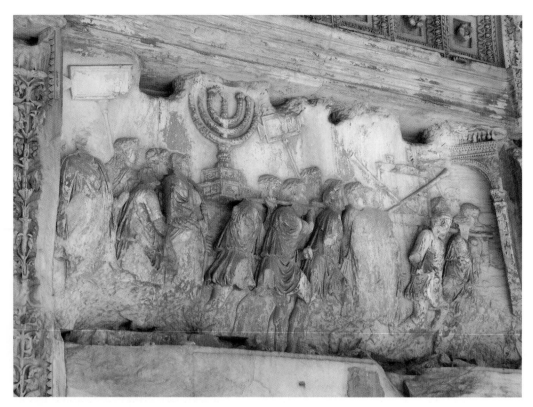

7.23 Relief of Spoils from the Temple in Jerusalem in the Triumphal Procession, Arch of Titus, Rome, after 81 CE. H 6 ft 7 in (2 m). Photo courtesy Steven L. Tuck.

7.24 Relief of Titus in triumphal chariot, Arch of Titus, Rome, after 81 CE. H 6 ft 7 in (2 m). Photo courtesy Steven L. Tuck.

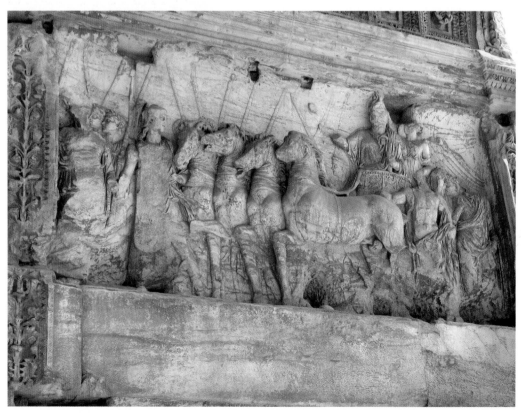

the use of shallow profiles and offset figures in an attempt to display depth. The overlapping and receding horses notably illustrate a convention found in Greek relief sculpture as early as the sixth century BCE.

Cancelleria reliefs

A later set of public reliefs, the Cancelleria reliefs, were found in the late 1930s under the Cancelleria Palace in Rome along with the *Vicomagistri* reliefs (Figure 6.14). The reliefs, datable to 93–96 CE, contain many elements familiar from the Arch of Titus panels, with the combination of divine and human figures and the subject of an imperial procession. Yet their very Classicizing style illustrates the range of styles of official art during Domitian's fifteen years of rule. This pair of marble relief panels was discovered leaning against an ancient Roman tomb, probably part of a stock of marble collected for later reuse. Scholars believe that they were removed from a building in Rome, probably shortly after Domitian's death, and they exemplify both high quality sculpture and the use and reuse of imperial state reliefs by successive emperors. Neither the desire to eliminate an unpopular emperor from public monuments nor the reuse of works were unique in Roman art. When an emperor was assassinated without heirs these two trends converge in the rapid recarving of his public images and erasing of his name from inscriptions. The modern name for this practice is *damnatio memoriae*, condemnation of memory.

The first relief, apparently showing the *adventus* of Vespasian to Rome, has Domitian greeting his father upon his return to Rome. Vespasian is recognizable in a toga and standing facing left near the right edge of the relief. A youthful Domitian, also in a toga, faces him. The remainder of the figures in the front rank standing on the groundline are lictors, priests, and priestesses, and Roman officials whose presence reinforces the rank and importance of the two principals. The figures in the back row are all divine. Victory can just be seen hovering behind Vespasian holding a laurel wreath over his head. Behind and flanking Domitian are the personifications of the Senate, a bearded mature man to his left, and the People of Rome, a young man to his right. *Virtus* is carved to the far left seated on a throne-like chair. The conventions of depth rely on Classical sculpture with the figures in the front rank all carved with three-quarter view heads while those in the upper, back rank have profile faces. The lack of any contextualizing landscape or architecture is also a Classicizing feature. Uniquely Roman, however, the sculptors have added details that explain the heights of the figures in the back rank using the throne and a footstool as supports.

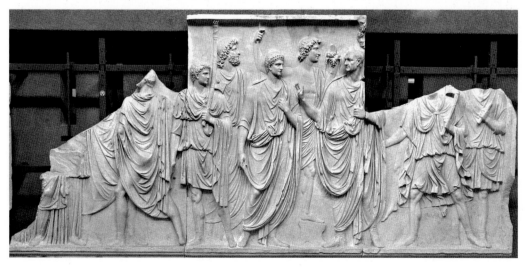

7.25 Cancelleria relief of *adventus* of Vespasian, Rome, 93–96 CE. Musei Vaticani, Rome. Marble, H 6 ¾ ft (2.06 m). Source: Rome101.com (a DBA of LiveSky, Inc.).

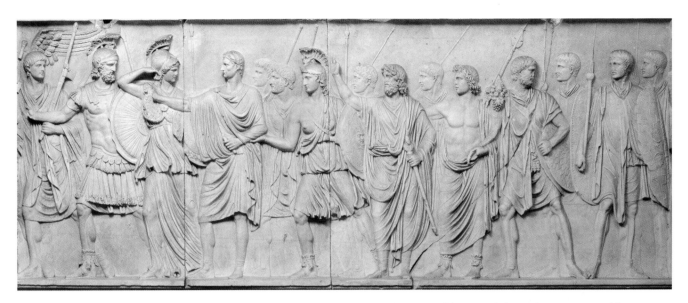

7.26   Cancelleria relief of *profectio* of Domitian, Rome, 93–96 CE. Musei Vaticani, Rome. Marble, H 6 ¾ ft (2.06 m). Source: © Araldo de Luca/Corbis.

FORM & FUNCTION
Personifications in Roman art

The use of personifications, the representation of non-human things as humans, is an integral element of Greek and Roman art. These figures, overwhelmingly female, play an important role in the arts allowing the depiction of a range of peoples, places, and things that would otherwise be almost impossible to portray. Categories of personifications include geographical and cosmological divisions (mountains, rivers, celestial bodies, the sky, sea, and heavens), ethnic groups and divisions of people (tribes, provinces, cities, and kingdoms), personal qualities (health, courage, clemency), abstract qualities (peace, love, victory, fear, inspiration, justice), and divisions of time (seasons, eternity, months, and time itself). In Roman art, particularly public art, personifications work as a means of defining place, time, and people allowing a readable statement of Roman power in a variety of media. The most common types found in Roman art are personifications of people and geographical areas in historical reliefs (Figures 6.4, 9.10). The Senate and People of Rome are commonly represented in public art (Figure 7.26). In more personal works of art such as mosaics and sarcophagi personifications serve to express notions of time, qualities, and beliefs, often without captions, their identities successfully expressed through attributes (Figures 10.17, 10.18).

profectio
a ritual departure, generally of a Roman commander from the city to war. It was essentially the opposite of the *adventus*, also taking place at the city gates.

The second Cancelleria relief portrays Domitian's *profectio* for the Sarmatian War of 93–95 CE. Many of the same figures can be seen escorting the emperor out of Rome as welcomed Vespasian in the paired relief, certainly a deliberate technique to connect the emperor to his father. Along with the human officials and soldiers, the personification of *Virtus* holds his elbow while the personifications of the Senate and People of Rome follow. Leading Domitian from the left can be seen Victory, Mars, and Minerva, the latter his particular patron deity. Again this relief has no architecture or landscape for context, but the figures here are displayed in a single rank with a pronounced isocephaly. Domitian's face is particularly striking since it looks nothing like his lifetime portraiture. In fact, the features are those of his successor, Nerva, and the recutting of the relief demonstrates the reuse of the reliefs after Domitian's death when Nerva was attempting to bolster his own position as emperor.

Tomb of the Haterii

An important, because rare, example of private relief sculpture from the period of Domitian is from the Tomb of the Haterii, found outside the Porta Maggiore at Rome. The reliefs show the continuity of traditional Italic sculptural subjects and conventions. One of the three major reliefs depicts a *collocatio*, the lying in state of the deceased that was a subject found throughout Greek, Lucanian, and Etruscan art although this is the only example known in Roman sculpture. For a wealthy family like the Haterius the *collocatio* took place in the atrium of the family home.

This relief shows a female member of the family on a *lectus* in an atrium. The architectural setting is indicated by a split scene with a cutaway of the building opened so that the interior and roof are both visible. Another Italic convention used is hierarchy of scale with the most important figures larger. In this case the deceased is the largest, followed by what must be members of her immediate family, husband and daughters, behind the *lectus*. The figures on the groundline in the foreground are smaller dependent on their status and relationship with the deceased. The immediate family is also on a groundline that should not exist if this were a visually consistent scene, another Italic convention. Finally, in the upper right a small scene that seems to show the deceased in life seated at a desk, perhaps composing her will, represents another Italic convention of episodic narrative with the main figure portrayed multiple times in different episodes in the same scene.

Architecture

Architecture under Domitian reveals two major trends, increasingly elaborate Classical decoration and revolutionary concrete construction, both of which began under Nero and continue under the emperors of the second century. The first is an expanded use of architectural decoration found on

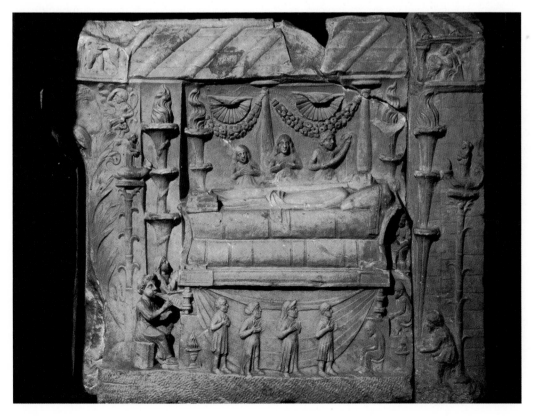

7.27 *Collocatio* relief, Tomb of the Haterii, Rome, *c.* 90–100 CE. Musei Vaticani, Rome. H 30 in (76.2 cm), marble. Source: © Heritage Image Partnership Ltd./Alamy.

ART AND LITERATURE
Flavian architecture and ekphrastic poetry

Poetry under the Flavian emperors is an important source for understanding the forms of public and private art and architecture. **Ekphrasis** plays a key role in this. In Flavian ekphrasis the emotions and associations art and architecture evoke make poetry a critical source for our understanding of the reception of Flavian art and architecture.

Martial (*c.* 38–104 CE) wrote epigrams under a number of powerful patrons at Rome beginning in *c.* 64 CE. His first book of these was the *Liber Spectaculorum*, which includes epigrams written to commemorate the inaugural games in the Colosseum in 80 CE. The first three poems serve as an introduction defining the achievement of the construction of the amphitheater and the games. Epigram 1 in the collection establishes the conventions of comparison by stating the superiority of the Flavian amphitheater over the pyramids, the walls and gardens at Babylon, the Temple of Artemis at Ephesus, the Altar of Horn on Delos, and the Mausoleum at Halicarnassus. These are six of the foreign buildings considered the Wonders of the World. The amphitheater is Rome's answer to all previous architectural wonders, and it surpasses them all: "All labor yields to Caesar's Amphitheater: Fame will tell of one work instead of them all" (*Spect.* 1.7–8).

In the next poems, Martial provides additional context to understand the amphitheater and its effect on the city. Epigram 2 advertises the Flavian intention of returning the land that was part of Nero's Golden House to the use of the people of Rome. The contrast between Nero seizing the vast acreage for his personal pleasure and the Flavians returning that land and, by building the Baths of Titus and the amphitheater, repurposing it for the pleasure of the entire populace couldn't be clearer: "Here . . . the hated halls of a cruel king used to gleam" (2.3) while now "the awesome bulk of the amphitheatre soars before our eyes" (2.5–6). Epigram 3 stresses that the audience for the amphitheater in Rome is drawn from across the Roman world and not just from Rome itself and certainly not only from among its upper classes: "What people is so far removed and so barbarous that there is no spectator from it in your city, Caesar?" (3.1–2). In one of his later poems, *Epigram* 8.36, Martial describes the palace of Domitian, again drawing flattering comparisons to previous Wonders of the World and even mythological figures. He reveals the contemporary imperial ideology of the emperor Domitian as the new Jupiter on earth surpassing the traditional Olympian gods, a notion that develops throughout the second century.

Martial's slightly younger contemporary, Statius (*c.* 45–96 CE), also composed poetry that employed extended ekphrasis. Statius' *Silvae* 4.2 serves as a thank you for a dinner invitation at Domitian's palace. Often dismissed as a work of shallow praise to a monarch, it actually reveals the notions of design and imperial ideology behind the construction of the palace through the comparison between Domitian and Jupiter and the catalog of imported marbles that decorated the palace, drawn from across the entire Roman world. Cataloging them indicates that Domitian's selection was intended to project Roman control over the edges of imperial territory as well as control over the resources necessary to bring these materials to Rome, a power that rested in the hands of the emperor. In *Silvae* 2.2, Statius employs these themes in a description of a visit to a *villa maritima* of Pollius Felix, overlooking the Bay of Naples. The villa is presented as a technological marvel demonstrating man's conquest of nature by overcoming the restrictions of the site and constructing a massive complex on the top of a cliff. The villa is a metaphor for the triumph of Roman morals and virtue over the natural world "where once the sun shone through clouds of dust and the way was wild and unlovely, now it is a pleasure to go." The extensive descriptions of Greek art and imported marbles show that what had once been celebrated by emperors for public spaces, as at Augustus' Temple of Apollo, was now appropriate for domestic spaces. It also reflects the superiority of the Roman system over foreign powers and cultures. Both nature itself and foreign cultures are tamed by Roman character and architecture.

traditional building forms. This is a very ornate Classicism and seems to be the design style chosen by Domitian or his architects for traditional building types such as temples. The style consists of expanded use of friezes of traditional type, such as egg and dart, bead and reel, or acanthus, but now cut and drilled more deeply and often with multiple friezes where in the past one would have served to decorate a temple entablature, for example. This leads to a profusion of decoration, which is richly detailed and more volumetric than in the past. Elements both architectural and decorative recede and project more than previously seen. The best extant example of this is seen on the entablature of the Temple of Vespasian and Titus in the Forum Romanum. The same style of work can be seen on Domitian's Forum Transitorium, laid out in the narrow space between the Temple of Peace and the Forum Augustum. While the poor preservation of the Arch of Titus makes it impossible to tell, this Classicism probably applied to it, as can be seen in the elaborate series of decorative friezes that frame the central sculptural relief of the apotheosis of the deified Titus inside the passageway.

Domitian's most influential architectural complex, however, was his palace on the Palatine Hill in Rome. While not the first palace built on the Palatine by an emperor, it was the largest and remains the best preserved. Later overbuilding, including wings of this palace, covers all the earlier palaces of Tiberius, Caligula, and Nero. The architect Rabirius was responsible for a massive complex which presented many challenges, including an irregular site and pre-existing buildings. He chose to create

ekphrasis
a rhetorical device consisting of a self-contained description often of an event or of a work of art or architecture.

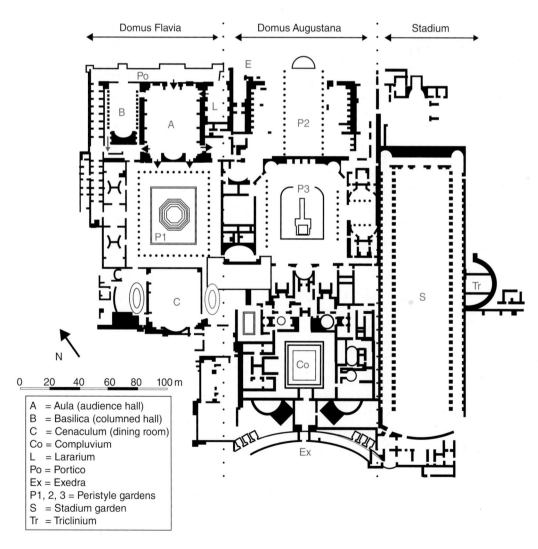

7.28 Plan of the Palace of Domitian, 92 CE, Palatine Hill, Rome, designed by the architect Rabirius. Cassius Ahenobarbus/Wikimedia Commons.

A = Aula (audience hall)
B = Basilica (columned hall)
C = Cenaculum (dining room)
Co = Compluvium
L = Lararium
Po = Portico
Ex = Exedra
P1, 2, 3 = Peristyle gardens
S = Stadium garden
Tr = Triclinium

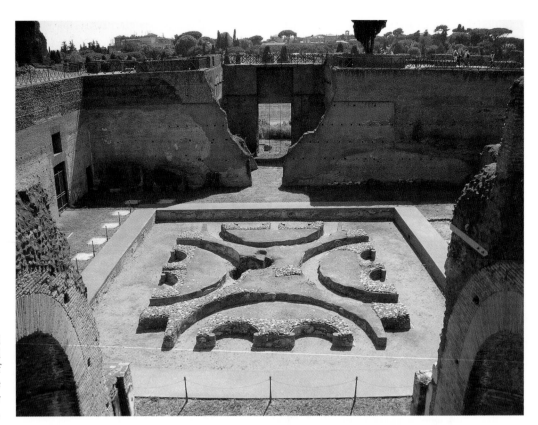

7.29 Garden with central fountain feature surrounded by suites of rooms, Palace of Domitian, 92 CE, Palatine Hill, Rome. Photo courtesy Steven L. Tuck.

a large complex which in places rises over six stories in height. Despite the lack of reliable artificial light, the rooms were not caverns. This was all possible owing to the use of brick-faced concrete as the primary building material.

In addition to adding light, the use of concrete changed the form of the rooms as well. Rabirius experimented primarily with curves, creating multiple spaces that were circular, semi-circular, or apsed. These often alternate with rectangular rooms, foreshadowing the alternating circular and square forms of second-century architecture. These revolutionary room shapes required complex roofing solutions for which traditional gabled roofs were not designed. He relied again on concrete with the result that the circular and semi-circular rooms are roofed with a variety of domes, segmented domes, and half domes while concrete barrel and cross vaults cover some of the rectangular rooms as well. Some of the suites are composed of sets of rooms directly connected with no hallways in between them, a very difficult problem for roofing, but one solved again by the use of concrete. Overall, the complex is boldly experimental and successful. It builds on the work of Severus and Celer in the Domus Aurea and creates new interior spaces that inspired the work of Apollodorus of Damascus and other second-century CE architects.

Concrete construction solved the problem of how to light the rooms at a time when no reliable source of artificial light existed. By using concrete to build great free-standing piers instead of solid walls for structural support, Rabirius created large openings of windows and lightwells in the walls so that light poured into all of the rooms of the various suites in the palace. Open garden spaces and lightwells alternate with suites of closed rooms so that both light and air move through the palace.

Interior climate control in the ancient world was limited. It mainly relied on architecture and setting to keep rooms comfortable in all seasons. Domitian's dining room, on the southwest side of the complex, could have been unbearable in the heat. Rabirius, however, included large windows

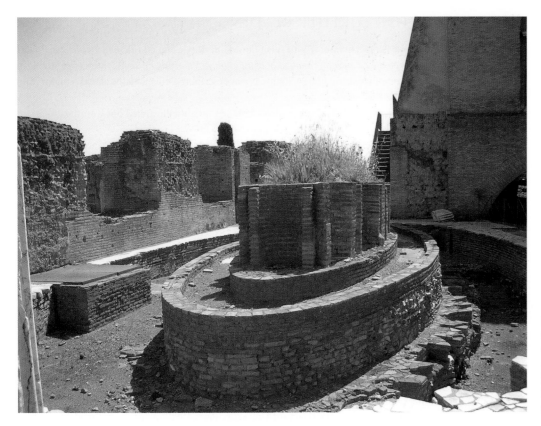

7.30 Fountain adjacent to the dining room (note large windows opening into the dining room on the left), Palace of Domitian, 92 CE, Palatine Hill, Rome. Photo courtesy Steven L. Tuck.

and, just in front of them, an elevated fountain. The prevailing winds from the west blew across the fountain and into the dining room acting as a non-technological form of air conditioning.

CONCLUSION

The art of the Flavian emperors represents an important period of tension, innovation, and transition. Many of the trends develop from their beginnings under the Julio-Claudians into more fully realized components of Roman art and architecture. The architectural revolution, begun under Nero, matures under Domitian with the design and construction of his palace by the architect Rabirius. Its new building forms and solutions to the longstanding problems of air and light in immense building will inspire architects over the next two centuries. The Classicism of Flavian traditional buildings, from the facade of the Colosseum to the entablature of the Temple of Vespasian and Titus in Rome, foreshadows the ornate architecture that has its more spectacular expression at Baalbek.

The sculptural reliefs of the Flavians demonstrate the tensions between Greek and Italic traditions. They also reveal the capability of sculptors to call upon elements of both styles to solve problems of depth and narrative that have hindered two-dimensional works for centuries. The mosaics from Roman Africa show the regional variations of style and subject found across the Roman world. They also provide a sense of images of Roman power as projected in public spectacle. The wall paintings found in Vesuvian lands demonstrate the assimilation of Greek subjects and styles of work into public and domestic settings even in small towns in the Roman world. And yet the uses to which these works are put show that they are effective reinforcements of Roman social, religious, and political structure, providing additional evidence of the inclusive nature of the Roman system.

SUGGESTIONS FOR FURTHER READING

Bettina Bergmann, "Painted Perspectives of a Villa Visit" in Elaine K. Gazda, ed., *Roman Art in the Private Sphere: New Perspectives on the Architecture and Decor of the Domus, Villa, and Insula* (University of Michigan Press 1991). This essay combines an analysis of Statius' poem describing a villa with the actual remains from Campanian villas.

Joanne Berry, *The Complete Pompeii* (Thames & Hudson 2007). A lavishly illustrated book on the city by an expert on the city effectively combines a coffee table book with scholarly insights.

Eve D'Ambra, *Private Lives, Imperial Virtues: The Frieze of the Forum Transitorium in Rome* (Princeton University Press 1993). An excellent work that contextualizes this work of relief sculpture from the forum with Domitian's program of cultural renewal in Rome.

Jodi Magness, "Some Observations on the Flavian Victory Monuments of Rome" in Derek B. Counts and Anthony S. Tuck, eds., *Koine: Mediterranean Studies in Honor of R. Ross Holloway*, 35–40 (Oxbow Books 2009). Provides a survey of the monuments and their meanings in this important category of Flavian public building and art.

Steven L. Tuck, "The Origins of Imperial Hunting Imagery: Domitian and the Redefinition of *Virtus* under the Principate." *Greece & Rome* 52.2: 221–245 (2005). Argues that hunting imagery in imperial art began at least as early as Domitian, contributing to a redefinition of *virtus*.

Michael Vasta, "Flavian Visual Propaganda: Building a Dynasty." *Constructing the Past*, 8.1, Article 10 (2008). http://digitalcommons.iwu.edu/constructing/vol8/iss1/10, accessed July 28, 2014. The author supplies a survey of Flavian dynastic art and the key subjects and themes that defined it with particular emphasis on the role of victory in Flavian public monuments.

Katherine E. Welch, *The Roman Amphitheatre: From Its Origins to the Colosseum* (Cambridge University Press 2007). Welch gives an architectural study of the amphitheater form including detailed analysis of Pompeii's early example and the Colosseum.

Paul Zanker, *Pompeii: Public and Private Life* (Harvard University Press 1998). A serious but readable analysis of aspects of life in Pompeii by a senior scholar who often advances innovative interpretations.

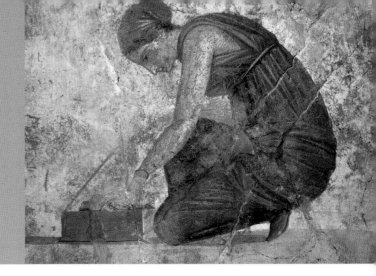

TRAJAN AND HADRIAN, 98–138 CE

Emperors from the Provinces

96–98 CE	Nerva as emperor
98–117 CE	Trajan as emperor
103 CE	Trajan's new harbor of Portus at Ostia begun
106 CE	Conclusion of the Dacian War; conquest of Petra and Nabatean kingdom
109 CE	**Adamclisi victory monument built**
112 CE	**Forum of Trajan inaugurated**
113 CE	**Column of Trajan dedicated**
114 CE	Parthian War begun; **Arch of Trajan, Beneventum**
117–138 CE	Hadrian as emperor
118 CE	**Villa of Hadrian begun**
120 CE	Hadrian's Wall begun
126 CE	**Pantheon completed**
130 CE	**Hadrianic roundels**

A History of Roman Art, First Edition. Steven L. Tuck.
© 2015 Steven L. Tuck. Published 2015 by John Wiley & Sons, Ltd.

This chapter concentrates on the art under emperors from Italica in the Iberian peninsula (modern Spain), Trajan and Hadrian. Their similar emphasis on the provinces reinforces the increasing role of these areas and foreshadows the decline of Rome in the imperial scheme. Their building projects in Rome are addressed but balanced by focus on the art and architecture from outside the city, including projects in many provinces around the empire. In terms of subject, the arts of Trajan and Hadrian are very different: Trajan's public art shows a relentless promotion of his image as a successful general waging a number of victorious wars. Hadrian in contrast added imagery of hunting as an imperial virtue onto a monument in Rome for the first time. Yet their art is stylistically so similar that scholars argue, and will certainly continue to argue, as to which emperor was actually responsible for many key works of sculpture from the period. The commitment to Classicizing figures and style no matter what the subject is found throughout the period. Even the traditional Roman form of the triumphal arch is, under Trajan, covered with sculpture that is Classical in style. Greek mythological sculpture survives from this period from public buildings where it was used to create metaphorical programs celebrating Roman power.

Architecturally, the separate trends of architecture seen earlier continue. The first is the continuing experimentation with concrete, explored first under Apollodorus of Damascus, Trajan's architect, and then under Hadrian himself, a skilled architect. The scale and range of innovative building forms in concrete reaches its zenith in this period thanks to these two men. Nevertheless, Classicizing trends also continue. Hadrian, the most philhellene of emperors, exploited traditional Greek forms in new ways and these two trends come together at his great experimental complex, the Villa of Hadrian at Tivoli.

NERVA, 96–98 CE

The collapse of the Flavian dynasty with the assassination of Domitian in September 96 CE left Roman government in a difficult situation with no natural successor to the office of *princeps*. The Senate selected Marcus Cocceius Nerva for the office and titles of the emperor. The elderly Senator Nerva, a sixty-six-year-old from Narnia, a small town in central Italy, was a figure of stability following the death of Domitian and a staunch supporter of senatorial positions. Nevertheless, his rule was inherently weak since he was elderly, infirm, without a son to create a dynasty, and faced the hostility of the army, who had benefitted from the rule of Domitian, in particular the Praetorian Guard, who were angered by Domitian's assassination. To bolster his rule, in October 97 CE Nerva selected and adopted Trajan, a skilled and popular Roman general, as his heir. This was a remarkable moment in Roman government and from 96 to 180 every emperor was selected by adoption, creating the non-dynasty known as the Five Good Emperors: Nerva, Trajan, Hadrian, Antoninus Pius, and Marcus Aurelius.

Nerva survived only a few more months after his adoption of Trajan, dying in January 98. He ruled for slightly less than sixteen months and, as a result, very little art can be attributed to him. His limited surviving portraiture shows a mature man with a long face, large hooked nose, thin lips, and some facial lines, notably around his mouth and forehead. His hair is notable as it ignores the Flavian style in favor of comma-shaped bangs across the forehead; it seems that Nerva is rejecting Flavian imagery in favor of deliberate associations with Augustus and his Julio-Claudian successors. He could hardly do otherwise since he became emperor after the assassination of the last Flavian, Domitian. The recarved and reused Domitianic images on the bronze equestrian statue from Misenum (Figure 7.19) and the Cancelleria relief (Figure 7.26) from the previous chapter are some of the best examples of his appearance in relief sculpture and sculpture in the round. While not precisely datable, they are thought either to date from his short reign or from the early years of Trajan's rule, when Trajan benefitted from reminders of the recently deceased Nerva, whom he deified. No works of architecture can be assigned to Nerva's reign. Although he dedicated the Forum Transitorium, which is occasionally referred to as the Forum of Nerva, nevertheless the design, decoration, and construction of the space are clearly Domitianic.

TRAJAN, 98–117 CE, AND HADRIAN, 117–138 CE

Trajan (Marcus Ulpius Traianus) was the first Roman emperor from outside of Italy; he was born in 53 CE in Italica in the province of Hispania Baetica. Prior to being named emperor, Trajan had a long and successful military career of over twenty years, culminating in military command and election to the highest offices in Rome under Domitian. His military experience and support from key units in the army, which Nerva himself lacked, was likely the primary reason Nerva settled on him as his adopted son and successor. When Nerva died in January 98 CE, Trajan was serving as governor of Germania Superior and in fact he spent the first year of his rule securing Roman power along the Rhine and Danube river frontiers. This attention to the frontiers was a product of his military training and a theme throughout his reign. Trajan remained an active military commander during his almost twenty years in office. He launched an invasion of Dacia, a large and wealthy kingdom north of the Danube in modern Romania, which he annexed as a province in 106 CE following two wars. His greatest war, however, was against the Parthian empire. The Parthian campaigns began in 114 CE and continued until his death in 117 CE, and resulted in the annexation of Armenia and short-lived conquest of the whole of Mesopotamia including the Parthian capital at Ctesiphon. Trajan's military victories led to the additions of Dacicus, Germanicus, and Parthicus into his imperial name.

Trajan's successful campaigns against the wealthy kingdom of Dacia and the Parthian empire resulted in tremendous plunder that funded an enormous program of public works. Roads, bridges, and harbors were constructed across the empire, with particular emphasis on Rome, Italica, and key ports in Italy, notably a new harbor basin at Ostia. At Rome Trajan's Forum and markets represent the culmination of his building program. Also, provisions were made for the poor as *alimenta*, special funds, were established for their maintenance. He was considered such a great emperor that he was referred to as the *optimus princeps*, the best emperor, and by the fourth century CE the Senate said of new emperors, may you be "more fortunate than Augustus and better than Trajan" (*felicior Augusto, melior Traiano*) (Eutropius, *Breviarium* 8.5.3).

Hadrian (Publius Aelius Hadrianus), was, like Trajan, a native of Italica and on the death of his father became a ward of Trajan. In 98 CE he carried the news of the death of Nerva to Trajan in Germany. Under Trajan he served in a number of key military and civilian offices. Hadrian's succession was uncertain as Trajan did not mark him out as heir prior to Trajan's final illness. Even more damaging, Trajan's wife signed the letter of succession allegedly dictated by Trajan on his deathbed. Women were not supposed to insert themselves into political matters. Many believed that Hadrian's succession was engineered by her rather than at Trajan's instructions, weakening his authority to rule. One of Hadrian's first major acts was to withdraw Roman forces from the Parthian territories invaded and occupied, but never stabilized, by Trajan in his final campaigns. This marked a major reversal of Trajan's foreign policy and foreshadowed Hadrian's eventual policy of imperial consolidation over expansion.

Despite its uncertain beginning, Hadrian's principate (117–138 CE) was long, largely stable, and marked by an attentive emperor dedicated to good government and personal inspection of the provinces, effectively extending Trajan's domestic policies. In fact, Hadrian spent about half of his twenty years of rule traveling the Roman provinces. He personally interviewed public officials, inspected tax records, and ordered new construction especially to fortify the Roman frontiers. Taxes were lowered or even forgiven on occasion as well. Even when in Italy he rarely lived at Rome preferring, like Tiberius before him, to reside at his villa at Tivoli in the countryside of Latium several miles outside

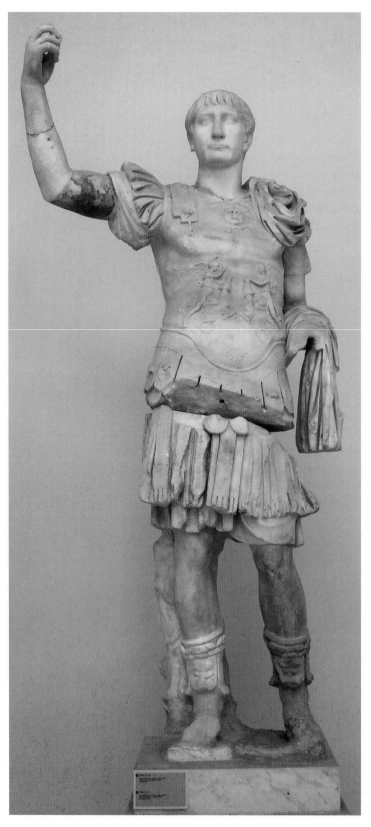

8.1   Portrait of Trajan as victorious general, *c.* 110 CE, Ostia. Museo Archeologico Ostiense. H 6 ft 4 ¾ in (1.95 m), marble. Photo courtesy Daniel Resheter.

the city. A dedicated philhellene, he was the first emperor since Nero fifty years earlier to publicly celebrate Greek culture in his personal life. This commitment to Greek culture and philosophy certainly influenced the form of his public art and architecture.

Portraiture of Trajan and Hadrian

Trajan's portraiture has more in common with that of Augustus than any of his more immediate predecessors, probably to create an association with the last emperor who greatly expanded Roman territory. He appears in his many extant images with a clean-shaven, calm, relatively smooth face topped by a cap of hair combed down straight all around. His hair seems to be a military style, often with variations on the bangs that allude to Augustus' imagery. The major difference between them is that Augustus appeared eternally youthful while Trajan seems to preserve his appearance in middle age, around forty-five when he took office as emperor. A full-length cuirassed image of him from Ostia is an excellent example of his portraits with echoes of the Augustus of Prima Porta in its dress and stance. The cuirass and military cloak over his left shoulder are elements of traditional Roman victory imagery while the paired Victories on the breastplate derive from Greek iconography and can be traced back to reliefs on the Athenian Acropolis in the fifth century BCE. His stance is a variation on Greek contrapposto as well.

Hadrian's portraiture differs from all previous emperors in one significant way: he is the first emperor to be portrayed wearing a full beard. Whether this was because of his desire to be seen as a Greek philosopher or to hide his acne scars – the ancient sources are not in agreement – it is important because it is a style followed by all emperors for the next one hundred years. In addition, it provided an opportunity for sculptors to explore the textural distinctions between hair and skin, and over the next eighty years we can see the development of their skills and techniques in distinguishing between smooth skin and increasingly volumetric hair and beards. Hadrian's hair is combed from the crown of his head, as was Trajan's, but in his case it falls in thick waves and terminates in curls along his forehead; in fact, one ancient source attributes these to the curling iron. Hadrian's portraiture is also similar to Trajan's in his agelessness. He appears throughout his life as he was when he came to power at forty-one.

This remarkable bronze statue was found by chance in 1975 (by a tourist with a metal detector), some 7 miles (12 km) south of Beth Shean (Scythopolis), at a site that was once a camp of the Sixth Roman Legion. The Sixth Legion was stationed here to crush the Bar Kokhba Revolt (132–135 CE) provoked by Hadrian's plan to build a temple of Jupiter on the remains of the Second Temple in Jerusalem destroyed by Titus. The statue is a standard one of a standing cuirassed emperor, here in a rarely surviving bronze version. This metal, unlike marble, was frequently melted down and reused. The head, cast in one piece, is one of the finest portraits of Hadrian and illustrates an artistic advance under Hadrian, the consistent carving of pupils making the eyes more expressive than before. The breastplate, probably reused from an earlier imperial statue, depicts a mythological battle, a subject rarely seen on cuirassed statues, perhaps selected here for a statue in a military camp and not a victory dedication. In this case, it is a scene of the final battle in Vergil's *Aeneid* as the Roman hero Aeneas defeats the opposing king Turnus.

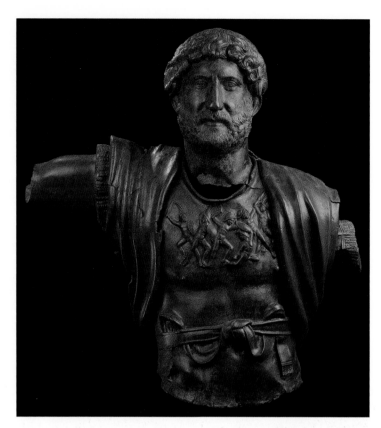

8.2 Bronze cuirassed portrait of Hadrian, *c.* 135 CE, from camp of the Sixth Roman Legion, near Tel Shalem, Israel. The Israel Museum, Jerusalem. H 35 in (89 cm). Source: Israel Antiquities Authority/ The Bridgeman Art Library.

Portraiture of empresses

Developments in female portraiture under Trajan and Hadrian can be illustrated with examples of portraits from Ostia of Plotina, Trajan's wife, and Sabina, Hadrian's wife. Plotina's portrait relies on the conventions of Trajan's with her oval, calm, ageless face and her smooth hair shallowly carved into separate locks. Notable as an extension of the Flavian styles is the fan-shaped bouffant component rising behind her bangs. Also of note is that her pupils are not carved or drilled, a convention that begins in imperial portraiture under Hadrian.

The hairstyle on Sabina's portraits differs from Plotina's and her Flavian predecessors and in fact establishes the precedent for imperial women's imagery for the remainder of the century. While her Classicizing face is consistent with the Trajanic pattern her hair is a rejection of the elaborate styles of the past thirty years. It is center parted and brushed back and fastened into a loose bun, ponytail or, in this case, chignon. Rather than the volume of hair seen earlier on the top of her head, she wears a diadem, sometimes simple but here a lunate one combined with a veil. This style is based on images of Classical Greek goddesses, in this case probably Venus. Other portraits of Sabina also specifically reference important goddesses including Juno and Ceres. This sort of combined identity of empresses and goddesses dates back to Livia, the wife of Augustus, and continues in imperial portraits into the third century CE.

Architecture

Trajan and Hadrian were both responsible for tremendous building programs across the entire Roman world, although you might be dubious of this given the sparse remains. Unfortunately for us, many of these were not the type of practical infrastructure that survives, nor do many ancient authors give detailed descriptions or analysis. Not many ancient authors spend their time describing remarkable sewer systems and the vaults of bath buildings. Nevertheless Trajan's primary architect, Apollodorus of Damascus, is credited with a phenomenal range and amount of design and building

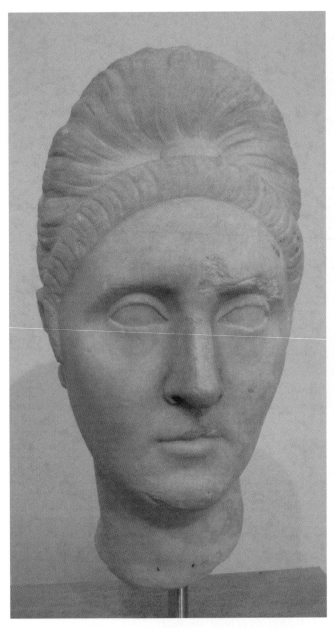

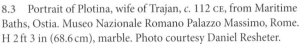

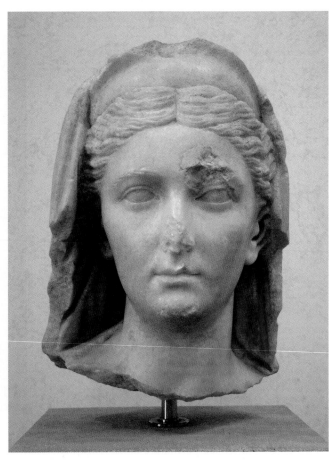

8.4   Portrait of Sabina, wife of Hadrian, *c.* 135 CE, from Maritime Baths, Ostia. Museo Archeologico Ostiense. H 14 in (35.6 cm), marble. Photo courtesy Daniel Resheter.

8.3   Portrait of Plotina, wife of Trajan, *c.* 112 CE, from Maritime Baths, Ostia. Museo Nazionale Romano Palazzo Massimo, Rome. H 2 ft 3 in (68.6 cm), marble. Photo courtesy Daniel Resheter.

work for Trajan including a massive bridge over the Danube to aid in the invasion of Dacia. Trajan's major construction project in the city of Rome is his Forum and markets, both believed to be the works of Apollodorus, and together responsible for reshaping the center of the city in antiquity.

The Forum of Trajan (Forum Traiani) was the fifth, largest, and final of the imperial fora. Trajan's relies on the basic design and building sets of each previous imperial forum, consisting of an open plaza surrounded by a portico, an emphasis on axiality and symmetry with an entrance on one short end, and a temple as the culminating monument at the opposite short end. The major buildings include a basilica, the Basilica Ulpia, two libraries, and the Column of Trajan. The design with its pairs of large hemicycles deliberately references the adjacent Forum of Augustus. An enormous volcanic stone firewall is also a feature adopted from Augustus' forum as was the use of an equestrian

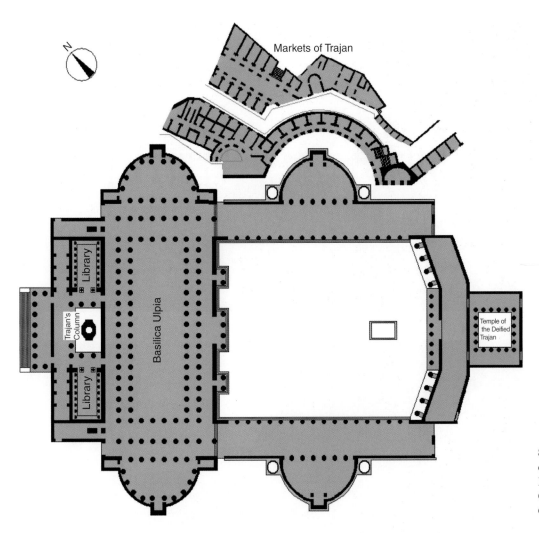

Markets of Trajan

N

Library

Library

Trajan's Column

Basilica Ulpia

Temple of the Deified Trajan

8.5 Plan of the Forum of Trajan (Forum Traiani), Rome, dedicated 113 CE. Cristiano64l/Wikimedia Commons.

statue of the emperor as the central decorative element in the plaza. In all of these components Apollodorus has arranged traditional building forms into a massive new, level space over 650 ft (200 m) in length. It was created by carving out the flank of the Quirinal Hill, a type of excavation also seen in Trajan's rerouting of the Via Appia at Terracina. Although badly preserved, the forum has been extensively studied and it is clear that the building forms rely heavily on the Classicizing styles of the late Flavians with ornate friezes and complex capitals and decorative elements on the traditional building forms. The decoration of the forum, addressed in detail below (Sculpture), is, however, unprecedented in its subject if not its theme, the victory over the Dacians, which paid for this construction. For the first time in the city of Rome the active prosecution of warfare is graphically portrayed as the primary means of celebrating a military triumph, establishing a precedent that will influence future public art for centuries.

The most remarkable and innovative of Trajanic architectural projects were the Markets of Trajan, which extend in six stories up the flank of the Quirinal Hill above the Forum of Trajan in space that presented enormous challenges for the architect, Apollodorus. Given the lack of reliable artificial light in the Roman world, a multi-story complex built against a cliff with no access, light, or air from the cliff side presents enormous challenges, particularly to the lower stories. Apollodorus turned to the materials and forms of the architectural revolution, building on the work of Rabirius and relying on brick-faced concrete to create an extraordinary complex of over one hundred and fifty individual shops and offices of rounded forms, barrel vaulted passages, and compound domed spaces supported by piers and lighted by enormous windows. The great **hemicycle** facade that makes up the

hemicycle
literally a half-circle. In architecture, a hemicycle is a wall, building, or architectural feature constructed in the shape of a half circle.

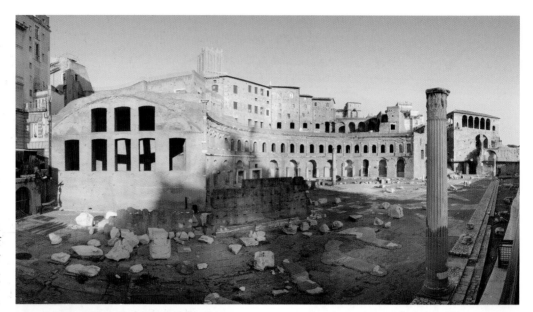

8.6   Markets of Trajan designed by Apollodorus of Damascus, *c.* 110 CE, view from the Forum of Trajan, Rome. Matthias Kabel/Wikimedia Commons.

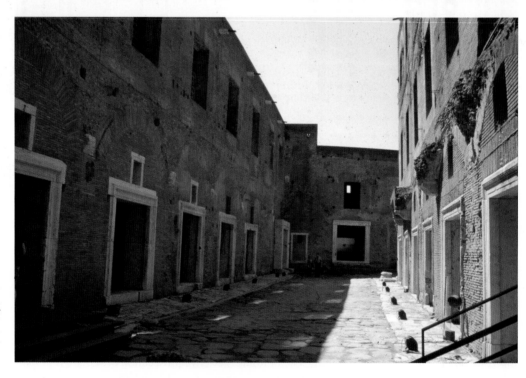

8.7   Street of shops, Markets of Trajan designed by Apollodorus of Damascus, Rome, *c.* 110 CE. Photo courtesy Steven L. Tuck.

ground floor facing Trajan's Forum demonstrates how the need for light drove the design. The semi-circular shape creates a longer building than a straight line would and the lower floor serves as a foundation for the upper floors.

Each of the shops has an open door surmounted by an open transom while each end of the ground floor terminates in a space lighted by great windows under a vaulted roof and a form of sky-light to carry the light into the interior spaces, passageways, and stairs. The upper stories are each stepped back from the lower ones. Rather than the lightwells and sunken courtyards of Domitian's palace, here smaller courtyards, windows, and skylights channel additional light into each level.

The central feature of the complex is what is known as the main market hall, a vaulted space over 91 ft (28 m) long with two stories of six shops on each level on each side of the hall. Those in the upper story are set back from the line of shops on the lower story, and fronted by a corridor with balustraded openings corresponding to the six bays of the central vault. This refinement creates an open space in front of the line of shops allowing light to pour into both stories of the hall. The vault is not a solid barrel vault, but is cross-vaulted, lifting the roof in each bay as an extra refinement to provide light into the space. Piers rather than columns support this utilitarian yet innovative structure, which uses concrete construction to offset the difficulties of the site creating a multi-story interior space of the type previously only seen in imperial palaces.

The Pantheon is the best-preserved surviving Roman temple. The name (from the Greek *pan* meaning all and *theon* meaning building of the gods) suggests that it was dedicated to all the gods, but nothing is known of any actual cult activity in it. It represents the culmination of the architectural revolution in Rome. Its revolutionary features include the extreme emphasis on the interior over the exterior, contrasting the pattern of traditional Roman temple architecture. In this case, the drab exterior was deliberately designed to hide the form of the interior. It is also designed as a central plan building, made possible by the vast concrete dome, contrasted with a traditional rectangular plan temple with an apse or statue niche in the rear wall. Finally, it exemplifies the revolutionary creation of space emphasizing light and height. The interior is also brightly

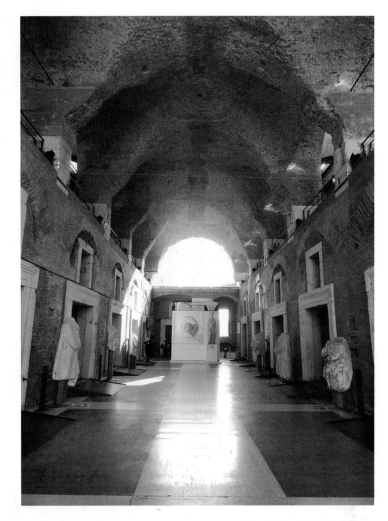

8.8 Main Hall, Markets of Trajan designed by Apollodorus of Damascus, Rome, *c.* 110 CE. Photo courtesy Daniel Resheter.

colored, clad in a variety of imported marbles, a feature of the style. Constructed under Hadrian, and many scholars believe designed by him personally, it dates after 126 CE and was a replacement for the Pantheon of Marcus Agrippa that stood on this spot until destroyed in the fire of 80 CE. The building faces due north to the Mausoleum of Augustus and consists of three elements: a porch, an intermediate block, and the rotunda.

The porch gives the building the facade of a traditional Roman temple with its high pediment hiding the dome behind. This was clearly the designer's intent, as a visitor approaching from the front would not see the vast dome from the exterior. In fact, this would have been even more effective in antiquity when the ground level was lower and the porch originally designed with taller columns. The dome was only visible from inside when one reached the front door. It creates a visual surprise of the type seen throughout Hadrian's architecture. This surprise was reinforced by the apparent replication of the original dedicatory inscription of 27 BCE, "M. AGRIPPA L.F. COS TERTIUM FECIT" ("Marcus Agrippa, son of Lucius, consul for the third time, made this"). The intermediate block between the porch and rotunda, patterned on the triumphal arch, seems designed to create access to the attic rooms while further screening the rotunda from viewers on the outside.

The rotunda is supported by a great concrete drum, which appears as a solid circular wall, but structurally is far more complex. The drum consists of eight great compound piers that alternate with seven niches and the entrance creating a rhythm along the interior wall. The niches alternate rectangular and semi-circular in form with only thin curtain walls behind them. The eight piers

(a)

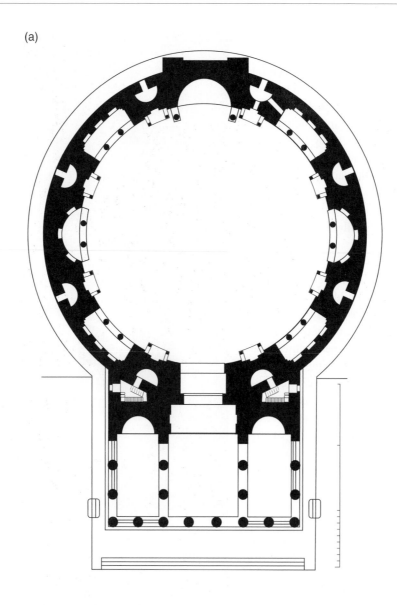

(b)

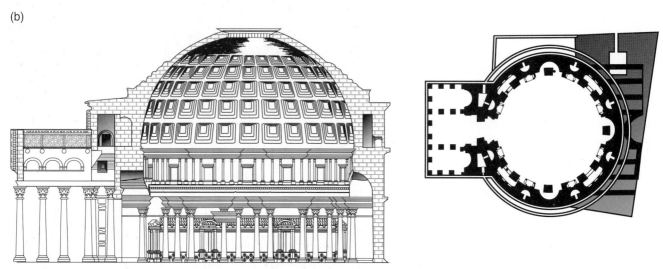

8.9a and 8.9b   Pantheon, Rome, after 126 CE, plan and section. (a) Plan: Georg Dehio/Gustav von Bezold: *Kirchliche Baukunst des Abendlandes*. Stuttgart: Verlag der Cotta'schen Buchhandlung 1887–1901, Plate No. 1. (b) Section: Lueger, Otto: *Lexikon der gesamten Technik und ihrer Hilfswissenschaften*, Bd. 5 Stuttgart, Leipzig 1907, S. 790–791. http://www.zeno.org/nid/20006070620.

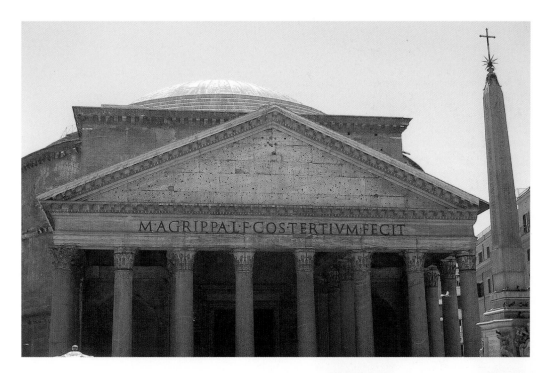

8.10 Pediment on the Pantheon, Rome, after 126 CE. Photo courtesy Steven L. Tuck.

support the entire weight of the structure. To lighten the load, the aggregate in the concrete, the coarse filler that is one component of concrete, is made of lighter materials as the drum rises. At the base of the walls where more support is needed, denser travertine is used, then tufa, broken up brick, and finally pumice, the lightest material, is found in the dome where it does not need to support any further superstructure.

The rotunda is roofed by a large dome, a perfect half sphere, 141 ft (43.2 m) or 144 Roman feet in diameter, which is exactly the height of the supporting drum, meaning that a sphere 144 Roman feet in diameter would fill the entire top half of the interior while resting on the floor just beneath the oculus. The oculus, the circular opening 29 ½ ft (9 m) in diameter at the top of the dome, is the only light source other than the open doors. The dome is the largest concrete dome constructed prior to the twentieth century and still the largest diameter dome of unreinforced concrete. It represents a remarkable technical achievement as the concrete appears to have been laid in a single batch, an accomplishment that still baffles architectural historians. The circular shape, emphasis on the interior over the exterior, the great dome, the light through the oculus, and the array of colored marbles all contribute to this as the quintessential building of the architectural revolution.

While the Pantheon can be seen as the culmination of the architectural revolution, the various buildings and suites of rooms at Hadrian's villa at Tivoli may be understood as the laboratory where he worked out his

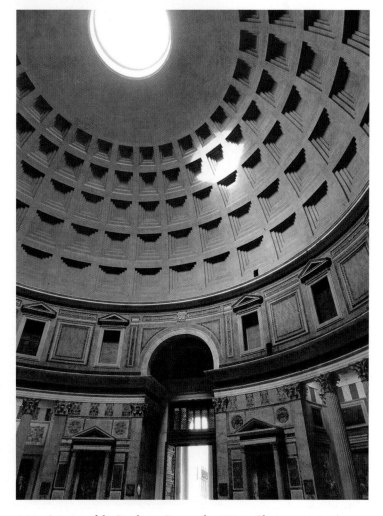

8.11 Interior of the Pantheon, Rome, after 126 CE. Photo courtesy Steven L. Tuck.

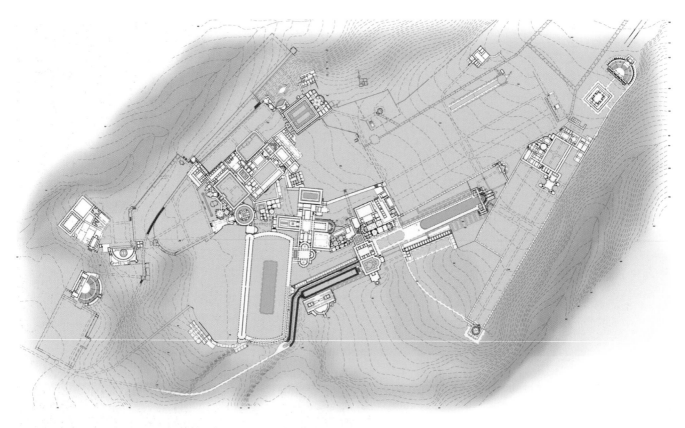

8.12 Plan of the Villa of Hadrian, Tivoli, Hadrianic. © 2012 by The Regents of the University of Virginia. All rights reserved.

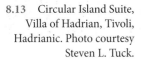

8.13 Circular Island Suite, Villa of Hadrian, Tivoli, Hadrianic. Photo courtesy Steven L. Tuck.

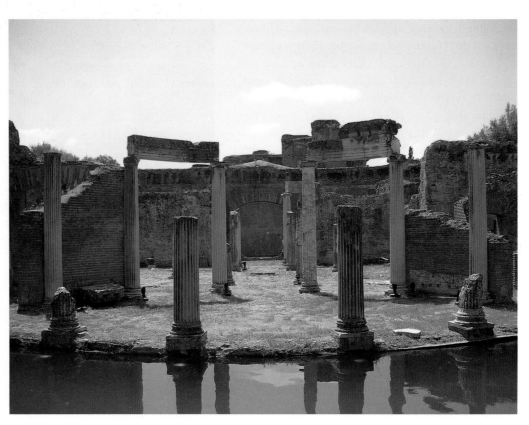

experiments in concrete and radical roofing systems. Many buildings in the complex were designed to evoke the memory of famous buildings and locations around the empire, creating a site where architecture, memory, and ideology intersect. The entire villa complex, constructed during Hadrian's principate and we believe by his design, is a series of scattered suites of rooms, enclosed spaces, and building complexes across a bare and fairly level stretch of land about 17 miles (28 km) from Rome and was the largest imperial villa in the Roman world.

One of the most architecturally sophisticated of the suites is the so-called Teatro Marittimo or Circular Island Suite. While not a theater, its actual use is still debated with some scholars considering it Hadrian's or Sabina's private apartment suite while others think it operated as an astronomical observatory. The suite is an exercise in the architecture of undulating curves and the creation of enclosed space with a minimum of supporting walls. It consists of a circular enclosure wall 144 ft (44 m) in diameter (almost exactly the same as the Pantheon), a surrounding ambulatory with portico, a moat, and a circular island filled with a series of undulating convex and concave rooms around a central courtyard with a fountain. The suite rejects the traditional reliance on axiality and symmetry in favor of spaces laid out with a compass, emphasizing segments of a circle as a design feature. As with other works of the archi-

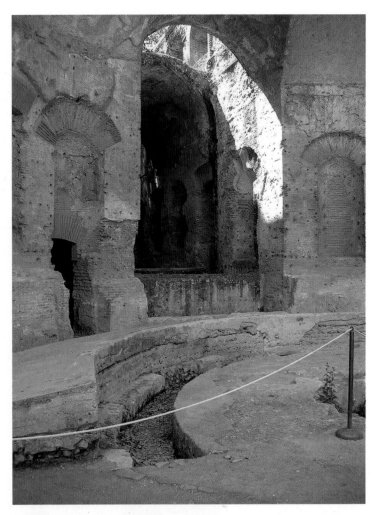

8.14 Serapeum dining complex, Villa of Hadrian, Tivoli, Hadrianic. Photo courtesy Steven L. Tuck.

tectural revolution, the goal here is the creation of spaces with a maximum of light, an exploration of centrally oriented, curvilinear design, and the freedom from heavy supporting walls. Experiments in roofing systems were also a major component, but better examined in what is referred to as the Serapeum, a dining complex with decoration inspired by the sanctuary of Serapis in Alexandria, Egypt.

Hadrian's Serapeum is located on almost the opposite edge of the villa complex and exemplifies an exploration of memory, history, and architectural innovation. The building faces a large artificial pool, called the Canopus after the canal at Alexandria in Egypt running between the Nile and the sanctuary of Serapis, which Hadrian visited on one of his travels. At the far end of the pool stands a semi-circular portico with statues of Mars, Mercury, and Minerva. Along the long side of the pool are four copies of the caryatids from the fifth-century BCE Erechtheion on the Athenian acropolis. These copies may have been rescued from Agrippa's burned Pantheon. On a square platform in the Canopus was a large sculpture group of Scylla similar in placement and design to the one at Tiberius' dining grotto at his villa at Sperlonga (Figure 6.8).

At the southern end of the canal is a small pool and just beyond that the complex of the Serapeum was built into the hillside. The primary audience for this display was the emperor and his guests who reclined on a large semi-circular dining couch facing the Canopus and the sculptural display in and around it. Immediately behind the couch is an artificial grotto perhaps evoking the dining context at Sperlonga. Here it is created with a great concrete half dome 72 ft (22 m) in diameter, exactly half that of the Pantheon. Not a true dome, it is a "melon" vault of which the nine radiating segments alternate in convex curve or flat sections. Hadrian's love of these segmented vault or dome structures is preserved in a famous anecdote. Hadrian offered advice on a building to Apollodorus of Damascus, who responded dismissively, "Go away and draw your melons" (Cassius Dio, *Roman History* 69.4).

That rhythmic flat and curved pattern continues along the back wall with eight statue niches with alternating semi-circular or square tops. The central wall area of the grotto is broken by a deep barrel vaulted chamber that recedes into the hillside. Its sidewalls have eight more alternating statue niches in which black basalt statues stood and it terminates in a large statue niche for a colossal white bust of Serapis with the facial features of Antinous. The design of the Canopus/Serapeum complex evokes the sanctuary of Serapis Hadrian rebuilt at Alexandria and the passing of Antinous who becomes the new deity worshipped here. All of this is created using the materials and building vocabulary of the architectural revolution.

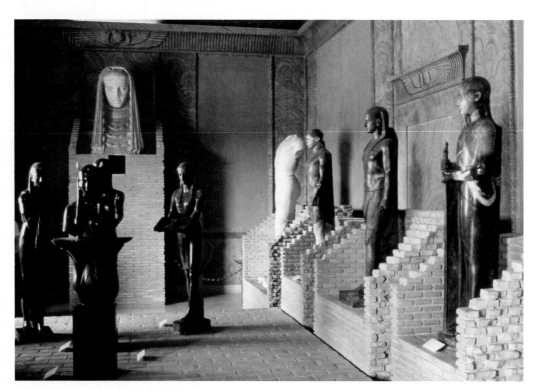

8.15 Sculpture from the Serapeum complex, Villa of Hadrian, Tivoli, Hadrianic. Musei Vaticani, Rome. Photo courtesy Steven L. Tuck.

HISTORICAL CONTEXT
Antinous

Another personal trait that influenced Hadrian's art and architecture was his mourning for Antinous. Antinous, a young man from Bithynia, was the emperor Hadrian's favorite companion and traveling partner. He was famed for his beauty and his relationship with Hadrian may have been sexual, replicating Greek practice where an older man takes a young man as a lover and companion. Antinous drowned in the Nile in 130 CE, either as a result of an accident or willingly giving up his life as a sacrifice to protect the emperor from a death prophecy. When he died Hadrian was distraught, as one source said, "weeping like a woman." In reaction to his loss, he deified Antinous, an unprecedented step for someone not a member of the emperor's family, and founded a cult that included sanctuaries, cities named in his honor, and a rich variety of images of Antinous created and displayed throughout the empire. Antinous was often depicted as an ideally beautiful young man, often with attributes of gods of resurrection such as Osiris and Dionysus.

SCULPTURE

Sculpture under Trajan and Hadrian follows the by now familiar categories of imperial sculpture including historical reliefs, free-standing statues, and relief works that celebrate the emperors, and mythological subjects drawn from Greek myth. The style of the works is in almost all cases very Classicizing, whether it is free-standing sculpture or reliefs, even when the monuments are traditionally Roman, such as triumphal arches. Perhaps the continuity of style found in their reigns owes its form partially to their long periods of rule and partially to their similar upbringing, outlook, and policies. Still, even forty years of very consistent rule did not result in an artistically homogeneous Roman world. The relief panels from the trophy of Trajan at Adamclisi contrast with the artistic product of the Hellenizing workshops in Rome. These demonstrate the need for local styles to communicate with a particular local audience, in that case on the eastern border of the Roman world.

Historical reliefs

The almost forty years of combined rule by Trajan and Hadrian saw the creation of an immense amount of public sculpture and especially of historical relief work. Without a doubt, the largest and most important of these works was the Column of Trajan, set up in his forum in Rome and still in situ and largely intact almost two thousand years later. Victory columns had been erected in Rome since the third century BCE, but none had ever been this large, elaborate, or highly decorated. It serves three purposes. First, its height records the depth of the excavation needed to create enough level space for building the forum complex. Second, it serves as a triumphal monument for the Dacian campaign. Third, although not originally intended, it served as a tomb for Trajan and his wife Plotina, whose cremated remains were placed in golden urns in a chamber in the base of the Column.

The Column is composed of three parts. The first, the base, contains the dedicatory inscription above the door allowing access into the chamber at the foot of the Column and to the 185 spiral stairs that continue up the entire Column. The exterior decoration on the base is of piles of captured arms, armor, and military trumpets carved in relief. Second, the top of the Column terminates in a capital, platform, and, originally, a bronze statue of Trajan, replaced in 1588 by one of St. Peter. Finally, the shaft of the Column itself is composed of drums of Luna marble stacked 100 Roman feet (96 British ft; 29.2 m) in height exclusive of its base and is decorated on the exterior by a visual record of Trajan's Dacian campaign carved in 23 spiral bands of *c.* 3 ft (1 m) in height filled with 2650 human figures. This unprecedented form of victory monument created the largest continuous narrative sculpture in Rome and inspired later imitations.

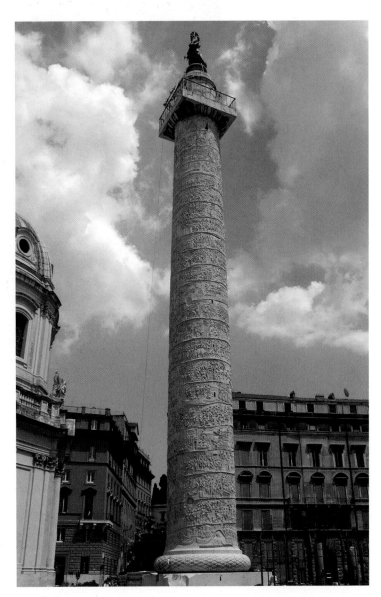

8.16 Column of Trajan, Rome, dedicated 113 CE. Photo courtesy Steven L. Tuck.

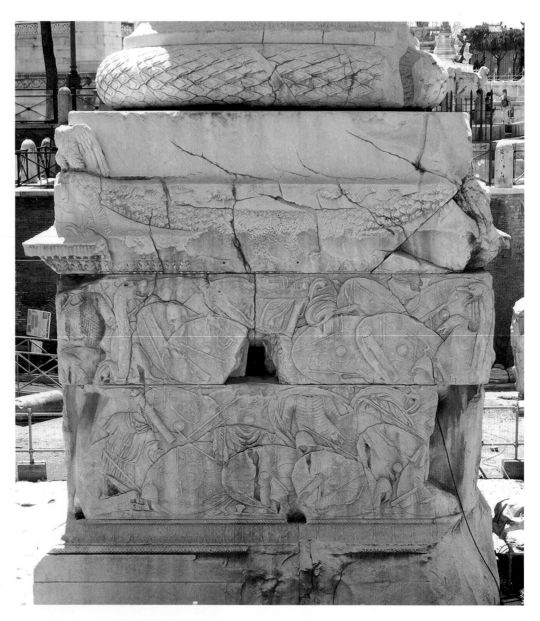

8.17 Base of the Column of Trajan, Rome, dedicated 113 CE. Photo courtesy Steven L. Tuck.

The relief field is divided into 155 separate scenes that narrate the key events in the Dacian Wars from the initial invasion to the death of the Dacian king, Decebalus. These scenes establish the process by which Trajan became the conqueror of Dacia, Dacicus as his new title states. They also changed the iconography of triumphal monuments by introducing scenes of active warfare into the canon of victory images in Rome.

Although there are some battle scenes (Figure 8.19 upper register) the overwhelming majority are not of battle, but of Trajan overseeing the various components of the invasion; often elevated and taller than his companions, he addresses troops (Figure 8.18 lower register), oversees battle (Figure 8.19 upper register), steers ships into harbor (Figure 8.18 top register), conducts sacrifices (Figure 8.19 lowest register), and supervises fort construction (Figure 8.19 middle register). The Augustan qualities of *virtus*, *clementia*, and *pietas* are all evident as the emperor leads troops, forgives defeated enemies, and sacrifices to the gods. The scenes utilize a combination of Roman generic imagery and Hellenistic artistic conventions. The reliefs, like a great deal of Roman marble sculpture, were originally painted in bright colors of red, blue, black, and yellow, which would have aided in their legibility.

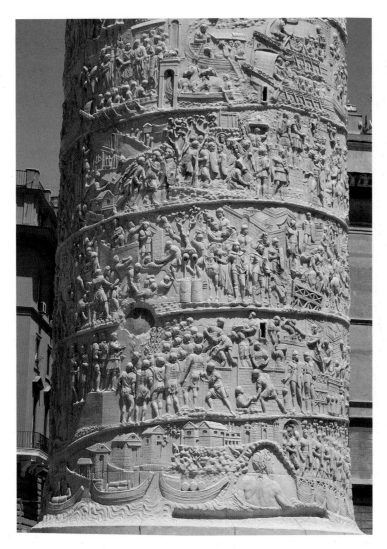

8.18 Spiral frieze of the Column of Trajan, Rome, dedicated 113 CE. Lowest registers on the south side. Photo courtesy Steven L. Tuck.

HISTORICAL CONTEXT
Cassius Dio on Trajan's Dacian Wars

When Trajan in his campaign against the Dacians had drawn near Tapae where the barbarians were encamped . . . he engaged the foe, and saw many wounded on his own side and killed many of the enemy. And when the bandages gave out, he is said not to have spared even his own clothing, but to have cut it up into strips. In honor of the soldiers who had died in battle, he ordered an altar to be erected and funeral rites to be performed annually. . . . Trajan . . . conducted the war with safe prudence rather than with haste and eventually, after a hard struggle, vanquished the Dacians. In the course of the campaign he himself performed many deeds of good generalship and bravery and his troops ran many risks and displayed great prowess on his behalf. . . . Decebalus, when his capital and all his territory had been occupied and he was himself in danger of being captured, committed suicide and his head was brought to Rome. (*Roman History* 68.14)

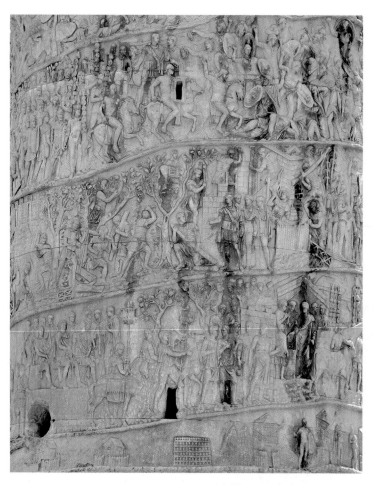

8.19 Spiral frieze of the Column of Trajan, Rome, dedicated 113 CE. Lowest registers on the north side. Photo courtesy Steven L. Tuck.

The individual figures have classicizing proportions (Figure 8.18 lower register), but appear in generic ways with mostly clean-shaven Roman soldiers in armor versus mostly bearded, trouser-wearing barbarians. Roman soldiers march, build, fight, and present Trajan with the heads of his enemies (Figure 8.19). Roman and native buildings are generalized into the recognizable dichotomy of Roman ashlar construction (Figure 8.18 and 8.19) or barbarian timber huts (Figure 8.19 bottom register). In many ways the scenes are similar to those on the Telephos frieze on the Great Altar at Pergamon; both display the conventional division of scenes by means of trees and other background features as well as landscape and architectural elements provide context.

Also from the forum complex are the panels of the Great Trajanic Frieze. Where these were displayed in the forum and the length the frieze originally extended are both unknown, but four panels of this 10 ft tall frieze are now found reused in the Arch of Constantine. Two of these demonstrate the continuity of iconography between the frieze and the Column, with the same images of battle and the presentation of Dacian heads to Trajan on each work. Unlike the Column, the Great Trajanic Frieze consists of generic scenes with no apparent overall narrative. One panel shows Trajan on horseback riding down an enemy soldier as another enemy kneels in surrender in front of his horse (Figure 8.22). In the right rear of the panel Roman soldiers present the emperor with Dacian heads. The composition has a parallel to the Alexander mosaic (Figure 4.21) with the convention of the victor moving from the left to the right, both on charging horses. Another Hellenistic element is the focus on the defeated enemy's suffering and death, a contrast to the Classical style which solely emphasized the victor.

The second panel pairs a battle scene on the right half, complete with kneeling barbarian, along with an *adventus* of the triumphant emperor Trajan on the left. The *adventus* episode demonstrates a number of components familiar from Flavian art. The slender Classicizing figures and the lack of contextualizing background are very similar to the presentation of the same subject on the Cancelleria reliefs (Figures 7.25, 7.26) from about twenty years earlier. In the *adventus* scene Trajan is crowned by Victory herself and guided by *Virtus* and *Honos* (Figure 8.23). Domitian on the Cancelleria reliefs was similarly accompanied by divine and human figures together. The chariot relief from the Arch of Titus (Figure 7.24) dating to *c.* 81 CE includes many of the same figures, both human and divine, with Victory crowning Titus as his chariot is led into Rome by *Virtus* and *Honos* personified. The remarkable continuity in sculptural vocabulary regardless of the form of the monuments is what ensured that Roman audiences could read the visual narrative without captions and grasp the meaning of a sophisticated political and military message.

Anaglypha Traiani

Another pair of relief large-scale panels are the Anaglypha Traiani (a modern name meaning "sculptural reliefs of Trajan"), from the Forum Romanum. This set of marble reliefs is unusually carved on both sides. Each has a *suovetaurilia* on the reverse and a different historical relief on the front,

VIEW FROM THE PROVINCES

Tropaeum Traiani: celebrating victory on the frontier

The Tropaeum Traiani, the Trophy of Trajan at Adamclisi, is a remarkable work of Roman art and architecture. Built in 109 CE on the Roman side of the Danube near the area of Trajan's Dacian conquest, it is a victory monument carefully designed to speak to both conqueror and conquered.

The elements designed for a Roman audience include the form of the monument and its dedicatory inscription. The monument is a large circular drum 124 ½ ft (38 m) in diameter topped by a conical roof with a large trophy of Dacian arms rising out of the center as the highest component. The design reflects the arms carved on the base of the Column of Trajan, but also copies elements of the Mausoleum of Augustus, probably to create an association between Augustus and Trajan as seen also in Trajan's portraiture. The poorly preserved dedicatory inscription in Latin was repeated at least twice on the base of the trophy feature, probably for a Roman audience. The opening reference to Mars Ultor created another implicit link between Trajan and Augustus, who initiated the worship of Mars Ultor.

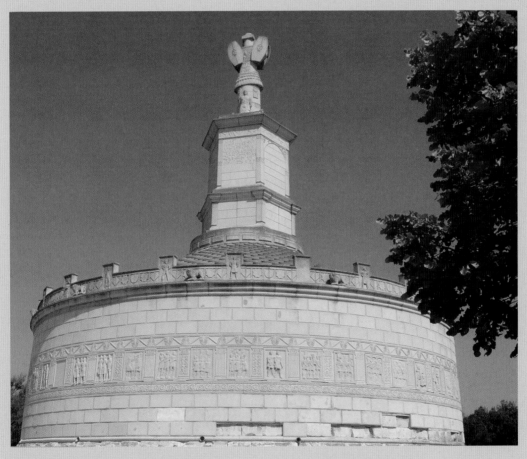

8.20 Adamclisi victory monument, 109 CE, reconstruction drawing, Adamclisi, Romania. Jgabios/ Wikimedia Commons.

(Continued)

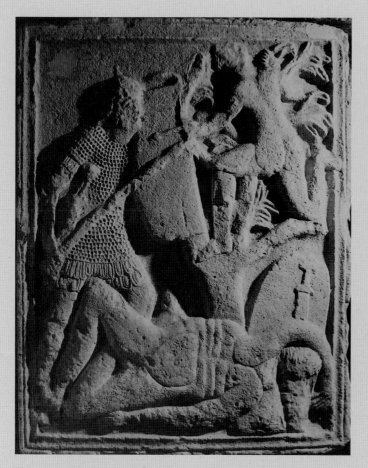

8.21   Relief panel, Adamclisi victory monument, 109 CE, Adamclisi, Romania. H 5 ft 2 in (1.58 m). CristianChirita/Wikimedia Commons.

The element that seems designed to convey a message of Roman power to a local audience is the sculptural decoration around the drum. The drum is decorated with fifty-four rectangular panels, often referred to as metopes, each carved with a figural relief of a scene of the Dacian War or its aftermath. The panels typically have scenes that use three or four figures to convey the narrative. Many of these are generic images of the types found on the Column of Trajan or the Great Trajanic Frieze, of Roman soldiers marching, leading bound prisoners, fighting against Dacians, or, in at least three examples, an equestrian Roman riding down a Dacian. The figures generally distinguish Roman from Dacian by dress or weapons. The Romans appear in military dress while the Dacians are often nude, and the characteristic legionary weapons are contrasted with the Dacian falxman, a curved blade with a handle long enough for a double-handed grip.

The panel of a Roman soldier and Dacian archer displays many of the qualities of the work, with Dacian nudity and armament contrasted with Roman legionary armor and weapons. The figures are non-Classicizing in style with irregular proportions, interior detail defined by simple lines rather than modeling of musculature, and poses that defy Classical conventions of balance and body movement. The figure in the foreground shows the frontality of this style and the figure of the archer in the tree combines profile legs with a full back view, a convention dating back to Greek Archaic art. It is notable, however, that the decorative borders that frame the figural panels are very Classicizing and demonstrate the capacity of the sculptors to carve in the style most current at Rome as seen on the contemporary Anaglypha Traiani. Based on that work, we have to reject the normal scholarly descriptions of these panels as crude, low quality work or the artists as ungifted. On the contrary, the art here is bold, powerful, and clear in the individual scenes as well as the overall narrative. The abstracted forms of figures in the panels probably reflect the visual expectations in the region and the bold and clear art that conveyed public messages to an audience unaccustomed to the conventions of Classicizing sculpture.

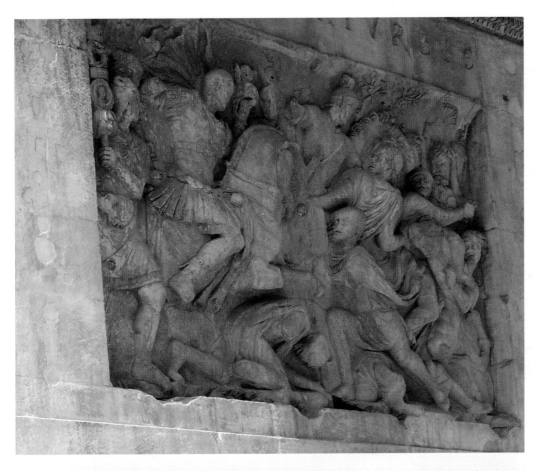

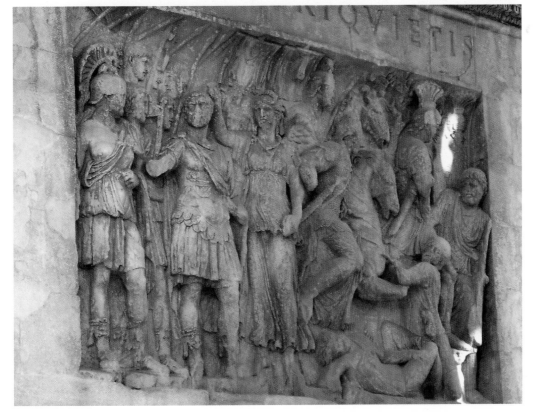

8.22 Trajan in battle, Great Trajanic Frieze, from the Forum of Trajan, Rome, Trajanic?. 9 ¾ ft (2.98 m). Photo courtesy Steven L. Tuck.

8.23 Trajan crowned by Victory, Great Trajanic Frieze, from the Forum of Trajan, Rome, Trajanic?. 9 ¾ ft (2.98 m). Photo courtesy Steven L. Tuck.

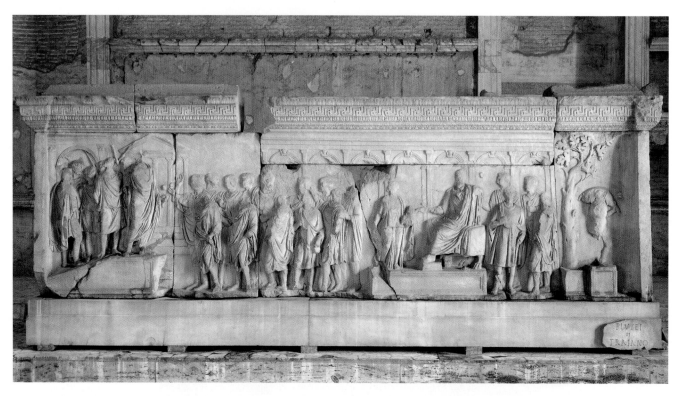

8.24   Trajan addressing a crowd in the Forum Romanum, Anaglypha Traiani, from the Forum Romanum, Rome, Trajanic?. H 5 ft 6 in (1.68 m). Source: Getty Images/ Universal Images Group/ Leemage.

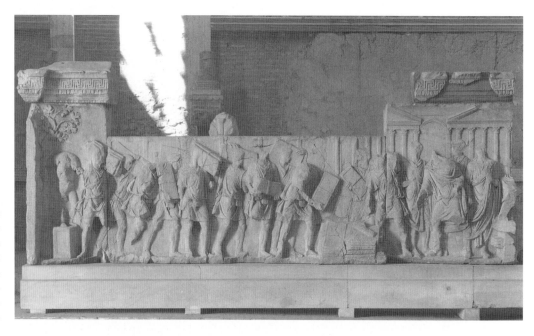

8.25   Burning of debt records in the Forum Romanum, Anaglypha Traiani, from the Forum Romanum, Rome, Trajanic?. H 5 ft 6 in (1.68 m). Source: Felbermayer, Neg. D-DAI-ROM 68.2785.

unified by their common setting in the Forum Romanum. Both demonstrate the qualities of classicizing Roman historical relief with figures that conform to Classical proportions, with the conventions of depth and movement familiar from earlier examples.

On the left of the first panel is an emperor, his head – and therefore identity – missing, standing on the rostra addressing a crowd of toga-clad Roman citizens (*adlocutio*). The right half of the relief is dominated by another scene of an emperor seated on a dais presenting an alimentary payment to a woman with two children, an infant which she holds and an older child by her side. This figure group may represent a statue, with the woman a personification of Italy, and not constitute a separate event taking place in the forum. The Basilica Aemilia fills the background while the fig tree and statue of Marsyas, distinctive and important monuments in the Forum Romanum, fill the right end of the panel.

The other relief shows a burning of tax records in the Forum Romanum. Trajan ordered this forgiveness of debts owed to the state treasury after the financially successful Dacian war. Nine Roman soldiers carry the bundles of records to a bonfire in the right center of the foreground where a Roman official lights them with a torch. The emperor oversees the scene from a **curule chair** on the right. The fig tree and Marsyas statue frame the panel on the left while in the background are the Basilica Julia and Temples of Saturn, Vespasian and Titus, and Concordia. The Classicizing style is seen most clearly in the slender proportions of the figures and the isocephaly displayed across the entire scene. Together the panels represent the most developed expression of Roman historical relief in a Classicizing style that survives from Rome.

curule chair
the chair on which senior magistrates such as consuls, praetors, censors, and all those with imperium were entitled to sit.

Eight tondi, round relief panels, from a missing Hadrianic monument in Rome are now attached to the Arch of Constantine. These panels are partially based on a series of bronze medallions struck under Hadrian with hunting scenes and inscriptions reading *Virtuti Augusti* – to the *Virtus* of the emperor. Together the tondi and medallions demonstrate the shift in the redefinition of *virtus* to include hunting. Rather than showing the stages of preparation for battle, battle itself, post-battle sacrifice to various deities, and the return following a successful battle, the tondi use the imagery of big game hunting to demonstrate Hadrian's virtues. Hunting imagery as an expression of power has a long history in the art of ancient Egypt as well as the art of the Assyrian and Persian empires.

The tondi include *pietas* as well as *virtus* with the emperor facing a bear, boar, and lion, and then sacrificing afterwards to Apollo, Hercules, Silvanus, and Diana. Dynasty is a secondary theme, with figures from Hadrian's court including his prospective successors and Antinous accompanying him in the episodes. Status in the Roman world is conveyed by one's attendants and Hadrian's portrayal here requires that he not appear alone, but with the status-conferring group, as seen with emperors in earlier historical reliefs such as the Column of Trajan, Arch of Titus, and the Ara Pacis. This group is not only in art, but would follow him in almost every context, including bathing in the large public bath complexes.

The reliefs on the Arch of Trajan at Beneventum, begun in 114 CE and finished in 118 CE under Hadrian, are not precisely historical. None seem designed to record particular events in his principate in a documentary manner. Although they use the iconography of historical reliefs, they are actually the largest set of ideological images from any single monument in the Roman world. They provide a very expansive statement of Trajan's foreign and domestic policies and achievements, personal attributes, and justification for rule. The Beneventum Arch is virtually identical in size and design to the Arch of Titus in Rome (Figure 7.22). It differs in its far more extensive sculptural decoration. The main body of the arch has eight large relief panels while the attic has four, two on each side flanking the inscription. In addition, a smaller frieze, very similar to the one on the Arch of Titus, fills the area just below the attic at the top of the body of the arch and the **spandrels** of the passage are also filled with personified Victory figures. The passage itself has three large panels, one on either side and a third in the top of the barrel vault. Smaller reliefs of Victories sacrificing bulls separate the main panels.

spandrels
the roughly triangular space between the curve of an arch and the surrounding molding that frames it. Spandrels on triumphal arches are usually filled with figures of Victory.

The major exterior panels memorialize some of Trajan's major accomplishments such as military campaigns, founding of colonies, creating his alimentary scheme, establishing harbors, reorganizing the army, and *adventus* into Rome as a new emperor. Many of the panels continue the Flavian style with Classicizing figures, but with the Italic tradition of including divinities and personifications within the scenes. In most, these figures provide setting as the personifications of Rome, the Senate,

SCHOLARLY PERSPECTIVE
Trajanic or Hadrianic sculpture: a debate about date

Some of the most difficult questions in Roman art involve the dates and responsibility for the relief sculpture on the Column of Trajan, the Anaglypha Traiani, and the Great Trajanic frieze. One of the key problems is that the Classicizing style in which they are carved is not in and of itself datable. Without some other internal feature or an external one such as an inscription or historical reference, these works could be either Trajanic or Hadrianic. The difference in date of ten or twenty years not only affects the dating of other similar and less prominent works, but changes our understanding of these sculptures and the themes and messages they are designed to communicate. These relief works have traditionally been assigned to Trajan, but recent scholarly work has questioned those attributions, concluding in each case that Hadrian was more likely to have created the works at the beginning of his reign in honor of Trajan. For the Anaglypha Traiani/Hadriani the subject and date are debated. With the emperor on the rostra and the one seated in the curule chair missing their heads, it is not certain whether they are the same figure. Instead of Trajan standing at the rostra addressing the crowd while facing a statue group of himself celebrating his alimentary program, the relief might portray Hadrian at the rostra in 118 CE announcing his extension of Trajan's program. Nothing preserved on the relief is conclusive. The second relief shows the burning of debt records in the Forum Romanum, clearly identified by the buildings in the background. Historical sources record a Hadrianic debt burning in 118 CE, but it took place in the Forum of Trajan. Many scholars conclude that the relief provides evidence of an otherwise unknown Trajanic debt burning that took place in the Forum Romanum, arguing that the specificity of the setting takes primacy over the lack of independent evidence of such a debt relief plan, especially given the almost complete lack of historical sources covering Trajan's rule.

The Great Trajanic Frieze and the Column of Trajan are the subjects of similar debates. In this case it is known that Hadrian did complete the Forum of Trajan, in fact dedicating its major temple to the Divine Trajan, which would not have been done in Trajan's lifetime. Scholars debate what other components of the forum might be Hadrianic. The subjects and iconography of the reliefs of the Great Trajanic Frieze are so consistent with those on the Column that many authors assume that both were created under the same emperor, whether Trajan or Hadrian. Hadrianic dating is based on the iconography of the scene of Trajan on horseback. Some scholars conclude that Trajan riding into battle without a helmet signifies his divinity. While it is certainly not a documentary image of an historical event, there are no antecedents for that image in imperial art supporting the divinity conclusion.

The spiral relief on the Column of Trajan is the largest and most important of these sculptures. The arguments for a Hadrianic date are complex but evidence cited includes the fact that the relief does not appear on Trajan's coins that show the Column. Time is also a factor and the need to carve the relief in situ after the Column was erected but before Trajan's death, the appearance of the arch erected at Ancona in 115 CE on the Column, and the use of the Column as Trajan's tomb lead those who favor the Hadrianic date to argue that the Column was carved under Hadrian when the tomb was added in 118 CE. The evidence for a Trajanic date is largely refutation of the Hadrianic arguments. Trajan's coins clearly show a spiral on the Column and given the minuscule size of a coin reverse any further indication of the relief would be practically impossible. There should have been time to carve the relief under Trajan in the eight years available. Finally, the dedicatory inscription records Trajan's offices and titles for the year 113 CE, indicating that it was in place by then, leaving four years to carve the reliefs in situ. Finally, unlike the Arch at Beneventum, there is no indication here of Hadrian inserting his image into the reliefs on either the Column or the Great Trajanic Frieze. To say that these questions are still unsettled is obvious. To say that they are unanswerable is to go too far. We outline them to demonstrate the extent of our knowledge and the current state of the field of Roman art history, but also with the understanding that a new approach or new evidence could put these problems in the solved category.

Amanda Claridge, "Hadrian's Column of Trajan." *Journal of Roman Archaeology* 6:5–22 (1993).

(a)

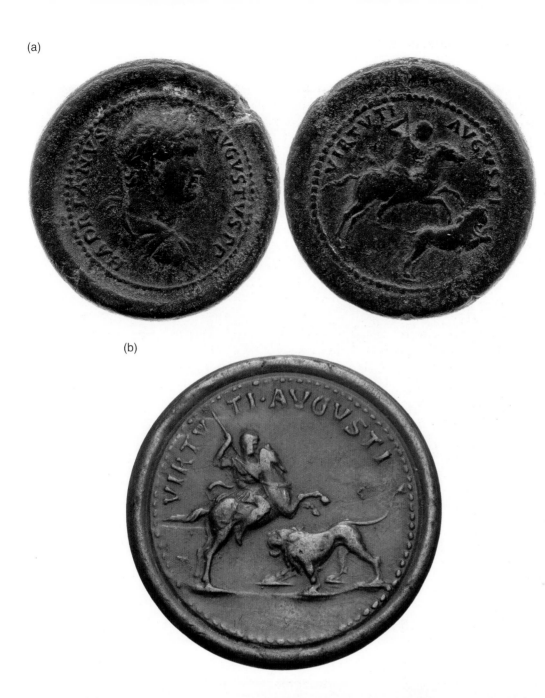

(b)

8.26a and 8.26b
Medallions of the *virtuti Augusti*, the manliness of the emperor Hadrian, 130–138 CE. (a) Source: © The Trustees of the British Museum. All rights reserved. (b) Source: © 2014. Photo Scala, Florence/BPK, Bildagentur für Kunst, Kultur und Geschichte, Berlin.

8.27 Tondi of Hadrian, 130–138 CE, from the Arch of Constantine, Rome. D 6 ft 6 in (1.98 m). Photo courtesy Steven L. Tuck.

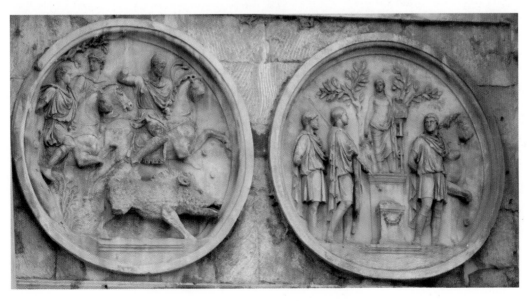

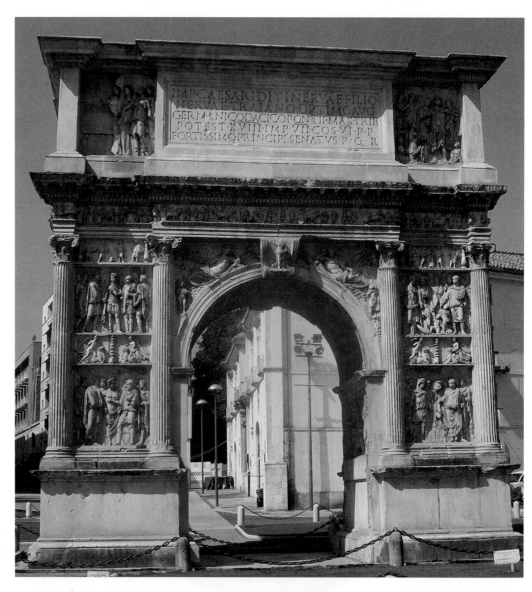

8.28 Arch of Trajan, Beneventum, 114 CE, marble. Photo courtesy Steven L. Tuck.

8.29 Sacrifice relief panel, Arch of Trajan, 114 CE, Beneventum, Italy. H 7 ft 10 in (2.39 m), marble. Photo courtesy Steven L. Tuck.

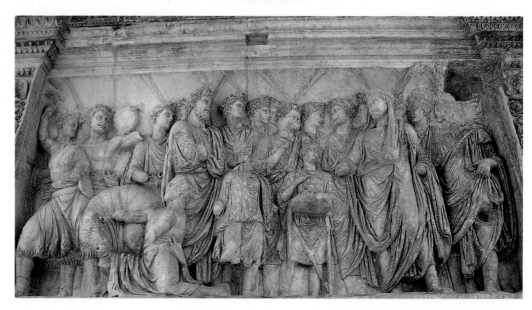

or the People. In others they actively engage the emperor, as when Jupiter holds out his thunderbolt to hand to Trajan, extending his authority to his agent on earth.

The panels in the passageway differ from those on the Arch of Titus in subject; the triumphal and historical aspects are muted in favor of more generic scenes. One on side Trajan presides at a sacrifice. This very Classicizing composition features all of the key figures including priests, *victimarii*, and attendants, all with precise isocephaly and the use of shallow profile heads to denote background figures. The object of the sacrifice is unclear, however, as there is no temple in the background or any other indicator of the deity involved. It is more an image of Trajanic piety than of a particular event.

The accompanying panel records the distribution of the alimentary payments to widows and orphans. The recipients fill the right half of the relief but many of the women wear crenellated crowns instead of contemporary headdresses indicating that they are personifications of communities rather than just generic individuals receiving the largesse. The panel in the barrel vault shows a standing Trajan in armor crowned with a wreath by Winged Victory herself, a motif depicted on the chariot panel on the Arch of Titus and the Great Trajanic Frieze.

The border of the panel is piled captive arms and armor as seen on the base of the Column of Trajan. Overall, the sculptural program on the arch is sophisticated, complex, and designed to reinforce all of the elements that made Trajan the *optimus princeps*.

Mythological sculpture

The amphitheater at Capua preserves the best evidence we have from the Roman world on the decoration of an amphitheater, an important and widespread building form. Architecturally it is virtually a copy of the Colosseum in Rome and was constructed immediately following it during the late first and early second centuries CE. Its final decoration, which may reflect the lost decorative program of

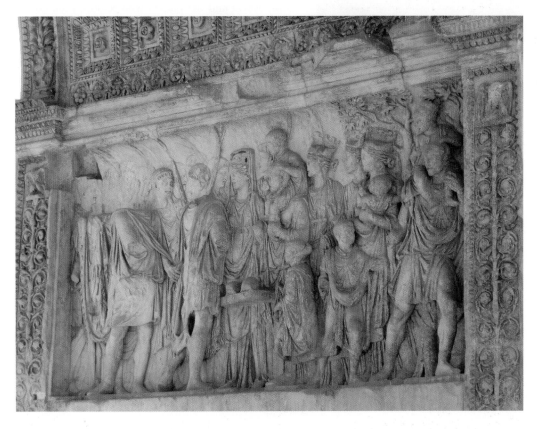

8.30 *Alimenta* relief panel, Arch of Trajan, 114 CE, Beneventum, Italy. H 7 ft 10 in (2.39 m), marble. Photo courtesy Steven L. Tuck.

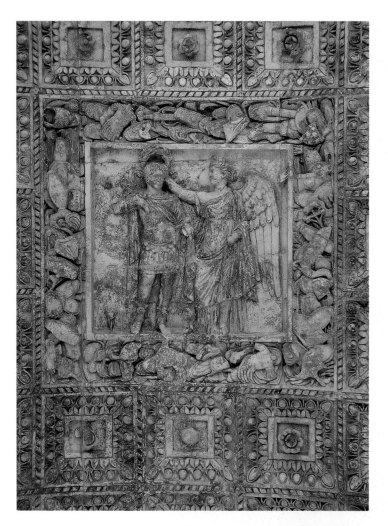

8.31 Keystone image of Victory crowning Trajan, Arch of Trajan, 114 CE, Beneventum, Italy, marble. Photo courtesy Steven L. Tuck.

the Colosseum, was installed under Hadrian. The decoration is a mix of free-standing and relief stone sculpture. On the exterior originally eighty protome heads of mythological figures projected from the keystones above the entrance arches on the ground floor of the facade. These took the place of the Roman numerals on the Colosseum and may have served the same purpose, labeling the entrances into the amphitheater. The second floor arcade on the facade contained sculptures of standing mythological figures. These may have matched the subjects of the protomes immediately below them. On the interior each entrance tunnel led to a passageway and stairs into the *cavea* or seating area. The eighty openings in those staircases were framed on the top and sides by marble balustrades. The flanking panels were largely relief portrayals of animals from the arena while the panels above the stairs were 6 ft (2 m) long panels of largely mythological figural scenes.

Of the original eighty facade sculptures only four remain: Mercury, Psyche, Venus/Aphrodite, and Adonis. With the exception of Psyche, all have specific associations with the events in the amphitheater and their selection may have been designed to reinforce the events taking place on the arena floor. Mercury was the *psychopompos* who guided the souls of the dead to the underworld and the person who removed the bodies of dead gladiators might have dressed as Mercury. Adonis was a famous mythological hunter, lover of Aphrodite, and tragically killed in a boar hunt, a story related by Ovid in his *Metamorphoses* book 10. The Venus demonstrates the very classicizing proportions and style of the figures, based on the fourth century BCE Classical sculpture from Athens. The figure's smooth and highly polished skin contrasts with the deeply carved and rougher drapery and hair, a pattern that is typical of the period. Her hairstyle and diadem are the type that served as a model for female portraiture of the period as seen in the sculpture of Sabina (Figure 8.4) and slightly later found on tomb portraits of elite Roman women.

The interior figural relief panels are more clearly related to events surrounding the games. Of the forty extant panels, ten show elements of the *pompa*, the formal procession that started a set of games, sacrifices taking place in the plaza outside the amphitheater and the magistrates arriving for games. The remaining thirty panels are all mythological subjects, yet the context for them is often given by architectural features of the amphitheater, notably the doorways leading into the building or the arena itself that show that the myths are not generic representations of these stories, but reenactments of them taking place in the arena in the course of a set of games. One of the best-preserved of these panels is a boar hunt, recognizable as the Calydonian Boar Hunt.

Atalanta leads the hunters with her bow followed by Meleager ready with a spear. A third hunter stands ready at the left next to an archway, the visual marker that this scene takes place in the arena and not in the wild. The standard animal hunts that opened a day's games in the arena became increasingly elaborate mythologically themed spectacles during the late first and second centuries CE. Caves were built over the trapdoors in the arena floor so animals could appear by surprise, an innovation of the Flavian period.

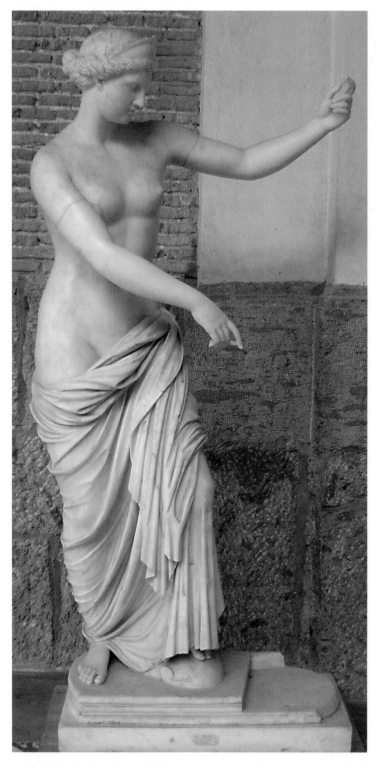

8.32   Venus statue from the facade of the amphitheater at Capua, Hadrianic. Museo Archeologico Nazionale di Napoli. Marble, 7 ¼ ft (2.2 m). Photo courtesy Steven L. Tuck.

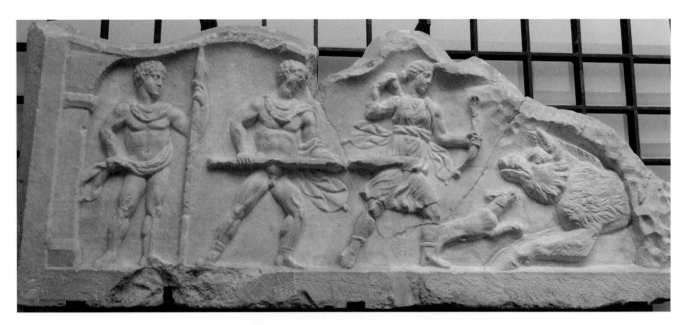

8.33   Calydonian Boar Hunt relief panel from the amphitheater at Capua, Italy, Hadrianic. H 40 in (1 m), marble. Photo courtesy Steven L. Tuck.

MORE ON MYTH
The Calydonian Boar Hunt

The boar hunt of this Greek myth was to kill a deadly rampaging boar sent by the goddess Artemis to the region of Calydon as punishment for neglecting her worship. In the myth the local king, Oeneus, sent for the greatest hunters in Greece offering them the animal's hide and tusks as prizes. According to various ancient versions of the myth as many as fifty heroic hunters joined in the hunt. Many of the Argonauts, who had sailed with Jason to find the Golden Fleece, answered along with Meleager, the king's son, Peleus, the father of Achilles, and a female hunter, Atalanta. Atalanta wounded the boar first with an arrow and Meleager killed it with a spear. She was offered the prize of its hide, angering some of the male hunters who claimed it and rejected the idea that a woman should get the trophy. Meleager killed two of his uncles who led that group. In response his mother had him killed. Also Peleus accidentially killed his host Eurytion.

Mosaics

One of the many contributions to ancient art created under the patronage of the Greek kings of Pergamon in the second century BCE was a type of pictorial mosaic referred to as *opus vermiculatum*, meaning "worm-like work," featuring tesserae so minuscule that the resulting mosaic, almost always an emblema or inset panel in the center of a floor, closely resembled a panel painting. These works often featured visual illusions of depth, trompe l'oeil elements, plays of light off water, or reflective vessels such as bronze pitchers.

The mosaic of doves perched on the rim of a bowl of water is the only mosaic from antiquity whose artist is named in literature. According to Pliny the Elder in his *Natural History* (36, 184) this was the work of Sosus of Pergamon, active in the second century BCE.

The mosaic is known from a number of copies in the Roman world, but the highest quality example was found in the villa of Hadrian at Tivoli; its quality, seen particularly in the rippling water, so high that some scholars believe it to be the original by Sosus. It exemplifies the Greek interest in replicating nature in their arts as well as the Hellenistic interest in portraying the ephemeral, as the composition has frozen in time the rippling water in the vase.

ART AND LITERATURE

The four major events in a day of games: the opening procession and sacrifice, morning hunts, lunch time prisoner executions, and concluding gladiatorial combats, are almost all found in the sculpture at Capua. The only missing component are the gladiators and they did not lend themselves to the theme of reinforcing state power as seen in the reliefs and literary descriptions of these events. Tertullian describes the opening procession in detail in *On the Spectacles* 7.2, "the unbroken train of images, the cars and chariots and conveyances for carrying them, the portable thrones and garlands and the attributes of the gods. Moreover, how many sacred rites are observed, how many sacrifices offered at the beginning . . ." For hunts literature again reflects the art as in the Calydonian Boar Hunt described by many ancient authors, but here perhaps inspired by Ovid's account in *Metamorphoses* 8, the longest and most popular version for Roman audiences. Varro (*De Re Rustica* 3) describes in particular the myth of Orpheus reenacted in an animal hunt. Many of the Capua reliefs illustrate labors of Hercules in the arena, a popular subject for reenacted hunts as later performed by the emperor Commodus and described in Roman literature.

The most elaborate mythological reenactment was used for the mid-day prisoner executions. From the time of Nero on we have ample literary evidence for prisoners being killed in ways that were based on Greek myths. Rather than simple executions by sword or fire, the myths of Dirce, dragged to death by a bull, of Icarus, falling from a great height, Prometheus, eaten alive by a bird, and Actaeon, torn to pieces by his own hunting dogs, were reenacted to add spectacle and entertainment value to this component of the games. These were so spectacular that they were a featured part of the inaugural games of the Colosseum in 80 CE, as Martial records in his book of poetry on the games.

In addition to the spectacular aspects of the myths, the scenes also reinforced Roman authority and values. All of the figures punished in the myths had committed acts of hybris, which challenged or threatened religious or political authority leading directly to their grisly deaths. These reenactments were therefore designed to be instructional to the tens of thousands of spectators. The reliefs at Capua preserve the only evidence of these prisoner executions as mythological reenactments in Roman art, all of which are recorded in literature. The reliefs include Icarus (Suetonius, *Life of Nero*, 12), Prometheus (Martial, *Book of Spectacles*, 7), and Actaeon (Tacitus, *Annals* 15). The myth of Actaeon, most familiar to Romans from Ovid's version, occurred while he was hunting (see More on Myth: Actaeon, in chapter 6) and accidentally saw the bathing Diana. As punishment she turned him into a stag and his dogs turned on him and tore him to pieces. The myth inspired Nero's punishment of the Christians, blamed for starting the Great Fire of Rome in 64 CE as Tacitus records, "First, Nero had self-acknowledged Christians arrested. Then, on their information, large numbers of others were condemned . . . . Their deaths were made farcical. Dressed in wild animal skins, they were torn to pieces by dogs . . ." (*Ann.* 15.44). The amphitheater reliefs at Capua demonstrate the power of myth in conveying the values of Roman government, even on a local level as at Capua, to an audience of Roman men.

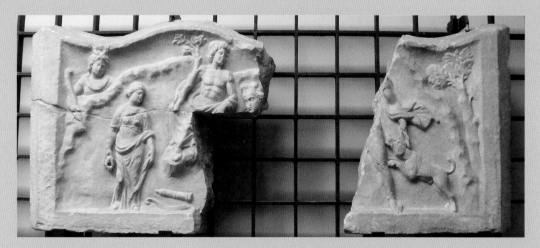

8.34   Actaeon relief panel from the amphitheater at Capua, Italy, Hadrianic. H 40 in (1 m), marble. Photo courtesy Steven L. Tuck.

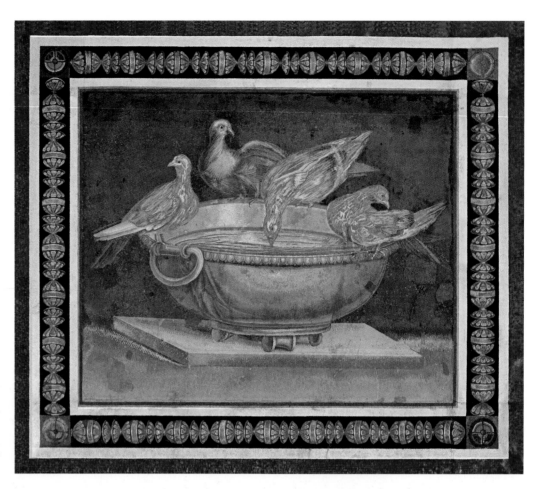

8.35   Dove mosaic from the Villa of Hadrian, Tivoli, Hadrianic. Now in the Musei Capitolini, Rome. 38 ½ in (98 cm) x 33 ½ in (85 cm). Photo courtesy Steven L. Tuck.

ANCIENTS ON ART
Sosus of Pergamon

Paved floors originated among the Greeks and were skillfully embellished with a kind of paint-work until this was super-seded by mosaics. In this latter field the most famous exponent was Sosus, who at Pergamon laid the floor of what is known in Greek as 'the Unswept Room' because, by means of small cubes tinted in various shades, he represented on the floor refuse from the dinner table and other sweepings, making them appear as if they had been left there. A remarkable detail in the picture is a dove, which is drinking and casts the shadow of its head on the water, while others are sunning and preening themselves on the brim of a large drinking vessel.(Pliny the Elder, *Natural History* 36. 184)

Unlike the Greek tradition of polychrome mosaic work, the Italian schools developed a tradition of black and white floor mosaics with a white background and black design. In many ways the use of a white background is the antithesis of the illusionistic tendencies of the Greek style, eliminating spatial cues and contextualizing details by pushing the design to the foreground on a flat plane. A non-figural example with geometric patterns is found in the guest quarters of Hadrian's Villa at Tivoli. The division of the floor into separate sections reflects use of the space. The more elaborate designs were in the center of the floor while the simpler panels were the sections of floor covered with furniture.

The large figural mosaic from a bath complex at Ostia illustrates the use of the black and white style for a pavement with mythological and documentary elements and some interesting features.

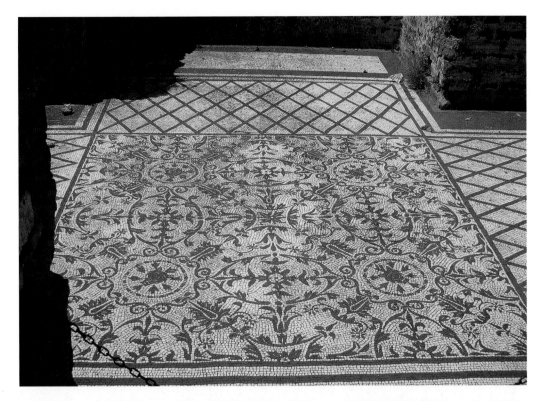

8.36 Black and white mosaic from the Villa of Hadrian, Tivoli, Hadrianic. Photo courtesy Steven L. Tuck.

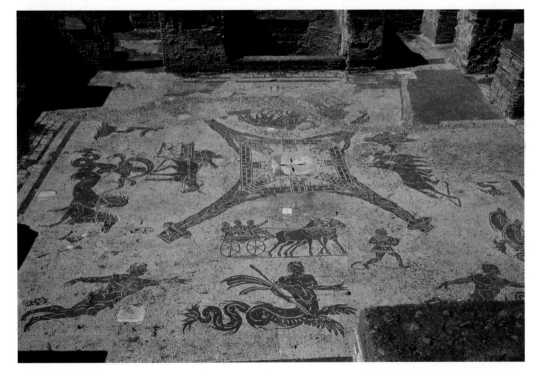

8.37 Black and white mosaic, Baths of the Cart Drivers, Ostia, *c.* 120 CE. Photo courtesy Steven L. Tuck.

The figures appear in two registers. The upper or inner one has four small vignettes of cart drivers, while the outer one includes swimmers, sea creatures, and nautical mythological figures. The selection of mythological water creatures is designed to reinforce the primary use of the space as a bathing complex. The organization of the mosaic so that each side has a groundline that faces one wall indicates the use of the space. Bathers walking around the room would engage the mosaic, both admiring the design and recognizing the cart drivers who are thought to be the benefactors who paid for the facility. In addition, the design in the center of the mosaic with male figures holding up masonry reflects the form of the building as it echoes the roof structure in the room. The mosaic really carries three different artistic perspectives: illusionary architecture, patron imagery, and mythological figures to define the use of the space.

CONCLUSION

The history of Roman art under Trajan and Hadrian is dominated by two contrasting trends, those of the further development of Classicizing art, which we saw develop under the Flavians and continue here most clearly in sculpture, and the rejection of the Classical seen in architecture in the works of the architectural revolution and in art in the Italic traditions and provincial work at Adamclisi. The real lesson is of the increasing use of the wide variety of artistic styles, materials, and themes in a range of particular contexts and venues. Trajan's public art relied heavily on that of Augustus for its models while Hadrian built on the Trajanic styles and subjects. The provincial limestone reliefs at Adamclisi share the same subjects with scenes from the Luna marble frieze on the Column of Trajan but each monument is designed for a particular place, use, and audience and the materials and styles are not interchangeable. Similarly the traditional building set and Classicizing architecture of the Forum of Trajan serves to reflect and build on the previous imperial fora, while the bold experiments in concrete construction found at the Villa of Hadrian at Tivoli extends the architectural revolution further than any other architect. Upon the death of Hadrian, the adoptive dynasty of the Five Good Emperors continues with Antoninus Pius and Marcus Aurelius. Under them the trends in art seen in this chapter can be traced in new works that rely heavily on the forms, styles, and media of those seen under Trajan and Hadrian.

SUGGESTIONS FOR FURTHER READING

Mary T. Boatwright, *Hadrian and the Cities of the Roman Empire* (Princeton University Press 2002). For the first time catalogues and analyzes Hadrian's benefactions to over 130 cities including imperial patronage of temples, tombs, and engineering projects.

Amanda Claridge, "Hadrian's Column of Trajan." *Journal of Roman Archaeology* 6:5–22, (1993). This article began a re-evaluation of the patronage of the Column of Trajan as well as other works attributed to Trajan.

Filippo Coarelli, *The Column of Trajan* (Colombo 2000). In addition to plates illustrating all of the scenes on the Column, it provides essays on the context, function, figurative structure, and history of this remarkable monument.

Mark Wilson Jones, *Principles of Roman Architecture* (Yale 2003). Part II of the book (pp. 161–213) provides detailed analysis of the design and construction of the Column of Trajan and the Pantheon.

E. La Rocca, *The Imperial Fora* (Latomus 1995). A thoughtful analysis of the design and use of the imperial forums by the former director of the sites.

Anne-Marie Leander-Touati, *The Great Trajanic Frieze: The Study of a Monument and of the Mechanisms of Message Transmission in Roman Art* (Svenska Institutet i Rom 1987). This book combines 130 pages of text with 56 plates of images to create an exhaustive study of the frieze, but also to explore notions of imperial art and the creation and projection of an imperial image.

William L. MacDonald, *The Pantheon: Design, Meaning, and Progeny* (Harvard University Press 2002). This work introduces one of the most important and influential buildings in world history. It presents in clear language not only a coherent summary of the history, description, and analysis of the building, but also a discussion of the influence the Pantheon exerted over later architecture.

Thorsten Opper, *Hadrian: Empire and Conflict* (British Museum Press 2008). A catalogue from a major exhibition on the life and art of Hadrian, which contains essays and descriptions of the full range of art and architecture under Hadrian. It explores these materials in the context of Hadrian's life, political and military activities, and wider cultural world.

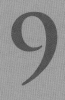

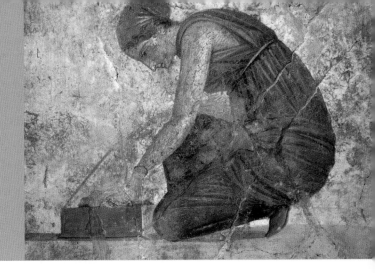

9

ANTONINE EMPERORS, 138–192 CE

From an Empire of Gold to One of Rust

138–161 CE	Antoninus Pius as emperor
140 CE	**Baths of the Seven Sages, Ostia**
147 CE	**Faustina the Younger portrait bust**
160 CE	**Hercules sarcophagus**
161–180 CE	Marcus Aurelius as emperor
161–169 CE	Lucius Verus, co-emperor with Marcus Aurelius
161–166 CE	Parthian War
161 CE	**Column of Antoninus Pius**
165 CE	Plague sweeps Rome; **Alcestis sarcophagus**
176 CE	**Arch of Marcus Aurelius begun**
180–192 CE	Commodus as emperor; **Portonaccio sarcophagus**
192 CE	**Column of Marcus Aurelius completed; Commodus bust**; Commodus appears in the Colosseum as Hercules
193 CE	Civil war and Year of the Six Emperors

A History of Roman Art, First Edition. Steven L. Tuck.
© 2015 Steven L. Tuck. Published 2015 by John Wiley & Sons, Ltd.

INTRODUCTION

The title of this chapter comes from the Roman historian, Cassius Dio, who wrote an eyewitness account about the dynasty of adoptive emperors and the disastrous succession of Marcus Aurelius by his son, Commodus. His full quote, "This matter must be our next topic; for our history now descends from an empire of gold to one of iron and rust . . ." (*Roman History* 72.36), indicates the scope of this chapter and also alludes to changes not only in the political situation, but also in the cultural. Throughout the period we see the decline in large-scale, innovative architecture and the shift from Rome-centered Classicizing art to provincial styles. As the first son to succeed his father as emperor in over one hundred years and the final emperor before the civil war of 192 CE, Commodus makes a convenient and noteworthy point of conclusion for the chapter.

With the death of Hadrian in 138 CE, the offices of the emperor passed peacefully to Titus Aurelius Fulvus Boionius Antoninus, known as Antoninus Pius. He was the adopted son of Hadrian and married to Faustina the Elder, the emperor Hadrian's niece. In fact, the succession was established for the future as well since Antoninus Pius adopted Marcus Annius Verus, the future emperor Marcus Aurelius, and Lucius, son of Aelius Verus, the future emperor Lucius Verus. Marcus Aurelius was further bound to Antoninus through marriage to his daughter, Faustina the Younger.

In many ways, Antoninus Pius was as successful an emperor as Trajan and Hadrian, but completely different from them in experience and personal behavior. His rule, from 138 to 161 CE, was the longest since Augustus, but he led no armies, invaded no foreign territories, and did not travel in the provinces. It has been calculated that he never came within five hundred miles of a Roman legion, although he authorized the conquest of part of northern Britain beyond Hadrian's Wall. Nevertheless, he ruled efficiently by writing letters from Rome and his villa at Lorium about 12 miles (20 km) from Rome. His competence is reflected in the largely peaceful empire and his success in ruling by correspondence is illustrated by his response to a threatened Parthian invasion. Retaliating against Trajan's invasion of Parthia, the Parthians planned an invasion of Roman-controlled territory. Antoninus Pius dissuaded them with a letter and the invasion was abandoned.

Marcus Aurelius and his co-emperor, Lucius Verus, had a far more difficult principate. They succeeded in 161 CE and ushered in the first truly shared rule by emperors, the *Concordia Augustorum*, the Harmony of the Augusti. Marcus Aurelius based his life and rule on the tenets of Greek Stoic philosophy and many of his daily musings are preserved for us in his *Meditations*. The circumstances of his rule must have tested his philosophy as he faced invasions from Germanic tribes, notably the Marcomanni, and the Parthian empire as well as revolts in Britain and Syria. In addition to military crises, he and Lucius Verus faced monetary crises, widespread economic problems, and an outbreak of plague that became a pandemic, sweeping through the empire and killing up to one third of the population, including perhaps Lucius Verus in 169 CE. The result of all of this uncertainty and conflict was very little building and a rise in interest in deities whose worship offered personal salvation such as Mithras, Isis, Dionysus, Christianity, and Hercules.

Upon the death of Marcus Aurelius in 180 CE, his son, Commodus, succeeded him as the last of the Antonine emperors. If it weren't for the eyewitness account of Cassius Dio, it would be easy to dismiss the senatorial criticism of Commodus since it follows the exact same pattern and some specific behaviors attributed to Domitian: increasing dictatorial rule, executions of political opponents, claims of plots against the emperor and so forth. Nevertheless, it seems certain that in his twelve-year rule Commodus demonstrated increasing attempts to directly and personally control Roman government and society, culminating in his plans in 192 CE to rename Rome, many of the legions, and the months in the calendar after himself. A conspiracy of household officials succeeded in arranging his assassination on December 31, 192 CE. January 1, 193 CE dawned with no emperor in power and led to civil war, the first since 69 CE.

The art of the Antonine emperors – Antoninus Pius, Marcus Aurelius, and Commodus – shows continuity with much of the Trajanic and Hadrianic period, but under Marcus Aurelius we begin to see the instability and insecurity that will mark the third century reflected in art. The imagery of war develops from that seen under Trajan to reveal the savagery of combat while portraiture seems to reflect the insecurity of the age. The portraiture of Commodus, for example, reveals his attempts at redefinition of the imperial role, perhaps building on the Greek associations found in the portraiture from Trajan to Lucius Verus. The impetus for the Greek-inspired art of the Antonine period is often credited, directly or indirectly, to the famously philhellene emperor Hadrian. The love of things Greek by any one man, however, even one as prominent as the emperor, cannot reasonably account for the rapid and widespread adoption of Greek subjects and styles in second-century CE art. When we realize that these trends began prior to Hadrian, another impetus must be sought and the coincidence of Classicizing art and the Second Sophistic indicates that it may be the key. The art of this period reflects a larger trend in culture than just imitation of the emperor and relied on the Second Sophistic for its existence and form. Throughout the public sculpture of the period, Classicizing tendencies are increasingly restrained in favor of traditions of imagery associated with Italic and provincial art.

ANTONINE PORTRAITURE

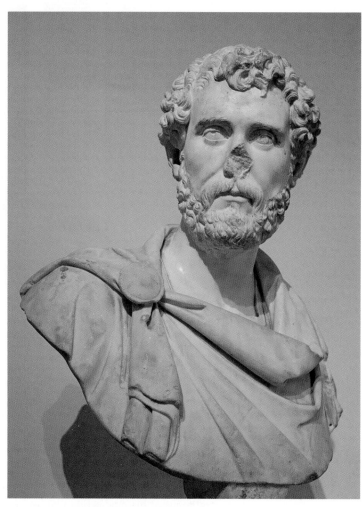

Both male and female portraiture under the Antonine emperors continues the trends seen in Hadrianic portraits. The emphasis on bearded, Classicizing male figures of idealized adulthood and modest women with hairstyles derived from Classical goddesses both expand and develop. Male hair and beards in particular demonstrate more volume, with the drill used to create deep curls and corkscrew locks of hair. Carved pupils are found inconsistently in Hadrianic period portraiture, but are a regular feature under the later Antonines. They are an element of the increasingly detailed sculpture using both the drill and chisel to create more lifelike figures.

Portraits of emperors and empresses

The portraits of Antoninus Pius as an idealized adult illustrate all of these features, with carved pupils and beard and head of hair patterned after Hadrian's portraits. As in Hadrian's portraits, the curly hair and beard are deeply carved and in fact in some places undercut, so that locks of hair are actually carved in the round not just in deep relief.

9.1   Bust of Antoninus Pius, *c.* 147–149 CE, Rome. Musei Vaticani, Rome. H 2 ft 5 in (73.7 cm), marble. Photo courtesy Daniel Resheter.

Each portrait of Marcus Aurelius with its long face, wrinkled forehead, hooded eyes, and distant gaze represents his features, but also demonstrates the development of marble carving technique and the very extensive use of drill work in the portraiture of the last part of his rule. The locks of the hair are now individually drilled with hollow cores and the center-parted beard falls into corkscrew curls.

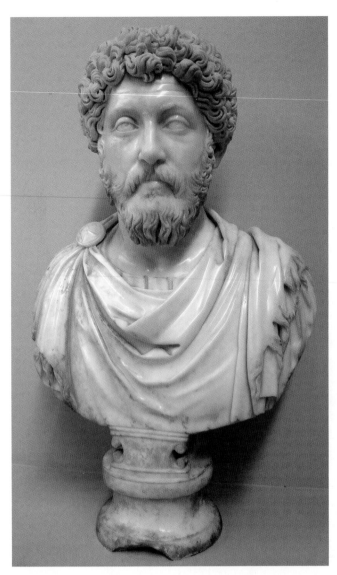

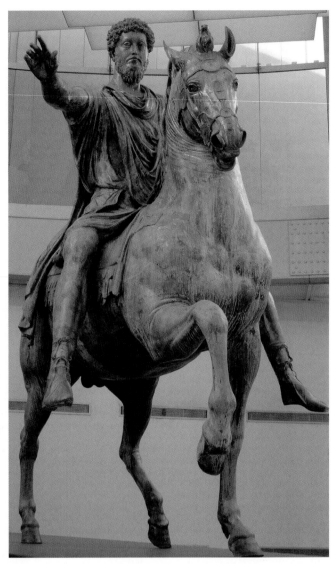

9.2   Bust of Marcus Aurelius as a victorious general, 170–180 CE, Rome. Musei Capitolini, Rome. H 2 ft 9 in (83.8 cm), marble. Photo courtesy Daniel Resheter.

9.3   Equestrian statue of Marcus Aurelius, 176 CE, Rome. Musei Capitolini, Rome. H 11 ft 6 in (3.5 m), gilded bronze. Photo courtesy Daniel Resheter.

The face reveals aging in the wrinkled forehead and deep bags under his eyes, perhaps a result of the myriad military, foreign, and domestic problems of his reign. In many ways this aging foreshadows the imperial portraits of the third century CE, which seem to deliberately reflect the problems of ruling the Roman world.

The best surviving portrait of Marcus Aurelius is the gilded bronze equestrian statue, the best-preserved example of this once common form of commemoration. It actually survives because of mistaken identity. In the Middle Ages it was preserved because it was thought to be a statue of Constantine, the first Christian emperor. It was so revered that Michelangelo used it as the central focus of his new urban plan on the Capitoline Hill. Only much later was it recognized as a portrait of Marcus Aurelius. It shows the emperor seated on horseback, wearing civilian dress, with his right hand outstretched in a gesture of clemency. Most scholars reconstruct the statue as part of a group with a fallen or kneeling German warrior or commander originally placed on the base in front of the horse. It is equally possible that the gesture is a more general one noting the end of the German campaigns and not directed at a specific figure, but representing the emperor's

HISTORICAL CONTEXT
Marcus Aurelius' Meditations

We have more statements from Marcus Aurelius explaining his personal philosophy than from any other emperor. His *Meditations*, which seem to have been compiled from his daily journals, reveal his Stoic philosophy on life and rule. They were written in Greek while he was on campaign in various wars and were written only for himself, not for publication, so they provide insight into his inner life, thoughts, and struggles. The twelve books include many observations consistent with Stoic philosophy, including:

> If you are pained by any external thing, it is not this that disturbs you, but your own judgment about it. And it is in your power to wipe out this judgment now. (8.47)

> . . . if there are gods, is not a thing to be afraid of, for the gods will not involve you in evil; but if indeed they do not exist, or if they are not concerned with human affairs, what is it to me to live in a universe devoid of gods . . . ? (2.11)

> The soul becomes dyed with the color of its thoughts. (5.16)

achievements and personal attributes. Similar to the bronze equestrian statue is a marble portrait bust of Marcus Aurelius in military dress.

The portraits of Faustina the Younger, wife of Marcus Aurelius and daughter of Antoninus Pius and Faustina the Elder, clearly age as she does. The earliest type dates to *c.* 147 CE when, at the age of seventeen, Faustina the Younger was named Augusta. Her broad, highly polished face has a small, closed mouth and wide-set eyes with drilled pupils and irises and heavy upper lids familiar from both male and female later Antonine portraits. Her hairstyle is a development of the Greek goddess type first seen under Sabina with her long straight hair centrally parted and divided into four layers on each side. All of these are gathered into a bun at the back of her head just above the neck.

Non-imperial portraiture

The influence of both male and female imperial images is demonstrated by the Antonine period pediment on the front porch of the Sacellum of the Augustales at Misenum, probably dating to *c.* 160 CE. The relief portraits of the patrons of the newly renovated shrine, Lucius Laecanius Primitivus and his wife, Cassia Victoria, fill the central wreath. Their facial features are apparently portraits while their hairstyles are self-conscious imitations of Marcus Aurelius and Faustina the Younger, with whom they associated themselves. Victoria wears the 147 CE hairstyle of Faustina the Younger while Primitivus' look is based directly on Marcus Aurelius' early portraits. Such imitation of imperial styles is found from the time of Augustus

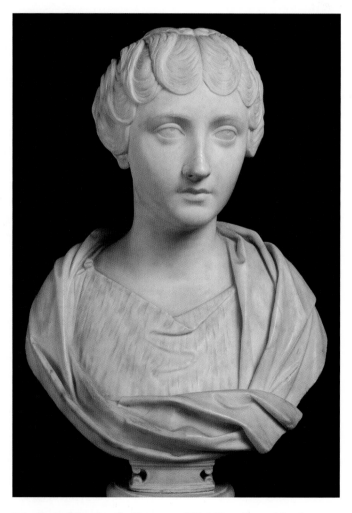

9.4 Bust of Faustina the Younger, *c.* 147–148 CE, Rome. Musei Capitolini, Rome. H 2 ft (61 cm), marble. Source: © Araldo de Luca/Corbis.

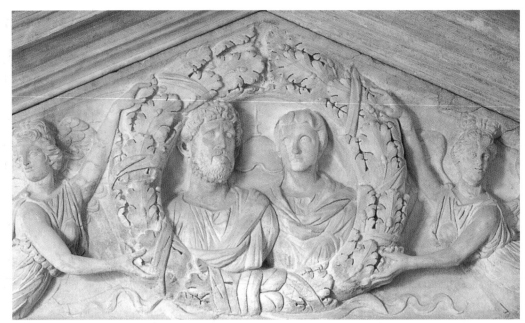

9.5   Pediment of Sacellum of the Augustales, Misenum with portrait busts of donors, Lucius Laecanius Primitivus and his wife, Cassia Victoria, 160 CE. Museo Archeologico dei Campi Flegrei, Baia. H 78 ¾ in (2 m) L 27 ft 5 in (8.35 m), marble. Photo courtesy Steven L. Tuck.

onward, but this is one of the clearest examples of both male and female portraits together inspired by the imperial family.

The use of paired funerary and commemorative portraits with ideological, mythological, or religious associations also becomes more common during the Antonine period. One of the types seen in multiple examples is the funerary portrait pair of a husband and wife as Mars and Venus. In this example the eclectic nature of the pairing is clear. The female portrait is based on the Venus from Capua (Figure 8.32) with the same pose and dress, but finished with the facial features of an unknown Roman woman and slightly adjusted to appear to engage with the male portrait. Her hairstyle is distantly based on the Venus, but seems most directly modeled on an Antonine empress, probably Faustina the Younger. The man is a variant on a well-known type of Mars, here heroically nude with only helmet and sword baldric. His hairstyle, and to a lesser extent his facial features, seem to rely on images of Antoninus Pius. Judging by the hairstyles, many scholars argue that this pairing may be based on an imperial model, but none survive to confirm that conclusion.

Not every portrait, however, was derived from imperial types. A bust of a man found in Athens and datable to the principate of Marcus Aurelius displays all the latest stylistic tendencies and carving techniques, notably the calm, adult, idealized features with the smooth skin contrasted with the deeply carved and drilled hair. In this case, however, the hair is separated into long, only slightly wavy locks that fall from the crown of his head in a mop of hair. His short beard has volume, but differs dramatically from the long corkscrew curls of the later Antonines, while his facial features have no specific Antonine allusions. It is a portrait that reflects contemporary technique and style but not imperial imagery.

This sculpture also illustrates a problem shared by much ancient art including the earlier chimera (Figure 3.18) and so-called Brutus (Figure 3.19) statues, lack of provenance. With no secure findspot giving context for the work what we can say about it is limited to stylistic discussion. Knowing that it was created, for example, for a tomb, a house, or display in a public building would convey much more information about sculptural display and use in antiquity. Regrettably, findspot information is rarely attached to works discovered in the Renaissance or that circulate through the art market.

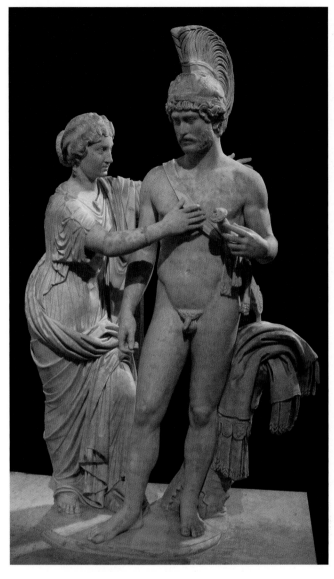

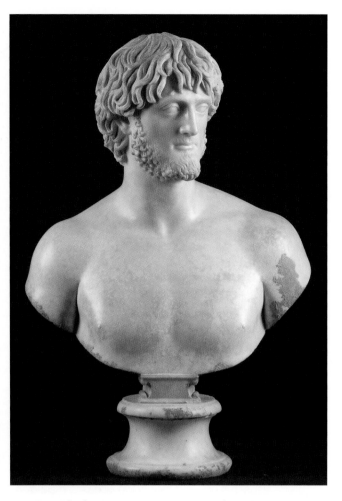

9.7   Bust of unknown man, *c.* 160–180 CE, Athens. H 32 in (81.3 cm), marble. Saint Louis Art Museum, Museum Purchase 299:1923.

9.6   Funerary portrait of man and woman as Mars and Venus, *c.* 155 CE, Rome. Musée du Louvre, Paris. H 6 ft 2 in (1.88 m), marble. Photo courtesy Daniel Resheter.

Commodus portraiture

One of the final and most spectacular of the Antonine portraits is a marble bust from Rome showing the emperor Commodus as Hercules, probably from the last year of his rule. His facial features, hair, and beard all develop from the images of his father, Marcus Aurelius.

Here are the hooded eyes, similar facial structure, hairstyle, and beard shape. The polish on the skin seems even finer and contrasts with the fuller hair and beard made possible by deeper drill work. He wears the lionskin and carries the club of Hercules. In his left hand he holds the Golden Apples of the Hesperides, representing the Labor of Hercules that brought the promise of eternal life, not for himself, but for those Romans who believe in him as a savior figure. The support at the base of the bust combines images of the globe for Roman global power, cornucopia for abundance, and a kneeling Amazonian figure for conquest over barbarians. The image is sophisticated and carries a complex political message to a Roman audience. Like Hercules, Commodus was the son of a god (the

A VIEW FROM THE PROVINCES
Portraits from Palmyra

Another private portrait reveals the style of art from the eastern provinces that would heavily influence art across the Roman world in the third century CE. This style is typically referred to as Palmyrene, after the city of Palmyra where the style originated. Palmyra was an oasis city on the important eastern trade routes midway between the Mediterranean ports of Tyre, Sidon, and Byblos, and the Euphrates river in Mesopotamia. It was absorbed into the Roman province of Syria under Tiberius. Thanks to the wealth of the caravan trade, the city expanded in size and importance in the second century CE. A massive building program with temples, streets, colonnades, and public buildings all in the local limestone transformed the city. Its architectural and sculptural style, which blended Greek, Roman, and Near Eastern traditions, spread throughout Syria and Phoenicia. In the third century CE the style spreads to Rome and the Severan building program at Leptis Magna in Roman Africa. Palmyra broke away from Roman rule in the mid third century CE until it was conquered and destroyed by the emperor Aurelian in 273 CE.

The Palmyrene style is best seen in the funerary relief portraits of its wealthy citizens, carved on the fine limestone slabs that covered their grave niches in mausolea. The images demonstrate the style's strong frontality, an emphasis on the head, which is carved in higher relief and in a larger scale than the body, oversized eyes, and careful attention to the attributes that distinguish the deceased such as jewelry, crowns, medallions, and amulets, all enhanced with paint.

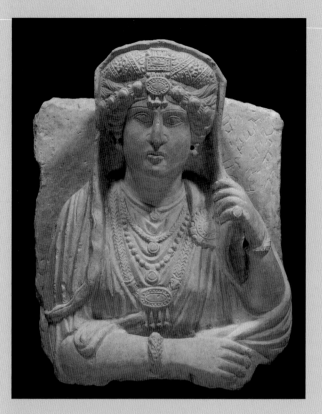

9.8   Funerary bust of Palmyrene woman in high relief, *c.* 200 CE, Palmyra. University of Pennsylvania Museum of Archaeology and Anthropology, B8904. H 19 ¾ in (50 cm), limestone. Source: Courtesy of Penn Museum, image # 8041.

This example is typical as a strictly frontal bust of the deceased carved in limestone with a large head and dramatic, oversized, carefully carved eyes. Her face ignores the contemporary imperial trend of wrinkles and sagging skin in favor of very broad planes for the surfaces of the face with no modeling of the flesh and an abstracted, almost schematic presentation of the facial features. Her hands are roughly carved. This is not because the portrait was unfinished, but because the sculptor was engaged with other elements. Detailed attention is lavished on her hair, dress, and jewelry, as is typical for the style. She is formally dressed and elaborately decorated in tunic, cloak, turban, veil, and jewelry. Her jewelry includes a jeweled ring on the smallest finger of her left hand, two spiral bracelets with studded decoration, drop earrings, four necklaces – three with circular pendants and the fourth with a large oval pendant and four drops, and a large circular jeweled brooch at her left shoulder. Typically for the style, the head receives even more attention. The turban is textured with rosettes and what appears to be a brocade pattern and the scallop edge of the veil is clearly carved. A complex brooch of rectangular and oval plaques and drops is pinned to the front of the turban while a string of large beads encircles her hair just below the turban. As with funerary sculptures in many cultures the Palmyrene images were meant to convey the status and position of the deceased. Here, unlike in most Roman tomb sculpture, that is conveyed by allusions to wealth, not public service or family obligations.

deified Marcus Aurelius), who was using his power to bring benefits to others. Commodus reinforced this message by appearing in the arena dressed as Hercules in grand staged animal hunts. His biographer records that he accepted statues of himself as Hercules and that offerings were made to his Hercules statues as to a god.

ARCHITECTURAL SCULPTURE

Compared to the amount of work under Trajan and Hadrian, very few large-scale buildings were constructed in Rome under the Antonines. Antoninus Pius lived quietly out of Rome at a villa while Marcus Aurelius spent most of his twenty years of rule fighting massive wars along Rome's frontiers. Those buildings we know of were mostly tombs, temples, altars, columns, arches, and other such forms designed to commemorate the lives and achievements of emperors. The vast majority of these have disappeared or survive only in ruins leaving behind only their decorative sculpture to give a sense of their original forms and political statements. One of the earliest of these is the Hadrianeum, Temple of the Divine Hadrian, constructed and dedicated under Antoninus Pius to honor his predecessor.

Relief sculpture honoring Hadrian and Antoninus Pius

Twenty-one reliefs with personified provinces and nine reliefs of captive arms and armor are preserved from the original decoration of the temple and surrounding portico. Each of the personified provinces stands isolated on a blank panel. The figures derive from Classical Greek art of personified ethnic groups borrowed by Greek artists from Persian art of the fifth century BCE. The shallow relief and frontality of each figure are not Classicizing nor found on the Hadrianic coin series that seems to have inspired them. These components, along with the use of a drilled outline surrounding each figure, are probably derived ultimately from Hellenistic art and most immediately from sculptural styles current in Roman Gaul, demonstrating the increased influence of provincial art in Roman public sculpture in the Antonine period. Vergil's *Aeneid*, written under Augustus, reinforces the celebration of Roman power of this type of display of conquered peoples. He describes how "the conquered nations walked in long procession in all their different costumes, and in all their different armor . . ." (*Aeneid* 8.724).

Antoninus Pius was himself deified upon his death and honored with a column erected by Marcus Aurelius and Lucius Verus. The column itself, a 50 ft monolith of red granite, was not carved, but its large base has relief scenes on three sides and a dedicatory inscription on the fourth side. The panel opposite the inscription portrays the apotheosis of Antoninus Pius and Faustina.

Flanked by two eagles, imagery of imperial apotheosis dating back to Augustus, the divine couple ride on the back of a *Genius* figure that probably represents *Aeternitas*, the personification of eternity

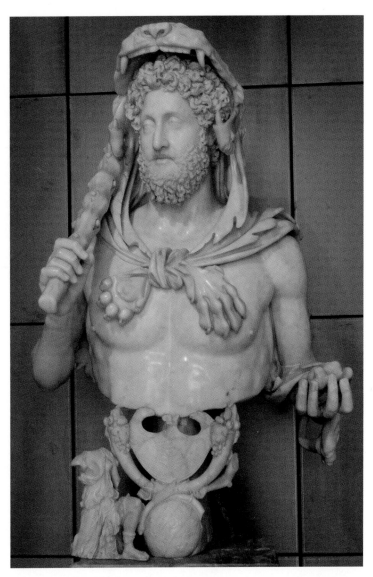

9.9 Bust of Commodus, *c.* 192 CE, Rome. Musei Capitolini, Rome. H 4 ft (1.22 cm), marble. Photo courtesy Daniel Resheter.

MORE ON MYTH
Golden Apples of the Hesperides

Retrieving the Golden Apples of the Hesperides was Hercules' most difficult and epic labor. They were kept in a walled garden on the edge of the world, guarded by a great serpent, Ladon, and the daughters of Atlas, the Hesperides. To find the garden Hercules wandered through large areas of Europe, Asia, and Africa. During these travels he encountered many obstacles and fought and questioned many individuals including the sea-god Nereus and Antaeus, the son of the earth-goddess. In Egypt he narrowly avoided being made a human sacrifice by King Busiris, one of the sons of Poseidon. Finally, with the help of the Titan Prometheus, he found the garden and convinced Atlas to retrieve the apples for him. In exchange he took over Atlas' burden, holding up the heavens. When Atlas returned with the apples, he refused to take back the heavens. Hercules tricked him into doing so by asking him to hold them for just a moment while he spread his lionskin to pad his shoulders. Then he took the apples to King Eurystheus and completed his quest. In an alternate version Hercules killed Ladon instead of employing Atlas to help him.

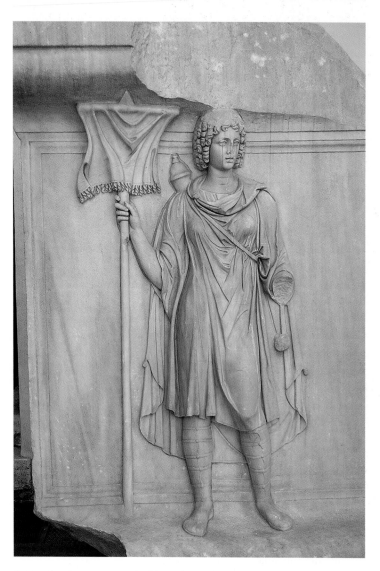

9.10 Captive province relief from the Hadrianeum, Rome, *c.* 145 CE. Musei Capitolini, Rome. H 6 ft 10 in (2.08 m), marble. Photo courtesy Steven L. Tuck.

found on commemorative coinage of Faustina. The scene is witnessed and given context by the figures below. To the left the personification of the Campus Martius, the specific location of their cremation and burial, is indicated by one of the Augustan obelisks erected in the area. To the right is the seated figure of Roma with her standard attributes as seen on many works of imperial art, notably the Ara Pacis Augustae. She raises her hand in the same gesture of approval used by the crowd to the emperor on the Anaglypha Traiani relief (Figure 8.24). All of the figures are carved with Classicizing proportions, poses, and features, with rounded forms, fully integrated anatomy, and deeply carved and drilled drapery.

The apotheosis panel differs dramatically from the two scenes that flank it. These two sides of the base are decorated with very nearly identical images of military units riding in a form of spectacular exercise known as a *decursio*, which might represent a portion of the funeral ceremony. On each side a cavalry unit circles a group of ten standing soldiers, two of whom hold military standards and, like the cavalry, wear tunics while the remainder are armed and armored. The conception and execution of the scene could not be more different from the apotheosis panel. Instead of a single perspective, the viewer gets a non-integrated view of the scene. Individual figures or small groups stand on their own groundlines rising up the field of the panel and violating classical conventions of space. Depth, notably in the standing soldier group, is indicated by figures in the background standing on their own raised sections of ground. The figures are very squat in proportion, and their internal definition is through linear detail instead of rounded forms. The

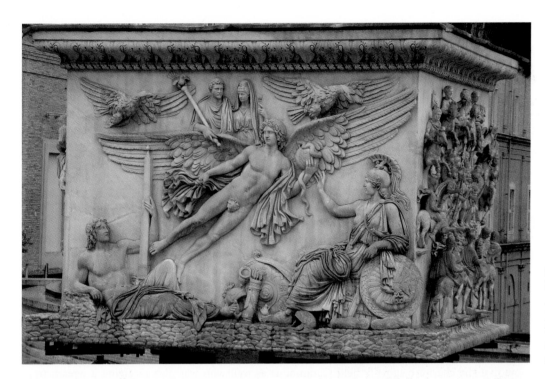

9.11 Apotheosis scene, base of Column of Antoninus Pius, Rome, 161 CE. Musei Vaticani, Rome. H 8 ft 1 ½ in (2.48 m), marble. Photo courtesy Steven L. Tuck.

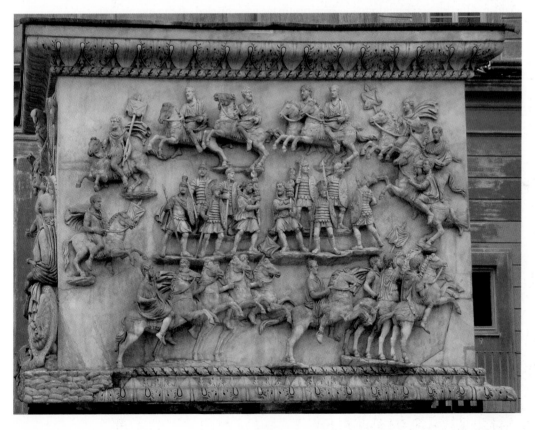

9.12 Military parade scene, base of Column of Antoninus Pius, Rome, 161 CE. Musei Vaticani, Rome. H 8 ft 1 ½ in (2.48 m), marble. Photo courtesy Steven L. Tuck.

entire scene reflects the Italic tradition as seen in the Amiternum relief rather than the Classicizing works we have come to expect of public art under the principate. The base is the first example of an imperial monument that uses the Italic style along with the Classicizing in a single work. It will not be the last.

Reliefs from victory monuments of Marcus Aurelius

Another of the missing Antonine monuments is an arch of Marcus Aurelius. Scholars debate whether the eleven extant relief panels actually come from one or two arches. What is clear is that the panels are consistently designed vertically oriented scenes that represent the achievements and personal qualities of Marcus Aurelius in very traditional ways. The qualities celebrated include those on the golden shield voted by the Senate to Augustus: justice, clemency, martial prowess, and piety. These are combined with traditional images of *adventus*, *adlocutio*, and many scenes related to activities around the Marcomannic wars. Two of the best examples of these are the Triumph and Clemency panels.

The Clemency panel shows Marcus Aurelius on horseback, portrayed very similarly to the gilded bronze equestrian statue in Rome, granting clemency to two Germans kneeling before him, presumably in the aftermath of his successful war against them. The scene, its composition with surrounding soldiers, and the setting established by flanking background trees, are all elements found on the Column of Trajan. Another panel represents a synoptic narrative of military victory combining two elements of the traditional imagery of the triumph into a single panel: passing through an arch and its conclusion at the temple of Jupiter. In this relief, Marcus Aurelius rides in the triumphal chariot with the figure of Victory hovering over him as the procession is about to pass through an arch, all elements found on the passageway relief of the same scene from the Arch of Titus. Here, however, is the added image of an unidentified temple in the background, perhaps evoking a victory temple. Note that the chariot originally held Commodus as well who was also receiving a wreath from Victory. After his assassination, however, his image was chiseled off the monument.

(a)

(b)

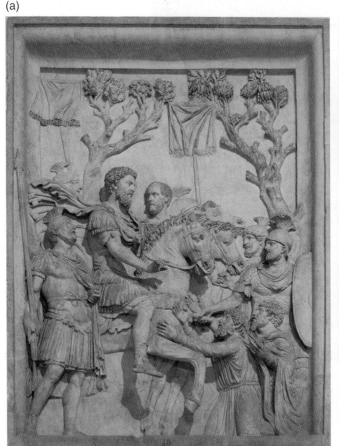
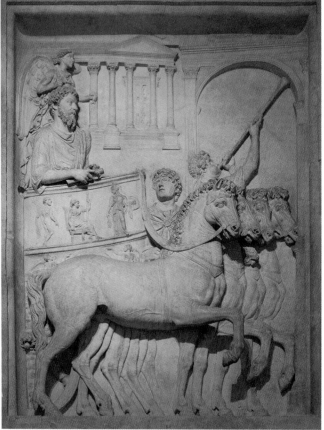

9.13a and 9.13b   Clemency and Triumph panels, Arch of Marcus Aurelius, Rome, 176–180 CE. Musei Capitolini, Rome. H 10 ft 6 in (3.2 m) W 7 ft 3 in (2.21 m), marble. Matthias Kabel/Wikimedia Commons.

The Column of Marcus Aurelius is the most important and intact of his architectural sculpture. Based closely in size, scale, placement, and decoration on the Column of Trajan (Figure 8.16), the Column of Marcus Aurelius is decorated with a sculptural frieze that depicts the Marcomannic and Sarmatian campaigns in the same way that Trajan's depicted the Dacian campaign. There are, however, some key differences.

This column has fewer spirals, the figures are carved in higher relief, and the scenes use more elements from Italic and provincial art. The figures are more often portrayed frontally with larger heads and squatter proportions than the Classicizing ones on the Column of Trajan. The smaller figures allow each scene to contain multiple registers rather than a single line of figures all on one groundline at the base of the spiral. The small group of figures that includes the emperor often appears on its own groundline separated from and elevated above the surrounding figures. This separation of the ruler from the ruled will continue to widen throughout the second to fourth centuries CE.

In addition, the tone differs from the Column of Trajan. Trajan's sculpture introduced images of the prosecution of war into Roman civic space for the first time, but the images on the Column of Marcus Aurelius show the brutality of war, including Roman forces burning native villages and decapitating bound prisoners. The subject of the suffering of the defeated ultimately derives from the Hellenistic victory monuments from the city of Pergamon, but here emphasizes the harrowing nature of warfare.

Reliance on spiritual intervention is also a factor in the war as a sudden rainstorm, seen in the appearance of a colossal rain god who destroys the barbarian enemy, averts military disaster. This differs dramatically from the image of the colossal personified Danube river on the Column of Trajan subdued by the force of Roman engineering in the great bridge of Apollodorus of Damascus (Figure 8.18 lowest register). A sense of uncertainty and pessimism seems to permeate throughout the images. As Marcus Aurelius himself wrote, in his daily *Meditations* (2.17), "All things of the body stream away like a river, all things of the mind are dreams and delusion; life is warfare, and a visit to a strange land; the only lasting fame is oblivion."

ARCHITECTURE

The Temple of Hadrian at Ephesus was dedicated by Publius Quintilius to Hadrian, Artemis, and the people of Ephesus perhaps prior to Hadrian's visit of 128 CE although in its final form it seems to date to after his death. The small, simple structure consists of just a pronaos (porch) constructed in marble and small cella or naos (shrine) of rubble construction. It contains elements seen in the baroque Classicizing architecture already examined from Rome. Buildings such as the Temple of the Divine Vespasian and Titus and the Forum Transitorium use the elaborate decoration of multiple friezes, projecting and receding elements, and

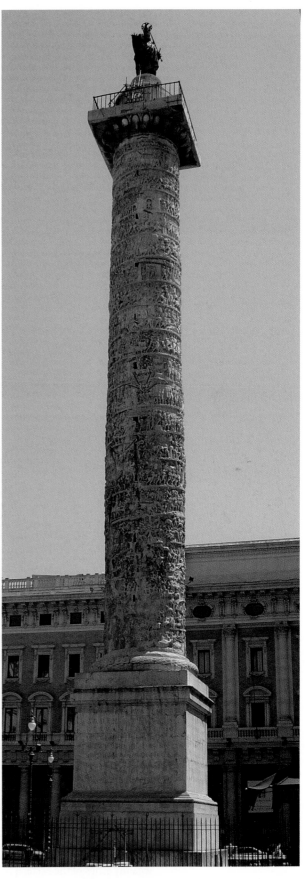

9.14 Column of Marcus Aurelius, Rome, overview, 180 CE, marble. Photo courtesy Steven L. Tuck.

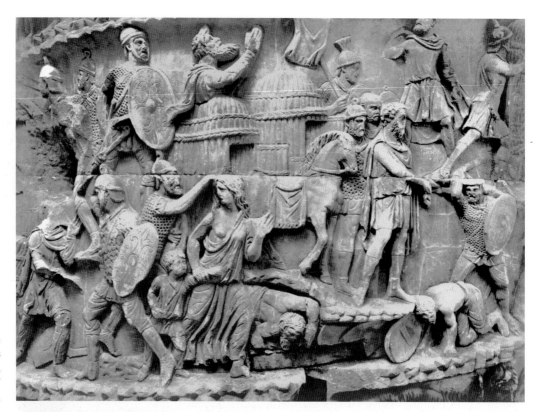

9.15 Village destruction scene, Column of Marcus Aurelius, Rome, 180 CE, marble. Source: Alinari/ The Bridgeman Art Library.

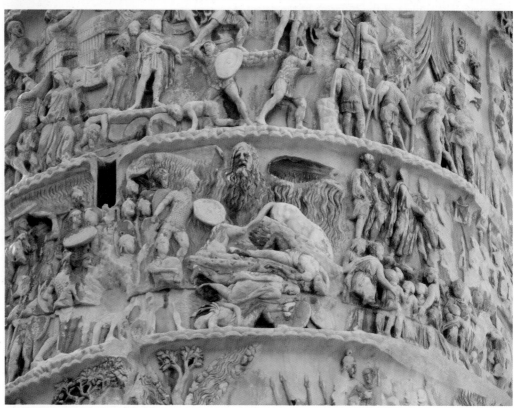

9.16 Storm god scene, Column of Marcus Aurelius, Rome, 180 CE, marble. Photo courtesy Steven L. Tuck.

classical sculpture that are seen as elements of this style. It exemplifies the style of architecture, often referred to as Syrian, that probably has its origins in Palmyra. It is found there and in the other wealthy cities of the eastern provinces in the second century CE as Palmyrene style spreads across the Roman world.

HISTORICAL CONTEXT
Cassius Dio, on the miracle of the rain

At a time when the Romans had run into danger in the battle the Heavenly Power most unexpectedly saved them. The Quadi had surrounded them and the Romans were fighting valiantly . . . and the barbarians ceased fighting, expecting to capture their enemies easily by heat and thirst. So they posted guards all about and hemmed them in to prevent their getting water anywhere, for the barbarians were far superior in numbers. The Romans fell into dire distress from their fatigue and wounds and the sun's heat and their thirst . . . when suddenly numbers of clouds rushed together and a great rain, certainly of divine origin, came pouring down. . . . when the rain poured down at first all bent their faces upwards and received it in their mouths. . . . The barbarians charging upon them, they drank and fought at the same time . . . they would have suffered some great damage from the enemy's onset had not violent hail and thunderbolts fallen upon the latter's ranks. In the same spot one might see water and fire descending from Heaven at the same time: the one side was being drenched and drinking, the other was being burned with fire and dying. (*Roman History* 72.8)

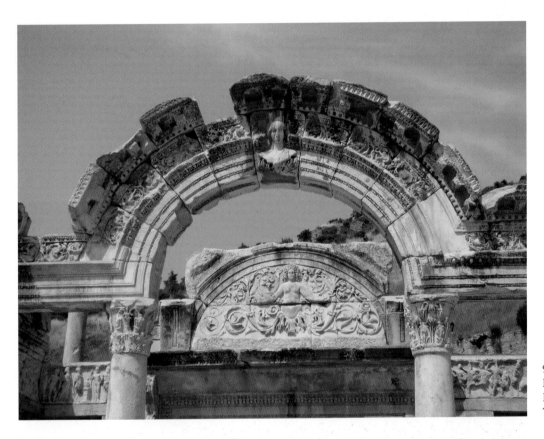

9.17 Temple of Hadrian, Ephesus, *c.* 140 CE, marble. Photo courtesy Francesca Tronchin.

The facade is highly three dimensional with the Syrian pediment with its central arch and broken pediment corners seen just above the square pilasters on the corners of the pediment. As with the portrait sculpture of the period, the drill is used to effect here to give a sense of depth and volume to the reliefs on the temple. The intent is arguably the opposite of the architectural revolution with the Syrian style's emphasis on traditional stone block construction, post and lintel supports, and the facade over the interior. The specific features of this temple include a Syrian arch in the outer pediment with multiple lines of frieze decoration. The keystone of the arch has a projecting protome bust of Tyche, the personification of the city, very similar to those busts found on the ground floor facade of the amphitheater at Capua. Inside the temple porch above the door into the temple itself, a carved **tympanum** is ornamented with a human figure, probably the Gorgon Medusa. She appears on the

tympanum
a semi-circular area over an entrance bounded by the lintel below and an arch above. It often contains sculpture, usually in relief.

central axis surrounded by symmetrical ornaments of spiraling acanthus leaves. The figure on the semi-circular panel is clearly apotropaic, but her appearance above the cella door is misleading. From a distance the curve of the tympanum fills the arch of the Syrian pediment and makes this figure appear as a part of that outer decoration as well. Only on approaching the porch does the three-dimensional nature of the facade become clear.

WALL PAINTING AND MOSAICS

Early Antonine interior decorative art is preserved at Ostia in the Baths of the Seven Sages. In addition to its wall paintings, the bathing complex had an enormous, high quality black and white floor mosaic and polychrome wall and ceiling mosaics, altogether giving evidence of the wealthy establishment with sophisticated decoration utilizing a range of contemporary arts. The Seven Sages wall paintings, which give their name to the entire complex, demonstrate the use of Greek models as well as humor in Roman wall paintings, especially those found in shops, bars, and baths.

The main feature of the wall decoration is the set of seven images in the Greek portrait tradition of seated sages or poets in the central register of each of the walls. Each man sits in a wooden chair, wearing a Greek tunic and mantle and carrying a stick. Each one is identified by a painted caption with his name and an aphorism in Latin mocking the various philosophers by referring to the activities of the latrine instead of an expected quote from Greek philosophy. Advice on treating constipation is found repeatedly. Next to the image of Chilon of Sparta, we can still read: VISSIRE TACITE CHILON DOCVIT SVBDOLVS (The cunning Chilon taught how to fart silently). This type of bathroom humor developed from violating the expectation of the viewer; the reader would see the Greek philosopher and read the caption assuming it would be a statement of philosophy only to receive something completely different.

The House of Jupiter and Ganymede at Ostia belongs to an *insula*, a block of houses, shops, and apartments that was built one street from the forum during the Hadrianic period and painted in its

insula
literally in Latin "island," refers to an apartment building that filled an entire block in a Roman city, with shops on the ground floor and apartments above.

9.18   Wall painting of Greek sages, *c.* 140 CE, Baths of the Seven Sages, Ostia. Overall height of painted room 17 ft (5.2 m). Source: © Anthony Majanlahti.

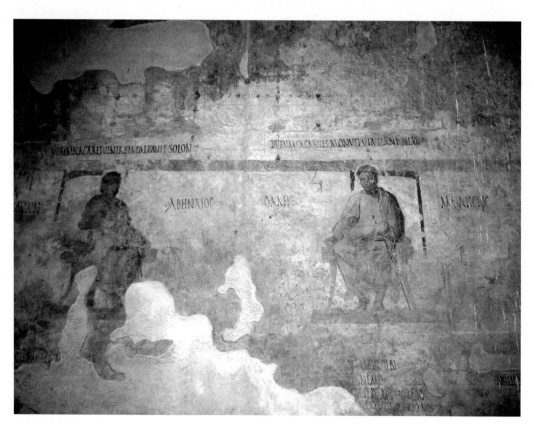

ART AND LITERATURE
Art and the Second Sophistic

The Second Sophistic was an intellectual movement lasting from the reign of Nero to *c.* 230 CE which saw an explosion in works of Greek literature based on the example of Greek, particularly Athenian, orators of the Classical period. The Sophists, authors and orators of the Second Sophistic, were cataloged by Philostratus in his *Lives of the Sophists*. Leading Sophists included Aelius Aristides, Dio Chrysostom, Herodes Atticus, Lucian, Philostratus, Plutarch, and Polemon of Laodicea. They were famous for their ability to compose and perform speeches for an audience, often with little or no preparation, effectively creating extemporaneous works of rhetoric to entertain large crowds of students or spectators.

In addition, the Sophists should be credited with the revival of the use and value of higher education in the Roman Empire during this period. Although the major Sophists were Greek, their audience included many elite Romans of all levels including emperors, for example Antoninus Pius and Marcus Aurelius. For a time Herodes Atticus received up to three letters a day from Marcus Aurelius, who also once waited three days to meet Aelius Aristides and another day before he was allowed to hear him speak.

The Sophists wrote repeatedly about art, providing verbal responses to the visual world. They were adept at the presentation of verbal pictures, known as ekphrasis. This notion of picturing a scene is key to their work. It also indicates that the written word had an impact in how the audience viewed a scene. Greek subjects had been used in Roman art for centuries of course. The change is in some new subjects, in the approach to them, in the celebration of the Athenian Classical world as opposed to the Archaic or Hellenistic, using Athenian styles and motifs specifically.

The Sophists were more than inspirational teachers and orators, they were also among the leading art patrons of the period, so it is not surprising that the styles and subjects in art should reflect their cultural contributions. Herodes Atticus, for example, endowed many buildings across the Roman Empire and paid for a great number of dedicatory statues as well.

The explosion of bearded images in the Antonine period has been attributed to the imitation of Hadrian's beard, but since many do not copy the specific style of Hadrian's they seem better understood as visual markers of the intellectual tradition of which Hadrian is only one example. The rise in statues, mosaics, and paintings of Greek and Roman local and imperial elites dressed in Greek himation, the distinctive mantle that Greeks wore instead of the Roman toga, reflects the inspiration of the Sophists. The result is a form of art, especially portraiture, with deliberately mixed Roman and Greek values and identities, not just among Greek inhabitants of the empire, but among the highest levels of Roman elites. Dio's *Rhodian Oration* 31 captures this mix of identities using mythological figures to convey what were also traditional Roman values. He cites notions of public service and *virtus* but illustrated with those "who had undergone great labors for virtue's sake, as they say Hercules did, and Theseus and the other semi-divine heroes of the past." He claims the result of this ideal is "This is the reason brave men are found on the battlefield wounded in front instead of having turned and fled." Here, as with the mythological sarcophagi, the models are Greek heroes not figures from Roman history.

The writings of Plutarch represent many of the main intellectual currents of this movement and he has been described as perhaps the most important author of the Second Sophistic. His work gives us an excellent example of the expectation that an informed Roman audience would be familiar with the works of the Sophists. The wall painting in the Bath of the Seven Sages at Ostia conforms to the subject of the Dinner of the Seven Sages in Plutarch's *Moralia* where he names the seven wise men: Thales, Bias, Pittacus, Solon, Chilon, Cleobulus, and Anacharsis. Images of Thales, Solon, Bias, and Chilon are preserved on the wall at Ostia. It seems clear that the Second Sophistic inspired the emphasis on Athenian style classicism of the first to third centuries CE. This cultural movement changed the forms of Roman portraiture, interior decoration, and possibly architecture over a hundred and fifty years until the Late Antique style finally fully develops in the third century CE.

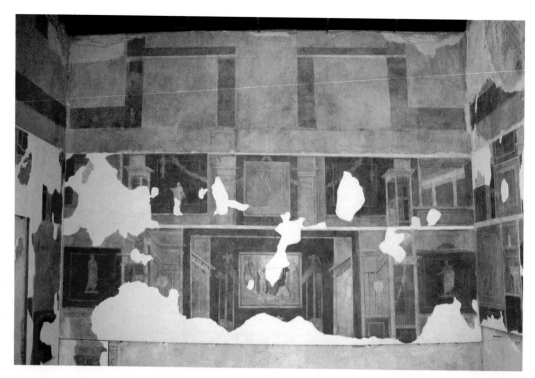

9.19 So-called *tablinum*, House of Jupiter and Ganymede, *c.* 180–190 CE, Ostia. 22 ft (6.75 m) x 28 ¾ ft (8.75 m), wall painting. Source: By permission of Soprintendenza Speciale per i Beni Archeologici di Roma.

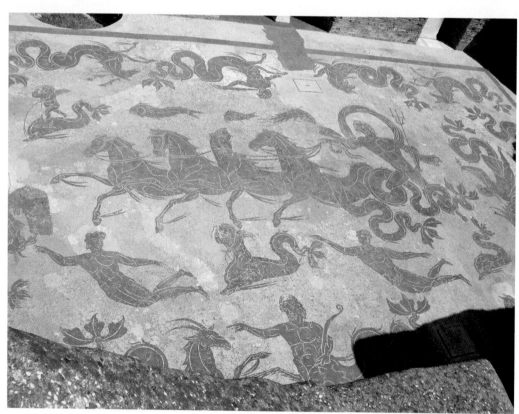

9.20 Black and white mosaic floor from the Baths of Neptune, Ostia, 139 CE. 59 ft 4 in x 34 ft 1 ½ in (18.1 m x 10.4 m). Photo courtesy Steven L. Tuck.

best-preserved phase under the Antonine emperors. In this period the building was decorated with high quality paintings, the details of which unfortunately had been applied to dry instead of wet plaster as was typical in true fresco and so have largely disappeared. This is the largest room in the House of Jupiter and Ganymede. It is larger than almost any of the reception rooms at Pompeii, and the largest extant painted surface at Ostia. The decoration on its east wall gives the name to the entire house. The wall represents a painting composition typical for the Antonine period. The traditional vertical and horizontal division of the wall into three zones has disappeared and along with it the use of three panel paintings per wall as seen in the reception rooms in the House of the Vettii. Instead there is a patchwork of panels of varying size with only a single large panel painting of Jupiter and Ganymede in the center of the lowest register. It is surrounded by individual figures: depictions of Dionysus, Flora, Venus rising from the sea, philosophers, poets, and maenads. Rather than the peopled architecture of the Pompeian Neronian paintings, the figures seem to float isolated in front of the panels that are meant to frame them much as the ethnic personifications from the Hadrianeum do.

The pavement from the Baths of Neptune at Ostia is an excellent example of Italian black and white mosaic work and the changes in that style of art over the course of the second century CE. The floor is filled with standard bathing establishment motifs of swimmers and sea creatures and mythological figures, many of which are identical to figures seen in the Baths of the Cart Drivers from the Hadrianic period at Ostia (Figure 8.37). Here they are more detailed, with white interior lines of tesserae used to show the outlines of overlapping figures and the main divisions of the body and also musculature, surface texture, and highlights. This mosaic is larger than that in the Baths of the Cart Drivers, with the figures in three registers rather than two, and a more formal and rigid composition including the use of symmetrical arrangement and axial organization with confronted figures on each side in the lower register. The central, isolated figure group is emphasized by hierarchy of scale with the main figure enormous compared to those around it. These elements will become more prominent as Roman art adapts into the third century CE.

SARCOPHAGI

One of the most important and remarkable cultural changes of the Roman world occurred in the second century CE. In a brief span of about forty years, Roman burial practice altered radically. At the beginning of the principate of Trajan about 90 percent of Romans were cremated upon death and buried in cineraria or ash urns while about 10 percent were buried with their bodies relatively intact in sarcophagi. By the death of Hadrian, those numbers were almost exactly reversed and sarcophagi, once rare in the Roman world, became common. A number of factors contributed to the explosion in the use of the sarcophagus in the Hadrianic and Antonine periods, including the increase in cults promising corporeal life after death, the example of Greek sarcophagi, and the existence of more Romans with sufficient wealth who were able to purchase these expensive items. Sarcophagi were generally large boxes carved from a single piece of marble with a matching lid. As a group they represent the largest component of private relief sculpture in the Roman world of the second through fourth centuries CE. Generally one of the long sides of the sarcophagus and the lid were carved into a scene or series of scenes, sometimes the short ends were carved as well.

Mythological sarcophagi

The use of the sarcophagus as a field for mythological relief sculpture differs dramatically from the example of the Scipio Barbatus sarcophagus (Figure 4.1) of the Republican period and instead relies on Greek models of figural sarcophagi dating back to the fourth century BCE.

The Orestes sarcophagus found in a tomb just outside Rome and datable to the late Hadrianic period displays many characteristics of the early decorative sarcophagi. The long side is a continuous narrative of scenes from the myth of Orestes. He appears three times along the relief, killing his mother Clytemnestra and her lover Aegisthus in episodes familiar from the tragedy of Aeschylus. The continuous scene is thought to derive from sculptural schools in mainland Greece, perhaps from

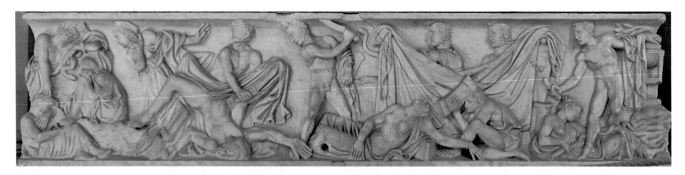

9.21 Orestes sarcophagus, *c.* 135 CE, Rome. Musei Vaticani Museo Gregoriano Profano #10450. L 6 ft 10 in (2.1 m), marble. Jastrow/ Wikimedia Commons.

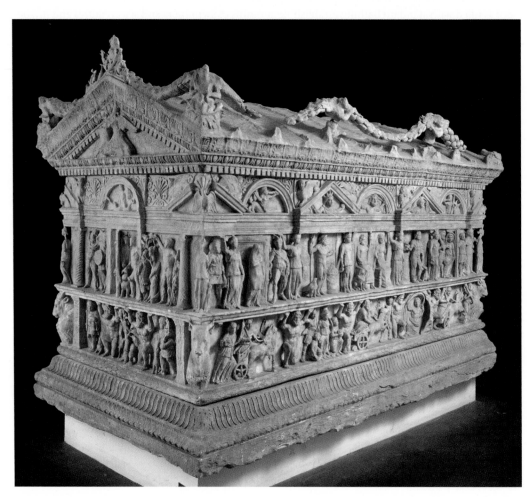

9.22 Velletri sarcophagus, *c.* 135–140 CE, Velletri, Italy. Museo Civico Archeologico Oreste Nardini, Velletri. L 8 ft 5 in (2.57 m) H 4 ft 9 in (1.45 m) D 4 ft 1 in (1.245 m), marble. Source: Araldo de Luca www. araldodeluca.com.

in or around Athens. The frieze on the lid is a later episode from the same myth from the tragedy, *Iphigenia in Tauris*, by Euripides. The combination of a Greek subject with very Classicizing forms matches the predominant style of sculpture at the time inspired by the Second Sophistic.

The Velletri sarcophagus, named for the community where it was found in Latium southeast of Rome, displays a very different approach to the organization of the relief on the side of a sarcophagus because of where it was made. The division of the field into multiple registers and the use of architecture to separate and frame scenes are elements of a school of sculpture from Asia Minor, modern Turkey. The registers are filled with 184 figures from a variety of mythological subjects including the twelve Labors of Hercules, Proserpine, and Alcestis. In the main register Hercules appears repeatedly

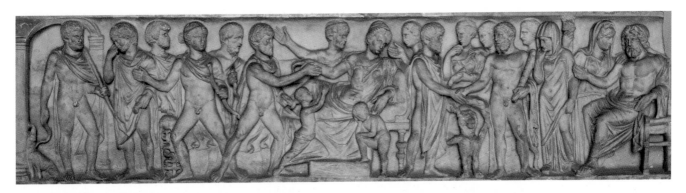

9.23 Alcestis sarcophagus from Ostia, *c.* 165 CE. Musei Vaticani, Rome. L 7 ft 9 ½ in (2.4 m) H 21 ¼ in (54 cm) D 36 ¼ in (92 cm), marble. Jastrow/Wikimedia Commons.

in episodic narrative as the labors are framed by columned architecture roofed with alternating semicircular or triangular pediments. The entire lid of the sarcophagus is designed like a roof, making the sarcophagus a notional temple, another element from the sculptural schools of Asia Minor. The figures may have been selected to reflect a wish for life after death. Proserpine and Alcestis both returned from the underworld in Greek myth. In the third century CE *Hymn to Hercules*, he is referred to as "Father of Time," "immortal," who "disarms death," epithets evoking his ability to bring the dead back to life.

The figures of Hercules and Alcestis make up the major narrative of a sarcophagus of *c.* 165 CE found at the city of Ostia, but probably originating from mainland Greece. As the major harbor for the city of Rome, Ostia was important to the spread of imported marble sarcophagi. Many are found here and most that ended up in the region probably passed through its harbor and warehouses. The story of Alcestis and her husband Admetus dominates the sarcophagus. In the myth Admetus was fated to die unless he could find someone to take his place, a role his wife, Alcestis, agreed to take. Hercules rescued the selfless Alcestis and returned her from the underworld. In this sarcophagus the deceased, a priestess of Magna Mater, Metilia Acte, and her husband, Junius Euhodus, appear as Alcestis and Admetus in the central scene of the relief. The plaque above the register with Acte's name and titles is supported by two Victory figures, a motif that becomes common in the Antonine period. The meaning of this type and others like it is explored in the Scholarly Perspectives box.

The Meleager sarcophagus, found outside of Rome and datable to about 180 CE, also exemplifies the Greek mainland style. It shows another mythological subject in a very different format and echoing different cultural movements. This is the Calydonian Boar Hunt of Greek mythology. The long end of the body of the sarcophagus holds a single large scene of a boar hunt with Meleager holding a spear and attacking the animal, which he will kill after it is wounded by Atalanta. The composition and carving of the sarcophagus is in the mainland Greek style. The artist has chosen to portray the anticipatory moment just prior to the boar's death, rather than the actual spearing, to heighten dramatic tension in the scene. The sarcophagus shows the spread of the boar hunt motif, which was the subject of one of the amphitheater reliefs at Capua (Figure 8.33) and one of Hadrian's tondi (Figure 8.27) where it displayed the *virtus* of the emperor.

Biographical sarcophagi

Another sarcophagus that reflects contemporary imperial public art is the Portonaccio sarcophagus.

One of the most spectacular of the Antonine sarcophagi is the Portonaccio sarcophagus of *c.* 180–190 CE. The lid has a biographical frieze of three scenes from the life of a Roman general: birth, wedding, and providing clemency to a captive barbarian commander. The general appears in

SCHOLARLY PERSPECTIVE
Sarcophagi – a search for meaning

A scholarly debate in Antonine art is the search for meaning in the scenes selected for Roman sarcophagi. Roman Republican tombs had images that displayed the status, identity, and values of the deceased. Later Christian sarcophagi carved with biblical scenes did likewise. Many scholars believe that sarcophagi scenes had meaning for the deceased or their families. For the Antonine period the tremendous number of subjects make such determinations difficult. For some subjects we may never know the reason behind their selection. For example, a small group of sarcophagi show episodes from the myth of Medea, including explicit scenes of her killing her sons and her husband, Jason's, chosen second wife, Creusa. These horrific scenes seem to have no connection to larger philosophical or religious trends or to indicate any desire for personal salvation or life after death. They may just display an enjoyment of the play by Euripides. For other subjects some patterns seem certain.

Some common scenes and motifs are apparently metaphors for life. Victory personified, chariot races, and ships sailing into harbor are all probably symbols of life and its successful conclusion. Victories often support the central portrait of the deceased or the epitaph panel as on the Alcestis sarcophagus from Ostia. Whether these motifs also convey a sense of afterlife is unclear, but the primary message seems to be a life successfully completed. That notion of a well-lived life seems to inspire the more explicitly biographical scenes such as battle sarcophagi, wedding scenes, and images of civic office.

The use of biographical details indicates that sarcophagi were considered appropriate venues to reference a person's life. That motivation may drive the selection of certain myths as well. The images of Admetus and Alcestis in the central scene of the Alcestis sarcophagus from Ostia are portraits of the couple, a form of self-identification with mythological figures also seen in the Mars and Venus statue pairs. The death and resurrection of Alcestis in the myth may refer to the couple's hope for life after death and the end of spousal separation with their reunion. There is no evidence that the myth has any more specific meaning to their lives or that Acte actually gave up her life for her husband.

Other mythological sarcophagi may represent sincere religious beliefs. Many subjects on Antonine and later sarcophagi are taken from the cults that promised life after death. These so-called mystery religions were a set of cults in the Roman world that shared common features including worship of deities who had demonstrated the ability to bring people back from the dead. The worship of these deities including Dionysus, Mithras, Hercules, Orpheus, and Isis gained popularity in the Antonine period. Images of Dionysiac revels, banquets, and meals might have been selected as appropriate images to be viewed during the funerary banquets that were held at Roman tombs several times a year.

The inclusion of Hercules as the explicit means by which Alcestis was resurrected and returned to her husband on earth makes him the primary figure who can grant resurrection. Dionysiac scenes are also common on marble sarcophagi and Dionysius' role in returning the dead from the underworld, beginning with his own mother, Semele, was well known. Images of Orpheus are less common but his ability to return people from the underworld made him an object of cult across the classical world. In all of these cases the selection of these images for sarcophagi could reveal the beliefs of those interred in them. Other Greek myths might have been selected to associate the deceased with a particular hero or mythological figure in their personal qualities if not the details of their life. The Orestes sarcophagus probably doesn't reflect a young man who killed his philandering, murderous mother, for which it seems there would not have been a large market, but one who displays filial devotion in revenging the death of his father.

Finally, there are so many images of death in these reliefs: motifs of untimely death, abduction by the gods, sorrowful partings, etc. These may simply reflect Roman pragmatism and a philosophical approach to death and dying. Epicureanism, the philosophy that advocated rejecting the fear of death, is quoted on some epitaphs and these images of death may reflect Epicurean beliefs. Or they might reflect Stoic philosophy with its contemplation of death. These images could illustrate passages in the works of the Stoic philosopher Seneca, "The point is not how long you live, but how nobly you live" (*Ep.* 101.15). That may be the overall lesson of the mythological scenes.

Michael Koortbojian, *Myth, Meaning, and Memory on Roman Sarcophagi* (University of California Press 1995).

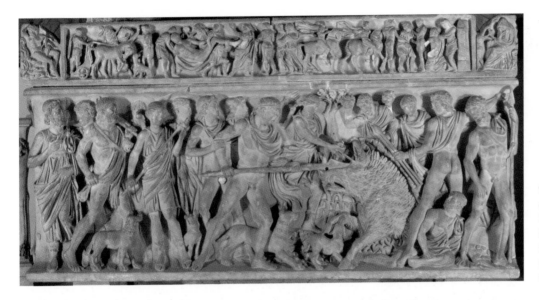

9.24 Meleager sarcophagus, *c.* 180 CE, Rome. Palazzo Doria Pamphili, Rome. L 8 ft 1 ¼ in (2.47 m) H 37 in (94 cm) W 3 ft 7 in (1.1 m), marble. Source: © Superstock/Superstock.

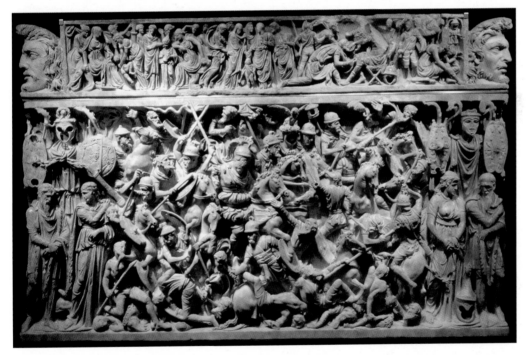

9.25 Portonaccio sarcophagus, *c.* 180–190 CE, Portonaccio. Museo Nazionale Romano Palazzo Massimo, Rome. H 5 ft ¼ in (153 cm), marble. Photo courtesy Steven L. Tuck.

all three scenes that were critical to his public and private identity as a Roman citizen, *pater familias*, and conquering general. The main body of the sarcophagus is a single battle scene based on the sculptural style, images, and motifs found on the battle sculpture of Marcus Aurelius from his Column and arches.

What looks at first glance like an image of the chaos of battle has a very clear underlying structure. Pairs of bound prisoners, one male and one female, stand under Roman trophies of arms and frame each side of the panel. The fighting men fill the field in groups of two or three in approximately three registers but with no visible groundlines. They seem to rise up in space much like the military parade figures on the base of the Column of Antoninus Pius. The central figure of the unidentified deceased is on a rearing horse with a surrendering barbarian under the horse's front hooves, a motif found on the Great Trajanic Frieze and the sculpture of Marcus Aurelius. His victory in this battle is portrayed as the central event of his life and evidence that the display of *virtus* through battle is still powerful,

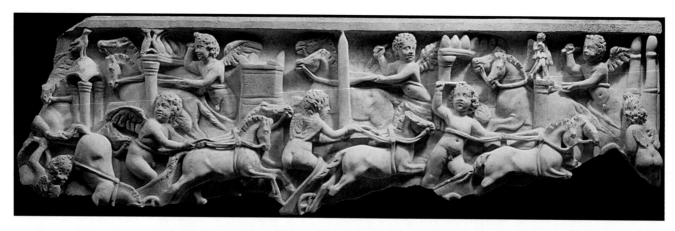

9.26 Front panel from a child's sarcophagus, *c.* 190 CE, eastern Roman world. Museum of Art and Archaeology, University of Missouri. H 15 ¾ in (40 cm) L 4 ft 6 ½ in (138 cm) W 7 in (18 cm), Greek marble. Courtesy of Museum of Art and Archaeology, University of Missouri-Columbia.

especially as it reflects the official sculpture of the Antonine period. This type of battle sarcophagus with biographical scenes remains popular for over a century.

Children's sarcophagi

Given a high infant and childhood mortality it should not be surprising that there were special sarcophagi for children. A portion of a child's sarcophagus shows the use of the relief field to represent a chariot race in a circus. The setting has many of the detailed decorations from the *spina*, the central divider of the Circus Maximus in Rome, including columns, an obelisk, the turning posts, and the lap markers shaped like eggs. An accident, a common occurrence in actual races, is also shown. The depth and three-dimensional carving allow for chariots on both sides of the track racing in both directions. The major change from the real world is the use of Eros figures as charioteers, the youthful characters presumably appropriate for a child's sarcophagus.

FAYUM MUMMY PORTRAITS

Portraits that covered the heads of mummies from the Fayum region in Egypt are the only preserved examples of panel painting, as opposed to wall painting, from the Roman world. Panel painting was the most highly respected form of ancient painting and these portraits give unique insight into the subjects and techniques of this type of art. The mummy portraits provide extraordinary evidence of the direct effect of Roman rule on Egypt as they represent a combination of Egyptian, Greek, and Roman traditions from the period of Roman occupation in Egypt from *c.* 30 BCE to the third century CE. The mummy portraits constitute about nine hundred extant bust images of individuals found attached to the fronts of mummies, largely from the Fayum area of Egypt. The vast majority are painted on wooden panels, some plastered and others with fabric stretched over them to hold the paint. These panels were then placed over the face of the deceased and held in place with the wrappings that covered the mummy prior to burial. Their burial in the dry sand of Egypt led to their almost perfect preservation.

The painting itself follows the Greek artistic tradition. Two types of paint are used, wax-based encaustic and egg-based tempera. The more common encaustic yields the more realistic portraits probably because it, like human skin, is translucent, allowing light to penetrate a short distance under the surface. It could also be worked for a longer period than the tempera, which dried very quickly.

TOOLS & TECHNIQUES
Encaustic painting

Encaustic (the term coming from the Greek word for burning) is a type of painting using hot wax that produced the most realistic of the Fayum portraits. In the most common form, a wooden panel was cut and prepared, either for painting on directly or first covered with a whitewash primer. The ground pigments were mixed into a medium, hot beeswax, which must have been melted to blend the pigments thoroughly. The beeswax may have been pure or had a resin added to lower the melting point and allow the painter to work more slowly, although the only description of encaustic painting technique from the ancient world, Seneca, *Epistle* 121.5, emphasizes speed, "the painter chooses with great speed between his colors which he has placed in front of him . . . and he goes back and forth between the waxes and the picture." The wax must have been heated to melting the entire time the painter was working. It was applied with a brush and a set of hard tools like small palette knives. As it cooled the wax-based paint could be layered and blended giving the work three-dimensional modeling as well as translucence mimicking skin.

In every case, the artists conformed to the conventions of Greek Classical art including use of the four-color palette (red, white, black, and yellow in various combinations), naturalistic portraiture, a single light source defining the subject through light and shadow, asymmetrical compositions with one side of the subject turned slightly to create a more dynamic image, and attributes such as jewelry and wreaths that serve to define the individual and his or her cultural identity including religious beliefs. Each of the paintings is an individual portrait, in many cases with the name of the deceased painted across the front. Computerized tomography (CAT) scans of a number of the mummies show as clearly as can be determined that they conform by sex and age to the portraits on each mummy, meaning that they are true portraits of particular people painted at or near their deaths, not just general images.

In addition to the Egyptian mummification and Greek art traditions, these portraits represent the Roman use of portraiture and ancestor images in homes, during funerals and on tombs. They also reflect the hairstyles contemporary to their creation. The earliest of the images here (early second century CE) is one of the best of the tempera portraits showing a woman, Aline, aged thirty-five, with gold and pearl jewelry added in stucco and wearing a white tunic with two purple stripes, all standard attributes. She turns slightly to the right with highlights on her cheek, forehead, neck, and ear created by a light source coming from her left. Her skin is modeled with short strokes of a brush or tool, but not blended since the fast-drying tempera would not allow that.

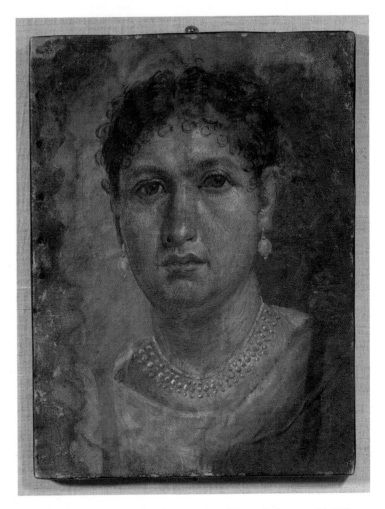

9.27 Fayum portrait of Aline from Arsinoe (Hawara), Egypt, *c.* 98–117 CE. Ägyptisches Museum Berlin. H 16 ½ in (42 cm), tempera on linen. Source: Photo: Juergen Liepe. © 2014. Photo Scala, Florence/BPK, Bildagentur fuer Kunst, Kultur und Geschichte, Berlin.

Aline's image differs dramatically from that of an Antonine woman also wearing a local tunic and elaborate jewelry. The green in the emeralds is the only exception to the four-color palette that was used by the artist. Her image is defined with a strong light source from her right seen in the highlights on her cheek and forehead. Her center-parted hair reflects the style of Faustina the Younger, the wife of Marcus Aurelius, but her facial features are definitely individual. In addition to her lavish jewelry indicating wealth she wears a gold wreath, an element of Greek funerary ritual associated with the worship of Orpheus. Actual gold wreaths have been found in the graves of followers of Orpheus, so this painted version represents that this woman believed in Orpheus and had hopes for a life after death, a popular and spreading belief in the second century CE.

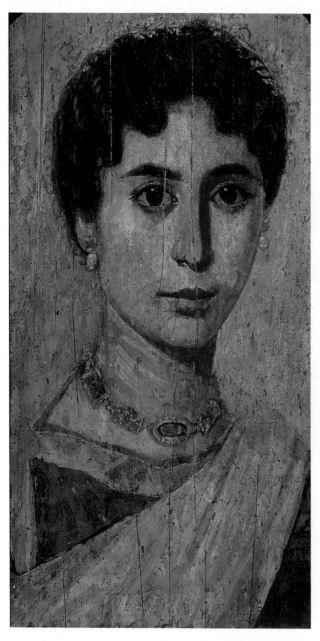 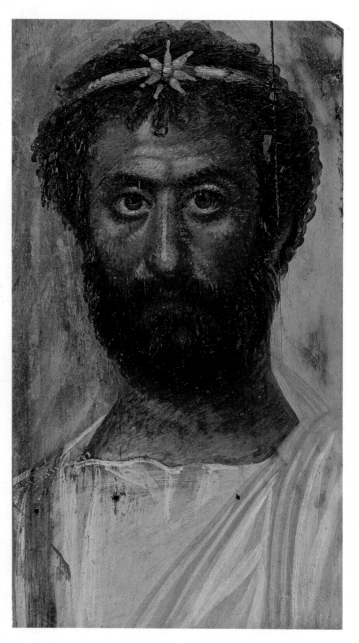

9.28 Fayum portrait of Antonine woman from Philadelphia, Egypt, *c.* 160–190 CE. British Museum, London. H 17 ⅜ in (44.2 cm) W 8 in (20.4 cm), encaustic on wood panel. Source: © The Trustees of the British Museum. All rights reserved.

9.29 Fayum portrait of a priest of Serapis from Arsinoe (Hawara), Egypt, *c.* 138–161 CE. British Museum, London. H 16 ¾ in (42.5 cm), encaustic on wood panel. Source: © The Trustees of the British Museum. All rights reserved.

A vivid early Antonine (138–161 CE) portrait of a man similarly combines contemporary imagery and personal belief in a unique image. The portrait shows a mature, bearded man dressed in the conventional white tunic, with one purple stripe visible over his right shoulder, and a mantle over his left. Unusually the light source is frontal with highlights along the ridge of the nose and evenly on both cheeks and the forehead. His hair and beard closely copy those on the statues of Serapis, a Greco-Egyptian deity whose worship became more popular and spread through the Roman world in the Antonine period. The three locks of hair on his forehead are standard elements of the iconography of Serapis that become part of the imagery of the emperor Septimius Severus (covered in the next chapter). The diadem and seven-pointed star indicate that this man was more than just a worshipper and establish his status as a priest of Serapis.

Another male portrait in encaustic wax, probably from the same area as the Antonine woman with the Faustina hairstyle, shows a boy whose name is given as Eutyches, freedman of Kasianos (Greek for the Roman name Casianus). The portrait is painted in the Greek style in the four-color palette. He faces the viewer in a three-quarter pose that emphasizes the right side of his face. A bright light from his right creates highlights on his right cheek, lips, and forehead and contrasting shadows along his left side. He wears the standard tunic with a mantle covering the purple stripes along his left side as seen in the previous male portrait. Eutyches differs from the other portraits we have seen in his youthfulness. His naturalistic features are plump and proportioned as an adolescent. His center-parted short locks of hair and his clean-shaven face both reflect standard features of portraits of youths in the Antonine period. This image uniquely has another name in the inscription. Added to the end of the name is Evandros followed by "I signed." This seems to indicate that an Evandros signed the panel, and was very likely the painter. If so, this Greek name is the only panel painter known whose work can be attributed from the ancient world. It also reinforces the conclusion that Greek artists created these works in the Greek artistic tradition for a Greco-Egyptian population whose imagery, social structure, and belief systems reflect the province of Egypt under Roman rule.

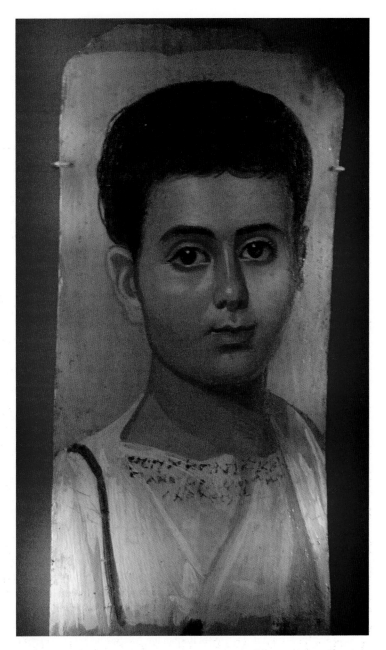

9.30 Fayum portrait of Eutyches, freedman of Kasianos from Philadelphia, Egypt, c. 190 CE. Metropolitan Museum of Art, New York. H 15 3/8 in (39 cm), encaustic on wood panel. Ad Meskens/ Wikimedia Commons.

CONCLUSION

With Roman art under the Antonines we seem to witness the collapse of the architectural revolution. The works of architecture that survive are traditional in form and material and conservative in design with the re-emphasis on the exteriors, as seen in the large amount of relief sculpture that survives from the outside of arches, columns, and similar public monuments. The bold experiments of the previous reigns are no longer of interest. In the area of sculpture the technical developments that allow carved and drilled pupils, drapery, and volumetric hair and beards are a key feature. These technical improvements seem to be driven by the need to more accurately portray the images of the emperors and others in the forms dominated by the Second Sophistic. The Greek garments, long hair, and beards of that intellectual movement are almost ubiquitous through the period. The most important innovation in sculpture is the explosion in the use of sarcophagi. Their large and small panels dominated by Greek mythological scenes provide us with a complex set of private art without parallel from any other period in Roman art. The meaning of these scenes is still debated, but that they have some meaning that perhaps reflects personal belief as well as wider cultural trends is without doubt. That these develop from sculptural schools around Athens and in the province of Asia means that like the Sophistic portraits they reflect a complex Greek and Roman identity. The Fayum portraits with their Greek, Egyptian, and Roman elements perhaps best exemplify that notion of a combined identity. The long Roman practice of cultural inclusiveness makes the images part of Roman art as well as provincial works that speak to an audience in a very limited area of the Roman world.

SUGGESTIONS FOR FURTHER READING

Martin Beckmann, *The Column of Marcus Aurelius: The Genesis and Meaning of a Roman Imperial Monument* (University of North Carolina Press 2011). In this study of the Column the author attempts to recreate the creative process that led to its creation including planning, construction, and carving. Includes also an analysis of the monument's meaning.

John R. Clarke, *The Houses of Roman Italy, 100 B.C.–A.D. 250: Ritual, Space, and Decoration* (University of California Press 1991). In case studies of seventeen excavated houses, Clarke demonstrates how patterns of Roman decoration signal the cultural, religious, and social imprints of the people who lived with them.

John R. Clarke, *Roman Black-and-White Figural Mosaics* (Penn State University Press 1990). Clarke explores these mosaics concentrating on Italy and the second-century material. His survey and analysis covers changes in composition and stylistic trends across these periods.

Euphrosyne Doxiadis, *The Mysterious Fayum Portraits* (Harry N. Abrams 1995). This book features over one hundred of the surviving one thousand ancient mummy portraits from Roman period Egypt. It sets the people and the paintings in their complex cultural, social, artistic, and geographical context, and describes the artistic techniques used to create them.

Diana E.E. Kleiner, *Roman Sculpture* (Yale 1992). Chapter 6 of this superb book surveys the sculpture of the Antonine period. It includes detailed description, analysis, and extensive bibliography for each work.

Michael Koortbojian, *Myth, Meaning, and Memory on Roman Sarcophagi* (University of California Press 1995). This study looks at two myths: Aphrodite and Adonis and Selene and Endymion, not only with respect to their appearance on Roman sarcophagi, but also with regard to the myths' significance in the greater fabric of Roman life. Moving beyond the examination of these sarcophagi as artistic achievements, he sets them in their broader historical and social contexts.

Edmund Thomas, *Monumentality and the Roman Empire: Architecture in the Antonine Age* (Oxford University Press 2008). This book is the first full-length study of architecture in the Antonine Age. It explores the public architecture of Roman Italy and both western and eastern provinces of the Roman Empire from the point of view of the benefactors who funded such buildings, the architects who designed them, and the public who used and experienced them.

Marcel van Ackeren, ed., *A Companion to Marcus Aurelius* (Wiley Blackwell 2012). Among the thirty-four chapters on elements of the life and times of Marcus Aurelius are five illustrated chapters, all written by prominent scholars, that cover his Column, equestrian statue, coins, portraits, and historical reliefs.

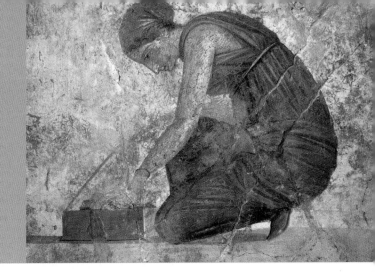

10

CIVIL WAR AND SEVERAN DYNASTY, 193–235 CE

Calm before the Storm

193–211 CE	Septimius Severus as emperor
193 CE	**Julia Domna portrait from Gabii**
197 CE	Invasion of the Parthian empire
200 CE	**Painted portrait of Severan family**
203 CE	Severan family's triumphal entrance into Lepcis Magna; **Arch of Septimius Severus dedicated in Rome; Forma Urbis Romae begun; Julia Domna portrait from Ostia**
204 CE	Celebration of the 950th anniversary of Rome; **Arch of the Argentarii erected**
211–217 CE	Caracalla as emperor
216 CE	**Baths of Caracalla dedicated; Farnese Bull and Farnese Hercules sculptures**
218–222 CE	Elagabalus as emperor
222–235 CE	Alexander Severus as emperor
c. 225 CE	**Achilles and Penthesilia sarcophagus**

A History of Roman Art, First Edition. Steven L. Tuck.
© 2015 Steven L. Tuck. Published 2015 by John Wiley & Sons, Ltd.

INTRODUCTION

The assassination of Commodus marked the end of the Antonine dynasty and led the Roman world into a period of uncertainty, bloodshed, and a protracted civil war. From all of that emerged a dynasty that was to rule the empire from 193–235 CE and represent the last stability the Roman world would know until Diocletian created the Tetrarchy (rule by four emperors) near the end of the century. Commodus was killed sometime after dark on December 31, CE 192 by a conspiracy composed of members of his family and court who feared that he would kill them on January 1, 193 CE when he had planned a grand public spectacle and announcement of his own greatly expanded powers, which was thought to include the deaths of the major elected officials. The conspirators immediately offered the position of emperor to Pertinax, a successful consul, general, and prefect. His rule ended on March 28 as he was in turn killed by the Praetorian Guard. They had no chosen successor, but essentially sold the position in an auction to Didius Julianus, a senior senator.

Meanwhile, when word of the death of Pertinax reached the provinces, three generals were also declared emperors by their troops. Pescennius Niger, governor of Syria, was backed by four legions, Clodius Albinus, governor of Britain, had three legions behind him, while Septimius Severus, governor of Upper Pannonia, had the support of the sixteen legions of the Rhine/Danube army. Thanks to his support base in the legions the outcome of the struggle for power was perhaps inevitable and on June 1, 193 CE the Senate officially invested Septimius Severus with the titles and offices of the emperor as his army approached Rome itself. In just over a year he defeated Niger in battle and had him killed and finally battled and defeated Clodius Albinus in 197 CE, solidifying his rule over the entire Roman world.

Septimius Severus was the first Roman emperor from Africa. He was born at Lepcis Magna, a great trading city on the coast of modern Libya. From there he entered the Roman army and, rising through the ranks, came to power holding a series of civic and military offices. He married his second wife, Julia Domna, in 186 CE. Daughter of the high priest of the sun god Elagabal at the sanctuary at Emesa, Syria, he selected her because her horoscope prophesied that she would marry a king. They had two sons, Caracalla, born in 188 CE, and Geta, born in 189 CE, who were brought up to create a dynasty and would rule with their father but fail to share power after his death. First emperor of the third century CE, Septimius Severus was also the last in the century to die peacefully in his bed, which he did in 211 CE urging his sons to "come to agreement between them, give money to the soldiers and do not regard any other men" (Cassius Dio, *Roman History* 79.2–3).

The second part of that deathbed statement became something of a motto for emperors in the third century as they looked to the army to establish and stabilize their rule, which the next chapter addresses more completely. Septimius also used the army to conduct foreign wars as a means of reinforcing his authority to rule and unifying the factions in the empire. Invasions of the Parthian empire Britain north of Hadrian's Wall, and in Africa seem intended to focus attention on external foes. The first part of the directive was based on Septimius' desire to create a dynasty, but was not strong enough to end the strife and competitiveness between Caracalla and Geta that led to Geta's assassination within a year. Each subsequent emperor of the Severan dynasty suffered a similar fate, as did every emperor of the third century until Diocletian. Nevertheless, the Severans managed to create a multi-generational dynasty based on blood and marriage, the first such since the Julio-Claudians in the first century CE.

TRENDS AND DEVELOPMENTS IN SEVERAN ART

Coming to power in a civil war, the Severans worked to bolster their public image as the Flavians had before them: by looking backward. Images of Septimius Severus and his immediate family deliberately extend the iconography and attributes of the Antonines, clearly as an attempt to associate their usurping dynasty with that one's reputation for stability and successful rule. By the time of Caracalla, however, the form of the third century CE portrait was established and the basis for the Late Antique style with its rejection of Greek tradition and Classicizing style was laid. The same trend is seen in historical relief sculpture where the Italic tradition dominates over the Classicizing styles of the past. The usual subjects (battle reliefs, victory displays, etc.) continue to be created, but their presentation is altered into a new style. In architecture the Syrian ornate style seen earlier at the Temple of Hadrian at Ephesus has spread as far as Roman Africa and it becomes the predominant style of the tremendous Severan building program at Lepcis Magna.

Portraiture

In no previous forty-year period have we seen such radical changes in portraiture as can be observed under the Severans. The early portraiture of the Severans illustrates their insecure succession with a series of images that reference the Antonines, creating the illusion that the Severans are an extension of that earlier, successful dynasty. Legally, they were since they arranged their own posthumous adoption by the long-dead emperor Marcus Aurelius in 195 CE. By the end of the dynasty it is clear that

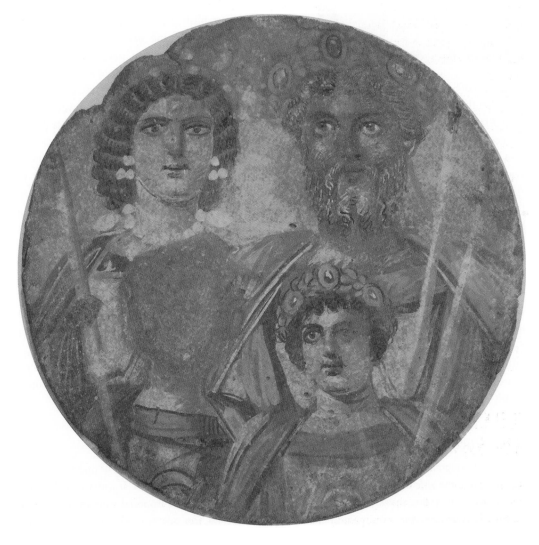

10.1 Portrait of Septimius Severus, his wife, Julia Domna, and sons, Caracalla and Geta, *c.* 200 CE, from Egypt. Staatliche Museen, Antiken-Sammlung, Berlin. H 12 in (30.5 cm) tempera on wood panel. Photo courtesy Francesca Tronchin.

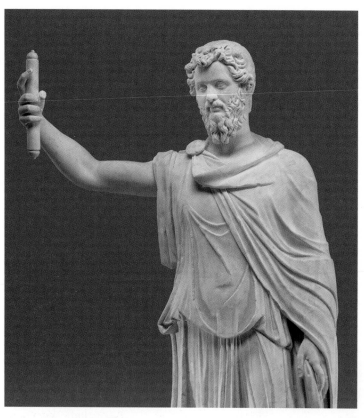

10.2 Portrait of Septimius Severus, *c.* 195–200 CE, Greek marble, Rome? Formerly in the collection of Vincenzo Giustiniani (1564–1637), now in the Virginia Museum of Fine Arts (67.50). Photo: Katherine Wetzel © Virginia Museum of Fine Arts.

Classicism is played out in favor of a more abstracted style which has been called restless, energetic, and perhaps even spiritual, the Third Century style. But at the beginning of the dynasty the Antonine style predominated and images of the full dynasty were common.

A unique surviving painted round portrait of the Severan family discovered in Egypt was done in tempera on a wooden panel in the same tradition and materials as the Fayum portraits introduced in the previous chapter. The elements of imperial portraiture that would become standard in the fourth century CE are already here at the beginning of the third. The individual figures are very frontal, with oversized eyes that do not engage the viewer, but gaze upward into the distance. Each of them is distinguishable from other Romans by the multiple attributes of rank including diadems, gold-bordered tunics, and cloaks, scepters and, in the case of Julia Domna, a pearl necklace and earrings that become standard for imperial women in later periods. The uncertainty of his succession and need to establish the position of his heirs led to Septimius Severus creating many dynastic portraits throughout his principate. This painting is joined by many coin portraits in pairs and groups, the reliefs on the arches of Septimius Severus at Rome and Lepcis Magna, and the Arch of the Argentarii at Rome. Note that the politics of the reign of Caracalla have altered this image. Geta's face in the lower left was erased from the painting after his death when, by order of his surviving brother, all of his public images and inscriptions bearing his name were destroyed or defaced.

The individual portraiture of Septimius Severus underwent many changes during his eighteen years of rule. The two major types include an Antonine-inspired portraiture based on that of Antoninus Pius and, most strongly, Marcus Aurelius. Elements of Aurelius' portraiture are seen in the curly hair and short, parted beard affected by Septimius. In these images Septimius is reaching back past the civil war in his public image program to associate himself with the successful emperors of the second century CE. In many ways, this Severan portraiture represents the end of the Antonine portrait tradition, which will be shortly replaced by an entirely new aesthetic. The second portrait type combines the image of the emperor with that of the Greco-Egyptian god, Serapis. The worship of Serapis had expanded from its origin in Alexandria throughout the Roman world under Hadrian with Hadrian's Serapeum images of Antinous. The imperial family visited the original sanctuary of the god during an inspection tour of Egypt in 199–200 CE and the Serapis portraiture postdates that visit. The Serapis images are readily identifiable by the long corkscrew locks of hair, generally four in number, that fall in bangs across the emperor's forehead. This portrait type also used the parted beard. All of the hair and beard is deeply carved and drilled. The eyes are drilled, with the pupils clearly articulated, generally looking up and into the distance as seen in the roundel portrait.

Portraiture of Julia Domna

Such a long reign and an emphasis on dynastic succession also led to the creation of many images of Julia Domna, the wife of Septimius Severus. Given her role as the mother of Caracalla and Geta it is perhaps not surprising that she became the most visible and powerful imperial woman since Livia, essentially ruling in cooperation with her eldest son, Caracalla. Her portraits fall into as many as six major types that divide into two broad categories, distinct by date. The earliest of these is from the very beginning of the rule of Septimius Severus, *c.* 193 CE.

This type was based on the portraits of Faustina the Younger, the wife of Marcus Aurelius. Julia Domna's facial features, with widely spaced eyes flanking a long nose, connected brows, and curving mouth with soft folds of skin at the corners, are portrayed consistently. She wears her hair in a heavy, center-parted helmet-shaped style with short hair loose front of her ears. The style terminates in a large bun at the base of her neck, very similar to Faustina the Younger's (Figure 9.4). The result is a formal imperial image that makes direct visual links between her and the previous, successful dynasty.

Julia Domna's later portraiture represents a departure from her previous imagery with different associations and attributes. Gone are the direct visual links to Antonine portraiture. She is recognizable from her distinctive facial features, but with major differences in her hairstyle. The style is no longer that of Faustina the Younger, but a softer, center-parted one with the hair falling in long folds on each side of her head to the base of her neck and then gathered and tucked back up under at her temples. Her mantle is pulled over her head as befits a priestess performing a ritual and she holds in her left hand poppies and stalks of wheat, attributes of the goddess Ceres. Images of Roman empresses as Ceres had their origins with Livia, wife of Augustus, and it is possible that Julia Domna is making a visual link back to Livia in this portrait. In any event, she is combining her identity with that of the goddess in a way that associates her with the abundance Ceres symbolizes.

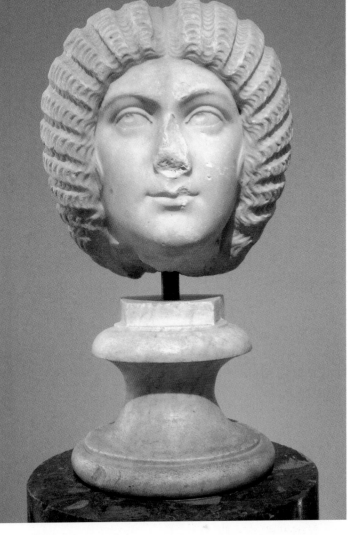

10.3 Portrait of Julia Domna, *c.* 193 CE, from Gabii, Italy. Musée du Louvre, Paris. H 24 ⅜ in (62 cm), marble. Photo courtesy Steven L. Tuck.

The slightly later portraits of the adult Caracalla demonstrate a rejection of the Antonine traditions and point the way to the portrait style of the remainder of the third century CE. The plasticity and volumetric portrayal of hair of the second century is replaced with a plasticity of skin. Hair and beards become gradually reduced as the figure's skin is explored with incised lines, chiseled wrinkles, and whiskers. The distant look and grave competence of the second-century CE portraiture are now replaced with a restless energy demonstrated in twisting necks, apparent internal conflict, and evidence of the concern for ruling the Roman world. This is portraiture that is simultaneously military, as demonstrated in the cropped hair and beard, and psychological. Modern viewers have no trouble seeing in this image the anger and hatred that led him to stab his brother to death. Whether Romans would see that as well is debated. Caracalla's broad face with its cleft chin is patterned with lines and creases that make a large X shape across his face with the legs of the X created by deep nasolabial grooves and the top half by forehead wrinkles. These combined with the drawn brows and slightly down-turned mouth give an intense but energetic expression, a far cry from the calm Classicism and competence of the second-century CE imperial portraits.

This is not to say that the Classical style of portraiture was at an end. The official portraits of Alexander Severus, the last emperor of the Severan dynasty (ruled 222–235 CE), evoke both the

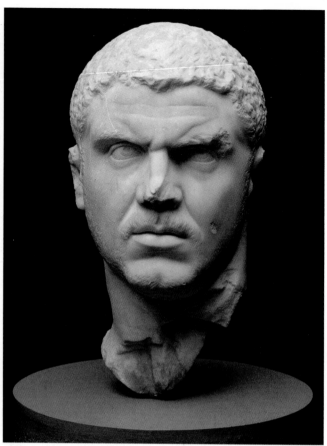

10.5   Portrait of Caracalla, *c.* 206–212 CE, Rome. Metropolitan Museum of Art, New York. Marble, H 14 ¼ in (36 cm). Source: Photo Schecter Lee. © 2014. Image copyright The Metropolitan Museum of Art/Art Resource/Scala, Florence.

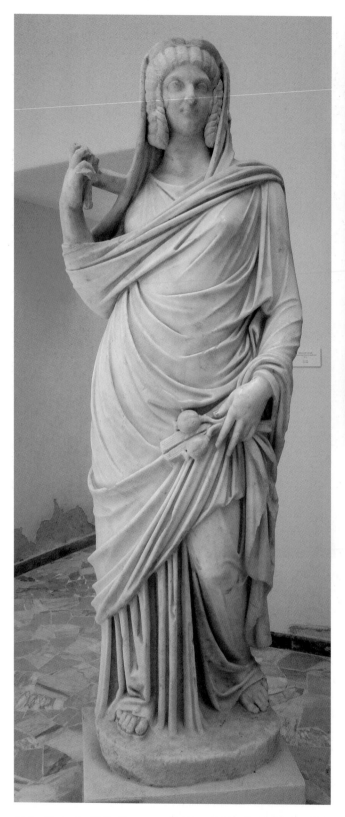

10.4   Portrait of Julia Domna as Ceres, *c.* 203 CE, from Ostia. Museo Archeologico Ostiense, Ostia, marble. Photo courtesy Daniel Resheter.

Antonine links and the psychological portraiture of the third century CE. Instead of the square face seen under Caracalla, Alexander's portraiture emphasizes a classical oval with full lips, smooth skin, and a closed, full-lipped mouth. The calm image is a sharp contrast to the imagery of his predecessors and successors. Nonetheless, the style also has elements of the new portraiture in the closely cropped hair chiseled into the shape of the skull and drilled eyes that glance to the side, conveying the sense of restlessness of the period and, perhaps unintentionally, the uncertainty of imperial rule in the third century CE.

Baths of Caracalla: Architecture and sculpture in Rome

The Baths of Caracalla were only one of a number of immense imperially sponsored bathing complexes in the city of Rome. The tradition started under Augustus with the Baths of Agrippa and continued throughout the first and second centuries CE under emperors as varied as Nero, Titus, and Trajan. These were the first great public baths built in over a century, following the Baths of Trajan. Under the Severans, both Septimius Severus and Caracalla were patrons of these enormous bathing establishments. Far more than just a place to bathe, the baths consisted of a huge block of bathing rooms, 702 ft (214 m) x 360 ft (110 m), surrounded by formal gardens laid out on a large terraced platform.

The entire complex was surrounded by a high wall. The bathing block was a spectacular building, huge in scale and lavishly covered with marble floors and wall panels. It was constructed of brick-faced concrete with a range of complex roofing systems including domes, half domes, cross vaults, and barrel vaults. In addition to the standard bathing suite of open air swimming pools as well as hot, warm, and cold water rooms, the baths had a series of varied climate rooms with a range of temperature and humidity combinations so that bathers could move through an array of climate-controlled spaces.

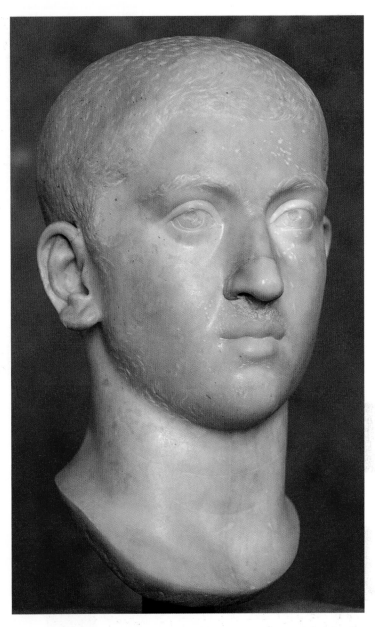

10.6 Portrait of Alexander Severus, 222–235 CE. Musée du Louvre, Paris. H 15 ¾ in (40 cm) marble. Marie-Lan Nguyen/Wikimedia Commons.

They also offered lecture halls, rooms for musical and poetic performances, libraries and reading rooms, and a host of athletic spaces for running, ball games, boxing, wrestling, and the full range of track and field events. The goal seemed to be to provide everything in one location to ensure opportunities to fulfill the ideal expressed in Latin: *mens sana in corpore sano*, "a sound mind in a sound body."

The decorative program of the baths consisted of over forty statues and many multi-colored mosaic floors. Many of these images can be seen as thematically appropriate to the baths including athletes, healing gods (doctors prescribed bathing activities for treating a wide range of illnesses), and Greek heroes. Others seem to have been selected only for scale.

The Farnese Bull Group, the largest statue group that survives from the Roman world, depicts the myth of Dirce and might have been commissioned for these baths. It is hard to imagine what

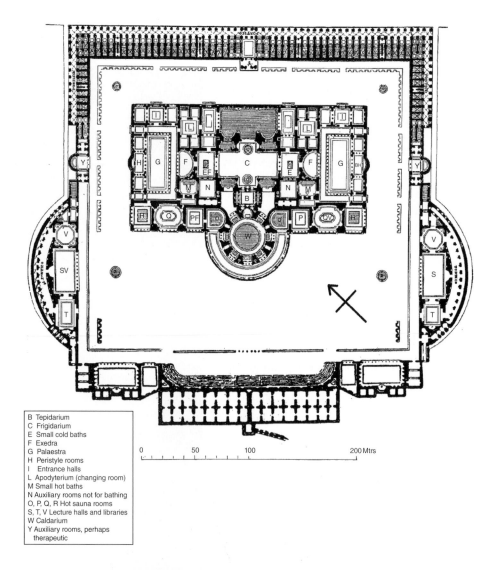

10.7 Baths of Caracalla, along the Via Appia, Rome, dedicated in 216 CE. Wilhelm Lübke, Max Semrau: Grundriß der Kunstgeschichte. Paul Neff Verlag, Esslingen, 14. Auflage 1908.

B Tepidarium
C Frigidarium
E Small cold baths
F Exedra
G Palaestra
H Peristyle rooms
I Entrance halls
L Apodyterium (changing room)
M Small hot baths
N Auxiliary rooms not for bathing
O, P, Q, R Hot sauna rooms
S, T, V Lecture halls and libraries
W Caldarium
Y Auxiliary rooms, perhaps therapeutic

0   50   100   200 Mtrs

10.8 Remains of the Baths of Caracalla, along the Via Appia, Rome, dedicated in 216 CE. Brick-faced concrete. Photo courtesy Steven L. Tuck.

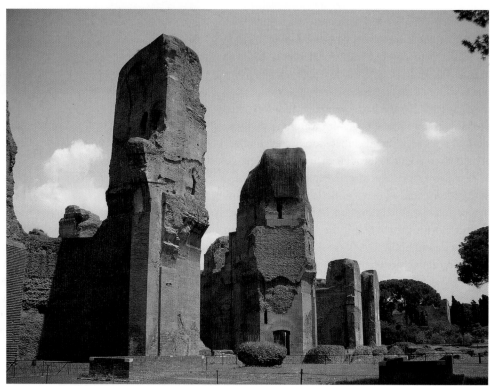

ANCIENTS ON ART
Baths of Caracalla

The Baths of Caracalla were his greatest building project and literary testimony reveals that the unprecedented scale of the concrete domes was the result of the earliest reinforced concrete in history. Like modern concrete it seems the dome was reinforced with metal bars throughout, a technique that would not be used again until the nineteenth century.

Among the public works which he left at Rome was the notable Bath named after himself, the cella soliaris of which, so the architects declare, cannot be reproduced in the way in which it was built by him. For it is said that the whole vaulting rested on gratings of bronze or copper, placed underneath it, but so great is its size, that those who are versed in mechanics declare that it could not have been built in this way. (*Historia Augusta*, The Life of Antoninus Caracalla 9.4–10)

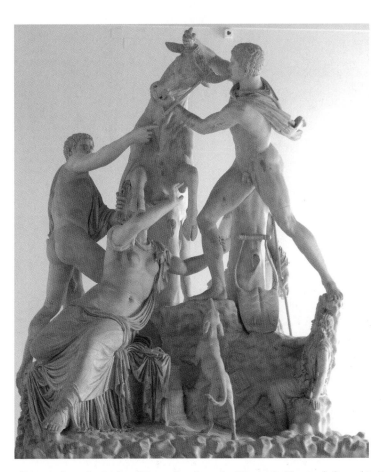

10.9 Farnese Bull group from the Baths of Caracalla, along the Via Appia, Rome, dedicated in 216 CE. Museo Archeologico Nazionale di Napoli. H 12 ft 1 in (3.7 m). Photo courtesy Steven L. Tuck.

other space would have been adequate. The group shows the punishment of Dirce who, having inflicted torments on Antiope, is tied to a mad bull by Antiope's sons to be dragged to death down a mountain. The subject is fairly common in Roman art and the theme of impiety punished is a familiar one from both public and private art. This sculpture is believed to be a copy of a famous version from the second century BCE by the Rhodian sculptors Apollonius and Tauriscus. Michelangelo had planned to alter the statue into an enormous fountain for the Farnese Palace in Rome, but that work was not completed.

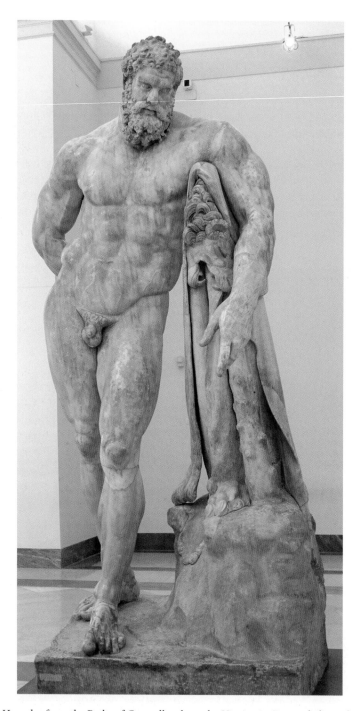

10.10 Farnese Hercules from the Baths of Caracalla, along the Via Appia, Rome, dedicated in 216 CE. Museo Archeologico Nazionale di Napoli. H 10 ft 4 ½ in (3.17 m). Photo courtesy Steven L. Tuck.

Similar in scale to the Farnese Bull is the Hercules from the Baths, signed by the sculptor Glykon of Athens. Based on the original by Lysippus, it was probably also specially commissioned for the Baths. The subject is common, showing Hercules with the Golden Apples of the Hesperides, the same episode used by Commodus in his Hercules statue (Figure 9.9). The many images of Hercules found in the baths were likely commissioned or selected to refer metaphorically to Caracalla whose identity was associated with Hercules from the time his father became emperor. The Hercules images include figures in the architectural sculpture as seen in the Severan buildings at Lepcis Magna in addition to multiple free-standing statues, most famously the Farnese Hercules.

ART AND LITERATURE
The Baths of Caracalla and literary descriptions of Roman bathing

Analysis of the baths as a setting for the projection of imperial identity is an important topic and raises the issue of active engagement with bath decoration by the bathers. Literary sources say little about this although many describe various sets of baths. Martial (9.75) and Statius (*Silv*. 1.5.13) both assign qualities of luxury to the Baths of Etruscus at Rome. Pliny the Younger gives a sense of the expectations of grandeur and opulence in his description of baths at villas at Laurentine and in Etruria (Pliny, *Ep*. 2.17.11; 5.6.25–27). One of the most important testimonies of awareness of decoration is an anecdote in the Mishnah (*Avodah Zarah* 3.4) about Rabban Gamaliel in the baths of Aphrodite. When a pagan asked how Gamaliel could tolerate the bathhouse's statue of the goddess, the rabbi said the sculpture didn't function as a deity, but rather was an ornament for the bath. Gamaliel reasoned that Romans would not walk around naked in front of a statue they intended to worship. The same principle may apply to the images of the imperial family often found in baths (Figures 8.3, 8.4). It is clear that the bathers would show an awareness of and react to the lavish decorative features in bathing complexes.

The baths also served a host of needs for quite probably thousands of Romans every day. These Romans left little record in the baths themselves, but the literary record provides a great deal of evidence of their activities and attitudes towards public bathing and bath facilities, although very little references the emperors who provided these complexes. Instead their bathing habits and concerns reveal these complexes as the stages for a variety of social, economic, and political interactions. One element of the baths that the literary sources make clear is the social mixing that took place. Cicero notes that upper class youths and slaves shared bathing facilities. Similar circumstances are recorded by later authors such as Plutarch (*Mor*. 288A) and Petronius (*Satyricon* 92) in whose novel an equestrian, a slave, a youth, and the narrator are in the bathing complex together. The wealthy in fact used the baths as they did the streets as a venue to demonstrate their wealth and power with an entourage, luxurious bathing accessories, or even by being carried around the complex in a litter as Lucian (*Nigr*. 34) records. This social mixing meant that members of all classes were thrown together in the baths, giving the lower classes access to the elite.

This access extended all the way to the person of the emperor. A famous anecdote from the life of the emperor Hadrian relates how, coming upon an army veteran rubbing his back against the wall of the bath because he didn't have a slave to rub it for him, Hadrian gave him a slave. At his next visit to the baths, he was faced with a line of veterans rubbing their backs on the wall in the hopes of also being given slaves (*Hadr*. 17.5–7). The story makes it clear that Hadrian visited the baths regularly with the expectation of engaging with regular Romans during those visits. The expectation of the Romans was that their emperor would also pay attention to them and on occasion grant their requests.

These engagements seem to have led to requests of the wealthy, often for invitations to dinner. The poet Martial records both sides of this process and reveals much about the activities in the baths as context. One of Martial's epigrams (12) describes the extraordinary attempts of a sycophant to ingratiate himself with a prospective dinner host. He joins a ball game to score points for his target, retrieves his lost balls from the dust, fetches drinks, wipes sweat from the man's brow, and praises and admires everything about his target. He compares his dirty towels to snow and his thinning hair to the locks of Achilles. He continues in a thousand ways until the dinner invitation comes through. The situation in the poem illustrates that the entire space of the bathing complex was a venue for social networking. Another poem by Martial (5) describes a former pursuer of dinner invitations turned avoider of Martial. It turns out that the man has found a better dinner table than Martial's to take advantage of. The association between the baths and dining, both in the baths and afterwards, is a consistent motif that argues for their central role in Roman social life.

Historical reliefs

A combination of factors including civil war, invasions, assassinations, and economic problems in the Roman world contributed to the construction of a very small number of large-scale public buildings in Rome under the Severan dynasty. Two of the most significant public monuments created under Septimius Severus in Rome were his triumphal arch in the Forum Romanum and the Arch of the Argentarii in the old Forum Boarium area near the Tiber. These are both important as examples of the Severan style of relief sculpture, which differs from that seen in the second century CE and marks the reemergence of Italic style in official art.

The Arch of Septimius Severus in the northwest corner of the Forum Romanum was a traditional form of victory arch dedicated in 203 CE in celebration of the Severan dynasty and their successful Parthian campaign that culminated with the taking of the Parthian capital in 198 CE. The use of a foreign campaign to legitimize rule in the wake of a civil war has already been seen in the public art of Augustus and Vespasian. In this case the form of the monument is a triple passage arch with a tall central passage flanked by two lower side passages built over the Via Sacra, the sacred way that triumphal processions used as they passed through the Forum and began to climb the Capitoline Hill just to the west of the arch.

The exterior of the arch is covered with three major surviving sculptural elements: a small frieze, reliefs on the pedestals that support the four free-standing columns on each side, and – most importantly as they demonstrate the developing Late Antique style – four large panels that flank the central passage above each of the side passage openings. To these was added a bronze dynastic triumphal group on the very top of the arch with Septimius Severus in a *quadriga* (four horse chariot), flanked by Caracalla and Geta each on horseback. The small frieze shows the triumphal procession of 202 CE. This type of narrow processional frieze is seen on the altar of the Ara Pacis Augustae and the attic story of the Arch of Titus as well. The reliefs on the pedestals all illustrate Roman soldiers escorting captured Parthians, presumably in the triumphal procession itself. Their placement, flanking the

10.11 Arch of Septimius Severus, Forum Romanum, Rome, 203 CE. Photo courtesy Steven L. Tuck.

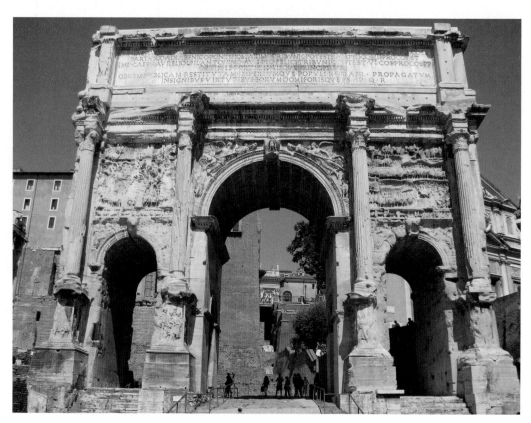

passages and at ground level, gives the effect of reenacting the triumph visually for those walking through the arch and catching sight of the figures.

The subject of the large panels, scenes of the actual prosecution of the Parthian War, derives from the model of Trajan's victory monuments, especially his column. They may also reflect the large paintings depicting battles and conquered territory carried in triumphal processions. It is notable that Trajan also mounted his own successful Parthian invasion and the arch might be as much an allusion to him as to the Parthian arch of Augustus that originally faced this from across the forum. Trajan was granted the name Parthicus while Septimius was named Parthicus Maximus, a clear imitation. Trajan's own triple passage arch survives only on reverses of his coins.

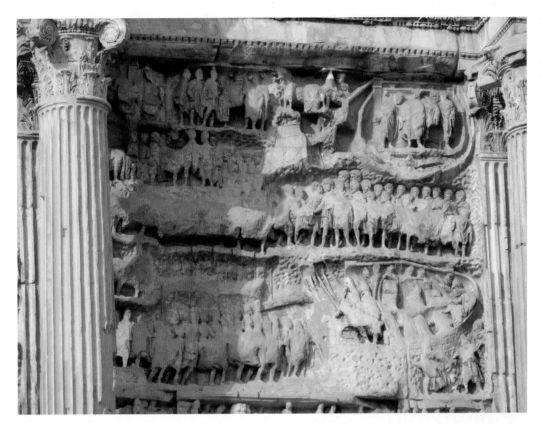

10.12 Panel 2, Arch of Septimius Severus, Forum Romanum, Rome, 203 CE. Photo courtesy Steven L. Tuck.

HISTORICAL CONTEXT
The Severan Parthian campaign

The Parthian empire (centered in modern Iraq and Iran) had been invaded by Trajan eighty years earlier. Julius Caesar had planned to invade it following his victory in civil war, like Septimius Severus probably hoping it would unify the Roman Empire with an external foe. The Severan campaigns were in 195 and 197–8 CE and as wars of annexation resulted in the first significant expansions of Roman territory since Trajan's Dacian campaign. The first campaign led to the creation of the province of Osrhoene. The second, a much larger invasion, saw Septimius Severus leading an army from the north down the Euphrates river and taking the important and wealthy cities of Seleucia and Babylon. The army then moved east crossing the Euphrates to attack, take, and sack the Parthian capital Ctesiphon, on the east bank of the Tigris river, 20 miles south of modern Baghdad. Here the Romans took a hundred thousand Parthians as captives and emptied the royal treasury. This campaign led to the annexation of a second new province, Mesopotamia, the heart of modern Iraq. The territories were eventually lost by Macrinus in 217 CE, never to be retaken.

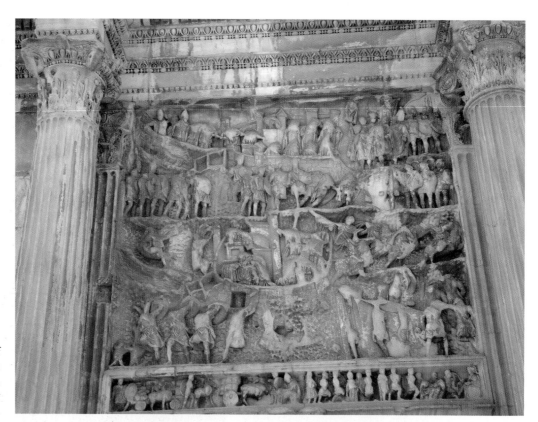

10.13 Panel 3, Arch of Septimius Severus, Forum Romanum, Rome, 203 CE. Photo courtesy Steven L. Tuck.

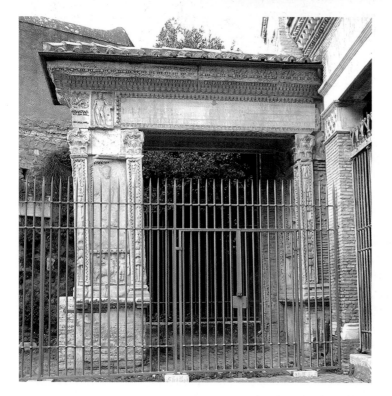

10.14 Arch of the Argentarii, Forum Boarium, Rome, 204 CE. Photo courtesy Steven L. Tuck.

Each of the panels differs dramatically in style from the historical reliefs of the second century CE victory monuments. Instead of large-scale figures filling the field and standing together on a common groundline, the composition features many small-scale figures populating a landscape in the Hellenistic rather than Classical tradition. Each panel features a number of registers created from multiple groundlines and groups of figures, each very squat and conforming to Italic rather than Classicizing conventions of scale. Also in Italic style is the overall composition with its split-perspective combining profile and bird's eye view in each frame.

In panel 3, for example, the profile figures of the Roman soldiers besiege a city in the center of the panel that is defined by its surrounding wall seen from above. The panels each continue and in fact extend the trend of isolating the ruler and his dynasty from other Romans. Where Trajan appeared addressing the army and surrounded by them, Septimius, as in the upper right corner of panel 2, is distinct from them in space as well as hierarchy of scale and his frontal presentation makes him more visible than the soldiers who are in profile. In some areas, for example in panel 3, the Italic convention of raising the figures in the second row of a group so that they are visible but above any groundline is used, creating figures that are apparently disembodied heads hovering over their comrades in the front row.

The Arch of the Argentarii in Rome is a unique structure and demonstrates the reception and transmission of imperial imagery in a private commission. The arch, actually a form of doorway created by a flat lintel supported by two rectangular piers leading into a private precinct, was commissioned by the Argentarii, bankers or silversmiths, in 204 CE. The inscription on the lintel says that it was erected in honor of the imperial family. While shrines, statues, and dedications to various imperial families are known, this is a particularly large example whose full extent and impetus both remain mysteries. Its exterior is covered with figural relief panels whose subjects reflect those of the Arch of Septimius Severus in the Forum Romanum: the Severan dynasty and the successful Parthian campaign. The arches also share many similar artistic conventions including frontal portraits, the use of hierarchy of scale and split-perspective, the combination of narrow processional and vertical figural friezes, and squat Italic proportions.

The flat, rather hieratic, frontality of the reliefs is demonstrated by the sacrifice panel of Septimius Severus and Julia Domna. The preserved scene does not reflect the original composition, however. The blank space to the right was originally filled with the image of Geta, removed after his death on orders of Caracalla. This so-called *damnatio memoriae*, condemnation of the memory, is an interesting example in privately commissioned rather than official art since it shows that Caracalla's order was followed in private art

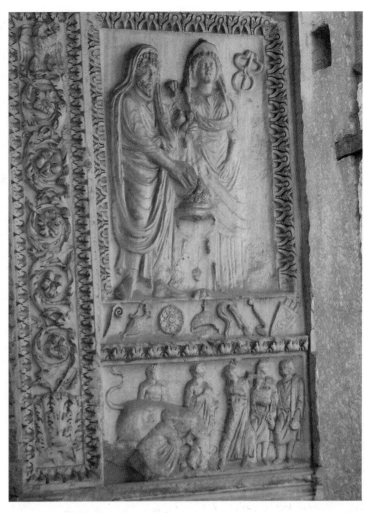

10.15   Panel of Septimius Severus and Julia Domna sacrificing, Arch of the Argentarii, Forum Boarium, Rome, 204 CE. Photo courtesy Steven L. Tuck.

caduceus
the wand, entwined by two serpents, generally carried by Mercury. As the protector of merchants, it is associated with commerce and business occupations.

as well. The result makes the panel appear asymmetrical. In fact all three of the figures were essentially frontal images that engage the viewer without interacting with each other. Note that Julia Domna, recognizable by her hairstyle, wears a tiara and carries a **caduceus**, both attributes serving to distance her from other Romans. She also appears taller than Septimius Severus to the left, violating the Classicizing convention of isocephaly and instead utilizing the Italic pattern of increasing the height of the person in the back of the scene for better visibility. Unlike earlier scenes of sacrifice, the imperial family here is completely isolated, stripped of the normal attendants who would be critical to this type of ritual, and continuing the trend of visually separating the dynasty from other Romans.

Mosaic art under the Severans

Although the arts of private sculpture and painting are not well preserved from the Severan period, floor mosaics, most from domestic contexts, do survive. The evidence provided by mosaics demonstrates a number of critical aspects of Roman art under this dynasty including regional developments in art, intersections of art with imperial policy, and lessons about the processes used to create this art.

A mosaic found at Merida in Spain illustrates the debt Rome owed to Greek art, in both subject and composition, and the Roman perspective on the shape and organization of the world and cosmos. This large mosaic consists of approximately fifty figures, most of them labeled in Latin, arranged in a world defined by cosmological and terrestrial zones within a rectangular field with an arched top.

SCHOLARLY PERSPECTIVE
The subject and meaning of the El Djem arena mosaic

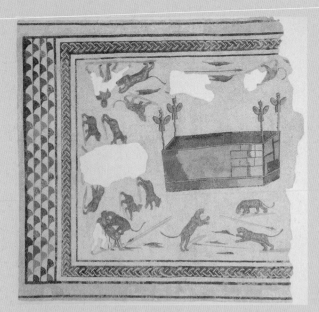

10.16   Arena mosaic from a Roman villa outside Thysdrus (El Djem, Tunisia), *c.* 203 CE. 16 ½ ft x 11 ½ ft (5 × 3.5 m). Photo courtesy Steven L. Tuck.

A large mosaic on the floor of a dining room from a palatial Roman villa outside Thysdrus (modern El Djem in Tunisia) illustrates a single scene of *damnatio ad bestias*, prisoner execution by animals in an arena in Roman Africa. The owner of the villa, his reason for displaying this, the location of the event, and the identities of the prisoners are all the subjects of scholarly discussion. The image on the mosaic, however, is fairly straightforward. The background is largely composed of white tesserae with the ground distinguished by occasional lines, shadows, and four scattered spears.

The center of the field is dominated by a large rectangular enclosure or structure with one opening in the visible short end. Each of the four corners terminates in a trophy that projects above the walls. Each trophy consists of a tree trunk hung with a tunic, helmet, and paired shields. The scene around the structure in the two-thirds of the mosaic that is preserved contains five human figures and twelve animals all standing oriented along the outside edge of the mosaic ranging along the three intact sides. The humans are clustered in the extant corners. In the first one an attendant supports a taller, lighter-skinned bound captive staggering backward under the attack of a large cat clinging to his body with claws in his thigh, chest, and shoulder as it bites his face. Blood pours down his body onto the arena floor beneath him. In the second a tall, lighter-skinned captive is held up by two attendants while a large cat has just begun to leap on him from the arena floor. Five of the animals are bears with their short muzzles, heavy bodies, and very short tails. The other animals are seven large spotted cats. The cats all appear to be leopards. The scene is similar but not identical to the Zliten mosaic prisoner executions (Figure 7.17). The prisoners are taller than their captors, lighter skinned, clean shaven, but with long droopy mustaches and blond hair shown volumetrically separated into rising locks. It has been argued that, rather than local prisoners, Germans, or generic barbarians that have been proposed, the Thysdrus *damnati* are precise images of Celts or Gauls as seen in Hellenistic and Roman art and as described by Diodorus Siculus:

> the Gauls are tall of body, with rippling muscles and white skin; their hair is blond not only by nature but also because they are accustomed to use artificial means to enhance its natural color. For they are always washing it in limewater, and they pull it back from the forehead to the top of the heard and the nape of the neck, so that they look like satyrs and Pans; for this treatment makes the hair look so heavy and coarse that it differs not at all from horses' manes. The nobles shave their cheeks but let their moustaches grow freely so as to cover their mouths. (5.28.1–3)

The trophies in the arena also display recognizably Celtic armor of the types shown on trophies in Roman art dating back to Julius Caesar. The appearance of Celts in an African arena is consistent with the imagery of Septimius Severus and Caracalla displaying prisoners following their campaigns in Britain and Parthia.

The bears reinforce this conclusion. Literary references record bears imported from Scotland to be hunted in the arena, as the scattered spears around them may symbolize. The scene may reveal Severan foreign and domestic policy: specifically, their conquests of lands north of Hadrian's Wall and the display and distribution of prisoners and wild animals to celebrate those conquests, particularly throughout the African provinces, probably in association with the Severan visit to the province in 203 CE. The patron of this mosaic was perhaps a local official connected to the games illustrated, perhaps the person directly in charge, or perhaps a political ally of the emperor proclaiming his association with this image. The location of the arena is still debated with some scholars favoring the closer Thrysdus and others the coastal city of Leptiminus.

Katherine M.D. Dunbabin, *Mosaics of the Greek and Roman World* (Cambridge University Press 1999), 101–129.

Along the base are nautical, terrestrial, and geographical ideas personified including Ocean, Calm, Navigation, and Abundance, and above them are Nature, the Seasons, the Euphrates, and the Nile, along with Portus and Pharos, the harbors of Ostia and Alexandria respectively. Just above are Mountains and Snow. These surrounded the now missing central figure of Eternity. Above the ground in the sky are the Sun, Clouds, and Winds, while across the top are the concepts of Heaven and Time. The use of personifications of geographical areas as well as abstract qualities, all labeled, is an element of mosaic work from the Roman east, but the use of Latin labels and the emphasis on the grain trade between Egypt and Italy and its vital harbors at Alexandria and Ostia demonstrates that this is not completely an eastern work but probably based on a design from the Roman east, such as the city of Antioch, where the use of such personifications is much more common. The mosaic displays a symbolic representation of the world and a completely different conception of space and composition than the El Djem mosaic. Like the Grand Camée (Figure 6.12) it organizes the world and the figures that define it into registers with the upper zone given to the celestial and the lower to the terrestrial. This contrasts dramatically with the El Djem mosaic that illustrates a particular scene in a single frame and episode. It shows, therefore, the transmission of artistic motifs and the spread of styles across the Roman world and the wide range of styles available for private patrons. The Roman conception of space and geography seen here is similar to those seen in the Classicizing art of the Augustan and Julio-Claudian periods, notably the breastplate of the Prima Porta Augustus (Figure 5.2) with its geographical and cosmological personifications. The use of personifications is found increasingly in Severan sarcophagi as well.

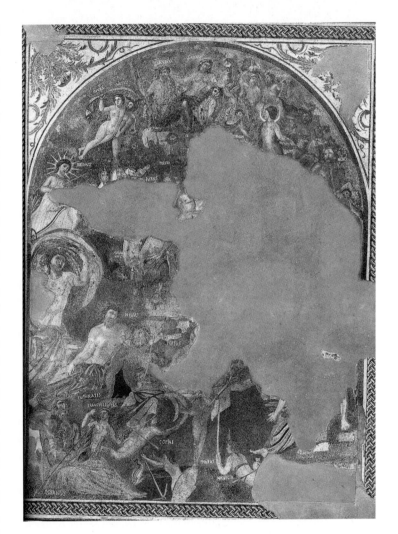

10.17 Cosmological mosaic, Emerita (Merida), Spain, Severan. 13 ¼ × 16 ⅝ ft (4.04 × 5.07 m). Source: © Consorcio Ciudad Monumental de Mérida/ J.M. Romero.

Sarcophagi

Sarcophagi continued to be an important component of burials in the Severan period and the most common form of privately commissioned sculpture under the dynasty. Many of the subjects and styles continued from the Antonine period and also reflected the contemporary developments in

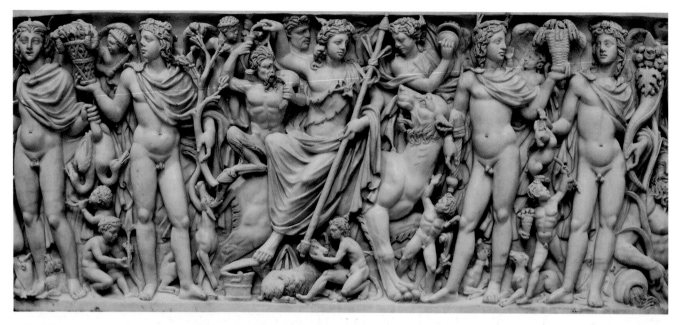

10.18 Dionysus and Seasons sarcophagus, 220–235 CE. Metropolitan Museum of Art, New York. Marble, H 34 x L 85 x W 36 ¼ in (86.4 x 215.9 x 92.1 cm). Marie-Lan Nguyen/Wikimedia Commons.

sculpture as seen in the official art of the Severans. For example, the use of elongated figures and distorted proportions to dramatic emotional effect is a standard feature of third-century CE sarcophagi. Portraits on sarcophagi reach their greatest popularity in this period. Scenes of specific mythological hunts, such as the Calydonian Boar Hunt, are replaced by generic lion hunts with symbolic but no narrative purpose. They instead serve to convey the virtues of the deceased or the notion of conquest of life crises. The deceased appears as a portrait of himself and not as Meleager or another mythological hero. Timeless and narrativeless figures and groups predominate with a rise in the number of abstract or personified figures. Timeless allegory prevails over mythological subjects as seen, for example, in the decline in the number of Hercules images. But other traditional images endure and are incorporated into these new themes. One such combination found repeatedly is Dionysus with the four seasons.

Images of the god Dionysus were one of the most popular subjects on second and third-century CE sarcophagi. The popularity of Dionysus is certainly due to his position as the object of a cult that promised its followers life after death. Dionysus demonstrated the ability to raise the dead in Greek myth on his mother, Semele. The rescue of his wife, Ariadne, from her abandonment on a small island is another form of Dionysiac rescue commonly seen on these sarcophagi. Among the deities whose followers were promised life after death Dionysus alone actively recruited followers through proselytizing. His great conversion pilgrimage was into India and his triumphant return to Greek lands is illustrated here as he rides a panther surrounded by his cultic supporters, many of whom are shown in the background or in smaller scale filling the field of the sarcophagus. The overall composition owes much to battle sarcophagi such as the Portonaccio sarcophagus (Figure 9.25). The four standing figures in the foreground are the personified Seasons, a popular motif of the period and perhaps indicating here the cycle of life, or life and death given the promise of resurrection that Dionysus brought. Although the figures of the Seasons and Dionysus are Classicized in dress, hairstyle, and isocephaly as is common in works of the late Severan dynasty, they are very flat and frontal with smooth skin and no defined musculature. This reduction of detail is a step towards the abstraction seen in fourth-century sculpture. It seems likely that the selection of Dionysus here reflects the personal beliefs of the deceased. More explicitly biographical sarcophagi reflecting life events, values, and identity are also found, some also mythologically based.

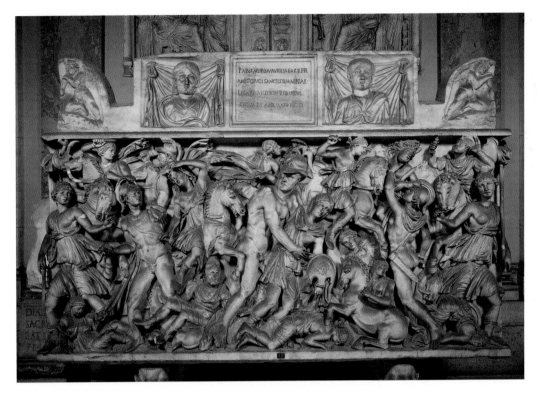

10.19 Sarcophagus with Achilles and Penthesilea, 225–235 CE, Rome. Musei Vaticani, Rome. H 3 ft 10 in (1.17 m). Source: © 2014. Photo Scala, Florence.

MORE ON MYTH
Achilles and Penthesilea

Penthesilea was an Amazon queen and daughter of the war god Ares who led an army of her female warriors to join in the defense of the city of Troy in the Trojan War. The myths say that she did this either for money or to redeem herself for killing her own sister, a sacrilege the Trojan king had purified her from. After the death of the Trojan hero, Hector, she aided the Trojans in battle, in some accounts for several days. She killed many Greeks including the Greek hero Makhaon. She then fought Achilles, who was struck by the queen's beauty at the moment of killing her, making the event a romantically tragic battle. After killing her, Achilles returned her corpse to the Trojans for honorable burial. For his love and honoring of her, Achilles was mocked by Thersites, whom he killed.

Many of the trends of sculpture, and mythological sarcophagi in particular, can be identified in a sarcophagus from the period of Alexander Severus found on the outskirts of Rome. The subject is based on Greek Classical Amazonomachy, the mythical battle between Greeks and Amazons. The overall composition is based on Antonine battle sarcophagi with figures filling the entire frame of the long side of the sarcophagus on illusionary groundlines as they move up the field. Six large-scale figures fill the foreground of the relief. Two Amazons and two Greeks are found on each side, symmetrically placed from the corners, three of them very frontal and planar in appearance. The Amazons share the dress of the personified Roma and *Virtus* on other sarcophagi from the same period. In the center are the two main figures, the Amazon queen, Penthesilea, and her opponent, Achilles.

Here the pair display portrait features suggesting that they represent a husband and wife, a pairing typically found in biographical sarcophagi from the second and third centuries CE. The use of this story of tragic murder and lost love for a married couple raises the question of just how closely sarcophagi reflect personal identity, values, and beliefs. In this case, it seems unlikely that we are seeing an exact parallel and instead, as with the Alcestis and Admetus sarcophagus, the sarcophagus represents the use of a mythological subject to convey the theme of premature death.

Forma Urbis Romae

The vast majority of the ancient city of Rome is lost to us forever. One work of art allows us to recover part of it, at least visually, and to understand how the Romans viewed their city. The large marble plan of Rome, generally referred to as the Severan Marble Plan or the *Forma Urbis Romae*, illustrated in minute detail the ground plan of all architectural features in the city at the time it was carved. This unique surviving map, incised onto 151 marble slabs that filled a wall in the Templum Pacis, originally measured *c.* 60 x 43 ft (*c.* 18 x 13 m). Currently only 1,186 fragments or about 10 percent of the original survive although an additional 10 percent was recovered and lost in the sixteenth century, surviving only in drawings made at that time.

The plan was carved on the marble slabs of the wall, then the lines and labels painted, under the rule of Septimius Severus sometime between 203 and 211 CE. The plan is almost unbelievably detailed and accurate including, as far as can be determined, ground plans of all buildings, fountains, gardens, walls, columns, and every built feature, public and private, within the city of Rome. Notably the plan only shows architecture so it effectively defines the city by the built environment of Rome with a total rejection of geographical or political features. The Tiber river, for example, appears only

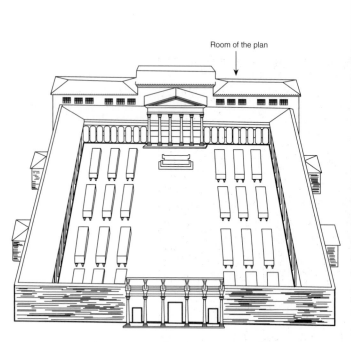

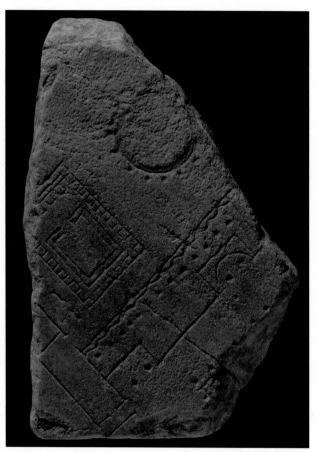

10.20 *Forma Urbis Romae* drawing of wall in Templum Pacis, Rome, 203–211 CE. Courtesy of the Penn Museum, image #The Lost Architecture of Ancient Rome (Reynolds, D.W.).

10.21 *Forma Urbis Romae* fragment showing temple complex, Rome, 203–211 CE. Source: Forma Urbis Romae Project, Stanford University.

as a blank space between rows of warehouses and buildings that line its opposite banks. The *pomerium*, the sacred boundary of the city defined by a line of stone markers, is also missing.

Many of the major public buildings are distinguished in ways that set them apart from the majority of the structures on the plan. While the walls of most buildings are represented by single lines, in the case of some notable buildings the walls were rendered in more detail. Examples include temples and the Septizodium, a Severan building adjacent to the Circus Maximus, built in 203, effectively informing us that the plan dates after its construction. The walls and column bases were carved in outline and recessed, often also depicted in red paint. They were also named with inscriptions that serve as captions. Examples include major entertainment buildings such as baths, the Circus Maximus and the Flavian Amphitheater (Colosseum), as well as temples including the Temple of the Deified Claudius, Temple of Castor, and Temple of Minerva. It is notable that the Severan building works, new or remodeled, were emphasized in scale, large labels, and perhaps in the paint scheme, so the plan itself was a display monument celebrating Severan metropolitan munificence.

Other than the outlines of a few major buildings, the depiction of architectural features is consistent across the plan. Doorways are usually shown as a break in the line of a wall; arcades are shown by dashed lines; colonnades are represented as lines of dots; indoor staircases are usually represented by a V or a triangle; outdoor stairways are typically indicated by a series of short perpendicular lines between two long parallel lines. The fragments that depict the Circus Maximus and Septizodium illustrate all of these conventions. The shops that filled the arcade on the exterior of the Circus show the distinction between major buildings like the Circus and their less significant construction. Their interior stairs and arcade facade are also illustrated accurately when compared to excavation records.

This is one of the great benefits of the plan. Its demonstrated detail and accuracy allow the study of the vast areas of Rome that cannot be excavated because of later structures that still exist or where the ancient buildings no longer survive. Especially important is that the plan preserves even buildings which leave no literary record. A superb example is the fragment of three atrium style houses. This style of Roman house is well known from Pompeii but no actual examples have

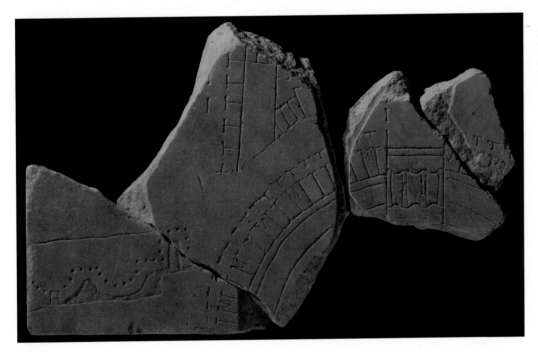

10.22 *Forma Urbis Romae* fragment showing Circus Maximus, Rome, 203–211 CE. Source: Forma Urbis Romae Project, Stanford University.

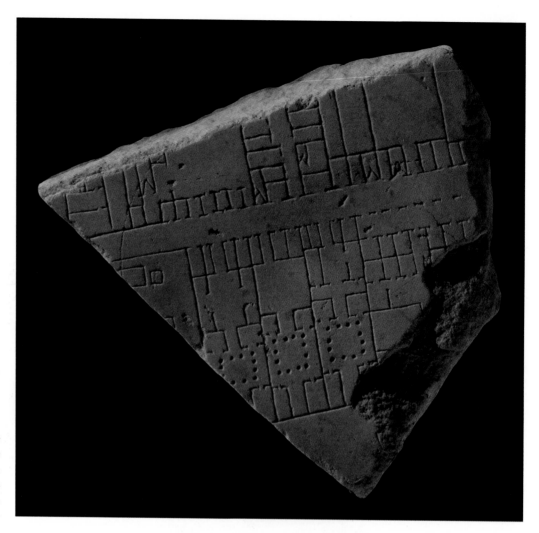

10.23 *Forma Urbis Romae* fragment showing three atrium houses, Rome, 203–211 CE. Source: Forma Urbis Romae Project, Stanford University.

HISTORICAL CONTEXT
Roman mapping tradition

The Forma Urbis Romae is the culmination of two longlived Roman practices, mapping and architectural drawings of buildings, both well known from literature, but neither with many surviving examples. The best-preserved maps, the Peutinger Table and Madaba Map Mosaic, date to the fifth or sixth century CE. The Peutinger Table probably derives from a map commissioned by Marcus Agrippa under Augustus. The Romans created maps, including cartographic wall paintings, that defined the empire by its built environment, notably paved roads, cities, and orthogonal field systems. Prominent topographic features were named to give context to Roman presence in and control over the known world. These maps were more schematic references to express the imperial world than aids to travel, although road networks and the cities they connected were correctly labeled. Architectural drawings, both floor plans and elevations, are found from the Roman world. Examples of full-size elevation drawings, used to aid construction, survive from the Pantheon and the amphitheater at Capua. Scale floor plans survive on marble and mosaic. Floor plans carved on marble were for non-professional audiences. Two plaques from Roman cemeteries show tomb complexes with accurate scale plans of buildings and gardens to provide evidence that the wishes of the deceased were followed faithfully.

been found in Rome. The plan preserves the only evidence that at least some Romans lived in this style of dwelling in the Severan capital.

The plan is the largest marble relief work of third-century CE Rome and is a purely decorative piece of art. In this way it varies from the few other building plans that survive from the Roman world. It deliberately illustrates places people would never see in person in a manner, placed high on the interior wall of a subsidiary room, that could not be closely examined. As the Column of Trajan celebrated his war visually in a way that could not be closely analyzed, the plan does the same for the city of Rome. For modern viewers the plan reveals in its relief images unique and important evidence for the Roman conventions of portraying space, architecture, and the range of urban environment. This illustration tells us that the Romans utilized a sophisticated set of conventions of depiction and expected that the viewers would understand and appreciate them.

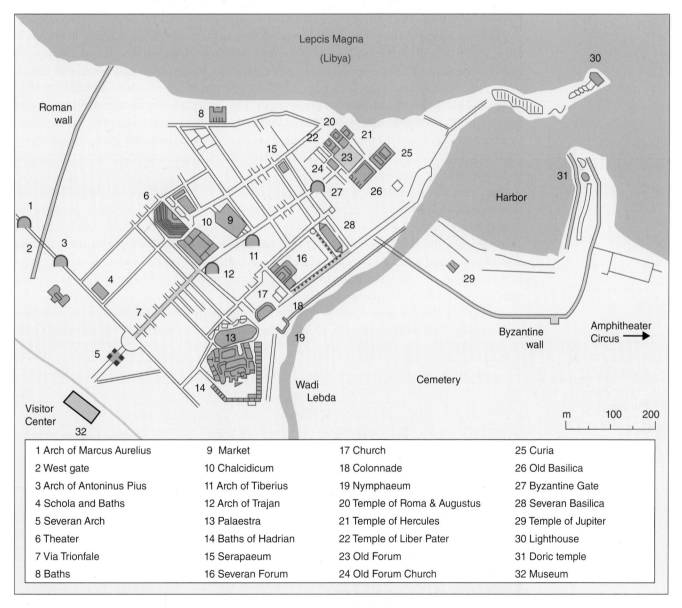

1 Arch of Marcus Aurelius	9 Market	17 Church	25 Curia
2 West gate	10 Chalcidicum	18 Colonnade	26 Old Basilica
3 Arch of Antoninus Pius	11 Arch of Tiberius	19 Nymphaeum	27 Byzantine Gate
4 Schola and Baths	12 Arch of Trajan	20 Temple of Roma & Augustus	28 Severan Basilica
5 Severan Arch	13 Palaestra	21 Temple of Hercules	29 Temple of Jupiter
6 Theater	14 Baths of Hadrian	22 Temple of Liber Pater	30 Lighthouse
7 Via Trionfale	15 Serapaeum	23 Old Forum	31 Doric temple
8 Baths	16 Severan Forum	24 Old Forum Church	32 Museum

10.24 Plan of Lepcis Magna, Libya with Severan buildings including the harbor marked, 196–206 CE. Hobe/Holger Behr/Wikimedia Commons.

Severan building program at Lepcis Magna

The building program under Septimius Severus at Lepcis Magna shows Severan emulation of Trajan's policies and aspirations with an understanding of Trajan's great harbor at Portus, his lavish use of arches, and his constructions in his own hometown of Italica in Spain. Embedded in the architectural forms in the Syrian provincial style is a message declaring Septimius Severus as the new Trajan – divinely led to rule and to conquer not just as Parthicus but as Parthicus Maximus.

Septimius Severus' decision to aggrandize his birthplace of Lepcis Magna through his extensive building program operates on many levels. First, one cannot overestimate the importance of announcing control of the resources of the empire through construction of an architectural wonder by a *princeps* whose position results from civil war. Many previous emperors pursued the same policy, including Augustus rebuilding the center of Rome and Vespasian building the Colosseum and complex of buildings associated with it. We should resist the temptation to think of this as merely personal interest in his place of birth. An emperor's presence, his local administrative actions, his public works, and his benefactions were all acts of imperial policy, rather than personal preference.

The first element of the Severan building program was the harbor, built to resemble Trajan's at Ostia, with a monumental lighthouse, small temples that flank the harbor mouth, and a large-scale podium temple on the shore opposite the harbor entrance, which served as a prominent central monument above the quays and anchorage. The inscription on the altar states its dedication both to Jupiter and to the victory and return of the Severans. The victory refers to the successful invasion of Parthia in 197 CE while the return is the 205 CE visit to the city by Septimius and his immediate family and court, which is in the form of a triumphal procession. From the harbor a colonnaded triumphal avenue over 65 ½ ft (20 m) wide and almost 1310 ft (400 m) long connects the harbor monuments to the new Severan forum complex.

The forum was a completely new civic space, *c.* 656 x 328 ft (200 x 100 m), designed to reflect the Forum of Trajan at Rome and to expand the city of Lepcis. It consists of three elements: a basilica like Trajan's Basilica Ulpia in Rome featuring two apses, and set transverse to the rest of the forum; a large open square surrounded by porticoes; and a tall podium temple to the *gens Septimia*, the dynasty of Septimius Severus. While the building set is largely an imitation of Trajan's work in Rome, the forms of the buildings are based on models from the far eastern provinces of the Roman Empire, starting with the broad colonnaded avenue.

The basilica itself has elements of the Syrian architectural style with an emphasis on the projecting and receding elements along its walls. Colossal free-standing columns on tall pedestals terminating

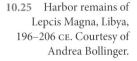

10.25   Harbor remains of Lepcis Magna, Libya, 196–206 CE. Courtesy of Andrea Bollinger.

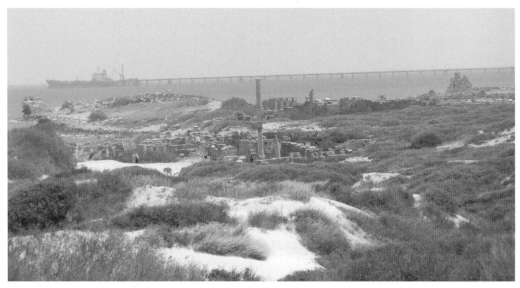

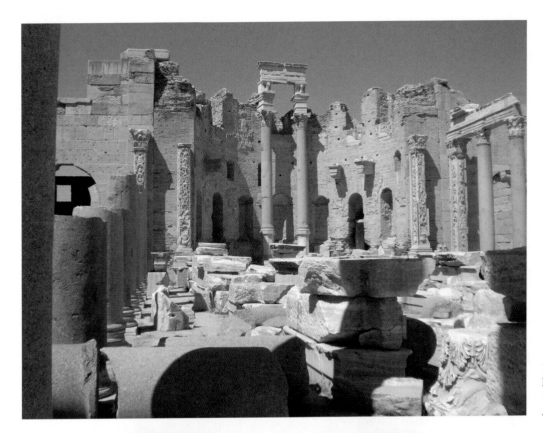

10.26   Severan Basilica, Lepcis Magna, Libya, 196–206 CE. Courtesy of Andrea Bollinger.

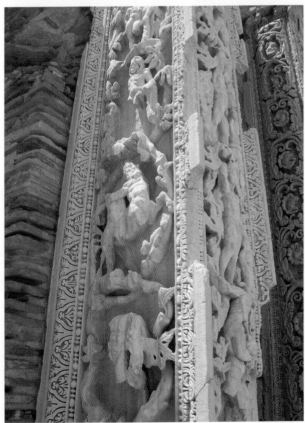

10.27   Detail of relief sculpture from the Severan Basilica, Lepcis Magna, Libya, 196–206 CE. Courtesy of Andrea Bollinger.

A VIEW FROM THE PROVINCES
The Severan arch at Lepcis Magna, 203 CE

The final element of the Severan program is in some ways – location and style – truly art from the provinces while in others – subject – it represents work from the city of Rome finally appearing in a provincial city. It is a large arch, in plan a tetrapylon, a four-sided arch, built over a crossroads. Each of the four facades shares architectural and sculptural elements common to the forum complex. The arched openings are elaborately decorated with sculpture. The arches

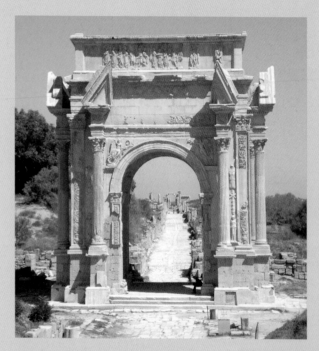

themselves spring from carved engaged square pilasters. Further pilasters decorate the exterior corners of the arch. Each facade has a pair of tall, free-standing columns on very tall pedestals that flank each opening. The columns here do not terminate in sections of architrave, however. Each architrave section above the capital supports a further free-standing architectural element: a section of a triangular pediment. These add to the dynamic three-dimensional qualities of the arch. The major figural work consists of four large horizontal reliefs, one in the attic story between the broken pediments on each side of the arch. Each relief panel features the Severan family participating in events that reinforce their power: triumph, procession, sacrifice, and Concordia Augustorum, the harmony of the emperors, a concept first seen under the Antonines.

One of the four relief panels depicts the entrance of the *Augusti* into the city in the manner of a Roman triumph: the central, frontal figure of Septimius Severus shares the triumphal *quadriga* with his sons Caracalla and Geta as he shared the religious monuments of the harbor with them. The lighthouse of Lepcis Magna provides the only architectural context in the scene as the

10.28 Overall view of Severan arch, Lepcis Magna, Libya, 203 CE. Marble. Courtesy of Andrea Bollinger.

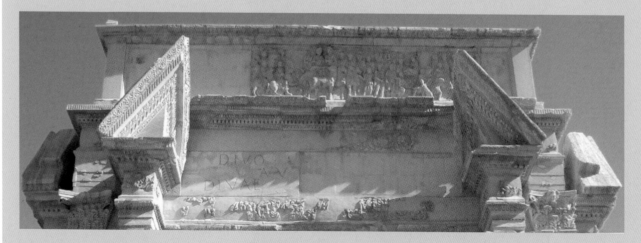

10.29 Attic triumph panel, Severan arch, Lepcis Magna, Libya, 203 CE. H 5 ft 6 in (1.68 m), marble. Courtesy of Andrea Bollinger.

Augusti pass through the harbor into the city. The lighthouse establishes the location of the triumphal procession as commencing along the Severan harbor from whence it will proceed along the monumental avenue to the forum.

Visually and ceremonially the two major public spaces in the city constructed under Severus are connected through this monument; the lighthouse acts as a marker for the beginning of the procession and as shorthand for the entire harbor project. It fills the position which on previous monuments would have been occupied by an arch as the architectural marker of a triumph, as on the spoils relief on the Arch of Titus (Figure 7.23), which shows the arch as the architectural context for the triumphal procession, in fact defining the procession as triumphal. The other details of the chariot, patron deities, emphasis on victory, and especially the presence of Parthian captives all reinforce the visual statement of triumph.

The multiple levels of meaning and deities into whose identity the Severans assimilated themselves were appropriate to mark the growth of the *princeps* from Parthicus to Parthicus Maximus. The monuments and messages also greatly expand the notion of triumph previously exclusive to Rome, a concept so important that one justification for Augustus' declaration of war on Mark Antony was that he held a triumph outside of Rome. The constructions at Lepcis Magna are a leading indicator of the future of the imperial government. Within a hundred years Rome would become primarily symbolic and the active capitals of the emperors were to be found at more strategic sites around the empire.

in sections of architrave above their capitals are essentially more developed examples of the type found on the Arch of Septimius Severus in the Forum Romanum. The colonnades end with engaged square pilasters along the walls of the basilica. The pilasters framing the apses are covered on three sides with deeply carved reliefs organized around scrolls issuing from chalices. Vine and acanthus leaves cover the scrolls, which interlock to form a series of roundels inhabited by animals and human figures. Scenes including figures from the myths of Hercules and Dionysus, the patron deities of Caracalla and Geta, fill the scrolls. The sculptors of this work probably came from Aphodisias in Asia Minor where carvings of a comparable subject, technique, and quality have been found. The Syrian ornate style carries over into the porticoes surrounding the open square of the forum as well. The columns of the portico have a type of Aeolic or East Greek capital, more common in Asia Minor. They do not support a flat architrave, but an arcade, a line of arches all around the square, a dramatic stylistic evolution not seen before in the province, also derived from eastern provincial models. Flat, frontal heads on shields filled the area over each capital in the spandrels of the arcade.

CONCLUSION

The Severan dynasty represents a critical moment in both Roman history and Roman art. As the last multi-generational dynasty in the western Roman Empire, it stands in a position on the threshold between the stability of the second century CE and the chaos of the later third. Dynastic portraiture reveals the tensions that abounded during the period, and the deliberate use of Antonine iconography and attributes in portraits of Septimius Severus and his immediate family illustrates his attempt to associate the dynasty, not with one that usurped power, but with one boasting a reputation for stability and successful rule. By the reign of Caracalla, however, the third-century CE portraiture appears fully developed with the techniques of dramatic, almost abstracted, energetic, or possibly anxious sculpture. The historical reliefs of the Severans in Rome and Lepcis Magna share this split between past and future with design elements of the Antonine battle reliefs combined with a return to more Italic images: flatter, more frontal, and increasingly abstracted figures. The Classicizing tradition is far from finished however and elements of it are still seen in a modified form in the portraiture and sarcophagi from the period of Severus Alexander. The Severan building program at Lepcis Magna perhaps gives a sense of what their buildings in Rome might have looked like had they survived. The combination of monument sets from the Roman tradition, repeated and layered references to Trajan, and the expansion of Syrian ornate style architecture all give a sense of a dynasty bent on referencing the past, but not directly copying it. The innovation combined with emulation that we see in Severan art and architecture gives the work a sense of vitality and vision that is effectively the last sense of confidence found in Roman art for at least fifty years.

SUGGESTIONS FOR FURTHER READING

Richard Brilliant, *The Arch of Septimus Severus in the Roman Forum* (American Academy in Rome 1967). The only book-length study of this critical Severan monument in English. It provides a systematic description and analysis of the sculptural program on the arch with particular attention to the innovative historical reliefs of the Parthian War.

Katherine M.D. Dunbabin, "The North African Provinces" in *Mosaics of the Greek and Roman World* (Cambridge University Press 1999), 101–129. Contains a detailed, well-documented survey of the major subjects and styles of mosaic work in the Roman African provinces.

Susann Lusnia, *Creating Severan Rome: The Architecture and Self-Image of L. Septimius Severus* (Collection Latomus 2012). This work explores Severan building programs and their use for dynastic propaganda in the city of Rome. It concentrates on urban planning and sculptural display as means of projecting self and dynastic identity.

Miranda Marvin, "Freestanding Sculptures from the Baths of Caracalla." *American Journal of Archaeology* 87: 347–384 (1983). Reconstructs the sculptural program of these baths including an analysis of the sculptures in their architectural setting. Reveals public taste in the grand bathing complexes of ancient Rome.

Simon Swain, Stephen Harrison, and Jas Elsner, eds., *Severan Culture* (Cambridge University Press 2007). This collection of twenty-seven essays on the Severan period by noted scholars includes chapters on themes and style in Severan art, metaphor, and identity in architecture, urban development, and the marble plan, and Septimius Severus as the new Augustus.

Stanford Digital Forma Urbis Romae Project (http://formaurbis.stanford.edu/). Quite possibly the ultimate resource on the marble plan, which contains all 1,186 surviving fragments online in high definition scans, images of the drawings of lost fragments, a searchable glossary and bibliography on the marble plan, and a digital slab map.

Janet Stephens, "Ancient Roman Hairdressing: On (Hair)pins and Needles." *Journal of Roman Archaeology* 21: 110–132 (2008). Argues against the common scholarly conclusion that elaborate Roman women's hairstyles required wigs. She recreates the hairstyles of Julia Domna among others using Roman hairpins and techniques.

J.B. Ward-Perkins, *The Severan Buildings of Lepcis Magna: An Architectural Survey* (Society for Libyan Studies 1993). Provides a systematic overview of the Severan building program in the hometown of Septimius Severus. It includes all of the major public buildings, their form and decoration, as well as the vital architectural sculpture of the entire collection of buildings and monuments.

11

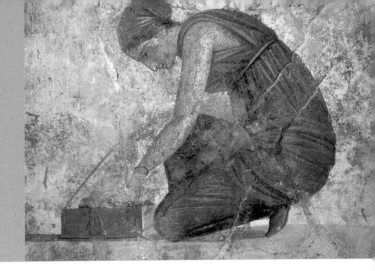

THE THIRD CENTURY AND THE TETRARCHY, 235–306 CE

Crisis and Renewal

238 CE	**Acilia sarcophagus**
244–249 CE	Philip the Arab as emperor; **portrait bust of Philip the Arab; Synagogue at Dura Europus**
249–251 CE	Decius as emperor; **portrait of Decius**
250 CE	**Mattei Lion Hunt sarcophagus**
253–260 CE	Valerian as emperor
260 CE	**Relief of Emperor Valerian kneeling before Shapur I**
260–270 CE	**Good Shepherd sarcophagus**
270–275 CE	**Aurelian wall built around Rome**
284–305 CE	Tetrarchy founded with Diocletian and Maximian as joint rulers
298–303 CE	**Arch of Galerius, Thessaloniki**
c. 300 CE	**Tetrarchs porphyry statue group; Villa of Piazza Armerina built**
303 CE	Tetrarchs visit Rome; **Decennalia monument dedicated**
306 CE	**Baths of Diocletian dedicated**

A History of Roman Art, First Edition. Steven L. Tuck.
© 2015 Steven L. Tuck. Published 2015 by John Wiley & Sons, Ltd.

THIRD-CENTURY EMPERORS AND THE TETRARCHY

The remainder of the third century after the death of Alexander Severus and the loss of the slightly stabilizing force of the Severan dynasty was a period of unprecedented chaos, military defeat, and social, economic, and political instability across the entire Roman world. Not all of the Roman world, all of the time, was affected by all of these crises. The ripple effects of them were felt across the entire Roman world to a greater or lesser extent depending on location. Italy, for example, was largely untouched by barbarian invasions, but badly damaged by civil war and economic instability. Although none of the Severan emperors after Septimius Severus had managed to die peacefully in their own beds, the pattern of assassination and usurpation now accelerated. Over the remainder of the century twenty-eight different men, the so-called "soldier-emperors," would be hailed as emperor and twenty-six of these would be murdered.

The Roman world that emerged from this period was vastly different from the one that entered it, as seen in every aspect of society including its art. The changes are best seen in the portraiture of the period, in which the portrayals of the emperors both in sculpture and coin portraits reflect the instability of the Roman world. Imperial images have been described as anxious, restless, insecure, and troubled. All these seem applicable to modern viewers. To the Romans they may have looked responsibly concerned or engaged, considering the troubles of the period.

After 235 CE, the general pattern of succession involved a military officer being proclaimed emperor by his troops, managing to rule, however briefly or over a small portion of the empire, and then being murdered by another usurper. Within this pattern were some particular events with larger consequences for the entire Roman world.

Philip the Arab, 244–249 CE

One of these emperors was Philip the Arab (244–249 CE), the first Roman emperor of Arab descent and an example of the expansion of citizenship and military and political opportunities under the empire. His portraiture relies on the pattern established under Caracalla, effectively rejecting the classicism of other Severans. His short-cropped hair and the X created by the lines on his face and brow are elements of Caracalla's military portraiture. The hair and beard are chiseled with small incisions and the turned head, deep eyes, and drilled pupils give an expressive and restless appearance to the work that seems to suggest psychological state.

Decius, 249–251 CE

Philip was assassinated and succeeded by Decius in 249 CE. Decius' portraiture shows the development of the expressive military trends seen under Philip. Now the emphasis is almost completely on the shape of the head and the surface decoration. There is no volume above the surface. The chiseled grooves have turned into deep trenches in his skin, as seen in the nasolabial grooves and in his forehead. Combined with the turned head and down-turned mouth he looks less like an energetic ruler than a pessimistic one. The restlessness looks like defensiveness or anxiety while the entire head is an abstracted image of a human skull. The image is typical of many of the imperial and elite portraits of the period and may reflect a Stoic acceptance of the nature of the struggles in the world, common in the culture at the time. In 251 CE Decius became the first Roman emperor to fall in battle against a foreign enemy, while fighting the Goths who had invaded across the Danube.

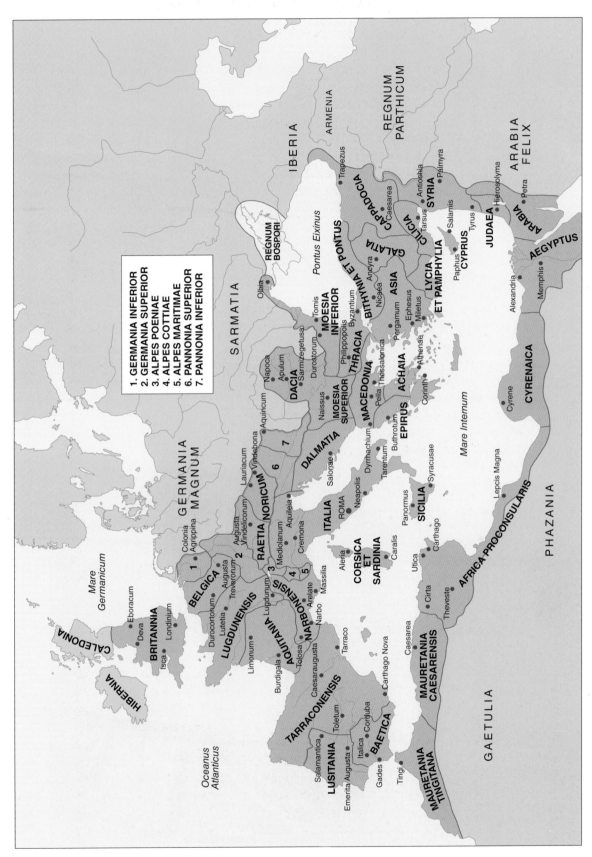

11.1a and 11.1b   Map of the Roman Empire of the third century with Tetrarchic capitals and breakaway regions labeled. (a) Andrei nacu/Wikimedia Commons.

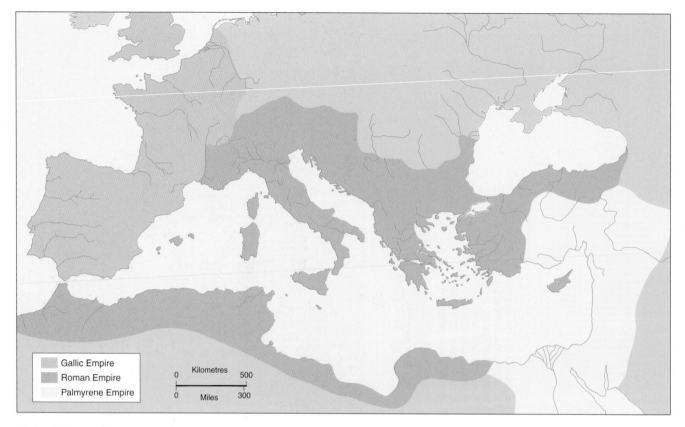

Gallic Empire
Roman Empire
Palmyrene Empire

Kilometres
0   500

0   Miles   300

11.1b   (*Continued*)

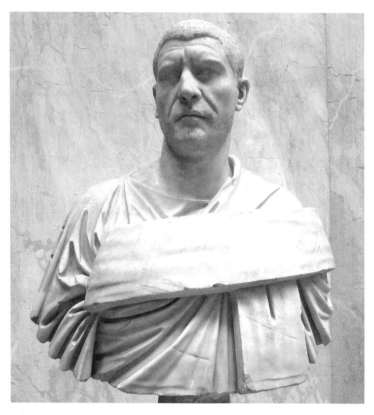

11.2   Portrait of Philip the Arab, 244–249 CE, Rome. Musei Vaticani, Rome. H 2 ft 4 in (71.1 cm), marble.
Photo courtesy Steven L. Tuck.

Valerian, 253–260 CE

The low point was reached, however, in the reign of Valerian (253–260 CE). In 260 CE Valerian became the first and only emperor to be captured and die in captivity abroad. He was captured by the Persian emperor Shapur I himself during Valerian's campaigns in the east against Persian incursions. A large-scale contemporary relief carved into a cliff at Naqsh-i Rustam in Iran depicts the victory over Valerian. The mounted Persian king of kings accepts the surrender of the kneeling Valerian whose portrayal, although executed on a Persian monument, follows third-century CE Roman conventions with his close-cropped hair and beard, tunic and military cloak. His laurel wreath diadem is an attribute found on imperial coinage indicating his rank as Roman emperor. The sculptors of the monument, perhaps with input from captive Romans, were as concerned to accurately depict Roman dress and military equipment as were the sculptors of the Adamclisi monument under Trajan (Figure 8.21). The figure is very flat in an awkward profile, but the folds of the cloak and the hem of the tunic echo Classicizing conventions for fabric.

Following this debacle the western empire was invaded by Alemanni, Franks, and Goths who rampaged through Germany, Gaul, Spain, and northern Italy while the central Roman authorities were powerless to help. The governor of Lower Germany, Postumus, was declared emperor by his troops in 260 CE and established a breakaway Roman empire in Britain, Gaul, Germany, and Spain. This Gallic Empire remained separate from the rest of the empire for at least fifteen years. Meanwhile in the east beginning in 261 CE a second breakaway kingdom centered at the important caravan city of Palmyra eventually grew to include the Roman territories around the eastern Mediterranean from Egypt in the south, the provinces of Judea, Syria, Arabia, Mesopotamia and into Asia Minor. This wealthy and strategically significant area was not reabsorbed into the main empire until 272 CE.

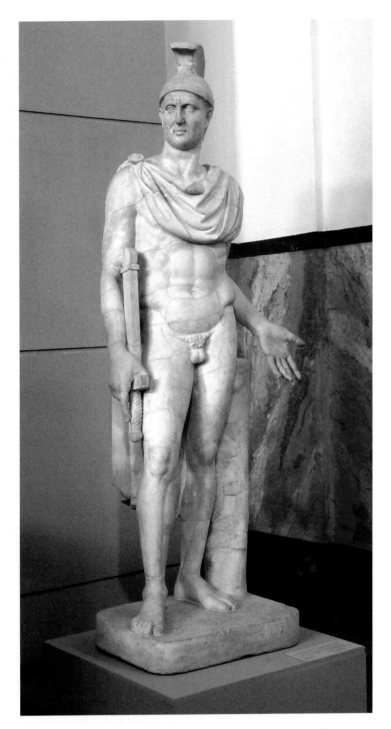

11.3 Portrait of Decius, 249–251 CE, Rome. Musei Capitolini. Marble, H 7 ½ ft (2.3 m). Photo courtesy Steven L. Tuck.

Aurelian, 270–275 CE

The first turning point for the empire in this series of disasters was the principate of Aurelian (270–275 CE). His relatively long reign allowed him to make great strides in recovering lost territory. He defeated many invaders in northern Italy and forced them back across the Danube. He then turned to the reconquest of the Gallic Empire, and finally, by the fall of 274 CE, to the defeat of the Palmyrenes and the restoration of the Roman Empire as it was under the Severans. Following his defeat of the invasions into Italy, Aurelian planned and began to build the first walls around Rome since those that followed the Gallic sack in 386 BCE. Although it is arguably a

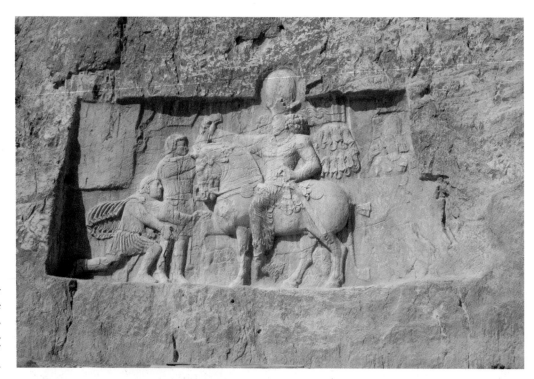

11.4 Relief of Emperor Valerian kneeling before Shapur I, after 260 CE, found at Naqsh-i Rustam, Shiraz, Iran. Ali Ganjei/Wikimedia Commons.

HISTORICAL CONTEXT

The captivity and death of Valerian

The Early Christian author Lactantius records the details of the capture, captivity, and death of Valerian. According to Lactantius (*de mortibus persecutorum* 5), Valerian was kept in wretched conditions and regularly humiliated by Shapur who used Valerian as a footstool, forcing the former emperor to crouch and present his back whenever Shapur wished to mount his horse. Another source relates that after he had endured this for a long time he offered Shapur a vast sum of money for his release. In reply Shapur had him killed by pouring molten gold down his throat, demonstrating Persian contempt for riches. Lactantius notes that death did not stop his humiliation. After he died he was skinned, his skin dyed purple, the color reserved for royalty, and placed on display in the temple of the gods as a permanent reminder of the great Persian victory. When Roman ambassadors came to negotiate with the Persians they were always shown the skin as a lesson in Persian power.

statement of imperial control and power, the walls are also indicative of the Roman government's uncertainty in defending the capital.

The walls were a massive brick-faced concrete construction over 12 miles in circuit, just over 20 ft (6 m) in height and 13 ft (4 m) thick at the base. They were pierced by eighteen gates with large gatehouses constructed of cut stone instead of concrete for strength. For their time, they were not the peak of military engineering but were quick to erect and considered sufficient to hold off invading tribes without siege equipment. In the fourth century CE their height was doubled, indicating the continuing unrest of the period. Aurelian's murder by high-ranking officers in the army, the cause of death of most third-century emperors, shows that the instability of the period would continue. In fact, the crises of the third century CE were not solved until the emperor Diocletian came to power in 284 CE and reorganized the Roman world.

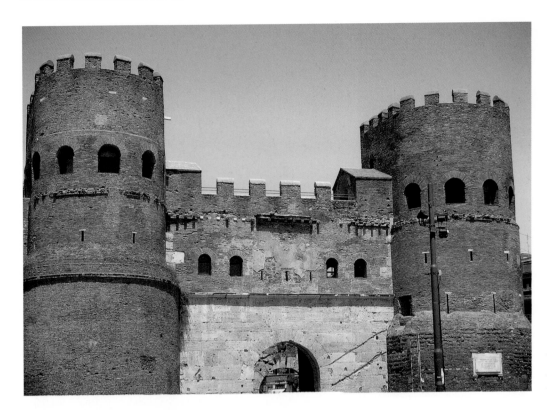

11.5   Gate in the Aurelian Wall, Rome at the Via Appia, 270–275 CE. Photo courtesy Steven L. Tuck.

Diocletian, 284–305 CE

Diocletian was seemingly another in the line of usurping generals of the third century CE. However, he came to power with a vision and a motivation to solve Rome's systemic problems. His comprehensive attempted reform of the entire Roman world and solutions to its military, political, economic, and social problems were not always successful but they gave the empire much needed stability and allowed his colleagues and successors to build on his work. For example, he was the first emperor to separate military and civilian authority in the Roman provinces and he subdivided the existing provinces into ninety-eight smaller ones. Never again could a local governor control enough resources to usurp power. His economic reforms, such as the edict on maximum prices (301 CE), were not successful, but his political and military ones largely were.

His greatest achievement was the creation of the Tetrarchy, the rule by four men. In 285 CE Diocletian raised another army officer, Maximian, to the rank of junior emperor or Caesar. In 286 CE he was raised to co-emperor or Augustus. He and Diocletian then each selected a Caesar, Maximian adopting Constantius and Diocletian adopting Galerius. These men became the Tetrarchs and their position, not the individual man, was the focus of their official imagery, notably portraiture.

A Tetrarchic portrait thought to be Diocletian provides one example. The imagery conveys power more than personality and is designed to distance the ruler from the ruled. The large diadem, a wreath with a central gem, is very similar to that worn by Septimius Severus on the painted Severan portrait (Figure 10.1). Here it is deeply drilled and undercut, emphasizing this feature and the rank it represents. The facial features, hair, and beard are somewhat generic and create an emphasis on the attributes of power, not on the person of the emperor. It could be a portrait of any of a number of emperors from the period. The aspect of the Tetrarchy that ensured stability was the succession plan it established. On May 1, 305 CE, after twenty years of rule, Diocletian and Maximian abdicated power simultaneously. Their joint retirement from office led to the promotion of their Caesars, Galerius and Constantius, as the new Augusti. They in turn each selected a new Caesar as an associate emperor.

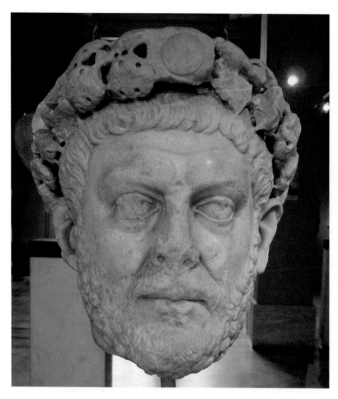

11.6   Diocletian (?) statue head, from Nicomedia, Turkey, 284–305
CE. Istanbul Archaeological Museum. Marble, H 15 ¼ in (39 cm).
Photo courtesy Francesca Tronchin.

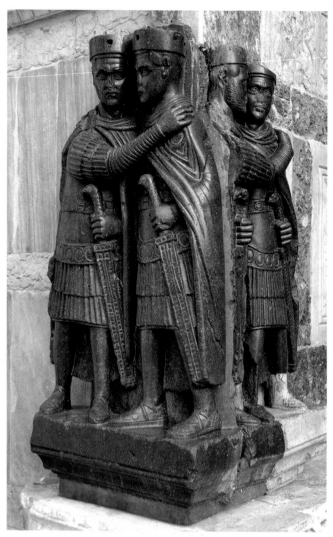

11.7   Tetrarchs statue group, *c.* 300 CE, from Constantinople, now
set into Basilica of S. Marco, Venice. H 5 ft 2 ½ in (159 cm), porphyry.
Photo courtesy Francesca Tronchin.

Diocletian and Maximian became the first Roman emperors to retire to private life, leaving behind a
greatly changed and more stable Roman empire.

The practical result of the Tetrarchy was that each emperor controlled a much smaller area,
approximately one quarter of the empire, and could respond more quickly and presumably more
knowledgably to their local problems. It also made assassination a useless strategy for usurpation. No
plot could target, kill, and overthrow four emperors in four distant areas of the Roman world
simultaneously. Four regional capitals at Nicomedia in northwestern Asia Minor, Thessalonica in
northern Greece, Mediolanum (modern Milan) in northern Italy, and Augusta Treverorum (modern
Trier) in Germany further reduced the importance of Rome and led to new venues and spaces that
required official art. The Diocletian portrait, for example, was found in Nicomedia.

The Tetrarchy

porphyry
a hard purple stone
quarried by the Romans at
one spot in Egypt, Mons
Porpyritis, and used
extensively by emperors
since its purple color
denoted royalty.

The iconic image of the Tetrarchs is a **porphyry** group portrait carved in Alexandria, found in a
Byzantine palace, and now in Venice. The rich purple color of the stone, a color generally reserved for
emperors, conveys the status of the rulers while the composition of paired figures in collegial embrace,

one Augustus and one Caesar – one senior and one junior emperor, parallels the political structure. Personal characteristics are absent in this group portrait. Each senior emperor is bearded while his junior emperor is clean-shaven. Otherwise the men are identically dressed in armor and military cloak with flat hats adorned by, now missing, gems. Their faces have lined foreheads and exceptionally large eyes with carved pupils, showing the continued emphasis on this feature in third-century CE portraiture. Each holds the handle of his sword with his left hand, indicating the source of their power.

COIN PORTRAITS OF THE THIRD CENTURY CE

The use of coins to promote the values and identity of Roman government is not new to the third century CE or even to the imperial period. Roman government officials had used coinage to transmit images to the Roman people since the middle Republic. Coins played a larger role in previous periods of instability, for example the civil war of 69 CE. In such times coins are the easiest way to transmit messages to parts of the populace, demonstrating their importance in transmitting the messages that underlie all of Roman art. In this unsettled and chaotic period, moreover, given the lack of other types of art, this traditional form of communication and display takes on a new significance, giving us key evidence for imperial art, portraiture, and artistic themes and imperial programs. A remarkable feature of the third century CE is the explosion in coin hoards. These large collections of buried coins, sometimes numbering in the tens of thousands, provide important evidence of the numismatic issues of otherwise barely recognizable emperors. In addition their very existence reinforces our conclusions about the insecurity felt by Roman citizens. They buried their life savings hoping to retrieve them at a later time, a strategy that failed for many Romans, particularly those along the frontiers where hoards are most often found.

Most imperial coins follow a set pattern with an obverse or face side dominated by a profile bust portrait of an emperor and captioned with his titles. The reverse is more varied but generally its image and simple inscription convey one aspect of the current ruler's foreign or domestic policy. In many cases these are celebrations of achievements such as welfare payments to the poor or specific military victories. In other cases, they represent aspirations.

A coin of the emperor Gordian III (238–244 CE) falls in the second category. The obverse shows the emperor in profile image wearing a breastplate, cloak, and radiate crown. This latter attribute is found first on coins of Nero associating him with the sun god, Helios. By the third century CE it can mark a coin of double value and is often used on portraits of new emperors, presumably giving them additional visual authority given their uncertain successions. The reverse shows winged Victoria, the personification of military victory, standing over a seated captive, with a palm branch of victory in

(a)

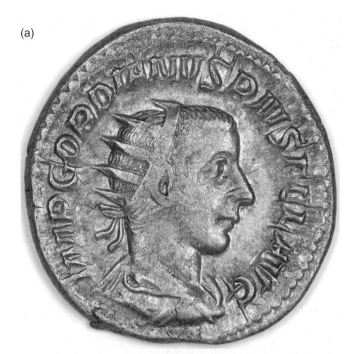

(b)

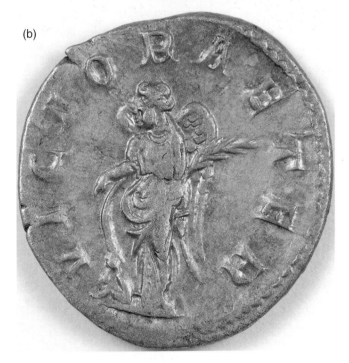

11.8a and 11.8b
Gordian III Mint: Rome
RIC vol IV.iii, p. 31, no. 154
1991.17.25 Collection:
University of Virginia Art
Museum, Antoninianus,
238–244 CE. Source:
Courtesy of The Fralin
Museum of Art at the
University of Virginia,
Museum Purchase,
1991.17.25.

her left hand. The caption, VICTOR AETER, names her as eternal victory, obviously an aspiration and not a proclaimed achievement, considering that Gordian's assassination resulted from a series of military defeats.

The power and importance of these images for establishing Roman authority is demonstrated by their use by Postumus, emperor (260–269 CE) of the breakaway Gallic Empire. He struck and distributed a series with reverses of standing female figures who personified traditional Roman values such as *Felicitas* (good luck), *Fides* (faith), *Fortuna* (good fortune), *Pax* (peace), and *Salus* (safety). This example shows Postumus very much as a typical third-century CE emperor in breastplate and military cloak with radiate crown on the obverse. The reverse has a standing *Providentia Augusta* (imperial foresight) holding a scepter and globe, an optimistic image of world power and one that is interesting for an empire that separated itself from Rome.

(a)   (b)

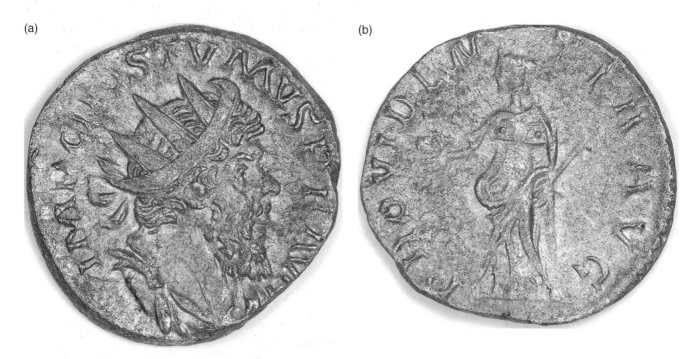

11.9a and 11.9b   Emperor Postumus, Mint: Lugdunum RIC vol V.ii, p. 341, no. 49 1991.17.238 Collection: University of Virginia Art Museum, Antoninianus, 260–269 CE. Source: Courtesy of The Fralin Museum of Art at the University of Virginia, Museum Purchase, 1991.17.238.

11.10   Constantius Caesar, Laureate bust right RIC 33a, RSC 291B Reverse: Tetrarchs sacrificing over tripod before archway in four-turreted enclosure, 293–305 CE. Classical Numismatic Group, Inc. http://www.cngcoins.com.

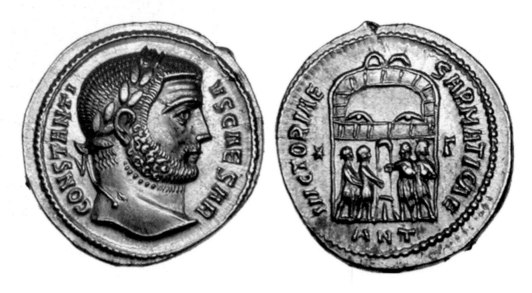

Under the Tetrarchs the traditional imagery of imperial coinage was adapted to account for their new form of government, creating imagery that celebrated each member of the four in the context of the entire group. A silver coin of Constantius, struck at Antioch in the east, provides evidence of this trend. The obverse shows the standard profile portrait of the bearded Caesar or junior emperor, wearing a laurel wreath with his name and title, Constantius Caesar. The reverse shows all four Tetrarchs sacrificing over a small altar in front of the arched doorway into an enclosure, possibly a fort or walled town. Tetrarchs sacrificing together is a motif found on much of their art including the reliefs we examine elsewhere in the chapter. The enclosure has four turrets, a symbol of the Tetrarchs and their military association. The text reads VICTORIAE SARMATICAE, commemorating a battle against the Sarmatians, a powerful group of people from modern day northern Iran. The victory is clearly presented as an achievement by the Tetrarchs as a group.

The final coin we will examine in detail was struck under Maximian. The obverse has the standard right-facing profile portrait of the emperor wearing a laurel wreath and a text of his name and titles. The reverse, however, is different in that it does not explicitly reference the emperor or the Tetrarchy.

The image is a walled military camp with four turrets on the top of the wall and an open gate. It reads VIRTVS MILITVM , the martial prowess of the soldiers. As a coin type it clearly recognizes and celebrates serving members of the military. As a political statement, however, it recognizes the basis for the power of the Tetrarchs, the competence and loyalty of the serving military. As such, it displays a remarkable awareness of their power and its foundations.

HISTORICAL RELIEFS

Thanks to the stability afforded the Roman world by the Tetrarchy, more large-scale monuments were built in this period than during the chaos of the earlier third century. This included historical reliefs that served to chronicle major events in the Tetrarchic administration. Many of these took very traditional forms, such as the Arcus Novus, a marble triumphal arch erected in Rome to celebrate the military victories in the east. Its sculptural decoration included captive barbarians, Victory figures crowning trophies, personifications, and a range of by now familiar images. Nevertheless,

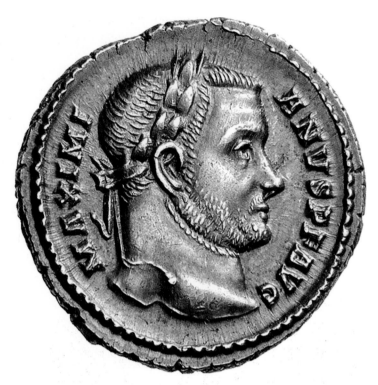

11.11 Emperor Maximian, obverse inscription: IMP C GAL VAL MAXIMIANVS PF AVG, Laureate bust right, 293–311 CE. Source: Ex Nomos, Auction 3, 10.05.2011, Lot 228.

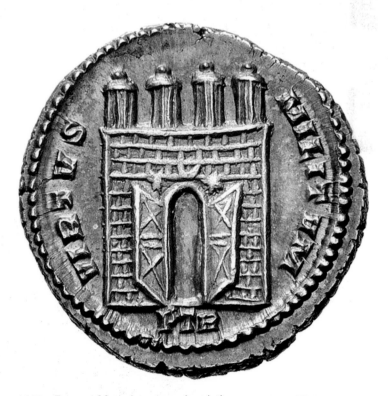

11.12 Emperor Maximian, reverse inscription: VIRTVS MILITVM, Camp gate with four turrets, gate half closed RIC VI 39, 293–311 CE. Source: Ex Nomos, Auction 3, 10.05.2011, Lot 228.

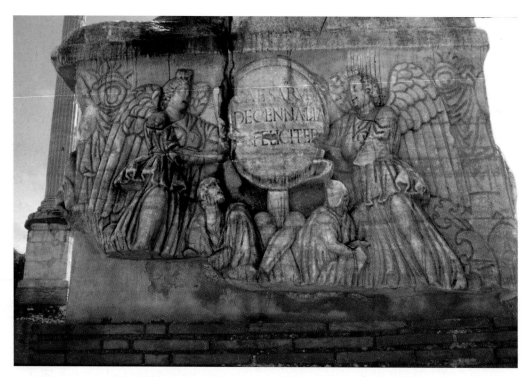

11.13   Victories inscribing shield, Decennalia base, 303 CE, Forum Romanum, Rome. W 5 ft 10 in (1.78 m), marble. Photo courtesy Steven L. Tuck.

the needs of the Tetrarchs to celebrate dynasty over individual achievement as seen in portraiture also change the forms of historical relief sculpture. Despite the rising importance of the Tetrarchic capitals in other regions, Rome was still the official capital and the site of some ceremonial events and commemorations.

Decennalia Monument, Forum Romanum, Rome, 303 CE

One of these commemorations was the Decennial, the celebration of ten years of full Tetrarchic rule in 303 CE. In honor of that event as well as Diocletian's Persian triumph – his sole visit to Rome, the Tetrarchs erected a series of five columns on tall, square pedestals in the Forum Romanum. Four of the columns terminated with statues of the Tetrarchs while the fifth supported a statue of Jupiter. All that currently remains is one of the pedestals with carved reliefs on all four sides. Like the form of the monuments, the subjects of the reliefs are very traditional: Victories inscribing a shield, a procession of Roman magistrates, a *suovetaurilia*, and a sacrifice taking place.

Although these are traditional subjects, the style of carving and the selection of images reflect contemporary needs and trends in art. The Victories relief is a variant of a scene on the Column of Trajan and has antecedents going back to Republican art. Here the image is very formal and symmetrical with paired Victories instead of the traditional one. It is carved in very shallow relief with flat figures having almost no modeling. The trophies in the background behind each Victory are completely flat and carved only with shallow channels. The figures also are outlined with broad lines that isolate them from the background. The inscription on the shield, CAESARUM DECENNALIA FELICITER, gives the occasion of the "happy Decennalia of the Caesars."

The procession scene consists of two rows of male figures walking to the left. The four men in the foreground wear the toga with a prominent *contabulatio*, the flat drapery fold that is prominent on third-century CE images of togate figures. Each holds a scroll in his left hand as his only extant attribute besides the toga. Although their heads, carved in higher relief than the rest of the relief, are missing, they are certainly images of the Tetrarchs. They are portrayed very frontal with little modeling; instead the interior details of the figures are defined by flat planes of fabric separated by

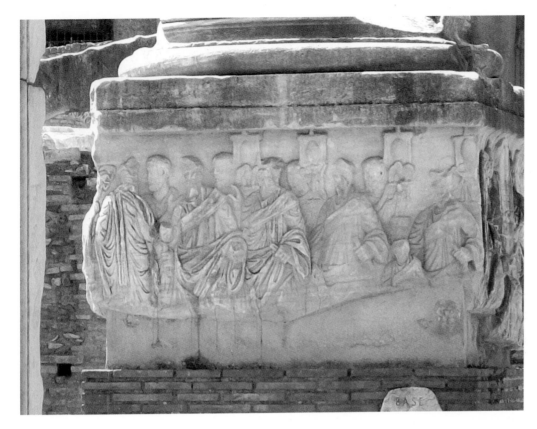

11.14 Procession of Tetrarchs, Decennalia base, 303 CE, Forum Romanum, Rome. W 5 ft 10 in (1.78 m), marble. Photo courtesy Steven L. Tuck.

channels. The background men are lined up offset from the Tetrarchs so that their faces are visible between the Tetrarchs, but in lower relief. They hold military standards decorated with eagles and personifications, probably each associated with the emperor they follow, completing their identity with a military component along with the civilian.

Arch of Galerius, Thessalonica, 303 CE

Almost simultaneously, Galerius, Diocletian's Caesar, erected a tremendous arch at his capital at Thessalonica that was dedicated in 303 CE. More than a simple triumphal arch, the structure was a complex octopylon (eight-pillared gateway) that spanned two intersecting colonnaded avenues.

The surviving piers are covered with marble slabs carved with scenes that reinforce the authority, various accomplishments, and civil and military identities of the Tetrarchs. All of the scenes are characterized by a rigid formality, with overall symmetry and a number of devices that promote the rulers above the ruled. For example, the Tetrarchs appear most often along the central axis of scenes, and the hierarchy of scale and use of subsidiary supporting or flanking figures draw attention visually to the importance of the rulers. The scenes are carved in horizontal registers whose proportions and layout resemble sarcophagus panels.

The best preserved of the relief panels is the set of three scenes on registers on the interior of the southwest pillar. The upper register (not illustrated) shows a variation on the *adventus* scene, called a translation, where the emperor Galerius is shown seated on a throne on the back of a cart moving from one city to another, probably entering Thessalonica. He is flanked by smaller-scale horsemen and greeted at the city gates by even smaller-scale standing figures holding their hands in gestures of acclamation. The central register is an image of Galerius on a rearing horse facing a similarly mounted Persian adversary. A barbarian kneels beneath the hooves of Galerius' horse. The motifs are familiar from the Great Trajanic Frieze (Figure 8.22) but here they are almost completely without any Classicizing elements. The hierarchy of scale and figures moving up the field in the background all rely on Italic sculptural traditions.

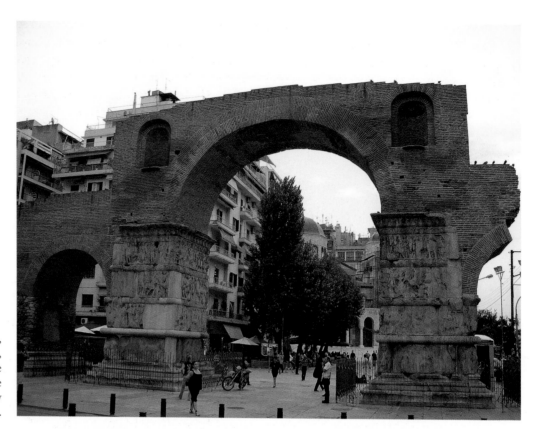

11.15 Arch of Galerius, 298–303 CE, Thessalonica, Greece. Brick-faced rubble structure clad in marble panels. Photo courtesy Steven L. Tuck.

11.16 Galerius on horseback and Tetrarchs enthroned reliefs, Arch of Galerius, 298–303 CE, Thessalonica, Greece. Marble. Photo courtesy Steven L. Tuck.

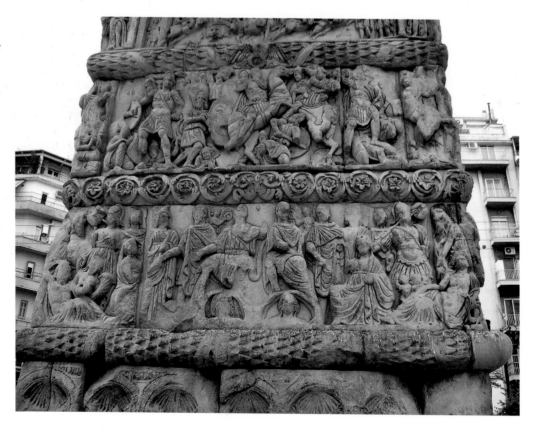

The lowest register shows the four Tetrarchs enthroned. The two Augusti are in the center flanked by their two Caesars. The entire group is flanked and in fact surrounded by a host of personifications, some of territories and celestial areas including Syria, Britain, Armenia, the Tigris and Euphrates rivers, others of qualities including *Honos* and *Virtus*. The entire composition is a statement of Tetrarchic power, its geographical extent, and the qualities on which it is based. The notion is familiar from works of Augustus, but the frontal, formal portraiture is consistent with this period.

Sarcophagi

Many of the observations in the previous chapter about sarcophagi under the Severans apply to those carved in the later third century CE as well. The styles closely reflect the official sculptural relief work of the Tetrarchic period. The subjects and overall themes are consistent with earlier practice including the use of biographical sarcophagi, battle scenes, distorted figures for enhanced emotional display and the reflection of personal belief in the images. Some of the sarcophagi that survive from the period fit into a number of scholarly categories. The Ludovisi sarcophagus (Figure 11.19), for example, can be analyzed as an example of biographical, battle, or personal belief sarcophagi.

The Acilia sarcophagus, found at the small town of Acilia outside Rome, is a badly damaged but amazingly high quality sarcophagus of the *lenos* (bathtub) shape. The sarcophagus is covered with a standing group of men, a few poorly preserved women, and one prominent boy or young man. The scene is a procession, similar to that on the Decennalia base, but here probably the *processus consularis*, the formal procession of a new consul into the Forum Romanum prior to take the oath of office. All of the figures are frontal and fill the entire panel of the sarcophagus in a single register. The men are all dressed in togas, which are deeply carved with realistically portrayed folds and carefully modeled drapery. All of the men, much like the soldiers and barbarians on the Ludovisi sarcophagus, have expressive faces and deeply drilled hair and beards. The boy by contrast has the large staring eyes and hair indicated by chiseled incision found on portraits of emperors and those who emulate them, such as the Mattei Lion Hunt sarcophagus. The Acilia sarcophagus provides evidence that the changes that occurred in sculpture, notably in the abstracted, surface-focused portraiture of the period do not reflect a lack of ability to carve Classicizing images. Rather, they represent a shift in the needs of the patrons, who are clearly commissioning this new style of portrait, and the resulting style captures the qualities required by the elite of the period.

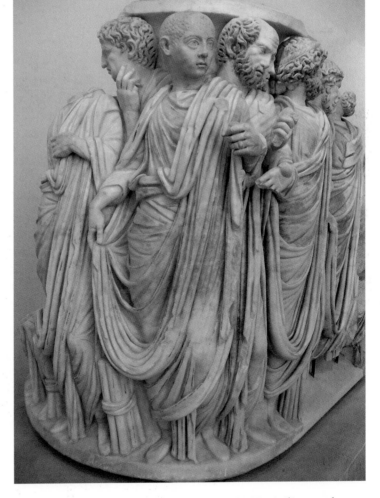

11.17 Acilia sarcophagus, *c.* 240 CE, Rome, Museo Nazionale Romano Palazzo Massimo, Rome. H 4 ft 11 in (1.50 m), marble. Photo courtesy Steven L. Tuck.

Lion hunts were a popular subject for sarcophagi in the third century CE. Considered by some scholars to belong to the biographical sarcophagi, it is perhaps better to consider them as symbolic representations adorned with portraits of the deceased. Unlike sarcophagi with explicit images of spouses and offices held, these seem to reflect symbolic rather than actual achievements. The Mattei

SCHOLARLY PERSPECTIVE
Spolia *and the reuse of art in the Roman world*

Spolia, Latin for spoils, refers to the reuse of art and architecture from previous periods in new works of art or monuments. This was a common practice in the entire period of Roman art, but seems to have accelerated in the third century CE. The meaning and motivation behind much of the reuse of art is debated and the fact of *spolia* itself causes a number of problems for art historians of the period particularly in attempting to trace the original date, form, and placement of the spoils. One issue scholars have continued to wrestle with is the meaning of the reused work in its new context. In some cases we conclude that the reuse is simply an expedient or way to make use of perfectly good existing material such as recutting a face or recarving a sculpture with new features. This is probably best seen in works of a disgraced emperor such as Domitian who was condemned by the Senate following his assassination. His facial features were recut to those of his successor, Nerva, on a number of monuments such as the Cancelleria reliefs (Figure 7.26) and the bronze equestrian statue from Misenum (Figure 7.19). These are thought to be expedient or pragmatic uses as the resulting works, in this case, associating Nerva with the long-dead Vespasian and Titus, make no sense historically or politically. This is certainly an association which Nerva made no use of in his other public arts.

Other forms of reuse are certainly symbolic. This tradition in Roman art has been noted in the display of captured armor and other material taken in war. But the reuse of Roman material by other Romans seems to carry meaning different than conquest. It can be an attempt to create a comparison between two Roman emperors or make some other putative connection. The Arcus Novus of the Tetrarchs mentioned earlier reused large-scale reliefs from an earlier monument in Rome to create a Tetrarchic display commemorating their Decennial. If this was a deliberate attempt to connect the Tetrarchs with previous emperors, the meaning is lost as we can no longer identify the patrons of the original monument. Suppositions range from Claudius to the Antonines, so clearly that did not get transmitted to us. And it may not have mattered to the contemporary Romans. We do not know. The same problem on a different scale occurs with the Acilia sarcophagus. Some scholars attribute the dramatic stylistic difference between the faces to reuse, arguing that the sarcophagus was made earlier and the one head was later recut, in *c.* 238 CE or, as some scholars conclude, 270 CE, resulting in a work with potentially a generation of difference between its phases of creation and use. It may represent a case of recutting and therefore *spolia* from Roman to Roman within the third century CE.

That brings us to the issue of determining the original date, form, and placement of the *spolia*. This is a constant and sometimes frustrating guessing game. The Cancelleria reliefs provide a case study in this since they might have originally been an altar surround, a balustrade, a boundary around a sacred object or space – any one of a number of possibilities. The Hadrianic hunting medallions are similarly difficult to pin down and demonstrate the use and problems of *spolia* from the biggest set of reused sculptures: the Arch of Constantine. Constantine reused a tremendous number of relief and free-standing sculptures on his arch, taken from monuments of three previous emperors, recutting the imperial portraits with his own features. The result is that the relief panels and figures, notably the Great Trajanic Frieze, cannot be restored. While we can recognize the frieze as Trajanic, where it came from, its full original meaning, and its date are all lost to us. That certainly doesn't stop scholarly speculation on these issues. But they may never be resolved. Finally, the Arch of Constantine shows the second type of reuse of *spolia*, the symbolic or ideological. The selection of art from the monuments of only three of the Five Good Emperors seems deliberate and a superb example of the reuse of *spolia* to create associations between the original and the secondary patrons.

D. Kinney, "Spolia. Damnatio and Renovatio Memoriae." *Memoirs of the American Academy in Rome* 42, 117–148 (1997).

Lion Hunt sarcophagus shows the deceased centrally placed on a rearing horse about to throw a spear at a roaring lion. His achievement is consciously portrayed as heroic as the distraught Romans in the background react to the possibility that the lion might kill the Roman on the ground under the horse's hooves. The deceased, with his close-cropped hair and stubbly beard, conforms to contemporary portrayals and differs from the tousle-haired men on the hunt with him. The notion

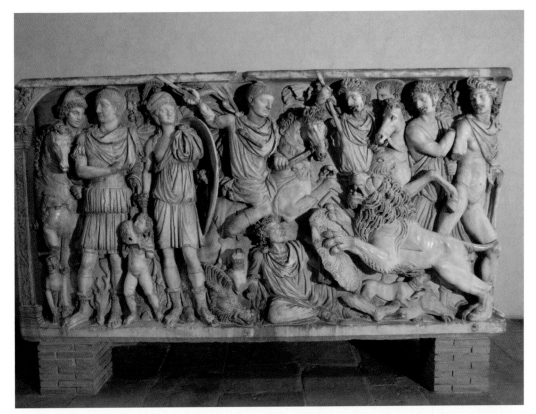

11.18 Mattei Lion Hunt sarcophagus, *c.* 250 CE, Rome. Musei Capitolini, Rome. L 7 ft 4 in (2.2 m) H 4 ft 4in (1.3 m), marble. Source: Collection du Musée Historique Saint-Rémi de Reims, 978.20171. Photo: Valérie Chopin.

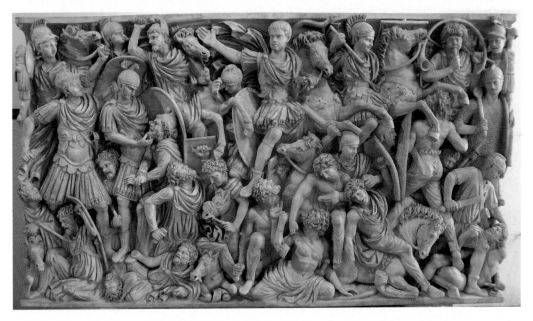

11.19 Ludovisi sarcophagus, *c.* 260 CE, Rome. The sarcophagus is in the Museo Nazionale Romano Palazzo Massimo, Rome and the lid (not illustrated) in the Römisch-Germanisches Zentralmuseum, Mainz. L 8 ft 11 ¼ in (2.73 m) H 5 ft (1.53 m) W 4 ft 5 ¾ in (1.37 m), marble. Photo courtesy Steven L. Tuck.

that this image represents the redefinition of *virtus* in the context of hunting rather than just battle is reinforced by the figures that fill the left side of the panel. Here the deceased is departing for the hunt with his horse and attendant beside him. The standing figure of *Virtus* herself leads him and serves to separate the two scenes and images of the man. At his feet is a small-scale captive barbarian, further blurring the line between battle and hunting.

The Ludovisi sarcophagus was discovered in 1621 just outside the gates of Rome. The large side of the sarcophagus presents a single panel scene of battle, a sarcophagus type first developed under Marcus Aurelius. In fact, it bears a number of strong similarities to the Portonaccio sarcophagus

(Figure 9.25) and to the Column of Marcus Aurelius, both created almost one hundred years earlier. The entire field is a single register showing a battle between Romans and barbarians. The bearded, shaggy-haired barbarians are clearly losing to the heavily armed and armored Romans. With the exception of the main figure in the upper central register, the battle is organized into small figure groups who fight, surrender, or are injured or captured. The barbarians display a range of facial expressions reflecting the emotions of their loss, injuries, and capture, consistent with the heightened emotional imagery of the third-century CE sarcophagi.

The main figure, however, differs dramatically from the other combatants and from his antecedent on the Portonaccio sarcophagus. He is disengaged from the battle and literally above most of it. He is portrayed on horseback, frontally, with no helmet or weapons and his right hand spread in a gesture that seems to denote personal triumph. Scholars debate the precise identity of the figure but all agree on two things. First, it is a portrait. Second, that the X incised on his forehead is probably a mark of his personal belief in a cult of personal salvation, indicating this is a victory over death and the problems of this world, which the rather generic barbarians around and below him might represent.

The three scenes on the lid are also statements of achievement and values, but more precisely biographical than the large scene on the sarcophagus, although some scholars see biography in the attributes of the barbarians, arguing that they represent German and Persian campaigns. The lid, bisected into two major scenes by the inscription plaque in the center, shows a portrait of a woman with a scroll, probably his wife, on the right. On the left is the deceased himself seated in a curule chair surrounded by soldiers and accepting barbarian captives including children in a standard scene of *clementia*, the Roman quality of mercy. Elements of this motif are found in the official art of Augustus and a number of second-century CE emperors and indicate his status as a Roman commander, possibly a member of one of the third-century CE imperial families. Beneath the inscription panel is another standard scene of captive barbarians symmetrically flanking a trophy of captured arms. This is another element of battle sarcophagi and official relief art of the second century CE. Altogether the sarcophagus and lid show the transmission of values and artistic motifs from the second century CE, biographical details of the life of the deceased and indications of personal belief in triumphant life after death.

ART AND LITERATURE
The Good Shepherd in Early Christian sculpture and literature

The traditions in Roman pagan art of illustrating fertility, abundance, and metaphorical images of deities all served to form the iconography of early Christian art as well. The imagery of Dionysus was particularly adaptable to Christian uses given the common themes of fields, wine, and harvest. In both Christianity and Dionysiac worship we encounter life after death explored metaphorically with fallow fields and vineyards. Partially from the needs of Christians to disguise their faith and partially from the traditions of metaphorical portrayals in art, the major images of Jesus were bucolic ones of the Good Shepherd, often surrounded by vines or harvest images, and derived from the Gospel of John 10:11 in which Jesus states "I am the Good Shepherd." The concept is based on Psalm 23 in which David says, "The Lord is my shepherd."

One of the earliest of these Good Shepherd images is found in the Catacombs of St. Callixtus in a space where funerary or memorial meals were eaten on the anniversary of a loved one's death. Here the Good Shepherd stands in a Classicizing contrapposto with a lamb across his shoulders, a pose seen as far back as Greek Archaic sculpture of the sixth century BCE. Here, rather than classical nudity, the figure is dressed in the tunic and leggings of a rural agricultural worker.

The idealized, youthful, clean-shaven Good Shepherd figure is found in a number of media during the third century CE including a half-lifesize marble statuette. The high quality of the marble and carving provide testimony of the spread

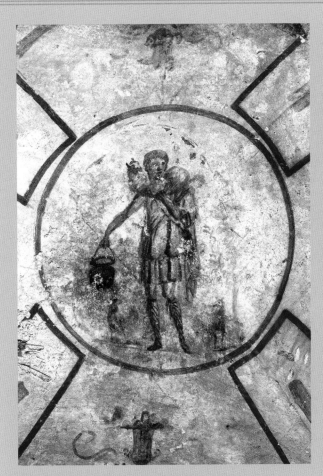

11.20　Good Shepherd ceiling painting, 3rd cent. CE, Catacombs of S. Callisto, Rome. Source: © 2014. Photo Scala, Florence.

of Christianity to the upper classes in Roman society. His dress, stance, and attributes match the wall painting. The face and hairstyle reflect the Seasons on the Seasons sarcophagus (Figure 10.18), placing him in the third-century CE sculptural tradition.

The youthful, idealized Good Shepherd group with lamb and flanking sheep and trees is the central element of a balanced, symmetrical relief panel on a sarcophagus found at Rome. To the left of the Good Shepherd group is a group of three men, two standing who flank a third who is larger in scale and seated, reading from a scroll. The type derives from a seated bearded philosopher, a motif emulated by elite Romans on second- and early third-century CE pagan sarcophagi. The flanking men

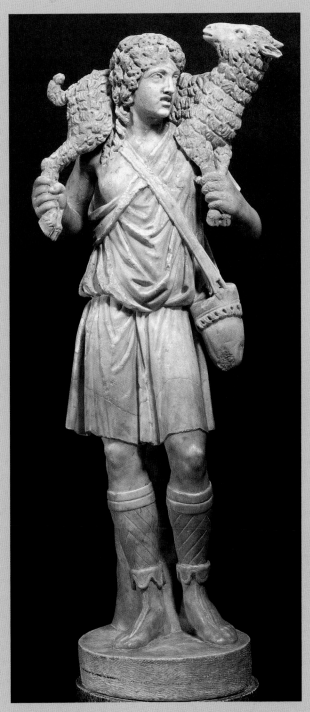

11.21　Good Shepherd statue, 3rd cent. CE, from Catacomb of Domitilla, Rome. Musei Vaticani, Rome. Marble, H 39 in (99 cm). Source: © 2014. Photo Scala, Florence.

turn to the seated one in apparent attention to what he reads from the scroll. These are balanced on the right by a group of three women. Again, two stand flanking a larger-scale seated figure. She, like her male counterpart, holds a scroll,

(Continued)

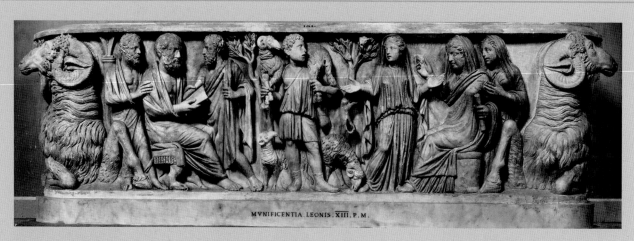

11.22   Sarcophagus of the Good Shepherd, 260–270 CE, from Via Salaria, Rome. Museo Nazionale Romano Palazzo Massimo, Rome. Source: Alinari Archives, Florence.

indicating love of wisdom, here Christian wisdom. The standing woman between her and the Good Shepherd turns to him with her arms outstretched, palms up in the Orans pose of prayer. The motif of paired male and female figures is found on biographical sarcophagi of married couples. In those earlier pagan versions the love of learning or literacy as a cultural marker is common. Here, the insertion of the Good Shepherd group as the central focus changes the meaning from love of philosophy or pagan poetry to one of love of Christian faith. The apparent eye contact between the Good Shepherd and the women on the right demonstrates their acceptance of his lessons and the redirection of Roman values from philosophy to Christian texts.

IMPERIAL ARCHITECTURE

The chaos and crises of the third century CE did not allow for much large-scale construction by emperors other than the Aurelian walls around Rome. The emperors by and large did not survive long enough to initiate, let alone complete, great building projects, nor did they control the resources necessary to bring together the people and materials to finish the lavishly decorated spaces that their predecessors built. Perhaps no better tangible evidence of the achievement of Diocletian survives than his baths in Rome, the first imperial bathing complex in the city since the Baths of Caracalla in 212 CE, and the largest ever constructed.

Baths of Diocletian

The Baths of Diocletian, built between 298 and 306 CE, like earlier imperial baths consisted of a large central bathing block with symmetrically organized rooms all within an immense walled enclosure that included formal gardens and exercise grounds. The bathing block measures 771 x 492 ft (235 x 150 m) and the entire complex 1168 x 1037 ft (356 x 316 m). According to one ancient author the baths could hold up to three thousand bathers, almost double the number that could use the Baths of Caracalla at one time.

The construction was all brick-faced concrete with a variety of roofing systems including domes, half domes, and barrel and groin vaults. The dome covering the *tepidarium*, for example, is a smaller

tepidarium
the warm water room in a Roman bath complex, usually the largest and most central room of the bathing suite.

(a)

(b)

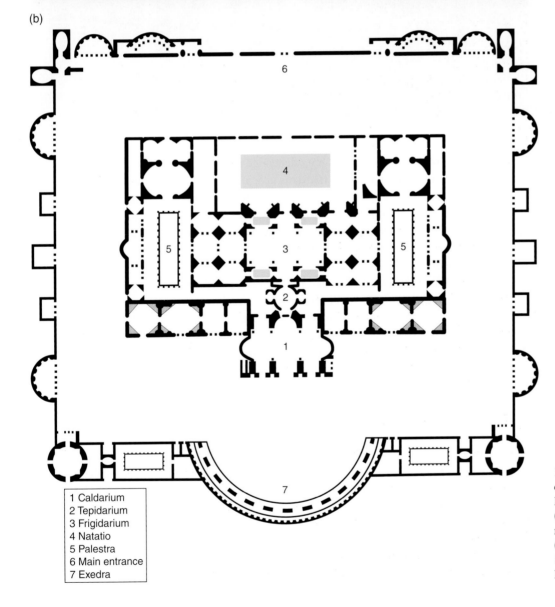

1	Caldarium
2	Tepidarium
3	Frigidarium
4	Natatio
5	Palestra
6	Main entrance
7	Exedra

11.23a and 11.23b Baths of Diocletian, 305 CE, Rome, overall plan. Source: (a) André Caron www. maquettes-historiques.net. (b) Lanciani, R., *Forma Urbis Romae*, 1893–1901. Plate X.

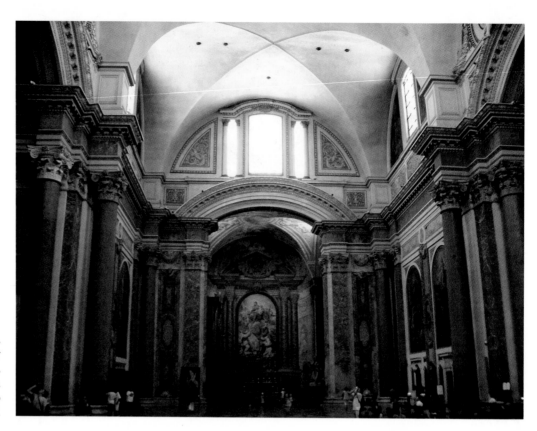

11.24 Baths of Diocletian, 305 CE, Rome, interior view of S. Maria degli Angeli, brick-faced concrete with marble veneer. Photo courtesy Steven L. Tuck.

frigidarium
the cold water room in a Roman bath complex, generally found in the core of the building away from the furnace or the sun.

version of the roof of the Pantheon, possibly a deliberate reference to Hadrian. In fact, the range of roofing systems finds its best parallel at Hadrian's villa at Tivoli. The scale was immense, with the central cruciform *frigidarium* measuring 216 ½ x 157 ½ ft (66 x 48 m) with a roofing system of three groin vaults, which rise 98 ft (30 m) from the floor. The interior walls up to the top of the walls at the base of the vaults were lined with polychrome marble veneers and free-standing granite columns on projecting brackets. Large windows with insulating glass filled the areas just below the roofing allowing raking light to penetrate the complex.

Enough of the main block survives today, notably repurposed by Michelangelo as the church of Santa Maria degli Angeli, that we can still experience the design, interior color, and the space created for the baths. The effect for Romans following the uncertainty of the third century CE was likely to have been reassuring. Those who experienced these baths would be faced with the lesson that the Tetrarchic system worked and that their government directly benefited these bathers as well as the large number of Romans employed in the construction of the complex.

Architecture and mosaics: Villa at Piazza Armerina, Sicily

The largest Tetrarchic building complex is not actually in the city of Rome or any of the Tetrarchic capitals. It is a large, sprawling villa complex in central Sicily near the town of Piazza Armerina, which gives its name to the villa. Although generally referred to as a villa, a rural residence, it can be considered a palace with a tremendous formal, lavishly decorated audience hall as the central element in the major building block. In fact the excavators concluded that it is the residence to which Maximian retired in 305 CE when he and Diocletian abdicated power in favor of their Caesars, a conclusion many scholars have cast doubts on in recent years.

The complex has features that are reminiscent of Hadrian's villa at Tivoli. It was constructed in a sprawling set of suites of rooms that are not orthogonally arranged. The four major groups of rooms and buildings are also not symmetrical nor is strict axiality enforced except in the immediate vicinity

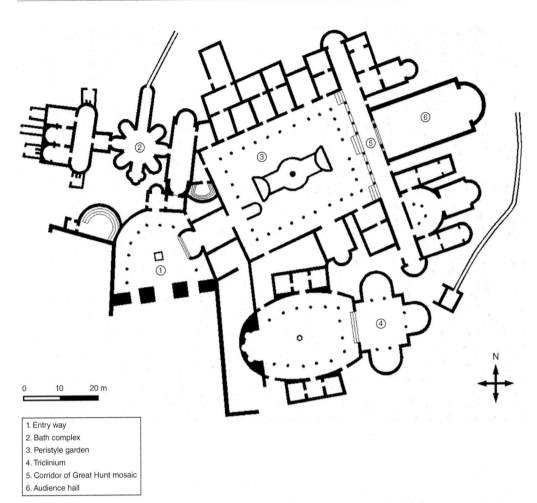

11.25 Villa at Piazza Armerina, Sicily, 305 CE. Experiencing Rome: A Visual Exploration of Antiquity's Greatest Empire, © 2008 The Teaching Company. Reproduced with permission of The Teaching Company, www.thegreatcourses.com.

0 10 20 m

1. Entry way
2. Bath complex
3. Peristyle garden
4. Triclinium
5. Corridor of Great Hunt mosaic
6. Audience hall

of the audience hall. Even the peristyle courtyard that precedes the audience hall is not a rectangle, as was standard, but a parallelogram with an off-axis entrance. The more organic organization suggests that, like Hadrian's villa, it was probably built over a period of time, perhaps during the last years of Maximian's rule. A number of the rooms feature unusual shapes similar to those found at Hadrian's villa, including rooms with multiple rounded lobes, semi-circular and central plan spaces as well as a formal entry court and a small bath complex. The scale is diminished from that seen earlier, but the effect is similar and suggests imitation of or reference to the larger villa. The decoration of the villa also carries allusions to earlier imperial residences. Great amounts of marble facing are found, including a very large opus sectile floor that covers the audience hall. In addition marble sculptures were placed in niches throughout the rooms, including an Apollo and Hercules in especially significant locations.

The Piazza Armerina villa is particularly significant as it preserves the largest set of floor mosaics from any building in the entire ancient world. It contains almost 37,675 square feet (3,500 square meters) of figurative floor mosaics of the very highest quality. The mosaics are closely related in style and subject to those from the period in nearby Roman Africa; especially notable are the genre and spectacle subjects, which are rarely found in other regions. Their appearance here is likely due to proximity and the commissioning of a large number of skilled workshops to undertake the tremendous amount of work necessary to create mosaic floors for the entire villa.

A wide range of subjects is found throughout the complex, falling into three broad categories: genre scenes (bathing, exercising, greeting guests, hunting, fishing), spectacular entertainments (chariot racing), and mythological scenes (Hercules, cupids, Odysseus, various deities, personifications of the Four Seasons). Although the subjects are broad, they are united by the overall theme of imperial power. The genre scenes, such as chariot racing, bathing, and greeting guests, provide visual

TOOLS & TECHNIQUES
Artistic training in the Roman world

We often refer to artistic workshops when discussing ancient art. There was no formal schooling for artists, instead they were all trained in an apprentice system organized around small groups called workshops. The best evidence for these is in the creation of mosaics and wall paintings. The workshops consisted of teams of 5–7 artists who worked together. Many of the workshops were family based and represented multi-generational organizations. In addition to family related by blood, slaves and former slaves were integrated into these workshops as well and were trained alongside free artists. The least experienced artists, probably the youngest, worked on tasks requiring the least skill while they practiced. Their training involved copying works by the head of the workshop or designs taken from pattern books. Innovation seems to have been largely discouraged and there was no concept of art for art's sake. As artists gained experience they would be given more creative tasks and more autonomy. Since most works of wall painting and mosaics were created on site, the majority of workshops were only active in a small area, leading to great regional differences in style and subject in many arts across the Roman world.

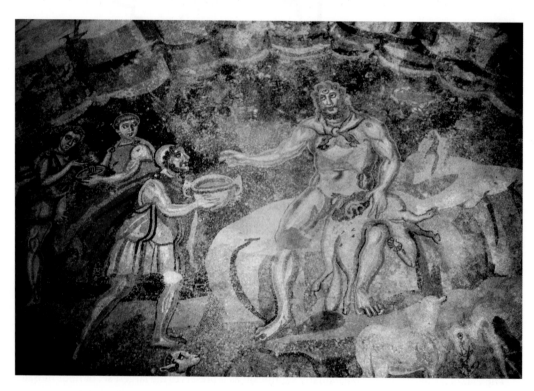

11.26   Odyssey mosaic, Villa at Piazza Armerina, Sicily, 305 CE. 25 ft (7.6 m) x 17 ft 1 in (5.22 m). Photo courtesy Steven L. Tuck.

displays of imperial beneficence and generosity. Even the mythological scenes may contain elements of ideological communication. The Hercules statue and mosaics may have been selected to reinforce Maximian's identity as the new Hercules, which is found in his art and particularly on his coinage. A less explicit but still important imperial scene is found on the floor near the audience hall.

The room immediately to the left of the audience hall contains a floor mosaic of a scene from book 9 of Homer's *Odyssey*. We the viewers are looking through the mouth of the cave of Polyphemus, the Cyclops. He is seated on a rock in the center right of the scene wearing only an animal skin and holding a disemboweled ram on his lap. With his right hand he reaches out for a cup of wine being offered by Odysseus. Two of his men are behind him in the background filling a second cup out of a

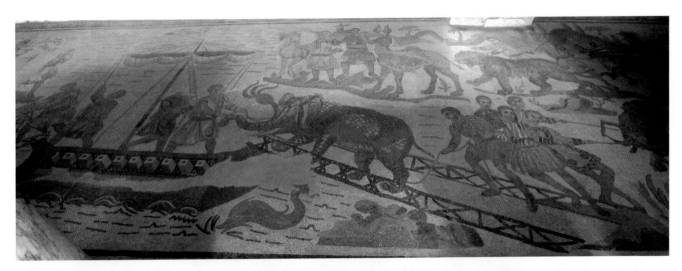

11.27   Animal capture scene, Great Hunt mosaic, Villa at Piazza Armerina, Sicily, 305 CE. Photo courtesy Steven L. Tuck.

wine skin. Five sheep fill the foreground of the scene. In a few key ways the portrayal of the event differs from Homer's account. The Cyclops is eating a ram and not a human and he, perhaps as a result of confusion on the part of the mosaicist, has three eyes rather than the typical one. This subject's connection to imperial domestic display dates back three hundred years to the villa of Tiberius, Rome's second emperor, at Sperlonga. At that villa the episode was displayed in sculpture in an actual cave, creating an image that reflected the space in which it was found. Perhaps a closer parallel to this scene is the Julio-Claudian villa at Punta Epitaffio where the sculpture group in the niche of the dining room was exactly this scene. Preserved from that group are an almost identical Odysseus holding out the wine cup and his companion with the wine skin.

The largest of the mosaics at Piazza Armerina, in fact the longest mosaic found from the ancient world, decorates the corridor outside the audience hall. At 200 Roman feet (*c.* 197 ft or 60 m) in length the Great Hunt mosaic seems designed for this ambulatory space. As a guest or a visitor awaiting an audience walked back and forth he or she would be faced with scenes of imperial power and beneficence as episodes of collecting animals for a great set of public games are depicted. The entire mosaic is organized geographically. The exedrae at either end have lunette-shaped mosaic scenes filled with personifications. The left lunette is the province of Mauretania and the right is India, each surrounded by characteristic animals. The animals being collected on the left side of the floor are all African while those on the right are Asian. In each half of the mosaic the animals and their cages are placed on board ships in different harbors. In the center they are offloaded, probably at the port of Ostia near Rome. Unlike the typical animal hunt scenes, such as on sarcophagi of the period, here the capture and transport of live animals by members of the Roman army shows the goal of collecting animals for a major set of games, probably at Rome. The geographical composition that underlies the mosaic has roots going back to the art of Augustus.

The use of the army makes it clear that this represents an aspect of imperial government at work. That notion is more explicit in the figure group of a nobleman, protected by two soldiers, who oversees the capture of the animals. The bearded nobleman has a lined forehead and large eyes and wears an elaborately embroidered cloak and a hat. His facial hair, features, and hat are identical to those of the Tetrarchs in the porphyry group sculpture. One of the soldiers has an ivy leaf on his shoulder badge, indicating that he belongs to the Legio Herculea of Maximian. Soldiers with shields protecting the emperor are common in Tetrarchic art and this is possibly Maximian personally overseeing the collection of animals. Altogether the mosaic represents a remarkable display of imperial power and generosity probably for an audience anticipating an encounter with the emperor himself immediately after viewing this.

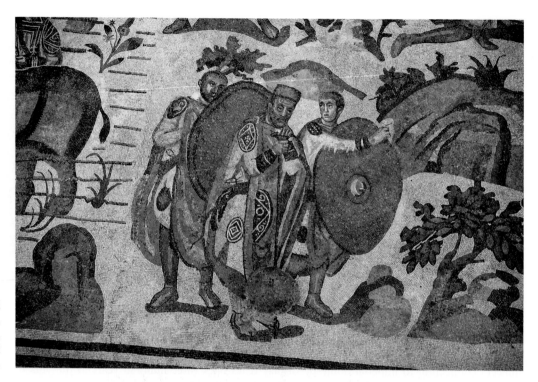

11.28   Detail of Command Group, Great Hunt mosaic, Villa at Piazza Armerina, Sicily, 305 CE. © Luigi Nifosi/Shutterstock.

Mosaics from the city of Antioch-on-the-Orontes in the Roman east

The region of the Roman east, notably Greece, Asia Minor, Egypt, and the Near East, had its own workshops of mosaic production. Like the examples from Roman Africa these were largely figural works in rich polychromy. Unlike them, the subjects were almost exclusively mythological, probably owing to the long Greek tradition in the area. They also have many more captions than African or Italian mosaics and these are almost always in Greek as well, indicating the primary language of the inhabitants of the area. Probably the finest examples and certainly the largest numbers of these come from the city of Antioch and its suburbs. Antioch-on-the-Orontes, modern Antakya in Turkey, was the most important city in the eastern part of the Roman Empire. Its position close to the troubled areas of Armenia and Parthia also increased its importance in the third century CE. It was also one of the most important centers of Christianity in this period. The mosaics that were found and excavated here are from a variety of building types including houses, villas, baths, and mausolea. They reveal the wealth and Greek culture of the community.

One of the best understood of the houses with extensive mosaics is the House of the Atrium at Daphne, a suburb of Antioch-on-the-Orontes. The house was redecorated at some point after the massive earthquake of 115 CE. Its *triclinium*, a formal dining room designed for three dining couches, has a pavement floor with geometric designs under the couches and four figural panels in the open floor. Three of these panels face the door into the room so guests see them as they enter.

The major panel, filling the floor for the width of the doorway, illustrates a drinking contest between Hercules and Dionysus. Two smaller panels of Dionysiac dancers flank it. The drinking contest mosaic has five figures: a reclining, apparently triumphant Dionysus and, to his left, the tanned kneeling Hercules still drinking. A flautist, a cupid, and a satyr join them. The foreground shows the discarded cups and the wine krater for serving wine in the contest. As the god of wine, Dionysus was, naturally, unbeatable and the mosaic should be understood as a mythologically themed cautionary tale against drunkenness of the type found repeatedly in Roman dining spaces. The message of moderation would be conveyed to every guest entering the *triclinium*.

TOOLS & TECHNIQUES

Creating mosaics

The vast majority of mosaics were laid out on site, requiring tremendous preparation of materials and the bedding to ensure that they did not crack and that once started the work could continue without delay. A foundation of rubble, above that *c.* 9 inches (22.8 cm) of mortar, followed by a layer of mortar and aggregate about 6 inches (15.2 cm) thick all made the mosaic bed. The mosaic itself was laid in a fresh layer of fine mortar that was laid as the work progressed. The mosaic itself was created by arranging anywhere from thousands to millions of small cubes called tesserae into the patterns that created pictures. Tesserae were generally natural materials, almost always limestone, marbles, or granite, sometimes terracotta, and rarely colored glass or clear glass backed with a layer of gold. The stone tesserae were made by sawing the raw material into sticks and breaking them to the right size with a hammer and chisel. To lay the mosaic a pattern, very often from a pattern book, was traced on the bedding and a thin layer of fresh mortar troweled in and the tesserae placed by hand. Once the mortar was dry the mosaic was ground smooth and polished.

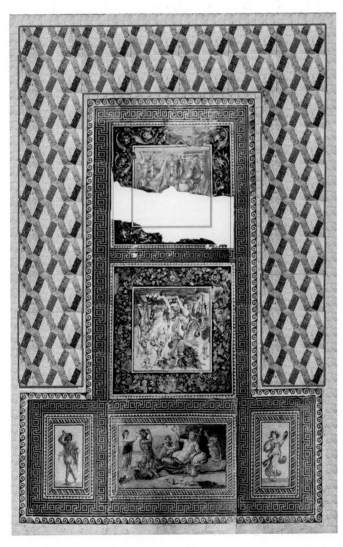

11.29 Overall view of dining room floor, 3rd cent. CE, in House of the Atrium, Daphne, outside Antioch-on-the-Orontes. 23 ½ ft x 15 ¾ ft (7.2 m x 4.8 m). Source: Worcester Art Museum, Worcester, Massachusetts. Image © Worcester Art Museum.

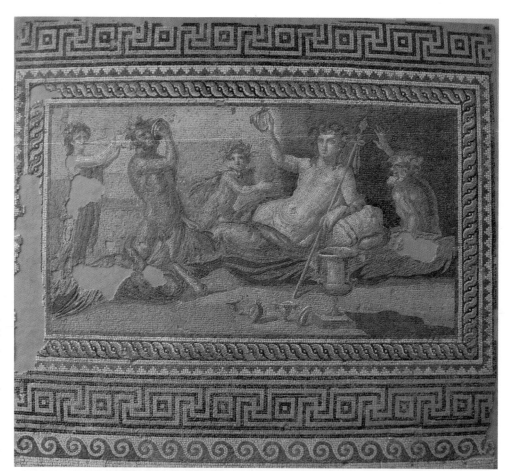

11.30 Hercules and Dionysus drinking contest mosaic, 3rd cent. CE, from House of the Atrium, Daphne, outside Antioch-on-the-Orontes. Worcester Art Museum, Worcester, Massachusetts. 72 ¼ × 73 ⅜ in (183.5 x 186.4 cm). Daderot/Wikimedia Commons.

11.31 Judgment of Paris mosaic, 3rd cent. CE, from House of the Atrium, Daphne, outside Antioch-on-the-Orontes. Musée du Louvre, Paris. 73 in (1.86 m) sq. Marie-Lan Nguyen/ Wikimedia Commons.

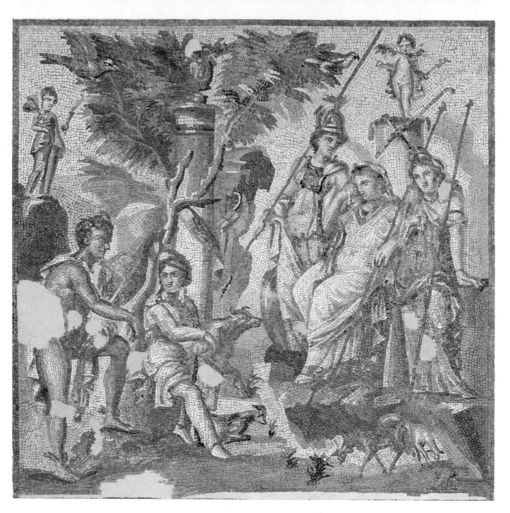

MORE ON MYTH
The Judgment of Paris

The story, one of the most popular of the ancient world, begins with the marriage feast of Peleus and Thetis to which Eris, the goddess of discord, was not invited. She threw one of the Golden Apples of the Hesperides inscribed "for the fairest" into the gathering. Three goddesses, Hera, Aphrodite, and Athena, all claimed the prize. They asked Zeus to judge between them. Too wise to judge a beauty contest between three members of his family, he suggested the Trojan prince, Paris, as judge since he had recently judged a contest involving the god Ares. Each goddess offered him a bribe. Athena, wisdom and skill in war, Hera, kingship over Europe and Asia, and Aphrodite, the most beautiful woman in the world. Paris awarded the prize to Aphrodite and then traveled to Greece to abduct or abscond with Helen, the wife of King Menelaus of Sparta. Helen and Paris fled back to Troy and the Greeks launched a great expedition, led by Agamemnon, brother of Menelaus, to retrieve Helen. In this they were aided by the spurned goddesses Hera and Athena. This, according to many ancient sources, was the origin of the Trojan War.

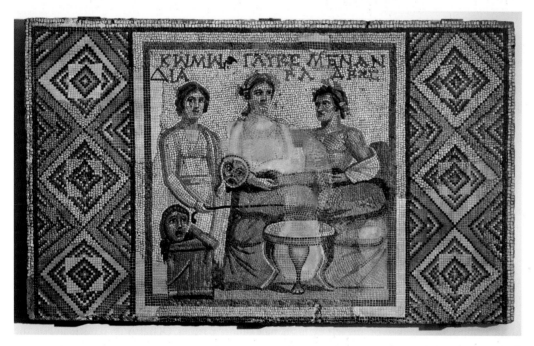

11.32 Menander, Glykera, and Comedy mosaic, 250–275 CE, House of Menander, Daphne, outside Antioch-on-the-Orontes. Princeton University Art Museum. 53 ⅛ x 88 ¾ in (134.9 x 225.4 cm). Source: Photo Bruce M. White. © 2013. Princeton University Art Museum/Art Resource NY/Scala, Florence.

The central panel facing the dining couches is a very detailed image of the Judgment of Paris. The scene is composed in a landscape that owes its origins to Hellenistic painting. The central background element of a column and tree are familiar from sacro-idyllic landscape paintings of the Augustan period from the walls of Pompeii. The figures fill the panel, with the goddesses in the upper right and Paris and Hermes in the lower left creating a sense of depth in the work and space in and around the figures. Behind them are statuettes of Cupid and Psyche reinforcing the theme of love and foreshadowing the eventual victory of Aphrodite. The complex depiction filled with intricate details would make a focal point for viewing and would facilitate discussion during a dinner. Here a wide Dionysiac border, again appropriate to a dining space, frames the figural panel.

Another dining room floor mosaic shows Menander, Glykera, and Comedy. In this panel the Greek playwright Menander (342–291 BCE) reclines on a dining couch with his mistress, Glykera. At the left stands a female figure labeled ΚΩΜΩΔΙΑ (Comedy), referring to Menander's plays. This personification holds theater props: a mask and a staff with a curved handle typically held by the

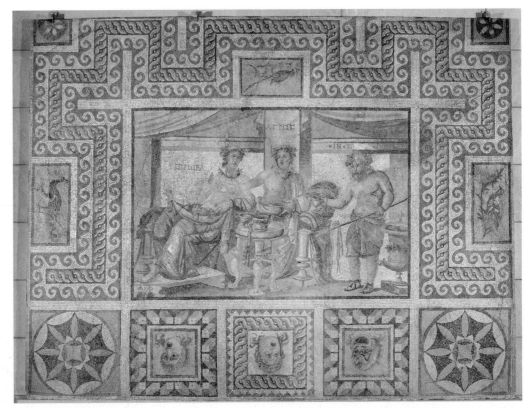

11.33 Mosaic of Opora, Agros, and Oinos, 3rd cent. CE, from the House of the Boat of Psyches, Daphne, Antioch-on-the-Orontes. Baltimore Museum of Art. 94 ½ in x 124 ½ in (dimensions include decorative border). Source: The Baltimore Museum of Art, Antioch Subscription Fund, BMA 1937.127. Photography by: Mitro Hood.

narrator on stage. Another mask rests upon the *scrinium* or case for books. Menander's plays certainly would have been performed in the theaters of Antioch-on-the-Orontes, and may have been performed here during banquets, selected for their subjects that often reflect drinking and dining or might provide a topic for learned conversation. Note that each of the figures is captioned above with a name in Greek, indicating the language of the audience as well as the expectation that the subject might not be immediately identifiable.

The sophisticated messages of these floor mosaics, their correspondence to the activities in the rooms where they are found, and the detail reminiscent of Greek painting are demonstrated by a mosaic in the House of the Boat of Psyches.

This scene depicts two figures reclining at dinner. The male, ΑΓΡΟΣ (fields), reclines in the center of the composition flanked on the left by his female dinner partner, ΟΠΩΡΑ (Harvest), and on the right by the servant ΟΙΝΟΣ (wine). The space is richly decorated and furnished with a dining couch, expensive table, and wine cups that would be recognizable to the viewers from their own surroundings. The slightly triangular composition with the male figure central, slightly higher, and emphasized by the pier behind him derives from Greek art traditions hundreds of years old. The personification of Wine is appropriately dressed as a Silenos, a follower of Dionysus, giving the scene an additional layer of meaning beyond dining and consideration of the fertility of the region. It creates a religious undertone for the mosaic crediting the wealth of the region to Dionysus as god of wine.

CONCLUSION

The chaos of the third century CE that led to twenty-five emperors in fifty years did not leave much time or resources to dedicate to official or state art or architecture. The few portraits that we have from the middle of the century demonstrate continuity in sculptural style and subject from the Severan

A VIEW FROM THE PROVINCES
The house church at Dura-Europos

The third century provides the earliest Christian paintings from an identifiable church. This house church was discovered at the city of Dura-Europos, an important and wealthy city on the edge of the Syrian desert and between the Roman and Persian empires. The city was invaded by the Romans in 165 CE in the Parthian War of Marcus Aurelius and destroyed in 256 CE during another Roman war, this time against the Sassanian Persians. The wall paintings in the house church date to 235 CE, almost contemporary with the last phase of a synagogue also found at Dura-Europos, which is decorated with tempera wall paintings that date to 244 CE. The church was renovated from a house into a Christian religious complex, which included a large assembly room, perhaps a classroom, and a baptistery, all organized around a central courtyard.

The wall paintings that decorated the baptistery are acknowledged as the earliest Christian paintings that survive from antiquity and, although fragmentary, these frescoes preserve some identifiable scenes. Notably they include the Good Shepherd, demonstrating the spread of this motif across the Roman world, as well as other scenes that directly illustrate passages from the Gospels and episodes from the life of Jesus. These include the Good Samaritan (Luke 10:25–37), Jesus healing a paralytic (Mark 2:1–12), Jesus and Peter walking on water (Matthew 14:22–33), and the three Marys visiting the tomb of Jesus (Mark 16:1).

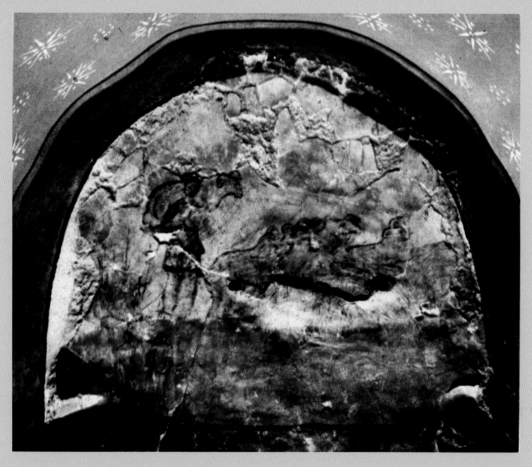

11.34   House church, Dura-Europos, wall painting, detail of the Good Shepherd with Adam and Eve, 235 CE. Yale University Art Gallery. Marsyas/Wikimedia Commons.

(Continued)

The Good Shepherd image shows the standard figure with a lamb over his shoulders. In the foreground, however, are small-scale images of Adam and Eve. They serve two visual purposes. First, they serve as links to the genealogy of Jesus traced back to Adam as listed in the Gospel of Luke (3:23–38). More importantly, perhaps, this combination of large-scale Good Shepherd and small-scale Adam reflects Paul's first letter to the Corinthians (15:22) in which he directly contrasts the two, "For as in Adam all die, so also in Christ all will be made alive." The text would be familiar to many if not most Christians and reinforces the context of the painting in the baptistery, a space for those being initiated into the Christian faith. These earliest surviving images of Jesus are evidence of the power of early Christianity in this desert community. The context of the house church is also significant as it was found in proximity to a contemporary Jewish synagogue as well as a Mithraeum, a thriving shrine for the worship of the widespread cult of the god Mithras, suggesting that the Christians were not in hiding but integrated into the community.

dynasty. The lack of state or historical reliefs speaks loudly about the lack of power over the imperial resources controlled by the Antonine and Severan dynasties. In a period when the largest work of state-sponsored architecture is a set of walls to protect the capital from attack, we do not need to look far for tangible evidence of the state of the Roman government. Private art, however, continued to be created, as evidenced by the marble sarcophagi of the third century CE, the Antioch mosaics, and the rise of Christian art. The latter may in fact be a product of the uncertainty of the period leading to a rise in the interest in cults that promised the certainty of life after death to people living in the deep insecurity of the third century.

The art and architecture of the Tetrarchy reflects the restabilization that their administration brought to the Roman world. The generic imagery of their portraiture symbolizes the new order and its emphasis on the position of the emperor over the person. That emphasis is clear in the official reliefs of the Tetrarchy with their joint appearances and the increased isolation of the emperors from the remainder of the Roman world. The artistic style of the period shows a rise in the Italic component of Roman relief over the Classicizing as the more abstracted style is selected to create a bold image that can speak to the vast majority of viewers, increasing numbers of whom were probably not educated in the iconography or nuances of the Classicizing tradition. The mosaics from the palace at Piazza Armerina as well as those in the houses and tombs at Antioch represent the survival of regional schools of art across the Roman world. In the case of mosaics we see that despite the myriad problems of the third century, individuals continue to commission these expensive works of art in multiple provinces. The Tetrarchy did not last, but it established a system that allowed the Roman world to recover from the chaos of the third century CE and led to the principate of the last emperor to rule over the entire, unified Roman world, Constantine.

SUGGESTIONS FOR FURTHER READING

Lawrence Becker and Christine Kondoleon, eds., *The Arts of Antioch: Art Historical and Scientific Approaches to Roman Mosaics and a Catalogue of the Worcester Art Museum Antioch Collection* (Princeton University Press 2005). The most detailed and systematic study to date of the mosaics from the important site of Antioch. This book includes recent work on mosaic materials, artistic techniques, glassmaking technology, stone quarries, workshops, trade, and patronage.

Jaś Elsner and Janet Huskinson, eds., *Life, Death and Representation: Some New Work on Roman Sarcophagi* (De Gruyter 2011). While not restricted to the third century, this collection of essays on sarcophagi includes many contributions that explore themes, subjects, and styles of the third century as well as those with continuity from the second to the fourth centuries.

Robin Margaret Jensen, *Understanding Early Christian Art* (Routledge 2000). Explores the iconography of early Christian art and problems in interpreting this art at the start of the Christian era. Includes a chapter on the use of Classical symbols and popular motifs.

Dale Kinney, "Spolia. Damnatio and renovatio memoriae." *Memoirs of the American Academy in Rome* 42: 117–148 (1997). Explores this important concept in the art and architecture of this period with many examples from public and private arts of the third century.

Christine Kondoleon, ed., *Antioch: The Lost Ancient City* (Princeton University Press in association with the Worcester Art Museum 2000). This exhibition catalogue includes descriptions and analysis of the mosaics from Antioch as well as contextualizing essays on houses and cultural identity in this vital eastern city.

Kurt Weitzmann and Herbert L. Kessler, *The Frescoes of the Dura Synagogue and Christian Art* (Dumbarton Oaks Studies, 28, 1990). Provides a panel-by-panel analysis of the synagogue frescoes as well as thoughtful discussion of their relationship to the art in the contemporary and nearby church at Dura and their influence in the wider world of Christian art.

R.J.A. Wilson, *Piazza Armerina* (University of Texas Press 1983). An interesting, readable, but lightly illustrated guide to this villa including descriptions of the mosaics, the highlight of the building.

Susan Wood, *Roman Portrait Sculpture, 217–260 A.D.: the Transformation of an Artistic Tradition* (Brill 1986). This thorough work charts the rise and development of the abstracted style of third-century portraiture. It traces it from the portraiture of Caracalla through the classicizing images of the late Severans until it becomes the dominant art of the soldier-emperors of the period.

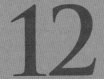

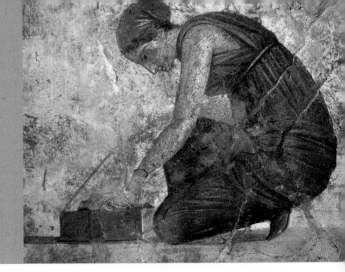

CONSTANTINE, 306–337 CE

Christian Empire and the Decline of the West

306 CE	Constantine declared emperor at York
310 CE	**Basilica at Trier built**
312 CE	Battle of the Milvian Bridge; **Arch of Constantine begun; Basilica Nova completed**
313 CE	Edict of Milan issued legalizing Christian worship
315 CE	**Colossal portrait of Constantine from the Basilica Nova**
324 CE	Final defeat of Licinius and unification of empire under the rule of Constantine
330 CE	**Porphyry sarcophagus of Constantina; Lullingstone mosaic;** founding of Constantinople
336–337 CE	**Bronze portrait of Constantine**
340 CE	**Low Ham Villa and mosaic**
359 CE	**Sarcophagus of Junius Bassus**
476 CE	Abdication of Romulus Augustulus, last emperor of the western empire
955–983 CE	Otto II, Holy Roman Emperor
1453 CE	Fall of Constantinople to Ottoman Empire
1806 CE	Arc de Triomphe commissioned in Paris
1865 CE	**Apotheosis of Washington fresco**

A History of Roman Art, First Edition. Steven L. Tuck.
© 2015 Steven L. Tuck. Published 2015 by John Wiley & Sons, Ltd.

U nder the emperor Constantine Roman art finally transforms into what we call today the Late Antique style. This development began at least in the middle of the second century as seen on the base of the Column of Antoninus Pius (Figure 9.12). The differences between that monument and the ones in this chapter may be noticeable, but certain elements are identifiable as foreshadowing the fourth century. I refer to these as the three Fs: art that is Flat, Frontal, and Formal. Sculptures are carved with shallow figures delineated with flat surfaces, channels, and grooves rather than rounded forms. The surviving art demonstrates an interest in controlling the perspective of the viewer, restricting the view to a frontal approach previously seen in Italic art of the early Roman Republic. Finally, art reasserts a formality with emphasis on axiality and symmetrical composition.

CONSTANTINE, THE FIRST CHRISTIAN EMPEROR

With the retirement of Diocletian and Maximian in 305 CE, the junior emperors in the Tetrarchy, Galerius and Constantius Chlorus, became the senior emperors. This pair continued the policies of their now retired predecessors but were not able to retire themselves. For once again, as in past dynasties, ambitious sons wished to succeed their fathers. Constantius supported his son, Constantine, while Maximian supported his son, Maxentius, as members of the Tetrarchy. The reintegration of dynastic succession into the Roman world destroyed the meritocracy of the Tetrarchy and led to civil war. It also ushered in the rule of the first Christian emperor, Constantine.

On the death of Constantius in 306 CE, his son, Constantine, was declared emperor by his troops. Marriage and shared titles held this new Tetrarchy together for a few years, but ambition for sole rule meant that civil war could only be postponed for so long. After years of conspiracies and intrigues the system collapsed with the death of Galerius in 311 CE. Constantine and Maxentius each proclaimed supreme power in the Roman west leading to an inevitable civil war in 312 CE. Constantine invaded Italy from the north, defeated Maxentius' armies and marched on Rome where Maxentius waited.

Rather than relying on the Aurelian walls to withstand a siege, Maxentius marched out to meet Constantine in battle. At the Milvian Bridge, north of Rome, the decisive battle was fought and

HISTORICAL CONTEXT
Constantine's conversion experience

One of the profound events in his life, Constantine's vision of the cross, is recorded by the historian and Christian bishop, Eusebius of Caesarea (263–339 CE), a contemporary and supporter of Constantine. It is often described as Constantine's conversion experience, but it might be better considered as the moment that he determined to support his official acts with Christian symbols. Eusebius wrote about the episode in both his *Life of Constantine* and *Ecclesiastical History*. He describes a critical occasion in 312 CE when Constantine was marching to meet Maxentius at the Battle of Milvian Bridge. He heard the words "In this, be victorious," a statement rendered in Latin as "*In hoc signo vinces*," and translated as "In this sign you will conquer." Looking at the sun the emperor saw a cross of light above it. The vision was reinforced by Christ appearing to Constantine in a dream. The sign is thought to have either been the cross of the crucifixion or a cross formed from the X and P, the Chi-Rho sign that made up the initial letters of Christ in Greek. Eusebius goes on to associate that moment with inspiring the *labarum*, the finial at the top of the pole that carried Constantine's battle standard, which incorporated the Chi-Rho sign.

Maxentius defeated and killed. In 313 CE Constantine met with and agreed to share power with Licinius, who ruled the eastern empire. This arrangement lasted until 324 CE when Constantine finally defeated Licinius, reunifying the Roman Empire under his sole rule. One of Constantine's great legacies was inaugurating a new capital for the empire in 330 CE at the site of the Greek city of Byzantium, which he renamed Constantinopolis (Constantinople, Istanbul as it is known today). With this act, the ruling power, which had been declining in Rome for years, was finally transferred away permanently. And a new center of power in the Roman world was founded in the eastern empire where it would last for another thousand years. After the fall of the western empire in 476 CE, the eastern or Byzantine Empire would continue until its final collapse in 1453 CE.

Portraiture

Like much about his rule, Constantine's portraiture is bold and differs dramatically from his immediate predecessors. Many of its major elements can be seen in two colossal images from Rome, one in marble and the other in bronze. The first and perhaps most important feature is the lack of a beard. Constantine is the first clean-shaved adult emperor since Trajan. This marks a dramatic contrast from the imperial portraits of the second and third centuries CE and is a deliberate reference back to Trajan or perhaps even to Augustus as a visual model. The image of Constantine as the new Trajan is striking and reflects a departure from the military imagery of the third century; it is found in his colossal portraiture as well as his public works, such as the reliefs on his arch in Rome.

The colossal marble portrait, which was originally displayed in the Basilica Nova in Rome and survives in fragments, was an **acrolithic** seated image of the emperor originally about 30 ft in height. Its features parallel those on his coinage after 313 CE including the very characteristic bowl haircut with bangs that curl towards the center of his forehead. The bowl cut and clean-shaven face are obviously similar to and probably directly based on Trajan's imperial portraits. The

acrolithic
a statue, usually large scale or even colossal in size, in which the body is constructed of a wooden framework covered with drapery and only the exposed limbs are carved stone.

12.1 Colossal portrait of Constantine the Great, *c.* 315 CE, from the Basilica Nova, Rome. Musei Capitolini, Rome. H 9 ft 9 ¾ in (2.97 m), marble. Photo courtesy Steven L. Tuck.

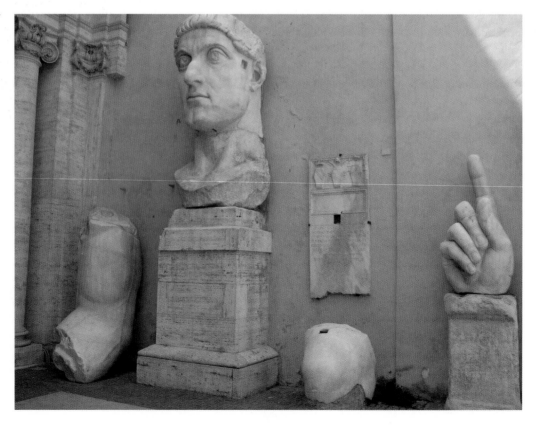

smooth face and forehead, closed mouth, and straight nose are all carved in simple planes in contrast to the creases, wrinkles, chisel marks, and curled lips prominent in third-century CE portraits. But they are all overwhelmed by the size and detail of his eyes. They are oversized and deeply cut to dramatically emphasize them as a feature. The result is an abstracted, almost geometric image, which encourages, almost requires, engagement with his eyes over any other feature. The simple planes of the face contrast with the naturalistic anatomical detail in the surviving fragments of arms and legs. Clearly the style of this new, bold, abstracted imagery is planned and not the result of any reduction in the ability of imperial sculptors to portray anatomical detail. The exact form of the statue and its attributes are not certain, but it was probably draped with bronze clothing and posed like the cult statue of Zeus at Olympia, one of the seven wonders of the ancient world. Seated on a throne in the west apse of the Basilica Nova, he held a staff or scepter in his right hand that, along with the colossal size, increased the grandeur and power of the image.

The colossal bronze portrait of Constantine has much in common with the marble one. It shares the bowl cut, but here with bangs that flip up in a continuous curl that frames the face. The facial features including the compact mouth and long hooked nose are also very similar. The major common feature is the emphasis on the eyes, here again oversized, very well defined, with the pupils and irises distinguished and comma-shaped brows that further draw attention to them. It however shows the gradual aging reflected in many of Constantine's later portraits including his coinage. It was probably produced near the end of his life, after 330 CE. Aging is seen subtly in a wrinkled forehead and lines framing the mouth and chin, again a feature found previously in Trajan's later public images. It is the largest surviving bronze head of any emperor and demonstrates Constantine's extensive public art program as well as his control of the resources to carry it out.

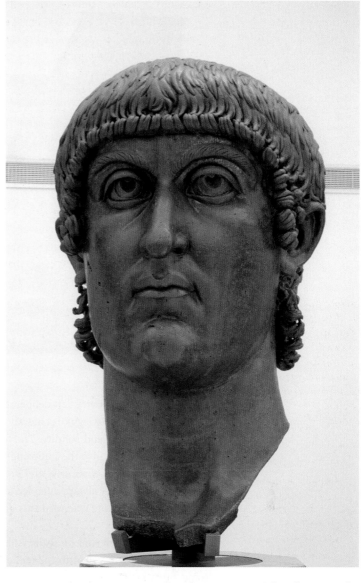

12.2 Colossal portrait of Constantine, *c.* 336 CE, Rome. Musei Capitolini, Rome. Bronze, H 5 ft 9 ½ in (1.77 m). Photo courtesy Steven L. Tuck.

Architecture at Trier: Building a provincial capital

Following his declaration as emperor in 306 CE Constantine took up residence at Augusta Treverorum, modern Trier in Germany. His residence here can be seen as a continuation of the third-century CE practice of emperors living and constructing capitals in the periphery of the empire rather than at Rome. His construction projects in the city demonstrate his attempts to turn it into an impressive imperial capital and foreshadow his later work on a greater scale at Constantinople. The importance of the city and its place near the frontier of the Roman world is confirmed by the remains of the four gates and walls that were designed to protect it, perhaps begun during the German wars of Marcus Aurelius. The Porta Nigra, the Black Gate, still survives as the largest and oldest surviving Roman city gate north of the Alps. It probably took its final form late in the Tetrarchic period.

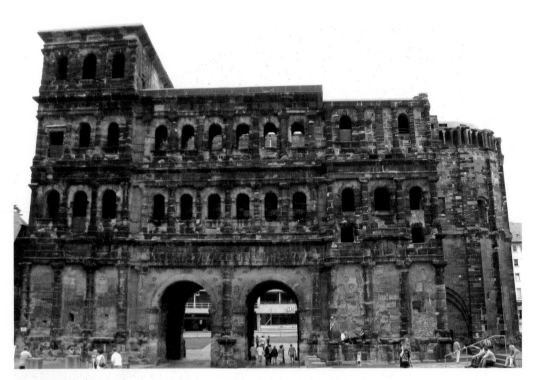

12.3 Porta Nigra, *c.* 300 CE, Trier, Germany. Sandstone. Photo courtesy Steven L. Tuck.

The rusticated masonry, left deliberately rough rather than chiseled to a smooth finish, is an element seen in the Porta Maggiore gateway of Rome built by the emperor Claudius in 52 CE (Figure 6.17) and conveys volume and solidity. The four-story semi-circular towers with engaged half columns and sculpted capitals give the imposing structure both a sense of volume as well as decoration that projects the identities of security and Roman culture to all who view it in this far northern province. The gate was probably always intended as much as a display of Roman power as a functional defense of the city. Constantine extended this display of Roman imperial identity in his bath complex and basilica.

The basilica is referred to as the Aula Palatina, or audience hall, which effectively describes its function as well as its debt to the audience chamber of Domitian in his palace on the Palatine in Rome. Such halls, as seen in the villa at Piazza Armerina, were the setting for appearances by the emperors and indicate the desire of rulers at this time to have a formal space for interactions with their audience.

The basilica at Trier from 310 CE is a rectangular building over 220 ft (70 m) long by 90 ft (27 m) wide with an interior height of over 98 ft (30 m), making it the largest surviving room from the Roman period. The rear of the building terminates in a large semi-circular apse that served to frame the seated emperor as he received his audience. The decoration of the interior emphasized this area as well. While the long interior walls were lined with marble revetment, the apse was covered with mosaic, which further distinguished it visually. The exterior of the building is plain brick with two superimposed stories of windows that terminate in semi-circular tops giving an appearance of a two-story structure. The recessed windows cause the intervening buttresses to appear to project more than they actually do, emphasizing the vertical lines and therefore the height of the building.

Inside, of course, it is all a single room, now more austere than its original form, since the hypocaust heating system in the floor no longer operates and the original decorations have been stripped. Nevertheless, it is a vast space that was designed to reflect the greatness of Constantine. The plain roof consisting of timber framing and a wooden coffered ceiling was a traditional type as seen in the

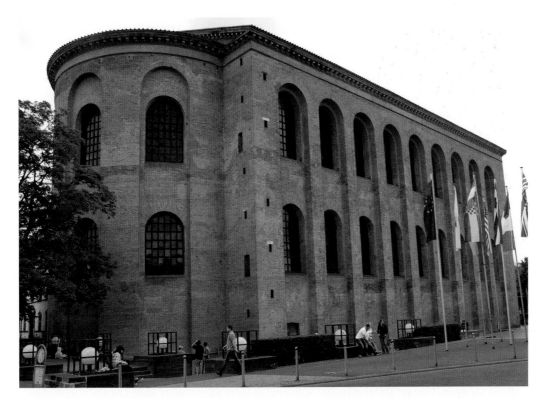

12.4 Exterior of the basilica, *c.* 310 CE, Trier, Germany. Brick. Photo courtesy Steven L. Tuck.

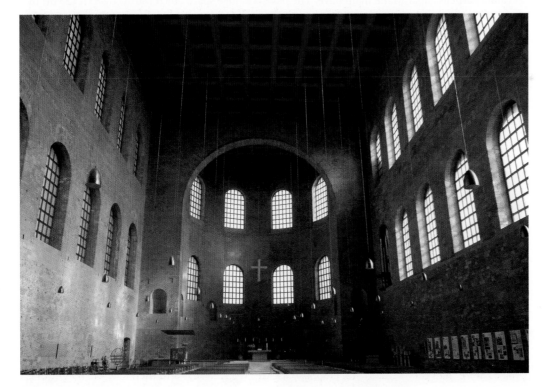

12.5 Interior of the basilica, *c.* 310 CE, Trier, Germany. Brick. Photo courtesy Steven L. Tuck.

basilica at Pompeii and the Basilica Ulpia in the Forum of Trajan, considered the finest basilica in Roman architecture. This timber framing was simpler than concrete vaulted structures seen in other imperial building programs. This cheaper, lower technology roofing becomes standard in the Christian basilicas built in and after the last years of Constantine's rule.

Architecture and sculpture at Rome: Augmenting the imperial capital and creating a dynasty

Although his building forms at Trier were certainly designed and executed as projections of imperial power, Constantine's greatest building program, at least until the founding of Constantinopolis, was at Rome itself, where he appropriated all of Maxentius' work, finishing buildings and dedicating them under his name alone. Part of this work was the usual sort of rebuilding and repair work expected of emperors, such as his restoration and expansion of the seating area of the Circus Maximus. It also included large-scale new construction, an element of imperial responsibility as established by Augustus. Before 315 CE he began the Baths of Constantine in Rome, the last of the immense imperial bath complexes in the city. This structure was similar in scale, rooms, and materials to the previous bathing establishments such as the Baths of Caracalla and Diocletian. It was constructed on the Quirinal Hill near the Markets of Trajan with huge walls of brick-faced concrete roofed with concrete vaults and domes of the type preserved in the Baths of Diocletian. This style of construction was also used for the Basilica Nova adjacent to the Forum Romanum.

Known as the Basilica of Maxentius, the Basilica of Constantine, or the Basilica Nova, this building, the largest basilica ever constructed in Rome, was begun under Maxentius and completed under Constantine after the Battle of the Milvian Bridge. Its form and materials relied not on traditional basilica columned hall construction, but on those of the imperial baths. In design the building has a tall central nave flanked by two side aisles. Each of the side aisles, one of which survives, measures 75 ft (23 m) by 56 ft (17 m) and was roofed with a set of three tremendous semi-circular concrete barrel vaults perpendicular to the main nave. The nave is a huge space 265 ft (80 m) by 83 ft (25 m) that rises 127 ft (39 m) to a roof created by a line of three immense concrete groin vaults.

The entire nave is supported by eight large piers, four at the corners and four in the center, instead of the more traditional line of columns that screened nave from side aisles in old-fashioned basilicas. The effect is a tremendous open space with no intervening supports to block the views of this spectacular interior. The nave terminates on the west end in a large semi-circular apse that held the colossal marble statue of Constantine, the focal point of the building, and a feature based on his basilica at Trier that Constantine added to the original design.

12.6   Basilica Nova, *c.* 315 CE, Rome, reconstruction drawing. Rome Reborn. © 2012 by Frischer Consulting, Inc. All rights reserved.

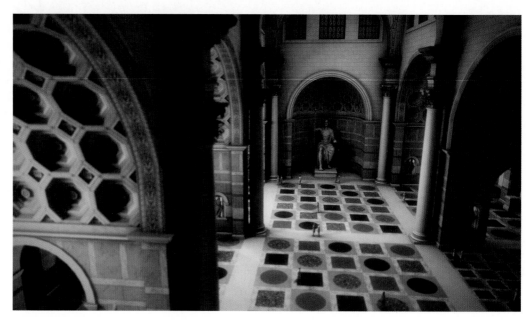

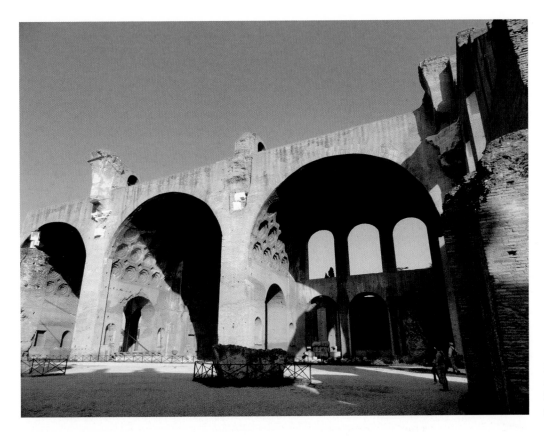

12.7   Basilica Nova,
c. 315 CE, Rome. Brick-
faced concrete. Photo
courtesy Steven L. Tuck.

HISTORICAL CONTEXT

Celebrating civil war

The erection of a monument celebrating a civil war was unprecedented in Rome even after a thousand years. The Roman attitude towards this is clearly stated by Valerius Maximus, a Latin writer of the time of Tiberius (14–37 CE), in his *Memorable Deeds and Sayings* 2.8.7:

> Even if someone had performed glorious deeds that benefitted the Republic during a civil war, he was not proclaimed an imperator on that account, no public thanksgivings were decreed, and he did not hold an ovation or triumph complete with chariot. Such victories might have been necessary, but it was felt that they were always tragic since they had been won by shedding the blood of our own people, not the blood of foreigners. … The Senate did not grant laurels to a man, nor did any man want to receive laurels, if a part of our state was in tears at his victory.

For Constantine, it was necessary not to refer to Maxentius by name in his triumph, but still the existence of the victory arch illustrating battles that a contemporary audience would have recognized, some from their participation in them, demonstrates that Roman culture had changed and that such celebrations were now at least tolerated.

Arch of Constantine

Another work in Rome from the early period of Constantine's rule is the Arch of Constantine. This triumphal arch is in some ways completely unprecedented while in other ways it relies on the most traditional forms. Its most unprecedented element is its subject. For the first time ever, a Roman emperor celebrated in a triumphal arch openly dedicated to commemorate victory in a civil war, in this case the war against Maxentius.

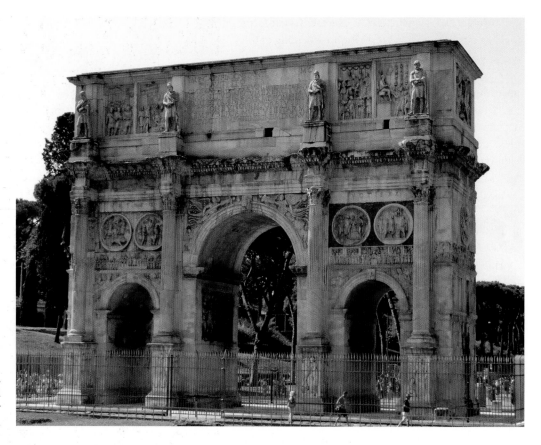

12.8 Arch of Constantine, 312–315 CE, Rome, general view. Photo courtesy Steven L. Tuck.

The subject is clear in the dedicatory inscription in which Maxentius is referred to as a faction, notably the same term Augustus used to refer to Mark Antony in his official documents describing their civil war. It also represents an early work in Constantine's rule, dating in the years immediately after the victory at the Battle of the Milvian Bridge in 312 CE when he was attempting to bolster his rule. To serve that purpose he created a work that made reference to some of Rome's greatest emperors, associating Constantine with Trajan, Hadrian, and Marcus Aurelius, reusing material from their public monuments and replacing the heads of these great emperors with his own portrait.

In design the arch is very traditional. A triple passage arch with a tall central passage flanked by two smaller ones, it resembles the Arch of Septimius Severus in the Forum Romanum and probably the lost arch of Marcus Aurelius as well. The decoration of the exterior also resembles previous arches with a dedicatory inscription in the attic, flying Victory figures in the spandrels of the main passage, and a host of sculptural relief panels. Unlike the major examples of public sculpture that survive, on the arch a large amount of the sculptural relief decoration is reused material, referred to as *spolia*. This reappropriated material includes relief panels and standing figures from public monuments of only three emperors: Trajan, Hadrian, and Marcus Aurelius. This seems a deliberate attempt to extend the meritocracy of the Five Good Emperors to include Constantine by creating a sort of extended dynastic display. Each of the large sides includes four Hadrianic tondi, the roundel images of Hadrian hunting and sacrificing. The attic of the arch also includes eight reliefs from a lost arch of Marcus Aurelius and colossal standing Dacian captive figures from Trajan's forum. Four sections of the Great Trajanic Frieze are found as well, two in the central passage and two on the attic, one each on both of the attic short exterior sides. All of these images show emperors, many with their facial features recut to those of Constantine, performing public, official, and praiseworthy acts such as warfare, hunting, sacrifice, arrival and departure ceremonies, and addressing crowds of civilians and the army. The figure of the emperor is often carved with a halo as well, reinforcing the divine authority that supported his rule. The themes conform to those established by Augustus at the founding of the principate: *virtus*, *pietas*, *iustitia*, and *clementia*.

The original Constantinian sculpture on the arch is mainly limited to three areas on each of the large sides: the spandrels of each entrance, the pedestals supporting the four freestanding columns on each side, and, most importantly, the frieze that runs in segments around the arch above the flanking passages. The figures in the spandrels include Victories, deities, and various personifications including river gods, Mars, Roma, and the Genius of the Roman People. There are also two Constantinian roundels on the Arch of Constantine attic ends. One features Sol ascending in a chariot and the other features Luna descending.

The pedestal reliefs are standard scenes of Victories with either captives or trophies or writing on shields as seen on many previous monuments such as the Column of Trajan. The sculptural style of the reliefs is even more abstracted than that seen under the Severans. The figures are flat with planar drapery distinguished, not by rounded folds, but by flat channels cut through the marble defining the forms. The figures are noticeably more frontal, heavier, and more shallowly carved than in past Classicizing examples. The frieze that circles the arch is notable for both subject and style. In subject it varies from the traditional triumphal procession and instead displays a combination of episodes from the war and official, ceremonial scenes in Rome. Like the Arch of Galerius and unlike previous public monuments such as the Column of Trajan, the arch as a whole and the frieze in particular does not present an integrated narrative. Instead, it has images of the war with Maxentius interspersed with panels displaying imperial virtues and stock scenes of public imperial actions. In style the frieze exemplifies the triumph of the Italic style over Classicizing and the rise of a new art referred to as Late Antique.

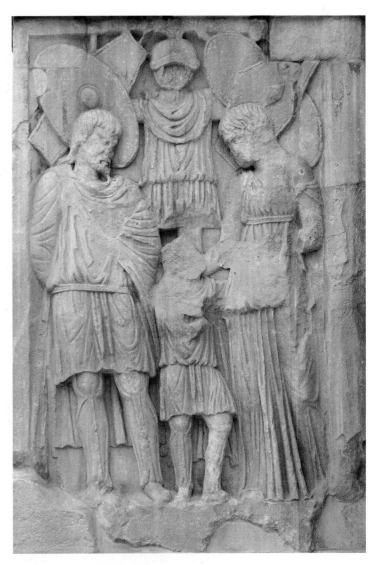

12.9 Arch of Constantine, 312–315 CE, Rome, captive barbarians and trophies frieze on pedestal. Photo courtesy Steven L. Tuck.

The components of the Late Antique style are seen in the two segments of the frieze on the north side of the arch above each of the side passages. One of these is an *oratio*, a scene of the emperor addressing the Roman people in the Forum Romanum. The same subject is found on the Anaglypha Traiani, which make an excellent contrast in style from the Classicizing to the Late Antique. In keeping with Italic artistic tradition, the scene is set with identifiable architecture providing context: two basilicas flank the rostra while the five-column Tetrarchic monument is seen above the heads of the figures on the speaker's platform. The composition and style differ dramatically from those seen in the Anaglypha. Centrality and axiality are used, along with the speaker's platform, to further define the emperor and to further distance him from the ruled. The figure of Constantine, now headless, is carved in the center of the rostra in higher relief and standing frontally, flanked by figures on the platform and in the forum whose attention is almost all on him. As seen in the overall sculptural program of the arch Constantine's authority is increased by associations between himself and previous emperors. Here statues of the seated Hadrian and Marcus Aurelius flank the rostra and the emperor. The proportions of the Romans in the scene are very different from those on the Anaglypha or the Hadrianic tondi above them. They are portrayed in squat, small-scale, reduced proportions,

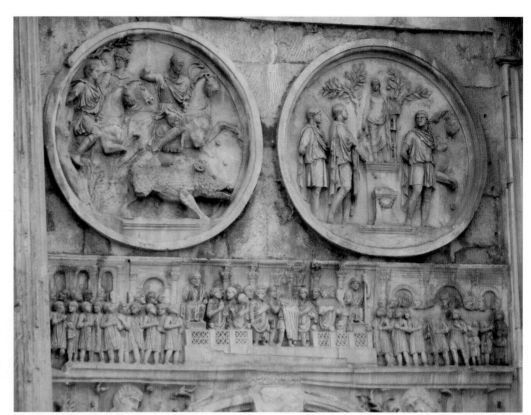

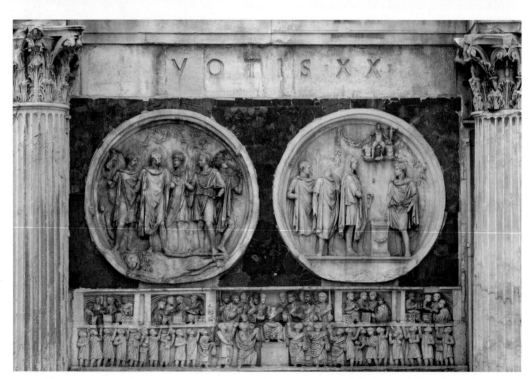

and in some cases the background figures in the two registers of spectators are represented only by heads. This reduction of figures represents a culmination in that development from the second to the fourth century as the slender, elongated Classicizing figures are replaced by these almost half their height and with very truncated proportions.

ART AND LITERATURE
Reconciling a Christian Constantine with his non-Christian art

The contemporary Christian authors on Constantine naturally emphasize signs and events that demonstrate his sincere Christianity, although these events rarely if ever appear in his official art. The Edict of Milan of 313 CE is the major statement of Constantine's favoritism towards Christianity as recorded by both Eusebius and Lactantius (250–325 CE). This edict reinforced religious tolerance throughout the Roman world, "now any one of these who wishes to observe Christian religion may do so freely and openly without molestation." It also restored to the Christians their property which had been seized in earlier persecutions, " … also other property, namely the churches … you will order to be restored without any hesitation or controversy at all." The edict essentially turns the apparatus of the state to the support and protection of the Christians with the expectation that the Christian God will reciprocate with his blessings. One of the closing statements of the edict is candid on that, "Let this be done so that, as we have said above, Divine favor towards us, which, under the most important circumstances we have already experienced, may, for all time, preserve and prosper our successes together with the good of the state." The foundation of Christian churches, such as St. Peter's Basilica in Rome in 326 CE and a variety of churches of Constantinopolis, perhaps provides evidence of state support for Christianity. Still, the evidence is mixed.

While Constantine founded St. Peter's in Rome, his foundation of the new capital was not the opportunity for a complete break from the traditional past. Its public areas were filled with non-Christian *spolia* demonstrating the cultural continuity of the New Rome. The sacred tripods from the sanctuary of Apollo at Delphi were placed in the hippodrome along with statues of Castor and Pollux. Statues of the Muses were brought from Mt. Helicon and placed in the Senate House while statues of Zeus from Dodona and Athena from Lindos were erected in front of it. An eclectic collection of over eighty statues, including Greco-Roman deities, Greek writers and philosophers, and Roman generals, decorated the large and popular Baths of Zeuxippus. The goal was clearly to transfer the expected decoration of public spaces to the new capital.

Constantine's clean-shaven portraiture differs from his predecessors, but is solidly within the imperial tradition, probably modeled on Trajan and Augustus. The fourth-century CE non-Christian emperor, Julian the Apostate, readopts bearded imagery to make visual connections to Greek philosophers, but that does not require that we consider Constantine's unbearded images as Christian. The colossal statue in the Basilica Nova shows no explicitly Christian attributes despite evidence of being revised late in his reign to include a scepter or staff. The coinage of Constantine, both its portraits and reverses, exemplify the continuity of traditional iconography. Personified virtues, Victory, Sol Invictus (unconquered sun), She-wolf and twins, military symbols, and so on show continuity with those images and themes that supported previous rulers. Considering the bronze coinage of Constantine, by one count of approximately 1,363 types known, less than 1 percent might have Christian symbols. Many of these symbols are a single letter, the Greek letter X, which was added by the local mint supervisor perhaps as a Christian symbol. The only definitive Chi-Rho symbols date to the final three years of Constantine's rule.

Perhaps the most ambiguous evidence of Christian public imagery is on the Arch of Constantine. The dedicatory inscription on the attic on both sides of the arch (Figure 12.8) refers to the "impulse of divinity" but seeing this as a thematic statement for the arch seems extreme, given the reliefs of Sol and Luna also on the attic. The inscription certainly makes a Christian reference, but not so the sculpture, either that carved under Constantine or the *spolia*. Notably absent is the *labarum*, the standard that Eusebius and Lactantius credit to Constantine with the X and P, known as the Chi-Rho, that surmounted it in Constantine's battles. The art and literary sources provide us with two very different images of the emperor. This was no doubt due to their very different audiences. The Christian authors wrote for Christian audiences who were eager to understand the signs that celebrated Constantine's Christian beliefs, while the majority of Romans who saw his art were reassured by the continuity in traditional subjects and forms that defined their cultural identity.

The matching segment of the frieze also on the north side of the arch shows a scene of *congiarium*, the distributions of money given periodically by the emperors to the Roman people, also shown on the Arch of Trajan at Beneventum (Figure 8.30). Trajan and Hadrian were famed for these distributions and Constantine himself gave one in 313 CE. Here all of the elements of the Late Antique style are used to portray the event. Constantine's high status is reinforced by many artistic conventions. He is essentially enthroned, seated like a statue on a high platform in the center of the composition, frontal and elevated above the standing Romans who surround him, senators in togas in his immediate company, and ordinary Romans further away. Hierarchy of scale also further distinguishes him. The Roman men and boys standing in a line in the lower register are even squatter than those in the *oratio* panel, creating further contrast between the ruler and ruled. This art celebrates the rule of a single individual, no longer the *primus inter pares*, first among equals, of Augustus, but closer to and the inspiration for the image of medieval kingship. In many ways the imagery reflects the way people would see Constantine in the apse of the basilica in Trier or in Rome, seated on a throne, if not a god then divinely inspired to rule.

Constantinian church and tomb architecture in Rome

The extent and variety of Constantine's Christian building program can be seen in two very different buildings, the basilica church of Old St. Peter's and Santa Costanza. The first of these is the church built beginning in 325 CE at the Vatican over the location believed to be the tomb of St. Peter which set a very important pattern for Christian churches up to the present day. The church was laid out using the simple, cheap, and easily reproducible form of the Roman basilica. A Roman temple was a poor building design for a church. Its small size, lack of windows, high podium, and inaccessible design all factored against the needs of a congregation for a large interior space with good light. The traditional basilica form, however, was designed for crowds of people, cheap to construct, and readily adaptable.

Old St. Peter's was in essence a five-aisled basilica, much like Trajan's Basilica Ulpia, consisting of a nave flanked on each side by two narrower side aisles, over 350 ft (110 m) in length. Marble columns, *spolia* from earlier buildings, separated the aisles and were the only luxurious materials. The

12.12 Old St. Peter's, Rome, *c.* 325 CE, plan. Locutus Borg (modified to English language by Amandajm)/Wikimedia Commons.

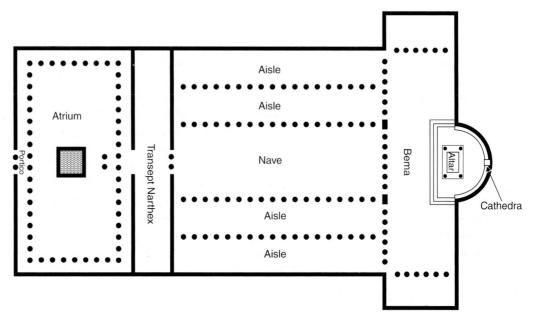

walls were rubble construction and the roofing system was all timber, making it a low cost and easy to replicate building form. The five doors allowed for the circulation of large numbers of people to visit the tomb of St. Peter, marked by a monument in an apse at the west end of the nave. The use of an apse to distinguish important space was seen previously in the basilica at Trier and the Basilica Nova. The major innovation to the basilica design is the addition of two chapels at the west end of the building beyond the ends of the aisles. This is the origin of the transept, a cross corridor that in medieval churches becomes the arms in the cross-shaped building plan. The transept served to widen that end of the church, separating it from the aisles, further distinguishing it architecturally and allowing better visibility and movement around the ritually significant areas. Old St. Peter's became a model plan for major churches across Europe for the next thousand years.

The second late Constantinian building in Rome, a much smaller-scale building, is now the church of Santa Costanza, but was originally designed as the tomb of Constantine's daughters, Constantina and Helena. The building differs in almost every possible way from the basilica plan of Old St. Peter's. It is an internally oriented, central plan building 74 ft (22 m) in diameter, constructed from concrete and lavishly decorated on the interior with mosaics and imported marble. The plan relies on a different but old Roman tradition of centrally organized buildings

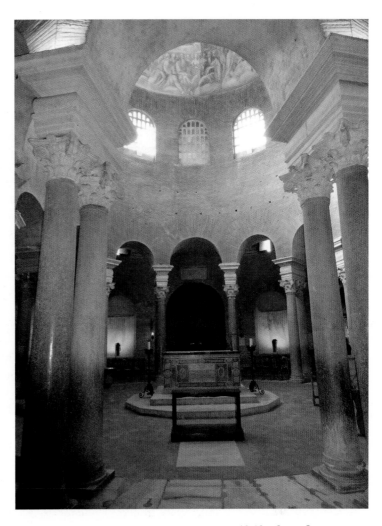

12.13 Santa Costanza, Rome, *c.* 325–350 CE, interior view. Photo courtesy Daniel Resheter.

roofed with concrete domes. Prominent examples include the Pantheon and the Circular Island in the Villa of Hadrian, Tivoli. The latter had the key element, found at Santa Costanza, of a circular ambulatory that surrounded the round central element, separated from it by a line of columns. At Santa Costanza that colonnade was created by twelve pairs of columns supporting segments of architrave. These provided the support for the drum that terminated in the central dome. The drum carried the dome high enough above the ambulatory to allow for twelve windows that created a light, open central area contrasting with the dark ambulatory. The addition of windows in the central space replaces the oculus found at the Pantheon and other early domed buildings, but still serves to emphasize that central space as more important than the darker and lower surrounding ambulatory.

The floor and the barrel vault that made up the roof of the ambulatory were covered with mosaics. These demonstrate the continuity of traditional pagan subjects in decorative art under Constantine. Various motifs familiar from earlier mosaics and probably selected from pattern books are found here including doves on a bowl of water, garlands, branches, and silver vessels. Large panels also contain clearly Dionysiac scenes including grapevines and Cupids making wine. The combination of wine and figures symbolic of erotic love were a staple of pagan art in virtually all media and their appearance here shows that those traditions continue far into Constantine's rule. It is possible that this imagery might have a second, hidden meaning for early Christians, as discussed in the Scholarly Perspective.

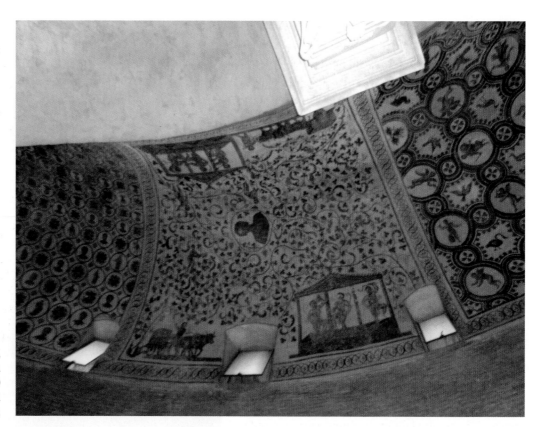

12.14 Vintage scenes, vault mosaic, Santa Costanza, Rome, *c.* 325–350 CE. Photo courtesy Daniel Resheter.

SCHOLARLY PERSPECTIVE
The iconography and ownership of imperial porphyry sarcophagi

Currently housed in the Vatican Museum are two large sarcophagi reconstructed from fragmentary remains, one of which was found in Santa Costanza.

One was decorated with images of Cupids harvesting, transporting, and stomping grapes to make wine. The vignettes on the long side take place within three large roundels created by grapevine tendrils. These motifs echo some in the ambulatory vault mosaics at Santa Costanza, her tomb. The images have a long tradition in Roman art, sometimes as general images of rural life, but especially in spaces and on objects used for the worship of Dionysus. Here the motif refers to the metaphor of Christ as the vine, his followers as the branches (John 15). The animals along the groundline on the long side of the sarcophagus, peacocks and a sheep, may also suggest a deeper meaning. The sheep was, of course, long an image associated with art of the countryside, rural areas, and bucolic poetry. References to Christ as the Good Shepherd and associated imagery in Christian catacombs and tombs dating back at least a century suggest that this is a form of hidden Christian iconography. Good Shepherd iconography from the third century CE often incorporated vines as well as sheep (Figure 11.22). The peacocks in the corners of the composition were a Christian image of resurrection, dating back at least into the early third century CE when they were found in the catacombs. Here they may show continuity from that earlier period of symbolic representation of Christian belief in funerary art. Some scholars argue that the sarcophagus, with its high quality sculpture and images that reflect early Christian iconography with covert images of Christian belief, may have been originally intended for St. Helena, the mother of Constantine. This explains why the combination of subjects matches those from the third century CE. It is likely that Helena, mother of Constantine, commissioned this long before her death at the age of eighty. Why she was

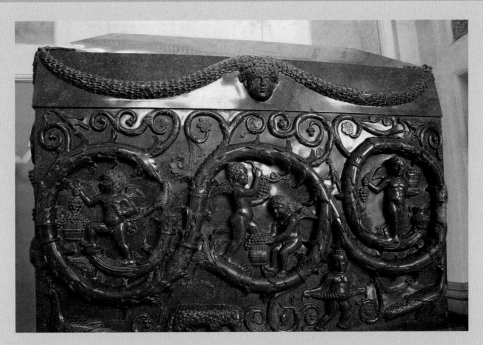

12.15   Porphyry sarcophagus of Constantina, 330–360 CE, from Santa Costanza, Rome. Musei Vaticani, Rome. L 7 ft 7 ½ in (2.3 m) W 5 ft 1 ¾ in (1.6 m) H 4 ft 2 3/8 in (1.3 m). Photo courtesy Steven L. Tuck.

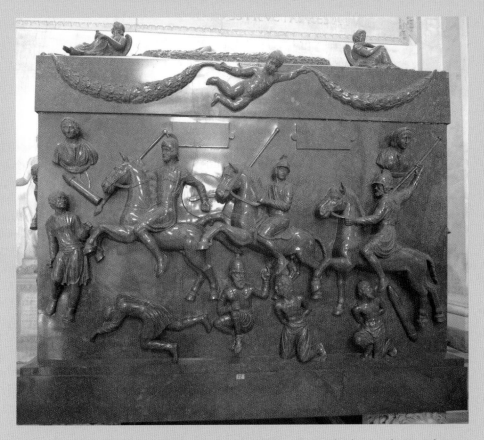

12.16   Porphyry sarcophagus of Helena, 330–360 CE, Mausoleum of Helena on the Via Labicana, Rome. Musei Vaticani, Rome. Photo courtesy Steven L. Tuck.

(Continued)

not laid to rest in it is not known, but it is possible that a more explicitly Christian tomb was prepared for her and that this porphyry sarcophagus, restricted to the imperial family, was used for Constantina.

The sarcophagus of Helena, mother of Constantine, raises even more suggestive possibilities based on its subject and style. Although often described as a battle sarcophagus, it is not. The scenes on both short sides and the one carved long side are Roman cavalry riding across the field of the sarcophagus with bound barbarian prisoners below them. On the long side are three cavalry on rearing horses taking up the center of the field with crouched, kneeling, or fallen barbarians, their hands bound behind their backs, below them along the groundline. The same subject fills the short ends as well although with standing barbarians instead of kneeling ones. The subject of a military parade of some fashion, perhaps triumphal or symbolic, has precedent on the base of the Column of Antoninus Pius (Figure 9.12). On both works of art the cavalry ride in a line with separate groundlines. In each case the imagery was used in the context of a funeral, since the Column of Antoninus Pius marked his tomb complex. Here the cavalry may be participating in some form of funeral games or a presentation of captives associated with another major imperial occasion such as a triumphal procession or an *adventus*.

This subject is problematic for the staunchly Christian mother of an emperor. The military imagery does not seem appropriate and is unprecedented for any in the imperial family but an emperor. Many scholars believe that this sarcophagus was originally intended for Constantine himself, designed and carved in Egypt, and then shipped to Rome for his burial. This is plausible and if accurate solves the problem of the subject. If this is the case, it provides evidence that Constantine, at least at one time, planned to be buried at Rome and not at Constantinople where he was eventually laid to rest. It is likely that these two porphyry sarcophagi were sculpted by the same workshop in Egypt and shipped to Rome where each was finally used for a different imperial burial than was originally intended.

Diana E.E. Kleiner, *Roman Sculpture* (Yale 1992), 455–458.

Silver vessels in the fourth century CE

Britain was invaded and added to the Roman Empire beginning in 43 CE under the emperor Claudius. Over the next century Roman occupation expanded until it reached a fixed border and frontier under Hadrian. The province became wealthy and prosperous and as an island avoided most of the chaos of the third century CE. In the fourth century CE Roman Britain was one of the wealthiest, most stable provinces with a large upper class of Romanized inhabitants and productive enough to export food to support other areas in the empire. Evidence of this wealth and elite residence abounds. The large number of villas, elite rural residences, shows the stability of the region, but perhaps the best evidence of high status culture is provided by the many silver vessels from the period that have been discovered in widely separate areas across Britain.

One of the most spectacular of these silver vessels is the Corbridge Lanx, a type of tray designed for display rather than actual use. The lanx was discovered in northern Britain near Corbridge in Northumberland (ancient Coriosopitum, site of a Roman town and military garrison). These display vessels were placed where guests in dining rooms could view them and so they made up part of the elite cultural display in Roman dining spaces to augment one of the most protracted of high status activities, the banquet. This lanx is a shallow, rectangular tray almost 20 in (50 cm) in length. The tray has a single scene with the god Apollo on the right standing before a shrine, holding his bow with his lyre propped at his feet. His sister Artemis enters the scene from the left. She is separated by an altar and tree from three goddesses who fill the center of the composition. Athena and Aphrodite stand and face Artemis while Hera sits and faces Apollo. In the foreground are landscape elements as well as animals associated with Artemis and Apollo and their myths. The scene is a variant of the Judgment of Paris where the three goddesses in the center contested for the golden apple as a prize

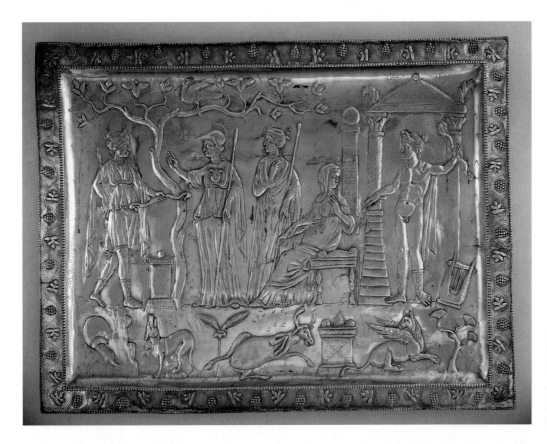

12.17 Corbridge Lanx, silver tray, 4th cent. CE. British Museum, London. L 20 in (50.6 cm). Source: © The Trustees of the British Museum. All rights reserved.

for the fairest, the divine beauty contest that led to the Trojan War. Along the rim a border of grapevine with alternating leaves and grape bunches frames the scene and adds a Dionysiac element to the decoration. The lanx is a fourth-century CE work probably from the eastern Mediterranean, perhaps the Roman province of Asia, and represents the continuity of elite culture across the empire at this period. It is a work in the Greek tradition in terms of subject and style with the composition and representation based on the conventions of Hellenistic landscape work.

Another example of domestic display silver is the Mildenhall treasure, a collection of twenty-seven pieces of fourth-century CE silver discovered near Mildenhall in Suffolk in eastern England. The three most important pieces all share Dionysiac motifs and were probably made as part of a set, a conclusion reinforced by the large beaded edging they have in common. These include two small silver plates, one of which shows Pan and a maenad playing instruments in a landscape while the second has a satyr and maenad dancing. All of the figures conform in pose and proportions to the conventions of Classical art from the fourth century BCE. Both are inscribed on the back with a Greek owner's name, indicating that they belong to one Eutherius. The third piece in this set is the so-called Great Dish, a large display platter also of silver and decorated in low relief and engraving with two registers of very high quality figures. The largest register of figures, arranged with the dish's edge as a groundline, is a line of Dionysiac figures, most of them dancing. Dionysus himself stands holding a bunch of grapes and accompanied by his typical panther while Pan, satyrs, and maenads dance and play instruments in the company of a drunken Hercules, a motif seen on mosaics from Antioch. An inner circle of figures contains only sea creatures including nymphs, a triton, and mythical marine creatures such as a sea-horse, and a sea serpent. The center of the dish is a medallion with the face of Oceanus, his wild hair and beard decorated with dolphins and seaweed. The central figure bears strong similarities in subject and style to the face on the pediment of the temple at Bath, an important Roman religious and healing sanctuary in Britain. The Great Dish from Mildenhall was probably imported to Britain from the eastern Mediterranean so it does not represent local art, but empire-wide art that reflects local taste.

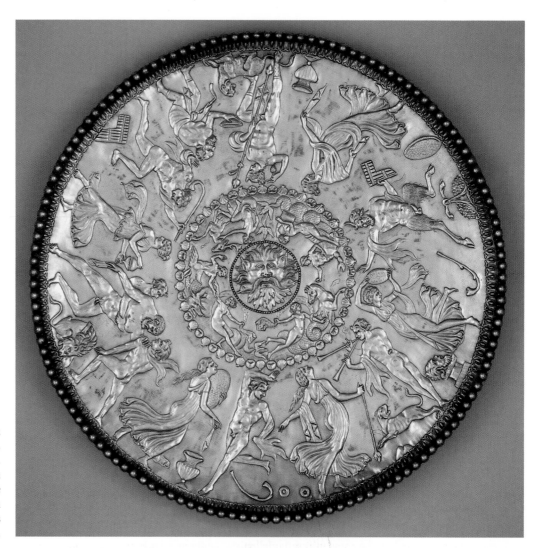

12.18 Great Dish from Mildenhall, 4th cent. CE. British Museum, London. Silver tray, D 23 ¾ in (60.5 cm). Source: © The Trustees of the British Museum. All rights reserved.

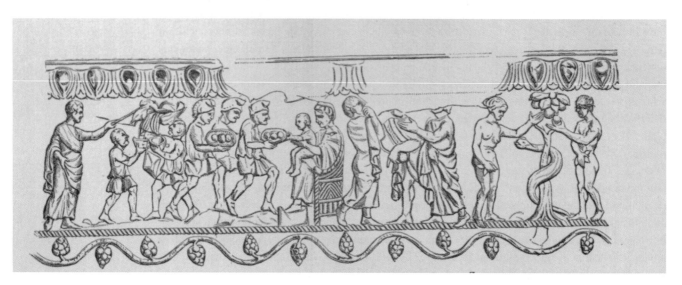

12.19 Traprain silver gilt flagon, 4th cent. CE, H 8 ½ in (21.6 cm), drawing after A. Curle, *Treasure of Traprain*, 1923, fig. 2. Photo courtesy Steven L. Tuck.

Both the Mildenhall and Corbridge treasures contained items with Christian significance, small objects inscribed with the Chi-Rho monogram of Christ's name. Silver vessels from the Traprain Treasure reveal even more about the spread of early Christianity and the use of ritual vessels in the early church. The treasure was found within the area of the ancient settlement on Traprain Law hill, in East Lothian, Scotland, far to the north of Roman territory. It consisted of over a hundred and fifty objects weighing just over 53 lbs., most of which had been crushed, cut, or hacked into pieces for convenient weighing and redistribution. These fourth-century CE objects were largely from three contexts: domestic silver for use and display, military items, and Christian items from a set of liturgical silver from a church. The vessels of church plate share the same forms of plates, cups, and wine pitchers as seen in the table service silver from the period. One of the silver-gilt wine jugs is decorated around its body in repoussé with four scenes, two each from books of the Hebrew and Christian Bibles. From left to right, Adam and Eve, the Betrayal of Christ, the Adoration of the Magi, and Moses striking water from the rock give us our best sense of the figural decoration of early Christian church utensils. The composition of the scenes is not chronological as might be expected from left to right, but might be designed to be "read" from right to left beginning with the Adam and Eve group. All of these scenes are known from other contexts, notably carved on early Christian tombs and painted on catacomb walls, but this is the earliest surviving use of them on metalwork or in a non-funerary context. In style the figures retain many Roman features. The Moses and the figures in the Betrayal of Christ scene wear togas, while Adam and Eve are presented in very Classicizing three-quarter poses in proportions familiar from Greek sculpture of the Late Classical period. While the jug is fourth century CE, the date of the treasure, based on coins to c. 410 CE, just after Roman government withdrew from Britain, provides evidence of the relations between Romans and the local populations beyond Hadrian's Wall as well as of the continued influence of Rome in the post-Roman period, as this hoard may have been payment to native troops or allies in the chaos of the Roman withdrawal from Britain in 410 CE.

Mosaics

One of the most sophisticated examples of Romano-British art work of the period was created about 330 CE for the *triclinium* of the Roman villa at Lullingstone in Kent, southeastern England. The floor in the dining room is covered with a large square floor mosaic mostly filled with geometric shapes, but has a central panel with the hero Bellerophon riding the winged horse, Pegasus, and slaying the monster, the Chimera. The scene is surrounded by four images of dolphins that fill out the scene but do not directly relate to it. The corners outside the frame of the Bellerophon scene contain roundels with busts of personifications of the four seasons, a common motif of the period. The major focus of the floor is a semi-circular apse in the center of one side with a separate mythological subject, the Rape of Europa.

The Rape of Europa mosaic shows the major scene of Europa abducted by Zeus in the form of a white bull who carries her away on his back against her will. A pair of Cupids, one of whom leads the bull as it apparently flies through the panel, flanks these figures. The movement of the bull is shown by its spread legs, Europa's billowing mantle, and the Cupid behind tugging on the bull's tail in an attempt to stop the abduction. The panel differs from the vast majority in not having a simple white background, but the lower portion of the panel is black, indicating the sea that they are traveling over. Unlike the same scene in Pompeian wall painting or mosaics from the eastern Mediterranean, only simple black lines that outline each figure and divide each element of anatomy and dress define the figures. The story of Europa was related by a great number of Classical authors, both Greek and Roman. This version probably owes its inspiration most directly to Ovid's *Metamorphoses*, his epic poem written under the emperor Augustus. He relates the abduction in a brief passage (book 2, 846–875) that emphasizes her fluttering drapery and the snow-white bull.

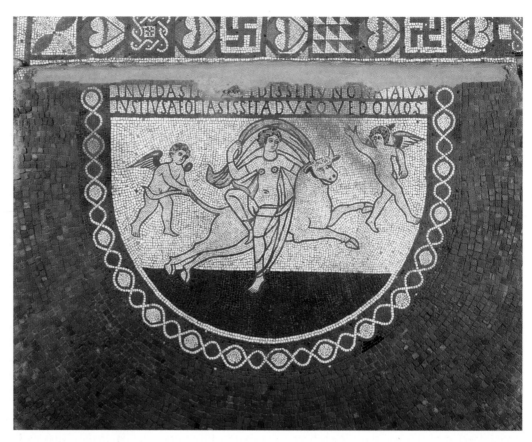

12.20 Lullingstone mosaic of Rape of Europa, *c.* 330 CE, Lullingstone, Kent. H 5 ft (1.52 m) W 8 ft (2.45 m). Source: London, English Heritage, 1991. © 2014. Photo Scala Florence/ Heritage Images.

MORE ON MYTH
Aeneas and Vergil's Aeneid

The myth of Aeneas told the story of the travels of this refugee from the Trojan War as he followed his fate to Italy. The son of the goddess Venus, he fled Troy as the Greeks sacked it, bringing with him his father, Anchises, his son, Ascanius, and the household gods. In some versions he also brought to Rome the sacred image of Athena. As did Homer's Odysseus, along the way he faced obstacles including many sent by Juno, who opposed his fated founding of a Trojan colony in Italy. Once he reached Italy, he married a local princess, Lavinia, daughter of Latinus, king of the Latins, and created a mixed community of Trojans and native Italians. One of the most commonly illustrated episodes from the story of Aeneas is his interlude in Carthage. Shipwrecked by a storm on the shore of North Africa he falls in love with and then abandons Dido, the queen of Carthage in order to fulfill his destiny in Italy. His romance with Dido was orchestrated by his mother, Venus, and through gifts presented to Dido by his son, Ascanius. Dido's subsequent suicide made the romantic story tragic and set up the later historical Carthaginian Wars.

A verse inscription set in the mosaic, very unusually for a floor mosaic, accompanies the episode. This couplet is above the apse mosaic, essentially separating it from the larger floor mosaic and serving as a caption:

INVIDA SI TAVRI VIDISSET IVNO NATATVS
IVSTIVS AEOLIAS ISSET CEVS QVE DOMOS
"If jealous Juno had seen the swimming of the bull,
she would with more justice have gone all the way to the halls of Aeolus."

A VIEW FROM THE PROVINCES
The Aeneid in Romano-British mosaics

Unlike the silver vessels that were imported into Roman Britain from the Mediterranean, mosaics in Britain as in other provinces were produced by local workshops and so reveal the art that artists created to satisfy the tastes and to fulfill commissions of local patrons. Based on ancient artistic training where an apprentice was trained in a workshop by more experienced artists, the result was an art that was very localized or at most regional in style. Given also that mosaics are heavy, made of stone, and almost all created on site where they were displayed, they represent one of the most regional styles of art. Consistent with the imported silver the mosaics in many villas, elite rural domestic spaces, use traditional Classical subjects. In fact, there is a group of mosaics that derive from not just Classical art or mythology but from specific literary accounts, notably created in a local Romano-British style demonstrating that they are not imported works, but products of local taste and art.

A villa in Low Ham, Somerset in southwestern England provides a unique example of a work by a regional mosaic workshop dated to *c.* 340 CE. The large square mosaic has five panels that show episodes in the story of Aeneas, the Trojan refugee, Roman founder and hero of Vergil's *Aeneid*. It is the only episodic narrative mosaic found in Roman Britain and the scenes are all from the story of Dido and Aeneas in the epic, which was written under the emperor Augustus over 400 years earlier. Four of the panels are from books 1 and 4 of the *Aeneid*: Aeneas sailing into Carthage where he will meet Dido; Dido and Aeneas meeting led by his son, Ascanius, and his mother, Venus; the couple riding to the hunt; and the couple embracing. The fifth panel is not a specific episode from the poem but a central image of Dido flanked by Cupids with torches: one raises his torch to indicate burning love while the other lowers his to show love extinguished. The style is very regional. The figures in each panel are recognizable by the standard iconography.

Aeneas, for example, wears a Phrygian hat showing his origin in Asia, but stylistically there is almost nothing here of the Classical tradition. The individuals are very two-dimensional in representation. They are defined by outlines rather than shadows and have no internal modeling or shading, which would give the bodies roundness and a sense of substance. Internally lines are used to define drapery, giving every figure and item stripes rather than shading and blended colors. There are also no explicit groundlines; figures hover in the field of the white background in the panel and

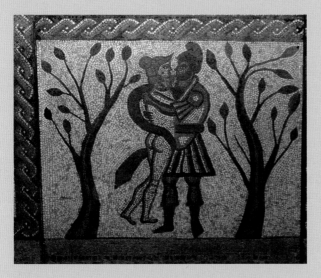

12.21   Low Ham mosaic of Dido and Aeneas, *c.* 340 CE. Museum of Somerset, Taunton Castle, Taunton. Full dimensions 13 ft 1 ½ in (*c.* 4 m) on a side. Udimu/Wikimedia Commons.

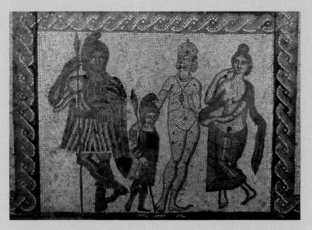

12.22   Low Ham mosaic, detail of Aeneas, Ascanius, Dido, and Venus, *c.* 340 CE. Museum of Somerset, Taunton Castle, Taunton. Full dimensions 13 ft 1 ½ in (*c.* 4 m) on a side. Udimu/Wikimedia Commons.

(Continued)

trees rise out of the bottom of the panel. The figures and the landscape are therefore incompletely integrated, leading to a sense that the figures hover in mid air or occupy a position on the front of a stage.

The continuity of Roman culture and its continued reference back to its major cultural markers is seen in the Vatican Vergil. This is the oldest manuscript of the works of Vergil and the oldest illustrated manuscript of any work of Classical literature. It is not intact, but probably originally included all three of Vergil's works of poetry, the *Aeneid*, *Georgics*, and *Eclogues*. Surviving are 76 pages out of the original 400, which contain 50 of the approximately 280 illustrations. The miniature paintings all illustrate episodes in the text, in many cases clearly based on pattern books judging by their parallels in earlier works in other media. The illustration of Dido sacrificing before the Temple of Juno relies on many of the same conventions as previous works of the same event. She stands over the altar with her mantle covering her head, assisted by two attendants in tunics and two *victimarii*, stripped to the waist, who prepare the animals. Behind Dido the Temple of Juno gives context to the scene and its open door reveals the cult statue so that the episode is not in doubt. All of these elements are found dating back to the Republican period in the Roman art of sacrifice. The illustration is very Classicizing with slender, Classically proportioned figures with much internal modeling and shading defining their forms. Weight is given to the figures through the use of shadows along the ground under each of them as well.

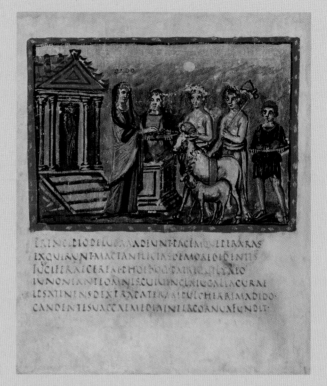

12.23   Image of Dido sacrificing, end of the 4th cent. CE, Vatican Vergil, Vatican, Biblioteca Apostolica, Cod. Vat. Lat. 3225. Fol. 33 v. Source: Vatican Library, Vatican City/The Bridgeman Art Library.

Like the scene below them, the structure, meter, and syntax of the couplet rely on Ovid's poetry. The verse, however, makes reference to the episode in book 1 of Vergil's *Aeneid* when Juno visits the west wind, Aeolus, bribing him to send a storm to scatter and sink Aeneas' fleet. The mosaic and couplet demonstrate the expectations this type of decoration put on the audience who would view them. Here is a space designed for elite, leisure activities – primarily banquet dining – with decoration that makes allusion to Greek mythology mediated through two works of Roman poetry from the time of Augustus over four hundred years earlier. And all without labels or captions to identify the subjects or sources, meaning that the viewers were expected to recognize the events and the sources referenced, even in allusion.

CONCLUSION

Constantine's thirty-year period of rule demonstrates some elements of remarkable continuity with the long traditions of Roman art. His triumphal arch in Rome closely resembles that of Septimius Severus almost exactly a hundred years earlier, while many of the subjects of its sculptural decoration are based on the public art of Augustus. His portraiture meanwhile makes deliberate reference to the hairstyle of Trajan. His basilica in Rome relies on the forms and materials of Roman bath complexes, demonstrating the continued use of these building forms and practices even when his bath complex no longer survives. In the non-imperial art we see evidence of a continuing elite Classical culture that extended into the fourth century CE and across the Roman world, as the mosaics and silver of Roman Britain reveal. In each artistic medium traditional Classical subjects, without identifying captions and with consistent iconography dating back hundreds of years, show that elite Romans in their dining spaces continued that expectation of cultural identity based on literature and myth from centuries earlier. It is perhaps notable that the late fourth century provides our only ancient commentary on the works of Vergil, written by Servius.

And yet changes are also strongly evident. The subject of the Arch of Constantine, Roman civil war, is unprecedented in all of Roman art for a triumphal monument. The style of the reliefs on the Arch of Constantine shows the conquest of the Late Antique style with their squat proportions, reduction of the non-elite human figures, emphasis on frontality, axiality, and symmetry, and celebration of the emperor by enhanced scale, central position, and architectural framework. That style with more simplified, abstracted figures and disregarding depth and illusions of space is found in the Christian art of the period, probably as a reaction against Classical art in both subject and style. The rise in the emphasis on the contributions of the periphery over the center in the building and artistic patronage of cities besides Rome culminates in the founding of a new capital at Constantinople.

These elements of the new subjects of Christian art, the shift of Roman government and patronage of public buildings to Constantinople and regional centers, and the new Late Antique style all become building blocks of the new medieval world that follows the fall of the western Roman Empire in 476 CE. Constantine's imagery of rule becomes the model for medieval monarchs while Constantinople becomes the great bastion of western civilization for the next thousand years. His legacy in art, architecture, and city construction proved the vitality of these forms and their power into succeeding generations.

EPILOGUE: THE FALL OF ROME AND THE RISE OF NEW ROMES

The Roman legacy in art is the subject of the final section of the book. The Roman Empire is widely regarded as one of the most successful, long-lasting, and certainly broad-ranging governmental forms in world history. Its success, of course, depended largely upon the visual aspect of the Roman world. It is through the visual that the Romans defined and projected their power, shaped their world, and announced their identities. These visual forms continued after the dramatic transformations of the pagan Roman world into a Christian medieval one were completed. It matters little whether one places the fall of Rome in 476 CE with the abdication of the last independent emperor of the west, Romulus Augustulus, or in 1453 CE and the fall of Constantinople. The forms continue in these Roman spaces. And not just the forms of art and architecture, but the organization of urban space and the themes that Romans used in their buildings. When later people adopted the forms, and by people I mean individuals as well as governments and nations, they were engaging with the ideas behind these visual elements. Rome became a lens through which later people saw and judged their own cultures. So, the study of the reception and emulation of Roman forms of art also allows us to study the reception of Roman culture and cultural values throughout history.

One of the great cultural changes of the fourth century CE was the legalization and increasing acceptance of Christianity. After the Edict of Milan legalized Christian worship in 313 CE it became more open and more entangled with the apparatus of the state, which supported it. That trend of increasing connections to the state and the preference for Christianity over paganism reached its conclusion under the emperor Theodosius (ruled 379–395 CE), the last emperor to rule over the

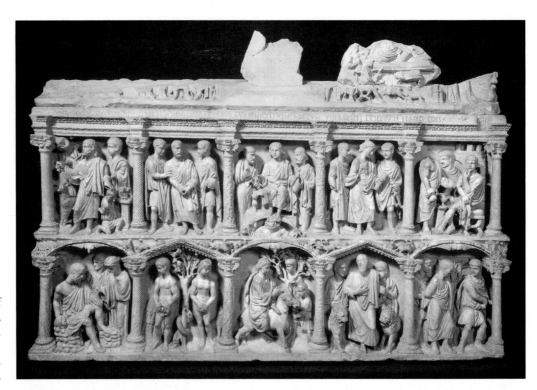

12.24 Sarcophagus of Junius Bassus, *c.* 359 CE, Rome. Musei Vaticani, Rome. L 8 ft (2.44 m) H 3 ft 11 in (1.18 m). Source: © 2014. Photo Scala, Florence.

eastern and western halves of the empire and the one who in a series of decrees finally made Christianity the official state church and forbade pagan worship. The life and career of Junius Bassus illustrates that period between Constantine and Theodosius when Christianity was becoming more open and official. Bassus, who died in 359 CE at the age of forty-two, was a Roman Senator and Praefectus Urbi (urban prefect of Rome, one of the highest offices in Roman government) who died a recent Christian, perhaps baptized on his deathbed as was customary in the fourth century CE. His sarcophagus, found at Old St. Peter's, was a very high quality, sophisticated work of art that retained the form of second-century CE columned sarcophagi from Asia Minor. Here the ten frames in two registers created by the columns are not filled with the standard Labors of Hercules, as seen on the Velletri Sarcophagus (Figure 9.22), but with biblical scenes cut in high relief with deep undercutting and extensive drillwork, making them almost three dimensional.

In the upper register from the left are the Sacrifice of Isaac, the Arrest of Peter, Enthroned Christ with Saints Peter and Paul, and two episodes from the Trial of Christ by Pontius Pilate. In the lower register are Job, Adam and Eve, Christ's entry into Jerusalem, Daniel in the Lion's Den, and the Arrest of Paul. The composition is traditionally Roman with the central images in each register the most important, emphasizing Christ, who is presented frontally in the upper central panel, not strictly a biblical story, but a *traditio legis*, the passing of laws by a lawgiver, an image found in Roman imperial art. The enthroned Christ takes the place traditionally filled by the emperor as he hands scrolls of the law to Saints Peter and Paul. The scenes in the upper register also develop a narrative from the Sacrifice of Isaac, considered a precursor to that of Christ, foreshadowing Christ's eventual sacrifice, which is not shown but anticipated by the scenes of his trial by Pontius Pilate.

In artistic style the reliefs owe more to the traditions of the second century CE than to the Constantinian innovations of the fourth. The figures are very Classicizing in their proportions, stances, and drapery with its deep folds and rounded profiles, which contrasts with the flat, drilled drapery more common in the fourth-century CE official reliefs. The architectural frames and the furniture within the scenes are all based on Classical examples. The alternating semi-circular and triangular pediments in the lower register are adapted from the Asian sarcophagus tradition as seen on the Velletri Sarcophagus (Figure 9.22). The figure of Christ is youthful and unbearded as seen in the Early Christian Good Shepherd images (Figure 11.21). Here, however, he is more formally portrayed as judge, associating him more strongly with Roman government and, perhaps, Junius Bassus himself. Christ is not quite completely associated with the emperor as his later images were, but this can be seen as an intermediate step as Christianity was now in an intermediate phase in its transition to official religion. The sarcophagus ends are relief scenes of putti performing seasonal tasks such as harvesting grapes. This subject in particular had strong pagan associations with the worship of Dionysus, but was adopted by Early Christians for sarcophagi as seen on the Good Shepherd sarcophagus from 260–270 CE (Figure 11.22) and on the porphyry sarcophagus of Constantina (Figure 12.15).

Tracing the reception of Roman imperial imagery through the later periods of art would be a book in itself, but perhaps one image can at least provide evidence of my earlier assertion that along with the forms, later people took the culture of Rome as well. Otto II, Holy Roman Emperor (ruled 973–983) is presented in this manuscript illumination as an enthroned monarch, a common composition in the Middle Ages and later.

For our purposes it is significant first that he was a German monarch who was proclaimed as a Roman emperor, a title that carried significant cultural weight. And of particular significance is that the image derives ultimately from those of Constantine and other late

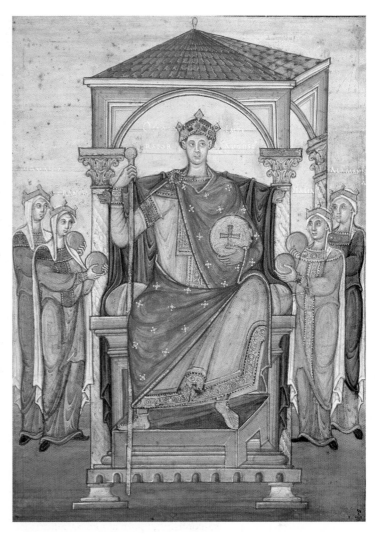

12.25 Otto II, Holy Roman Emperor (973–983 CE), manuscript illumination from the Registrum Gregorii, c. 983 CE. Musée Condé, Chantilly, France. Source: Musee Conde, Chantilly, France/ Giraudon/The Bridgeman Art Library.

Roman emperors. Comparing it to the *congiarium* relief of Constantine enthroned on the Arch of Constantine (Figure 12.11) makes this clear. Otto II is presented frontally with a dramatic hierarchy of scale emphasizing his importance. The figures flanking him direct the viewers' attention to him as they symbolically support his rule. His position on the central axis elevated and framed also parallels that of Constantine on the *oratio* and *congiarium* reliefs on his arch. The portrait, if such a word can be used of such a generic image, of Otto II reflects and extends the subjects and forms of Roman art of the ruler over six hundred years into the future.

One of the most powerful and wide-ranging forms that we see from ancient Rome is the gateway. When considering gates and arches in ancient Rome they can be classified together as armatures of celebration whatever their precise form. These are repeated throughout the later history of architecture, and not just in the western world, but across the globe from every European country to North and South America and across Asia from Constantinople in the west to Korea in the east. Almost all of these are set up as individual monuments and whether they are set in piazzas or at crossroads, much as the Romans did, they generally articulate space and urban forms to create passages and sightlines of celebration. Of the many thousands built across the world over the past two thousand years, perhaps a very traditional one can stand for all here, the Arc de Triomphe in Paris.

Commissioned in Paris in 1806 by the Emperor Napoleon to commemorate his victories and the men who fought in the Napoleonic Wars, the arch is a very traditional adaptation of a Roman single passage arch. Although much larger, it has the same proportions as the Arch of Titus (Figure 7.22),

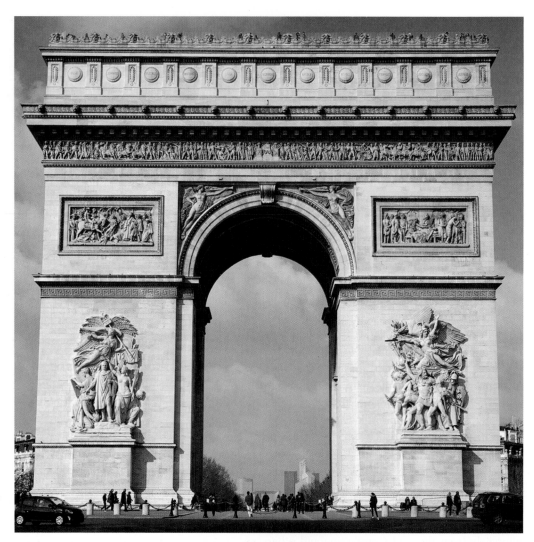

12.26 Arc de Triomphe, commissioned in Paris by Napoleon, 1806. Photo courtesy Steven L. Tuck.

the oldest surviving triumphal arch in Rome. In addition to the proportions it has carved Victories in relief in the spandrels of the arch, a strongly articulated attic story above, and sculptural relief panels as well as a continuous frieze. The designer, Jean Chalgrin, adapted material from other ancient victory monuments including a triglyph metope frieze with a line of thirty shields across the attic story, each engraved with the name of a victorious battle, a motif used in Greek and Roman victory monuments, notably votive temples. He also did not conclude the arch with a culminating statue group, which originally topped the Arch of Titus, but does not survive, so the form here follows the surviving examples of Roman triumphal arches not their original design. A Roman triumphal monument seems a natural form for an imperial power whose leader emulated Roman titles and examples in his presentation of himself and his rule.

To fully appreciate the emulation of Roman visual vocabulary, its extent, and the notion of the interconnections, Washington D.C. provides a remarkably developed example. There we see the self-consciously modeled Roman government adopted Roman forms of architecture and monumentalization because those forms come with the ideas of government embedded in them. The forms and the lessons that they transmit matter. The layout of the city directly emulates Roman urban forms in its buildings and monuments. These include the Jefferson Memorial, an adaptation of the Pantheon, and the Supreme Court building, based on the Temple of Jupiter Capitolinus in Rome. Perhaps one of the best examples is the U.S. Capitol, a tremendous building in terms of

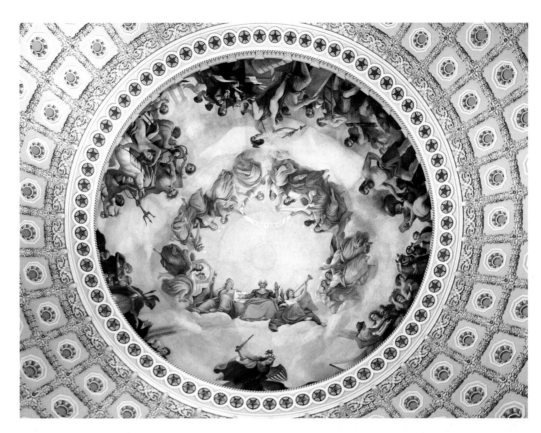

12.27 *Apotheosis of Washington* fresco, interior of the Capitol Dome, 1865, by Constantino Brumidi. U.S. Capitol, Washington D.C. Raul654/Wikimedia Commons.

scale. Its placement on a hill, Capitol Hill, is an attempt to visually dominate the area around it, perhaps as the name suggests based on the Temple of Jupiter Capitolinus but also reminiscent of the temple at Terracina. Unlike the temples, the centerpiece of the U.S. Capitol building is a great Roman-inspired dome.

From the interior the space created by the dome is called the rotunda, a space that reached its final form after the second building campaign concluded in 1866. On the walls around the rotunda are eight large historical paintings, four are subjects of the revolutionary war and four are scenes of early exploration of America. Above all of it is a very large fresco by a painter born and trained in Rome, Constantino Brumidi, that fills the interior of the dome. In figures up to 15 ft (5 m) tall, designed to be seen from the floor over 180 ft (60 m) below, he painted *The Apotheosis of Washington*.

The notion of apotheosis, the bodily ascent into heaven, is a standard Roman idea that was attributed to Roman rulers as far back as Romulus and was continued by many emperors, as seen on the Arch of Titus (Figure 7.22). Here the fresco is divided, like an ancient Roman work, into two registers. In the center is the risen George Washington flanked by personifications, female as was standard for ancient Rome, Liberty and Victory on either side of him, and all of them surrounded by thirteen female figures who stand for the thirteen original colonies. We have examined a Roman example of geographical personifications from the Temple of the Deified Hadrian (Figure 9.10). Six groups of figures make up the outer register. Directly below Washington is War with Freedom and an eagle, symbol of Zeus as well as the United States, defeating Tyranny. The other five groups are organized around key American themes and Roman gods, recognizable by their attributes and hierarchy of scale, passing their knowledge along to famous Americans, shown in smaller scale. Science is personified by Minerva, Marine by Neptune, Commerce by Mercury, Mechanics by Vulcan, and Agriculture by Ceres. The overall effect is one of the transmission of Roman culture and values directly to the United States through the gods.

These four examples, in relief sculpture, manuscript illumination, architecture, and fresco, can hardly begin to do justice to the reception of Roman art through the centuries and across cultures since the fall of Rome. What they can do, however, is demonstrate that those forms do continue and that the themes and messages that they transmit continue to matter as well to those who are commissioning and viewing this art up to the present day. It is popular (among academics at least) to debate how much we owe to Rome, how like Rome we are, and what these deliberate, explicit associations really mean. As you reflect on these visual forms of Roman culture, I hope that you will continue that discussion informed by your understanding of the visual culture of the Roman world with an awareness of its transmission to us today.

SUGGESTIONS FOR FURTHER READING

Jonathan Bardill, *Constantine, Divine Emperor of the Christian Golden Age* (Cambridge University Press 2012). The book explores the emperor's image as conveyed through literature, art, and architecture, and shows how Constantine reconciled the tradition of imperial divinity with his monotheistic faith. It demonstrates how the traditional themes and imagery of Roman rulers were exploited to portray the emperor as the savior of his people and to assimilate him to Christ.

Jaś Elsner, *Art and the Roman Viewer: The Transformation of Art from the Pagan World to Christianity* (Cambridge University Press 1995). Based on ancient art images and texts, Elsner presents a fresh analysis of why the arts of Late Antiquity moved away from Classical naturalism towards spiritual abstraction. This shows how an understanding of Roman viewing practices greatly deepens our insight into this fundamental transformation.

Allan Greenberg, *Architecture of Democracy* (Rizzoli 2006). A work that links the forms of American government buildings with their Classical, especially Roman, forms and meanings.

Elizabeth Hartley et al., eds., *Constantine the Great: York's Roman Emperor* (York Museums and Gallery Trust 2006). Catalogue from an exhibition at York, it includes essays and material that focuses on the art, coinage, and design under Constantine with an emphasis on the western empire, especially Britain.

R. Ross Holloway, *Constantine and Rome* (Yale University Press 2004). This work examines the building program and public art of Constantine in the city of Rome. It establishes his context as the first Christian emperor and gives detailed attention to the arches, basilicas, baptistery, and the tomb of St. Peter.

Fraser Hunter and Kenneth Painter, eds., *Late Roman Silver. The Traprain Treasure in Context* (The Society of Antiquaries of Scotland 2013). The authors provide fresh insights into the Traprain hoard and bring together a challenging series of perspectives on the nature of late Roman society and economy, and its relationship to the non-Roman world. Their work also explores important yet relatively unknown hoards and groups of material from Britain and the Continent.

Elizabeth Struthers Malbon, *The Iconography of the Sarcophagus of Junius Bassus* (Princeton University Press 1990). Malbon explores the sarcophagus of Junius Bassus not only as a magnificent example of mid-fourth-century sculpture but also as a treasury of early Christian iconography clearly indicating the Christianization of the Roman world and the Romanization of Christian art. She explores its iconography in the fourth-century context and reveals the fluid distinction between pagan and Christian images.

Roger Rees, ed., *Romane Memento: Vergil in the Fourth Century* (Duckworth 2004). Amid the rise of Christianity, the changing status of the city of Rome, and the emergence of the new governing classes, Vergil remained a foundation of Roman identity. This collection of essays explores the ways in which Vergil was read, understood, and appropriated and the many ways in which his works continued to enrich Roman culture in the fourth century.

J. Weisweiler, "From Equality to Asymmetry: Honorific Statues, Imperial Power, and Senatorial Identity in Late-Antique Rome." *Journal of Roman Archaeology* 25: 319–350 (2012). This article explores the evidence from statue bases to explore the impact of imperial withdrawal and the formation of the Late Roman state on the senatorial aristocracy in Rome in the fourth century CE.

GLOSSARY

acrolithic: a statue, usually large scale or even colossal in size, in which the body is constructed of a wooden framework covered with drapery and only the exposed limbs are carved stone.

acroterion: a decorative ornament, such as a statue, placed on the roof of a temple, usually above the front pediment but could also be spaced along the ridgeline.

adlocutio: a public address by an emperor to the army or citizens, shown by the right arm raised in salute.

adventus: arrival ceremony conducted by civil and religious officials, usually after a military campaign, welcoming a commander or emperor back into Rome. These occurred formally at the city gate.

aedicular niche: a structural framing device in architecture that creates a space designed like a shrine, usually with a frame surround and roof structure above.

apotheosis: to become a god, often shown as the elevation to divine status through bodily ascension or the moment the figure is welcomed into the company of the gods.

apotropaic: literally "to ward off evil," usually with designs, often grotesque, frightening, and incorporating serpents, placed on the outsides of buildings or objects to protect those within from harm.

Archaistic: a style of art imitating or reviving elements of Greek Archaic art (600–480 BCE). It was a popular revivalist style in Roman free-standing and relief sculpture.

arcuated pediment: also known as a Syrian pediment, combines the standard triangular pediment with a semi-circular arch which usually fills the center of the pediment.

atmospheric perspective: artistic device to create a sense of depth in painting by shifting the background colors to the blue side of the spectrum and painting distant objects paler.

atrium: the main or central room of a Roman house, usually directly accessible from the front door.

barrel vault: a cylindrical architectural feature formed by extending an arch along an indefinite length, creating a solid roofing system that is essentially a continuous arch.

basilica: a Roman building characterized by a central hall with flanking aisles and often a porch on one end and a raised tribunal on the other, often used for law courts.

biclinium: a Roman dining room or space with two dining couches rather than the usual three found in a *triclinium*.

bulla: amulet worn by Roman boys like a locket designed to protect them from harm until they came of age and stopped wearing it.

caduceus: the wand, entwined by two serpents, generally carried by Mercury. As the protector of merchants, it is associated with commerce and business occupations.

caldarium: hot room in a Roman bath complex. It usually featured a heated pool and radiant heat from the walls and floor.

capite velato: Latin, meaning "with covered head," referring to the act of covering one's head while performing a sacred ritual.

caryatid: a female figure used in place of a column to support the entablature of a building.

cella (pl. cellae): the inner room of a temple. It served primarily to house the cult statue. It could also hold votive objects and ritual items such as vessels and braziers.

chthonic: literally "of the earth," refers to anything, usually a god or other powerful being, that dwells under the earth or draws its power from the earth.

clerestory: the upper level of a building, seen in basilicas, that rises above the roof level of the outside aisles. Pierced with windows it floods the central aisle with light.

contrapposto: counterpoise, gives a figure a dynamic but relaxed pose by alternating weight-bearing and free arms and legs coupled with hips and shoulders held at slight angles.

corona civica: the civic crown, a wreath of oak leaves, a tree sacred to Jupiter, awarded to Roman citizens who saved the lives of other citizens in battle.

cryptoporticus (pl. *cryptoportici*): a vaulted covered passageway, usually open along one side, that creates the support for a building above. Often used to create large platforms for a Roman temple or villa.

curule chair: the chair on which senior magistrates such as consuls, praetors, censors, and all those with imperium were entitled to sit.

dado: the lower portion of the wall of a room, often distinctly decorated with panels or painted in contrasting colors.

dentil frieze: a series of closely spaced projecting rectangular blocks that make a molding on a building usually at the top of the wall just below the roofline.

ekphrasis: a rhetorical device consisting of a self-contained description often of an event or of a work of art or architecture.

entablature: architectural term for the part of the building above the columns including cornice, moldings, and friezes.

episodic narrative: a narrative structure in which a series of events or episodes occur with the same main character, generally portrayed in each episode.

Etrusco-Italic: refers to architecture, especially temples, shared by cultures of central Italy. The temples generally featured tall podiums, deep front porches, wide roofs, small cellas, and rooftop sculptures.

exedra (pl. exedrae): in architecture semi-circular recesses or bays often roofed with a half dome.

A History of Roman Art, First Edition. Steven L. Tuck.
© 2015 Steven L. Tuck. Published 2015 by John Wiley & Sons, Ltd.

frigidarium: the cold water room in a Roman bath complex, generally found in the core of the building away from the furnace or the sun.

hemicycle: literally a half-circle. In architecture, a hemicycle is a wall, building, or architectural feature constructed in the shape of a half circle.

herm: a type of Greek statue, originally of Hermes, with a squared stone pillar supporting a carved upper body and head; used as boundary markers in Greek cities and sanctuaries.

hierarchy of scale: an artistic convention in which higher status or more important figures are portrayed as larger than lower status or subsidiary figures in a scene.

hieros gamos: from Greek, literally "holy marriage," may refer to a marriage between a god and goddess, for example Jupiter and Juno, or to a ritual re-enactment of that by elites.

horror vacui: from Latin meaning "fear of empty space," the filling of the entire surface of a work with details, often ones that are extraneous to the narrative or the main scene.

imbrication: an overlapping pattern like roof shingles or fish scales.

insula: literally in Latin "island," refers to an apartment building that filled an entire block in a Roman city, with shops on the ground floor and apartments above.

isocephaly: artistic convention of portraying figures, whether seated or standing, with all of their heads on the same level.

lectus: Roman couch used by the elite to recline while dining, sleeping, and to display the body in a funeral.

loggia: a roofed gallery open on one side and generally supported by columns, often found on an upper floor of a building.

mimesis: literally "to imitate" in Greek, especially refers to the goal of accurate representation of the human and natural world in art.

necropolis (pl. necropoleis): from Greek, literally "a city of the dead." Refers to the extramural cemeteries often mimicking real cities organized by family tombs shaped like houses, sometimes with roads, sidewalks, and drains.

negotium: Latin term for business (literally "not leisure"), including both public and private business.

obsonia: literally spoils or prizes, prepared food as a subject for painting in Hellenistic art.

oculus: from the Latin meaning "eye," refers to a circular open skylight in the center of a dome to provide light into the building.

opus incertum: a facing of irregularly shaped, fist-sized tufa stones commonly applied to concrete structures in the late second and early first centuries BCE.

opus sectile: literally "cut work." Refers to the decorative use of cut stone, usually colored imported marble, in patterns to create decorative floor and wall treatments.

Orientalizing: style of art based on ideas, forms, and materials from the Near East and Egypt. In Greek art, it dominates the period 700–600 BCE.

orthogonal planning: the type of city plan in which the streets run at right angles to each other, forming a grid.

orthostates: squared stone blocks of greater height than depth. These upright standing stones were used to make the bases of walls and then topped with courses of smaller cut stones.

otium: Latin term for leisure, it includes time spent on reading, writing, and academic activities, including rest. Often associated with the Roman villa as the space for *otium*.

paradeisos: a walled park where wild animal hunts took place. A Persian concept adopted by the Greeks after the conquests of Alexander the Great.

pediment: the triangular gable found below a pitched roof on either end of a building. On ancient temples these were often filled with sculptures or relief decoration.

peripteral: refers to a building, usually a temple, with a single row of columns surrounding it.

peristyle: refers to a structure with columns that enclose it, such as a peristyle temple with columns on all four sides of the exterior or a peristyle courtyard with colonnaded porches on all four sides.

pinacotheca: literally a picture gallery. In Roman houses a room decorated with mural paintings that replicate Greek panel paintings, often copies or variations of famous pictures.

polychromy: the use of many colors in decoration, especially in architecture and sculpture. Refers to the brightly painted multi-colored buildings and sculptures of the ancient world.

pomerium: the sacred boundary of Rome. In legal and religious terms Rome consisted only of that part of the city within it. Burials were forbidden inside the *pomerium*.

porphyry: a hard purple stone quarried by the Romans at one spot in Egypt, Mons Porphyritis, and used extensively by emperors since its purple color denoted royalty.

post and lintel architecture: a building system with a horizontal feature (lintel) supported by two vertical features (posts or columns) to create open space such as rooms or doorways.

Praetorian Guard: the bodyguard of the Roman emperors, formed by Augustus. They guarded the emperor, his palaces, and sometimes acted to remove or create emperors.

profectio: a ritual departure, generally of a Roman commander from the city to war. It was essentially the opposite of the *adventus*, also taking place at the city gates.

protome: a form of art that consists of a frontal view of an animal head or human bust.

provenance: the place of origin or earliest known history of something. In art it can refer to the chain of ownership of a piece from origin to the present day.

pseudoperipteral: refers to a building that mimics the peripteral colonnades that completely surrounded Greek temples. It has a porch with free-standing columns but engaged half columns around the sides and back.

psychopomp: *psychopompos*, literally "guide of souls," a descriptor of the god Mercury who guided the souls of the newly dead into the underworld.

quadriga: four-horse chariot, used for chariot racing and by successful generals in triumphal processions. A general in a *quadriga* was a common subject in victory monuments.

register: division of an artistic field into parallel columns or rows. These, usually horizontal bands, act as groundlines and aid in creating narrative.

repoussé: a type of artwork, generally of metal, that features a design in raised relief created through hammering the material from the reverse side.

scaenae frons: the elaborate background for a Roman theater stage, usually two or three stories in height with multiple entrances, balconies, and alternating projecting and receding elements articulated with columns.

spandrel: the roughly triangular space between the curve of an arch and the surrounding molding that frames it. Spandrels on triumphal arches are usually filled with figures of Victory.

sulcus primigenius: The ritual furrow plowed to mark the *pomerium* and the subsequent line of walls at Rome by Romulus and later by other Romans at Rome and its colonies.

suovetaurilia: a sacrifice made up of a bull, sheep, and pig, traditionally made to Mars, it was one of the oldest and most sacred Roman rituals.

symposium: a Greek elite male drinking party at which men would recline on couches to drink wine, listen to entertainment, sing, or discuss philosophical, cultural, or political topics.

tablinum: a room in the Roman house off the atrium and directly opposite the front door. It was the major formal reception room, used to receive clients and conduct business.

tepidarium: the warm water room in a Roman bath complex, usually the largest and most central room of the bathing suite.

terminus post quem: literally "time after which" referring to the notion that a datable object or event only tells us the date after which something might have occurred.

tesserae: small handcut cubes of stone used to make mosaics.

torque: large neck ring, often made of twisted strands of gold wire, worn by elite ancient Celts or Gauls.

triclinium: Roman dining room laid out for nine diners reclining on three couches (in Greek: *tri cline*) from which the room gets its name.

triglyph-metope frieze: element of Doric architecture with rectangular panels (metopes), often used for sculpture, separated by projecting blocks (triglyphs) with three vertical portions separated by two channels.

triumphal procession: victory parade granted by the Senate to a conquering general, who rode in a *quadriga*. It began at the city gates and concluded at the Temple of Jupiter.

trompe l'oeil: literally, "to fool the eye." A technique in art to create the optical illusion of objects existing in three dimensional space.

tumulus (pl. tumuli): a type of tomb with a mound raised over it. Etruscan examples cover chamber tombs that belonged to extended families. Large tumuli resemble small hills.

tympanum: a semi-circular area over an entrance bounded by the lintel below and an arch above. It often contains sculpture, usually in relief.

veristic: from the Latin *verus* meaning "true," refers to a style of exaggerated naturalism or hyper-realism found in Roman portraits, often to emphasize the age-dependent virtues of the subject.

Victory: based on the Greek Nike, a winged female personification of Roman success in war or sports, identifiable by the palm branch and victor's crown she often carries.

votive: something offered in fulfillment of a vow. These range from small statuettes to pieces of armor or altars or temples, all demonstrating the piety of the dedicant.

xenia: guest gifts, a class of paintings described by the Roman architectural author Vitruvius, including provisions such as poultry, eggs, vegetables, fruit, and the like.

GUIDE TO FURTHER READING

Books on Roman Arts in General, Aesthetics, Theory, Art Historical Approaches

Sorcha Carey, *Pliny's Catalogue of Culture: Art and Empire in the Natural History* (Oxford University Press 2003).

James Cuno, *Who Owns Antiquity?: Museums and the Battle over Our Ancient Heritage* (Princeton University Press 2008).

Eve D'Ambra and Guy P.R. Metraux, eds., *The Art of Citizens, Soldiers, and Freedmen in the Roman World.* BAR International Series 1526 (Archaeopress 2006).

Jaś Elsner, *Art and Text in Roman Culture* (Cambridge University Press 1996).

David Fredrick, *The Roman Gaze: Vision, Power, and the Body* (Johns Hopkins University Press 2002).

Niels Hannestad, *Roman Art and Imperial Policy* (Aarhus University Press 1986).

Natalie Boymel Kampen, *Family Fictions in Roman Art* (Cambridge University Press 2009).

T.M. Kristensen and B. Poulsen, eds., *Ateliers and Artisans in Roman Art and Archaeology. Journal of Roman Archaeology* supplementary series, 92. (Journal of Roman Archaeology 2012).

Jerome J. Pollitt, *The Art of Rome, 753 B.C.–A.D. 337: Sources and Documents.* rev. ed. (Cambridge University Press 1983).

Steven Rutledge, *Ancient Rome as a Museum: Power, Identity, and the Culture of Collecting* (Oxford University Press 2012).

Rabun Taylor, *The Moral Mirror of Roman Art* (Cambridge University Press 2008).

Architecture

Jean Pierre Adam, *Roman Building: Materials and Techniques* (Routledge 2001).

James C. Anderson, Jr., *Roman Architecture and Society* (Johns Hopkins University Press 1997).

E.M. Orlin, *Temples, Religion, and Politics in the Roman Republic* (Brill 1997).

L. Richardson, Jr., *Pompeii: An Architectural History* (Johns Hopkins University Press 1988).

Ingrid Rowland and Thomas Noble Howe, *Vitruvius: Ten Books on Architecture* (Cambridge University Press 1999).

Henri Stierlin, *The Roman Empire: From the Etruscans to the Decline of the Roman Empire* Taschen's World Architecture vol. 1 (Taschen 1996).

Rabun Taylor, *Roman Builders: A Study in Architectural Process* (Cambridge University Press 2003).

Roger B. Ulrich and Caroline K. Quenemoen, eds., *A Companion to Roman Architecture* (Wiley-Blackwell 2013).

J.B. Ward-Perkins, *Roman Imperial Architecture* (Yale University Press 1994).

Sculpture

Yaron Z. Eliav, Elise A. Friedland, and Sharon Herbert, eds., *The Sculptural Environment of the Roman Near East: Reflections on Culture, Ideology, and Power* (Peeters 2008).

Jane Fejfer, *Roman Portraits in Context* (Walter de Gruyter 2008).

Elaine K. Gazda, ed., *The Ancient Art of Emulation: Studies in Artistic Originality and Tradition from the Present to Classical Antiquity* (University of Michigan Press 2002).

Rachel M. Kousser, *Hellenistic and Roman Ideal Sculpture: The Allure of the Classical* (Cambridge University Press 2008).

Brenda Longfellow, *Roman Imperialism and Civic Patronage: Form, Meaning and Ideology in Monumental Fountain Complexes* (Cambridge University Press 2011).

Brian Christopher Madigan, *The Ceremonial Sculptures of the Roman Gods* (Brill 2012).

Carol Mattusch, *The Villa dei Papiri at Herculaneum: Life and Afterlife of a Sculpture Collection* (J. Paul Getty Museum 2005).

Marina Prusac, *From Face to Face: Recarving of Roman Portraits and the Late-Antique Portrait Arts* (Brill 2011).

Peter Stewart, *Statues in Roman Society: Representation and Response* (Oxford University Press 2003).

Paul Zanker and Bjorn C. Ewald, *Living with Myths: the Imagery of Roman Sarcophagi* (Oxford University Press 2013).

Painting and Mosaics

Katherine M.D. Dunbabin, *Mosaics of the Greek and Roman World* (Cambridge University Press 1999).

Katherine M. D. Dunbabin, *The Mosaics of Roman North Africa: Studies in Iconography and Patronage* (Oxford University Press 1978).

Rachel Hachlili, *Ancient Mosaic Pavements: Themes, Issues, and Trends* (Brill 2008).

Hetty Joyce, *The Decoration of Walls, Ceilings, and Floors in Italy in the Second and Third Centuries A.D.* (Giorgio Bretschneider 1981).

Roger Ling, *Ancient Mosaics* (Princeton University Press 1998).

Roger Ling, *Roman Painting* (Cambridge University Press 1991).

Eric Moormann, *Divine Interiors: Mural Paintings in Greek and Roman Sanctuaries* (Amsterdam University Press 2011).

A History of Roman Art, First Edition. Steven L. Tuck.
© 2015 Steven L. Tuck. Published 2015 by John Wiley & Sons, Ltd.

D.S. Neal and S.R. Cosh, *The Roman Mosaics of Britain*. 4 vols. (Society of Antiquaries, 2002, 2006, 2009, 2010).

Umberto Pappalardo, *The Splendor of Roman Wall Painting* (J. Paul Getty Museum, 2009).

David Parrish, *Season Mosaics of Roman North Africa* (Giorgio Bretschneider 1984).

L. Richardson, Jr., *A Catalog of Identifiable Figure Painters of Ancient Pompeii, Herculaneum, and Stabiae* (Johns Hopkins University Press 2000).

Frank Sear, *Roman Wall and Vault Mosaics, Römische Mitteilungen* Ergänzungsheft 23 (F.H. Kerle 1977).

Houses, Villas, and Domestic Décor

John Bodel, "Monumental Villas and Villa Monuments." *Journal of Roman Archaeology* 10: 5–35 (1997).

Elaine Gazda, ed., *Roman Art in the Private Sphere: New Perspectives on the Architecture and Decor of the Domus, Villa, and Insula* (University of Michigan Press 1991).

Shelly Hales, *The Roman House and Social Identity* (Cambridge University Press 2003).

Ray Laurence and Andrew Wallace-Hadrill, eds., *Domestic Space in the Roman World. Journal of Roman Archaeology* Supplement 22 (Journal of Roman Archaeology 1996).

Eleanor Winsor Leach, *The Social Life of Painting in Ancient Rome and on the Bay of Naples* (Cambridge University Press 2011).

Francesca Tronchin, ed., *Arethusa*, special edition, *Collectors and the Eclectic: New Approaches to Roman Domestic Decoration* 45.3 (2012).

Andrew Wallace-Hadrill, *Houses and Society in Pompeii and Herculaneum* (Princeton University Press 1994).

Metalwork, Glass, Gems, and Coins

Chris Entwistle and Noël Adams, eds., "*Gems of Heaven*": *Recent Research on Engraved Gemstones in Late Antiquity, AD 200–600* (British Museum Press 2011).

Stuart James Fleming, *Roman Glass: Reflections on Cultural Change* (University of Pennsylvania Museum 1999).

Martin Henig, *Catalogue of the Engraved Gems and Finger-rings in the Ashmolean Museum. Volume 2: Roman*. BAR International Series 1332 (Archaeopress 2004).

Philip V. Hill, *The Monuments of Ancient Rome as Coin Types* (Batsford 1989).

Catherine Johns, *The Hoxne Late Roman Treasure: Gold Jewellery and Silver Plate* (British Museum Press 2010).

Catherine Johns, *The Snettisham Roman Jeweller's Hoard* (British Museum Press 1997).

Ruth E. Leader-Newby, *Silver and Society in Late Antiquity: Functions and Meanings of Silver Plate in the Fourth to Seventh Centuries* (Ashgate 2004).

Erika Manders, *Coining Images of Power: Patterns in the Representation of Roman Emperors on Imperial Coinage, A.D. 193–284* (Brill 2012).

E. Marianne Stern, *Roman Mold-blown Glass: The First through Sixth Centuries* (L'Erma di Bretschneider in association with the Toledo Museum of Art 1995).

INDEX

A History of Roman Art, First Edition. Steven L. Tuck.
© 2015 Steven L. Tuck. Published 2015 by John Wiley & Sons, Ltd.